ROGER RUSSELL
36 F
HALIFAX, N.S.
ph: 479-2293

# MANAGING ORGANIZATIONAL BEHAVIOR

JOHN WILEY & SONS

New York • Chichester
Brisbane • Toronto • Singapore

# MANAGING ORGANIZATIONAL BEHAVIOR

**John R. Schermerhorn, Jr.**
Southern Illinois University at Carbondale

**James G. Hunt**
Texas Tech University

**Richard N. Osborn**
Battelle Human Affairs Research Centers
of the Battelle Memorial Institute

Production Supervisor **Ellen P. O'Neill**
Copy Editor **Joan Knizeski**
Photo Researcher **Elyse Rieder**
Text & Cover Design **Sheila Granda**
Cover Art **Jorge Hernandez**



**Library of Congress Cataloging in Publication Data**

Schermerhorn, John R.
Managing organizational behavior.

Includes index.
1. Organizational behavior. 2. Management.
I. Hunt, James G., 1932– II. Osborn, Richard.
III. Title.
HD58.7.S34 658 81-16267
ISBN 0-471-04497-0 AACR2

Printed in the United States of America

10 9 8 7 6 5 4 3 2 1

*For Ann, with all my love and gratitude.* **John**
*This one's for Mom and Dad.* **Jerry**
*To Judy with Love.* **Dick**

# ABOUT THE AUTHORS

JOHN R. SCHERMERHORN, JR., is Associate Professor of Administrative Sciences and Associate Dean of the College of Business and Administration at Southern Illinois University at Carbondale. John holds a Ph.D. in Organizational Behavior from Northwestern University, and previously taught at Tulane University and the University of Vermont. He has prior work experience in personnel and hospital administration and is most concerned in helping the discipline of organizational behavior serve the needs of practicing managers. He is professionally active in management training and consultation with organizations in the United States and abroad, is a member of the Academy of Management and other professional associations, and publishes regularly in scholarly journals.

JAMES G. (Jerry) HUNT is Professor of Business Administration and Coordinator of the Management Area at Texas Tech University. Jerry's Ph.D. in business is from the University of Illinois, and he has taught at Southern Illinois University at Carbondale, West Virginia Tech, Millikin University, the University of Illinois, and the University of Texas. An internationally known researcher on leadership, he is editor of seven state-of-the-art books in the leadership area and has published widely in the field of organizational behavior. As a scholar, he is committed to increasing the scientific rigor of organizational behavior research. Jerry is a Fellow of the Academy of Management, member of the editorial review boards of the *Academy of Management Review* and the *Journal of Business Research,* an active member of several professional associations, and co-author of *Organization Theory: An Integrated Approach.*

RICHARD N. OSBORN is a research scientist at the Battelle Human Affairs Research Centers of the Battelle Memorial Institute. His doctorate is from Kent State University, and he previously taught at Southern Illinois University at Carbondale. Dick is the author of over fifty articles and papers on organizations, organizational environments, leadership, and strategic management. His theoretical work examines environmental and organizational factors associated with leadership effectiveness. He presently heads an investigation of management and organization factors affecting the safety of nuclear power plants. Dick is an active member of the Academy of Management and is the incoming President of the Midwest Academy of Management. He is co-author of *Organization Theory: An Integrated Approach.*

# PREFACE

Most college textbooks are written for the instructor. This book is different. While we don't neglect the instructor, the book's emphasis is on getting the student in an introductory course in organizational behavior (OB) involved as he or she completes the assigned reading. *Managing Organizational Behavior* is written in a conversational manner that incorporates a number of special features designed to help students interact with its contents. These features are explained in detail in our memo to the students which precedes Chapter 1.

While we use a conversational writing style, we have not sacrificed rigor or content. You will find the text includes the well-known models in the field, some of the controversies (though without overwhelming the student), and a reasonable review of significant empirical work. In other words we've tried to strike a balance between readability and scholarship for the introductory student.

We invite you to peruse the Contents. The book covers both micro and macro OB topics. In addition to major sections on individuals, groups, and interpersonal processes, there are three chapters on the organization and its environment, as well as supplementary modules on research methods and the history of OB. A final integrating chapter briefly reviews the book as a whole with a view toward personal career planning.

*Managing Organizational Behavior* is designed for instructional flexibility in the sequencing of topics. While the Contents follows an individual-group-organization sequence, it is written so that other patterns may be used without sacrificing understanding. Furthermore, the four chapters on interpersonal processes in Part Five may be used individually at any point in the course according to your preferences.

We have made the book as self-contained as possible. Special features designed to elicit reader involvement include chapter opening anecdotes or articles, Management Application Questions, Checkpoints, Newslines, and examples of What Managers Do and What Consultants Do. In addition, each chapter concludes with an Exercise or Case, The Manager's Vocabulary which is a glossary of important terms and names, and a set of thought questions.

To further enhance the learning experience for the student and to make the instructor's job easier, we've provided an extensive instructor's manual. It includes, among other things, a number of different course schedules using alternative topic sequencing, chapter highlights and teaching suggestions, supplementary lectures, transparency masters, objective and essay examination questions and answers, additional cases, and sample assignments for individual and group projects.

For our acknowledgments we start with three student reviewers. We felt that the creation of a student-oriented book required substantial student input at various stages of the writing process. Barbara LaLancette, University of Vermont, and Catherine Chiarello and Linda Gereg, Southern Illinois University at Carbondale, were most helpful in this regard.

Among our colleagues, we would like especially to acknowledge Michael Hutt of Miami (Ohio) University and Edwin Greif of the University of Vermont who encouraged the initiation of this project; Ogden Hall, University of New Orleans, and Harold P. Welsch, DePaul University, who provided helpful reviews in the initial stages of the manuscript; and Larry Michaelson, University of Oklahoma, Douglas Simpson, California State University at Fresno, and Steven Kerr, University of Southern California, who reviewed the manuscript in the book's final stages. To all of these persons we extend a sincere thanks.

In addition to this very fine help from students and colleagues, we were most fortunate to have the secretarial assistance of Lynn Wells, University of Vermont, and Vicki Avery, Julie Jenkins, Linda Harris, Julie Nance, and Brenda Wells, all at Southern Illinois University at Carbondale. The Battelle Memorial Institute deserves our appreciation for administrative and technical help provided through the Battelle Human Affairs Research Centers. Our graduate assistants Gary Styzens and Mardi Von Hermann were also indispensable.

The staff at John Wiley & Sons was most helpful in the various stages of production. We thank them for their support. Our editor Rick Leyh deserves special recognition for his emphasis on quality and determination to see the project through to its conclusion.

Finally, we recognize our families. *Managing Organizational Behavior,* though exciting to write, has taken more time from them than we care to remember. Thanks to Ann Schermerhorn, Donna Hunt, Judy Osborn, and the children for their forbearance.

John Schermerhorn
Jerry Hunt
Dick Osborn

# CONTENTS

# MEMORANDUM

TO: The Reader
FROM: John Schermerhorn, Jerry Hunt, Dick Osborn
SUJECT: You and This Book

Most people, whether they like it or not, have to work for a living. They must produce or provide goods or services of value to someone else if they are to obtain the basic requirements of life, and a few luxuries as well. Oh yes, there are alternative lifestyles that downplay the economic necessity implied in this argument. Some people join communes, others just "drop out," while some simply rely on the good will of parents or friends for their support. But for you, probably, and for us, certainly, work is the basis of our livelihoods. We spend a large part of our lives working, and we should, therefore, know as much as possible about it.

## On Becoming a Manager

This book is about people at work in organizations. Reading it should help you to understand the many events that give meaning to your day-to-day work experiences. You will probably become a particular type of worker—a **manager,** a person in a work organization who is responsible for the performance of one or more other people.

Being a manager is a special type of personal challenge. Think about your own work experiences. Can you remember a time when you felt especially uncomfortable because you had to ask someone to do a rather unpleasant task, or a task that you knew they just did not want to do? Such anxiety or discomfort is typical in situations where one person must direct the work activities of others. This is a leadership challenge faced by all managers. What is your style of leadership? How effective is it? What should be your style of leadership? The learning experiences in this book will help you to answer these and other related questions.

## The Book in Perspective

Two points about this book and our purpose in writing it for you are especially important. First, please recognize that people act as managers in many different types of organizations. The issues, concepts, theories, and insights of this book are relevant to work activities in organizations of all types. Thus, there is a useful learning experience contained in these pages, regardless of where you plan to work—be it in business, education, government, health services, or social services. We have written for people who are going to work and to be managers in any of these occupational settings.

Second, we are committed to providing you with an active learning experience that will leave you with insights and knowledge that will help you in actual practice. This is not a theory book. There is a lot of theory in it, but the theory is explained and then applied to help you perform more effectively in an actual managerial capacity. To take full advantage of the learning experiences offered in this book, however, you must read carefully and stay involved. When we ask you to do something, such as complete an inventory of your leadership style, please do it. Such requests are designed to ensure learning outcomes that are as closely tailored to your own needs as possible.

Simply put, we have written this book:

1. For people who will serve as managers in all types of organizational and occupational settings.
2. To emphasize the practical application of theory, and to help you to perform more effectively as a manager.
3. As a self-contained learning experience that uses your active participation as a way of increasing comprehension by tailoring the material to fit personal needs.

## Key Features of the Book

We describe here the special features that make this a reader-oriented book. Consider each feature carefully so that you can take full advantage of the learning opportunities represented by each when they appear throughout the text.

### Practical Reference Points

We want you to know what is happening in the real world of management. Four special features in this book are designed to help you to make these important theory-into-practice transitions. These features include:

**Management Applications Question:** A question posed at the beginning of each chapter to highlight a critical, practical issue underlying the topics presented in the chapter.

**Newsline:** Excerpts from recent newspapers and news magazines that give examples of the application of text material and of the current "problems" or "opportunities" that challenge managers to act effectively.

**What Managers Do:** Examples of actual responses by managers to specific problems or opportunities.

**What Consultants Do:** Examples of actual responses by consultants to problems or opportunites faced by managers.

When you encounter these features in reading, consider them carefully. Some may prove useful as topics for term papers or special projects. Others may become topics for class discussion. It would be interesting, for example, to learn if anyone has experienced events described in a *Newsline* or in *What Managers Do,* or to find out if your professor agrees or disagrees with what is described in *What Consultants Do.* Asking questions can lead to a richer learning experience and help to draw forth an informative dialogue with your instructor.

## Learning Aids

There is more to this book than just these features. The book is and should be an academic instrument as well. You must read to expand your knowledge and to build personal theories that will apply to a wide variety of managerial situations. Neither this nor any other book can anticipate all work situations and provide the action guidelines to solve all of your future problems. Thus, our task is to help you develop a knowledge base that can be used to analyze any situation, develop a set of feasible responses, and choose and implement the best response systematically. This capability requires you to be familiar with the concepts and theories, and their implications, that most textbooks merely present to the reader. We will do more, with the help of the following learning aids.

**Planning Ahead:** Specific statements at the beginning of each chapter that describe the key topics to be discussed.

**Checkpoints:** Periodic places in the text where we ask you to pause to reconsider if you have understood the meaning of key terms or concepts previously covered, or to work on a special case or example.

**Summary:** A review at the end of each chapter that briefly outlines the key theories and concepts introduced in the reading.

**The Manager's Vocabulary:** A listing at the end of each chapter of key terms and their definitions, as well as important names.

Once again, each of the above features is specially chosen to help you to learn more when reading this book. Please take full advantage of them. Planning Ahead will give you a feel for the most important learning outcomes in each chapter. This should be especially useful when you read a chapter for the first time. Checkpoints will keep you up to date on key terms and concepts as they are introduced. They are opportunities to analyze and test yourself, and thereby reinforce what you've learned.

The Summary and The Manager's Vocabulary are additional chances to review a chapter and to consider whether you have covered it sufficiently. These features should be of special help when you study for exams.

## A Final Comment

*Managing Organizational Behavior* is more than a textbook. It is a learning instrument. It actively involves you in a learning process. You must think as you read. Think about yourself, the experiences you have had, and your aspirations. Think about other people, such as co-workers, classmates, and your instructor. Ask about their feelings and experiences to compare them with your own. Above all, read enthusiastically. These many special features provide "interactive" aspects which make this book different from other texts. For true interaction to occur, however, you must work as hard at using the book as we have in writing it. If you do this, we think you'll enjoy the learning every bit as much as we did the writing!

# MANAGING ORGANIZATIONAL BEHAVIOR

# PART ONE

## INTRODUCTION

### THE MANAGER'S GOAL

**To Accept Responsibility for Managing the Work Activities of Other Persons.**

### YOUR LEARNING OBJECTIVE

**To Develop an Appreciation for Work and for the Organization as a Work Setting.**

## Chapters in this Part of the Book

A **manager** is a person in an organization who is responsible for the performance of one or more subordinates. Being a manager is a special type of challenge. People are key resources of organizations, and managers must ensure that these human resources are well utilized. Simply put, a manager's job is to get things done through people.

**Organizational behavior** is the study of individuals and groups in organizations. This body of knowledge is important to all practicing managers. Good managers plan ahead to foresee human resource problems and opportunities and, to direct individual and group behavior to foster the most productive results. They use a knowledge of organizational behavior to understand work situations, and then to predict and control their consequences.

This book is designed to familiarize you with organizational behavior as a knowledge base, and to introduce you to this understanding-prediction-control discipline. What follows is a case written in a prediction format. It is presented in a series of segments that end with prediction questions asking you to think about what you expect to find in the next segment. The case involves a college professor and his relationships with a university. Read the case and answer the questions we ask. Compare your responses to our viewpoints on the case. This is a chance to explore your awareness of the key elements of organizational behavior.

# The Case of the Missing Raise[1]

It was late February, and John Lloyd had just completed an important long distance telephone conversation with Professor Fred Massie, Head of the Department of Management at Central University. During the conversation John accepted an offer to move from his present position at Private University, located in the East, to Central in the Midwest as an Assistant Professor. John and his wife Marsha then shared the following thoughts.

**John:** "Well, it's final."

**Marsha:** "Oh, hon, it's been a difficult decision, but I know it will work out for the best."

**John:** "Yes, however, we are leaving many things we like here."

**Marsha:** "I know, but remember, Professor Massie is someone you respect a great deal and he is offering you a challenge to come and introduce new courses at Central. Besides, he will surely be a pleasure to work for."

**John:** "Marsha we're young, eager and a little adventurous. There's no reason we shouldn't go."

**Marsha:** "We're going dear."

*Early Fall* John Lloyd began the fall semester eagerly. The points discussed in his earlier conversations with Fred were now real challenges, and John was teaching new undergraduate and graduate courses in Central's curriculum. Overall, the transition to Central had been pleasant. The nine faculty members were warm in welcoming him, and John felt it would be good working with them. John also felt comfortable with the performance standards that appeared to exist in the department. Although it was certainly not a "publish or perish" situation, Fred had indicated to John during the recruiting process that research and publications would be given increasing weight along with teaching and service in future departmental decisions. This was consistent with John's personal belief that a professor should live up to each of these responsibilities. Although there was some conflict in evidence among the faculty over what weighting and standards should apply to these performance areas, John sensed some consensus that the multiple responsibilities should be respected.

## QUESTIONS

1. Fred Massie is the "manager" so far in the case. What type of a "boss" do you feel he will be for John? What type of a relationship will they have?
2. What level of work performance do you predict for John? Why?

   high    medium    low

### Our Viewpoint

Organizational behavior recognizes the importance of the joining-up process, that is, the events that result in the individual entering the organization as a place of employment. In this case, John and his wife each felt they were giving up some positive things in the move to Central, but they also anticipated certain benefits. Although John and Marsha seem to have adapted well, we might wonder if the trade-offs between the losses and gains may affect John's behavior in the new job.

***Continuing On*** It was April, and spring vacation time. John was sitting at home reflecting upon his experiences to date at Central. He was pleased. Both he and Marsha had adjusted very well to Midwestern life. Although there were things they both missed from their prior location, she was teaching in a very pleasant school and they found the rural environment of Central very satisfying. John had also received positive student feedback on his fall semester courses, had presented two papers at a recent professional meeting, and had just been informed that two of his papers would be published by a journal. This was a good record and John felt satisfied. He had been working hard and it was paying off.

*May* The spring semester had ended and John was preoccupied. It was time, he thought, for an end-of-the-year performance review by Fred Massie. This anticipation had been stimulated, in part, by a recent meeting of the College faculty in which the Dean indicated that a 7% pay raise pool was now available for the coming year. He was encouraging department chairpersons to distribute this money differentially based on performance merit. John had listened closely to the Dean and liked what he heard. He felt this meant that Central was really trying to establish a performance-oriented reward system. Such a system was consistent with John's personal philosophy and, indeed, he taught such reasoning in his courses.

Throughout May, John kept expecting to have a conversation with Fred Massie on the above topics. One day, the following memo appeared in his faculty mailbox.

MEMORANDUM

TO: Fellow Faculty
FROM: Fred
RE: Raises for Next Year

The Dean has been most open about the finances of the College as evidenced by his detail and candor regarding the budget at the last faculty meeting. Consistent with that philosophy I want to provide a perspective on raises and clarify a point or two.

The actual dollars available to our department exclusive of the chairman total 7.03%. In allocating those funds I have attempted to reward people on the basis of their contribution to the life of the Department and the University, as well as professional growth and development. In addition, it was essential this year to adjust a couple of inequities which had developed over a period of time. The distribution of increments was the following:

| | | | |
|---|---|---|---|
| 5% or less | 3 | 7+%–9% | 3 |
| 5+%–7% | 2 | More than 9% | 2 |

## QUESTIONS

Think about Fred's memo:

1. What effect will it have on the faculty?
2. What effect will it have on John?
3. What does it tell you about Fred's "style" as a manager?

*Continuing On* John read the memo with mixed emotions. Initially, he was upset that Fred had obviously made the pay raise decisions without having spoken first with John about his performance. Still, John felt good because he was sure to be one of those receiving a 9+% increase. "Now," he mused to himself, "it will be good to sit down with Fred and discuss not only this past year's efforts, but my plans for next year as well."

John was disappointed when Fred did not contact him for such a discussion. Furthermore, John found himself frequently involved in informal conversations with other faculty members who were speculating over who received the various pay increments.

*June* One day Carla Block, a faculty colleague, came into John's office and said she had asked Fred about her raise. She received a 7+% increase, and also learned that the two 9+% increases had been given to senior faculty members. John was incredulous. "It can't be," he thought, "I was a top performer this past year. My teaching and publications records are strong, and I feel I've been a positive force in the department." John felt Carla could be mistaken and waited to talk the matter out with Fred.

A few days later another colleague reported to John the results of a similar conversation with Fred. This time John exploded internally. He felt he deserved just reward.

The next day John received a computerized notice on his pay increment from the Accounting Office. His raise was 7.2%. That night, after airing his feelings with Marsha, John telephoned Fred at home and arranged to meet with him the next day.

## QUESTIONS

1. What do you expect to happen at this meeting between Fred and John?
2. How would you begin the meeting if you were Fred?
3. What is your prediction about John's reaction to the meeting? Why?

   positive      negative      mixed

*Continuing On* Fred Massie knocked on the door to John's office and entered. The greetings were cordial. John began the conversation. "Fred, we've always been frank with one another and now I'm concerned about my raise," he said. "I thought I had a good year, but I understand that I've received just an average raise." Fred Massie was a person who talked openly, and John could trust him. He responded to John in this way.

> Yes, John, you are a top performer. I feel you have made great contributions to the Depart-

> ment. The two 9+% raises went to correct "inequities" that had built up over a period of time for two senior people. I felt that since the money was available this year that I had a responsibility to make the adjustments. If we don't consider them, you received one of the three top raises, and I consider any percentage differences between these three very superficial. I suppose I could have been more discriminating at the lower end of the distribution, but I can't give zero increments. I know you had a good year. It's what I expected when I hired you. You haven't let me down. From your perspective I know you feel you earned an "A," and I agree. I gave you a "B+". I hope you understand why.

John sympathized with Fred's logic and felt good having spoken with him. Although he wasn't happy, he understood Fred's position. His final comment to Fred was this. "You know, it's not the absolute dollar value of the raise that hurts. It's the sense of letdown. Recently, for example, I turned down an extensive consulting job that would have paid far more than the missing raise. I did so because I felt it would require too many days away from the office. I'm not sure my colleagues would make that choice."

## QUESTIONS

1. What do you now predict in terms of John's behavior?
2. What do you predict for other faculty in the department?
3. Think ahead to the coming academic year. Will John be a higher performer? Why or why not?

***Continuing On*** In the course of a casual summer conversation, Carla mentioned to John that she heard two of the faculty who had received 4+% raises had complained to Fred and the Dean. After lodging the complaints they had received additional salary increments. "Oh great," John responded to himself, "I thought I had put this thing to rest." He knew that this information would bother him and rekindle some of the irritation he had felt earlier.

About three weeks later, John, Fred, Carla, and another colleague were in a meeting with the Dean. Although the meeting was on a separate matter, something was said which implied that Carla had also received an additional pay increment. John confronted the Dean and learned that this was the case. Carla had protested to Fred and the Dean, and they raised her pay on the justification that an historical salary inequity had been overlooked. Fred was visibly uncomfortable as a discussion ensued on how salary increments should be awarded and what had transpired in the department in this respect.

Fred eventually excused himself to attend another meeting. John and the others continued to discuss the matter with the Dean and the conversation became increasingly heated. Finally, they each rose to terminate the meeting and John felt compelled to say one more thing. "It's not that I'm not making enough money," he said to the Dean, "but I just don't feel I received my fair share, especially in terms of your own stated policy of rewarding faculty on the basis of performance merit."

With that remark, John left the meeting. As he walked down the hall to his office, he said to himself, "Next year there will be no turning down consulting jobs because of a misguided sense of departmental responsibility."

## Our Viewpoint

Now the Dean is in the act too. Disgruntled faculty are complaining to the Department Head and then taking the issue up with his boss, the Dean. And then, there's John. He's back to his consulting agenda again. We hear him say that he can spend any extra time in one of two ways: (1) for the university or (2) in private consulting. We also hear him say that his choice is to consult. He seems to feel that the payoffs for doing "extra duty" for the university just aren't there. As a result, he is opting to reduce his university-oriented work efforts in the future.

The Dean in the case will evaluate Fred on how well the Department of Management performs. Fred's challenge is to meet his responsibility by creating a work environment within which faculty members, as human resources, want to and are able to achieve high performance. Obviously, Fred is currently feeling the full weight of this managerial challenge. He should feel threatened if John and others really do reduce their work efforts.

If Fred had been more sensitive to the developing case dynamics and more capable of analyzing them in a systematic fashion, he might have predicted the resulting feelings and behaviors of his faculty. Once predicted, appropriate action could have been taken to facilitate desirable work outcomes and minimize undesirable ones.

## MANAGING ORGANIZATIONAL BEHAVIOR

Organizational behavior (let's call it *OB* from now on), is a body of knowledge that addresses many of the issues in "The Case of the Missing Raise." Simply put,

OB is a knowledge base —used by→ managers —to accomplish→ good human resource utilization

Most managers face dilemmas similar to Fred's. What Fred lacked, and what all managers need, is a systematic means of analyzing work situations. Learning about OB can help you develop this capability. Remember:

1. OB provides managers with a way of systematically thinking about the behavior of people at work.
2. OB provides managers with a vocabulary of terms and concepts that allow work experiences to be clearly analyzed, shared, and discussed.
3. OB provides managers with techniques for dealing with the problems that commonly occur in work settings.[2]

### NOTES

[1] "The Missing Raise," ICCH #9-477-752; prepared by Dr. John R. Schermerhorn, Jr. as a basis for class discussion rather than to illustrate either effective or ineffective handling of an administrative situation.

[2] Developed from Larry L. Cummings, "Towards Organizational Behavior," *Academy of Management Review*, Vol. 3 (January 1978), pp. 90–98.

# 1

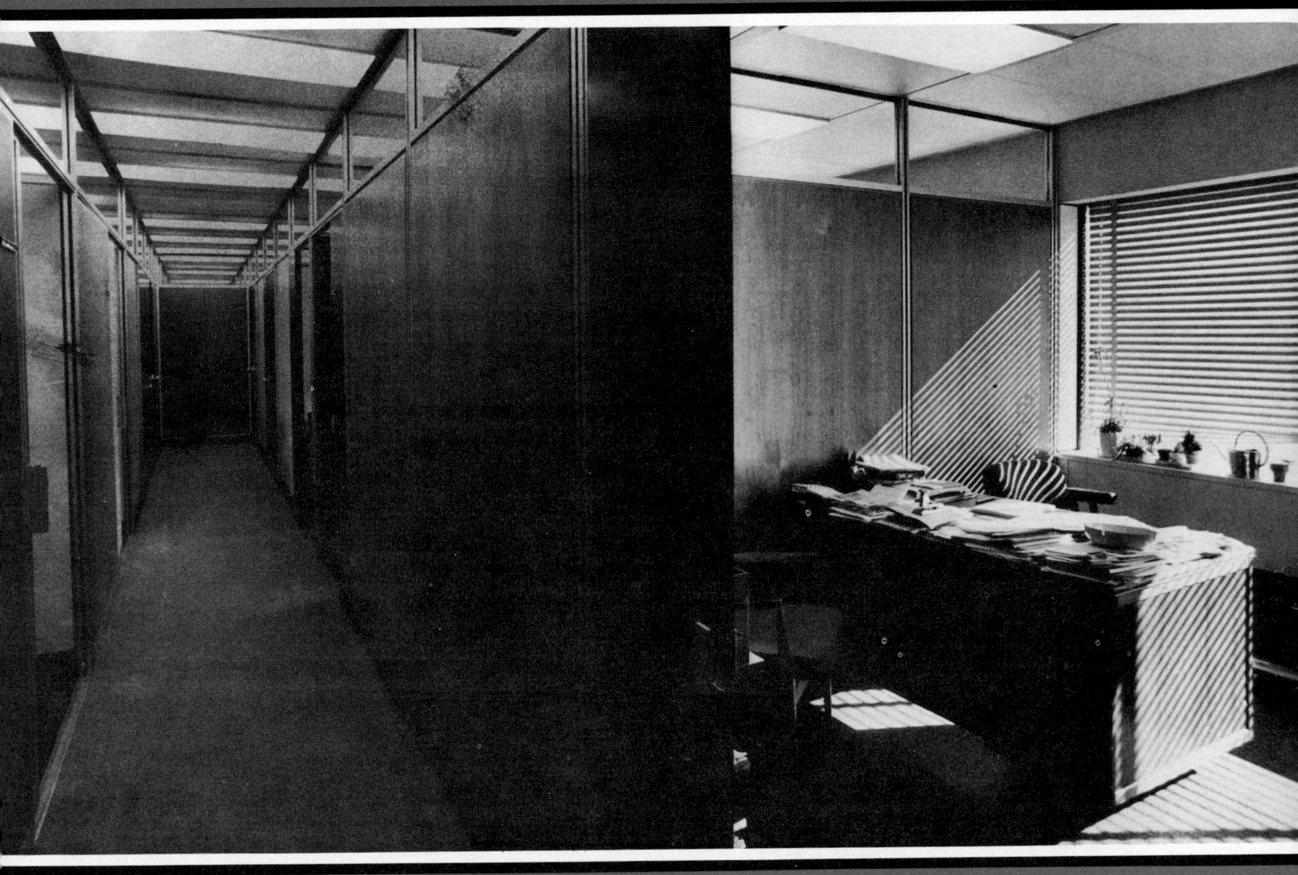

# ORGANIZATIONAL BEHAVIOR AND THE MANAGER

# BOSSES LIST MAIN STRENGTHS, FLAWS DETERMINING POTENTIAL OF MANAGERS

A recent *Wall Street Journal*/Gallup survey of 782 chief executives from the nation's largest corporations reports the following strengths and weaknesses of practicing managers.[1]

### HIGH ACHIEVERS

**Some Traits Chief Executives Cite As Most Important for Advancement**

| | Large Firms | Medium Firms | Small Firms |
|---|---|---|---|
| Integrity | 36% | 27% | 24% |
| Ability to get along with others | 32 | 36 | 34 |
| Industriousness | 25 | 23 | 24 |
| Intelligence | 25 | 14 | 10 |
| Business knowledge | 23 | 25 | 24 |
| Leadership | 15 | 12 | 10 |
| Education | 5 | 7 | 1 |

### WEAK MANAGERS

**Some Traits Chief Executives Cite As Failings of Subordinates**

| | Large Firms | Medium Firms | Small Firms |
|---|---|---|---|
| Limited point of view | 23% | 24% | 9% |
| Inability to understand others | 21 | 14 | 11 |
| Inability to work with others | 18 | 14 | 14 |
| Indecisiveness | 16 | 12 | 10 |
| Lack of initiative | 9 | 9 | 10 |
| Failure to take responsibility | 7 | 6 | 6 |
| Lack of integrity | 3 | 5 | 4 |

### MANAGEMENT APPLICATIONS QUESTION

Think about what it means to be a manager. What special challenges do managers face? How can a knowledge of organizational behavior help you to be successful in mastering these challenges in your future career as a manager?

## PLANNING AHEAD

**After reading this chapter and participating in the recommended learning experiences, you will be thoroughly familiar with the following topics.**

**Organizations**
**Managers in Organizations**
**What Managers Do**
**Scientific Thinking and the Manager**
**Learning About OB**
**The Manager's Challenge, OB, and this Book**

Good managers are problem solvers. They continually analyze work situations to locate problems to be solved, develop solutions to these problems, and implement the solutions.[2] We have seen the importance of this three-step process in the Case of the Missing Raise discussed in the Part One introduction. If Fred Massie had noticed sooner that potential problems existed in his department, he could have acted to solve the problems and avoid the undesirable events that occurred.

Good problem solvers know what to look for in work situations and how to understand what they find. This, for example, is a process for which physicians are carefully trained. During a physical exam the doctor systematically asks questions and is quick to note where one condition (such as a recurrent sore on a finger) may be symptomatic of a problem that requires further medical attention (e.g., treatment for a small skin cancer). Further diagnostic work and possible medical treatments follow.

Managers need similar diagnostic and action abilities. Instead of such things as sores and headaches, the manager's problem indicators include absenteeism, turnover, tardiness, negative attitudes, poor quality work, and declining work quantity on the part of employees. These problem symptoms are among the many issues encompassed in the study of organizational behavior. Just as every qualified physician has been schooled in the medical sciences, so too should the practicing manager be schooled in OB.

This book is written to acquaint you with OB as a knowledge base and to help develop your problem-solving capability as a manager. **Our specific goal is to help you learn how to utilize individuals and groups as the human resources of organizations.** This first chapter formally introduces the concepts of "organization" and "manager," discusses managerial work, and shows how the many topics covered throughout the book combine into a meaningful study of organizational behavior and the manager.

## ORGANIZATIONS

An **organization** is a collection of people working together in a division of labor to achieve a common purpose. This definition fits a wide variety of fraternal groups, clubs, voluntary organizations, and religious bodies, as well as entities such as businesses and government agencies. We are most interested in the organizations people belong to as employees. These are called work organizations.

### Why Do Organizations Exist?

Organizations exist because individuals are limited in their physical and mental capabilities. This logic is as old as the Bible, as the following example shows.

#### Moses and Jethro[3]

Some time after leading his people out of Egypt, Moses camped at the base of the Mountain of God. His days were consumed by making the many decisions required to maintain the tribe. Moses took care that the flock had proper food and clothing. He listened to their concerns, settled their disputes, and responded to all of those who came before him inquiring about God. Moses was a manager and his responsibilities were enormous.

Moses was fortunate to be joined in this camp by his father-in-law, Jethro. After observing Moses' daily routine, the wise counsel Jethro commented, "Thou wilt surely wear away, both thou and this people that is with thee; for this thing is too heavy for thee; thou are not able to perform it thyself alone."

Jethro went on to give Moses the following advice. He counseled Moses to select other persons to assist him in these many managerial chores. He further suggested that these people be given the responsibility to rule over groups of thousands, hundreds, fifties, and tens. Finally, he encouraged Moses to let them judge the small matters for the people under their control and to only bring the large matters to him.

Jethro, in effect, gave Moses a way to organize his people. Moses' "organization" involved the appointment of certain people as managers, and the grouping of the other members of the tribe under these managers. The result found Moses in a new position of responsibility, as shown in Figure 1.1.

Experiences similar to Moses' occur over and over again as organizations emerge in many different settings. In most cases the situation lacks the benefit of consultation such as that provided by

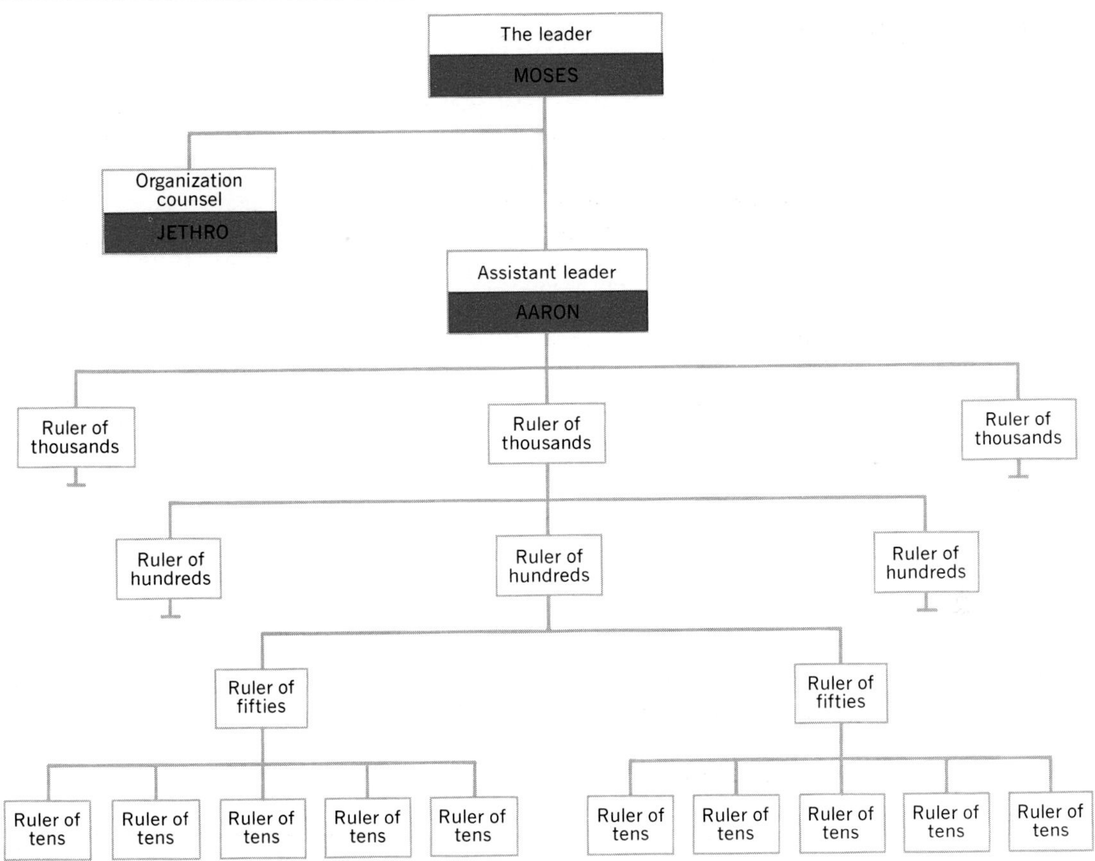


**FIGURE 1.1** Moses' organization. (Source: *New Ways of Managing Conflict* by Jane Likert and Rensis Likert. Copyright © 1966. Used with permission of McGraw-Hill Book Company.)

Jethro. Inevitably, though, organizations develop to accomplish work tasks that are beyond individual capabilities.

## Organizations as Open Systems

One way to analyze organizations is to view them as open systems as well as social systems. Because organizations involve people and ultimately depend upon the efforts of people to perform, we call them social systems. Although people are the human resources of organizations, organizations are more than people. They also include the machinery, equipment, raw materials, facilities, and money that allow people to produce some good or service. These are the physical resources of organizations.

As **open systems,** organizations transform human and physical resources received as inputs from their environments into goods and services that are then returned to the environment for consumption. The goods or services are the final products of a resource transformation process. Their production is made possible by the direct interaction of the organization with its environment.

Take, for example, a company producing electronic parts for computers. Figure 1.2 views this organization as an open system. People are human resource inputs which become part of a transformation process. They work with and combine various physical resource inputs to create a finished product. Both the physical and human resources are obtained from the external environment. Together, these resources are transformed by the organization into computer parts which are consumed by members of the environment. In this business example, the price paid by the consumers for the computer parts becomes an important monetary resource input to the organization. The company's ability to sell components today is what enables it to produce more components tomorrow.

It is often useful to view organizations and their subcomponents as open systems which transform resource inputs into product outputs.

## Ingredients of Organizations

Thus, organizations are working combinations of physical and human resources. Beyond that, they involve a purpose, division of labor,

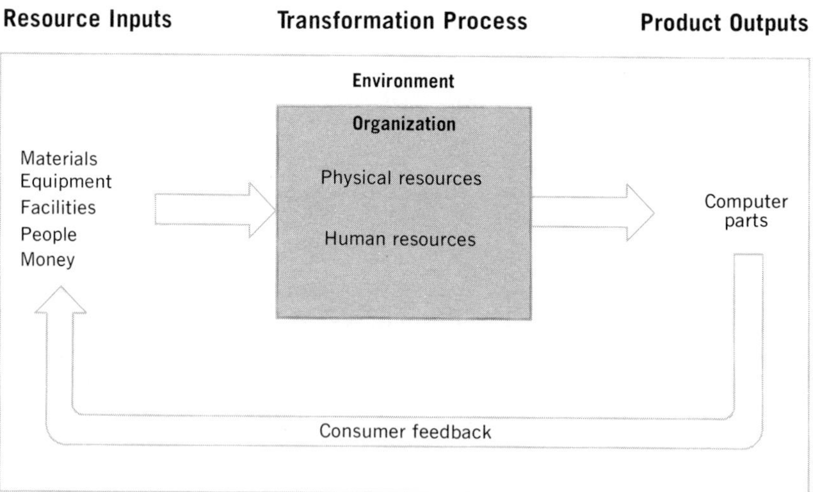


**FIGURE 1.2** A manufacturing company as an open system.

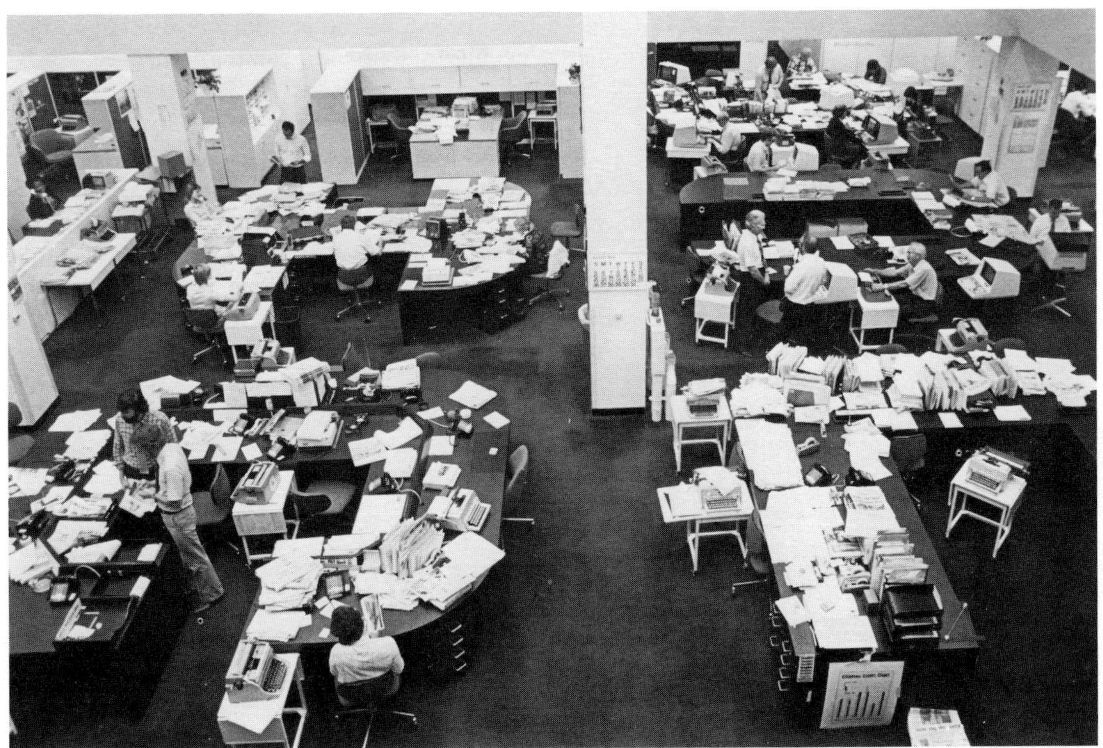

Inside an organization.

and hierarchy of authority. We briefly introduce each of these ingredients below. They are discussed in greater detail later, in Part Four of the book.

## Purpose

The **purpose of an organization** is to produce a good or service. Businesses, for example, produce consumer goods and services such as automobiles, appliances, recreational opportunities, gourmet dining, and accommodations. Nonprofit organizations produce services with public benefits, such as health care, education, judicial processing, and highway maintenance.

## Division of Labor

The essence of any organization is human effort. The process of breaking work into small components that serve the organization's purpose and to be done by individuals or groups is called the **division**

**of labor.** It is through the division of labor that organizations mobilize the work of many people to achieve a common purpose.

## Hierarchy of Authority

**Authority** is the right to command other persons. Managers have authority over their subordinates. When organizations divide labor into small components, something must be done to coordinate the resulting efforts to ensure that they combine and accomplish the organization's purpose. A **hierarchy of authority,** wherein work positions are arranged in order of increasing authority, facilitates this coordination. Persons of higher authority are able to make decisions that result in the proper coordination and direction of work activities at lower levels.

## Synergy in Organizations

The division of labor results in **means-end chains** which link the work efforts of individuals and groups to an organization's purpose. Let's begin by thinking of the organization's purpose as the end sought by top management. Using a division of labor, those executives immediately under the chief executive each have a set of goals. These become the means for accomplishing the end represented by the chief executive's view of the organization's purpose. The division of labor is then followed on down through the organization so that the goals at each level become the means for accomplishing ends at the next higher level. Thus, the means-end chain links the organization's purpose with the contributions of individuals and groups at various organizational levels.

Looked at another way, we can figuratively show a means-end chain as

Individual efforts $\xrightarrow[\text{to}]{\text{contribute}}$ group efforts $\xrightarrow[\text{to}]{\text{contribute}}$ the organization's purpose

There is something more, however, to the organization as a collection of means-ends chains. **Synergy** is the creation of a whole that is greater than the sum of its parts. You might think of it as the potential to make 2 + 2 equal something greater than 4. Synergy in organizations occurs when people work well together to pursue a common purpose through a division of labor and hierarchy of authority. It is facilitated by effective managerial behavior. Synergy occurs when

Organizational accomplishments $\xrightarrow{\text{are more than}}$ group accomplishments $\xrightarrow{\text{are more than}}$ individual accomplishments

## MANAGERS IN ORGANIZATIONS

Now that we share an understanding of organizations and their key ingredients, it is possible to speak more precisely about what it means to be a manager. Earlier, we identified a **manager** as a person in a organization who is responsible for the performance of one or more subordinates. Managers are identified by various job titles: Supervisors, principals, deans, general managers, presidents, and group leaders are a few examples. All managers, regardless of their titles, require a knowledge of organizational behavior to perform successfully. This includes an initial understanding of the manager's work setting and the basic challenge it represents.

### The Manager's Work Setting

The manager is in charge of a work unit. A **work unit** is a task-oriented group in an organization that includes the manager and his or her immediate subordinates. Examples include departments in a university, divisions of a corporation, branches of a bank, and wards in a hospital. Even the college classroom can be considered a work unit, with the instructor as its manager.

A manager's immediate concerns are work unit **task performance,** the quality and quantity of work produced, and **human resources maintenance,** the attraction and continuation of a viable work force. This latter notion focuses a manager's attention on such things as individual job satisfaction, job involvement, grievances, absenteeism, and turnover, as well as work performance. Without proper maintenance of the people who do the work, no work unit or organization will be able to perform at consistently high levels over time. *Newsline 1.1* on "job burnout" exemplifies the importance of human resource maintenance in work settings.

## NEWSLINE 1.1

### Job Burnout

Jack T. works long hours, but his department's productivity is low. Everybody else, he says, is to blame. Jack dropped out of college at the age of 20 because of financial problems. When he first started work as a salesman, he worked harder to get ahead than his college-educated peers. He was spotted as bright and aggressive. He kept getting promotions until he became a regional sales manager. He earns a salary that permits him to pay for a suburban home, membership in a country club that his wife uses for tennis and bridge, and college for his two children.

But he's blocked in his job, and he knows it. The national sales manager, whom Jack once stood a chance of succeeding, won't retire. So far as he's concerned, Jack's peers, the other regional sales managers, some of them younger and more aggressive, are getting the pick of new salesmen hired by the company. Jack looks upon his own staff as the culls. He knows that it's only a matter of time before the "baby boom brighties" in his company are going to force him out. He has high blood pressure.

Jack is a victim of "job burnout," a newly recognized syndrome that is thought to be costing employers a large if unmeasured amount of time and effort, and thus productivity. Sufferers generally show symptoms of chronic fatigue, low energy, irritability, and a negative attitude toward themselves and their jobs. Burnout is a specific set of symptoms brought on by severe or chronic stress directly related to the job rather than to personal difficulties, such as divorce, death of a spouse, money problems, or aging. Burnout more often affects employees who deal extensively with other people on the job.

Christina Maslach, Associate Professor of Psychology at the University of California at Berkeley, says burnout has three phases. In the first, she says, "There is emotional exhaustion, a feeling of being drained, used up, of having nothing more to give. Secondly, there is a cynicism, a callous, insensitive regard for people, a 'don't-knock-yourself-out-anymore-for-others' attitude." Finally, the burnout person comes to believe that he or she has been unsuccessful and all job effort has been fruitless.

Source: Adapted from Jerry E. Bishop, "The Personal and Business Costs of 'Job Burnout'," *The Wall Street Journal* (November 11, 1980), p. 31.


Task performance and human resource maintenance are the key work unit results sought by a manager. This book addresses these results as they relate to individual, group, and organization-level outcomes. Figure 1.3 summarizes these three levels of concern for the manager.

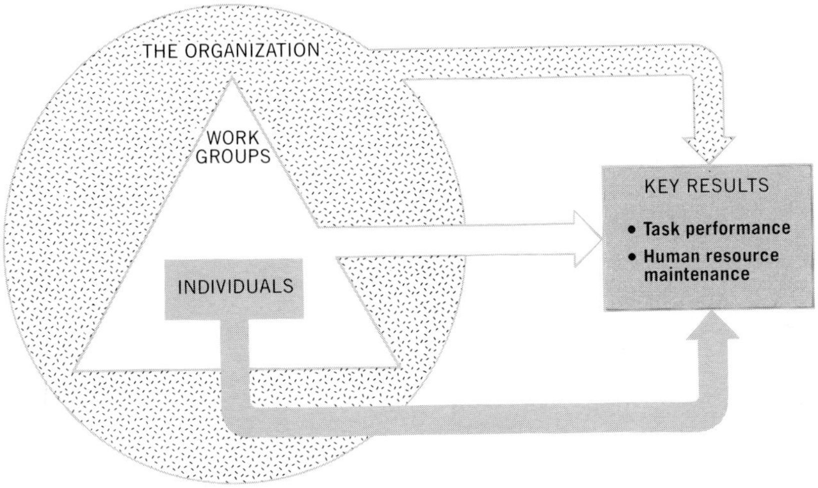

FIGURE 1.3 Key results in the manager's work setting.

## The Manager's Challenge

Most managers are simultaneously subordinates and superiors. Think about this statement and what it can mean. As subordinates, managers are held accountable by their superiors (or "bosses") for the performance and maintenance of their work units. Herein lies the **manager's challenge: At the same time that they are held accountable by their superiors for work unit results, managers are dependent upon the efforts of their subordinates to make these results possible.**

This last sentence says a great deal. Assume you are the production manager of a department making components for an electronic computer. Look at the diagram in Figure 1.4. This diagram depicts your manager's challenge. At the same time that you are held accountable by the plant superintendent for the production of electronic computer components, you depend upon the contributions of 25 subordinate employees to make this performance possible. You are responsible for work that is in large part produced by someone else! This reality is most evident on those days when the unit fails to meet its production quota. When this happens, the superintendent doesn't ask the employees what went wrong; he or she goes directly to you and asks the questions! You can't say, in return, "but my subordinates are the ones who didn't do the work." It is the manager's job to ensure that work unit performance and human resource maintenance are accomplished.

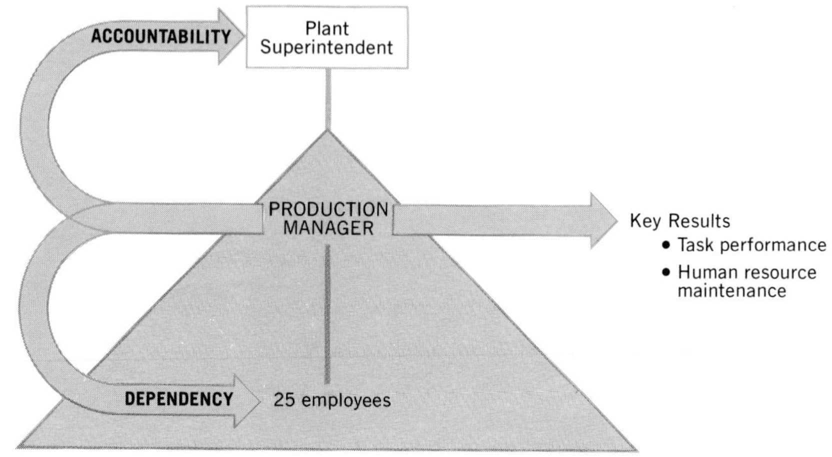


**FIGURE 1.4** A production manager's challenge in an electronics firm.

# WHAT MANAGERS DO

**Organizational behavior,** as stated earlier, is the study of individuals and groups in organizations. This book shows how and where a knowledge of OB can help you to master the manager's challenge as shown in Figure 1.4. Before moving further into the substance of the book, it will be helpful for you to reflect a bit on the nature of managerial work. The following discussion overviews some important managerial skills, the functions of management, and the interpersonal relationships of managers.

## Managerial Skills

A knowledge of OB can help to develop your problem-solving capabilities. It can help you to learn what to look for at work and how to correctly interpret what you see. Beyond this, however, you must have the skills to turn this acquired understanding into effective action.

A **skill** is the ability to translate knowledge into action that results in the desired performance.[4] This is the real bottom line for every practicing manager. Table 1.1 outlines some of the skills that educators feel should be taught to future managers. These skills are well covered in the chapters to follow.

**Table 1.1 Some "Teachable" Managerial Skills**

*Interpersonal relations*—Ability to enter into and maintain effective peer relationships with other persons in the work setting.
*Leadership*—Ability to deal with subordinates, to motivate and train, to help, to deal with authority and dependency problems.
*Conflict-resolution*—Ability to mediate between conflicting parties, to resolve disturbances and to negotiate differences with others.
*Information-processing*—Ability to collect information, to organize information for decision-making purposes, to disseminate information.
*Decision-making*—Ability to know when a decision is needed, diagnose a situation, plan an approach, search for solutions, evaluate potential consequences, and select an alternative.
*Resource-allocation*—Ability to distribute physical, financial, human, and personal resources among competing demands.
*Entrepreneurism*—Ability to recognize problems, implement solutions, and take advantage of opportunities for constructive change.
*Introspection*—Ability to understand one's job and staff, and to learn through self-study and awareness.

Source: Developed from discussions by Henry Mintzberg, *The Nature of Managerial Work* (New York: Harper & Row, 1973), pp. 188–193; and Robert L. Katz, "Skills of an Effective Administrator," *Harvard Business Review* (September-December 1974), pp. 90–102.

## The Managerial Functions

Theorists have traditionally identified five managerial functions: Planning, organizing, staffing, directing and controlling.[5] Table 1.2 defines each function and also gives an example of the responsibility each holds for the practicing manager.

Planning: A basic management function.

**Table 1.2 The Five Functions of Management**

| Function | Managerial Example |
|---|---|
| *Planning*—Selecting future goals and directions, and identifying ways to achieve them. | A college dean predicts declining enrollments for full-time students and suggests that the faculty give increased attention to adult education programs. |
| *Organizing*—Arranging the productive contributions of human and physical resources. | A special division for adult education is established, with a full-time coordinator. This person is given an office, staff allocation, and substantial budget. |
| *Staffing*—Finding, selecting, hiring, and maintaining human resource inputs. | The coordinator advertises for secretarial and teaching help. Interviews are held, references checked, and job offers made. |
| *Directing*—Guiding and supervising the work efforts of the persons. | Staff members are engaged in a variety of activities designed to prepare and implement evening courses for local adults. Special attention is given to meeting time deadlines. |
| *Controlling*—Monitoring performance and taking corrective action. | The coordinator monitors progress by carefully evaluating the new courses and discussing possible modifications with the teaching faculty. |

The study of OB contains practical implications for each of the managerial functions. Supplementary Module A at the end of this book traces the origins of these functions and the history of OB. Primarily, however, this book concentrates its attention on managerial responsibilities in the organizing, staffing, and directing areas. Other courses, such as personnel management, principles of management, and organization theory can round out your in-depth study of all five functions. A capstone course in administrative or business policy can be especially useful in integrating all of these areas of study.

## Interpersonal Relationships of Managers

Managers apply their skills and fulfill their functional responsibilities while maintaining a complex set of relationships with other persons. These interpersonal relationships, depicted in Figure 1.5, include contacts with subordinates, peers elsewhere in the organization, and the boss. They may also include contacts with outsiders such as clients and resource suppliers.

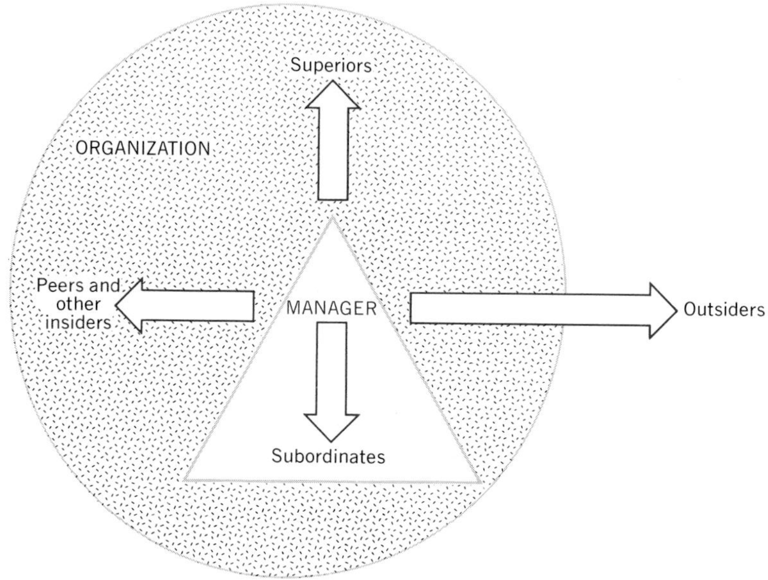


**FIGURE 1.5** Interpersonal relationships of managers.

Checkpoint

How would you estimate a typical manager would allocate time to these various relationships as shown in Figure 1.5?

_____% with subordinates
_____% with boss
_____% with peers and outsiders
100% = total time in contacts

You probably allocated most of a manager's time to contacts with subordinates. After all, they are the human resources upon whom the manager is most dependent for work unit performance. Actually, managers have been found to spend one-third to one-half (48%) of their time with subordinates, 7% of their time with their bosses, and one-third to one-half (44%) of their time with peers and outsiders.[6]

In the final analysis, managers are busy people whose work is never really done. This reality is evident in the accompanying *What Managers Do 1.1*. Even though these interpersonal relationships are time-consuming to maintain, they enable managers to gain and transfer the information needed to make good decisions while fulfilling their many responsibilities. OB is very concerned with interpersonal relationships and their managerial implications.

## WHAT MANAGERS DO 1.1

### The Chief Executive's Work

A study of chief executives found no break in the pace of activity during office hours. The mail (average of 36 pieces per day), telephone calls (average of 5 per day), and meetings (average of 8) accounted for almost every minute from the moment these people entered their offices in the morning until they departed in the evening. A true break seldom occurred. Coffee was taken during meetings, and lunchtime was almost always devoted to formal or informal meetings. When free time appeared, ever-present subordinates quickly usurped it. If these managers wished to have a change of pace, they had two means at their disposal—the observational tour and the light discussions that generally preceded scheduled meetings. But these were not regularly scheduled breaks and they were seldom totally unrelated to the issue at hand—managing the organization. The quantity of work to be done, or that the manager chooses to do, during the day is substantial and the pace is unrelenting.

Why do managers adopt this pace and workload? One major reason is the inherently open-ended nature of the job. The manager is responsible for the success of the organization, and there are really no tangible mileposts where one can stop and say, "Now my job is finished." The engineer finishes the design of a casting on a certain day, the lawyer wins or loses a case at some moment in time. The manager must always keep going, never sure when he or she has succeeded, never sure when the whole organization may come down because of some miscalculation. As a result, the manager is never free to forget the job, and never has the pleasure of knowing, even temporarily, that there is nothing else to do. Managers always carry the nagging suspicion that just a little bit more might be contributed. Hence, they assume an unrelenting pace in their work.

Source: Abridged and adapted from Henry Mintzberg, *The Nature of Managerial Work* (New York: Harper & Row, 1973), pp. 30, 39, 72. 

## SCIENTIFIC THINKING AND THE MANAGER

Given the complexity of their jobs, managers frequently look for ways of simplifying and doing them better. Advice comes from many sources and includes written materials available in bookstores and libraries, as well as verbal admonitions from friends and recognized "experts." It may also include newspaper articles such as the one excerpted at the beginning of this chapter. The informed manager will be discriminating and selective in taking such advice and in implementing it in actual practice. Consider, for example, the following case.

## Better Management, Inc.

Joan Brady, a representative of Better Management, Inc. was telling Don Black, the director of personnel for Osdo Corporation, about a new management training package her firm was offering. It was based, she said, on lengthy interviews with five outstanding company presidents whose combined work experience comprised more than 150 years.

The interviews had taken over a year to complete. They were analyzed to create a set of assessment materials which firms could use to determine the strengths and weaknesses of their managers. Better Management, Inc. was prepared to conduct the assessments and then to offer a training program capable of correcting any weaknesses so identified.

The assessment procedure begins by identifying the personal traits of a firm's managers. It then compares them to a profile of successful managers developed from interviews with the renowned chief executive officers. Don noticed that the traits were neatly listed and carefully defined. He was also impressed that each of his managers could be profiled for strengths and weaknesses. He worried, though, whether or not Better Management's assessment and training package really had all the answers.

Checkpoint

1. What do you think about the assessment ideas? Why?
2. Would you purchase these materials and the training program for Osdo? Why or why not?

As impressive as Joan's proposal may seem, the manager skilled in scientific thinking would scrutinize it very carefully. Table 1.3 evaluates Joan's proposal on a checklist of scientific thinking. The ideal profile is shaded, and you can readily see that the training program of Better Management, Inc. must be questioned for its lack of adequate scientific foundations. What follows is a brief comparison of scientific versus common-sense thinking.[7]

**Table 1.3 Checklist for Scientific Thinking**

| | Yes | No |
|---|---|---|
| 1. Systematic and controlled data collection? | ____ | X |
| 2. Systematic testing of alternative explanations? | ____ | X |
| 3. Metaphysical explanations avoided? | ____ | X |

▒ = Ideal response for scientific theory.

X = Evaluation for the Better Management, Inc. assessment and training package.

## Characteristics of Scientific Thinking

Start by considering the source of the data used by Better Management. It makes common sense that successful executives are in a good position to identify the traits of a successful manager. However, this source of data is anecdotal; that is, the executives are simply reminiscing and using recollections to identify the desirable managerial traits. Although this may appeal to our common sense, the sophisticated student of OB and the informed manager would insist on a more **systematic and controlled process of data collection.**

Second, scientific thinking is concerned with **systematically testing proposed explanations** and in systematically examining relationships among variables. This includes considering more than one possible explanation for a given question or event, and trying to locate the most feasible one and rule out the less feasible alternatives.

In our example none of these things was done. First, the only explanation given for managerial success was selected personal traits. Other variables with the potential to also affect success, such as the availability of resources, economic conditions, nature of the organization, and so on were completely neglected. Because of this, even if we find a relationship between the selected traits and managerial success, we can't be sure that there are not other factors with at least as good and perhaps better explanations for success.

Finally, scientific thinking is **unwilling to accept metaphysical explanations.** These are arguments that cannot be subjected to scientific proof. "It is God's will," is one example of metaphysical reasoning. In Better Management, Inc., attributing success to such traits as "charisma" or "gutsiness" are basically metaphysical arguments since these traits are hard to measure and test.

As a manager you will be better able to analyze work situations and evaluate the advice and suggestions of others if you develop your scientific thinking. This book presents many insights developed by scholars who apply scientific methods to the study of OB. Supplementary Module B at the end of the book acquaints you in more detail with their research methods. As you proceed with your studies and with the practice of management, give special attention to this need to discriminate scientific from common-sense thinking. When in doubt, use the checklist in Table 1.3 to test the rigor of your thoughts.

## LEARNING ABOUT OB

**Learning** is a change in one's behavior that occurs as a result of experience. Your learning about OB only begins with the pages of this book. It will continue in the future as you benefit from actual work experiences. The challenges of learning from both types of situations are substantial enough that we take time now to systematically consider them.

Experiential learning is a means of helping people to initially learn and then continue to learn about OB.[8] The learning sequence involves an initial experience and subsequent reflection. Theory-building follows to explain what took place, and this theory is tested through experimentation at the next opportunity.

This book is a formal opportunity for you to learn more about OB. It is also written to capitalize on the values of experiential learning. Your other course activities will complement the book to help you to take full advantage of the experiential learning cycle. Figure 1.6 shows how the various aspects of a typical OB course facilitate learning.

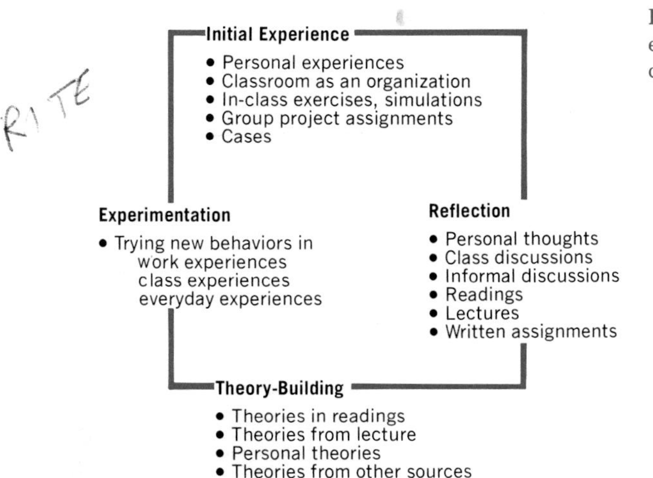


**FIGURE 1.6** Experiential learning in an OB course.

Figure 1.6 assigns to you a substantial responsibility for learning. Along with your instructor we can offer special cases and exercises to provide you with initial experience. We can even stimulate your reflection and theory-building by presenting theories and discussing their practical implications. Sooner or later, however, you must become an active participant in the learning process. You, and only you, can do the active experimentation required to complete the learning cycle.

## THE MANAGER'S CHALLENGE, OB, AND THIS BOOK

Chapter 2 continues our discussion of managers and organizations with a focus on people at work. Having concluded Chapter 1, you are now well prepared to address the more fundamental topics in the study of OB. As you proceed to Chapter 2, the final chapter in Part One, remember that

OB is a knowledge base —used by→ managers —to accomplish→ good human resource utilization

The remainder of the book is divided into the four additional parts summarized in Figure 1.7. Each part presents insights which can help you to become a successful manager.

Part Two focuses on understanding individuals in organizations. Chapter 3 reviews individual differences such as aptitudes, abilities, age, sex, and personalities. Chapter 4 introduces various motivation theories, while Chapters 5 and 6 acquaint you with how managers can use the theories to allocate rewards and design jobs to achieve high levels of task performance and human resource maintenance for their subordinates.

Part Three shifts attention to understanding the group as a human resource of organizations. Chapters 7, 8, and 9 discuss the dimensions of group behavior, explore the activities and sentiments of individuals engaged in group dynamics, and identify various means of managing groups to achieve the desired results of task performance and human resource maintenance.

Part Four focuses on understanding the organization as a total system. Chapter 10 presents the common features of organizations as work settings. They include the organization's environment, technology, and size. Chapter 11 reviews various designs for organiza-

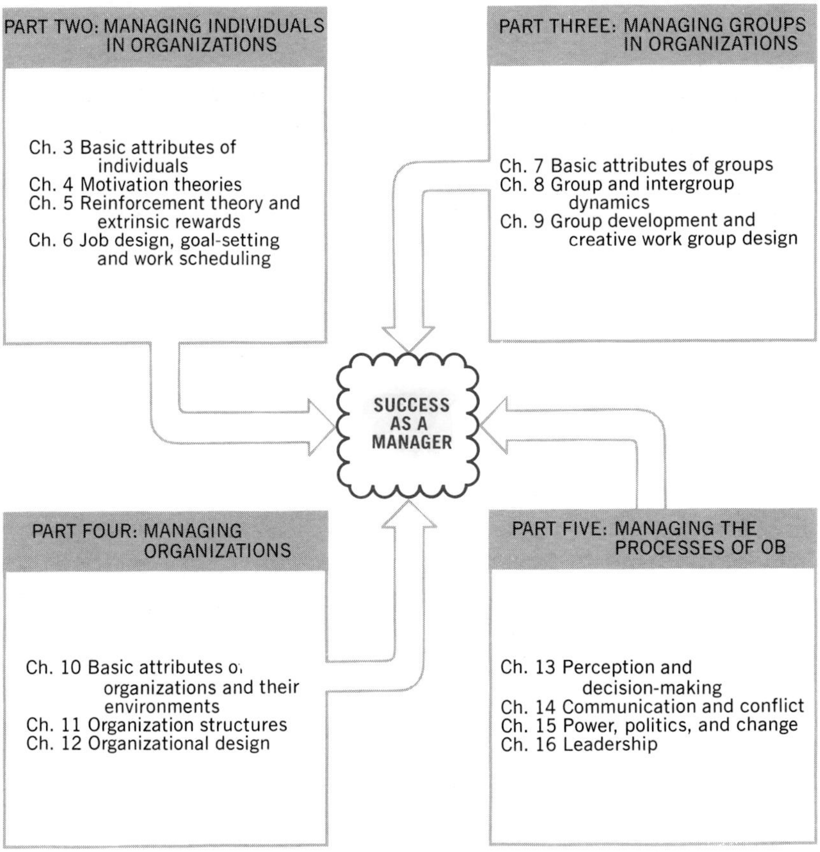

PART TWO: MANAGING INDIVIDUALS IN ORGANIZATIONS

Ch. 3 Basic attributes of individuals
Ch. 4 Motivation theories
Ch. 5 Reinforcement theory and extrinsic rewards
Ch. 6 Job design, goal-setting and work scheduling

PART THREE: MANAGING GROUPS IN ORGANIZATIONS

Ch. 7 Basic attributes of groups
Ch. 8 Group and intergroup dynamics
Ch. 9 Group development and creative work group design

SUCCESS AS A MANAGER

PART FOUR: MANAGING ORGANIZATIONS

Ch. 10 Basic attributes o, organizations and their environments
Ch. 11 Organization structures
Ch. 12 Organizational design

PART FIVE: MANAGING THE PROCESSES OF OB

Ch. 13 Perception and decision-making
Ch. 14 Communication and conflict
Ch. 15 Power, politics, and change
Ch. 16 Leadership

**FIGURE 1.7** The major elements in the study of OB.

tional structures, while Chapter 12 extends these concepts to engage you in activities which explore ways of configuring organizations to best achieve their performance purposes and properly maintain human resources.

Part Five treats the important processes of OB through which managers transfer this knowledge of individuals, groups, and organizations into action. Chapters 13 and 14 deal with perception, decision-making, communication, and conflict resolution. Chapter 15 treats power, politics, and change. Chapter 16 examines various leadership theories. It goes on to develop a comprehensive model which emphasizes both the horizontal and vertical dimensions of leadership as key aspects of managerial behavior.

Finally, Part Six of the book contains one short and concluding chapter. In Chapter 17 we review the major elements in the study of OB and suggest some of the critical issues which you will face in planning for a future and successful managerial career.

## SUMMARY

Managers are the hearts of organizations. Organizational behavior is a knowledge base that enables managers to help their organizations perform. Organizations rely on both human and physical resources for their continued functioning. To combine successfully the two types of resource inputs into product or service outputs, managers must understand organizations as work settings. The components of an organization include its purpose, its division of labor, and the hierarchy of authority.

The manager heads a work unit which links subordinates through means-end chains with the total organization. The manager is also responsible for how the work unit functions as an organization in and of itself. Key results sought by managers are task performance and human resource maintenance at the individual, group, and organizational levels.

Managers share a common challenge. On the one hand, they are held accountable by superiors for work unit performance. On the other hand, they are largely dependent upon their subordinates to do the required work. Thus, managers need special skills to fulfill the management functions and achieve success in their required interpersonal relationships. Ultimately, the good manager is able to understand and predict human behavior in organizations. Insights into organizational behavior and the discipline of scientific thinking will help you to achieve this important capability.

## THINKING THROUGH THE ISSUES

1. Managers are often described as the "people in the middle" or as having "two masters—the organization and subordinates." Are these descriptions truly appropriate? Why or why not?

2. Why would anyone who knows that he or she will end up in the position described in Question 1 want to be a manager?

3. Assume that the classroom is an organization. Draw a diagram of the "manager's challenge" faced by your instructor.

4. Choose an organization with which you are familiar. Diagram it as an open system such as the one shown in Figure 1.2. Explain how the concepts of purpose, division of labor, and hierarchy of authority apply to this organization.

5. How do the managerial skills listed in Table 1.1 help the

manager to fulfill the functional responsibilities of planning, organizing, staffing, directing, and controlling as described in Table 1.2?

6. Choose a managerial job with which you are familiar. Complete the "managerial examples" column of Table 1.2 for this job to show how it involves activities relating to the five managerial functions.

7. Look at the syllabus provided for your OB course. How does it use and require you to use the various stages in the experiential learning model?

8. Reread the newspaper clipping in the Introduction to this chapter. How would the scientifically thinking manager react to this list of managerial "strengths" and "flaws"? Why?

## EXERCISE: "MY BEST MANAGER"

### Purpose:

To help you to reflect seriously on the attributes of a good manager; to allow you to share your views with others, and to compare their thoughts with yours; and, to provide an opportunity for you to get to know other participants in the course and to learn about their work experiences.

### Time:

30 to 40 minutes.

### Procedure:

1. Make a list of the attributes that describe the **best** manager you have ever worked for. If you have trouble identifying with an actual manager, make a list of the attributes you would like the manager in your next job to have.

2. Convene as a member of a small group composed of four to eight other persons who have also completed Step 1. Go around the group with everyone sharing his or her list. Discuss any points of special interest, similarity, dissimilarity, disagreement, and so on.

3. Create one list that combines all of the unique attributes of the "best" managers represented in your group. Make sure that you have all attributes listed, but list each only once. You should place a check mark next to any that were reported by two or more members. Have one of your members prepared to present the list in general class discussion.

4. After all groups have finished Step 3, spokespersons should report to the total class. The instructor will make a running list of the "best" manager attributes as viewed by the class.

5. Feel free to ask questions and discuss the results.

## THE MANAGER'S VOCABULARY

**Authority** The right to command other persons.
**Division of Labor** The process of breaking work into small components that serve the organization's purpose, and to be done by individuals or groups.
**Hierarchy of Authority** The arrangement of work positions in order of increasing formal authority.
**Human Resource Maintenance** The attraction and continuation of a viable work force.
**Learning** A change in behavior that occurs as a result of experience.
**Manager** A person in an organization who is responsible for the performance of one or more subordinates.
**Means-End Chains** Link the work efforts of individuals and groups to an organization's purpose.
**Open Systems** Transform human and physical resources received as inputs from their environments into goods and services that are then returned to the environment for consumption.
**Organization** A collection of people working together, in a division of labor, to achieve a common purpose.
**Organizational Behavior** The study of individuals and groups in organizations.
**Organizational Purpose** To produce a good or service.
**Skill** The ability to translate knowledge into action that results in the desired performance.
**Synergy** The creation of a whole that is greater than the sum of its parts.
**Task Performance** The quality and quantity of work produced.
**Work Unit** A task-oriented group in an organization that includes the manager and his or her immediate subordinates.

### Notes

[1]From Frank Allen, "Bosses List Main Strengths, Flaws Determining Potential of Managers," *The Wall Street Journal,* November 14, 1980, p. 25.

Reprinted by permission of The Wall Street Journal, copyright © Dow Jones & Company, Inc., 1980. All rights reserved.

[2]Harold J. Leavitt, "Future Directions in Organizational Behavior," *The Teaching of Organizational Behavior,* Vol. I (December 1975), pp. 9–13.

[3]Adapted from "The Second Book of Moses, Called Exodus," Chapter 18, *The Holy Bible.* (Philadelphia: A. J. Holman Company, 1942), pp. 88–89.

[4]Robert L. Katz, "Skills of an Effective Administrator," *Harvard Business Review,* Vol. 52 (September-October 1974), p. 94.

[5]See for example Harold Koontz, C. O'Donnell, and H. Weihrich, *Management,* Seventh Edition (New York: McGraw-Hill, 1980); and L. Kozmeir, *Principles of Management: A Programmed Instructional Approach,* Third Edition (New York: McGraw-Hill, 1974).

[6]Henry Mintzberg, *The Nature of Managerial Work.* (New York: Harper & Row, 1973), p. 46.

[7]Modified from a treatment by Fred N. Kerlinger, *Foundations of Behavioral Research,* Second Edition (New York: Holt, Rinehart and Winston, 1973) pp. 3–5.

[8]David A. Kolb, "On Management and the Learning Process," in David A. Kolb, Irwin M. Rubin, and James M. McIntyre, *Organizational Psychology: A Book of Readings,* Second Edition (Englewood Cliffs, N.J.: Prentice-Hall, 1974), pp. 27–42.

# 2

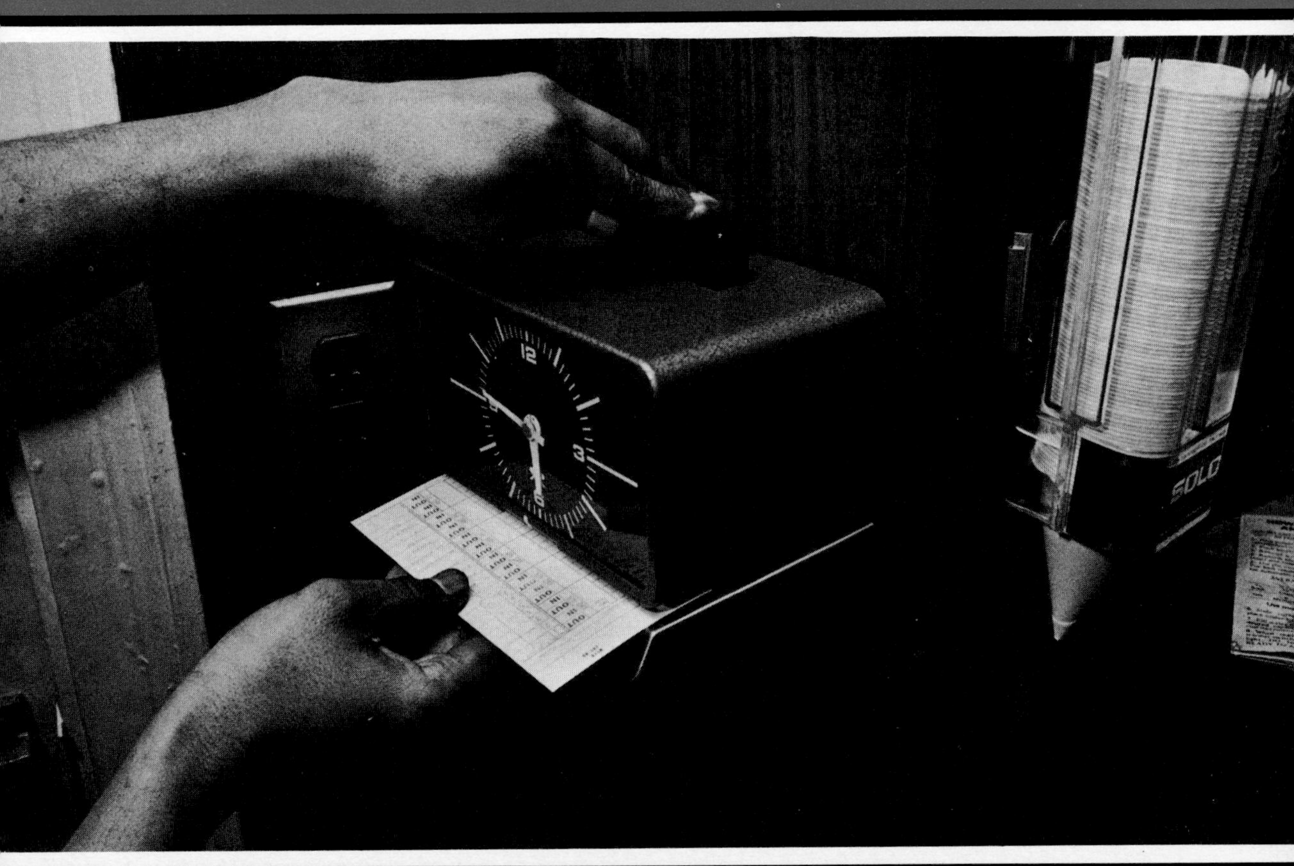

# PEOPLE AT WORK

# STUDS TERKEL LOVES HIS WORK
## but he says you don't

The following is an excerpt from an interview by *MBA Magazine* with Studs Terkel, famous contemporary author.[1] It raises some interesting issues about people at work.

**MBA:** We've heard you say—on several occasions—that work as we know it is an instrument of violence against the individual. That's a strong charge. How do you know it's true?

**Terkel:** I ride the bus, the Michigan Boulevard bus in Chicago, and I look at people's faces. I see the bank teller, the elevator operator, the secretaries, the guys who work on the assembly lines, when they come home at night. They're tired. They're beaten. There's a fatigue. It isn't the satisfying tiredness of a day well spent, but the fatigue of another day killed.

**MBA:** What about their bosses?

**Terkel:** I look down in the cars alongside the bus, and I see the managers and the executives. They sit behind their wheels with their teeth gritted, smoking one cigarette after another, looking as though they were furious. If getting caught on one little stoplight makes them *that* furious, there's something else going on: violence to the spirit—as well as the body. These execs, they *think* they have control, but they don't. They're always worried about being taken over by a conglomerate or a bigger company, or about having to fire someone they don't want to fire, or about being fired themselves.

**MBA:** In your book, *Working,* you interviewed 150 or so workers, blue and white collar, and it seemed that none of them liked their jobs.

**Terkel:** Oh, the great majority of people don't get any satisfaction from their work. Now, when I'd interview, very often, at the beginning, people would say, "Oh, I like my job." There was one woman, a switchboard operator at a Holiday Inn, she started out, "I like my work . . . I like it." And then, she started talking: "You know, they don't even know me. People take me for granted. I'm the center of this huge communications hub, but they talk to me like I'm nothing. You know what I'd like to do sometime? I'd like to take all those plugs out and goof 'em and switch 'em around. And one night, when people ring, I'd like to say, 'Marriott Inn. Marriott.' " So I asked her why she wanted to do that, and she answered, "I don't know. To make the night go faster."

### MANAGEMENT APPLICATIONS QUESTION

What is the meaning of work—to people in general, to those persons who may serve as your future subordinates, to you?

## PLANNING AHEAD

**This chapter explores the meaning of work and its implications for individual job satisfaction and performance. The learning activities of the chapter address the following topics.**

**Work**
**The Psychological Contract**
**The Meaning of Work**
**Job Satisfaction**
**Herzberg's Two-Factor Theory**
**The Satisfaction-Performance Controversy**
**Work and Non-Work**

The quality of life is everyone's concern, and the quality of work is an important component in the quality of life for most of us. This reality makes Terkel's observations on the quality of work in America most ominous. Indeed, his book *Working*[2] (which we highly recommend for reading) will leave you with a rather pessimistic view of work and the contribution it makes to people's lives. Because people at work are your concern as a manager, we need to carefully think through some basic issues relating to the quality of work.

## WORK

**Work** is an activity that produces value for other people.[3] It is what people do in exchange for things they value, but cannot provide for themselves. Work is a transaction that results in a mutually beneficial linkage between an individual and an organization. **Managerial work** is to direct the activities of subordinates so that the production goals of the work unit and organization are best served, and so that the subordinates are adequately maintained as human resources. This is what managers do in return for pay and other valued rewards.

To obtain a better understanding of the nature of work, we begin by focusing on the psychological contract. We then devote the rest of the chapter to a detailed look at job satisfaction in the workplace. Included here is the all-important examination of the relationship between satisfaction and performance, and between satisfaction and other aspects of human resource maintenance.

# THE PSYCHOLOGICAL CONTRACT

You are probably familiar with the word "contract" as it reflects on relations between labor unions and organizations employing their members. Such a contract is usually quite formal. Contract negotiations may cover such items as pay, work hours, vacations, and seniority rights, among others.

There is another, less formal contract which relates every employee to his or her work organization. A **psychological contract** is the set of expectations held by the individual and specifying what the individual and the organization expect to give to and receive from one another in the course of their working relationship.[4]

## Exchange of Values

The psychological contract specifies the exchange of values that causes the individual to work for the organization, and causes the organization to employ that person. During the time when the individual is being recruited by the organization, this exchange is an anticipated one. Later, during actual employment, anticipations are either realized or not realized. Needless to say, part of the manager's job is to ensure that both the individual and the organization continue to receive a fair exchange of values under the psychological contract.

## Inducements and Contributions

Figure 2.1 depicts the reciprocal character of this individual-organization exchange relationship. The individual offers **contributions** or work efforts of value to the organization's production purpose. These contributions make the individual a true resource to the organization. We can say at this point that these contributions are valued by the organization because of the various needs that it has.

Those things that the organization gives to the individual in return for contributions are called **inducements.** The term means exactly what it implies. To induce participation, the organization offers the individual things of value. As with the organization, individuals value these inducements in accord with their responsiveness to one or more individual needs.

When the individual and the organization both feel the exchange is fair, a state of inducements-contributions balance exists. Imbalance occurs in the individual's favor when inducements are greater than contributions; it occurs in the organization's favor when contributions are greater than inducements. This concept of balance, or

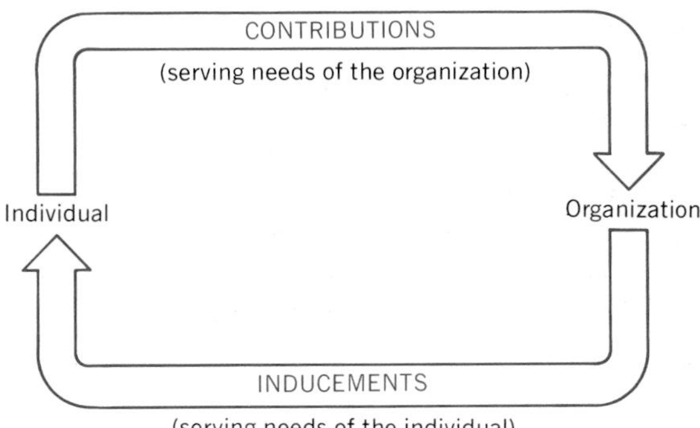


**FIGURE 2.1** The inducements-contributions exchange between the individual and the organization.

imbalance, is important to the manager. In the Case of the Missing Raise discussed in the Introduction to Part One, for example, John Lloyd felt his psychological contract was not being fulfilled with Central University. His inducements seemed less than his contributions. Apparently, too, he felt this imbalance could be resolved by reducing his contributions. For John's manager, Fred, this is not a desirable outcome, as Central would lose some of John's potential as a human resource of the organization. Fred needs to be a better manager of the psychological contracts of his subordinates.

### Managing Psychological Contracts

In a sense, the rest of this book is designed to increase your ability to successfully manage the psychological contracts of your subordinates. The importance of realistic and healthy psychological contracts for yourself and your subordinates should not be underestimated. In fact, some organizations hire consultants to help achieve this goal. An example is provided in *What Consultants Do 2.1*.

## THE MEANING OF WORK

Work can certainly be more than a source of pure economic livelihood for people. But it is the inability of work to achieve this broader level of meaning that is being damned by Terkel in the comments used to introduce this chapter. There are data in support of his concerns. Table 2.1, for example, shows that, in one sample, most of the employees in other than professional occupations would not choose the same work again. A majority of both white-collar and blue-collar

## WHAT CONSULTANTS DO 2.1

### Clarifying Psychological Contracts

Three new college engineering graduates were hired as junior managers in a manufacturing plant of a large corporation. For three months they participated in a training program. A senior manager was concerned that the trainees "get up to speed" as quickly as possible and that they be prepared to negotiate and explore expectations with their "first bosses." He also wanted to receive feedback from them on the training program, to acquaint the other top managers with the trainees, and to help the trainees feel a part of the management team.

A consultant was hired to conduct a twelve-hour session designed to accomplish these goals. Four senior managers, three supervisors, and the three trainees participated in the sessions, which were held over three days and involved the following activities:

- Questionnaires were completed beforehand by each participant to summarize their expectations regarding the give and take between the trainees, their eventual first bosses, and the organization.
- The first session began with contract-setting exercise that resulted in the participants setting goals for the session, establishing individual roles, and making an agenda.
- The consultant gave a brief lecture on the concept of the psychological contract.
- Participants were then divided into groups of senior managers, supervisors, and trainees to develop lists of "mismatches" from their own experiences.
- The groups presented their lists and engaged in a discussion of the issues.
- The session closed with the total group problem-solving on the issue "What can we do better concerning our joining-up process?"

Source: Adapted from a case described by John P. Kotter, "The Psychological Contract: Managing the Joining-Up Process." Copyright ©1973 by the Regents of the University of California. Reprinted from *California Management Review,* volume XV, no. 3, pp. 96 and 97 by permission of the Regents.

workers felt this way. Findings such as this have led to some concern for the prevalence of "white-collar woes" and "blue-collar blues" in our society.[5]

The extent to which job dissatisfaction actually exists among workers, however, is a subject of continued debate. One scholar reviewed the results of numerous surveys and concluded that most people were neither extremely satisfied nor extremely dissatisfied; rather, most workers are either moderately satisfied with their jobs or just barely dissatisfied.[6] The accompanying *Newsline 2.1* seems to support this conclusion.

**Table 2.1 Percentages in Occupational Groups Who Would Choose Similar Work Again**

| Professional and Lower White-Collar Occupations | % | Working-Class Occupations | % |
|---|---|---|---|
| Urban university professors | 93 | Skilled printers | 52 |
| Mathematicians | 91 | Paper workers | 42 |
| Physicists | 89 | Skilled autoworkers | 41 |
| Biologists | 89 | Skilled steelworkers | 41 |
| Chemists | 86 | Textile workers | 31 |
| Firm lawyers | 83 | Blue-collar workers, cross section | 24 |
| Lawyers | 83 | Unskilled steelworkers | 21 |
| Journalists (Washington correspondents) | 82 | Unskilled autoworkers | 16 |
| Church university professors | 77 | | |
| Solo lawyers | 75 | | |
| White-collar workers, cross-section | 43 | | |

Source: Reprinted from *Work in America: Report of a Special Task Force to the Secretary of Health, Education and Welfare,* the MIT Press, Cambridge, Mass. 1973.

## NEWSLINE 2.1

### Job Dissatisfaction May Not be as Rampant as Some Have Suspected

A survey released by the Conference Board, a private business research group, discloses that 87% of Americans are happy with their work (59% are "satisfied" and 28% "very satisfied"). About 10% of workers are "dissatisfied" with their jobs, and 3% are "very dissatisfied." Says a board spokesman: "Most working conditions are pleasant and current pay scales allow for a comfortable standard of living. . . . It appears today's work place provides a reasonably high degree of psychic satisfaction."

The survey also finds that the older workers get and the more money they make, the happier they are with their jobs. Only 13% of those in the $5,000-a-year income bracket say they are "very satisfied" with their jobs. In the $25,000-and-up category, 39% term their workaday life "very satisfactory."

Source: *The Wall Street Journal* (July 20, 1978), p. 1. Reprinted by permission of The Wall Street Journal, 

The debate over whether people are really satisfied or dissatisfied with their work is likely to continue. It is also one that is unlikely to be resolved. This is really of little concern to you as a practicing manager. For the manager, the key fact is that some workers achieve a sense of satisfaction with their jobs, while others do not. The manager's task is to discover what work means to individual subordinates at given points in time and to strive to help to make that meaning as positive as possible.

To help the manager master this task, the OB literature reports research on the concept of "job satisfaction." This concept recognizes that the ultimate meaning of work to an individual will be determined by such things as the tasks performed, the organization and the work unit within which the job exists, and the co-workers and other persons with whom the individual interacts. The manager is in a position to influence each of these factors to varying degrees.

## JOB SATISFACTION

**Job satisfaction** is the degree to which an individual feels positively or negatively about the various facets of the job tasks, the work setting, and relationships with co-workers.

### Measuring Job Satisfaction

Researchers go to great lengths to create good measures of job satisfaction. One straightforward approach is to simply ask people to respond orally or in writing to a question such as this.

How satisfied are you with your present job?

| not at all | | somewhat | | extremely |
|---|---|---|---|---|
| 1 | 2 | 3 | 4 | 5 |

Checkpoint

Let's measure your "job" satisfaction. Circle the response in the previous question that best reflects your feelings so far about one of your courses. Assume everyone else in the class also answers the question for the same course. Suppose, too, that your instructor collects and summarizes the responses. What would the instructor know if the average of all responses to the question was 3.5? Is this a good, bad, or in-between satisfaction score?

Actually, it is very hard to say if the 3.5 is good or bad as a satisfaction score. It is hard to know whether or not people share the same meanings for the terms "somewhat" and "extremely." Furthermore, it is likely that there are some aspects of the course that you find to be more satisfying than others. Perhaps you had a hard time deciding how to respond to the course satisfaction question because of this.

Your instructor would really like to know what he or she can do

Think of your present work. What is it like most of the time? In the blank beside each word given below, write

__Y__ for "Yes" if it describes your work
__N__ for "No" if it does NOT describe it
__?__ if you cannot decide

**WORK ON PRESENT JOB**

_____ Routine
_____ Satisfying
_____ Good
_____ On your feet

Think of the pay you get now. How well does each of the following words describe your present pay? In the blank beside each word, put

__Y__ if it describes your pay
__N__ if it does NOT describe it
__?__ if you cannot decide

**PRESENT PAY**

_____ income adequate for normal expenses
_____ insecure
_____ less than I deserve
_____ highly paid

Think of the opportunities for promotion that you have now. How well does each of the following words describe these? In the blank beside each word put

__Y__ for "Yes" if it describes your oppportunities for promotion
__N__ for "No" if it does NOT describe them
__?__ if you cannot decide

**OPPORTUNITIES FOR PROMOTION**

_____ promotion on ability
_____ dead-end job
_____ unfair promotion policy
_____ regular promotions

Think of the kind of supervision that you get on your job. How well does each of the following words describe this supervision? In the blank beside each word below, put

__Y__ if it describes the supervision you get on your job
__N__ if it does NOT describe it
__?__ if you cannot decide

**SUPERVISION ON PRESENT JOB**

_____ impolite
_____ praises good work
_____ influential
_____ doesn't supervise enough

Think of the majority of the people that you work with now or the people you meet in connection with your work. How well does each of the following words describe these people? In the blank beside each word below, put

__Y__ if it describes the people you work with
__N__ if it does NOT describe them
__?__ if you cannot decide

**PEOPLE ON YOUR PRESENT JOB**

_____ boring
_____ responsible
_____ intelligent
_____ talk too much

**FIGURE 2.2** Sample items from the job descriptive index (JDI). (Source: The Job Descriptive Index is copyrighted by Bowling Green State University. The complete forms, scoring key, instructions, and norms can be obtained from Dr. Patricia C. Smith, Department of Psychology, Bowling Green State University, Bowling Green, Ohio, 43404. Reprinted with permission.)

to improve the course and raise the average satisfaction score. Once again, the single question measure of job or course satisfaction proves deficient, since it gives the instructor no insight into what facets of the course could be improved upon. It is also deficient because it is not as reliable as multiple items in measuring the same concept. That is, single item measures are answered less consistently than those with more items.

Because of problems like the above, researchers try to use multi-item measures of various facets of work that can become sources of satisfaction and dissatisfaction. A sample of items from one of the more established measuring instruments is provided in Figure 2.2.

The instrument is called the Job Descriptive Index, or JDI for short.

The JDI measures five facets of job satisfaction: the work itself, quality of supervision, people on present job (co-workers), promotion, and pay. Each of these facets can be a source of meaning in work, and each represents a possible inducement to work. Instruments like the JDI are important to both researchers who are interested in learning about the sources of job satisfaction and its consequences, and to managers who are interested in predicting and controlling these outcomes. Frequent references to the concept of job satisfaction and to instruments such as the JDI will be made in the material ahead.

## The Consequences of Job Satisfaction

The job satisfactions of a manager's subordinates are important because of the various consequences with which they may be associated. Table 2.2 lists some of these consequences as they correspond to the facets of satisfaction measured by the JDI. Here, we are especially concerned to establish what these consequences may mean in terms of the manager's ability to take full advantage of the individual as a human resource of the organization. In effect, managers must be concerned with two decisions individuals make about their work and work organizations: the decision to belong, and the decision to perform.

### Job Satisfaction and the Decision to Belong

One response of people whose psychological contract expectations are unconfirmed is to leave organizations soon after joining them. Confirmation of these expectations by the organization, by contrast, is a source of job satisfaction.[7] When early job satisfaction is experienced as a result of psychological contract fulfillment, we can expect people to want to remain with their work organizations. Thus, managers must be concerned not only with inducing capable people to join their organizations, but also with continuing to induce them to stay.

There is good evidence that links job dissatisfaction with individual decisions to leave organizations. In general, research indicates that workers who are dissatisfied with work are more likely than satisfied ones to terminate their employment.[8] Employee turnover is of immediate concern to managers. When subordinates terminate their employment, human resources are missing that would otherwise contribute to the work unit's production purpose. The resulting loss in production and/or the need to replace the missing personnel can prove costly.

**Table 2.2 Sample Consequences of High and Low JDI Satisfactions of Employees**

| JDI Facets | High Satisfaction | Low Satisfaction |
|---|---|---|
| Work itself | Come early; stay late; stay on job | Seek transfer; be absent or late; quit |
| Supervision | Seek company of; accept demands and advice; stay on job | Avoid; complain and argue; reject demands and advice; file grievance; quit |
| Co-workers | Approach; conform to norms; stay on job | Avoid; argue with; be absent; quit |
| Promotion | Increase effort; raise aspirations; stay on job | Decrease effort; lower aspirations; quit |
| Pay | Modify effort depending on pay-performance connection; stay on job | Complain; solicit competing offer; modify effort depending on pay-performance connection; quit |

Source: Abridged from E. A. Locke, "Job Satisfaction and Job Performance: A Theoretical Analysis," *Organizational Behavior and Human Performance,* Vol. 5 (1970), p. 496.

You must be careful in thinking through this relationship between job satisfaction and employee rates of turnover. There are times when turnover can be of value to the organization. It can, for example, be an opportunity to bring replacements with creative ideas and new energy into the work unit.[9] Thus, there may be instances when a manager should encourage turnover, rather than to try to prevent its occurrence.

In summary, remember that job satisfaction is an individual work outcome of major significance to managers. Job satisfaction is important because

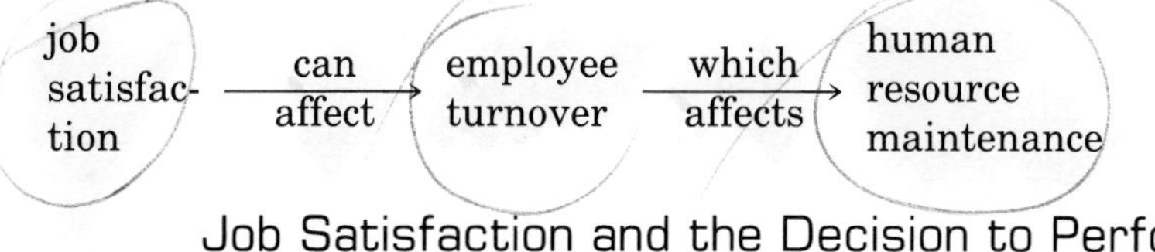

## Job Satisfaction and the Decision to Perform

Somewhere near a Ford Motor Company plant in Dearborn, Michigan, a tavern displays the sign[10]

> I Spend Forty Hours a Week Here
> —Am I Supposed to Work Too?

This sign communicates a simple but potent message to the manager:

It is one thing for people to decide to join and to stay with the work organization; it is quite another for them to work hard to perform well while they are there!

Performance is another key outcome of individual work behavior that is of major concern to managers. We defined performance generally in Chapter 1. Now, more specifically, we may think of **performance,** or productivity, as it is often called, as a summary measure of the quantity and quality of contributions made by an individual or group to the production purposes of the work unit and the organization. Individual work performance is of obvious importance to the manager. As the performance of individual subordinates rises or falls, work unit performance will also be affected. Because the manager is held accountable for work unit performance, one of his or her goals becomes to maximize performance among subordinates.

It seems logical that job satisfaction and work performance should be related to one another. The presumption, however, raises the question that turns managers' hair grey. It is also a question steeped in controversy among the OB scholars who seek to find its answer. **What causes high individual work performance?** We know that job satisfaction is one possible cause of turnover. Can we also say that job satisfaction causes individual work performance? Read on for the answers.

## HERZBERG'S TWO-FACTOR THEORY[11]

Frederick Herzberg is a psychologist who believes that job satisfaction is a cause of work performance. He has developed one of the most frequently praised and criticized theories in OB, the two-factor theory. Herzberg began his research by asking workers two straightforward questions:

1. "Tell me about a time when you felt exceptionally good about your job."
2. "Tell me about a time when you felt exceptionally bad about your job."

After analyzing almost four thousand responses to these questions, Herzberg and his associates developed the two-factor theory. They noticed that persons responding to the two questions identified different things as sources of satisfaction and dissatisfaction in their work. A summary of the actual data is presented in Figure 2.3.

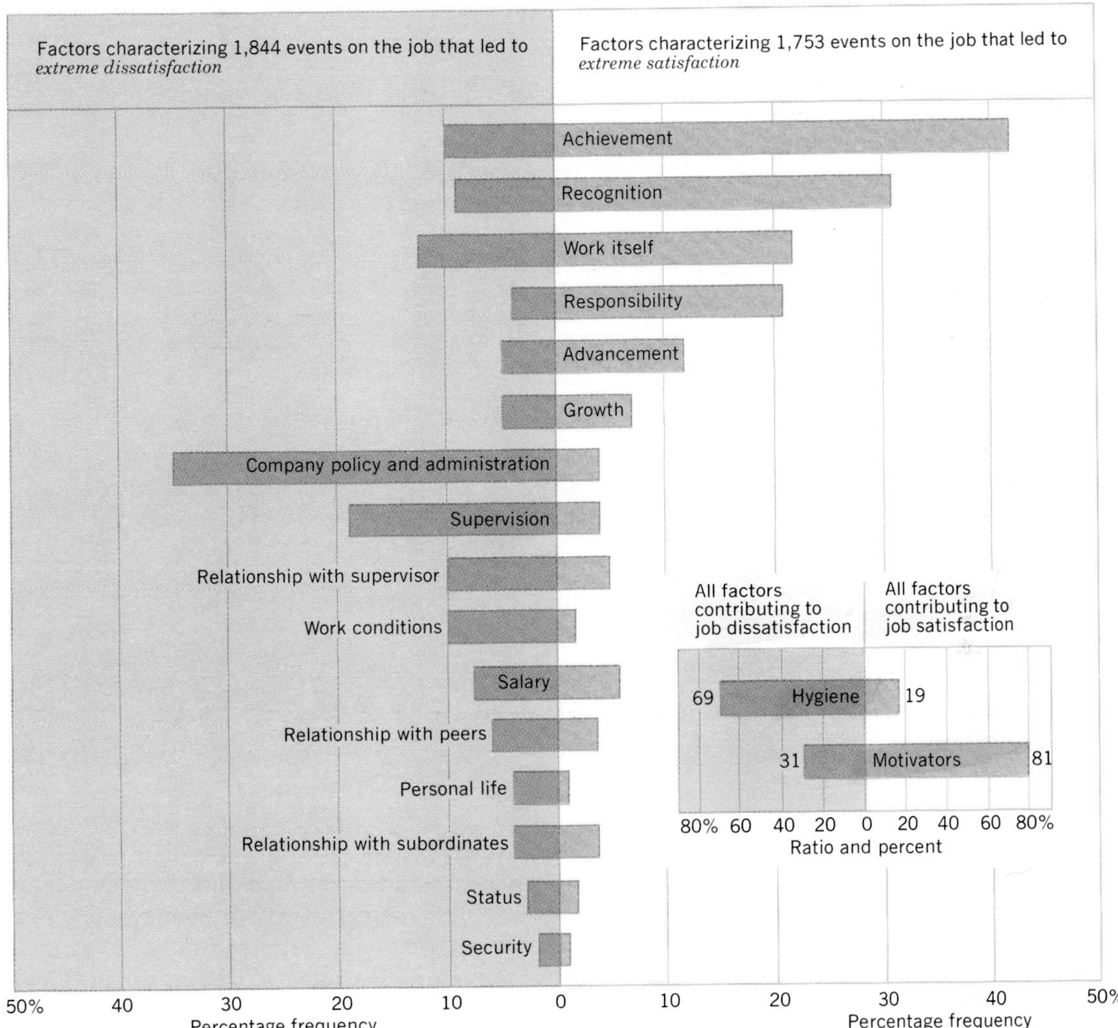


**FIGURE 2.3** Sources of satisfaction and dissatisfaction as reported in 12 investigations. (Source: Adapted from Frederick Herzberg, "One More Time: How Do You Motivate Employees?" *Harvard Business Review,* Vol. 46, January–February, 1968, p. 57. Copyright © 1968 by the President and Fellows of Harvard College; all rights reserved.)

## Hygiene Factors

Items appearing as sources of **job dissatisfaction** in Herzberg's research were found to be associated with the **job context.** That is, job dissatisfaction was linked more to the work setting than to the work itself. Herzberg refers to the sources of job dissatisfaction as **hygiene factors.**

A job hygiene factor—the comfortable lounge.

The hygiene factors are shown on the left side of Figure 2.3. They include such things as working conditions, interpersonal relations, organizational policies and administration, supervision, and salary. "Salary," you say? Yes, Herzberg views salary as a hygiene factor. The implications of this classification are most important. You may think, for example, that paying people more by raising their base salaries will create job satisfaction and increase performance. You might make a similar argument that improved work conditions (e.g., special offices, air conditioning) will do the same. Herzberg disagrees. The essence of this disagreement establishes the two-factor logic upon which his theory is based.

In the two-factor theory, job satisfaction and dissatisfaction are considered totally separate dimensions. Hygiene items only affect job dissatisfaction. Improving hygiene factors in the workplace can reduce the level of dissatisfaction felt by workers, but the improvement will not contribute to job satisfaction. The hygiene factors should be viewed by managers as follows:

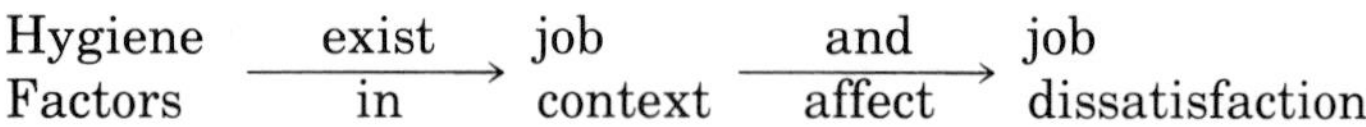

**Table 2.3 Sample Hygiene Factors found in Work Settings**

| Hygiene Factors | Examples |
|---|---|
| Organizational policies, procedures | attendance rules<br>vacation schedules<br>grievance procedures<br>performance appraisal methods |
| Working conditions | noise levels<br>safety<br>personal comfort<br>size of work area |
| Interpersonal relationships | co-worker relations<br>customer relations<br>relationship with boss |
| Quality of supervision | technical competence of boss |
| Base salary | hourly wage rate, or salary |

Table 2.3 gives examples of hygiene factors found in many work settings. Look, too, at *Newsline 2.2*. You may find it somewhat shocking. Yes, there are organizational policies and procedures that people can find quite upsetting, even if they really like their jobs!

## Satisfier Factors

Remember, Herzberg argues that improving a hygiene factor such as working conditions cannot make people satisfied with their work. It will only prevent them from being unhappy. To improve **job satis-**

## NEWSLINE 2.2

### No More Hands up on Assembly Line

IMLAY CITY, Mich. (AP)—Hamill Manufacturing Co. has agreed to stop requiring assembly line workers to raise their hands for permission to go to the bathroom, a union spokeswoman said Wednesday.

Ruth Union of United Auto Workers Local 481 said the company also agreed to pay back wages to workers who were suspended for refusing to follow the rule.

The company's four hundred employees make seat belts for Ford Motor Company. Employees recently staged a one-day work stoppage to protest the rule and a mass of unresolved grievances.

Source: The Associated Press as appearing in the *Burlington Free Press*, Burlington, Vermont (July 7, 1977). Reprinted by permission.

**faction,** the manager's attention must shift to **satisfiers.** These satisfiers are listed on the right side of Figure 2.3, and are part of **job content,** that is, they relate to what people actually do in their work.

Adding satisfiers to people's jobs is the link to performance in Herzberg's theory. He argues that managers can create opportunities for subordinates to experience such things as a sense of achievement, recognition, responsibility, advancement, and growth in the course of their performance. When these opportunities are absent from work, Herzberg feels that workers will neither experience job satisfaction nor perform their best. According to the logic of the two-factor theory,

## Two-Factor Dynamics

Two principles summarize the two-factor dynamics discussed above.

1. Improvements in hygiene factors can prevent and/or help eliminate job dissatisfaction; they cannot help to improve job satisfaction.
2. Improvements in satisfier factors can create job satisfaction; they cannot prevent job dissatisfaction.

You may be uncomfortable with these principles, especially the last one. It implies that a person can simultaneously experience job satisfaction and dissatisfaction. Because Herzberg considers job satisfaction and dissatisfaction to be separate dimensions, this is, in fact, possible under the theory. People at work can fall into any one of the four possibilities shown below.

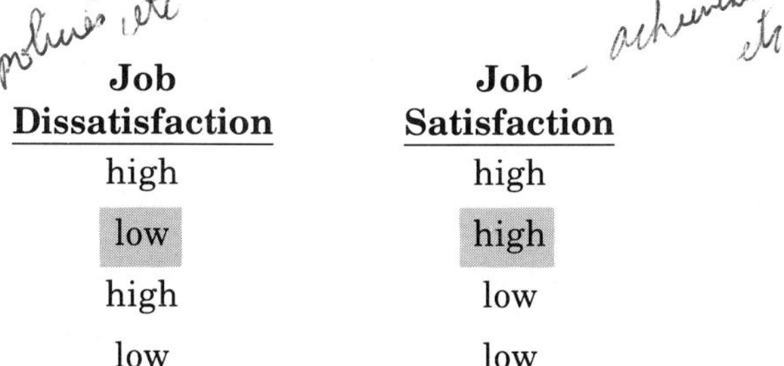

| Job Dissatisfaction | Job Satisfaction |
| --- | --- |
| high | high |
| low | high |
| high | low |
| low | low |

The least appealing situation for the manager is to have subordinates experiencing low satisfaction and high dissatisfaction; the most appealing is high satisfaction and low dissatisfaction. In any event, the manager's goal under the two-factor theory is to minimize job dissatisfaction and to maximize job satisfaction. To do this, he or she must remember that dissatisfaction is treated by improved hygiene factors. Once good hygiene eliminates dissatisfaction, however, managers are advised to shift their attention to satisfiers if they are to create job satisfaction. Failure to successfully do so will leave workers in jobs that are low in dissatisfaction, but which are also low in satisfaction.

## The Research

OB scholars debate the merits and demerits of the two-factor theory. Herzberg's continuing research and that of his followers support the theory.[12] Other researchers have used different research methods and find they are unable to confirm the theory. It is therefore criticized as method-bound, as being supportable only when Herzberg's original methodology is used.[13]

This is a serious criticism. The discipline of the scientific approach requires that theories be verifiable when different research methods are used. Some who review the research on the two-factor theory are somewhat forgiving in this regard. They defend the underlying logic of the theory, and call for future researchers to exert greater effort to test the theory with new and more sophisticated methodologies.[14]

## Practical Implications

With all this debate, you may ask if the two-factor theory is still useful. We think it is in terms of the discipline it provides in managerial thinking. Many organizations and their managers allocate considerable time, attention, and other resources to things that Herzberg would consider hygiene factors. Special office fixtures, piped-in music, special lounges for breaks, and even high base salaries are examples. The two-factor theory suggests caution in expecting too much from these investments. After all, you would still be taking the same OB course even if seated in a plush chair, located in a pleasant conference room, and with a group of good friends as companions. Regardless of classroom surroundings, the instructor must eventually deal with the content of the course in order to provide you with an increased desire to perform well. The same implication applies in other work settings.

Herzberg's theory is perhaps even more useful because it is associated with a specific technique for building satisfiers into job content. This technique is called job enrichment, and we give it special attention in Chapter 6.

## THE SATISFACTION-PERFORMANCE CONTROVERSY[15]

One offshoot of the debate over the two-factor theory is a more fundamental controversy illustrated by the following conversation.[16]

> As Ben walked by smiling on the way to his office, Ben's boss remarked to a friend: "Ben really enjoys his job and that's why he's the best damn worker I ever had. And that's reason enough for me to keep Ben happy." The friend replied: "No, you're wrong! Ben likes his job because he does it so well. If you want to make Ben happy you ought to do whatever you can to help him further improve his performance."

The core issue here is, does job satisfaction cause performance? Will managerial efforts designed to increase a person's job satisfaction cause that person's work performance to improve? Will a decline in job satisfaction cause a corresponding decrease in individual performance?

The previous questions introduce the satisfaction-performance controversy, a debate that involves three alternative points of view:

1. Satisfaction causes Performance (S→P)
2. Performance causes Satisfaction (P→S)
3. Rewards cause both Performance and Satisfaction (R→P, R→S)

### Argument: Satisfaction Causes Performance (S→P)

If this argument is true, managers should improve the job satisfaction of subordinates to increase their work performance. Herzberg's two-factor theory is consistent with this tradition. The position is a legacy of early research studies (e.g., the Hawthorne studies described in Supplementary Module A at the end of the book), and is typically associated with the "human relations movement." A classic example is the quotation,

> management has at long last discovered that there is greater production, and hence greater profit *when* workers are satisfied with their jobs.[17]

### The Research

Reviews of research on the S→P hypothesis consistently indicate that there is no simple and direct relation between individual job satisfaction at one point in time and work performance at a later point in time.[18] This conclusion is well respected among OB scholars, even though some continue to suggest that the S→P relationship may exist to various degrees depending upon the exact situation.[19] These alternative views continue to be debated,[20] and justify our use of the qualifiers "simple" and "direct" in summarizing the research evidence.

### Current Thinking

As researchers and as managers, we should recognize that job satisfaction alone is probably not a consistent predictor of individual work performance. It may well be, however, an important component of a larger set of variables that together can predict performance, and it may predict performance for certain persons. Finally, regardless of whether or not job satisfaction causes work performance, it is a part of human resource maintenance and is therefore an important work result in its own right. Managers should seek to create job satisfaction among their subordinates as something desirable in and of itself.

## Argument: Performance Causes Satisfaction (P→S)

If this argument is true, managers can promote job satisfaction by helping subordinates achieve higher levels of work performance. Rather than trying to create job satisfaction first, the manager's attention, according to this argument, would be shifted directly to performance. Given performance, job satisfaction and its positive contribution to human resource maintenance are assumed to follow.

Typical reasoning in support of the performance-causes-satisfaction argument follows.[21] When high performance is followed by a valued reward, satisfaction occurs. Thus, a manager can create satisfaction by first establishing conditions under which a person can achieve high performance, and then by properly rewarding the person for this performance. Figurative[illegible]aking,

| Work performance | $\xrightarrow[\text{by}]{\text{followed}}$ | individually valued rewards | $\xrightarrow[\text{produce}]{\text{will}}$ | satisfaction |
|---|---|---|---|---|

### The Research

Research studies report an empirical relationship between individual performance measured at one time and later job satisfaction.[22] This relationship is typically stronger than the one between initial job satisfaction and later work performance. The most provocative line of present inquiry is an attempt to examine the role of rewards as an intervening variable in the P→S hypothesis. Two open questions remain in this regard: How should rewards be best allocated?

Do variables other than rewards also intervene in the P→S relationship?[23] Chapters 4, 5, and 6 will deal rather specifically with these questions. Suffice it for now to recognize that researchers are seeking answers to them.

## Current Thinking

The P→S hypothesis is important to OB, not because it resolves the satisfaction-performance controversy, but because of the provocative research and managerial implication with which it is associated. This hypothesis appropriately focuses a manager's attention on how he or she rewards performance. Rewards are within a manager's capability to control. As inducements to work, they are also fundamental to the individual's psychological contract. The ultimate payoff from a well-managed system of rewards may well be

Performance followed by rewards $\xrightarrow[\text{create}]{\text{can}}$ job satisfaction $\xrightarrow[\text{reduce}]{\text{and}}$ turnover

The elegance of this managerial strategy is diminished, however, by the absence of an impact by the rewards and/or job satisfaction on performance. While research seems to question that satisfaction can cause performance, the potential for reward to cause performance has captured the attention of scholars.

## Argument: Rewards Cause Both Satisfaction and Performance (R→S, R→P)

This final argument suggests that a proper allocation of rewards can influence both individual job satisfaction and work performance. If true, the argument provides a missing ingredient in the managerial strategy just discussed.

## The Research

The evidence on the R→S and R→P hypothesis is encouraging. Laboratory experiments have found that subjects receiving higher rewards for performance report greater job satisfaction. Furthermore, rewarding subjects in proportion to their level of initial performance (i.e., high rewards for high performance, low for low) is positively associated with later work performance.[24] While giving a low performer a small reward may lead to initial dissatisfaction, this research indicates that such action is also likely to lead to higher performance in the future.

The managerial implications are straightforward. If you are only interested in creating high job satisfaction, pass out high rewards. If you are interested in high work performance as well, allocate rewards in proportion to performance. This recommendation is supported by research on the relationship between pay as the reward and both job satisfaction and performance.[25] We will examine this issue of managing merit pay and other rewards in Chapter 5. It is a most challenging topic!

### Current Thinking

This final argument in the satisfaction-performance controversy is the most compelling. From a practical point of view, it focuses the manager's attention on work rewards as things which can be viewed to affect both the job satisfaction and work performance of subordinates. Theory-wise, the hypothesis also raises such new and useful research questions as

- What determines the reward values individuals will attach to various work-related outcomes?
- What else in addition to rewards will or can affect work performance?

Chapter 4 responds to the first of these questions; Chapter 3 responds to the latter. As you read on, remember that empirical research does suggest that

- Job satisfaction can predict turnover.
- Job satisfaction is not a good predictor of work performance.
- Performance-related rewards can influence job satisfaction and future work performance.

## WORK AND NONWORK

Throughout this chapter we have discussed work and its meaning for the individual. Our concern has been to examine the meaning of work so that you, as a manager, can influence subordinates to make high-level performance contributions to the organization and achieve a high level of human resource maintenance in the process. Before concluding our discussion of people at work, however, we want you to realize that there is a broader social value associated with work that makes any manager's responsibilities even more complex.

We said earlier that the "quality of work is an important component in the quality of life." Consider the following comments of a steelworker.[26]

> When I come home, know what I do for the first twenty minutes? Fake it. I put on a smile. I got a kid three years old. Sometimes she says, "Daddy, where've you been?" I say, "Work." I could have told her I'd been in Disneyland. What's work to a three-year-old kid? If I feel bad, I can't take it out on the kid. Kids are born innocent of everything but birth. You can't take it out on your wife either. That is why you go to a tavern. You want to release it there rather than do it at home. What does an actor do when he's got a bad movie? I got a bad movie every day.

These comments show how a person's work experiences can affect their nonwork lives as well. That is, the quality of work may affect the quality of life. This potential transfer effect is especially important given the high value which many people now attach to their leisure time activities (see *Newsline 2.3*).

## NEWSLINE 2.3

### People Surveyed on Work and Leisure as Sources of Personal Satisfaction

When asked to compare work and leisure as sources of satisfaction, a survey of American workers responded as follows:

21% feel work means more than leisure.

60% say that while they enjoy their work, it isn't their major source of satisfaction.

19% report being so tired from work that it isn't even a minor source of satisfaction.

Source: Data reported in Daniel Yankelovich, "The New Psychological Contracts at Work," *Psychology Today* (May 1978), pp. 46–50.

Every employee of a work organization lives two overlapping lives, a work life and a nonwork life. The environment created by managers for people at work may have consequences that extend beyond the time an individual spends in the work setting. Managers should be fully aware that the quality of any individual's life, even their own, can be heavily influenced by the quality of life at work. Poor management can decrease the quality of life, not just the quality of work life. Perhaps good management can increase both!

The full impact of this last point is illustrated by the fact that the latest edition of a classic book on the social psychology of organizations now includes a chapter on "Work and Health."[27] The authors argue that work may have "unintended consequences" that carry over to affect the mental health of the individual. This point is dramatic. It may well be, for example, that the root cause of many prevailing social ills, such as rising criminal assault rates, drug abuse, spouse and child abuse, alcoholism, and suicide may trace in part to the inability of people to find work that is meaningful and/or compatible with their nonwork interests.[28] While this may seem to be an extreme position, it deserves thought.

## SUMMARY

Two themes dominate this chapter. The first is the concept of work and what it can mean to people. We have defined work, discussed it as a form of exchange between the individual and the organization, and identified how it can affect the overall quality of people's lives. We hope this chapter has left you with the feeling that being a good manager is of value not only to you and the organization, but also to society as well.

The second theme of the chapter focuses your attention on job satisfaction and its relationship to job performance. We have defined job satisfaction and found dissatisfaction to be one cause of employee turnover. Frederick Herzberg's two-factor theory of job satisfaction has focused your attention on hygiene factors as sources of dissatisfaction and on satisfier factors as sources of satisfaction. In going on to examine the satisfaction-performance controversy, we have concluded that job satisfaction alone is probably not a good predictor of work performance. Rather, we have resolved that managers should consider satisfaction and performance as two separate but equally important work results affected by the allocation of work-related rewards.

We continue to examine the determinants of each of these key results in each major Part of the book. In Part Two, which follows, we address them from the individual's point of view. For now, recall that

1. Well-allocated rewards can increase job satisfaction and encourage people to seek high levels of performance.
2. The quality of people's work lives is an important component in the overall quality of their lives in general.

## THINKING THROUGH THE ISSUES

1. Suppose that you are the chairperson to whom your course instructor reports. What do you think the instructor's psychological contract with the organization looks like?

2. What can a manager safely assume about the job satisfactions of subordinates in his or her work unit?

3. We have argued that ". . . as the performance of individual subordinates rises or falls, work unit performance will also be affected." However, the relationship between individual performance and work unit performance can be affected by synergy. Explain this last statement.

4. If researchers are correct in their current tendency to think that job satisfaction is *not* a good predictor of work performance, why should managers be interested in the job satisfaction of their subordinates at all?

5. Why should Studs Terkel enjoy his work, if, as he claims, other people don't enjoy theirs?

6. Use Herzberg's two-factor theory to identify possible sources of dissatisfaction-satisfaction in a job with which you are familiar.

7. Explain and defend a managerial strategy for increasing the satisfaction and performance of persons employed in the job described in Question 6.

8. Choose a current newspaper or magazine article, or TV news report, that reports on the deterioration in the quality of work life. Explain how this deterioration may spill over to affect the quality of people's lives in general. What can be done to correct the situation?

## EXERCISE: THE MEANING OF WORK

### Purpose:

To explore the meaning of work for persons employed in various occupations, and to examine the managerial implications of these findings.

### Time:

50–75 minutes class time; 4 hours preparation outside of class.

### Procedure:

1. Refer back to Table 2.1. Choose one or more of the occupational categories represented in the table.

2. Interview at least three persons who are locally employed full-time in each of these occupations. Ask them the following questions,

- If you could do it all over again, would you choose the same occupation again?
- Why? or Why not?

3. Make a complete copy of the Job Descriptive Index (JDI) items in Figure 2.2. Ask these persons to answer the job satisfaction questions.

4. Ask these persons any questions which you feel will shed further light on the meaning of work for them. Such questions might include,

- What do you like most about your work?
- What do you like least about your work?
- What is the relation between the demands of your job and your personal life?

5. In your assigned group, share your results with those of other students. Combine everyone's results to create a group version of Table 2.1 and a tally of responses to the JDI questions. Prepare a further summary of any interesting findings revealed by your supplementary questioning.

6. Be prepared as a group to report your summary results to the rest of the class.

7. The instructor will lead a discussion on the results and identification of their managerial implications.

## THE MANAGER'S VOCABULARY

**Contributions** Individual work efforts of value to the organization's production purpose.

**Hygiene Factors** Sources of job dissatisfaction that are found in the job context.

**Inducements** Things that the organization gives to the individual in return for contributions.

**Job Enrichment** A technique for building satisfier factors into job content.

**Job Satisfaction** The degree to which an individual feels positively or negatively about the various facets of the job tasks, the work setting, and the relationships with co-workers.

**Managerial Work** To direct the activities of subordinates so that the production goals of the work unit and organization are best served, and so that the subordinates are adequately maintained as human resources.

**Performance** A summary measure of the quantity and quality of contributions made by an individual or group to the production purposes of the work unit and organization.

**Psychological Contract** The set of expectations held by the individual and specifying what the individual and the organization expect to give and to receive from one another in the course of their working relationship.

**Satisfier Factors** Sources of job satisfaction that are found in the job content.

**Two-Factor Theory** A theory separating hygiene or job context factors as sources of job dissatisfaction from satisfier or job content factors as sources of job satisfaction.

**Work** An activity that produces value for other people.

## Important Names

**Frederick Herzberg** Author of the two-factor theory.

## Notes

[1]From "Studs Terkel Loves His Work, But He Says You Don't," an interview in *MBA*, Vol. 10 (June 1976), pp. 41–44.

[2]Studs Terkel, *Working* (New York: Avon Books, 1975).

[3]*Work in America: Report of a Special Task Force to the Secretary of Health, Education and Welfare* (Cambridge, Mass.: MIT Press, 1973), p. 3.

[4]Modified from John P. Kotter, "The Psychological Contract: Managing the Joining Up Process," *California Management Review*, Vol. 15 (Spring 1973), pp. 91–99.

[5]*Work in America,* op. cit., pp. 29–40.

[6]Robert L. Kahn, "The Meaning of Work: Interpretation and Proposals for Measurement," in Angus Campbell and Phillip E. Converse (eds.), *The Human Meaning of Social Change* (New York: Russell Sage Foundation, 1972), pp. 173–174.

[7]James D. Portwood and Edwin L. Miller, "Evaluating the Psychological Contract: Its Implications for Employee Job Satisfaction and Behavior," *Academy of Management Proceedings* (August 1977), pp. 109–113.

[8]You might think that satisfaction and absenteeism would also be related to each other. The latest research evidence indicates that this is not necessarily the case. See, for example, Frank J. Smith, "Work Attitudes as Predictors of Attendance on a Specific Day," *Journal of Applied Psychology, 62* (1977), pp. 16–19.

[9]Barry M. Staw and Greg R. Oldham, "Reconsidering Our Dependent Vari-

ables: A Critique and Empirical Study," *Academy of Management Journal,* Vol. 21 (1979), pp. 539–559.

[10]Justin Gooding, "Blue-Collar Blues on the Assembly Line," *Fortune* (July 1970), p. 69.

[11]The complete two-factor theory is well explained by Herzberg and his associates in Herzberg, Bernard Mausner, and Barbara Bloch Synderman, *The Motivation to Work,* Second Edition (New York: John Wiley & Sons, 1967) and Frederick Herzberg, "One More Time: How do You Motivate Employees?," *Harvard Business Review,* Vol. 46 (January–February 1968), pp. 53–62. This discussion is based on both sources.

[12]See the collection of studies reported in Frederick Herzberg, *The Managerial Choice: To be Efficient and to be Human* (Homewood, Ill.: Dow Jones-Irwin, 1976).

[13]Robert J. House and Lawrence A. Wigdor, "Herzberg's Dual-Factor Theory of Job Satisfaction and Motivation: A Review of the Evidence and a Criticism," *Personnel Psychology,* Vol. 20 (Winter 1967), pp. 369–389; Steven Kerr, Anne Harlan, and Ralph Stogdill, "Preference for Motivator and Hygiene Factors in a Hypothetical Interview Situation," *Personnel Psychology,* Vol. 27 (Winter 1974), pp. 109–124.

[14]Valerie M. Bockman, "The Herzberg Controversy," *Personnel Psychology,* Vol. 24, No. 2 (Summer 1971), pp. 155–189; Benedict Grigaliunas and Yoash Wiener, "Has the Research Challenge to Motivation-Hygiene Theory Been Conclusive? An Analysis of Critical Studies," *Human Relations,* Vol. 27 (1974), pp. 839–871.

[15]For a complete discussion of this controversy, see Charles N. Greene, "The Satisfaction-Performance Controversy," *Business Horizons,* Vol. 15 (October 1972), pp. 31–41; and, Charles N. Greene and Robert E. Craft, Jr., "The Satisfaction-Performance Controversy Revisited," in Kirk Downey, Don Hellreigel, and John Slocum (eds.), *Organizational Behavior: A Reader* (St. Paul, Minn.: West Publishing Co., 1977), pp. 187–201.

[16]Greene, op. cit., p. 31.

[17]Willard E. Parker and Robert W. Kleemeier, *Human Relations in Supervision: Leadership in Management* (New York: McGraw-Hill, 1951), p. 10, as cited in Donald P. Schwab and Larry L. Cummings, "Theories of Performance and Satisfaction: A Review," *Industrial Relations,* Vol. 7 (1970), pp. 408–430.

[18]Arthur H. Brayfield and Walter H. Crockett, "Employee Attitudes and Employee Performance," *Psychological Bulletin,* Vol. 52 (1955), pp. 415–422; Schwab and Cummings, op. cit.; Victor H. Vroom, *Work and Motivation* (New York: John Wiley & Sons, 1964).

[19]Dennis Organ, "A Reappraisal and Reinterpretation of the Satisfaction-Causes-Performance Hypothesis," *Academy of Management Review,* Vol. 2 (1977), pp. 46–53.

[20]Peter Lorenzi, "A Comment on Organ's Reappraisal of the Satisfaction-Causes-Performance Hypothesis," *Academy of Management Review,* Vol. 3 (1978), pp. 380–382.

[21]See, for example, Lyman W. Porter and Edward E. Lawler, III, *Managerial Attitudes and Performance* (Homewood, Ill.: Irwin, 1968).

[22]Donald D. Bowen and J. P. Siegel, "The Relationship Between Satisfaction and Performance: The Question of Causality," *Proceedings of the Annual Convention of the American Psychological Association*, 1970; and Charles N. Greene, "A Causal Interpretation of the Relationship Among Pay, Performance and Satisfaction," paper presented at the Annual Meeting of the Midwest Psychological Association, 1972, both cited by Greene and Craft, op. cit.

[23]Greene and Craft, op. cit.

[24]David J. Cherrington, H. Joseph Reitz, and William E. Scott, Jr., "Effects of Contingent and Noncontingent Reward on the Relationship Between Satisfaction and Task Performance," *Journal of Applied Psychology*, Vol. 55 (1971), pp. 531–536.

[25]Charles N. Greene, "Causal Connections Among Manager's Merit Pay, Job Satisfaction, and Performance," *Journal of Applied Psychology*, Vol. 58 (1973), pp. 95–100.

[26]Terkel, op. cit., p. 7.

[27]Daniel Katz and Robert L. Kahn, *The Social Psychology of Organizations*, Second Edition (New York: John Wiley & Sons, 1978).

[28]Edwin A. Locke, "The Nature and Causes of Job Satisfaction," pp. 1297–1349 in Marvin D. Dunnette (ed.), *Handbook of Industrial and Organizational Psychology* (Chicago: Rand McNally College Publishing Company, 1976).

# PART TWO

# MANAGING INDIVIDUALS IN ORGANIZATIONS

## THE MANAGER'S GOAL

**To Facilitate High Levels of Individual Performance and Job Satisfaction.**

## YOUR LEARNING OBJECTIVE

**To Develop a Capability for Analyzing Systematically the Behavior of Individuals at Work; and to Identify Action Alternatives for Relating Them More Productively and with Greater Satisfaction to Their Jobs.**

## Chapters in this Part of the Book

Now that you are sensitive to the need for managers to be good at understanding, predicting, and controlling behavior in organizations, the following case is most appropriate. This case involves people working in a manufacturing situation. It is presented in a prediction format so that you can further develop your analytical capabilities. The case introduces the full range of issues we will discuss in Part Two on individuals in organizations.

# The Hovey and Beard Company Case[1]

The Hovey and Beard Company manufactured a variety of wooden toys including animals, pull toys, and the like. The toys were manufactured by a transformation process that began in the wood room. There, toys were cut, sanded, and partially assembled. Then the toys were dipped into shellac and sent to the painting room.

In years past, the painting had been done by hand, with each employee working with a given toy until its painting was completed. The toys were predominately two-colored, although a few required more than two colors. Now, and in response to increased demand for the toys, the painting operation was changed so that the painters sat in a line by an endless chain of hooks. These hooks moved continuously in front of the painters and passed into a long horizontal oven. Each painter sat in a booth designed to carry away fumes and to backstop excess paint. The painters would take a toy from a nearby tray, position it in a jig inside the painting cubicle, spray on the color according to a pattern, and then hang the toy on a passing hook. The rate at which the hooks moved was calculated by the engineers so that each painter, when fully trained, could hang a painted toy on each hook before it passed beyond reach.

The painters were paid on a group bonus plan. Since the operation was new to them, they received a learning bonus which decreased by regular amounts each month. The learning bonus was scheduled to vanish in six months, by which time it was expected that they would be on their own—that is, able to meet the production standard and to earn a group bonus when they exceeded it.

## QUESTIONS

1. Assume that the training period for the new job set-up has just begun. What change do you predict in the level of output of the painters? Why?

   increase    decrease    stay the same

2. What other predictions regarding the behavior of these painters do you make based upon the situation described so far?

*Continuing On* By the second month of the training period, trouble developed. The painters learned more slowly than had been anticipated, and it began to look as though their production would stabilize far below what was planned. Many of the hooks were going by empty. The painters complained that the hooks moved too fast, and that the engineer had set the rates wrong. A few painters quit and had to be replaced with new ones. This further aggravated the learning problem. The team spirit that the management had expected to develop through the group bonus was not in evidence except as an expression of what the engineers called "resistance." One painter, whom the group regarded as its leader (and the management regarded as the ringleader), was outspoken in taking the complaints of the group to the supervisor. These complaints were that the job was messy, the hooks moved too fast, the incentive pay was not correctly calculated, and it was too hot working so close to the drying oven.

### Our Viewpoint

"Problems"—this is what you should have predicted! This is a perfect example of where "management" institutes a change in people's jobs without consulting those to be affected, and without thinking ahead to anticipate the consequences of the change for the people involved. The actual work performance of the individual painters and the work unit as a whole has decreased. In addition, the workers are complaining about the new job arrangement. Some have even quit. Productivity and employee satisfaction are down.

## QUESTION

1. What would you recommend that the responsible manager do now? Why?

*Continuing On* A consultant was hired to work with the supervisor. She recommended that the painters be brought together for a general discussion of the working conditions. Although hesitant, the supervisor agreed to this plan.

The first meeting was held immediately after the shift was over at four o'clock in the afternoon. It was attended by all eight painters. They voiced the same complaints again: the hooks went by too fast, the job was too dirty, and the room was hot and poorly ventilated. For some reason, it was this last item that seemed to bother them most. The supervisor promised to discuss the problems of ventilation and temperature with the engineers, and a second meeting was scheduled. In the next few days the supervisor had several talks with the engineers. They, along with the plant superintendent, felt that this was really a trumped-up complaint, and that the expense of corrective measures would be prohibitively high.

The supervisor came to the second meeting with some apprehensions. The painters, however, did not seem to be much put out. Rather, they had a proposal of their own to make. They felt that if several large fans were set up to circulate the air around their feet, they would be much more comfortable. After some discussion, the supervisor agreed to pursue the idea. The supervisor and the consultant discussed the idea of fans with the superintendent. Three large propeller-type fans were purchased and installed.

The painters were jubilant. For several days the fans were moved about in various positions until they were placed to the satisfaction of the group. The painters seemed completely satisfied with the results, and the relations between them and the supervisor improved visibly.

The supervisor, after this encouraging episode, decided that further meetings might also prove profitable. The painters were asked if they would like to meet and discuss other aspects of the work situation. They were eager to do this. Another meeting was held, and the discussion quickly centered on the speed of the hooks. The painters maintained that the engineer had set them at an unreasonably fast speed and that they would never be able to fill enough of them to make a bonus.

The discussion reached a turning point when the group's leader explained that it wasn't that the painters couldn't work fast enough to keep up with the hooks, but that they couldn't work at that pace all day long. The supervisor explored the point. The painters were unanimous in their opinion that they could keep up with the belt for short periods if they wanted to. But they didn't want to because if they showed they could do this for short periods then they would be expected to do it all day long. The meeting ended with an unprecedented request by the painters: "Let us adjust the speed of the belt faster or slower depending on how we feel." The supervisor agreed to discuss this with the superintendent and the engineers.

The engineers reacted negatively to the suggestion. However, after several meetings it was granted that there was some latitude within which variations in the speed of the hooks would not affect the finished product. After considerable argument with the enginees, it was agreed to try out the painters' idea.

With misgivings, the supervisor had a control with a dial marked "low, medium, fast" installed at the booth of the group leader. The speed of the belt could now be adjusted anywhere between the lower and upper limits that the engineers had set.

## QUESTIONS

1. What changes do you now expect in the level of output of the painters? Why?

   increase decrease stay the same

2. What changes do you expect in the feelings of the painters toward their work situation? Why?

   more positive more negative no change

3. What other predictions do you make about the behavior of the painters?

*Continuing On* The painters were delighted, and spent many lunch hours deciding how the speed of the belt should be varied from hour to hour throughout the day. Within a week the pattern had settled down to one in which the first half hour of the shift was run on a medium speed (a dial setting slightly above the point marked "medium"). The next two and a half hours were run at high speed, and the half hour before lunch and the half hour after lunch were run at low speed. The rest of the afternoon was run at high speed with the exception of the last 45 minutes of the shift, which was run at medium.

The constant speed at which the engineers had originally set the belt was actually slightly below the "medium" mark on the control dial. the average speed at which the painters were running the belt was on the high side of the dial. Few, if any, empty hooks entered the oven, and inspection showed no increase of rejects from the paint room.

Production increased, and within three weeks (some two months before the scheduled ending of the learning bonus) the painters were operating at 30 to 50% above the level that had been expected under the original arrangement. Naturally, their earnings were correspondingly higher than anticipated. They were collecting their base pay, earning a considerable piece rate bonus, and still benefiting from the learning bonus. They were earning more now than many skilled workers in other parts of the plant.

## Our Viewpoint

The supervisor's meeting with the painters appears to have been worthwhile. Productivity is up, satisfaction is up and, for the individual painters, earnings are up. These three results suggest an ideal work situation in which individuals perform at high production levels, are satisfied, and are well rewarded.

## QUESTIONS

1. How do you feel about the situation at this point?

2. Suppose you were the supervisor. What would you expect to happen next? Why?

*Continuing On* Management was besieged by demands that the inequity between the earnings of the painters and those of other workers in the plant be taken care of. With growing irritation between the superintendent and the supervisor, the engineers and supervisor, and the superintendent and engineers, the situation came to a head when the superintendent revoked the learning bonus and returned the painting operation to its original status: the hooks moved again at their constant, time-studied, designated speed. Production dropped again, and within a month all but two of the eight painters had quit. The supervisor stayed on for several months, but, feeling aggrieved, then left for another job.

### Our Viewpoint

It seems a manager's job is never done! Do you remember Chapter 1, when we discussed how managers spend their time? They spend a lot of it *outside* of the work unit, and they do so for a purpose—to support the unit within the larger context of the total organization. The Hovey and Beard case is a good example of how the rest of the organization interfered with what seemed to be a very satisfied and productive work unit. Perhaps this interference could have been prevented through astute managerial action. The fact that it did occur reinforces the manager's need to be very aware of the total organization as a work setting.

## SUMMARY

There are numerous issues in the Hovey and Beard Company case which highlight the challenges of managing individuals as human resources of organizations. The four chapters in Part Two of this book should give you many insights into how to deal with these challenges. Specifically, you may look forward to studying about individual attributes, motivation theories, rewards, reinforcement principles, job designs, goals, and work schedules, among other related topics. As you move through these chapters you will find an increasing emphasis on applications which can help you to become a better manager of individuals as human resources of organizations.

### NOTE

[1]Abridged and adapted from chapter 10 "Group Dynamics and Intergroup Relations" by George Strauss and Alex Bavelas (under the title "The Hovey and Beard Case"). From *Money and Motivation,* edited by William F. Whyte. Copyright ©1955 by Harper & Row, Publishers, Inc.

# 3

# BASIC ATTRIBUTES OF INDIVIDUALS

# YOUNGER EMPLOYEES APPEAR TO HAVE MUCH LESS NEED TO LEAD OR SUCCEED

The following report appeared recently in the *Wall Street Journal*.[1]

An AT&T study of more than two hundred recently hired college graduates finds they have considerably less interest in climbing the corporate ladder than did their counterparts 25 years ago. AT&T researchers Douglas Bray and An Howard also discover that today's younger workers "don't want to take charge in group situations." "Those two things together make us very concerned" about future management, Bray adds.

An Opinion Research Corp. poll of about two hundred firms shows workers under age 30 among the most dissatisfied with their jobs and employee benefits; they also are the most critical of their company compared with others. The best time to communicate with these workers, the survey found, is the first year of employment. That's when their attitudes toward their employer are the most favorable.

One bright spot in the AT&T survey: Young workers are just as interested in doing a good job as they were 25 years ago.

**MANAGEMENT APPLICATIONS QUESTION**

This newspaper clipping highlights the difference age might make in affecting individual work performance and job satisfaction. What other individual attributes, in addition to age, should you be concerned about as a manager?

## PLANNING AHEAD

**The reading and other learning experiences in this chapter will familiarize you with the following topics.**

**The Individual Performance Equation**
**Personality**
**Demographic Characteristics of Individuals**
**Competency Characteristics of Individuals**
**Psychological Characteristics of Individuals**
**Managing Individual Differences**
**A Final Word on Individual Attributes**

People are different! Accordingly, it is important for you to stop and ask how age and other differences among individuals may influence their performance and satisfactions at work. Specifically, what things must a manager be concerned about when attempting to influence individual performance? This question introduces the concerns addressed in this chapter. Our discussion begins with an individual performance equation which identifies major influences on job performance. The rest of the chapter looks in some detail at each component of the equation, and gives special attention to several of the more talked about attributes of individuals.

# THE INDIVIDUAL PERFORMANCE EQUATION

The individual performance equation is:

$$\text{Performance} = \begin{matrix}\text{individual}\\ \text{attributes}\end{matrix} \times \begin{matrix}\text{work}\\ \text{effort}\end{matrix} \times \begin{matrix}\text{organizational}\\ \text{support}\end{matrix}$$

This equation views performance to be the result of the personal attributes of individuals, the work efforts they put forth, and the organizational support which they receive. A manager must understand how each of these factors, alone and in combination, affects performance.

## Individual Attributes

There are three broad categories of attributes which create individual differences relevant to our study of OB: demographic characteristics (age, for example), competency characteristics (i.e., aptitude/ability), and psychological characteristics (e.g., extroverted-introverted orientations). The potential for these characteristics to influence job performance as well as human resource maintenance is illustrated by the AT&T example. Of course, the importance of the various attributes depends on the nature of a job and its task requirements. Managerially speaking, the challenge is summarized as follows.

$$\text{Individual attributes} \xrightarrow[\text{match}]{\text{must}} \text{task requirements} \xrightarrow[\text{facilitate}]{\text{to}} \text{job performance}$$

If a manager is to do well in matching jobs and workers, he or she must understand the characteristics of persons in his or her own work unit. Later in the chapter we will describe the major categories of individual attributes in more detail and show how managers can relate them to performance. By the time our discussion is finished you will be quite comfortable in answering the Management Applications Question which introduced this chapter. For now, simply be aware that individual attributes, along with work effort and organizational support, are an important part of the individual performance equation.

## Work Effort

Suppose a manager has a subordinate whose individual characteristics fit the task requirements as closely as possible. Can we predict that the individual will be a high performer? If the answer to this question were "yes," the manager's job would be greatly simplified. Unfortunately, the answer is "no." The reason traces to the important variable we call work effort. See Cartoon 3.1 for additional clarification.

In order to achieve high levels of performance, even people with the requisite individual attributes must try to perform, that is, they must put forth adequate work effort. Consider the college classroom. In your present course, for example, the chances are that the actual abilities, ages and social backgrounds of you and your colleagues are quite similar. Does that mean that your instructor can expect the same level of performance from everyone? "Certainly not," is our reply, and the typical end of the course grade distribution supports our position. But why is this so? Why, as you look around the class, will performance vary when the individual characteristics of students are pretty much the same? Once again, the answer is effort. Some students work harder at their learning tasks than others.

Instead of using the term "effort," your response to our question may have been different. Perhaps you said, "performance will vary because some students are more motivated than others." **Motivation**

*"What puzzles me is how he's gotten four weeks behind in his work when he's only been here two days."*

Reprinted from Mgr. Magazine, 1977.

**to work** is a term used in OB to describe the forces within an individual that account for the level, direction, and persistence of effort expended at work. This definition links motivation to work effort, not to work performance. The distinction is important.

Motivation predicts effort. Effort, along with individual attributes and organizational support, predict performance. A highly motivated person is one who exerts substantial effort to serve the production purposes of the work unit and the organization. An unmotivated person is one who exerts only minimum effort in this regard.

The concept of motivation is a most significant addition to our study of individual work performance. Earlier, we described people who had the requisite individual attributes to perform, but didn't put forth the effort required to achieve high performance results. They were not motivated to do so. The converse example is just as real. Some people are very motivated, meaning they work very hard and put a lot of effort into their jobs, but still don't achieve high levels of performance. The performance equation suggests this might occur because of a lack of fit between individual characteristics and task requirements, or inadequate organizational support, or both.

Thus, managers must develop good strategies for positively influencing the motivation to work of their subordinates. Exertion of effort is an individual perogative. A manager cannot do a subordinate's work. This is the essence of the manager's challenge—being held accountable for work that someone else has to do. As a manager, you will be very interested in understanding individual motivation as a way of fostering maximum work efforts. Chapter 4 offers many insights in this regard.

## Organizational Support

The third component of the individual performance equation is support from the organization. Even the person whose individual characteristics satisfy job requirements and who is highly motivated may not be a good performer unless there is adequate support in the workplace. Some of the obstacles which may interfere with a person's attempt to do a good job are:[2]

- Lack of time
- Inadequate tools, equipment, facilities
- Unclear instructions
- Unfair levels of expected performance
- Lack of sufficient formal authority
- Uncooperative co-workers
- Poorly defined work methods and procedures

You have probably experienced how such lack of organizational support can intrude on work performance. Having to rush a job because of a short deadline, not having the best tools, or not receiving clear instructions are not uncommon occurrences. In fact, you might argue that such failures of support are often found in the college classroom. They can include unrealistic due dates for assignments, inability to get library reference material, and not getting a clear statement of what the instructor is looking for in the first place.

All such problems share a common theme. They direct a manager's attention to the question, "How well does the organization support a motivated and capable individual as he or she seeks to perform the assigned job?"

Managers must ensure that organizational support does exist in the work setting. This book treats several of the more important dimensions of such support. In Part Three we discuss how the work group can provide or withold support for individual task performance and similarly influence human resource maintenance. Part Four

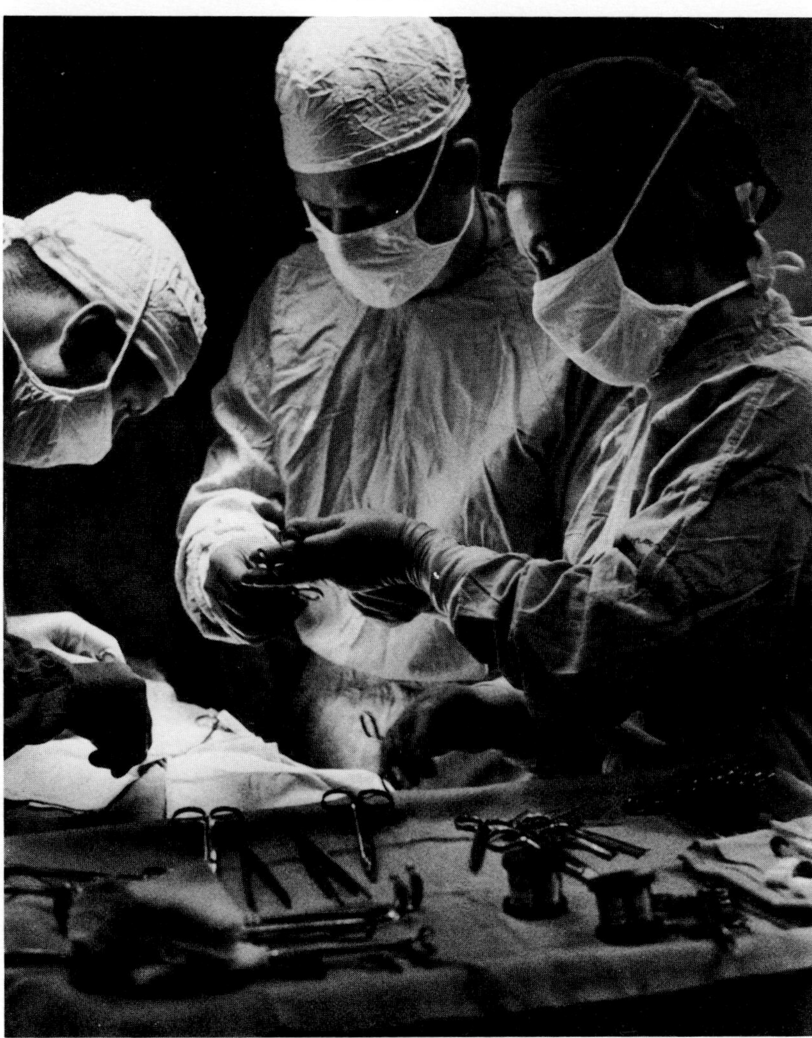

Good tools support people in their work efforts.

deals with organizational size, structure, and technology, all of which are additional sources of support. Finally, Part Five includes a treatment of leadership which, when provided by the manager and other key persons in the work setting, becomes an additional and very significant support mechanism.

In summary, remember that

1. A manager is often in a position to control levels of organizational support.
2. A manager should take the initiative to ensure that the proper level of support is provided to individuals in the work unit.

**Table 3.1 Management Implications for Variables in the Individual Performance Equation**

| Variable | Key Factors | Managerial Implications |
|---|---|---|
| Individual attributes | Demographic, competency, and psychological characteristics | To do a good job recruiting, selecting, and training employees. |
| Work effort | Motivation to work | To do a good job of allocating work-related rewards. |
| Organizational support | Work group dynamics; organization, size, structure, and technology; resources, goals, leadership | To do a good job planning, organizing, directing, and controlling work flows and the work setting. |

## A Manager's Viewpoint on Work Performance

Table 3.1 summarizes the action implications associated with each major variable in the individual performance equation. To ensure the presence of capable people, a manager must do a good job of recruiting, selecting, and training subordinates. Motivating workers to put forth maximum effort at work is accomplished through a good allocation of rewards. This was a major conclusion of our discussion in Chapter 2 of the satisfaction-performance controversy. Proper work planning, organizing, and direction are ways of ensuring that organizational support exists in the form of group, organizational, and leadership factors.

The manager's responsibility in facilitating individual work performance is summarized in Figure 3.1. In the figure, individual at-

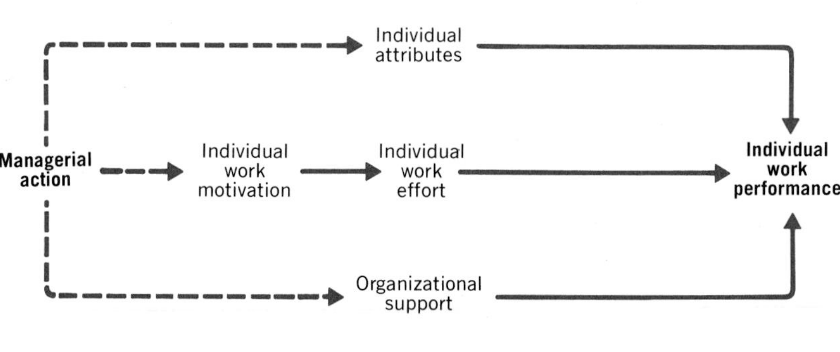


**FIGURE 3.1** Individual work performance as seen from the manager's viewpoint.

tributes, work effort, and organizational support are shown as the three primary determinants of performance. The manager is in a position to work directly with all three factors, although work effort is actually approached through the intervening variable of motivation.

Finally, recall that the individual performance equation shows a multiplicative relationship between individual attributes, work effort, and organizational support. This means that for performance to be high, all three factors must be present to a substantial degree. If any one or more is low or absent (e.g., if there is a lack of fit between individual characteristics and job requirements), the value of the others as positive influences on performance will be compromised.

## PERSONALITY

People frequently talk about one another's "personality." You have certainly heard about and perhaps even taken a "personality" test. But think; how many different interpretations are there for the term?

We consider **personality** to be the overall profile of basic attributes which, together, distinguish one individual from the next. Managers, therefore, can think of the personalities of other persons in the work setting as their unique blendings of individual attributes. Figure 3.2 shows three sets of characteristics important to this view of personality—demographic, competency, and psychological factors. A discussion of each of these components can help you to understand individual differences better and to account for them in the various decisions you will make as a manager.

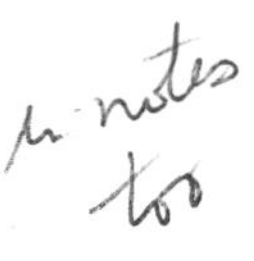

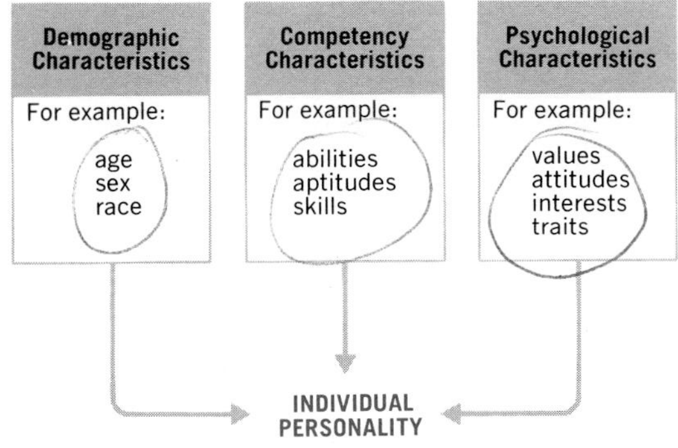


**FIGURE 3.2** The components of individual "personality."

# DEMOGRAPHIC CHARACTERISTICS OF INDIVIDUALS

**Demographic characteristics** are background variables which have helped shape what a person has become. Some are current, such as a person's socio-economic status; others are historical, such as where and how many places a person lived in growing up, size of family, family socio-economic status, and the like.

The demographic variables, in particular, are often the source of inappropriate generalizations or misconceptions. "Young people are lazy and lack ambition," "men are cold and insensitive," "blacks are better athletes," are a few of the more common examples. Managers who fall prey to such misconceptions lose sight of individual differences and can make erroneous judgments in their day-to-day work responsibilities. This problem is so serious that the federal government has enacted Equal Employment Opportunity legislation to protect people from such discrimination. *What Managers Do 3.1* gives you a good idea of how this legislation affects managers in one university setting.

Chapter 13 investigates the use of demographic characteristics in negative stereotyping of people by age and sex. Thus, we save a detailed treatment of this perceptual phenomenon for that chapter. What follows is a very brief synopsis of how misconceptions about three widely discussed demographic variables—age, sex, and race—may conflict with actual research insights. This section is offered to help you increase your sensitivity to individual attributes in working with other persons, as opposed to being prone to sweeping generalizations in these interpersonal contacts.

## Age

The newspaper clipping which introduced this chapter suggests the following as characteristics of younger versus older employees: less interest in advancement, don't want to take charge, and lower job satisfaction. But what do we find when we look at scientific evidence comparing older and younger workers? Research reveals fewer differences than many people think.

Take intelligence, for example. Early evidence suggests a decrease in intelligence with age. Recent research says this isn't so and, in fact, suggests that general intelligence and verbal ability increase with age. This is particularly true of persons at higher occupational, educational, and intellectual levels.[3]

## WHAT MANAGERS DO 3.1

### Employment Interviewing Guidelines for Supervisors

The following table summarizes some advice given by the personnel department of a large university to all supervisors. It shows what may and may not be asked of job candidates in a selection interview in order to comply with the guidelines of the Equal Employment Opportunities Commission (EEOC).

| Subject | Do NOT ask | OK to Ask |
|---|---|---|
| Age | Questions showing preference for specific age group. | Date of birth, proof of true age. |
| Family | About family planning, family size, children's ages, child care plans, spouse's employment, or salary. | Freedom to travel if job requires, meeting work schedule requirements. *All* applicants for a position must be asked the same questions. |
| Handicaps | General questions that bring out information that is not job related | Whether person has sensory, mental, or physical handicaps that relate to ability to perform job. |
| Marital status | Whether person is married, single, separated, divorced, engaged. | Nothing |
| National origin | About ancestry, birth place of applicant, parents, or spouse. | Ability to speak, read, or write English or a foreign language if the job requires. |
| Religion | About religion. | Anticipated absences from the job. |

Although intelligence doesn't decrease with age, some other physical characteristics do. Advancing age may bring decreased visual perception and a slowing of muscular responses. These changes could affect worker performance in tasks emphasizing speed and dexterity.

Older workers do seem to be more satisfied with various aspects of the work place than are younger workers. This supports AT&T's views as reported in the introductory news clipping. Older persons may also be more committed or loyal to the organization and have better attendance records. One exception is in fast-changing fields where older workers are likely to be less satisfied due to a feeling that their skills are becoming obsolete and are not keeping up with job demands.[4]

## Sex

Male-female differences are a much talked-about subject today. Summarized research shows that there are generally less performance-related differences between women and men than most people think. For example, there are no consistent male-female differences in sociability, suggestibility, self-esteem, learning ability, and analytical skills. There are also no differences in vocational interests, leadership, problem-solving ability, capabilities, cooperation, competition, motivation, or job satisfaction.[5]

Given all these similarities, where are the differences? It appears that females tend to be higher in verbal abilities, while males are higher in spacial-visual and mathematical abilities, and that males tend to be more aggressive.[6] *Newsline 3.1,* however, shows that research and considerable debate still continue on these topics as well.

A key question with which any manager must be concerned is the implications of male-female differences for organizations and management practices. As a manager, you would be wise not to

A woman in a traditionally male dominated occupation.

## NEWSLINE 3.1

### Do Males Have a Math Gene?

Can girls do math as well as boys? All sorts of recent tests have shown that they cannot. Most educators and feminists have blamed this phenomenon on socialization—arguing that because girls are told they can't do well in math, they develop "math anxiety" and don't. But last week, a new study appeared that explains the difference mainly in genetic terms. The authors' conclusion: "Sex differences in achievement in and attitude toward mathematics result from superior male mathematical ability."

The researchers admit that their results do not rule out "other environmental explanations," but they do address one commonly held idea: that boys are encouraged to like math more than girls. The psychologists used attitude questionnaires which showed, said Benbow, that "our girls like math just as much as boys" and that they did not believe math would be less useful in future careers.

The study's conclusions have drawn fierce objections from those who believe that environment, not genes, is the culprit. Says Shelia Tobias, the feminist author of "Overcoming Math Anxiety": "If your mother hates math and your father tells you not to worry your pretty little head about it, do you think that a math test would be an accurate measure of your ability?" Stephen Ivens, research director for the College Entrance Examination Board in New York City, agrees that there is a significant difference between boys' and girls' math scores, but he also maintains that environment is a factor. "If we reward girls differently," Ivens says, "the differences will probably decrease."

Patricia Lund Casserly, a senior research associate with the Educational Testing Service, which produces the SAT's, is among those who believe that results are what really count. "The question of genetic differences doesn't matter to me," she says. "The question is, can girls learn math, can girls make fine scientists and engineers?" The answer is yes.

Source: From Dennis A. Williams with Patricia King, "Do Males Have a Math Gene?," *Newsweek* (December 15, 1980), p. 73.

anticipate organizationally significant sex differences. At the very least, sex differences aren't great enough to justify the discrimination in job opportunities and careers which have traditionally existed between females and males. More is said on this issue when "sex-role stereotypes" are discussed in Chapter 13.

## Race

The most talked-about of possible racial differences are between blacks and whites. One of the more interesting debates relates to differences in athletic capabilities. Consider the following excerpts from a newspaper article reporting interviews with O. J. Simpson and John Mackey, two famous black athletes. O. J.'s comments came first.

> We are built a little differently, built for speed—skinny calves, long legs, high asses are all characteristic of blacks. That's why blacks wear long socks. We have skinny calves and short socks won't stay up. I'll argue with any doctor that physically we're geared to speed, and most sports have something to do with speed.[7]

The newspaper article goes on to say:

> In locker rooms, it is commonly agreed that blacks have bigger hands, arms, and for physiological reasons, are possessed of more speed, quickness and agility . . . There are all sorts of theories. Blacks are built differently. Blacks are more "hungry" and the two quickest ways out of poverty are sports and entertainment. Then too, there is the matter of environment, or what you did when you were a kid. It is a theory supported by John Mackey, a great tight end for Baltimore who has said: "I was chasing rabbits as a kid, and I could outrun any white guy who was just jogging up and down the street. When they turn loose African athletes who have been chasing, say, Cheetahs, then they will rewrite the record books. It's not because they're black, but because of what they've been doing!"

Among the more controversial racial discussions are those concerning differences in intelligence and ability. A substantial debate, for example, continues to rage as to the validity and significance of IQ tests on which whites tend to score higher than blacks.[8] Elsewhere, evidence suggests that blacks tend to be more ambitious and upwardly mobile than whites. Blacks also want work that provides higher income, but seem less interested than whites in work that provides a sense of accomplishment.[9]

It is still to be determined exactly what black-white differences exist, and to pinpoint if they are truly inherent in the races or are caused purely by discrimination and environment. In the end result, racial differences among people may be far less significant than the feelings people of various races have for one another. This latter point will be a continuing challenge for any manager.

## Conclusion

Demographic characteristics in general, and the three discussed here in particular, can be used to broadly classify differences among people. However, these factors should be assessed very carefully, and always with an awareness of the more specific characteristics they represent. For example, a manager might find that women performed better than men on an assembly task. The reason for this will probably not be an inherent sex difference, but a difference in skill. Rather than recruiting only women for the job, it would be far better to screen male and female applicants for the requisite skills. Thus, the issue becomes more a question of "competency" than "demography." A manager should always keep this point in mind when considering the significance of differing demographic characteristics among workers.

## COMPETENCY CHARACTERISTICS OF INDIVIDUALS

The term "competence" describes the aptitude and ability characteristics so important to individuals at work. **Aptitude** represents the capability to learn something. **Ability** reflects an existing capacity to perform the various tasks needed for a given job.[10] Aptitudes, in fact, are potential abilities. Abilities are skills which an individual already possesses.

Competency is an important consideration when a manager is initially hiring or selecting individuals to do a job. Once people with the appropriate aptitudes or abilities have been selected, then on-the-job and continuing education or training activities can be used to develop or enhance the required job skills. Among the more important aptitudes and abilities are basic mental, motor, and physical competencies.

### Mental Competencies

Each of us is acquainted with various tests used to measure mental aptitudes and abilities. Some provide an overall "IQ" score (e.g., the Stanford-Binet IQ test). Others provide measures of more specific competencies required of people entering various educational programs or career fields. Surely you have taken the ACT or SAT college entrance tests. Perhaps you plan to take a test for graduate study in law, medicine, or management. All such tests seek to measure mental aptitude or ability and thereby facilitate the screening and selection of applicants. Of course, there is some controversy over the validity of such tests and of the significance accorded to test score trends over time. Table 3.2 gives you an idea of the different kinds of mental abilities that can be measured as part of the job recruitment and selection process.[11] College grades, by the way, are often used by potential employers as indicators of a person's mental competencies. *Newsline 3.2* offers some thoughts on how the reported "grade inflation" is viewed by corporate recruiters.

**Table 3.2 Sample Mental Abilities and Motor Competencies Used in the Job Recruitment and Selection Process**

| | Description | Example |
|---|---|---|
| *Mental Abilities* | | |
| Perceptual speed | To perceive visual similarities and differences quickly and accurately. | Selecting the design in a series that is different from the others. |
| Numerical ability | To be speedy and accurate in making simple arithmetic computations such as adding, subtracting, multiplying, dividing. | Making change at a cash register. |
| Verbal comprehension | To understand the meanings of words and their relationships to each other; to comprehend readily what is read or heard. | Understanding and answering customer inquiries. |
| Inductive reasoning | To be able to discover a rule or principle and apply it in solving a problem. | Determining what is to come next in a series of numbers or words. |
| *Motor Competencies* | | |
| Multi-limb coordination | Ability to coordinate movements of a number of limbs simultaneously. | Packing a box with both hands. |
| Response orientation | Ability to make correct and accurate movements in relation to a stimulus under highly speeded conditions. | Flicking a switch when a warning horn sounds. |
| Manual dexterity | Skillful arm and hand movements in handling large objects under speeded conditions. | Placing blocks rapidly into a form board. |
| Finger dexterity | Skillful manipulation of small objects with the fingers. | Screwing a nut on a small bolt into a tight space. |

Source: Summarized from a discussion of Thurstone by Marvin D. Dunnette in Marvin D. Dunnette (ed.) *Handbook of Industrial and Organizational Psychology;* (Chicago: Rand McNally, 1975) and Edwin A. Fleishman, "The Description and Prediction of Perceptual-Motor Skill Training." In R. Glaser (ed.) *Training Research and Education.* (Pittsburgh: University of Pittsburgh Press, 1962).

## NEWSLINE 3.2

### Question of Degree? "Grade Inflation Alters Some Firms' Hiring Practices"

That's the finding of a survey of corporate recruiting officials conducted by a University of Mississippi research team. Of the 53 companies (out of 100 sent questionnaires) that responded to the survey, 87% said college grading standards have deteriorated over the last decade. And 49% were changing their hiring practices as a result.

Of those in the latter category, half said they're relying more on class rank than on grade point average in evaluating job candidates, while 31% have become more selective about the schools at which they recruit. Some say they're developing their own tests to help them evaluate applicants. Employers "don't have the confidence in the quality of the college degree that they once had," says survey director Milton Pressley.

Source: *The Wall Street Journal* (March 13, 1979), p. 1. Reprinted by permission of The Wall Street Journal, 

## Motor and Physical Competencies

In addition to mental competencies, researchers are also interested in the motor and physical proficiencies which can affect people's performance and behavior at work. Table 3.2 gives examples of motor competencies relevant to certain jobs.

Important physical competencies include static strength, the maximum force that can be exerted against external objects (e.g., lifting weights), and stamina, the capacity to sustain maximum effort requiring cardiovascular exertion (e.g., a hundred-yard dash).[12] Once again, the relevance of these competencies varies from job to job. It is up to the manager to establish where and how a given competency becomes important.

Checkpoint

Test yourself before going further. Assume you have a task where a person unpacks objects from a box and places them in one of five different kinds of bins. The person receives a new box every thirty seconds and must place each empty box in a stack five feet from the unpacking area. Select and justify the most relevant motor proficiencies from Table 3.2. Are there other needed proficiencies that do not seem to be covered in the table?

## PSYCHOLOGICAL CHARACTERISTICS OF INDIVIDUALS

The third category of individual attributes in which we are interested is **psychological characteristics.** While there is a wide range of these characteristics, they share a common tendency to predispose an individual to behave in predictable ways. These predispositions can have a substantial influence on behavior. Extroverted salespersons, for example, are likely to see things differently than introverts and to be seen differently by others. These differences will influence their behavior and the sales they are able to generate.

Psychological characteristics help to complete the picture of someone's personality. They are an additional source of differences among individuals that managers can use to better understand their employees.

In treating psychological characteristics, we'll start with a general look at values, attitudes, interests, and traits. Then we'll illustrate two personality characteristics of special importance in the study of OB: internal-external orientation and problem-solving style.

### Values and Attitudes

**Values and attitudes** are similar in that they both are beliefs about what is or is not appropriate. Values are broader, however, and cut across specific situations to which attitudes are tied. "Free enterprise is better than a welfare state," is an attitude. "It's not whether you win or lose, but how you play the game," is a value. Values are more enduring than attitudes.[13] Table 3.3 shows an example of items used by researchers to measure the degree to which a person believes in the value of the individual versus society. Such values have been shown to differ among people from different countries and would also be expected to differ among individuals at work.[14]

### Interests

**Interests** are personal likes and dislikes toward different activities. While values, attitudes, and interests are all concerned with preferences, interests lack the "ought" feature of values and attitudes. Such a "morally right" feeling is not necessary for an interest. The interests of most importance to managers are those relating to people's vocational and job preferences. These have been shown to have a bearing on success in a given job area.[15] You may have completed the Strong Vocational Interest test or the Kuder Preference Record in trying to determine the best choice for your major in college. These

**Table 3.3 The Individualism Dimension**

| Collectivist | Individualist |
|---|---|
| In society, people are born into extended families or clans who protect them in exchange for loyalty. | In society, everybody is supposed to take care of himself/herself and his/her immediate family. |
| "We" consciousness holds sway. | "I" consciousness holds sway. |
| Identity is based in the social system. | Identity is based in the individual. |
| There is emotional dependence of individual on organizations and institutions. | There is emotional independence of individual from organizations or institutions. |
| The involvement with organizations is moral. | The involvement with organizations is calculative. |
| The emphasis is on belonging to organizations; membership is the ideal. | The emphasis is on individual initiative and achievement; leadership is the ideal. |
| Private life is invaded by organizations and clans to which one belongs; opinions are predetermined. | Everybody has a right to a private life and opinion. |
| Expertise, order, duty, and security are provided by organization or clan. | Autonomy, variety, pleasure, and individual financial security are sought in the system. |
| Friendships are predetermined by stable social relationships, but there is need for prestige within these relationships. | The need is for specific friendships. |
| Belief is placed in group decisions. | Belief is placed in individual decisions. |
| Value standards differ for in-groups and out-groups (particularism). | Value standards should apply to all (universalism). |

Source: Reprinted, by permission of the publisher, from "Motivation, Leadership, and Organization: Do American Theories Apply Abroad?," Gert Hofstede, *Organizational Dynamics* (Summer, 1980), 

and other similar inventories compare a person's interests with those of persons unsuccessful in various occupational areas. Presumably, an interest profile consistent with those common to persons in a given occupation is predicted to lead to success in that career field.

Like psychological characteristics in general, values, attitudes, and interests are important because of the predispositions toward behavior which they indicate. As a manager, you will be interested in trying to build on these predispositions in order to increase individual performance and human resource maintenance.

## Traits

**Traits** are "any distinguishable and relatively enduring ways in which one individual differs from another."[16] Traits are things held in common by individuals, but which differ in amount among them. Researchers are working to establish a listing of key traits that can be used to profile ideal personalities for various jobs. One of the best developed of these "trait-factor" approaches to personality is sampled for you in Figure 3.3. It includes "source traits" defined by their stability and usefulness in profiling many different occupations. The figure also shows a profile for airline pilots on the selected trait-factors.

## Psychological Characteristics of Special Research Interest

Our earlier treatment of psychological characteristics focused on a broad range of individual differences. Now let's narrow the focus and look at two specific psychological characteristics which illustrate variables currently receiving a lot of attention in the study of OB: internal-external orientation and problem-solving style.

### Internal-External Orientation

The **internal-external orientation** measures the extent to which a person feels able to affect his or her life.[17] People have general expectancies about whether events are controlled primarily by themselves, which indicates an internal orientation, or by outside forces, characteristic of an external orientation. "Internals" believe they control their own fate or destiny. "Externals" believe that much of what happens to them is uncontrolled and determined by outside forces.

Two examples of questionnaire items from a twenty-nine item inventory which has been shown to separate internals from externals are:[18]

1. a. Many of the unhappy things in people's lives are partly due to bad luck.
   b. People's misfortunes result from the mistakes they make.
2. a. As far as world affairs are concerned, most of us are the victims of forces we can neither understand nor control.
   b. By taking an active part in political and social affairs, the people can control world events.

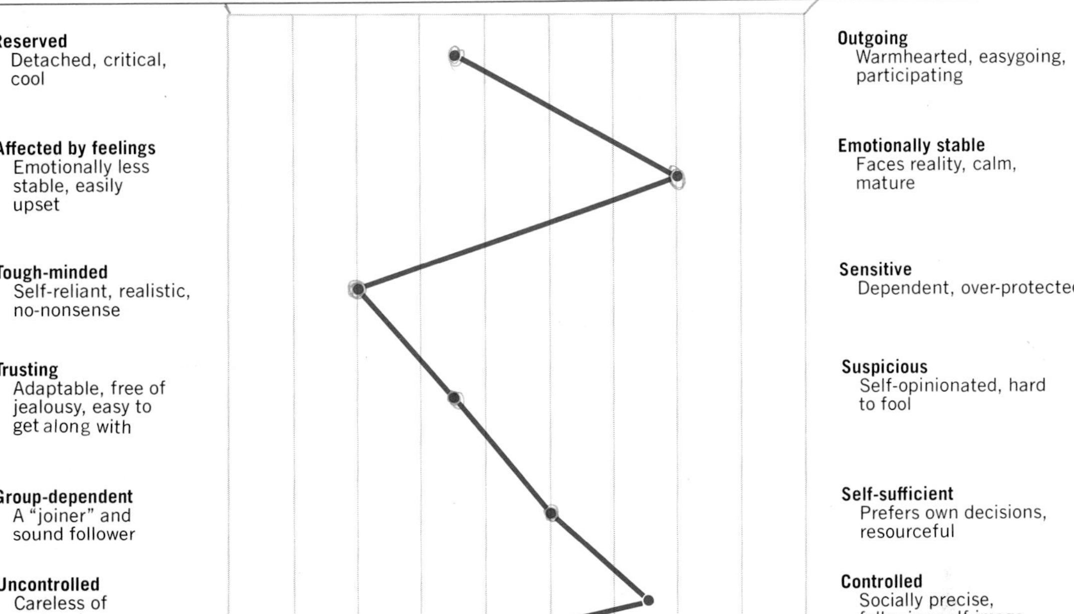


**FIGURE 3.3** Sample items from the Cattell trait-factor profile for airline pilots. (Source: Adapted from Raymond B. Cattell, "Personality Pinned Down," *Psychology Today,* July, 1973, p. 44, and Ledford, J. Bischof, *Interpreting Personality Theories,* Second Edition. New York: Harper & Row, 1970, pp. 464–466.)

In the complete inventory, answers 1a and 2a reflect an external orientation; 1b and 2b show an internal orientation.

Some ways in which externals and internals have been found to differ are summarized in Table 3.4. As you look at the table, ask yourself how these differences might be of importance in various jobs which people may hold.

## Problem-Solving Styles[19]

Another psychological characteristic is **problem-solving style,** the way in which a person goes about gathering and evaluating information in solving problems and making decisions.

### Checkpoint

What follows is the Problem-Solving Diagnostic Questionnaire.[20] Please respond to each item. There are no "right" or "wrong" answers.

**Table 3.4 Some Ways in Which Internals Differ from Externals**

| | |
|---|---|
| Information processing | Internals make more attempts to acquire information, are better at information retention, are less satisfied with amount of information they possess, are better at utilizing information and devising processing rules. |
| Job satisfaction | Internals are more satisfied, less alienated, and less rootless. |
| Self-control and risk behavior | Internals exhibit greater self-control, are more cautious, engage in less risky behavior. |
| Expectancies and results | Internals see stronger relationship between what they do and what happens to them, expect working hard leads to good performance, feel more control over how to spend time, perform better. |
| Preference for skill versus chance achievements | Internals prefer skill-achievement outcomes; externals prefer chance achievements. |
| Use of rewards | Internals more likely to use personally persuasive rewards and power bases; less likely to use coercion. |
| Response to others | Internals are more independent, more reliant on own judgment, less susceptible to influence of others, they resist subtle influence attempts and are more discriminating in information acceptance. Information is more likely to be accepted on own merits rather than based on prestige of its source. |
| Leader behavior | Internals prefer participative leadership; externals prefer directive. |

Source: Summarized from E. J. Phares, *Locus of Control: A Personality Determinant of Behavior* (Morristown, N.J.: General Learning Press, 1973); T. R. Mitchell, C. M. Smyser, and S. E. Weed, "Locus of Control: Supervision and Work Satisfaction," *Academy of Management Journal,* Vol. 18 (1975), pp. 623–631; and A. D. Szilagyi and H. P. Sims, "Expectancies and Locus of Control Across Multiple Occupational Levels," *Journal of Applied Psychology, 60* (1975), pp. 638–640.

## Problem Solving Diagnostic Questionaire

**PART I.** Circle the response that comes closest to how you usually feel or act.

1. Are you more careful about:
   A. people's feelings
   B. their rights
2. Do you usually get on better with:
   A. imaginative people
   B. realistic people
3. Which of these two is the higher compliment:
   A. he is a person of real feeling
   B. he is consistently reasonable
4. In doing something with

many other people, does it appeal more to you:
   A. to do it in the accepted way
   B. to invent a way of your own
5. Do you get more annoyed at:
   A. fancy theories
   B. people who don't like theories
6. It is higher praise to call someone:
   A. a person of vision
   B. a person of common sense
7. Do you more often let:
   A. your heart rule your head
   B. your head rule your heart
8. Do you think it is a worse fault:
   A. to show too much warmth
   B. to be unsympathetic
9. If you were a teacher, would you rather teach:
   A. courses involving theory
   B. fact courses

**PART II.** Which word in each of the following pairs appeals to you more? Circle A or B.

10. A. compassion   B. foresight
11. A. justice   B. mercy
12. A. production   B. design
13. A. gentle   B. firm
14. A. uncritical   B. critical
15. A. literal   B. figurative
16. A. imaginative   B. matter-of-fact

**PART III.** Use this key to score your problem-solving style. Count one point for each listed response on the following six scales. Then total the number of points recorded in each column. Instructions for classifying your scores are indicated below.

| Sensation | Intuition | Thinking | Feeling |
|---|---|---|---|
| 2B ______ | 2A ______ | 1B ______ | 1A ______ |
| 4A ______ | 4B ______ | 3B ______ | 3A ______ |
| 5A ______ | 5B ______ | 7B ______ | 7A ______ |
| 6B ______ | 6A ______ | 8A ______ | 8B ______ |
| 9B ______ | 9A ______ | 10B ______ | 10A ______ |
| 12A ______ | 12B ______ | 11A ______ | 11B ______ |
| 15A ______ | 15B ______ | 13B ______ | 13A ______ |
| 16B ______ | 16A ______ | 14B ______ | 14A ______ |
| Totals | | | |

Checkpoint

Write *intuitive* in the margin if your intuition score is equal to or greater than your sensation score. Write *sensation* if sensation is greater than intuition. Write *feeling* in the margin if feeling is greater than thinking. Write *thinking* if thinking is greater than feeling. When thinking equals feeling, you should write feeling if a male and thinking if a female.

In the problem-solving process, information gathering and evaluation are separate activities. Information gathering is the process by which a person organizes stimuli or data for use. Styles of information gathering vary from sensation to intuitive. **Sensation-type individuals** prefer routine and order, and emphasize well-defined details in gathering information. **Intuitive-type persons** prefer the big picture, like solving new problems, and dislike routine.

Evaluation involves making judgments about how to deal with information once it has been collected. Styles of information evaluation vary, from an emphasis on feeling to an emphasis on thinking.

**Table 3.5 Four Problem-Solving Styles**

| Personal Style | Action Tendencies |
|---|---|
| Sensation-Feeling (SF) | Focus on possibilities but approach them through interpersonal analyses.<br>Prefer dealing with theoretical or technical problems.<br>Enjoy positions that are ill-defined and require abstract skills.<br>Consider a number of options and problems simultaneously. |
| Intuitive-Feeling (IF) | Rely on general views, broad themes, and feelings.<br>Avoid specifics.<br>Decentralize decision making and maintain few rules and regulations. |
| Sensation-Thinking (ST) | Emphasize external facts, details, and certainty.<br>Use a scientific approach to decisions.<br>Develop rules and regulations for judging people's performance.<br>Concentrate on short-term, realistic goals. |
| Intuitive-Thinking (IT) | Show concern for here-and-now human problems.<br>Structure organizations for the benefit of the individual.<br>Emphasize detailed facts about people rather than tasks. |

Source: Adapted from Don Hellriegel and John W. Slocum, "Problem-Solving Style, Storytelling and Organization Design: Interesting Comparisons," *Southwest Division Academy of Management Proceedings* (1976), pp. 85–89.

**Feeling-type individuals** are oriented toward conformity and try to accommodate themselves to other people. They try to avoid problems that might result in disagreements. **Thinking-type people** use reason and intellect to deal with problems. They downplay emotional aspects in the problem situation.

When these two dimensions of information gathering and evaluation are combined, the matrix of problem-solving styles shown in Table 3.5 results. The table contains descriptions of four basic problem-solving styles: Sensation-Feeling (SF), Intuitive-Feeling (IF), Sensation-Thinking (ST), and Intuitive-Thinking (IT). By referring back to the last *Checkpoint* which indicates your preference on each of these dimensions, you can locate yourself in Table 3.5. How accurate do you feel the description is for you?

Researchers suggest that people with particular problem-solving styles may be better suited to certain jobs than others. For instance intuitive-feeling or intuitive-thinking individuals are likely to be better counsellors than sensation-feeling or sensation-thinking individuals. Given a fit between the problem-solving style and the information processing requirements of a job, a person should be more productive and satisfied than when there is a lack of fit.

## MANAGING INDIVIDUAL DIFFERENCES

Now that several of the basic attributes of individuals have been identified, let's explore how they can be managed to promote high performance and human resource maintenance. When there is an appropriate fit between individual characteristics and job requirements for each subordinate, a manager will have provided the work unit with a great boost in its performance potential. In fact, researchers report being able to predict as much as 30 to 50% of the variation in individual performance by these variables alone.[21] The remainder of the performance variation remains to be explained by the factors of work effort and organizational support, as well as unknown factors which haven't yet been discovered in OB research.

Thus, managers are advised to staff their work units with individuals of appropriate characteristics such that, given proper support and a motivation to work, they will be very productive. *What Managers Do 3.2* explains how one company tries to do this by improving on its selection and recruitment procedures for managerial employees. This staffing challenge involves (1) identifying individual attributes, and (2) determining the selection requirements of any jobs under their control.

## WHAT MANAGERS DO 3.2

### The Motorola Approach to Selecting Managers

Motorola, the giant Chicago-based electronics firm, is developing a systematic program for the selection and development of its future managers. The approach looks like this:

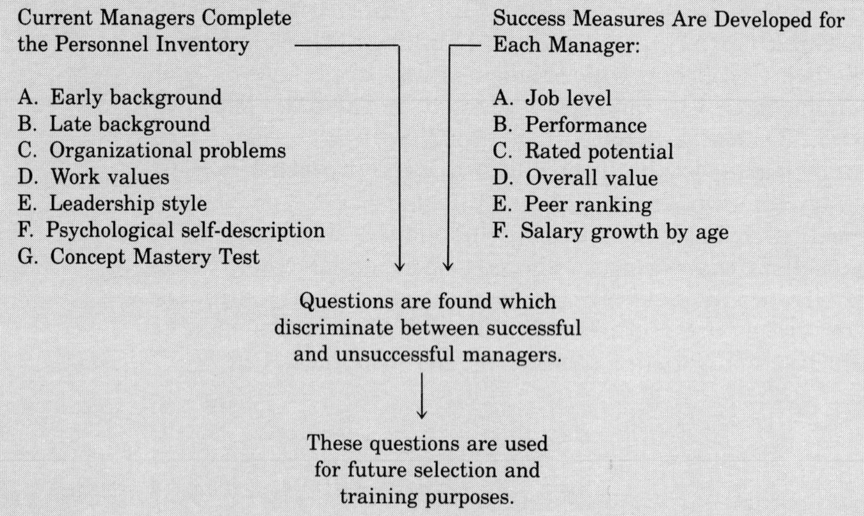

Current Managers Complete the Personnel Inventory

A. Early background
B. Late background
C. Organizational problems
D. Work values
E. Leadership style
F. Psychological self-description
G. Concept Mastery Test

Success Measures Are Developed for Each Manager:

A. Job level
B. Performance
C. Rated potential
D. Overall value
E. Peer ranking
F. Salary growth by age

↓

Questions are found which discriminate between successful and unsuccessful managers.

↓

These questions are used for future selection and training purposes.

Source: Adapted from Paul J. Patinka, "One More Time: Are Leaders Born or Made? From *Crosscurrents in Leadership* by James G. Hunt and Lars L. Larson. Copyright © 1979 by the Southern Illinois University Press. Reprinted by permission of Southern Illinois University Press.

## Identifying Individual Attributes

Information about individual differences can come from the individuals themselves (e.g., completing a job application form or taking a special test), from direct observations by the manager (such as a recruiting or performance appraisal interview), and from organizational records (e.g., a personnel file).

Employment applications typically provide background information thought to be relevant to future job performance. These application forms range from the simple to the very complex. Many of the latter use what is called a bio-data approach. This involves a wide range of questions covering the applicant's past and present background and are designed to be scored together as scales or dimensions in much the same manner as test questions.[22] Carefully developed bio-data approaches can be very good predictors of job performance. Sample bio-data items for several such scales are shown in Table 3.6.

Tests are another information-gathering device. Aptitude and ability tests are usually of the pencil and paper type, but tests may extend into skill or aptitude demonstrations as well. Many organizations are using formal assessment centers to identify promising managerial candidates. Here, candidates are engaged in a variety of cases, exercises, and simulations. Trained observers then score and evaluate individual performance, and make recommendations for future job placements or training programs.[23] *What Managers Do 3.3* reports on the use of assessment centers.

Interviews are still another means of information collection which may identify things not as readily obtained by other means. They may be used, for example, to gauge an applicant's interpersonal abilities or personal appearance.

Managers will typically use a combination of the above approaches to try to obtain information about people's individual attri-

**Table 3.6 Sample Bio-Data Items**

| Dimension | Questions or Items[a] |
|---|---|
| Personal | Age, marital status, number of years married, age when first child born, length of time at last address |
| Background, general | Occupation of father, occupation of mother, stable or transient home life |
| Educational | Education, educational level of wife, education finances—extent of dependence on parents, major field of study—high school |
| Employment experience | Previous occupations (general type of work, previous selling experience, length of time unemployed) |
| Skills | Does repair work on own car, number of machines that a person can operate |
| Socio-economic level (financial status) | Number of creditors, number of accounts with stores, make and age of auto owned |
| Social | Club memberships (social, community, campus, high school), offices held in clubs |
| Interests | Prefer outside to inside labor, hobbies |
| Personal characteristics, attitudes expressed | Willing to relocate or transfer, drive, stated job preferences |

[a]These are designed to be answered in terms of yes-no or multiple choice formats for scoring purposes.

Source: Adapted from Craig E. Schneier and Richard W. Beatty, *Personnel Management Today* (Reading, Mass.: Addison-Wesley, 1978), pp. 249–251.

## WHAT MANAGERS DO 3.3

### Measuring Executive Muscle

A growing number of organizations are using formal assessment centers to evaluate managerial abilities. Executives are selected for participation in a variety of simulated management situations. Trained observers then develop critiques of managerial strengths and weaknessess, and design programs of personal development for promising candidates. The following excerpt describes one person's experience in an assessment center exercise.

The executive bends over his desk, obviously under pressure. He has suddenly been named to replace the personnel director of a large manufacturing company who has suffered a heart attack while on vacation. He has been asked by a vice-president to spend a few hours on the weekend going through his predecessor's in-basket, where a number of pressing matters have been piling up. The thirty separate items in the basket involve subordinates and superiors—none of whom he knows well—in his own and other departments. Nearly all the items require some attention, and often a decision. There's a request for a vacation at an awkward time; an important conference scheduled for the day he formally arrives; a new organizational development program; recruitment problems; an imminent deadline for next year's department budget; a dubious travel voucher; and numerous complaints about promotions, women's rights, and the shortage of clerical help.

For background guidance, the new personnel director's secretary has prepared a few reference materials on the company's organization and policies. Beyond that, he's on his own. Since it's Saturday, there's no one else in the office to consult with, and the switchboard is closed. His new boss will obviously be watching his performance very carefully; his new colleagues will be equally curious about the way he takes over. All his decisions must be put into notes or memos, since he will be away and unreachable for the following week—which complicates many of his choices. It is now one o'clock in the afternoon. He has three hours to work before leaving for the airport.

Source: Berkely Rice, "Measuring Executive Muscle," *Psychology Today* (December 1978), p. 95.

butes. Once a person is on the job, the manager will then try to supplement the initial fit between person and job by encouraging high levels of work effort and providing needed organizational support. Training may also be used to help turn aptitudes into abilities and/or to maintain abilities over time.

### Determining Selection Requirements

It is during the hiring process that managers have the first opportunity to take action ensuring good individual-to-job fits among their subordinates. Listed below are several steps which can help the manager establish recruitment and selection criteria to be used in this staffing process.[24]

1. Study the job(s) in order to identify individual characteristics that might be related to performance success. Conduct a formal job analysis to provide a specific description of job duties. Draw up an accompanying job specification to summarize the characteristics which a person in the job should possess.
2. Decide on how you are going to measure job applicants on the key characteristics. If finger dexterity is important, for example, how will it be measured?
3. Obtain the information on a large group of job applicants (preferably thirty or more). Hire candidates from this group without referring to the data on differing individual characteristics.
4. Obtain data concerning the job performance (or other "success" measures) of all these people.
5. Determine the actual relationship between individual characteristics and performance success. Compile the set of characteristics which is the best predictor of desired job outcomes.
6. If possible, repeat the process again with a different group of applicants. This cross-validation will minimize the possibility that your original findings were due to chance.
7. Use the resulting profile of individual characteristics when selecting future applicants for this particular job.

## A CONCLUDING WORD ON INDIVIDUAL ATTRIBUTES

The specific attributes we've covered have been illustrative rather than exhaustive. We've simply tried to sensitize you to some examples of individual attributes that can be important. There are many others which might be important, depending upon the nature of the manager's work group. A key consideration is the extent to which a manager can determine job requirements for the jobs in his or her unit. If this can be done, then the importance of various attributes can be determined using techniques similar to those we have discussed.

We should also point out that the techniques are discussed in considerably more detail in personnel texts. Just as this chapter has sensitized you to the importance of various kinds of attributes without providing an exhaustive list, so too has it sensitized you to techniques for determining the importance of various attributes without spelling these out in detail.

Finally, though we've emphasized the importance of individual attributes in selection and placement, that is not their only use. They are very important in day-to-day work unit interactions. You'll want to keep them in mind throughout the rest of the book and especially in Part Three, which deals with groups. As we will show, the mix of individual attributes across the groups' members has much to do with what happens in the group and the way the group performs.

## SUMMARY

This chapter has introduced the individual performance equation.

$$\text{Performance} = \frac{\text{individual}}{\text{attributes}} \times \frac{\text{work}}{\text{effort}} \times \frac{\text{organizational}}{\text{support}}$$

The equation focuses your attention on individual attributes, work effort, and organizational support as three primary determinants of individual performance at work.

The study of motivation, defined as the forces within the individual that account for the level and direction of work effort, and organizational support have been reserved for the coming chapters. The bulk of our present discussion has dealt with individual characteristics and how managers can best take them into account in seeking to develop desirable work behaviors among their subordinates.

Three categories of basic individual attributes have been specified: demographic, competency, and psychological characteristics. The notion of personality has been introduced as the sum total of any one individual's unique profile on such personal characteristics.

Demographic characteristics include age, sex, and race, among others. Our discussion has included examples of how these factors are both correctly and incorrectly assumed to be a source of performance variations at work. Competency has been defined to include ability and aptitude factors. We have looked closely at mental characteristics and motor/physical competencies in this regard. Several examples have been used to show how organizations and their managers attempt to identify and measure these factors as part of their hiring and staff training programs. This latter point applies as well to our look at values, attitudes, and interests as key psychological characteristics of individuals.

We have concluded the chapter by showing how managers attempt to use a knowledge of individual differences to obtain a proper fit between individuals and their jobs. When this matching is done well, researchers suggest that quite a bit of the variation in individual performance can be accounted for. Matching individual attributes and jobs is an important first step in managing individuals at work. Given this preliminary understanding, Chapter 4 will now direct your attention to various motivation theories which attempt to explain effort as a second key variable in the individual performance equation.

## THINKING THROUGH THE ISSUES

1. Present the individual performance equation and use an example to show how each of the three major variables must be present if high performance is to be truly facilitated in the work setting.
2. List some forms of organizational support. Show how a lack of organizational support for teaching might inhibit the otherwise capable and motivated instructor from doing a good job in the classroom.
3. State and defend a list of demographic characteristics that might be associated with high performance as a research scientist and assembly-line worker. Do the same for competence and psychological characteristics.
4. Find an example from a newspaper or magazine of improper age, sex, or race discrimination in employment. Analyze and explain why such discrimination occurs and state how it might be eliminated.
5. Do you believe that entrance tests (e.g., SAT, GMAT) are useful and fair as screening devices for selecting applicants to colleges and various professional shools? Why or why not?
6. Make a list of the psychological characteristics you expect to be associated with success as a manager. Defend your list.
7. Assume you are trying to select students who are especially suited to do well in an OB class.
   a. Show how you might modify the "hiring" steps summarized in the chapter so that they would help in the selection process.

**b.** Indicate some possible individual attributes that you think might be important and show how you would use these attributes in student selection.

8. We have all heard someone described as having a "good" personality. What might that mean, and what would some managerial implications be, given the way the term has been described in the chapter?

## CASE: REVERSE DISCRIMINATION[25]

At a meeting of all management personnel, the legal advisor to the Rampart Insurance Company spoke on the subject of employee discrimination with special emphasis on subjects relating to employees of minority groups and female employees. Essentially the message was that there should be no discriminatory decisions by managers relating to the selection and hiring process, promotion policies, seniority, recognition, vacations, work loads, and so forth.

The managers of the company accepted the advice seriously, and under a climate established and implemented by the president, administered the philosophy vigorously. In some cases, women who had good performance records, equal seniority with men, and other minimal qualifications were promoted to supervisory positions, even though they might be married, have several children, and could not work overtime when needed. In other cases, employees who were classed as members of minority groups were purposely rated high on employee evaluation reports so a basis could be established for justifying a forthcoming promotion.

After about a year had passed, other nonmanagement employees gave signs that they were upset, dissatisfied, and angry about the newly introduced managerial philosophy. When no attention was given to their statements that they were now being discriminated against, and when no action came forth when they requested a hearing with the president, the informal leaders of the group posted a notice on all bulletin boards which read as follows:

All employees who are dissatisfied with present management practices and who desire to meet and discuss the organization of an independent union or discuss the possibility of affiliating with a national union, please sign below.

### Question

What would you do now as President? Why?

## THE MANAGER'S VOCABULARY

**Ability** The capacity to perform the various tasks needed for a given job.

**Aptitude** The capability to learn something.

**Attitude** A specific belief about what is or is not appropriate (e.g., "free enterprise is better than a welfare state").

**Demographic Characteristics** Background variables (e.g., age, sex, race) which help shape what a person becomes over time.

**Internal-External Orientation** the extent to which people feel able to affect their lives.

**Interests** Likes and dislikes toward different activities.

**Motivation to Work** The forces within an individual that account for the level, direction, and persistence of effort expended at work.

**Personality** The overall profile or basic attributes which together distinguish one individual from the next.

**Problem-Solving Style** The way in which a person goes about gathering and evaluating information in solving problems and making decisions.

**Psychological Characteristics** Psychological factors which predispose an individual to behave in predictable ways.

**Trait** Any distinguishable and relatively enduring way in which one individual differs from another.

**Value** A broad belief about what is or is not appropriate (e.g., "it's not whether you win or lose, but how you play the game that counts").

## Notes

[1]"Younger Employees Appear to Have Much Less Need to Lead or Succeed," *The Wall Street Journal* (December 8, 1980), p. 1. Reprinted by permission of *The Wall Street Journal,* copyright © Dow Jones & Company, Inc., 1980. All rights reserved.

[2]Charles N. Greene, "The Satisfaction-Performance Controversy," *Business Horizons,* Vol. 15 (October 1972), pp. 31–42.

[3]J. B. Miner and M. G. Miner, *Personnel and Industrial Relations,* Third Edition (New York: Macmillan, 1977).

[4]Ibid.

[5]Ibid.

[6]Ibid.

[7]Dallas Times Herald, July 19, 1977.

[8]A. R. Jensen, *Educability and Group Differences* (New York: Harper and Row, 1973).

[9]Miner and Miner, op. cit., 1977.

[10]Larry L. Cummings and Donald P. Schwab, *Performance in Organizations: Determinants and Appraisal* (Glenview, Ill.: Scott, Foresman and Co., 1973) p. 8.

[11]M. D. Dunnette, "Basic Attributes of Individuals in Relation to Behavior in Organizations," in M. D. Dunnette (ed.), *Handbook of Industrial and Organizational Psychology* (Chicago: Rand McNally, 1976).

[12]E. A. Fleishman, *The Structure and Measurement of Physical Fitness* (Englewood Cliffs, N.J.: Prentice-Hall, 1964).

[13]M. A. Brown, "Values—A Necessary but Neglected Ingredient of Motivation on the Job," *Academy of Management Review,* Vol. 1. (1976) pp. 15–23.

[14]P. E. Connor and B. W. Becker, "Values and the Organization: Suggestions for Research," *Academy of Management Journal,* Vol. 18 (1975) pp. 550–561.

[15]B. Berelson and G. A. Steiner, *Human Behavior: Shorter Edition* (New York: Harcourt, Brace and World, 1967).

[16]J. P. Guilford, *Personality* (New York: McGraw-Hill, 1959).

[17]J. B. Rotter, "Generalized Expectancies for Internal Versus External Control of Reinforcement," *Psychological Monographs,* Vol. 80 (1966) Whole No. 609, pp. 1–28.

[18]Ibid.

[19]This section based on a discussion by Don Hellriegel and John W. Slocum, Organizational Behavior, Second Edition (Minneapolis: West Publishing Company, 1976a): and, D. Hellriegel and J. W. Slocum, "Problem-Solving Style, Storytelling and Organization Design: Interesting Comparisons," *Southwest Division Academy of Management Proceedings,* (1976b) pp. 85–89.

[20]Adapted/reprinted from Hellriegel and Slocum, op. cit., 1976a, p. 222. Copyright © 1976, West Publishing Co. All rights reserved.

[21]J. P. Campbell, M. D. Dunnette, E. E. Lawler, III, and K. E. Weick, *Managerial Behavior, Performance and Effectiveness,* (New York: McGraw-Hill, 1970).

[22]W. A. Owens, "Background Data," in M. D. Dunnette (ed.), 1976.

[23]Miner and Miner, op. cit., 1977.

[24]This section is based on a discussion by Miner and Miner, op. cit., 1977.

[25]John M. Champion and John H. James, *Critical Incidents in Management,* Third Edition © Richard D. Irwin, Inc., 1963, 1969, and 1975, pp. 246–247. All rights reserved. Used with permission.

# 4

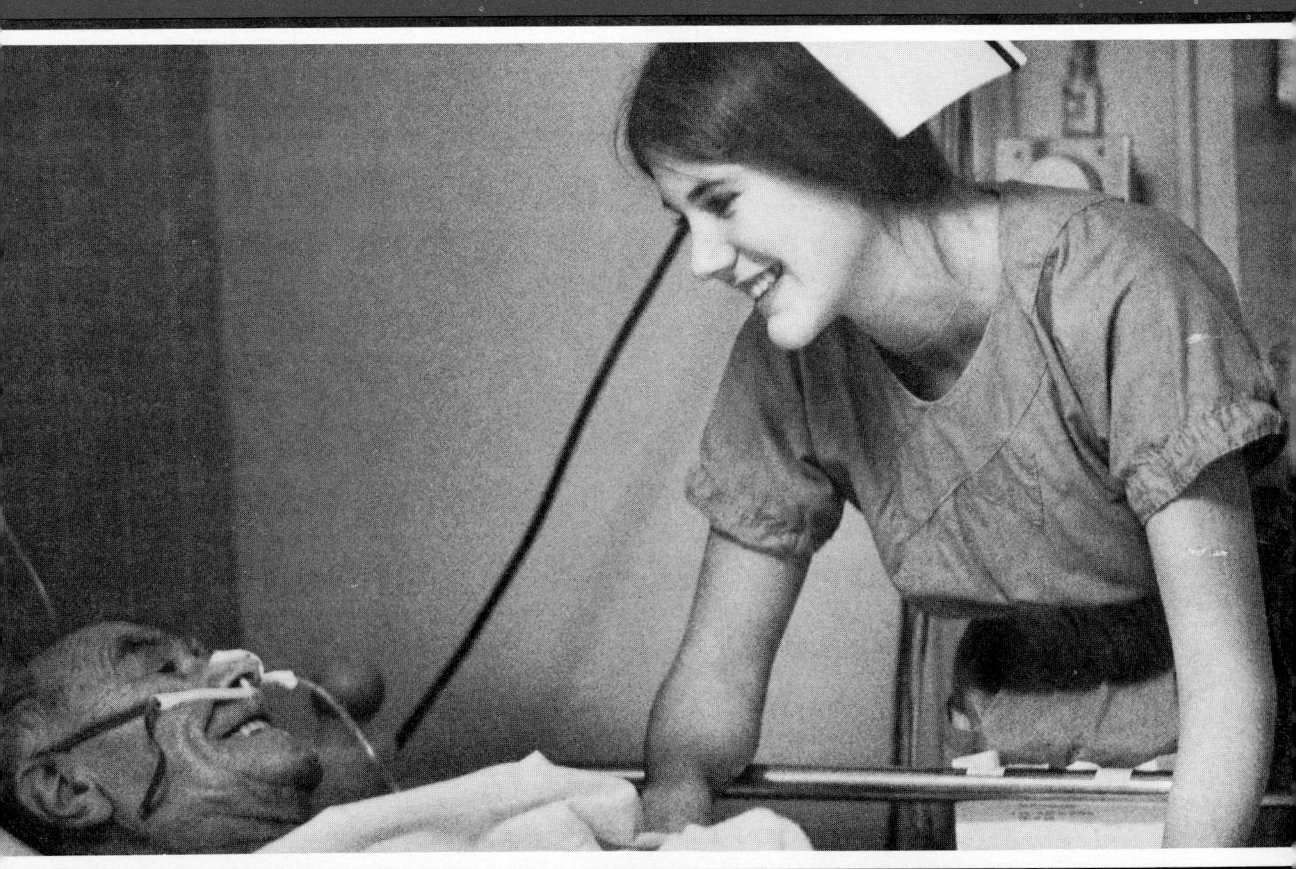

# MOTIVATION THEORIES

# A PARABLE[1]

Once upon a time there was a donkey standing knee-deep in a field of carrots, contentedly munching away. A wise farmer wanted the donkey to pull a loaded wagon to another field, but the donkey would not walk over to the wagon. So the wise farmer stood by the wagon and held up a bunch of carrots for the donkey to see. But the donkey continued to contentedly munch away on carrots in the field.

"But what," you ask, "do donkeys and carrots have to do with my goal of learning how to manage organizational behavior?" The question is well chosen. Look, though, at the accompanying Cartoon 4.1 from the cover of a magazine distributed by a large corporation to its supervisory personnel. Simply put, managers use a variety of "carrots" as "rewards" in their attempts to promote job performance and good human resource maintenance among subordinates. Often these attempts are no more successful than were the farmer's efforts in the parable.

The carrot . . . and the stick?
Reprinted from Mgr. Magazine, 1977. Drawing by Bill Basso.

**MANAGEMENT APPLICATIONS QUESTION**

What do you think people value as work rewards, and how should rewards be allocated by managers to achieve the desired levels of individual performance and job satisfaction?

## PLANNING AHEAD

**The following topics in the present chapter offer learning opportunities which will help you to respond to the Management Applications Question.**

**Types of Motivation Theories**
**Maslow's Hierarchy of Needs Theory**
**McClelland's Acquired Needs Theory**
**Questions and Answers on the Content Theories**
**Equity Theory**
**Expectancy Theory**
**Predicting Performance and Satisfaction**

The Management Applications Questions asks what managers must know and do if they are to be successful at using rewards to promote high performance and job satisfaction in the work unit. This chapter is an opportunity for you to examine motivation theories which respond to this question. These theories are an important foundation for the ideas to be developed throughout the rest of this book.

# TYPES OF MOTIVATION THEORIES

Theories of work motivation are largely grounded in the field of psychology. Psychologists, in turn, rely substantially upon the philosophical tradition of hedonism, that is, the view that people seek to maximize pleasure and minimize pain in their day-to-day lives, in their theory-building efforts. Two categories of motivation theories evolve from this starting point to become of immediate concern to us: content theories and process theories.

## Content and Process Theories

The **content theories** of motivation offer ways to profile or analyze individuals to identify their needs or motives. We use **needs and motives** interchangeably to mean physiological or psychological deficiencies which an individual feels some compulsion to eliminate. Content theories lend insight into people's needs, and thus help a manager to understand what people will and will not value as work rewards. The theories of Maslow and McClelland are singled out later as two of the better-known representatives of the "content" orientation.

Content theories are sometimes criticized as being static and descriptive. The **process theories** offer a more dynamic alternative. They strive to provide an understanding of the thought or cognitive processes that take place within the minds of people and which act to influence their behavior. We will discuss two process theories that offer significant managerial implications: the equity theory and the expectancy theory.

The content and process motivation theories complement rather than compete with one another. While the content theories are less directly linked with work efforts than job satisfactions, the process theories are directly concerned with work efforts and their performance implications. Ultimately, we will use expectancy theory to combine the insights of the content and process theories in a way that is most useful to the practicing manager.

## Mastering Motivation Theories

As we turn now to examine selected theories of motivation, remember that you must not only master the pure theories but also recognize their implications for managerial thought and action. No one theory has yet been proven to dominate all others. Thus, every theory must be carefully studied to derive its implications for predicting and controlling behavior in organizations. Accordingly, we have organized this chapter to help you master successfully the three following goals in studying motivation theories.

| Goals | Chapter Support |
|---|---|
| 1. To examine each theory in its pure form (e.g., to learn about Maslow's theory). | Each theory will be described with an emphasis on managerial usefulness. |
| 2. To critically evaluate each theory (e.g., to identify the limitations of Maslow's theory). | A summary will be provided to detail key research results and scholarly opinions relating to the theory. |
| 3. To create a personal theory of work motivation (e.g., to create a theory that seems useful to you for understanding individuals at work). | The theories will be compared for their similarities and differences. Then we offer an integrative theory. |

## INTRODUCING THE CONTENT THEORIES

Content theories use individual **needs** to help in the understanding of job satisfaction and work behaviors. Needs reflect either physiological or psychological deficiencies. Hunger, for example, is a physiological need; desire for emotional support is a psychological need. Needs are an additional aspect of individual attributes which complement the demographic, competency, and psychological characteristics which we discussed in Chapter 3. Because needs are so important to individuals at work, we give them separate and detailed attention here.

Although content theorists disagree somewhat concerning the exact nature of these needs, they do agree that

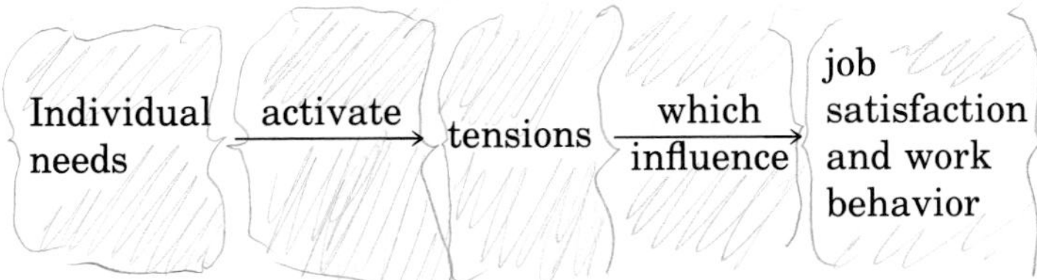
Individual needs
activate
tensions
which influence
job satisfaction and work behavior

Stated even more precisely, content theorists suggest that the manager's job is to create work environments that respond positively to individual needs. Such things as poor performance, undesirable behaviors, and/or decreased satisfactions can be partially explained in terms of "blocked" needs, or those which are not satisfied on the job. Also, the motivational value of rewards can be analyzed in terms of "activated" needs to which a given reward either does or does not respond. In our introductory parable, for example, the farmer failed in this latter regard. The moral is that neither donkeys nor human beings work for rewards when their needs for them are already satisfied!

To allocate rewards successfully, the content theorists argue that managers must understand

1. How individuals differ in what they need from their work experiences.
2. What can be offered to these individuals in response to their needs.
3. How to create work environments that give people the opportunity to satisfy their needs by contributing to the task performance of the work unit and organization.

## MASLOW'S HIERARCHY OF NEEDS THEORY

According to Abraham Maslow, humans share a concern for five levels of need satisfaction from their life experiences: physiological, safety, social, esteem, and self-actualization.[2] These five need levels

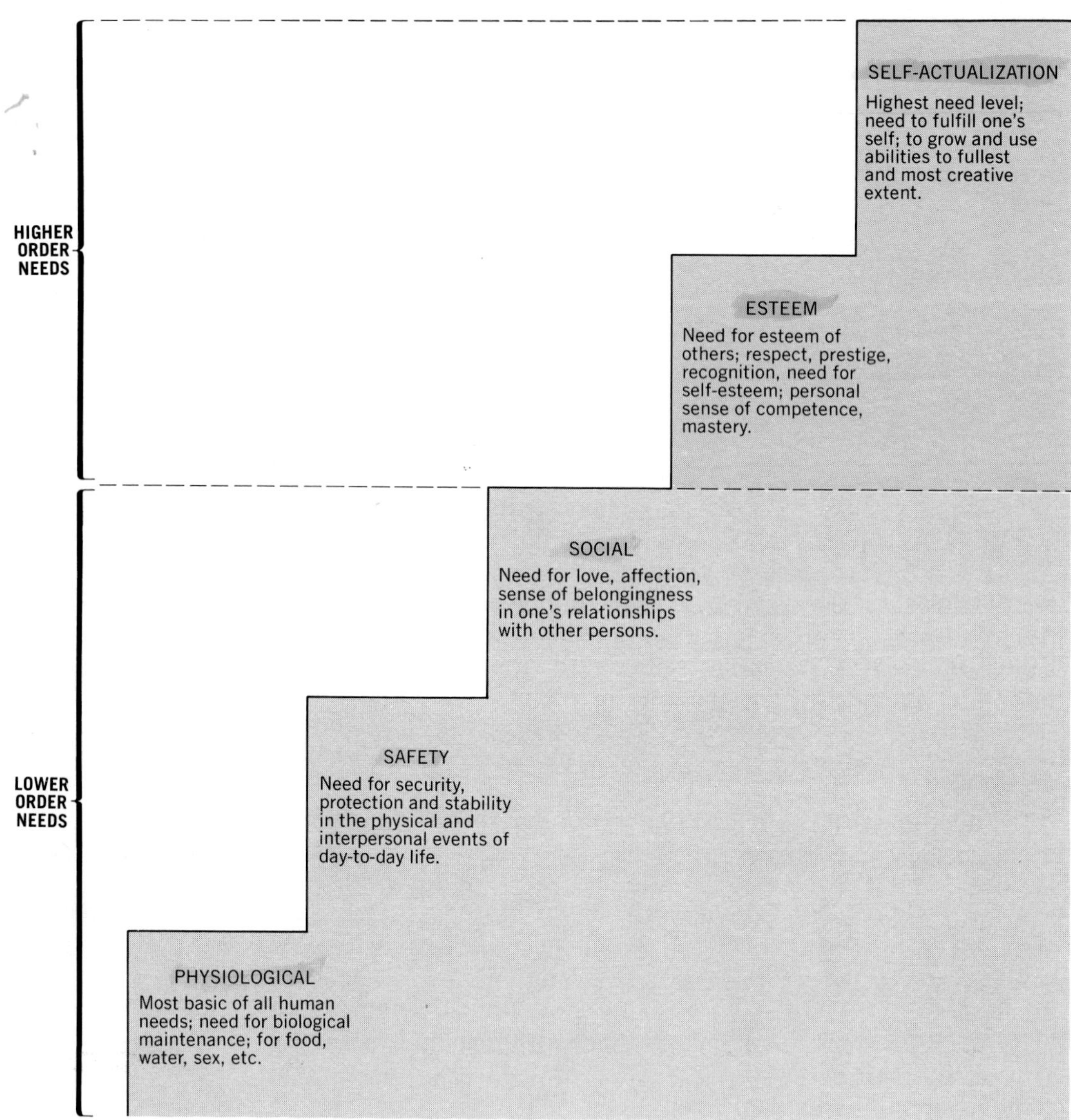

HIGHER ORDER NEEDS
LOWER ORDER NEEDS
SELF-ACTUALIZATION
Highest need level; need to fulfill one's self; to grow and use abilities to fullest and most creative extent.
ESTEEM
Need for esteem of others; respect, prestige, recognition, need for self-esteem; personal sense of competence, mastery.
SOCIAL
Need for love, affection, sense of belongingness in one's relationships with other persons.
SAFETY
Need for security, protection and stability in the physical and interpersonal events of day-to-day life.
PHYSIOLOGICAL
Most basic of all human needs; need for biological maintenance; for food, water, sex, etc.

**FIGURE 4.1** Maslow's hierarchy of needs.

exist in the hierarchy of importance shown in Figure 4.1. The figure also describes each need and classifies it as being of a lower or higher order.

As a manager, it is important for you to become familiar with how various aspects of the work setting relate to individual needs as described by Maslow. Some facets of work subject to managerial control are listed in Table 4.1 along with needs to which they may respond.

## Theory Dynamics[3]

Maslow's theory assumes that individual needs affect behavior in accord with two basic principles.

> **The Deficit Principle:** A satisfied need is not a motivator of behavior; people act to satisfy "deprived" needs, that is, needs for which a satisfaction "deficit" exists.

**Table 4.1 Sample Work Setting Responses to Individual Needs**

| Need Level | Related Aspects of Work Settings |
|---|---|
| Self-Actualization | Challenging job<br>Creative task demands<br>Advancement opportunities<br>Achievement in work |
| Esteem | Merit pay increase<br>High status job title<br>Supervisory recognition<br>Responsibility<br>Important job |
| Social | Compatible work group<br>Personable boss<br>Friendships at work |
| Safety | Safe working conditions<br>Fringe benefits<br>Job security |
| Physiological | Heat<br>Air conditioning<br>Base salary<br>Working conditions |

Source: from *Organizational Behavior and Performance* by John N. Ivancevich, Andrew D. Szilagyi, Jr., and Marc J. Wallace, Jr., p. 105. Copyright © 1977 by Goodyear Publishing Co., Inc. Reprinted by permission.

> **The Progression Principle:** The five need categories exist in a strictly ordered hierarchy of prepotency; a need at any one level only becomes activated once the next lower level need has been satisfied.

A deprived need causes a deficit that dominates individual attention and determines behavior. Once this deficit is satisfied, progression up the hierarchy occurs and the next higher-level need is activated. When the level of self-actualization is reached, the individual continues to be motivated, by concerns for self-fulfillment. The more this need is satisfied, the stronger it grows. The deficit and progression principles cease to operate at the highest level of need, self-actualization.

## The Research

Research identifies some tendency for higher-order needs to increase in importance over lower-order needs as individuals move up the managerial hierarchy.[4] Other studies report that needs vary according to a person's career stage,[5] organization size,[6] and even geographical location.[7]

The deficit and progression principles, however, cannot be verified.[8] There is no consistent evidence that the satisfaction of a need at one level will decrease its importance and increase the importance of the next higher need.[9] As a result, some theorists have tried to modify Maslow's theory and make it more realistic in terms of day-to-day individual behavior. One of the most promising among these latter efforts is the E.R.G. (existence, relatedness, growth) theory of Clayton Alderfer.

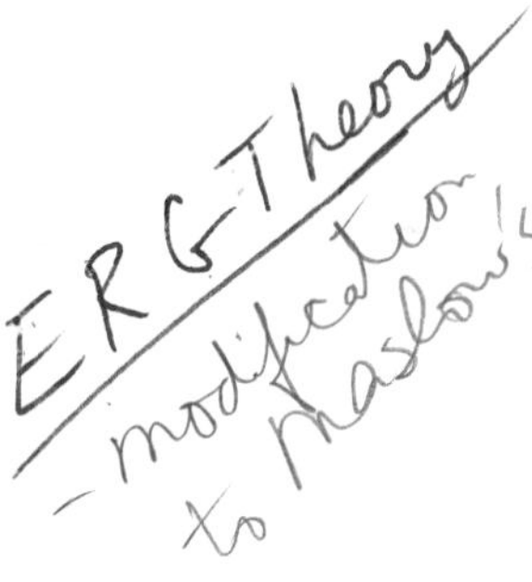


## Alderfer's Modification[10]

E.R.G. theory differs from Maslow's theory in three basic respects. First, E.R.G. theory collapses Maslow's five need categories into three: **Existence needs** relate to people's desires for physiological and material well-being; **relatedness needs** represent desires for satisfying interpersonal relationships; **growth needs** are desires for continued personal growth and development. Second, E.R.G. theory does not assume that lower-level needs must be satisfied before higher-level needs become activated. Finally, E.R.G. theory includes a unique "frustration-regression" principle whereby an already-satisfied lower-level need is felt to become activated when a higher-level need cannot be satisfied.

Alderfer's research lends support to the E.R.G. theory. Future research will help to establish whether or not this is the best form of a hierarchy of needs theory. For now, E.R.G. theory is useful as another means of understanding the needs and behaviors of people at work.

## McCLELLAND'S ACQUIRED NEEDS THEORY

In the late 1940s, the psychologist David I. McClelland and his co-workers began experimenting with the Thematic Apperception Test (TAT for short) as a way of measuring human needs. The TAT asks people to view pictures and write stories about what they see.

Checkpoint

One TAT picture is presented in Photograph 4.1. What short story would you write about it?

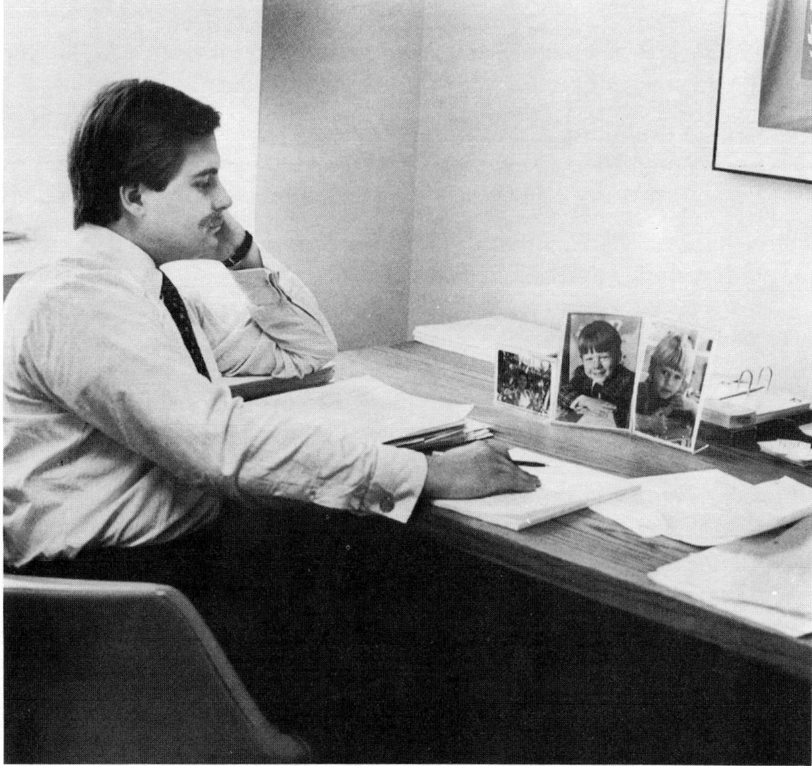

Man looking at desk photo.

## Three Types of Acquired Needs[11]

In one case, McClelland tested three executives using a similar photograph. One wrote of an engineer who was daydreaming about a family outing scheduled for the next day. Another described a designer who had picked up an idea for a new gadget from remarks made by his family. The third saw an engineer who was intently working on a bridge-stress problem that he seemed sure to solve because of his confident look.[12] Compare your response to those of the executives. Do you note any similarities?

McClelland distinguishes three themes that appear in such TAT stories. Each theme corresponds to an underlying need that he feels is important for understanding individual behavior. These needs are:

**Need for Achievement** (nAch): the desire to do something better or more efficiently, to solve problems, or to master complex tasks.
**Need for Affiliation** (nAff): the desire to establish and maintain friendly and warm relations with other persons.
**Need for Power** (nPower): the desire to control other persons, to influence their behavior, to be responsible for other people.

Let's go back to the picture of the man sitting at his desk. McClelland scored the stories given by the three executives as follows.[13]

| | |
|---|---|
| Person dreaming about family outing: | nAch = +1 |
| Person pondering new idea for gadget: | nAch = +2 |
| Person working on bridge-stress problem: | nAch = +4 |

Think back to your own story. To what degree does it reflect needs for achievement, affiliation, and power?

McClelland's basic theory is that these three needs are acquired over time and as a result of life experiences. People are motivated by the needs, and each can be associated with individual work preferences. The theory encourages managers to learn how to identify the presence of nAch, nAff, and nPower in themselves and other people, and to be able to create work environments that are responsive to the respective need profiles.

Two applications of the theory are especially relevant to you as a manager. First, nAch, nAff, and nPower complement the needs identified in Maslow's hierarchy and Alderfer's E.R.G. theory. Thus, they help you to understand people in their work settings. Acquired needs theory is especially useful, since each need is directly associated with a set of individual work preferences as summarized in Table 4.2. Second, if these needs are truly acquired, it may be possible

**Table 4.2 Work Preferences of Persons High in Need for Achievement, Affiliation, and Power**

| Individual Need | Work Preferences | Example |
|---|---|---|
| High need for Achievement | Individual responsibility<br>Challenging but achievable goals<br>Feedback on performance | Field sales person with challenging quota and opportunity to earn individual bonus |
| High need for affiliation | Interpersonal relationships<br>Opportunities to communicate | Customer service representative; member of work unit subject to group wage bonus plan |
| High need for power | Control over other persons<br>Attention<br>Recognition | Formal position of supervisory responsibility; appointment as head of special task force or committee |

to acquaint people with the need profiles required to be successful in various types of jobs. McClelland reports some success in terms of stimulating people's needs for achievement, and he is currently working on a program that helps managers to adopt need profiles found to be associated with successful executives.[14]

### The Research

McClelland's research supports the work preferences of the three need types as described in Table 4.2. Additional research lends special insights into the work preferences of a high nAch person.[15] But there is only a limited amount of research which relates the various needs to performance outcomes and which examines whether or not efforts to help people acquire specific needs make them more successful in certain jobs or occupations.[16]

## QUESTIONS AND ANSWERS ON THE CONTENT THEORIES

The content theories focus on human needs as a way to understand and predict work attitudes and behaviors. Even though the terminology differs, there is a substantial similarity in what the theories offer as a frame of reference for understanding these needs. Let's look at some questions you may have regarding the content theories and their managerial implications.[17]

***"How many different individual needs are there?"***
Research has not yet defined the complete listing of work-related individual needs. Each of the needs we have discussed has been found to be especially useful by OB scholars. As a manager, you can use these needs as a point of departure for understanding the many different needs that people may bring with them to the work setting.

***"Can one work outcome satisfy more than one need?"***
Yes, some work outcomes or rewards can satisfy or block more than one need. Pay is a good example. It is a source of performance feedback for the high need achiever. Pay can also be a source of security, as well as a way to satisfy physiological and social needs.

***"Is there a hierarchy of needs?"***
Research evidence fails to support the existence of a precise five-step hierarchy of needs as postulated by Maslow. Rather, the evidence seems to suggest that it is more legitimate to picture needs operating in a more flexible hierarchy, such as the one in E.R.G. theory. Also, it appears useful to distinguish between lower-order and higher-order needs in terms of motivational properties.

***"How important are the various needs?"***
Research is inconclusive as to the importance of various needs. Individuals probably vary in this regard. Also, they may value needs differently at different times.

***"What is the manager's responsibility as defined by the content theories?"***
Although their details vary, each content theory generally suggests that the manager is responsible for creating a work environment within which individual subordinates find opportunities to satisfy their important needs. To the extent that some needs are acquired, the manager's responsibility may also include acquainting subordinates with the value of needs to which the work setting can positively respond.

In summary, it is suggested that

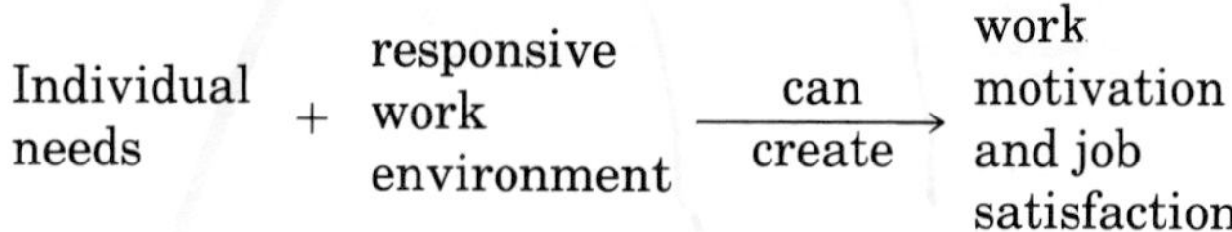
Individual needs
+
responsive work environment
can
create
work motivation and job satisfaction

## EQUITY THEORY

Do you remember the parable used to introduce this chapter? It said something about farmers, donkeys, and carrots, if you recall. Let's spin the parable around another time.

> *Second Parable*[18]
>
> Once upon a time there were six donkeys hitched to a wagon pulling a heavy load up a steep hill. Two of the donkeys were not achievement oriented and decided to coast along and let others do most of the pulling. Two others were relatively young and inexperienced, and had a difficult time pulling their share. One of the remaining two suffered from a slight hangover from consuming fermented barley the night before. The sixth donkey did most of the work.
>
> The wagon arrived at the top of the hill. The driver got down from his seat, patted each of the donkeys on the head, and gave six carrots to each. Prior to the next hill climb, the sixth donkey ran away.

An equity dynamic operates in the new parable, and it has affected the behavior of the sixth donkey. From a donkey's perspective, the moral of the story is to never be the sixth donkey if everyone gets six carrots! From a manager's point of view, similar equity dynamics can affect people's behavior in the work unit whenever rewards are being allocated. How would you like to lose your best worker under conditions such as those described in the parable? Fortunately, a manager can use equity theory to help avoid such undesirable consequences.

### The Equity Comparison

Equity theory is a process motivational theory whose origins lie in studies of social comparison. We know it best through the writings of J. Stacy Adams.[19] He argues that felt inequity is a motivating state of mind. That is, when people feel a sense of inequity in their work, they will be aroused to remove the discomfort and restore a sense of felt equity to the situation. Inequities exist whenever people feel that the rewards or inducements (e.g., "carrots!") received for their work inputs or contributions are unequal to the rewards other persons appear to have received for their inputs. For the individual, the equity comparison or thought process that determines such feeling is

$$\frac{\text{Individual rewards}}{\text{Individual inputs}} \underset{\text{to}}{\overset{\text{compared}}{\longleftrightarrow}} \frac{\text{Others' rewards}}{\text{Others' inputs}}$$

## Resolving Felt Inequities

A **felt negative inequity** exists when an individual feels he or she has received relatively less than others in proportion to work inputs. **Felt positive inequity** exists when an individual feels he or she has received relatively more than others. Both negative and positive inequity are motivating states. When either exists, the individual is predicted to engage in one or more of the following behaviors in order to restore a sense of equity.[20]

1. Change work inputs.
2. Change rewards received.
3. Leave the situation.
4. Change the comparison points.
5. Psychologically distort the comparisons.

Equity theory, for example, predicts that people who feel under-rewarded or over-rewarded for their work will act to restore a sense of equity. The research of Adams and others, largely accomplished in laboratory settings, lends tentative support to this prediction.[21] People who feel overpaid (felt positive inequity) have been found to increase the quantity or quality of their work, while those who are underpaid (felt negative inequity) do the opposite. The research is most conclusive in respect to felt negative inequity.[22]

## Managing the Equity Dynamic

Figure 4.2 shows that the equity comparison actually intervenes between a manager's allocation of rewards and his or her impact on the work behavior of subordinates. Rewards that are received with feelings of equity can foster job satisfaction and performance; rewards received with feelings of negative inequity can damage these key work results. The burden lies with the manager to take control of the situation and make sure that any negative consequences of the equity comparison are avoided, or at least minimized when rewards are allocated.

The following guidelines can help you to maintain control of the equity dynamic in your work unit.

1. Recognize that an equity comparison will likely be made by each subordinate whenever especially visible rewards such as pay, promotions, and so on are being allocated.
2. Anticipate felt negative inequities. Carefully communicate to each individual your evaluation of the reward, an appraisal of the performance upon which it is based, and the comparison points you consider to be appropriate.

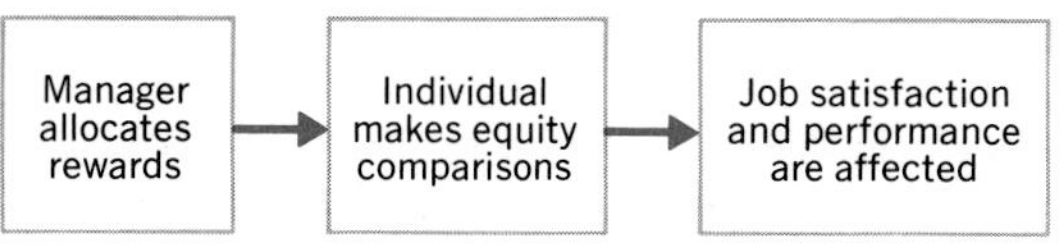
Manager allocates rewards
Individual makes equity comparisons
Job satisfaction and performance are affected

**FIGURE 4.2** The equity comparison: An intervening variable in the rewards, satisfaction, and performance relationship.

Remember, feelings of inequity are determined solely by the individual's interpretation of the situation. Thus, the assumption that every employee in a work unit will view their annual pay raise as fair is incorrect. It is not how a manager feels about the allocation of rewards that counts; it is how the individuals receiving the rewards feel or perceive them that will determine the motivational outcomes of the equity dynamic. Indeed, this whole area of perception is so important that we devote a large part of Chapter 13 to it.

## EXPECTANCY THEORY

In 1964, a book by Victor Vroom covering an expectancy theory of work motivation made an important contribution to the OB literature.[23] The theory seeks to predict or explain the task-related effort expended by a person. The theory's central question, and one of both theoretical and managerial relevance, is: what determines the willingness of an individual to exert personal effort to work at tasks that contribute to the production purposes of the work unit and the organization?

### The Theory

Expectancy theory argues that work motivation is determined by individual beliefs regarding effort-performance relationships and the desirabilities of various work outcomes that are associated with different performance levels. Simply put, the theory is based on the logic: "People will do what they can do when they want to."[24] It may help you to keep expectancy theory in proper managerial perspective by remembering that

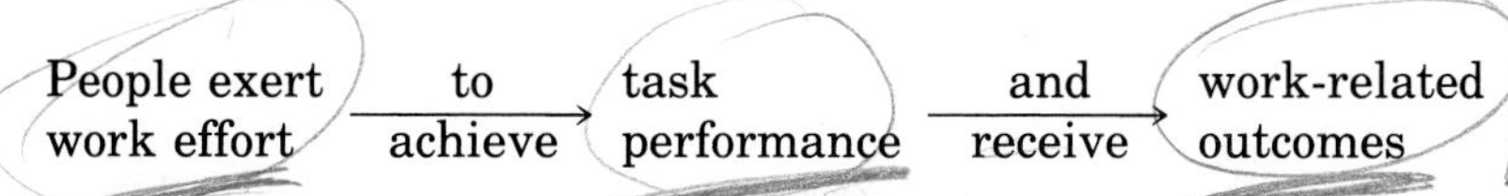
People exert work effort
to achieve
task performance
and receive
work-related outcomes

Recall that the theory asks, when and under what conditions will people put forth maximum work efforts in support of the organization's production purposes? To answer this question, Vroom argues that managers must know three things.

_____________ 1. The person's belief that working hard will enable various levels of task performance to be achieved.

_____________ 2. The person's belief that various work outcomes or rewards will result from the achievement of the various levels of work performance.

_____________ 3. The value the individual assigns to these work outcomes.

## Example

Figure 4.3 presents a schematic example of the expectancy theory. The individual is pictured as making a decision on how much effort to expend at work. In the figure, the individual may elect to follow Path A (working hard to achieve a high performance level), or path B (working less hard and achieving a low performance level). Obviously, a manager would like to encourage, that is, motivate, this person to choose Path A.

Under the theory, the first question the individual asks is "can I achieve different performance levels as a result of my work efforts?" Once this question is answered, attention shifts to the work outcomes that may be associated with each performance level. In the example, a high merit pay raise and social ostracism by co-workers follow the achievement of high performance. By contrast, a lower performance level results in an average pay raise and strong group support from co-workers. Finally, the person must evaluate each work outcome, such as considering a high merit raise as very desirable and social ostracism as very undesirable.

**Checkpoint**

Given what you know about expectancy theory, do you expect the person in this example to elect the high performance path or the low performance path? We will return to examine your answer in a moment.

## Key Terms

The previous example clarifies the thought process as a foundation of expectancy theory. Individuals are viewed as making conscious decisions to allocate their behavior toward work efforts and serve self-interests. The example helps you to anticipate the three key terms in expectancy theory.

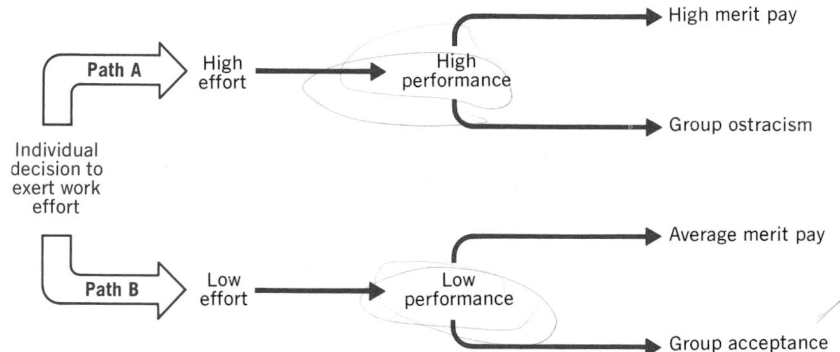


**FIGURE 4.3** An example of individual thought processes as viewed by expectancy theory.

**Expectancy:** The probability assigned by an individual that work effort will be followed by a given level of achieved task performance. Expectancy would equal "0" if it was felt impossible to achieve the given performance level; it would equal "1" if a person were 100% certain that the performance could be achieved.

**Instrumentality:** The probability assigned by the individual that a given level of achieved task performance will lead to various work outcomes. Instrumentality also varies from "1" meaning the reward is 100% certain to follow performance, to "0" indicating there is no chance that performance will lead to the reward.[25]

**Valence:** The value attached by the individual to various work outcomes. Valences form a scale from −1 (very undesirable outcome) to +1 (very desirable outcome).

Checkpoint

Go back to the three points listed above as things Vroom says managers should know. Each point represents a different term in the expectancy theory. Write the correct term in the space provided to the left of each point. Use the previous definitions to check your answers.

## Multiplier Effect

To predict which work path would be pursued by the individual in the example, you need to know how these three components of expectancy theory interrelate to affect motivation. Vroom posits that motivation ($M$), expectancy ($E$), instrumentality ($I$), and valence ($V$) are related to one another by the equation

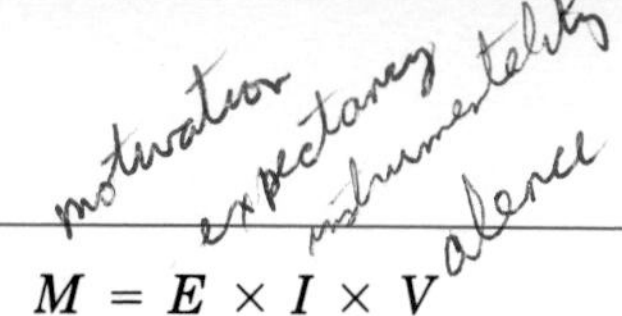

$$M = E \times I \times V$$

The equation states that motivation to work results from expectancy times instrumentality times valence. This multiplicative relationship means that the motivational appeal of a given work path is drastically reduced whenever any one or more of expectancy, instrumentality, or valence approaches the value of zero. Conversely, for a given reward to have a high and positive motivational impact as a work outcome, the expectancy, instrumentality and valence associated with the reward must all be high and positive.

Suppose a manager is wondering whether or not the prospect of earning a merit pay raise will be motivational to a subordinate. Expectancy theory predicts motivation to work hard to earn the merit pay will be *low* if:

1. Expectancy is low—a person feels that he or she can't achieve the necessary performance level.
2. Instrumentality is low—the person is not confident a high level of task performance will result in a high merit pay raise.
3. Valence is low—the person places little value on receiving a merit pay increase.
4. Any combination of the above.

The multiplier effect requires managers to act to maximize expectancy, instrumentality and valence when seeking to create high levels of work motivation among subordinates through the allocation of certain work rewards. A "zero" at any location on the right side of the expectancy equation will result in "zero" motivation. Figure 4.4 puts the expectancy theory terms into such a managerial frame of reference.

## Multiple Expectancies

Expectancy theory is able to accommodate multiple work outcomes in predicting motivation. Going back to the earlier case, merit pay was not the only work outcome affecting the individual's decision to exert high or low levels of work effort. Relationships with co-workers were also a part of each work path. Expectancy theory takes multiple outcomes into consideration in the following expanded version of the expectancy equation.

$$M_i = \sum_j [(E \times I)_{ij}(V)]$$

$$i = 1, n \text{ work effort paths}$$

$$j = 1, n \text{ effort-performance-outcome chains}$$

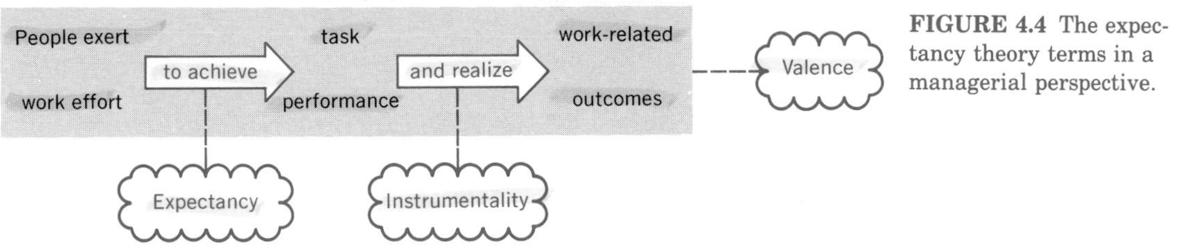


**FIGURE 4.4** The expectancy theory terms in a managerial perspective.

This equation states that motivation to exert effort along a given work path (e.g., high effort) is determined by the combined sum of the values of all effort-performance-outcome chains related to that path. For example, recall the high effort Path A from Figure 4.3. Two effort-performance-outcome chains appear for this path: a merit pay chain and a group ostracism chain. These chains are reproduced in Figure 4.5. Sample numerical values of the expectancies, instrumentalities, and valences for each chain are indicated by parentheses.

Now, let's apply the prior equation to Figure 4.5 and compute the motivational force assigned by the individual to this high effort work path. The equation basically means that the motivation to exert high effort equals the value of the pay chain plus the value of the group chain.

In mathematical notation, this reduces to

$$M_{\text{high effort}} = (E \times I \times V)_{\text{pay}} + (E \times I \times V)_{\text{group}}$$

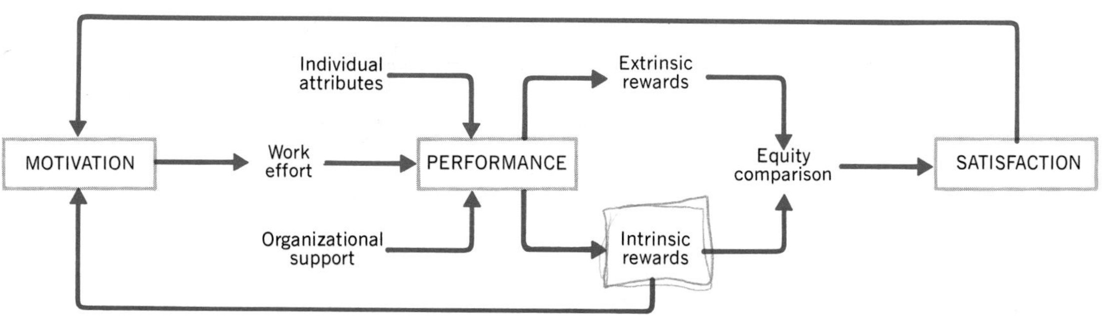


**FIGURE 4.5** Predicting individual work performance and satisfaction.

By substituting in the numerical values of *E, I, V,* we get

$$M_{\text{high effort}} = (1 \times 1 \times 1)_{\text{pay}} + (1 \times 1 \times -1)_{\text{group}}$$
$$M_{\text{high effort}} = (1)_{\text{pay}} + (-1)_{\text{group}}$$
$$M_{\text{high effort}} = 0$$

Thus, because of the multiplier effects and multiple expectancies, individual motivation to pursue this high performance path is zero! Is this result consistent with your earlier prediction back in the earlier *Checkpoint*? Even though merit pay was both highly valued and considered accessible to the individual, its motivational power was cancelled out by the countervailing negative effects of high performance on the individual's social relationships with his or her co-workers. One of the advantages of expectancy theory is its ability to help managers to take into account such multiple consequences when trying to determine the motivational value of various work rewards to individual subordinates.

Checkpoint

When the expectancy equation is applied to the low effort path from the example in Figure 4.3, a different result occurs. You should be able to verify that $M_{\text{low effort}} = .5$. Work this example through using the same methods we chose for the high effort path. Remember, on this path the valence of an average merit pay increase is .5; the

**Table 4.3 The Managerial Implications of Expectancy Theory**

| Expectancy Term | The Individual's Question | Managerial Implications |
|---|---|---|
| Expectancy | "Can I achieve the desired level of task performance?" | Select workers with ability<br>Train workers to use ability<br>Support ability with organizational resources<br>Clarify performance goals |
| Instrumentality | "What work outcomes will be received as a result of the performance?" | Clarify psychological contracts<br>Communicate performance → reward possibilities<br>Confirm performance → reward possibilities by making actual rewards contingent upon performance |
| Valence | "How highly do I value the work outcomes?" | Identify individual needs or outcomes<br>Adjust available rewards to match these |

valence of group acceptance is 1. Expectancy theory therefore predicts this person to be a low performer based upon the available work outcomes and their individual consequences.

## Managerial Applications

We've summarized the managerial implications of Vroom's expectancy theory in Table 4.3. Basically, expectancy logic argues that a manager must try to understand individual thought processes and then actively intervene in the work situation to control them. This control includes trying to maximize work expectancies, instrumentalities, and valences that support the organization's production purposes. Said differently, a manager should strive to create a work environment such that work contributions serving the organization's needs will also be valued by the individual as paths toward desired personal outcomes or rewards.

Table 4.3 shows that a manager can influence expectancies by selecting individuals with proper abilities, training people to use these abilities, supporting people with abilities by providing the needed resources, and clarifying desired task goals. Instrumentality is influenced by clarifying performance reward expectations in the psychological contract, by communicating revised performance → reward expectations specific to a given situation, and by confirming performance → reward expectations through direct action, that is, by actually rewarding desirable performance once it occurs. Finally, managers can influence valence by being sensitive to individual needs. This is where the content theories can be of great benefit to you. Once these needs are understood, rewards can be adjusted to respond more adequately to them.

## The Research

The research on expectancy is voluminous, and good review articles are available.[26] Although the theory has received substantial support, specific details, such as the operation of the multiplier effect, remain subject to question. Rather than charging that the underlying theory is inadequate, however, researchers indicate that their inability to generate more confirming data may be caused by problems of methodology and measurement. Thus, while awaiting the results of more sophisticated research, OB scholars seem to agree that expectancy theory is a useful source of insight into work motivation.

One of the more popular modifications of Vroom's original version of the theory distinguishes between extrinsic and intrinsic rewards as two separate types of possible work outcomes.[27] **Extrinsic rewards** are positively valued work outcomes that are given to the individual by some other person in the work setting. An example is pay. A worker typically does not pay himself or herself directly; some representative of the organization administers the reward. **Intrinsic rewards,** on the other hand, are positively valued work outcomes that are received by the individual directly as a result of task performance. They do not require the participation of another person. A feeling of achievement after accomplishing a particularly challenging task is one example of an intrinsic reward. This distinction is important because each type of reward demands separate attention from a manager seeking to use rewards to increase motivation. We discuss these differences very thoroughly in Chapters 5 and 6, that follow.

## PREDICTING PERFORMANCE AND SATISFACTION

Let's integrate the various motivation theories into one predictive model of individual job performance and satisfaction. We'll begin with the individual performance equation (see Chapter 3) and then proceed in building-block fashion. The equation directs our attention to individual attributes, work effort, and organizational support as three variables that influence individual performance. Simply put,

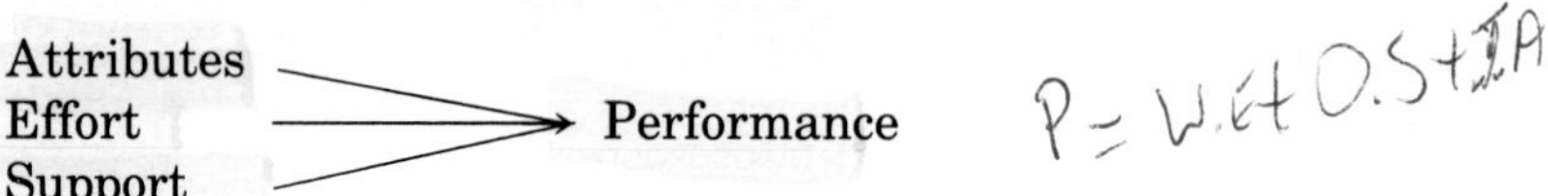


Recall, too, that we went on to say that because the individual alone controls his or her work effort, the manager attempts to influence effort through the concept of motivation. Thus, the above relationships can be modified to

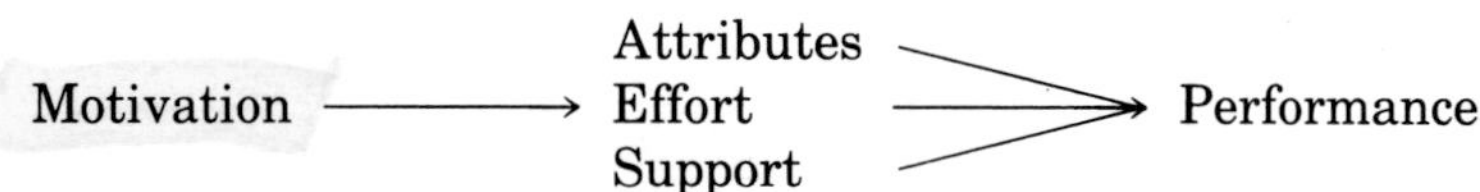


Note further, however, that managers are also interested in promoting high levels of individual satisfaction as a part of their concern for human resource maintenance. Remember, too, that we concluded our Chapter 3 review of the satisfaction-performance controversy by

noting that when rewards are allocated on the basis of past performance (i.e., when rewards are performance-contingent) they can cause both future performance and satisfaction. Figuratively speaking,

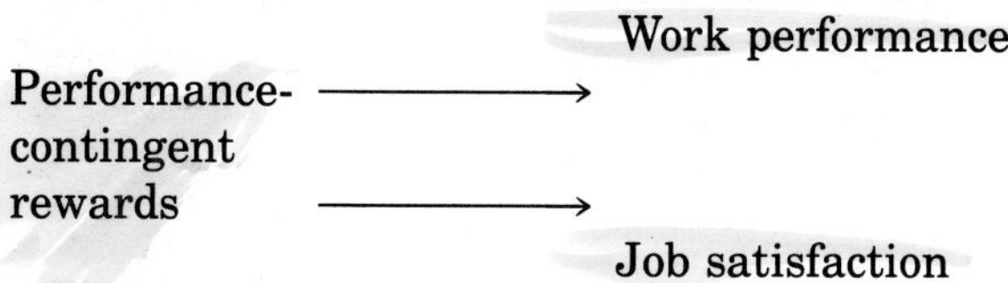


We have used the logic of expectancy theory to integrate these latter ideas with insights of the other motivational theories, and create the predictive model of individual performance and satisfaction shown in Figure 4.6. In the figure, performance is determined by individual attributes, work effort, and organizational support. Individual motivation directly determines work effort, and the key to motivation is the manager's ability to create a work environment that positively responds to individual needs and goals. Whether or not a work environment proves motivating depends upon the availability of rewards. When the individual experiences intrinsic rewards for work performance, motivation will be directly and positively affected. Motivation can also occur when job satisfactions result from either extrinsic or intrinsic rewards that are felt to be equitably allocated. When felt negative inequity results, satisfaction will be low and motivation reduced.

Figure 4.6 is a modification of Vroom's original expectancy theory that is based on the foundation of the individual performance equation. It includes a key role for equity theory and recognizes job performance and satisfaction as separate, but potentially interdependent, work results. The content theories enter the model as the

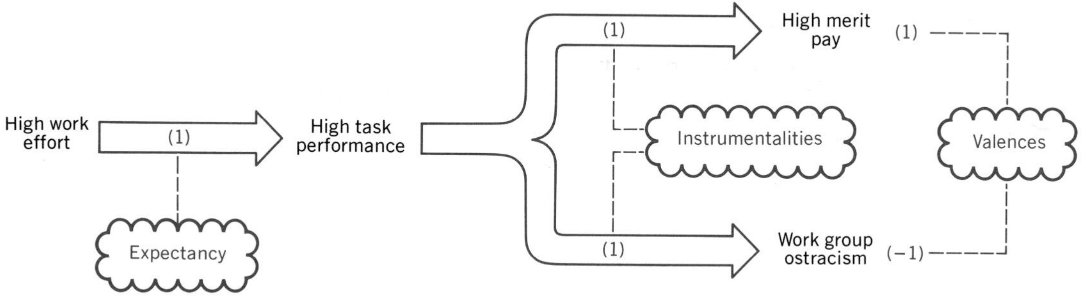


**FIGURE 4.6** The high effort work path in the expectancy example.

manager's guide to understanding individual attributes and identifying the needs which give motivational value to the various work rewards allocated by the manager.

## SUMMARY

This chapter introduces selected content and process theories of work motivation. Although the theories differ, each is useful in offering implications for management practice. They are likely to be especially useful when integrated into a personal theory that can best meet your needs as a manager. We have described one example of our integrated theory in Figure 4.5.

The management of work motivation begins with an ability to identify and understand individual needs. The content theories of Maslow and McClelland are helpful in this regard. The process theories go further in helping you to learn still more about what motivates people to apply their work efforts to support the organization's production purpose. Equity theory introduces the important dynamic of social comparison. Expectancy theory focuses our attention on the role of expectancies, instrumentalities, and valences in determining motivation to work.

Expectancy theory proves of special value as a way of integrating the multiple insights of the content and process theories. Thus, our final discussion has specified an integrated theory that can be used by managers to predict individual job performance and satisfaction, and to generate ideas on how to achieve these two key work results.

As we have shown, a manager must try to create a work setting that is a motivating stimulus to its individual members. One of the key aspects of any work setting is the pool of available work rewards. As a manager, you will need to be good at allocating these rewards. Chapters 5 and 6 build on this theme as it applies to rewards in both their extrinsic and intrinsic forms. Before you press on, though, consider a final parable.

*Final Parable*[28]

> Once upon a time a farmer had six donkeys and a barn full of carrots, which she kept under lock and key. At the end of a day of wagon pulling, the farmer looked back over the day's performance of each donkey. To one of the donkeys she said, "You did an outstanding job; here are six carrots." To four of the others, she said, "Your performance was average;

here are three carrots." To the remaining donkey she said, "You didn't pull your share of the load; here is one carrot."

Another day of wagon pulling dawned. The top donkey, having been properly rewarded, began the day in high spirits. The thoughts of the remaining donkeys were consumed with how they might earn more carrots through their efforts that day. The farmer had carrots available, but they had to be earned.

## THINKING THROUGH THE ISSUES

1. What is the key difference between the approaches taken by the content and process theories concerning their explanations of work motivation?

2. Two OB theorists are discussing the topic of work motivation. One says "motivation can never come from the boss," while the other states "if people aren't motivated, managers are to blame." How can each position be defended? How can the two positions be reconciled with one another?

3. Suppose you are a manager and find yourself with one group of subordinates who apparently seek higher-order need satisfactions at work, and another group that seems concerned only with lower-order needs. What would you do to motivate each group of subordinates? Why?

4. Refer back to the Case of the Missing Raise discussed in the introduction to Part One. Make a needs profile for John Lloyd based on the evidence presented in the case. Explain how John's manager, Fred Massie, could use this knowledge to increase John's motivation to work.

5. If David McClelland is right, and it is possible to stimulate certain needs in people, what is the managerial significance of this finding?

6. Choose an example of how the equity dynamic has affected your behavior as a student. What guidelines would you suggest to instructors that could help them to minimize the negative consequences potentially associated with this equity dynamic?

7. Explain the managerial significance of the final parable.

8. What is one major modification that you would make to the model of motivation to work presented in Figure 4.6 to increase its usefulness to practicing managers?

## CASE: PERFECT PIZZERIA[29]

Perfect Pizzeria in Southville, in deep southern Illinois, is the second largest franchise of the chain in the United States. The headquarters is located in Phoenix, Arizona. Although the business is prospering, it has employee and managerial problems.

Each operation has one manager, an assistant manager, and from two to five night managers. The managers of each pizzeria work under an area supervisor. There are no systematic criteria for being a manager or becoming a manager trainee. The franchise has no formalized training period for the manager. No college education is required. The managers for whom the case observer worked during a four-year period were relatively young (ages 24 to 27) and only one had completed college. They came from the ranks of night managers or assistant managers, or both. The night managers were chosen for their ability to perform the duties of the regular employees. The assistant managers worked a two-hour shift during the luncheon period five days a week to gain knowledge about bookkeeping and management. Those becoming managers remained at that level unless they expressed interest in investing in the business.

The employees were mostly college students, with a few high school students performing the less challenging jobs. Since Perfect Pizzeria was located in an area with few job opportunities, it had a relatively easy task of filling its employee quotas. All the employees, with the exception of the manager, were employed part time. Consequently, they worked for less than the minimum wage.

The Perfect Pizzeria system is devised so that food and beverage costs and profits are set up according to a percentage. If the percentage of food unsold or damaged in any way is very low, the manager gets a bonus. If the percentage is high, the manager does not receive a bonus; rather, he or she receives only his or her normal salary.

There are many ways in which the percentage can fluctuate. Since the manager cannot be in the store 24 hours a day, some employees make up for their paychecks by helping themselves to the food. When a friend comes in to order a pizza, extra ingredients are put on the friend's pizza. Occasional nibbles by 18 to 20 employees throughout the day at the meal table also raise the percentage figure. An occasional bucket of sauce may be spilled or a pizza accidentally burned. Sometimes the wrong size of pizza may be made.

In the event of an employee mistake or a burned pizza by the oven man, the expense is supposed to come from the individual. Because of peer pressure, the night manager seldom writes up a bill for the erring employee. Instead, the establishment takes the loss and the error goes unnoticed until the end of the month when the inventory is taken. That's when the manager finds out that the percentage is high and that there will be no bonus.

In the present instance, the manager took retaliatory measures. Previously, each employee was entitled to a free pizza, salad, and all the soft drinks he or she could drink for every 6 hours of work. The manager raised this figure from 6 to 12 hours of work. However, the employees had received these 6-hour benefits for a long time. Therefore, they simply took advantage of the situation whenever the manager or the assistant was not in the building. Though the night manager theoretically had complete control of the operation in the evenings, he did not command the respect that the manager or assistant manager did. This was because he received the same pay as the regular employees; he could not reprimand other employees; and he was basically the same age or sometimes even younger than the other employees.

Thus, apathy grew within the pizzeria. There seemed to be a further separation between the manager and his workers, who started out as a closely knit group. The manager made no attempt to alleviate the problem, because he felt it would iron itself out. Either the employees that were dissatisfied would quit or they would be content to put up with the new regulations. As it turned out, there was a rash of employee dismissals. The manager had no problem in filling the vacancies with new workers, but the loss of key personnel was costly to the business.

With the large turnover, the manager found he had to spend more time in the building, supervising and sometimes taking the place of inexperienced workers. This was in direct violation of the franchise regulation, which stated that a manager would act as a supervisor and at no time take part in the actual food preparation. Employees were not placed under strict supervision with the manager working alongside them. The operation no longer worked smoothly because of differences between the remaining experienced workers and the manager concerning the way in which a particular function should be performed.

Within a two-month period, the manager was again free to go back to his office and leave his subordinates in charge of the entire operation. During this two-month period, the percentage had returned to the previous low level and the manager received a bonus each month. The manager felt that his problems had been resolved and that conditions would remain the same, since the new personnel had been properly trained.

It didn't take long for the new employees to become influenced by the other employees. Immediately after the manager had returned to his supervisory role, the percentage began to rise. This time the manager took a bolder step. He cut out any benefits that the employees had—no free pizzas, salads, or drinks. With the job market at an even lower ebb than usual, most employees were forced to stay. The appointment of a new area supervisor made it impossible for the manager to "work behind the counter," since the supervisor was centrally located in Southville.

The manager tried still another approach to alleviate the rising percentage problem and maintain his bonus. He placed a notice on the bulletin board, stating that if the percentage remained at a high level, a lie detector test would be given to all employees. All those found guilty of taking or purposefully wasting food or drinks would be immediately terminated. This did not have the desired effect on the employees, because they knew if they were all subjected to the test, all would be found guilty and the manager would have to dismiss all of them. This would leave him in a worse situation than ever.

Even before the following month's percentage was calculated, the manager knew it would be high. He had evidently received information from one of the night managers about the employees' feelings toward the notice. What he did not expect was that the percentage would reach an all-time high. That is the state of affairs at the present time.

### Questions

1. Consider the situation where the manager changed the time period required to receive free food and drink from 6 to 12 hours of work. Try to apply each of the motivational approaches discussed in this chapter to explain what happened. Which of the approaches offers the most appropriate explanation? Why?
2. Repeat question 1 for the situation where the manager worked beside the employees for a time and then later returned to his office.
3. Repeat question 1 for the situation as it exists at the end of the case.
4. Establish and justify a motivational program based on one or a combination of motivation theories to deal with the situation as it exists at the end of the case.

## THE MANAGER'S VOCABULARY

**Content Theories** Offer ways to profile or analyze individuals to identify the needs which motivate their behavior.

**Existence Needs** Desires for physiological and material well-being.

**Esteem Needs** Desires for ego gratification in the forms of self-esteem and reputation.

**Expectancy** The probability assigned by the individual that work effort will be followed by a given level of achieved task performance.

**Extrinsic Rewards** Positively valued work outcomes that are given to the individual by some other person in the work setting.

**Felt Inequity** A work situation in which the individual feels his or her rewards received in return for work contributions made are relatively less (felt negative inequity) or relatively more (felt positive inequity) than those received by others.

**Growth Needs** Desires for continued personal growth and development.

**Higher-Order Needs** Esteem and self-actualization needs in Maslow's hierarchy.

**Instrumentality** The probability assigned by the individual that a given level of achieved task performance will lead to various work outcomes.

**Intrinsic Rewards** Positively valued work outcomes that are received by the individual directly as a result of task performance.

**Lower-Order Needs** Physiological, safety, and social needs in Maslow's hierarchy.

**Need** A physiological or psychological deficiency which the individual feels some compulsion to eliminate.

**Need for Achievement (nAch)** The desire to do something better, to solve problems, or to master complex tasks.

**Need for Affiliation (nAff)** The desire to establish and to maintain friendly and warm relations with other persons.

**Need for Power (nPower)** The desire to control other persons for personal (need for personal power) or social (need for social power) ends.

**Physiological Needs** The basic desire for biological maintenance.

**Process Theories** Seek to understand the thought processes that take place in the minds of people and which act to motivate their behavior.

**Relatedness Needs** Desires for satisfying interpersonal relationships.

**Safety Needs** The desire for security, protection, and stability in day-to-day life.

**Self-Actualization Needs** The desire to fulfill one's self, to grow, and to use one's abilities to their full and most creative extent.

**Social Needs** The desire for love, affection, and a sense of belongingness in one's relationships with other persons.

**Valence** The value attached by the individual to various work outcomes.

## Important Names

**Abraham Maslow** Created the hierarchy of needs theory.

**Clayton Alderfer** Modified Maslow's work to create the E.R.G. theory.

**David McClelland** Developed the managerial applications of acquired needs theory.

**J. Stacy Adams** Applied equity theory to work situations.

**Victor Vroom** Introduced the expectancy theory of motivation.

## Notes

[1]Adapted from Dale McConkey, "The 'Jackass Effect' in Management Compensation," *Business Horizons,* Vol. 17 (June 1974), pp. 81–91.

[2]Abraham H. Maslow, "A Theory of Human Motivation," *Psychological Review,* Vol. 50 (1943), pp. 370–396.

[3]This discussion on Maslow's theory is reported in Abraham H. Maslow, *Eupsychian Management* (Homewood, Ill.: Richard D. Irwin, 1965); Abraham H. Maslow, *Motivation and Personality,* Second Edition (New York: Harper & Row, 1970).

[4]Lyman W. Porter, "Job Attitudes in Management: II. Perceived Importance of Needs as a Function of Job Level," *Journal of Applied Psychology,* Vol. 47 (April 1963), pp. 141–148.

[5]Douglas T. Hall and Khalil E. Nougaim, "An Examination of Maslow's Need Hierarchy in an Organizational Setting," *Organizational Behavior and Human Performance,* Vol. 3 (1968), pp. 12–35.

[6]Lyman W. Porter, "Job Attitudes in Management: IV. Perceived Deficiencies in Need Fulfillment as a Function of Size of Company," *Journal of Applied Psychology,* Vol. 47 (December 1963), pp. 386–397.

[7]John M. Ivancevich, "Perceived Need Satisfactions of Domestic Versus Overseas Managers," *Journal of Applied Psychology,* Vol. 54 (August 1969), pp. 274–278.

[8]Mahmoud A. Wahba and Lawrence G. Bridwell, "Maslow Reconsidered: A Review of Research on the Need Hierarchy Theory," *Academy of Management Proceedings* (1974), pp. 514–520.

[9]Edward E. Lawler, III, and J. Lloyd Suttle, "A Causal Correlational Test of the Need Hierarchy Concept," *Organizational Behavior and Human Performance,* Vol. 7 (1973), pp. 265–287.

[10]See Clayton P. Alderfer, "An Empirical Test of a New Theory of Human Needs," *Organizational Behavior and Human Performance,* Vol. 4 (1969), pp. 142–175; and, Clayton P. Alderfer, *Existence, Relatedness, and Growth* (New York: Free Press, 1972); and Alderfer, Robert E. Kaplan, and Ken A. Smith, "The Effect of Variations in Relatedness Need Sat-

isfaction on Relatedness Desire," *Administrative Science Quarterly,* Vol. 19 (1974), pp. 507–532.

[11]Sources pertinent to this discussion are David C. McClelland, "Business, Drive and National Achievement," *Harvard Business Review,* Vol. 40 (July–August 1962), pp. 99–112; David C. McClelland, "That Urge to Achieve," *Think* (November-December 1966), pp. 19–32; G. H. Litwin and R. A. Stringer, *Motivation and Organizational Climate* (Boston, Mass.: Division of Research, Harvard Business School, 1966), pp. 18–25.

[12]George Harris, "To Know Why Men Do What They Do: A Conversation with David C. McClelland," *Psychology Today,* Vol. 4 (January 1971), pp. 35–39.

[13]Ibid.

[14]David C. McClelland, *The Achieving Society* (New York: Van Nostrand, 1961); McClelland, op. cit., 1966; and, David C. McClelland and David H. Burnham, "Power is the Great Motivator," *Harvard Business Review,* Vol. 54 (March-April 1976), pp. 100–110.

[15]Richard M. Steers, "Task-Goal Attributes, nAchievement, and Supervisory Performance," *Organizational Behavior and Human Performance,* Vol. 13 (1975), pp. 392–403.

[16]H. A. Wainer and I. M. Rubin, "Motivation of Research and Development Entrepreneurs: Determinants of Company Success," *Journal of Applied Psychology,* Vol. 53, (1969) pp. 178–184, and David C. McClelland and D. Winter, *Motivating Economic Achievement* (Glencoe, Ill.: Free Press, 1971).

[17]This section is based, in part, on a discussion by Edward E. Lawler, III, in *Motivation in Work Organizations* (Monterey, Calif.: Brooks/Cole Publishing Company, 1973), pp. 30–36.

[18]McConkey, op. cit.

[19]See, for example, J. Stacy Adams, "Toward an Understanding of Inequity," *Journal of Abnormal and Social Psychology,* Vol. 67 (1963), pp. 422–436; J. Stacy Adams, "Inequity in Social Exchange," in L. Berkowitz (ed.), *Advances in Experimental Social Psychology,* Vol. 2 (New York: Academic Press, 1965), pp. 267–300.

[20]Ibid.

[21]Paul S. Goodman and Abraham Friedman, "An Examination of Adams' Theory of Inequity," *Administrative Science Quarterly,* Vol. 16 (1971), pp. 271–288.

[22]W. Clay Hamner, Jerry Ross, and Barry M. Staw, "Motivation in Organizations: The Need for a New Direction," in Dennis W. Organ (ed.), *The Applied Psychology of Work Behavior* (Dallas: Business Publications, Inc., 1978), pp. 224–249.

[23]Victor H. Vroom, *Work and Motivation* (New York: John Wiley & Sons, Inc., 1964).

[24]Gerald R. Salancik and Jeffrey Pfeffer, "A Social Information Processing Approach to Job Attitudes and Task Design," *Administrative Science Quarterly,* Vol. 23 (June 1978), pp. 224–253.

[25]Strictly speaking, Vroom's treatment of instrumentality would allow it to vary from $-1$ to $+1$. We use the probability definition here and the 0

to +1 range for pedagogical purposes. This connection remains consistent with the basic motion of instrumentality.

[26]Herbert G. Heneman, III, and Donald P. Schwab, "Evaluation of Research on Expectancy Theory and Predictions of Employee Performance," *Psychological Bulletin,* Vol. 78 (July 1972), pp. 1–9; Terrence R. Mitchell, "Expectancy Models of Job Satisfaction, Occupational Preference and Effort: A Theoretical, Methodological, and Empirical Appraisal," *Psychological Bulletin,* Vol. 81 (1974), pp. 1053–1077; Mahmoud A. Wahba and Robert J. House, "Expectancy Theory in Work and Motivation: Some Logical and Methodological Issues," *Human Relations,* Vol. 27 (January 1974), pp. 121–147; Terry Connolly, "Some Conceptual and Methodological Issues in Expectancy Models of Work Performance Motivation," *Academy of Management Review,* Vol. 1 (October 1976), pp. 37–47; Terence Mitchell, "Expectancy-Value Models in Organizational Psychology," in N. Feather (ed.), *Expectancy, Incentive and Action* (New York: Erlbaum and Associates, 1980).

[27]Lyman W. Porter and Edward E. Lawler, III, *Managerial Attitudes and Performance* (Homewood, Ill.: Richard D. Irwin, 1968).

[28]McConkey, op. cit.

[29]Adapted from a case assignment prepared by Lee Neely for Professor James G. Hunt, Southern Illinois University at Carbondale. The case appears in John E. Dittrich and Robert A. Zawacki (eds.), *People and Organizations: Cases in Management and Organizational Behavior,* pp. 126–128. © Business Publications, Inc., 1981. All rights reserved. Used by permission.

# 5

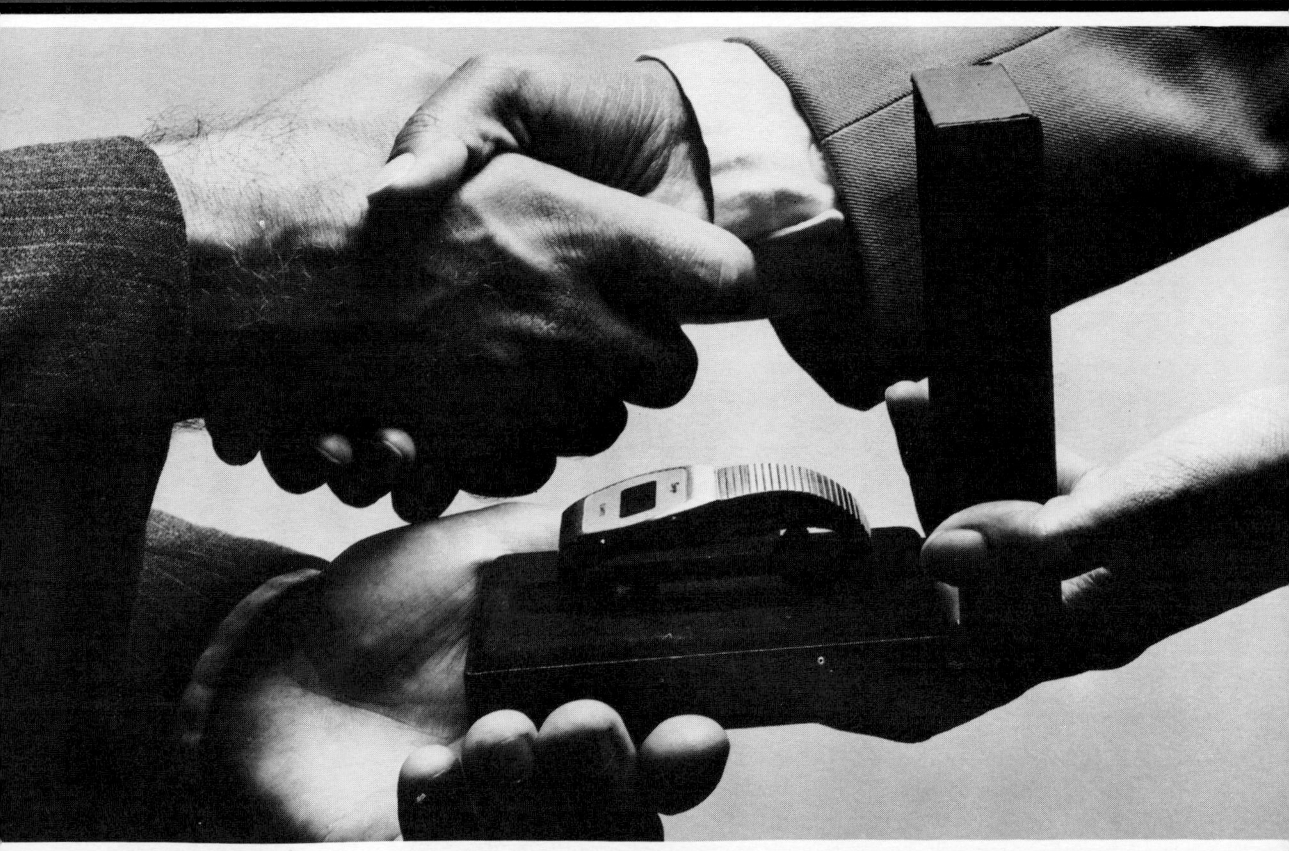

# REINFORCEMENT THEORY AND EXTRINSIC REWARDS

# ALEXEI AND THE GULAG ARCHIPELAGO

The following excerpt on life in the prison camps of the Soviet Union appeared in *The Wall Street Journal*.[1]

> Alexei's drinking problem, for example, began with another problem that troubled the commandant of his labor camp. "He had a quota of copper to be mined, but how could he meet it?" explains Alexei, almost sympathetically. "What incentive have the prisoners got to work? He can't give them money. He can't give them freedom. So he comes to them and says, 'All right, what do you guys really want to do this job?' And the only answer is vodka. So we got it. And we all got drunk. All the time."

The problem faced by Alexei's prison commandant is one that is shared by all managers, i.e., to provide rewards that will encourage other persons to exert maximum effort in support of an organization's production purpose.

### MANAGEMENT APPLICATIONS QUESTION

Cartoon 5.1 illustrates a popular alternative, pay, to the vodka used by Alexei's commandant to resolve this dilemma. How will you manage work rewards so that they will be motivating to your subordinates?

## PLANNING AHEAD

**The learning activities in this chapter will help you to learn more about reinforcement theory and extrinsic work rewards. The important topics you will study include the following.**

**Extrinsic Work Rewards**
**Reinforcement Theory**
**Organizational Behavior Modification**
**Positive Reinforcement**
**Extinction**
**Punishment**
**Multiple Meanings of Pay**

Good managers try to promote high levels of work performance and human resource maintenance among their subordinates. One key to effective action is the manner of allocating work rewards. Alexei's commandant, discussed in the chapter introduction, appears to have mastered this challenge in a rather extreme set of circumstances. Every manager has access to many different kinds of rewards. Some managers, however, will do better than others at using these rewards to create desired behaviors on the parts of other persons in the work setting.

# EXTRINSIC WORK REWARDS

**Extrinsic work rewards** are positively valued work outcomes that are given to the individual by some other person in the work setting. The manager is a source of extrinsic work rewards for his or her subordinates. A listing of extrinsic rewards which are often at a manager's disposal is presented in Table 5.1. Some other extrinsic rewards that come immediately to mind are verbal praise and recognition, status symbols, promotion, and pay. Of course, not all recognition is of positive value. See *Newsline 5.1* for example. We'll discuss this point later.

Your immediate interest is to learn how to use extrinsic rewards well enough to promote performance and human resource maintenance, especially job satisfaction, on the part of your subordinates. Reinforcement theory is a useful starting point for this.

**Table 5.1 Examples of Extrinsic Work Rewards**

| Contrived On-the-Job Rewards | | | | Natural Rewards | |
|---|---|---|---|---|---|
| Consumables | Manipulatables | Visual and Auditory | Tokens | Social | Preferred Activity |
| Coffee break treats | Desk accessories | Office with a window | Profit sharing | Friendly greetings | Special job assignment |
| Food baskets | Company car | Piped-in music | Stock options | Invitations to coffee/lunch | Extended breaks |
| Christmas turkeys | Watches | Redecoration of work environment | Movie passes | Solicitations of suggestions | Personal time off with pay |
| Company picnics | Trophies | Private office | Paid-up insurance policies | Compliment on work progress | Work on personal project on company time |
| Beer parties | Commendations | Feedback about performance | Vacation trips | Smile | |

Source: Adapted from *Organizational Behavior Modification* by Fred Luthans and Robert Kreitner, © 1975 Scott, Foresman and Company, p. 101. Reprinted by permission.

## REINFORCEMENT THEORY

**Reinforcement theory** is one that views human behavior as being determined by its environmental consequences. If you recall, each of the content and process motivation theories in Chapter 4 used a cognitive explanation of behavior. That is, they are concerned with explaining "why" people do things, such as to satisfy needs, pursue positive valences, or resolve felt inequities. The reinforcement theory, by contrast, is acognitive. It avoids this necessity of looking within the individual and examining such thought processes. It does so by focusing attention on the environment and its consequences for the individual. Consider the following example.[2] A person walking down the street finds a $10 bill. Thereafter this person is observed to spend more time looking down when out walking. The question is, "why?"

**The Cognitive Explanation:** The person continues to look down frequently because of the high value held for money. Because the person reasons that more money may be found by looking down, he or she has decided to look down more frequently when out walking in the future. The observed behavior, i.e., "looking down," follows a conscious decision to do so by the individual.

**The Reinforcement Explanation:** When the initial behavior of looking down occurred, it was reinforced by the presence of a

## NEWSLINE 5.1

### Billy Carter Receives Fillmore Award

Billy Carter has been chosen as the recipient of the 1980 Millard Fillmore Mediocrity Medal, bestowed annually by a Colorado Springs, Colo. group that says it is dedicated to mediocrity.

Phil Arkow, vice president and founder of the Society for the Preservation of Millard Fillmore, Last of the Whigs, said picking President Carter's younger brother for the distinction was no easy matter.

"The middle management committee had its hands full with nominees, everyone from Bert Parks to the unknown who replaced Bert Parks," Arkow said. "We're not picking on Jimmy (Carter) because he's a lame duck. We're picking on Billy because he's an albatross."

The 13th U.S. president, Fillmore was responsible for the first postage stamp.

Last year's winner was Johnny Carson's sidekick, Ed McMahon.

Source: The Associated Press as reprinted in *The Southern Illinoisan* (December 21, 1980), p. 5.

$10 bill. Having once been reinforced by this environmental consequence, the behavior becomes more likely to occur in the future.

## The Law of Effect

The example shows that the reinforcement orientation avoids making assumptions about individual thought processes in order to explain behavior. Rather than looking at "values," "reasons," and "decisions," reinforcement theory views present behavior, such as looking down while walking, as being determined by the environmental response to past behavior (e.g., being presented by a $10 bill after having looked down while out walking). The basis for this argument and the foundation for reinforcement theory is expressed in Thorndike's "law of effect."[3] Simply put, this law states

> behavior that results in a pleasing outcome will be likely to be repeated; behavior that results in an unpleasant outcome is not likely to be repeated.

The relationship between the law of effect and the management applications question which introduced this chapter is straightforward. Those outcomes or environmental consequences which are considered by reinforcement theory to determine individual behavior are extrinsic rewards. Thus, one way to increase your ability to successfully manage rewards is to understand the special implications of reinforcement theory as they apply to the work setting. Hopefully, you may develop the capacity to creatively manage rewards, as illustrated in *Newsline 5.2*.

## Operant Conditioning

**Operant conditioning** is a term popularized by the noted psychologist B. F. Skinner.[4] It is the process of controlling behavior by manipulating its consequences. You may think of operant conditioning as learning by reinforcement.

## NEWSLINE 5.2

### Well Pay

*Bonuses for just showing up*

Sick pay is one of those necessary and sensible corporate institutions that are often abused. If an employee is hung over or simply does not feel like working because it is a lovely day, he can call in with a feigned case of the blahs. That escape hatch from the workday world is being mildly threatened by a newfangled idea aimed at throwing dedicated malingerers into a dilemma: well pay.

Now being tried in several small and medium-size companies on the West Coast, well pay rewards people for doing what they are supposed to do: go to work regularly and on time. Some results have been impressive. Reports James Parsons, 59, president of Parsons Pine Products of Ashland, Ore., maker of nearly 80% of the nation's wooden mousetrap bases: "Our absenteeism has dropped 30%, and our tardiness is almost zero." Parsons' incentive: an extra day's pay at the end of every month to workers who are punctual. Reichhold Chemicals' fiberglass manufacturing division in Irwindale, Calif., offers half an hour's extra pay for each week a worker completes a full shift without illness or absence. The bonuses are called "sweet pay" (for Stay at Work, Earn Extra Pay).

Most employees like the idea, but some workers and union leaders seem skeptical. Says Mildred Corriveau, a vocational nurse at one of the 151 nursing homes owned by Pasadena's Beverly Enterprises, whose employees get 5% bonuses each month for showing up on time: "It's not enough money to persuade a person to come to work. I think we will still have as much diarrhea as we used to." For some folks, no reward can match the luxury of loafing.

Source: *Time* (August 7, 1978), p. 67. Reprinted by permission from *Time,* the Weekly Newsmagazine; Copyright © Time, Inc., 1978.

Often, operant conditioning is associated with animal behaviors. Skinner, for example, taught pigeons to play "pingpong" by rewarding them with food when they exhibited behaviors appropriate to the game. **Behavior modification** is the term used to describe a set of techniques for applying operant conditioning to the control of human behavior. You have probably read about "behavior mod," as it is often called, in the popular press. It has received widespread application in education and is now gaining special attention for its value in work settings.

**Organizational behavior modification,** "OB Mod," for short, is the "systematic reinforcement of desirable organizational behavior and the nonreinforcement or punishment of unwanted organizational behavior."[5] There are four strategies of OB Mod: positive reinforcement, negative reinforcement, punishment, and extinction. Let's look at these in some detail.[6]

**Positive Reinforcement:** Increasing the frequency of or strengthening a desirable work behavior by making it contingent with the occurrence of a desirable consequence.

> ***Example***—A manager nods to express approval to a subordinate after she makes a useful comment during a staff meeting.

**Negative Reinforcement:** Increasing the frequency of or strengthening a desirable work behavior by making it contingent with the avoidance of an undesirable consequence.

> ***Example***—A manager who has been nagging a worker every day about his performance doesn't nag when the daily production quota is met one day.

Checkpoint

Before reading further, make sure that you understand the difference between positive and negative reinforcement. Both of these OB Mod strategies seek to encourage desirable behavior. They just go about it differently. Check back to be sure this difference is clear to you.

**Punishment:** Decreasing the frequency of or weakening an undesirable behavior by making it contingent with the occurrence of an undesirable consequence.

> ***Example***—A manager docks an employee's pay when he reports late for work one day.

**Extinction:** Decreasing the frequency of or weakening an undesirable behavior by making it contingent with the removal of a desirable consequence.

> ***Example***—a person is becoming disruptive by breaking established work rules. She receives social approval for these acts from co-workers. The manager counsels the co-workers to stop giving this approval. Soon after, the disruptive behavior is discontinued.

The four OB Mod strategies are illustrated in Figure 5.1. This example shows how a nursing supervisor uses each of the strategies to direct employee work behavior toward desirable record-keeping practices. Notice that both positive and negative reinforcement are used to strengthen desirable behavior when it occurs; punishment and extinction are applied to undesirable behaviors in an attempt to decrease the frequency of their occurrence.

Each of the OB Mod strategies may be used in combination with one another, as well as singly. The following discussion will increase your understanding of these strategies from both theoretical and practical viewpoints.

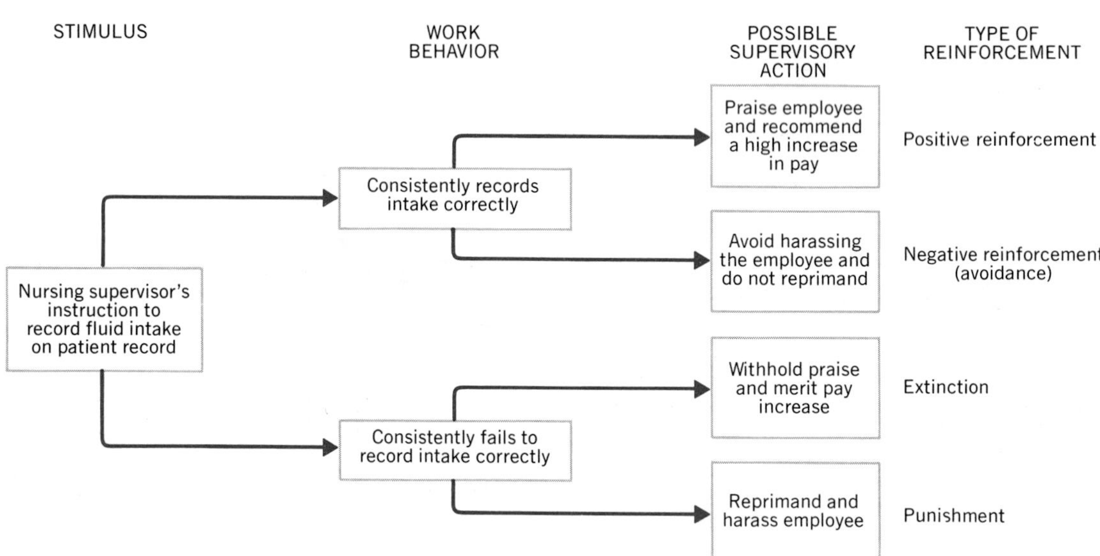


**FIGURE 5.1** Directing behavior through reinforcement. (Source: From *Organizational Behavior and Performance* by John M. Ivancevich, Andrew D. Szilagyi, Jr., and Marc J. Wallace.

## POSITIVE REINFORCEMENT

Positive reinforcement is an OB Mod strategy advocated by Skinner and his followers. *What Consultants Do 5.1* illustrates the range of Skinner's advice in this latter regard. To do positive reinforcement well in the work setting, however, you must first be aware of the wide variety of things in the organization that have potential reward value (see Table 5.1). Then you need to know when the allocation of a reward will have this desired effect. Two laws guide managerial action in this latter regard: the law of contingent reinforcement and the law of immediate reinforcement.[7]

> **The Law of Contingent Reinforcement:** In order for a reward to have maximum reinforcing value, it must be delivered only if the desired behavior is exhibited. This law indicates that rewards given indiscriminately by managers, that is, noncontingently, will not act as positive reinforcers.

## WHAT CONSULTANTS DO 5.1

### B. F. Skinner's Advice on OB Mod and Major League Baseball

Peggy Lamson has done a series of articles about the Boston Red Sox. The other day I suggested that she discuss with the manager a plausible technique of breaking up a batting slump. My guess is that a player is told what he is doing wrong or shown movies or videotapes of himself as he strikes out or grounds out easily. I suggested that, instead, he be shown a short film of himself hitting home runs. A videotape device in the back of the dugout could have short cassettes for each player. He is to look at his film a few minutes before batting.

Why do I think it will work? It could be a kind of imitation, but a more likely effect should be eliminating some of the current aversive effects of the slump. The player would say that he "feels better about himself" as a batter. Slight tensions in posture and movement might follow.

Later it occurred to me that it might work for shortstops and others who have been making errors. Let them see themselves playing brilliantly.

And just now I saw the significance in my own case. After reading some of my own published writing (it almost always seems good to me because I have kept at it until it is good according to my standards), I write freely and energetically for some time.

Source: From the book *Notebooks, B. F. Skinner,* by Robert Epstein. Copyright © 1980 by B. F. Skinner. Published by Prentice-Hall, Inc., Englewood Cliffs, N.J. 07632.

**The Law of Immediate Reinforcement:** The more immediate the delivery of a reward after the occurrence of a desirable behavior, the greater the reinforcing effect on behavior. The longer a manager delays in rewarding a desired behavior, the less likely the reward will act as a positive reinforcer.

## A Case of Positive Reinforcement

Taken together, the two prior laws require that you give rewards as immediately as possible and contingently upon desired behavior, if they are to serve as positive reinforcers in the work setting. Try your hand in this example.

### The Assembly-Line Supervisor[8]

A new young manager finds herself in charge of a group of workers on an automobile assembly line. This work unit is expected to produce components at a standard rate of seventy-two per hour. Actual performance has been running around forty-five per hour. The manager's boss is holding her accountable for the production discrepancy.

Checkpoint

How would you analyze and approach this case from a reinforcement point of view? How would this be analyzed from the approach of a manager using the insights of the cognitive (content and process) motivation theories?

In actual fact, the manager called her subordinates together and asked them what could be done to get production up to standard. They decided that an extra "break" might justify the increased effort. A deal was made; *if* the workers produced seventy-two units within an hour's time, then they could use the remaining time in the hour as a break. The results were immediate and positive. Within a week the work unit was producing up to standard and taking a twenty-five minute break every hour!

Checkpoint

Let's use this example to check your understanding of reinforcement terminology. For the workers, the possibility of an hourly break was a (1) ____________. When the break was provided as a result of the production standard being met, it became a (2) ____________. Because the break was given only when the production standard was met, the law of (3) ____________ was satisfied; because the break closely followed the accomplishment of the production standard, the law of (4) ____________ was also satisfied.

The correct answers are (1) extrinsic reward, (2) positive reinforcer, (3) contingent reinforcement, (4) immediate reinforcement. Refer back to our previous discussion to check your answers.

To continue the case . . . after these results were realized, it became obvious to both the manager and her subordinates that the situation

The coffee break.

couldn't continue. Higher management and the other work units would not tolerate this group taking a 25-minute break every hour. Another deal was made: when the group reached 92 units an hour, the remaining time in the hour could be used as a break. As a result of this agreement, the work unit was soon able to take a 10-minute break in almost every hour.

This manager used her reinforcement theory well. The result was that she was able to associate a desirable consequence, the work break, with behavior appropriate to organizational goal attainment, the 72-unit per hour production rate. It is also significant that the break was only one of a number of possible rewards the manager may have tried to use as a positive reinforcer. Wisely, she obtained information from the workers before choosing among the alternative rewards. As a result, the break was highly valued by the workers and proved to be a powerful positive reinforcer of a key work result.

**Epilogue** There is still another part of this case that deserves attention. One day, a vice-president showed up to see this group, about whom all sorts of glowing performance reports were being made. Unfortunately, the visit occurred at "break time" and the VP "hit the roof." Everyone was ordered back to work on the premise that "working" and not "breaking" was what they were being paid for. The group did go back to work, but production immediately fell back below the 72-unit standard.

Our Viewpoint

This epilogue should bring to mind a similar result that was observed in the Hovey and Beard Company case which introduced this part of the book. It demonstrates once again the need for every manager to recognize that a work unit cannot be treated in isolation from the organization as a whole. Later, in Part Four of the book, we'll return to this issue of "total system integration" to help you to avoid outcomes such as the one just depicted.

## Shaping

The supervisor in the previous example could also have used another form of positive reinforcement to achieve the desired level of production. **Shaping** is the creation of a new behavior by the positive reinforcement of successive approximations to the desired behavior. Recall that the work unit was originally producing at 45 units per hour, while 72 per hour was the desired goal. A shaping strategy would be to reward the subordinates with verbal praise and recognition each time they produced more than 45 units in an hour, 51 units, for example. As production increased, reinforcement would then be given only when production surpassed the previous highest level. Eventually, this rewarding of successive approximations to the desired production goal, that is, shaping, should lead to the accomplishment of the goal. Once production arrived at the standard level, continued positive reinforcement would then be used to stabilize behavior at this new performance.

## Scheduling Reinforcement

Positive reinforcement can be given according to continuous and intermittent schedules.[9] Table 5.2 describes a number of reinforcement schedules falling into the two categories. The schedules are important because of the different effects they may have on behavior. To succeed with a shaping strategy, for example, reinforcement should be given on a continuous basis until the desired behavior is achieved. Then an intermittent schedule should be used to maintain the behavior at the new level.

**Continuous reinforcement** administers a reward each time a desired behavior occurs. In **intermittent reinforcement,** behavior is rewarded only periodically. Although there is some controversy in the research on reinforcement schedules,[10] one reviewer concludes that a manager can expect that:[11]

1. Continuous reinforcement will draw forth a desired behavior more quickly than will intermittent reinforcement; but, continuous reinforcement will be more costly in terms of the consumption of rewards.
2. Behavior that is acquired under an intermittent schedule will last longer upon the discontinuance of reinforcement, than will behaviors acquired under a continuous schedule.

Intermittent reinforcement can be given according to fixed or variable schedules. **Fixed interval schedules** provide rewards at the first appearance of a behavior after a given time has elapsed; **fixed ratio schedules** result in a reward each time a certain number of the behaviors has occurred. The weekly paycheck is a fixed interval reward, whereas meeting a sales quota and then receiving an appropriate commission is a fixed ratio reward.

Variable reinforcement schedules offer rewards at random, rather than on a regularly scheduled basis. A **variable interval schedule** rewards behavior at random times, while a **variable ratio schedule** rewards behavior after a random number of occurrences. The variable schedules are considered to result in more consistent patterns of desired behaviors than fixed reinforcement schedules.[12]

**Table 5.2 Schedules of Reinforcement**

| Schedule | Description | Example | Effects on Behavior |
|---|---|---|---|
| Continuous | Reinforcer follows every response. | A manager watches an employee learning to use a new machine; praise is given each time the process is done perfectly. | Rapid and positive influence on behavior; behavior weakens rapidly when reinforcement is stopped. |
| Intermittent | Reinforcer does not follow every response. | | Slow in establishing a desired behavior; but behavior is more permanent when reinforcement stops. |
| Fixed interval | The first response after a specific period of time has elapsed is reinforced. | A paycheck is received at the end of a week's work; a grade is received at the end of a semester. | Produces an uneven response pattern varying from a very slow, unenergetic response immediately following reinforcement to a very fast, vigorous response immediately preceding reinforcement. |
| Fixed ratio | A fixed number of responses must be emitted before reinforcement occurs. | A person is paid on a "piece-rate," for example, for every 10 units produced a certain amount of pay is received; "commission" sales. | Tends to produce a high rate of response which is vigorous and steady. |
| Variable interval | The first response after varying or random periods of time have elapsed is reinforced. | A manager takes periodic but unscheduled walks around the unit; compliments are given to employees displaying desirable work behaviors. | Tends to produce a high rate of response which is vigorous, steady, and durable. |
| Variable ratio | A varying or random number of responses must be emitted before reinforcement occurs. | A worker's output is checked at random according to the number of units produced; when quality is 100%, a small monetary bonus is paid. | Capable of producing a high rate of response which is vigorous, steady, and durable. |

Source: Adapted from *Organizational Behavior Modification,* by Fred Luthans and Robert Kreitner. © 1975 Scott, Foresman and Company. p. 81. Reprinted by permission.

## Guidelines for Positive Reinforcement

To use operant conditioning properly and to ensure that the allocation of extrinsic work rewards has the desired positive reinforcement effects, a manager should:[13]

1. Clearly identify the desired behaviors, i.e., determine what specific behaviors will result in positive contributions by the work unit to organizational goal attainment.

2. Maintain an inventory of extrinsic rewards that have the potential to serve as positive reinforcers for members of the work unit.
3. Recognize individual differences as to which rewards will actually have positive value for subordinates.
4. Let subordinates know exactly what must be done to receive a desirable reward. Set clear targets, and give performance feedback.
5. Administer the extrinsic rewards contingently and immediately upon the appearance of the desired behaviors. Make sure that the reward is given only if the desired behavior occurs.
6. Administer the extrinsic rewards wisely in terms of scheduling the positive reinforcement.

## EXTINCTION

**Extinction** is the withholding of reinforcement for a behavior that has previously been positively reinforced. Whereas positive reinforcement seeks to establish and maintain desirable work behaviors, the goal of extinction as an OB Mod strategy is to weaken and eliminate undesirable ones! How would you apply this new strategy to the following case?

### A Case of Extinction[14]

The president of Alpha Company is worried. One of her bright young assistants is developing a problem behavior that could eventually erode his credibility. At the weekly staff meeting, Jason has started acting more like a comedian than an aspiring executive. He interjects "one-liners" and makes "wisecracks" with increasing frequency during discussions. As a result, the meetings are often disrupted. The president is becoming annoyed and is especially concerned because Jason's behavior has gotten worse during the last month.

Checkpoint

Remember, reinforcement theory views a behavior as a product of its environmental consequences. If you were the president of Alpha, how would you use reinforcement theory to analyze this situation?

Being wise in the ways of reinforcement theory, the president decided not to reprimand Jason. Rather, she tried to analyze his behavior in terms of the environmental consequences which it produced for him.

She reasoned that his behavior must be receiving some sort of positive reinforcement. At the next two meetings, she closely observed Jason's disruptive behavior and its results. She noticed that two other staff members usually acknowledged Jason's remarks with smiles and by nodding approval. In fact, the president noticed that Jason immediately looked to these persons each time after making one of his disruptive comments.

In terms of reinforcement theory, the president has found that Jason is being positively reinforced by these two persons for a behavior that is organizationally undesirable. Given this diagnosis, the president decided on a strategy of extinction. She went to Jason's two colleagues and asked them to avoid approving his disruptive behavior. They did so. In future meetings the frequency of his "joking" decreased dramatically.

### Extinction and Positive Reinforcement

Extinction can be especially powerful when combined with positive reinforcement. In fact, this is what actually occurred in the above case. Extinction caused Jason to stop making disruptive comments. However, the president was still concerned that Jason maintain and even increase his useful contributions. Whenever such a valuable comment was made, therefore, she provided him with immediate acknowledgement and approval. These extrinsic rewards had a positive reinforcing effect on desirable behavior. Thus, the combined strategy of extinction and positive reinforcement is a most useful tool for managers.

## PUNISHMENT

There is another strategy besides extinction that managers can use to eliminate undesirable behavior. **Punishment** is administering an unpleasant consequence contingent upon the occurrence of an undesirable behavior. To punish an employee, a manager may deny the individual a valued extrinsic reward, such as praise or even merit pay; or the manager may administer an adversive or obnoxious stimulus, such as reprimand or monetary fine. It is just as important to understand punishment as an OB Mod strategy as it is to understand the principles of positive reinforcement. Like the other strategies, however, punishment can be done poorly or it can be done well. Your goal, of course, is to know when to use this strategy, and then to know how to do it well.

## Problems with the Punishment Strategy

Problems may accompany a manager's use of punishment. Three potential ones deserve special mention.[15]

1. Although a behavior may be suppressed as a result of punishment, it may not be permanently abolished. An employee, for example, may be reprimanded for taking unauthorized work breaks. The behavior may stop, but only when the manager is visible. As soon as the threat of punishment is removed from the situation, such as when the manager is no longer present, the breaks may occur once again.
2. The person who administers punishment may end up being viewed negatively by others. A manager who frequently punishes subordinates may find that he or she has an unpleasant effect on the work unit even when not administering punishment. This manager has become so associated with punishment that his or her very presence in the work setting is an unpleasant experience for others.
3. Punishment may be offset by positive reinforcement received from another source. A worker may be reinforced by peers at the same time that punishment is being received from the manager. Sometimes the positive value of such peer suppport may be strong enough to cause the individual to put up with the punishment. Thus, the undesirable behavior continues. As many times as a student may be verbally reprimanded by an instructor for being late to class, the "grins" offered by other students may well justify the continuation of the tardiness in the future.

Does all of this mean you should never punish? No. The important things to remember are to do punishment selectively, and then do it right. Consider the following case.

## A Case of Punishment

Peter Jones is a forklift operator in a warehouse.[16] This is the highest paid nonsupervisory job in the firm. It is considered a high-status job, and it took Pete 5 1/2 years to work himself into the position. Unfortunately, he is prone to "show off" by engaging in a variety of unsafe driving habits which violate federal safety codes. Pete's manager "chews him out" regularly, but the unsafe driving continues.

Pete's boss analyzed the situation from a reinforcement perspective. He sought to determine what environmental consequences were associated with Pete's unsafe driving habits. As you may have predicted, he found that the undesirable behavior was typically followed by laughter and special attention from the other warehouse workers. He decided that it would be impossible to enlist their aid to implement a strategy of extinction similar to the one followed by the president of Alpha.

The next time Pete was observed to drive unsafely, Pete's boss took him off the forklift truck and reassigned him to general warehousing duties for a period of time. When allowed back on the forklift, Pete drove more safely. Finally, a true punishment had been found.

### Punishment and Positive Reinforcement

Punishment can also be combined with positive reinforcement. Pete, for example, could now be positively reinforced when observed to drive safely. Then he would know exactly what is wrong and the unpleasant consequences associated with it, and what is right and the pleasant consequences with which it may be associated. This combined strategy is advantageous in that it may help a manager to avoid the first problem identified above; having an undesirable behavior suppressed for a period of time, but not abolished.

### Guidelines for Punishment

The following guidelines are useful for managers using punishment as an OB Mod strategy.[17]

1. Tell the individual what is being done wrong; clearly identify the undesirable behavior that is being punished.
2. Tell the individual what is right; the desirable alternative to the behavior which is being punished should be clearly established.
3. Punish in private; avoid public embarassment by punishing someone in front of others.
4. Punish in accord with the laws of contingent and immediate reinforcement; make sure punishment is truly contingent upon the undesirable behavior and follows its occurrence as soon as possible.
5. Make the punishment match the behavior; be fair in equating the magnitude of the punishment with the degree to which the behavior is truly undesirable.

## REINFORCEMENT THEORY IN SUMMARY

We have introduced you to reinforcement theory, its supporting concepts, and its possible work applications as summarized in the concept of OB Mod. Before leaving this approach to managing extrinsic rewards, however, we would like to place the theory in a summary perspective. We need to discuss three remaining issues to do this: the accolades, the research, and the value dilemmas associated with the applications of reinforcement theory to work settings.

## Accolades

Testimony to the potential payoffs associated with the use of operant conditioning techniques in work settings is shown in Table 5.3. Note that the users include some rather substantial corporations. Further testimony to the popularity of the reinforcement orientation is evidenced by the growing number of consulting firms which specialize in OB Mod techniques. A typical approach which these experts follow when working with a client is outlined in *What Consultants Do 5.2*.

## WHAT CONSULTANTS DO 5.2

### Applying Behavior Modification Techniques to Industry

Carl Pitts Associates of Del Mar, California, is a management consulting firm. It guarantees clients savings which will double the firm's $15,000 fee in one year. A typical consulting program involves the following two steps.

**Step 1** A series (typically a three-day session) of "diagnostic," meetings are held between managers and their employees.

- Mutual needs and problems are discussed.
- Problem solutions are proposed.
- Performance standards and important tasks are clarified.
- Employees give the managers lists of reinforcers which could be used to modify the employees' behaviors.

**Step 2** The performance of employees is then observed by their managers who give frequent feedback and positively reinforce desired behaviors.

At Western Air Lines, for example, records are kept on the percentage of calls that actually result in flight reservations. This information is given to the reservation clerks on a daily basis. The supervisors praise clerks for asking callers for their reservations. The ratio of sales to calls has increased from one in four to one in two as a result of the program.

Source: This example reported in *Business Week* (January 23, 1978), p. 57.

**Table 5.3 Results of Positive Reinforcement Programs in Selected Organizations**

| Organization | Participants | Program Goals | Reinforcers Used | Results |
|---|---|---|---|---|
| Michigan Bell-Operator Services | 2000 of 5500: Employees at all levels in operator services | a. Decrease turnover and absenteeism<br>b. Increase productivity<br>c. Improve union-management relations | a. Praise and recognition<br>b. Opportunity to see oneself become better | a. Attendance performance improved by 50%<br>b. Productivity and efficiency has continued to be above standard |
| Michigan Bell-Maintenance Services | 220 of 5500: Maintenance workers, mechanics, first- and second-level supervisors | Improve<br>a. Productivity<br>b. Quality<br>c. Safety<br>d. Customer-employee relations | a. Self-feedback<br>b. Supervisory feedback | a. Cost efficiency increase<br>b. Safety improved<br>c. Service improved<br>d. No change in absenteeism<br>e. Satisfaction with superior and coworkers improved<br>f. Satisfaction with pay increased |
| B. F. Goodrich Chemical Co. | 100 of 420: Manufacturing employees at all levels | a. Better meeting of schedules<br>b. Increase productivity | a. Praise and recognition<br>b. Freedom to choose one's own activity | Production has increased over 300% |
| General Electric | 1000: Employees at all levels | a. Meet EEO objectives<br>b. Decrease absenteeism and turnover<br>c. Improved training<br>d. Increase productivity | Social Reinforcers (praise, rewards and constructive feedback) | a. Cost savings can be directly attributed to the program<br>b. Productivity has increased<br>c. Worked extremely well in training minority groups and raising their self-esteem<br>d. Direct labor cost decreased |

Source: Reprinted, by permission of the publisher, from "Behavior Modification on the Bottom Line," W. C. Hamner and E. P. Hamner, *Organizational Dynamics,* Vol. 4 (Spring 1976). 

## Criticisms

The same *Business Week* article from which we abstracted the *What Consultants Do 5.2*[18] was the object of rather severe criticism from a newspaper columnist. He takes a rather dim view of the trend toward behaviorism in management and says that "the chances are that behavior modification will work no better than a hundred other schemes executives have tried out in the past."[19] The skepticism in this comment leads to an inquiry into the exact status of research on this topic.

## Research

Research on the work applications of reinforcement theory is open to criticism. First, many "success" stories like the examples in Table 5.3 are single cases, analyzed by using nonexperimental research designs. It is hard to conclude definitively that the observed results were "caused" by reinforcement dynamics. In fact, one critic argues that the results may well have occurred only because specific performance goals were clarified and workers were individually held accountable for their accomplishment.[20]

Clearly, the role of reinforcement theory in OB requires further empirical examination and more sophisticated research designs. Like many OB approaches, the theory has strong advocates,[21] as well as critics.[22] We, too, join in the calls for more research. However, we expect that the results will mainly refine our knowledge of the OB Mod strategies rather than dramatically change existing insights. The power of operant conditioning techniques seems well confirmed. Their worth in applications to work settings also seems clearly established. Future research will probably tell us how, as managers, to better use reinforcement theory. That we should be using it already seems established.

## Value Dilemmas

The history of reinforcement theory is replete with debates over the ethics of controlling human behavior. From the manager's standpoint, there is concern that the use of operant conditioning principles ignores the individuality of people, restricts people's freedom of choice, and ignores the fact that people can be motivated by other than extrinsic work rewards.[23]

Advocates of OB Mod attack the problem straight on. They would agree that behavior modification involves the control of behavior. But, they would also go on to argue that behavior control is an irrevocable part of every manager's job. "Managers manipulate people all the time," they might say. The real question is, "How effective are you as a manipulator and what ends do you foster with your manipulation?"

Let's consider these value dilemmas. It's inevitable that a manager influences the behavior of other people. In fact, this influence must be done well if the manager's challenge is to be met successfully. The real question may well be not whether it is ethical to control behavior, but whether it is ethical not to control behavior well enough that both the goals of the organization and the individual are served.

Workers on strike for more pay.

## MANAGING PAY AS AN EXTRINSIC REWARD

Making pay allocation decisions will be one of the challenges you face as a manager of extrinsic work rewards. We'll use an examination of pay as a means of integrating our inquiry into the management of extrinsic work rewards.

### Multiple Meanings of Pay

Pay is a complex reward whose many facets can have important effects on work attitudes and behavior. Consider, for example, the negative consequences of pay dissatisfaction shown in Figure 5.2.

#### Pay and Job Satisfaction

Newspapers and other popular media frequently report on the status of pay satisfaction among various segments of the work force. One report that you may want to discuss further with your instructor is *Newsline 5.3*. A manager must understand why pay is important to people if he or she is to use it effectively as an extrinsic reward.

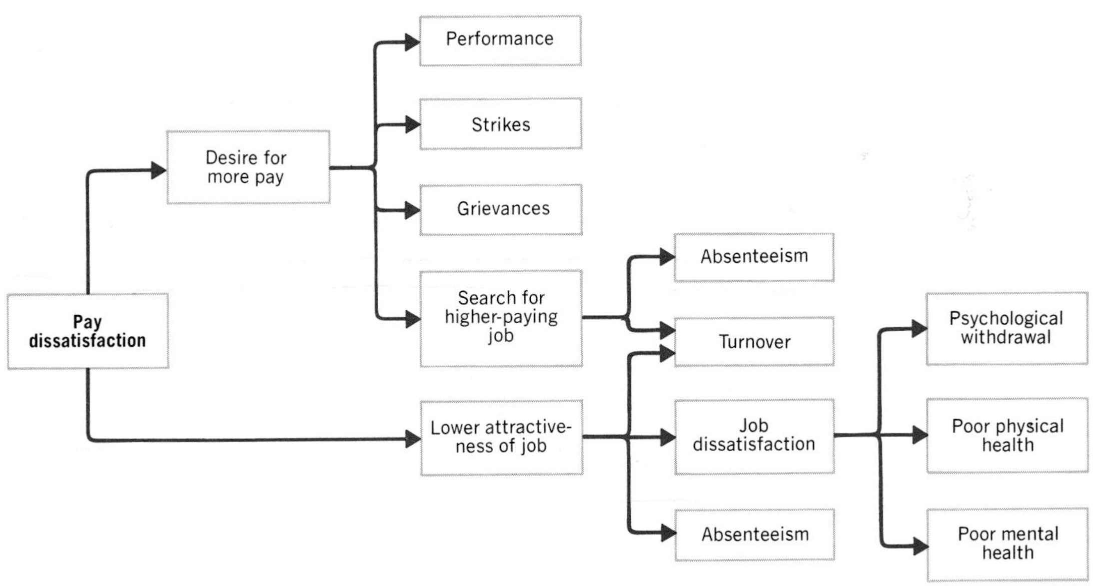


**FIGURE 5.2** The consequences of pay dissatisfaction. (Source: From *Pay and Organizational Effectiveness: A Psychological View* by Edward E. Lawler, III. Copyright © 1971 McGraw-Hill Book Company. Used with permission of McGraw-Hill Book Company.)

## NEWSLINE 5.3

### Professors Wince as Their Pay Falls Behind Inflation and Other Professional Pay

A study by the American Association of University Professors says salaries for faculty members who didn't change jobs increased 6.7% last year. Adjusted for inflation, that's 1%. The previous year, the figure was 0.5%. Fordham reports its salary increases have fallen behind inflation. At the University of Texas, pay was increased only 3.4% in two years; officials there say professors' buying power is behind 1970 levels.

The slippage is attributed to the recent high inflation, shrinking enrollments and a glut of profs in some fields. Concerns mount over universities' ability to recruit top talent, especially in the financial and scientific fields. Some Ph.D.s who would start at $15,000 at Ohio State, says an official there, could get twice that in private industry.

To ease the burden on younger personnel, Oberlin College in Ohio has given junior faculty members higher percentage wage raises than full profs.

Source: *The Wall Street Journal* (May 16, 1978), p. 1. Reprinted by permission of The Wall Street Journal, 

Table 5.4 summarizes the multiple meanings of pay as derived from three theories discussed earlier, Maslow's hierarchy of needs theory, McClelland's acquired needs theory, and Herzberg's two-factor theory.

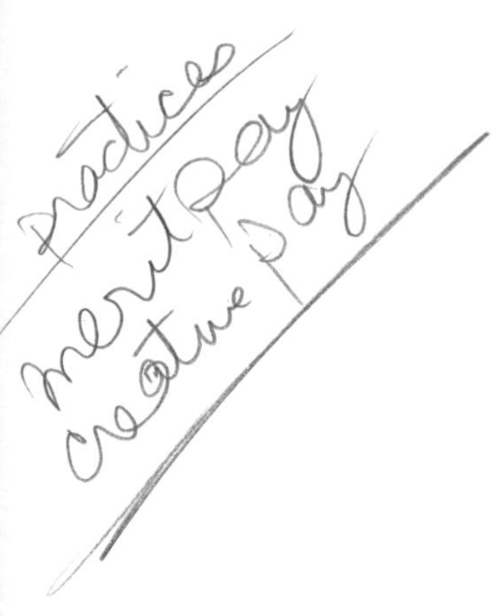

## Pay and Job Performance

Other theories giving insight into the meanings of pay as they relate to job performance are summarized in Table 5.5. Each of the theories, expectancy, equity, and reinforcement, implies that pay can serve as a motivator of work effort when it is properly managed. Taken together, they suggest that managers should make pay rewards contingent upon the desired behaviors, and allocate pay rewards in ways that maximize that positive consequences and minimize the negative consequences of the equity dynamic. Let's now look at two issues that are significant in respect to these latter challenges: merit pay and creative pay practices.

### Merit Pay

Research generally concludes that, in order for pay to serve as a source of work motivation, high levels of work performance must be viewed as the path through which high pay can be achieved.[24] Merit pay is the attempt to make pay contingent upon performance. Al-

**Table 5.4 The Multiple Meanings of Pay as Viewed from a Job Satisfaction Perspective**

| Theory | The Meaning of Pay |
|---|---|
| Hierarchy of needs theory | Pay is a unique work reward that can satisfy all types of individual needs. It is a direct way of satisfying lower-order needs. Pay can also provide access to various avenues of higher-order need satisfaction, e.g., the prestige of a high pay level can be a source of ego-fulfillment. |
| Acquired needs theory | Pay is important to the high need achievers because it serves as performance feedback and as a measure of goal accomplishment. When pay incentives are offered as group bonuses, they will be especially attractive to the high need affiliators. A person high in Power may value pay as a means of buying indicators of prestige, or as a way of controlling other people. |
| Two-factor theory | Pay represented by a person's base salary or wage rate is a hygiene factor. When pay is considered too low, dissatisfaction occurs. But high pay alone is not a source of work motivation. Pay can be a motivator when it occurs as a merit increase that gives special recognition to the individual for a job well done. |

**Table 5.5 The Multiple Meanings of Pay as Viewed from a Performance Perspective**

| Theory | The Meaning of Pay |
|---|---|
| Equity theory | Pay is an object of social comparison. People are likely to compare their pay and pay increases to those received by others. When felt inequity occurs as a result of such comparisons, work effort may be reduced in the case of negative inequity or increased in the case of positive inequity. |
| Expectancy theory | Pay is only one of many work rewards that may be valued by individuals at work. When valence, instrumentality, and expectancy are high, pay can be a source of motivation. The opportunity to work hard to obtain high pay will, however, be viewed in the context of other effort-outcome expectancies and the equity dynamic. |
| Reinforcement theory | Pay is one of the extrinsic rewards that a manager may use to direct the work behavior of subordinates. Through the techniques of operant conditioning, pay can be used as a positive reinforcer when the laws of contingent and immediate reinforcement are followed. |

though research supports the logic and theoretical benefits of merit pay, it also indicates that the implementation of merit pay plans is not as easy as we might expect.[25] *Newsline 5.4* attests to the presence of such difficulties in actual practice.

To work well, a merit pay plan should[26]

- Be based on realistic and accurate measures of individual work performance.
- Create a belief among employees that the way to achieve high pay is to perform at high levels.
- Clearly discriminate between high and low performers in the amount of pay reward received.
- Avoid confusing "merit" aspects of a pay increase with "cost of living" adjustments.

## NEWSLINE 5.4

### Merit Pay for Top Federal Workers Could Face Some Shakedown Problems

Federal agencies begin a new merit pay system next October for supervisors and certain managers. As many as 160,000 workers could get increases of up to 20% if they meet certain performance standards. But a General Accounting Office report warns that many agencies may not be prepared to administer the merit plan. It recommends more training of those who will give the raises and more advance details on what the plan's goals are.

The Office of Personnel Management, which oversees agencies' plans, asserts that it has made preparations. It says it conducted a five-day course for agency designers of merit plans and prepared a two-day program for covered employees so agencies can explain the system. It also has sought private-sector advice on merit plans.

Source: *The Wall Street Journal* (April 21, 1981), p. 1. Reprinted by permission of The Wall Street Journal, 

## Creative Pay Practices

Managers turn to a variety of creative practices to increase the positive value and minimize the negative consequences of pay plans. "Setting your own pay" is an extreme example illustrated in *Newsline 5.5*. Although you may not agree with the merits of this approach,

## NEWSLINE 5.5

### Boss Has Brainstorm

*Workers set own pay*

Arthur Friedman, an appliance dealer in Oakland, California, had a brainstorm. His idea was to let workers set their own pay, working hours, and vacation schedules. He told them to just let the bookkeeper know what they were worth. They would then be paid accordingly.

For a month after Friedman announced the policy no one asked for a raise. Then his wife Merle asked for $1 per hour more. Other employees asked for $50 and $60 more a week. One delivery truck driver demanded a $100 increase. This man had not been an especially good worker. After the raise, however, Friedman claimed things changed dramatically. The resentment about his prior pay had been cleared up. As a result he showed up early and worked extra hard.

Friedman claims his employees showed restraint and maturity in using the system. Their wages rose to a level just slightly higher than the level suggested by the union to which they belonged. In five years, there was no turnover and the use of sick days was very low. About his system Friedman says, "It takes faith. If you don't have it, or your employees don't believe you have it, it will never work."

Source: Reprinted Courtesy of *The Boston Globe:* "Boss Has Brainstorm: Workers Set Own Pay," by Martin Koughan, February 16, 1975.

the fact that it has been tried may stimulate your imagination. If you're timid, consider the alternatives of "cafeteria-style" and "lump sum" plans as a means of increasing motivation and raising satisfaction with pay.

## "Cafeteria-Style" Pay Plans

The total compensation package of an employee includes not only direct pay but also any fringe benefits which are paid for by the organization. Often these fringe benefits add an equivalent of 10 to 40% to a person's salary. It is argued that organizations need to allow for individual differences when developing such benefit programs.[27] Otherwise, the motivational value of this indirect form of pay incentive is lost. One proposal is to let individuals choose their total pay package by selecting benefits from a range of options made available by the organization. These cafeteria-style plans allow workers to select benefits according to needs. A single worker, for example, may prefer quite a different combination of insurance and retirement contributions than a married person. The predicted result is increased motivational benefit from pay as an extrinsic work reward.

### "Lump-Sum" Pay Increases

Do you know what an annual pay raise of $1,200 (the actual size of one of our recent raises) is worth when spread over 52 pay checks? It means exactly $23.08 per week! This figure is reduced substantially when taxes and other deductions are made. It is argued that this deflation of a pay increase compromises its motivational value to the individual.[28] An interesting alternative is to let people elect to receive the increase in one or more lump-sum payments. The full increase may be taken at the beginning of the year and used for some valued purpose (e.g., a down payment on a motorcycle, or a sizeable deposit in a savings account). Or a person might elect to take one-half of the raise early and get the rest at the start of the winter holiday season. In either case, the motivational significance of the pay increase is presumably enhanced by allowing the individual to receive it in larger doses and realize the most positive significance possible.

## SUMMARY

The significance of extrinsic work rewards can be summed up this way. Every manager will want to make sure that his or her use of extrinsic rewards promotes individual job performance and human resource maintenance as desirable work results. There are many types of extrinsic rewards. Thus, a manager must know which extrinsic rewards are available for allocation, and know how to allocate them to achieve the desired impact on performance and job satisfaction.

The predominate theme of this chapter has been that, to manage extrinsic rewards well, managers must allocate them on a performance-contingent basis, using the basic principles of reinforcement theory. As the heart of OB Mod, reinforcement theory offers a set of strategies for applying the techniques of operant conditioning to work settings. We have discussed OB Mod with special emphasis on three such strategies: positive reinforcement, extinction, and punishment.

Pay is an especially important extrinsic reward because of the multiple meanings with which it is associated. Previous theories of motivation are valuable in helping a manager identify these meanings. Yet there will be many challenges to be met when a manager actually seeks to employ extrinsic rewards, such as pay, to promote satisfaction and performance in his or her unit. Our discussion of creative pay practices demonstrates the lengths to which some organizations and their managers have gone to try to realize maximum motivational gains from their investments in rewards. This special case of pay illustrates quite well the multi-faceted challenge of managing work rewards. Remember,

> . . . money is one tool among many for managing motivation. It is a treacherous tool because it is deceptively concrete, tempting many managers to neglect other variables in the work situation and climate that really affect productivity. In the near future, there will be less and less excuse for neglecting these variables . . . .
>
> David I. McClelland[29]

## THINKING THROUGH THE ISSUES

1. Is there really a difference between the cognitive and reinforcement explanations of individual work behavior? Why or why not?
2. Identify the extrinsic rewards available to a college professor and of use in influencing student behavior. Develop a similar list for one or more work situations with which you are familiar.
3. Describe a reinforcement example that you have noticed in a work setting. How do you explain its effects?
4. Do you believe in the power of positive reinforcement when rewards other than pay are used as the potential reinforcers? Defend your answer.
5. When do you feel a manager is justified in using punishment as a behavior modification strategy?
6. Do you agree or disagree with those critics who claim the use of OB Mod strategies by managers is an unethical control of human behavior? Why or why not?
7. What does pay mean to you as a possible extrinsic reward for work? What are the implications of this meaning for the person who will be your boss?
8. Is there a future for "set-your-own" pay practices? Why or why not?

# EXERCISE: MANAGING MERIT PAY

## Purpose:

This exercise will allow you to experience the choices faced by managers when they make pay raise decisions. It will help you to review some of the theoretical issues involved in attempts to use pay as a motivator, and to apply these issues in a realistic and practical work setting.

## Time:

50 minutes.

## Procedure:

1. Reread the "Case of the Missing Raise" in Part One of the book. In the rest of this exercise you are to act in the role of Fred Massie, Management Department Head at Central University. Assume that it is the conclusion of the next academic year. Your task is to make pay raise allocations to your faculty for the coming year.

2. *Background Information:* There are eight faculty members in your department. They are listed below along with brief assessments of their work records during the past academic year. The College Dean has informed you that the pay increase available to your department is 7% of the existing wage budget. This gives you $16,170 to allocate as you see fit. The Dean has encouraged you to allocate the pay increases as fairly as possible and in a manner that will encourage faculty members to seek high levels of performance.

*Carla Black* Single, age 32, no children, 4 years with Central. Carla has published two fine articles during the year and has received outstanding course evaluations. You find her to be a productive faculty member who readily accepts administrative chores. She fulfills all obligations well.

*John Lloyd* Married, age 32, one child, 2 years with Central. John has published one article and presented two papers at professional meetings. He gets fine ratings from students and is well respected by his peers. You feel that John does his job very well. It appears that John also does a lot of consulting work. He is reported to have a job offer from another university that promises a substantial boost in salary.

*Harlan Mayne* Married, age 47, three children, 18 years with Central. Harlan is not a researcher and he is not popular with students. He does a good job on committee assignments and other administrative duties. Harlan appears to be well liked by his colleagues and is always willing to teach a wide variety of courses. He spends a lot of time with his family.

*Michael Lott* Married, age 56, six children, 22 years with Central. Students frequently complain about Michael's deficiencies as an instructor. His one published book is now 12 years old. He willingly serves on university committees and makes fine contributions during faculty meetings. Recently, Michael's oldest son was in a tragic automobile accident. It has been a costly financial drain for the family.

*Gene Hooper* Single, age 38, no children, 8 years with Central. Gene is a difficult personality to work with, and only seems interested in his personal research and specialized courses. He publishes frequently, three articles in the past year alone, and the few students who major in his area of study give him high course appraisals. Gene works long hours and is frequently observed to be in his office on weekends and even on holidays.

*Greer Smith* Married, age 26, no children, 1 year with Central. Greer is a new faculty member who is quite research-oriented. She has published one article and has two papers scheduled for presentation at professional meetings. Her course appraisals are high, but you find her to be very friendly with her students; too friendly, in fact. There is some question in your mind as to the academic rigor of her courses. Last weekend, you observed her having dinner with a group of students in a local night club.

*Josephine Jones* Married, age 46, two children, 14 years at Central. Josephine did not produce any research in the past year, and she receives consistently low student course appraisals. She spends very little time in her office, and avoids administrative work whenever possible. Josephine is a very warm and likeable person.

*Frank Boone* Divorced, age 37, no children, 7 years with Central. Frank works hard on his research but did not get anything accepted for presentation or publication during the past year. The same pattern has repeated itself for the last two or three years. He seems very diligent about his course preparations, but the students give him very low ratings. Frank has suffered a loss of self-confidence since his recent divorce, and seems to feel that everything is going against him.

**3.** Make an individual decision about the percentage raise you would give to each of the above faculty members. The overall percentage increases should average out to no more than the $16,170 ceiling imposed by the Dean. Individual raises can go from 0% to as high a figure as you feel able to defend.

**4.** Convene in a group of four to eight persons. Share your raise decisions with them. As a group, decide on a new set of raises and be prepared to report them to the rest of the class. Make sure that the group spokesperson can provide the rationale through which each person's raise was determined.

5. The instructor will call on each group to report its raise decisions. After some discussion, your instructor will give you the "expert's" decisions. More discussion will follow.

## CASE: PERFECT PIZZERIA REVISITED

Refer to the Perfect Pizzeria Case included at the end of Chapter 4. Use the reinforcement theory as explained in the present chapter to re-analyze key events in the case.

### Questions

1. How do you analyze, in reinforcement terms, the situation where the manager changed the time period required to receive free food and drink from 6 to 12 hours? Explain, in particular, the employees' reactions to this adjustment.
2. What were the reinforcement implications of the manager working beside the employees for a while, and then returning to his office?
3. How do you explain, in reinforcement terms, what happened at the end of the case?
4. What can now be done by way of a reinforcement program to deal with the situation at the end of the case?

## THE MANAGER'S VOCABULARY

**Behavior Modification** A set of techniques for applying operant conditioning to the control of human behavior.

**Extinction** Decreasing the frequency of or weakening an undesirable behavior by making it contingent upon the removal of a desirable consequence.

**Extrinsic Work Rewards** Positively valued work outcomes which are given to the individual by some other person in the work setting.

**Law of Contingent Reinforcement** In order for a reward to have maximum reinforcing value, it must be delivered only if the desired behavior is exhibited.

**Law of Immediate Reinforcement** The more immediate the delivery of a reward after the occurrence of a desirable behavior, the greater the reinforcing effect on behavior.

**Negative Reinforcement** Increasing the frequency of or strengthening a desirable work behavior by making it contingent upon the avoidance of an undesirable consequence.

**Operant Conditioning** The process of controlling behavior by manipulating its consequences.

**Organizational Behavior Modification (OB Mod)** The systematic reinforcement of desirable organizational behavior and the nonreinforcement or punishment of unwanted organizational behavior.

**Positive Reinforcement** Increasing the frequency of or strengthening a desirable work behavior by making it contingent upon the occurrence of a desirable consequence.

**Punishment** Decreasing the frequency of or weakening an undesirable behavior by making it contingent upon the occurrence of an undesirable consequence.

**Shaping** The creation of a new behavior by the positive reinforcement of successive approximations to the desired behavior.

## Important Names

**E. L. Thorndike** Expressed the "law of effect" which became a foundation for reinforcement theory.

**B. F. Skinner** Popularized the use of operant conditioning to modify animal and human behavior.

## Notes

[1]Excerpted from Neil Ulman, "Alexei and the Gulag Archipelago," *The Wall Street Journal,* (Thursday, September 30, 1976), p. 22. Reprinted by permission of the Wall Street Journal, copyright © Dow Jones & Company Inc., 1976. All rights reserved.

[2]Edward L. Deci, *Intrinsic Motivation* (New York: Plenum Press, 1975), pp. 7–8.

[3]E. L. Thorndike, *Animal Intelligence* (New York: Macmillan, 1911), p. 244.

[4]For some of B. F. Skinner's work see *Walden Two* (New York: Macmillan, 1948), *Science and Human Behavior* (New York: Macmillan, 1953), and *Contingencies of Reinforcement* (New York: Appleton-Century-Crofts, 1969).

[5]Fred Luthans and Robert Kreitner, "The Role of Publishment in Organizational Behavior Modification (OB Mod)," *Public Personnel Management,* Vol. 2 (May/June 1973), p. 157.

[6]Fred Luthans and Robert Kreitner, *Organizational Behavior Modification* (Glenview, Ill.: Scott, Foresman and Company, 1975), p. 15.

[7]Both laws are stated in Keith L. Miller, *Principles of Everyday Behavior Analysis* (Monterey, Calif.: Brooks/Cole Publishing Company, 1975), p. 122.

[8]Adapted from Harry Wiard, "Why Manage Behavior? A Case for Positive Reinforcement," *Human Resource Management* (Summer 1972), pp. 15–20.

[9]See Luthans and Kreitner, op. cit., 1975.

[10]See, for example, Chris J. Berger, "An Empirical Test of Operant Conditioning and Expectancy Theory Accounts of Reinforcement Parameters in Work Behavior," working paper, Krannert School of Management, Purdue University (1978).

[11]Stephen F. Jablonsky and David L. Devries, "Operant Conditioning Principles Extrapolated to the Theory of Management," *Organizational Behavior and Human Performance,* Vol. 7 (April 1972), pp. 340–358.

[12]Ibid.

[13]Adapted in part from W. Clay Hamner, "Using Reinforcement Theory In Organizational Settings," pp. 388–395 in Henry L. Tosi and W. Clay Hamner (eds.), *Organizational Behavior and Management: A Contingency Approach* (Chicago: St. Clair Press, 1977).

[14]Adapted from Luthans and Kreitner, op. cit., 1975, pp. 125–126.

[15]See Jablonsky, op. cit., p. 345.

[16]Adapted from Luthans and Kreitner, op. cit., 1975, pp, 127–129.

[17]Adapted in part from Luthans and Kreitner, op. cit., 1973; and Hamner, op. cit.

[18]"Productivity Gains from a Pat on the Back," *Business Week* (January 23, 1978), pp. 57–59.

[19]Nicholas Von Hoffman, "Motivating the Workers," *Burlington Free Press* (February 3, 1978), p. 7.

[20]Edwin A. Locke, "The Myths of Behavior Mod in Organizations," *Academy of Management Review,* Vol. 2 (October 1977), pp. 543–553.

[21]See, for example, Hamner, op. cit.; Luthans and Kreitner, op. cit., 1975; and Nord, op. cit.

[22]See, for example, Locke, op. cit.

[23]Hamner, op. cit.

[24]Edward L. Deci, "Paying People Doesn't Always Work the Way you Expect it To." *Human Resource Management* (Summer 1973), pp. 28–32; Charles N. Greene and Philip M. Podsakoff, "Effects of Removal of a Pay Incentive: A Field Experiment," *Academy of Management Proceedings* (August 1978), pp. 206–210.

[25]W. Clay Hamner,"How to Ruin Motivation with Pay," *Compensation Review,* Vol. 7 (Third Quarter 1975). pp. 17–27; Greene and Podsakoff, op. cit.

[26]Adapted, in part, from Edward E. Lawler, III, *Pay and Organizational Effectiveness* (New York: McGraw-Hill Book Company), p. 309.

[27]Edward E. Lawler, III, "Workers can Set Their Own Wages Responsibly," *Psychology Today,* Vol. 10 (February 1977), p. 109.

[28]Ibid.

[29]David C. McClelland, "Money as a Motivator: Some Research Insights," The McKinsey Quarterly (Fall 1967), p. 41.

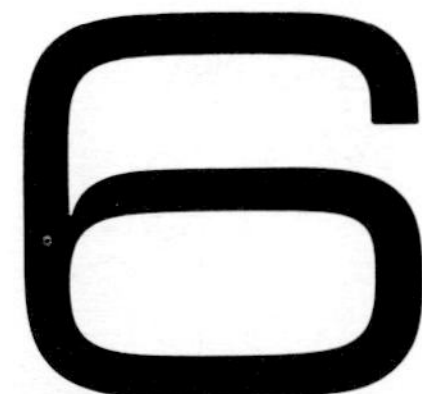

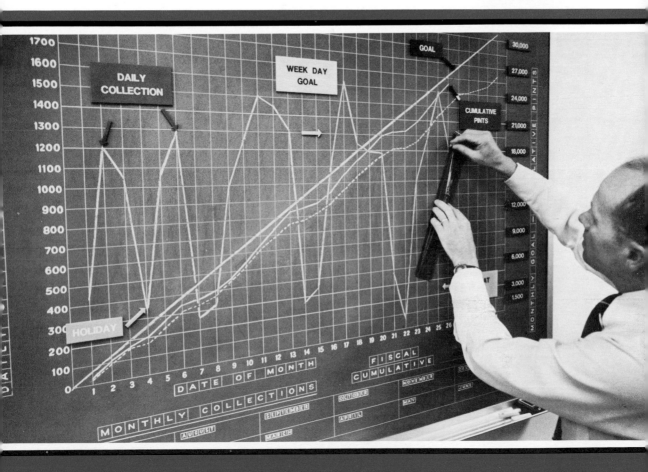

# JOB DESIGN, GOAL-SETTING, AND WORK SCHEDULING

# TURNING CONFUSION INTO ORDER[1]

An old man lived on a street where boys played noisily every afternoon. One day the din became too much, and he called the boys into his house. He told them he liked to listen to them play, but his hearing was failing and he could no longer hear their games. He asked them to come around each day and play noisily in front of his house. If they did, he would give them each a quarter. The youngsters raced back the following day and made a tremendous racket in front of the house. The old man paid the boys and asked them to return the next day. Again they made noise, and again the old man paid them for it. But this time he gave each boy only 20 cents, explaining that he was running out of money. On the following day, they got only 15 cents each. Furthermore, the old man told them, he would have to reduce the fee to 5 cents on the fourth day. The boys became angry and told the old man they would not be back. It was not worth the effort, they said, to make noise for only 5 cents a day.

Any manager would do well to seek the counsel of this wise man. He not only knows the value of extrinsic rewards, he also understands their unique power in relationship to intrinsic rewards. We will untangle this folktale and establish its managerial implications in the pages that follow.

**MANAGEMENT APPLICATIONS QUESTION**

How will you use intrinsic rewards and other aspects of the work setting as additional resources for promoting job performance and human resource maintenance within your work unit?

## PLANNING AHEAD

**After reading and participating in the learning activities provided in this chapter, you will develop new and creative responses to the management applications question. The topics you will study include the following:**

**Intrinsic Work Rewards**
**Job Design in Theory**
**Job Design in Practice**
**A Diagnostic Approach to Job Enrichment**
**Goal-Setting**
**Alternative Work Schedules**

Don't dismiss the introductory folktale too lightly. The message is an important one. Managers must be good at using both extrinsic and intrinsic rewards to promote performance and satisfaction in their work units. In this chapter we'll take a detailed look at the managerial challenges of intrinsic rewards. Then we will provide thoughts on how both intrinsic and extrinsic rewards can be integrated into a workable motivation strategy by a focus on job design, goal-setting and work scheduling.

# INTRINSIC WORK REWARDS

**Intrinsic work rewards** are those rewards which are received by the individual directly as a result of task performance. These are "rewards over which the employee has a high degree of self-control and that are an integral part of the work itself."[2] An intrinsic reward, in contrast to an extrinsic reward, which is externally controlled, results directly from task accomplishment.

## Examples of Intrinsic Rewards

One example of an intrinsic work reward is the feeling of achievement that a person gets when a challenging task is completed. In the introductory folktale, "playing noisily in the street" initially provided the children with intrinsic rewards. They achieved satisfaction directly from their play and not because of someone else's outside evaluation of the experience. As soon as the old man started paying the children to play, however, an extrinsic reward was introduced into the situation.

The emphases in the examples below highlight intrinsic rewards experienced by people in their work.[3]

| | |
|---|---|
| Teacher: | "The money I earn as a teacher is nothing; but I really enjoy teaching a student a new idea." |
| Machinist: | "The company doesn't give me a darn thing; but I take pride in producing a quality product." |
| Social worker: | "My working conditions are bad and my co-workers are boring; but I get a real sense of satisfaction out of helping my clients." |

## Managerial Implications

When we discussed extrinsic rewards, the conclusion was reached that they should be awarded contingent upon work performance. The manager was viewed as an agent of the organization; as a person responsible for allocating extrinsic rewards such as pay, promotion,

A teacher motivated in his work.

and verbal praise to employees. To serve in this capacity, a manager must be good at evaluating performance, maintaining an inventory of valued work rewards, and giving these rewards to employees in proportion to their performance contributions.

The management of intrinsic work rewards is an additional challenge for the manager. The manager still acts as an agent of the organization, but now, he or she must design jobs for individual subordinates so that intrinsic work rewards become available as a result of exerting work efforts on assigned tasks.

There is a natural tendency at this point to assume that every manager should design every job to provide every employee maximum opportunity to experience intrinsic work rewards. This is not a good assumption. Indeed, this chapter will help you to understand

- When people may desire intrinsic work rewards.
- How to design jobs for people who desire intrinsic work rewards.
- How to motivate those people who do not desire intrinsic work rewards.

## JOB DESIGN IN THEORY

Our investigation of the sources of intrinsic motivation begins with the job itself. What, really, is a "job?" We all have them, but can we define the term? A **job** is one or more tasks that an individual performs in direct support of the organization's production purpose. The key word is "tasks." In fact, **intrinsic motivation** is essentially task motivation, i.e., a desire to work hard solely for the pleasant

DOONESBURY

by Garry Trudeau

What do you want in a job?

experience of task accomplishment. When a job is properly designed, both task performance and job satisfaction should be facilitated. Additional human resource maintenance aspects, such as turnover, may also be influenced.

**Job design** is "the deliberate, purposeful planning of the job, including any or all of its structural or social aspects."[4] This definition encompasses both the specification of task attributes and the creation of a work setting for these attributes. The manager's responsibility is to design both task attributes and work settings that will prove to be motivational for the individual employee. Figuratively speaking, job design is properly done when

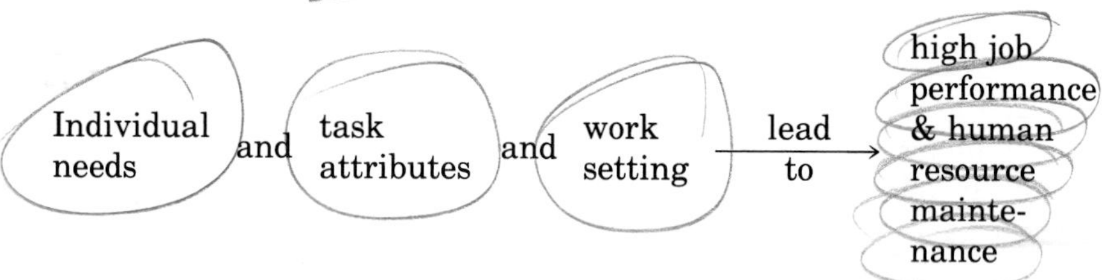
Individual needs
and
task attributes
and
work setting
lead to
high job performance & human resource maintenance

Chapter 4 provided various theories to help you to assess the needs of individual workers. Here, we'll discuss job simplification, enlargement, rotation, and enrichment as possible strategies for the design of task attributes. We will also discuss goal-setting and alternative work schedules as key aspects of work setting designs.

# JOB DESIGN IN PRACTICE

We can surely agree that job designs are important to the individual employee. Two questions, however, remain to be answered. What are some of the alternative strategies of job design? And which of these strategies provides more intrinsic work rewards for the employee? Let's answer these questions by example.

## A Case in Job Design[5]

Charles Krug is a competent person who is motivated by social satisfactions. He likes to participate in interesting conversations, and he feels good when being helpful or stimulating to other persons. How do you think Charles will react to each of the following job designs?

## The Assembly Line Job

Charles reports to a work station on an assembly line. The product is electric toasters. A partially assembled toaster passes in front of Charles on as conveyor belt every 2½ minutes. Charles puts plastic handles on each toaster and then lets the conveyor take the unit to the next work station. Everyone gets a 10-minute break in the morning and afternoon. There is a one-half hour lunch period. Charles works by himself in a rather noisy and cluttered setting.

Checkpoint

Note below your predictions for Krug's performance and satisfaction in this work setting.

| | | | |
|---|---|---|---|
| Job Satisfaction: | low | moderate | high |
| Job Performance: | low | moderate | high |

## The Modified Assembly Line Job

Charles reports to work on the same assembly line. Now, however, a toaster comes to Charles' station every 12 minutes and he performs a greater number of tasks. He adds the sides to the assembly, puts on the two handles, and installs the "light-dark" selection switch. Periodically, Charles changes stations with one of the other workers and does a different set of tasks. In all other respects, the work setting is the same as in the first job described.

Checkpoint

Mark your predictions once again.

| | | | |
|---|---|---|---|
| Job Satisfaction: | low | moderate | high |
| Job Performance: | low | moderate | high |

## The Team Assembly Job

Charles is part of a team responsible for assembling electric toasters. The team has a weekly production quota, but makes its own plans for the speed and arrangement of the required assembly processes. The team is also responsible for inspecting the quality of the finished toasters and for correcting any defective units. These duties are shared among the members and are discussed at numberous team meetings. Charles has been selected by the team as its plant liasion. In addition to his other duties, he works with people elsewhere in the plant to ensure a smooth supply of component parts to his team.

Checkpoint

Make a final set of predictions for Krug in this last job.

| | | | |
|---|---|---|---|
| Job Satisfaction: | low | moderate | high |
| Job Performance: | low | moderate | high |

Now, we can identify the following categories of job design strategies which are available to managers: job simplification, job enlargement and rotation, and job enrichment. Each of these strategies has its merits and demerits. A manager must learn when and how to employ each to its proper advantage.

Checkpoint

By the terms alone, you should be able to associate each job design strategy with its application in the Charles Krug example. Go back and note which job design strategy best describes each of Krug's previous job titles (the assembly line, modified assembly line, and team assembly jobs). Read on to verify your answers.

## Job Simplification

**Job simplification** involves standardizing work procedures and employing people in very clearly defined and specialized tasks. Charles Krug's first assembly line job was simplified. The machine-paced automobile assembly line is a classic example of this job design strategy. *Newsline 6.1* is one person's description of what it can be like to work on such a job.

Table 6.1 summarizes some of the potential advantages and disadvantages of job simplification. The disadvantages reported in this table are quite consistent with the Newsline. They are prone to

**Table 6.1 Expected Advantages and Realized Disadvantages of Machine-Paced Assembly Lines**

| Potential Advantages | Potential Disadvantages |
|---|---|
| Increased economy because: | Economy gains not realized because: |
| ■ Jobs require little training<br>■ Jobs staffed by low-skilled people<br>■ Workers interchangeable among jobs | ■ Absenteeism high<br>■ Turnover high<br>■ High wages required to attract workers |
| Production quality and quantity easily controlled. | Production quality suffers because workers become bored and frustrated. |

Source: From *Motivation in Work Organizations,* by E. E. Lawler. Copyright © 1973 by Wadsworth, Inc. Reprinted by permission of Brooks/Cole Publishing Company. Monterey, California.

## NEWSLINE 6.1

### The Grueling Life on the Line

Henry Belcher is a 40-year-old welder. His work day begins at 6 A.M., when the assembly line begins and cars move past his work station at the rate of 62 per hour. The noise is deafening and Belcher can't even talk to his co-workers less than three feet away. Even if he could be heard, he doesn't have time to talk. His job is to pound out dents and reweld defective seams in less than a minute for each car.

The work is tiring, but Belcher only gets one 11-minute break in the morning. At 10 A.M. the line stops for a 30-minute lunch. There isn't enough time to go to the cafeteria, so he eats from a bag. Often, he eats while standing in a line of men waiting to use the urinals. It's hard to leave the assembly line, so a chance to visit the bathroom can't be missed.

A whistle sounds at 10:30 A.M. to end the lunch break. Belcher works four more hours with one 12-minute break and leaves at 2:30. His pay is approximately five times the minimum wage per hour. About his job, Belcher says, "Everything is regulated. No time to stop and think about what you are doing; your life is geared to the assembly line. I have lost my freedom."

Source: Reported in "The Grueling Life on the Line," *Time*, Vol. 96 (September 1970), pp. 70–71.

emerge when a simplified job proves inconsistent with individual needs. In the example of Charles Krug, an important social need was thwarted by his first assembly line job. Thus, we would predict that his job satisfaction would be low and that he would be frequently absent. Boredom may lead to a high error rate, and his overall performance will probably just good enough to prevent him from being fired!

## Job Enlargement and Job Rotation

The job enlargement and job rotation strategies of job design seek to increase the variety of tasks performed by a worker. Task variety is assumed to offset some of the disadvantages of job simplification and thereby increase job performance and satisfaction for the individual.

**Job enlargement** increases task variety by combining into one job two or more tasks which were previously assigned to separate workers. The only change in the original job design is that a worker does more different tasks than previously. **Job rotation** increases task variety by periodically shifting workers among jobs involving different tasks. Job rotation can be arranged according to almost any time schedule, such as hourly, daily, or weekly.

Work on an assembly line.

Charles Krug's second job on the modified assembly line is an example of job enlargement with occasional job rotation. Rather than doing only one part of the toaster assembly task, he did three. Furthermore, he occasionally changed jobs with another worker to complete a different phase of the assembly process.

Because job enlargement and rotation reduced some of the monotony of Krug's original assembly line job, we would expect an increase in both his satisfaction and performance. Satisfaction should remain at a moderate level, however, since the job still doesn't provide a strong response to Krug's social needs. In addition, although quality should increase as boredom is reduced, low intrinsic motivation and lingering absenteeism are also likely to keep job performance at a moderate level.

## Job Enrichment

Frederick Herzberg (see his two-factor theory discussed in Chapter 2), feels it is illogical to expect high levels of motivation among employees whose jobs are designed according to the rules of simplification, enlargement, or rotation. "Why," he asks, "should a worker become motivated when one or more 'meaningless' tasks are added to previously existing ones or when work assignments are rotated among equally 'meaningless' tasks?"[6] Rather than pursuing one of these job design strategies, therefore, he recommends that managers practice job enrichment.

**Job enrichment** is the practice of building motivating factors into job content.[7] This job design strategy differs from the previous ones in that it seeks to expand job content by adding some of the planning and evaluating duties normally performed by the manager to the subordinates' job. These changes are referred to by Herzberg as a "vertical loading" of the job tasks.

Charles Krug's final job in the team assembly situation contains elements of job enrichment. The team is now responsible for doing some of the planning and evaluating work, typical managerial tasks, as well as for the actual assembly of toasters. Charles should find this arrangement especially satisfying for the intrinsic rewards it provides in response to his strong social needs. He should get added satisfaction from acting as the team's plant liaison because his assigned tasks bring him into regular contact with other people. This increase in intrinsic motivation should result in high levels of both job satisfaction and performance.

The seven principles guiding Herzberg's approach to job enrichment are listed in Table 6.2. Note that each principle is an action guideline designed to increase the presence of one or more motivating factors in the content of a job. Remember too, that in the job enlargement and rotation strategies managers retain all responsibility for work planning and evaluating. The job enrichment strategy, by con-

**Table 6.2 The Principles of Job Enrichment**

| Principle | Motivators Involved |
|---|---|
| 1. Remove some controls while retaining accountability | Responsibility and achievement |
| 2. Increase the accountability of individuals for own work | Responsibility and recognition |
| 3. Give a person a complete natural unit of work (module, division, area, and so on) | Responsibility, achievement, and recognition |
| 4. Grant additional authority to an employee in his activity, provide job freedom | Responsibility, achievement, and recognition |
| 5. Make periodic reports directly available to the worker rather than to the supervisor | Recognition |
| 6. Introduce new and more difficult tasks not previously handled | Growth and learning |
| 7. Assign individuals specific or specialized tasks, enable them to become experts | Responsibility, growth, and advancement |

Source: Copyright © 1968 by the President and Fellows of Harvard College; all rights reserved. Reprinted by permission of the Harvard Business Review, "One More Time: How do You Motivate Employees?" by Frederic Herzberg, January–February, 1968.

trast, involves vertical loading which allows subordinates to share in these planning and evaluating responsibilities, as well as to do the actual work.

## Summary: A Continuum of Job Design Strategies

The various strategies of job design are arrayed on a continuum in Figure 6.1. This figure summarizes how the strategies differ as sources of intrinsic work rewards. The availability of intrinsic rewards is lowest for task attributes associated with simplified jobs, and highest for enriched jobs. Since we are interested in learning how to manage intrinsic rewards and thereby promote motivation to work, we now turn our attention to a deeper look at job enrichment.

**FIGURE 6.1** A continuum of job design strategies.

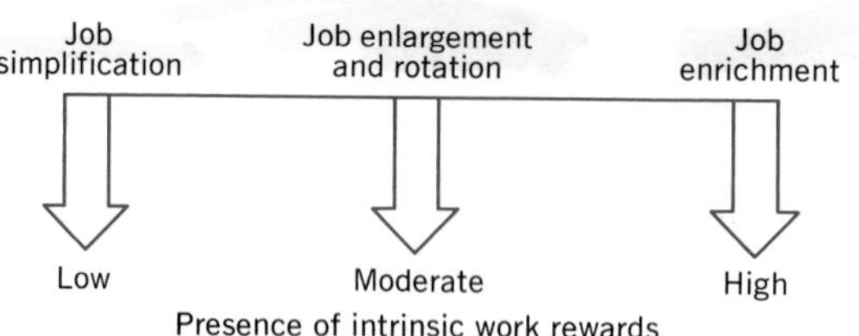

## A DIAGNOSTIC APPROACH TO JOB ENRICHMENT

In 1971, Richard Hackman and Edward Lawler reported a theory that attempted to identify when jobs will provide high levels of intrinsic work motivation. Their theory was tested in a sample of telephone company employees, with positive results.[8]

### The Theory[9]

The current version of this theory is shown in Figure 6.2. Five core job characteristics are identified as being task attributes of special importance to job designs. A job that is high in the core characteristics is said to be enriched. The core job characteristics and their definitions are

**Skill Variety:** The degree to which a job requires a variety of different activities in carrying out the work and involves the use of a number of different skills and talents of the employee.

**Task Identity:** The degree to which the job requires completion of a "whole" and identifiable piece of work, that is, one that involves doing a job from beginning to end with a visible outcome.

**Task Significance:** The degree to which the job has a substantial impact on the lives or work of other people elsewhere in the organization or in the external environment.

**Autonomy:** The degree to which the job gives the employee substantial freedom, independence, and discretion in scheduling

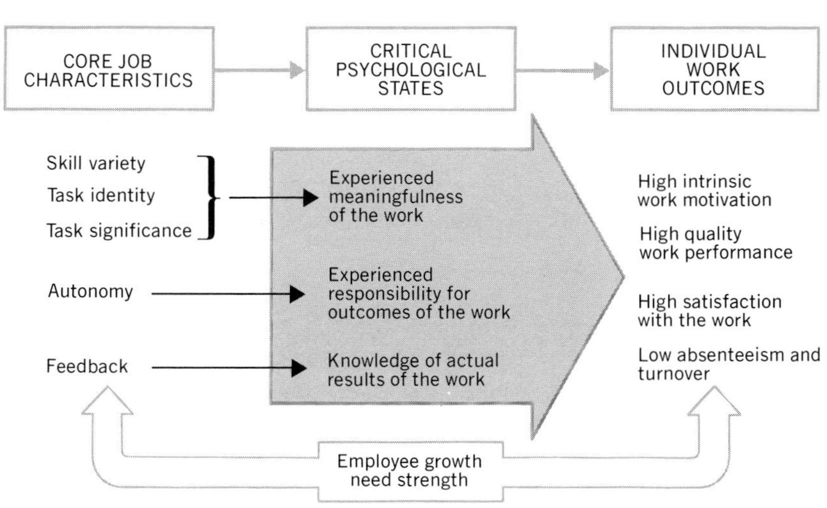


**FIGURE 6.2** Core job characteristics and individual work outcomes. (Source: Adapted from J. Richard Hackman and Greg R. Oldham, "Development of the Job Diagnostic Survey," *Journal of Applied Psychology,* Vol. 60, 1975, p. 161. Used by permission.)

the work and in determining the procedures to be used in carrying it out.

**Feedback from the Job Itself:** The degree to which carrying out the work activities required by the job results in the employee obtaining direct and clear information on the results of his or her performance.

Hackman and his colleagues argue further that three critical psychological states must be realized in order for people to develop intrinsic work motivation: (1) experienced meaningfulness in the work, (2) experienced responsibility for the outcomes of the work, and (3) knowledge of actual results of the work activities. These psychological states represent intrinsic work rewards which are hypothesized to occur, and to influence later performance and satisfaction, when the core job characteristics are present in the job design. These relationships are all detailed in Figure 6.2

The theory recognizes that the five core job characteristics will not affect all people in the same way. Employee growth need strength, as shown in Figure 6.2, is considered a most important source of individual variation. The theory predicts that people with strong growth needs will respond positively to enriched jobs, while people low in growth need strength will have negative reactions and find enriched jobs a source of anxiety. These predicted relationships are summarized in Figure 6.3.

This diagnostic approach to job enrichment has been examined in a variety of work settings, including bank, dental, corrections department, and telephone employees, among others.[10] The results are promising, but still tentative. Researchers generally indicate that

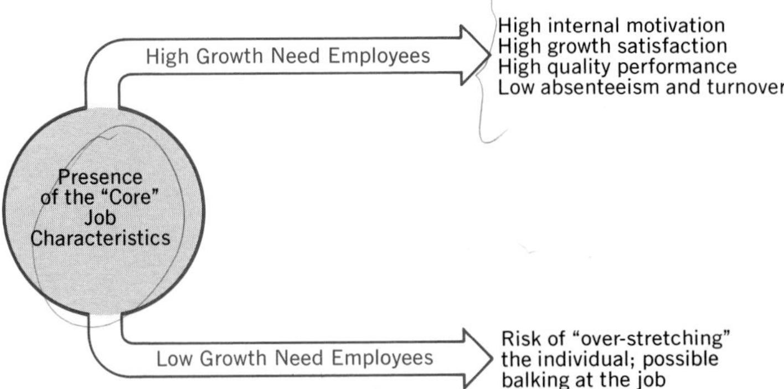


**FIGURE 6.3** Growth needs and the "core" job characteristics. (Source: J. Richard Hackman, Greg Oldham, Robert Janson, and Kenneth Purdy, "A New Strategy for Job Enrichment. Copyright © 1975 by the Regents of the University of California. Reprinted from *California Management Review,* Vol. XV, no. 3, pp. 96 and 97 by permission of the Regents.)

1. Growth need strength is a key variable that may predict how different people will react to jobs high in the core characteristics.
2. Jobs high in these characteristics are likely to increase job satisfaction, especially among high growth need employees.
3. Jobs high in these characteristics may lead to improved work performance.

## Implementing the Diagnostic Approach

A diagnostic approach to job enrichment holds promise for the practicing manager. To make sure that you fully understand the concept, work through the following case.

### Travelers Insurance Company[11]

The company depends heavily upon computerized information processing. This information is generated from keypunched cards that serve as input to the computer. The keypunch operators' job is to transfer data onto punched cards from printed or written documents supplied by user departments.

Requests for keypunching come from many departments within the company. These requests are received in the keypunch unit by assignment clerks who review the requests for accuracy, legibility, etc. Rejected requests are sent to the unit supervisor, who corrects the problems through direct contact with the user departments. Accepted requests are parceled out to keypunch operators in batches requiring approximately one hour of punching time.

The operators are supposed to punch exactly the information on the input documents, even when obvious coding mistakes exist. A verifier then checks all punching for accuracy as measured against the supporting documents. Any punching errors are randomly assigned back to the operators for correction.

Checkpoint

1. Use the scale below to assess the keypunch operator's job on each of the five core job characteristics.

| | | |
|---|---|---|
| Skill Variety | low | high |
| Task Identity | low | high |
| Task Significance | low | high |
| Autonomy | low | high |
| Feedback | low | high |

2. Based on your analysis of the job, what do you predict in terms of the operators' job performance and satisfaction?

| | | | |
|---|---|---|---|
| Job Satisfaction: | low | moderate | high |
| Job Performance: | low | moderate | high |

## Continuing On

Travelers Insurance Company became concerned because the keypunch operators were apathetic and sometimes hostile toward their jobs. Error rates were high, and absenteeism was frequent. If you predicted low performance and satisfaction, you were right!

The company next hired a professional consulting firm to look into the situation. The consultants concluded that the motivating potential of the keypunch job was low. Specifically, they identified the following weaknesses.

**Skill Variety:** There was none. Only a single skill was involved, the ability to accurately punch the data recorded on input documents.

**Task Identity:** It was virtually nonexistent. Keypunch batches were assembled to provide an even work load in the unit, but did not create whole and identifiable jobs for the operators.

**Task Significance:** None was apparent. The keypunching operation was a necessary step in providing service to the company's customers. The individual operator, however, was isolated by an assignment clerk and a supervisor from any knowledge of what the operation meant to the use department, let alone its meaning to the ultimate customer of the company.

**Autonomy:** There was none. The operators had no freedom to arrange their daily tasks to meet production schedules, or to resolve problems with the user departments, or even to correct, while punching, information that was obviously wrong.

**Feedback:** There was none. Once a punching batch left the operator's hands, he or she was not guaranteed feedback on its quality, since punching errors were randomly assigned back to the operators.

Checkpoint

Compare your predicted profile of job characteristics with the one determined by the consultants. Resolve any conflicts by referring back to the definitions of the job core characteristics, and by rereading the job description as detailed in the case.

## Continuing On

The consultants ultimately decided to enrich the job design. Initially, however, they did so only for some operators. The jobs of the others were left unchanged so as to serve as a control group. This quasi-experimental procedure was followed to provide evaluative data as to whether or not the enriched job was beneficial for the company and the operators. Thus, a decision could be made to abandon the program if it was not working, or to revise it in a constructive fashion.

The actual changes made by the consultants to enrich the keypunch operator's job included the following.

1. (________________): The random assignment of work batches was discontinued. Instead, each operator was assigned continuing responsibility for certain accounts, either user departments or specific recurring jobs. Now all work for a given account always goes to the same operator.

2. (________________): Some planning and evaluating duties were included along with the central task of keypunching. These changes are elaborated upon as we discuss additional changes below.

3. (________________): Each operator was allowed direct contact with keypunch clients. The operators, not the assignment clerks, now inspect input documents for correctness and legibility. When problems arise, the operator, not the supervisor, takes them up with the client.

4. (________________): The operators are provided with a number of additional sources of data about their performance. The computer department now returns incorrect cards to the operators who punched them, and operators correct their own errors. Each operator also keeps a personal file of punching errors. These can be reviewed to determine trends in the frequency and types of errors being made. Each operator receives a weekly computer printout summarizing errors and productivity. This report is sent directly to the operator, rather than to the supervisor.

5. (________________): Operators now have the authority to correct obvious coding errors on input documents. They also set their own punching schedules and plan their daily work, as long as they meet deadlines. Some competent operators have been given the option of not having their work verified.

The above changes illustrate five implementation concepts that are central to the diagnostic approach to job enrichment. These concepts indicate that, to improve upon the five core job characteristics, a manager must be skilled at combining tasks, forming natural work units, establishing client relationships, vertical loading, and opening feedback channels.[12] The relationship between these implementation concepts and the core job characteristics is shown in Figure 6.4.

---

### Checkpoint

Go back to the report of changes made by the consultants. Each change represents one of the implementation concepts just described. Write the name of each concept in the space corresponding to its

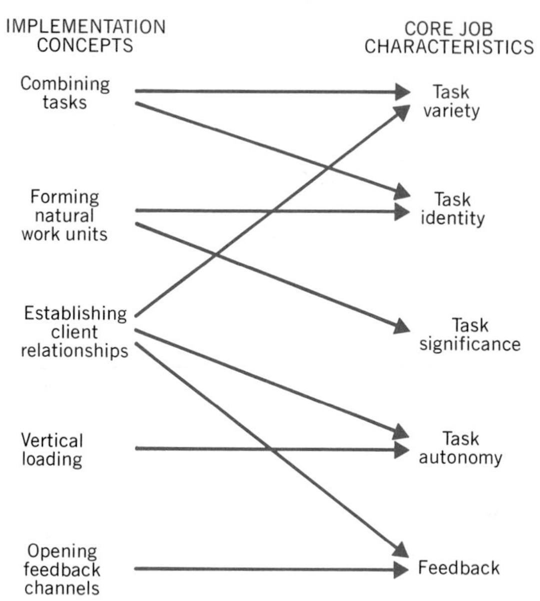


**FIGURE 6.4** Implementation concepts and the core job characteristics. (Source: Adapted from J. R. Hackman, et al., "A New Strategy for Job Enrichment." Copyright © 1975 by the Regents of the University of California. Reprinted from *California Management Review,* Vol. XV, no. 3, pp. 96 and 97 by permission of the Regents.)

correct description. (The correct answers are: 1. natural unit of work, 2. task combination, 3. client relationships, 4. feedback, 5. vertical loading.)

## Questions and Answers on Job Enrichment

There are probably a number of questions which are in your mind concerning job enrichment. Answering these questions gives us a way of summarizing the previous discussion and orienting you to the remaining issues to be covered in this chapter.

**Question:** "Is it expensive to do job enrichment?"

Job enrichment can be very costly. It is unlikely that the enrichment of the keypunch operator's job cost very much. But, only one phase of a job enrichment project at AT&T cost over $25,000 because of required facility rearrangements.[13] In many cases it is the nature of the work flow technology that makes job enrichment costly.

**Question:** "Can job enrichment apply to groups as well as individuals?"

Yes. In fact, automobile manufacturing is a good example. In Chapter 9 we'll discuss some innovative efforts that have been made to redesign into enriched work groups the automobile assembly line at a Volvo plant in Sweden. The technological changes were extremely expensive, and U.S. automakers have questioned their cost-benefit value. The enrichment of group tasks is possible, however, in many types of settings. Chapter 9 discusses a number of these creative work group designs.

**Queston:** "Will people demand more pay for doing enriched jobs?"

Herzberg argues that if employees are being paid a truly competitive wage or salary (i.e., if pay dissatisfaction does not already exist), then the intrinsic rewards of performing enriched tasks will be adequate compensation for any increased labor required. Other researchers are more skeptical. A study reports that 79% of the people in one company whose jobs were enriched felt that they should have been paid more.[14] A manager must be cautious on this issue. Any job enrichment program should be approached with due consideration given to pay as an important program variable.

**Question:** "What do the unions say about job enrichment?"

It's hard to speak for all unions. Suffice it to say that the following comments made by one union official do sound a note of caution for the manager.[15]

> ". . . better wages, shorter hours, vested pensions, a right to have a say in their working conditions, the right to be promoted on the basis of seniority, and all the rest. That's the kind of job enrichment that unions believe in. And I assure you that that's the kind of job enrichment that we will continue to fight for."

**Question:** "Should everyone's job be enriched?"

No, not everyone's job should be enriched. The informed manager will make very careful decisions when considering job enrichment as a way of promoting satisfaction and performance in the work unit. Cost, technological constraints, and work group and union opposition may make it difficult to enrich some jobs. Furthermore, the logic of individual differences suggests that not everyone will want an enriched job. The people most likely to have positive reactions to job enrichment will be those high in need for achievement,[16] those who hold middle-class working values,[17] and/or those seeking higher-order growth need satisfactions at work.[18] It also appears that job enrichment will be most advantageous when workers are not dissatisfied with hygiene factors found in the job context[19] and have the levels of training, education, and intelligence required to do the enriched job.[20]

**Question:** "What are some summary guidelines for doing job enrichment?"

The guidelines for implementing a program of job enrichment include:

1. Consider a job to be a candidate for job enrichment only when evidence exists that job satisfaction and/or performance is either deteriorating or open for improvement.
2. Proceed with job enrichment only when each of the following conditions is met:[21]
   a. Employees view their jobs as deficient in one or more of the core job characteristics.
   b. Extrinsic rewards and job context are not causing dissatisfaction.
   c. Cost and other potential constraints do not prohibit the types of job design changes necessary to result in enrichment.
   d. Employees view the core job characteristics with high and positive valences.

## NEWSLINE 6.2

### The World of Work as Seen by a Worker

Robert Schrank, author of *Ten Thousand Working Days* (Cambridge, Mass.: MIT Press, 1978), has spent most of his sixty years working as a laborer, farm hand, machinist, union organizer, business executive, and city official. He has been described as "one of the few experts on manual labor who has actually done very much of it."

Schrank says, "I am skeptical of people who tell factory workers their jobs can become creative, autonomous, challenging and self-actualizing . . . A production worker simply cannot decide on his own that the engine coming down the line should have four cylinders instead of eight, or that a car body should be red instead of blue." As a result, Schrank is not enthusiastic about job enrichment. After observing one experiment where people worked in pairs to assemble entire engines, he commented—"I was wondering, if I assembled one hundred or two hundred, maybe four hundred engines, what would the challenge be?"

The real challenge, according to Schrank, is to provide such workers with some of the amenities usually accorded only to managers and professionals, for example, setting their own work schedules.

Source: Adapted from Roger Ricklefs, "The World of Work as Seen by a Worker," *The Wall Street Journal* (May 26, 1978), p. 19; and Robert Schrank, "How to Relieve Worker Boredom," *Psychology Today* (July 1978), pp. 79–80.

3. Whenever possible, set up a controlled experiment (see Supplementary Module B) to evaluate the results of job enrichment.[22] This gives the manager an opportunity to discontinue the job design strategy or make constructive changes to increase its value.
4. Expect that enrichment will also affect the job of the supervising manager. He or she will normally be asked to delegate duties to subordinates. Some managers are threatened by this requirement, and they can become anxious or feel frustrated. These managers may require help to make the required personal work adjustments if such undesirable consequences are to be avoided.[23]

> **Question:** "What lies 'beyond' job enrichment as additional aspects of job design that should receive a manager's attention?"

*Newsline 6.2* reminds us that other aspects of the work setting are also important job design variables. In the remainder of this chapter, we'll examine two characteristics of work settings which are especially subject to managerial control: Task goals and work schedules. Proper attention to these variables can extend a manager's job design activities beyond job enrichment.

## GOAL-SETTING

Without proper goals, employees may suffer a direction problem. For example:[24]

> Several years ago, the Minnesota Vikings' defensive end, Jim Marshall, very alertly gathered up the opponent's fumble and then, with obvious effort and delight, proceeded to carry the ball some fifty yards into the wrong end zone.

Clearly, Jim Marshall did not lack intrinsic motivation! Unfortunately, though, he failed to channel his work energies toward the right goal. Similar problems are found in many work settings. They can be eliminated, or at least reduced, by the proper setting and clarification of task goals.

### Goal-Setting Theory

**Goal-setting** is the "process of developing, negotiating, and formalizing the targets or objectives that an employee is responsible for accomplishing."[25] Incorporating goal-setting into job designs results in specific task objectives for each individual. The presence of these objectives is important because of the motivational consequences with which they may be associated.

Edwin A. Locke has developed a set of assertions as to the motivational properties of task goals.[26] Locke's research, and that of others,[27] tends to support his predictions that

1. Difficult goals will lead to higher performance than less difficult ones.
2. Specific goals will lead to higher performance than very general ones (such as "do your best").
3. Goals will motivate people to higher performance only when they are accepted.

This last finding is of special interest to managers. Unless your subordinates accept their task goals, you can't expect to receive a motivational advantage. Research suggests that people will be more inclined to accept goals when they feel the goals are reasonable (i.e., expectancy is high), and when they see a clear relationship between goal attainment and desirable work outcomes (i.e., high instrumentality).[28] Once again, we find the basic tenets of expectancy theory are powerful aids in explaining work behavior!

## Combining Goal-Setting and Job Enrichment

One job design approach that combines goal-setting and job enrichment is shown in Figure 6.5. This approach integrates the use of

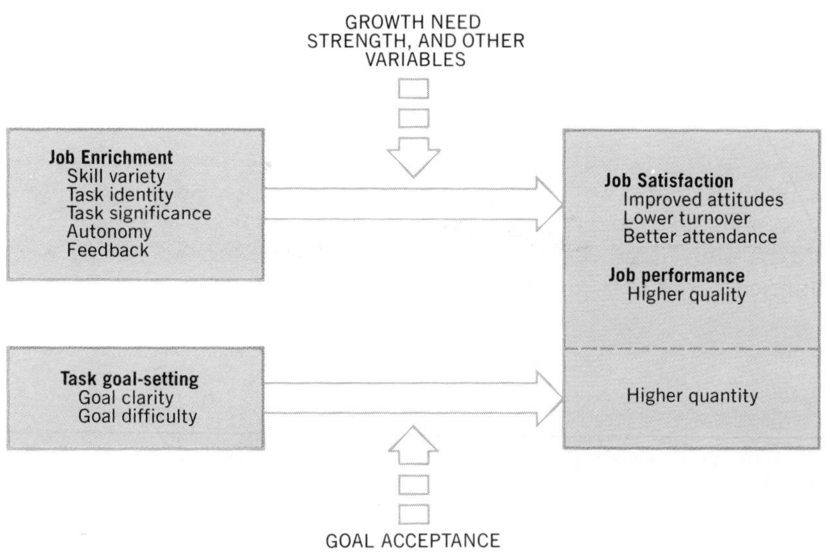


**FIGURE 6.5** An integrated model of job design. (Source: Adapted from Denis D. Umstot, Terrence R. Mitchell, and Cecil H. Bell, Jr., "Goal Setting and Job Enrichment: An Integrated Approach to Job Design," *Academy of Management Reivew, Vol. 3,* October 1968, p. 377. Used by permission.)

task goals and the enrichment of task attributes as ways of promoting job performance and satisfaction, respectively.

## ALTERNATIVE WORK SCHEDULES

Another way that work settings may be modified is to rearrange employee work schedules. A manager should recognize at least three alternatives to the traditional eight-hour per day/five days per week work schedule: the compressed work week, flexible working hours, and job sharing. Each of these approaches shares a common concern for making the work day and its time requirements more compatible with individual needs and non-work activities.

### The Compressed Work Week

A **compressed work week** is any scheduling of work that allows a full-time job to be completed in fewer than the standard five days.[29] The most common form of the compressed work week is the "4–40," that is, forty hours of work accomplished in four ten-hour days. A 4–40 schedule for a work unit of two employees is shown in Table 6.3. As the table shows, one result of the 4–40 is that employees have three consecutive days off from work each week.

This added time off is the source of most benefits that are associated with compressed work week plans, including

| The Organizational Benefits | The Individual Benefits |
|---|---|
| lower absenteeism | more leisure time |
| higher performance | lower commuting costs |
| better human resource maintenance | high job satisfaction |

The disadvantages may include increased fatigue and family adjustment problems for the individual, and increased scheduling problems and possible customer complaints for the organization.[30] Another

**Table 6.3 A Sample "4–40" Work Schedule**

| Employee | Mon. | Tues. | Wed. | Thurs. | Fri. | Sat. | Sun. |
|---|---|---|---|---|---|---|---|
| Smith | on | on | on | on | off | off | off |
| Jones | off | on | on | on | on | off | off |

possible constraint is union opposition. See *Newsline 6.2* for more details.

## Flexible Working Hours

Would you believe that there is a work schedule which is loaded with advantages, but has few disadvantages? Read the list of advantages below, then read on.[31]

| **Organizational Benefits** | **Individual Benefits** |
|---|---|
| lower absenteeism | more leisure time |
| reduced tardiness | shorter commuting time |
| reduced turnover | higher job satisfaction |
| higher work commitment | greater sense of responsibility |
| higher performance | greater ease of scheduling personal affairs |

The work schedule to which the above benefits are assigned is called **flexible working hours,** defined as "any work schedule that gives employees daily choice in the timing between work and non-work activities.[32] A typical flexible working hour schedule is depicted in Figure 6.6. Employees are required to work four hours of "core" time. They are then free to choose their remaining four hours of work from among flexible time blocks.

Flexible working hours, or "flextime," increases individual autonomy in work scheduling. Early risers may choose to come in early and leave at 4 P.M.; late sleepers may choose to start at 10 A.M. and leave at 6 P.M. In between these two extremes are opportunities to attend to such personal affairs as dental appointments, home emergencies, visiting the bank, etc. Proponents of this scheduling strategy argue that the discretion it allows workers encourages them to develop positive attitudes and increase commitment to the organization. Both research[33] and case reports (see *Newsline 6.4*) tend to support this position.

## Job Sharing

Another alternative work schedule is **job sharing.** This occurs when one full-time job is assigned to two persons who divide the work

| Flexible time | Core time | Flexible time | Core time | Flexible time |
|---|---|---|---|---|

7 A.M. 10 A.M. 12 noon 2 P.M. 4 P.M. 6 P.M.

**FIGURE 6.6** A sample flexible working hours scheme.

## NEWSLINE 6.3

### Four-Day Work Week?

*Experts disagree sharply on whether it has a future*

Once hailed as the wave of the future, the compressed work week (four days, 40 hours) has run up against union opposition, restrictive overtime laws, and employer scheduling problems. The Labor Department says only 27% of U.S. workers are on the job fewer than five days a week. And only 2% of employers surveyed by Georgetown University Professor Stanley Nollen and consultant Virginia Martin were considering adopting a compressed work week.

But a study by the University of Michigan and the Society of Manufacturing Engineers points the other way. In a survey of 125 manufacturing managers, 65% thought that a four-day week should be in effect at 50% of the nation's major industries in the future. They varied on how soon; the median year was 1987.

Source: *The Wall Street Journal* (July 25, 1978), p. 1. Reprinted by permission of The Wall Street Journal, 

## NEWSLINE 6.4

### Simmonds Precision Experiment Works

VERGENNES—The Instrument Systems Division of Simmonds Precision Inc. employs more than 900 workers in Vergennes and about 100 in Bellows Falls. The firm, which produces fuel-guaging systems for aircraft, began experimenting with flexitime three years ago.

But the company took the biggest leap of faith last January, when it instituted the practice in its production departments, according to plant manager Frank Cirello. "Everyone we talked to said you couldn't make flexitime work in production functions," said Cirello. "But having done it there, we knew we could do it everywhere."

And on Oct. 30, Simmonds opened flexitime to all but 180 workers. Those 180 work at a separate Vergennes plant, where limitations of equipment availability prevent flexible scheduling.

Cirello said fears the new scheduling freedom would cause harsh burdens on supervisors have proved to be largely unfounded.

Abuse of the system—late arrival and early departure—similarly has been negligible, he said. "If you have people with a strong work ethic—and we do—you can do this sort of thing."

Not only does the flexitime increase morale and productivity, but it provides "insurance" for workers to adjust their schedules according to seasons, and more importantly, any emergencies that might arise, he said.

Reaction among the Simmonds workforce appears highly positive.

Wayne Goddette, a senior designer with 20 years at the firm, said he uses the time for such things as yard work, errands or dental appointments.

"And a lot of the guys have used the early hours to go fishing or leave early to get in a bit of hunting before the sun goes down," Goddette said.

Bud Clapper, group leader in the soldering station, said flexitime is a "great morale booster." The only problem he sees is making sure there is coverage throughout the day.

Simmonds' workers may begin anytime between 6 and 8 A.M. and leave between 2:30 and 4:30 P.M. They need not declare their starting time in advance.

In practice, however, "we are all creatures of habit and most workers have settled into routines which fit their particular needs, saving the flexitime for emergencies," Cirello said.

As assembler Elizabeth Steadman said, "It's so fantastic. I'm surprised they didn't start the program before this!"

Source: *The Burlington Vermont Free Press* (November 19, 1978), p. 7D.

according to agreements made between themselves and with the employer.[34] Job sharing often occurs were each person works one-half day, although it can also be done on such bases as weekly or monthly sharing arrangements.

Organizations can benefit from job sharing when they are able to attract talented people who would otherwise be unable to work. An example is the qualified schoolteacher who is also a parent. This person may feel unable to be away from the home a full day, but able to work a half-day. Through job sharing, two such persons can be employed to teach one class. Many other opportunities for job sharing exist.

## SUMMARY

We can now pull together the accumulated insights of this second part of the book. Remember, your learning objective has been

> to develop a capability for analyzing systematically the behavior of individuals at work; and to identify action alternatives for relating them more productively and with greater satisfaction to their jobs.

The capability to analyze individual behavior at work was established in the first two chapters of Part Two. Chapter 3 looked in detail at basic attributes of individuals, while Chapter 4 discussed various motivation theories. These theories led into Chapter 5, which introduced reinforcement theory and its insights for managing extrinsic rewards. In the present chapter, we have looked in depth at intrinsic rewards as a means of promoting individual job performance and human resource maintenance through proper job design. Figuratively speaking, we conclude that

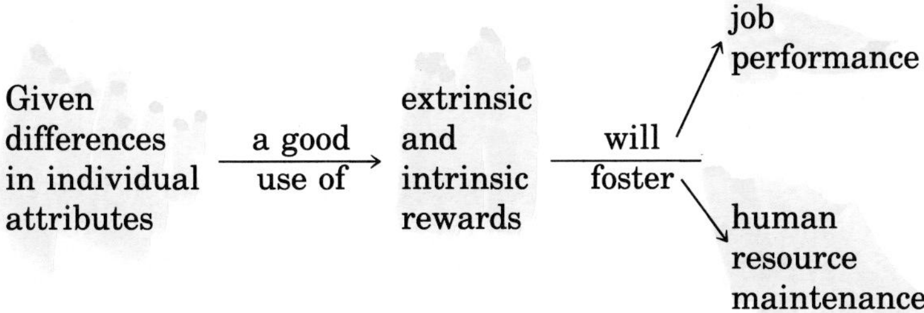


More specifically, this chapter suggested job enrichment as an alternative to job simplification, enlargement, and rotation, as a strategy for increasing the availability of intrinsic rewards in jobs. The diagnostic version developed by Hackman and his colleagues recognizes that people high in growth, or higher-order, need strengths respond most favorably to job enrichment. To enrich a job, they argue that tasks should be altered to increase the presence of five core characteristics of job content: skill variety, task identity, task significance, autonomy, and feedback.

Two characteristics of work settings that may also affect individual motivation are the presence of task goals and the nature of the work schedule. Managers are encouraged to use goal-setting and to examine compressed work weeks, flexible working hours, and job sharing as alternative work schedules for employees.

Clearly, the responsibility of managers for allocating work rewards is a bona-fide reality. Managers can either use work rewards to maximum advantage, or use them poorly. The challenge to you is clear-cut. To be good at using work rewards as a way of relating people more productively and with greater satisfaction to their jobs, it is important to:

1. Maintain an inventory of possible work rewards.
2. Remain continually aware of different individual work needs.
3. Allocate extrinsic rewards on a performance-contingent basis and according to reinforcement principles.
4. Design jobs so that task attributes, task goals, and work schedules are properly matched with individual work needs.

Finally, consider this thought, expressed by one worker about jobs in general.

> I think most of us are looking for a calling, not a job. Most of us, like the assembly line worker, have jobs that are too small for the spirit. Jobs are not big enough for people.
>
> Nora Watson, a worker[35]

## THINKING THROUGH THE ISSUES

1. Go back to Charles Krug's assembly line job described earlier in the chapter. Write a profile of the type of person you feel would be satisfied and productive in this job. Defend your profile and describe its managerial implications.
2. Look back to the union official's comment on job enrichment listed earlier. Why do you think the official feels this way? Do you think this opinion would be shared by most union members? Why or why not?
3. In what types of situations would job enlargement and/or job rotation be preferred to job enrichment as job design strategies?
4. Is goal-setting a managerial strategy that is only useful when applied in conjunction with job enrichment? Why or why not?
5. What are the three conditions cited by Locke as creating motivational properties for task goals?
6. If flexible working hours is such a positive work schedule, why aren't all organizations using it?
7. Extrinsic and intrinsic rewards present quite different challenges to managers who seek to make use of them. What are these differences and what are their implications for managers?
8. What does the closing quotation mean to you? What should it mean to the practicing manager?

## EXERCISE: DOING JOB ENRICHMENT[36]

### Purpose:

To allow you to practice job enrichment; to compare your results to a consultant's actual solution; to increase your sensitivity to the many practical issues which a manager must be prepared to face when implementing job enrichment as a job design strategy.

## Time:

50 minutes.

## Procedure:

1. Working individually or in your assigned group, develop a list of changes that could enrich the position described below. Remember that Herzberg suggests the following guidelines for approaching such a task:

   **a.** Approach the job with the conviction that it *can* be changed.
   **b.** Brainstorm a list of possible changes *without* regard to their practicality.
   **c.** Screen the list to *eliminate:*

      1. Suggestions involving hygiene factors.
      2. Generalities that fail to represent substantive change directions (e.g., "give them more responsibility").
      3. Suggestions that represent horizontal rather than vertical loading.
      4. Technological impossibilities.

2. Once you have a list of suggestions for doing job enrichment, be prepared (or designate someone in your group) to report these ideas to the rest of the class.

3. The instructor will record your suggestions on the blackboard and use them as a basis for further discussion on the job enrichment concept. Since this is a real case, he or she will provide you with the consultant's actual recommendations. These will stimulate additional discussion.

## Position Description:

*Title* Stockholder Correspondent

*Location* Company Headquarters

*Duties* Working in the assigned location, a stockholder correspondent will answer letter inquiries received from stockholders requesting information on such things as stock transfer procedures, dividend policies, purchases, or dispositions, etc. The correspondent will:

- Receive inquiries assigned by the supervisor in a quantity sufficient to meet the standard daily production quota.
- Match each inquiry with standardized responses catalogued in a loose-leaf binder according to type of request.
- Draft letter responses to the inquiries based on the standardized format.
- Submit completed letter drafts to the typing pool for final

preparation and eventual transmittal to the supervisor for proofreading, signature, and mailing.

- Correct any letters previously drafted and found inappropriate or incorrect by the supervisor.
- Refer back to the supervisor for assignment to a specialist those unique inquiries which fail to fit a standardized response.
- Ask the supervisor for assistance on any especially difficult inquiries.
- Perform additional duties as assigned by the supervisor.

## CASE: WORK REDESIGN IN AN INSURANCE COMPANY[37]

The executive staff of a relatively small life insurance company was considering a proposal to install an electronic data processing system. The proposal to install the equipment was presented by the assistant to the president, John Skully. He had been charged with studying the feasibility of the equipment after a management consultant had recommended a complete overhaul of the jobs within the company.

The management consultant had been engaged by the company to diagnose the causes of high turnover and absenteeism. After reviewing the situation and speaking with groups of employees, the management consultant recommended that the organization structure be changed from functional to client basis. The change in departmental basis would enable management to redesign jobs to reduce the human costs associated with highly specialized tasks.

The present organization included separate departments to issue policies, collect premiums, change beneficiaries, and process loan applications. Employees in these departments complained that their jobs were boring, insignificant, and monotonous. They stated that the only reason they stayed with the company was because they liked the small company atmosphere. They believed the management had a genuine interest in their welfare, but felt that the trivial nature of their jobs contradicted that feeling. As one employee said, "This company is small enough to know almost everybody. But the job I do is so boring that I wonder why they even need me to do it." This and similiar comments led the consultant to believe that the jobs must be altered to provide greater motivation. But he also recognized that work redesign opportunities were limited by the organization structure. He therefore recommended that the company change to a client basis. In such a structure each employee would handle every transaction related to a particular policyholder.

When the consultant presented his views to the executive staff, they were very much interested in his recommendation. And, in fact, the group agreed that his recommendation was well founded. They noted, however, that a small company must pay particular attention to efficiency in handling transactions. The functional basis enabled the organization to achieve the degree of specialization necessary for efficient operations. The manager of internal operations stated: "If we move away from specialization, the rate of efficiency must go down because we will lose the benefit of specialized effort. The only way we can justify redesigning the jobs as suggested by the consultant is to maintain our efficiency; otherwise there won't be any jobs to redesign because we will be out of business."

The internal operations manager explained to the executive staff that despite excessive absenteeism and turnover, he was able to maintain acceptable productivity. The narrow range and depth of the jobs reduced training time to a minimum. It was also possible to hire temporary help to meet peak loads and to fill in for absent employees. "Moreover," he said, "changing the jobs our people do means that we must change the jobs our managers do. They are experts in their own functional areas but we have never attempted to train them to oversee more than two operations."

The majority of the executive staff believed that the consultants' recommendations should be seriously considered. It was at that point that the group directed John Skully to evaluate the potential of electronic data processing (EDP) as a means to obtain efficient operations in combination with the redesigned jobs. He had completed the study and presented his report to the executive staff.

"The bottom line," Skully said, "is that EDP will enable us to maintain our present efficiency, but with the redesigned jobs, we will not obtain any greater gains. If my analysis is correct, we will have to absorb the cost of the equipment out of earnings because there will be no cost savings. So it comes down to what price we are willing and able to pay for improving the satisfaction of our employees."

## Questions

1. What core characteristics of the employees' jobs will be changed if the consultants' recommendations are accepted? Explain.
2. What alternative redesign strategies should be considered? For example, job rotation and job enlargement are possible alternatives; what are the relevant considerations for these and other designs in the context of this company?
3. What would be your decision in this case? What should the management be willing to pay for employee satisfaction? Defend your answer.

## THE MANAGER'S VOCABULARY

**Compressed Work Week** Any scheduling of work that allows a full-time job to be completed in fewer than the standard five days.

**Flexible Working Hours** Any work schedule that gives employees daily choice in the timing between work and non-work activities.

**Goal-Setting** The process of developing, negotiating, and formalizing the targets or objectives that an employee is responsible for accomplishing.

**Intrinsic Motivation** Task motivation, that is, a desire to work hard solely for the pleasant experience of task accomplishment.

**Intrinsic Work Rewards** Those rewards which are received by the individual directly as a result of task performance.

**Job** One or more tasks that an individual performs in direct support of the organization's production purpose.

**Job Design** The deliberate, purposeful planning of the job, including any or all of its structural or social aspects.

**Job Enlargement** Increasing task variety by combining into one job tasks which were previously assigned to separate workers.

**Job Enrichment** The practice of building motivating factors into job content.

**Job Rotation** Increasing task variety by periodically shifting workers among jobs involving different tasks.

**Job Sharing** One full-time job is assigned to two persons who divide the work according to agreements made between themselves and with the employer.

**Job Simplification** Standardizing work procedures and employing people in very clearly defined and specialized tasks.

### Important Names

**Richard Hackman and Edward Lawler** Developed a diagnostic approach to job enrichment based on five core job characteristics.

**Edwin Locke** Specified a goal-setting theory of work motivation.

### Notes

[1]Adapted from Margie Cassady, "The Tricky Business of Giving Rewards," Reprinted from *Psychology Today Magazine.* Copyright © September 1974, Ziff-Davis Publishing Company.

[2]William W. Notz, "Work Motivation and the Negative Effects of Extrinsic Rewards," *American Psychologist,* Vol. 6 (September 1975), p. 884.

[3]Ramon J. Aldag and Arthur P. Brief, "The Intrinsic-Extrinsic Dichotomy:

Toward Conceptual Clarity," Academy of Management Review, Vol. 2 (1977), pp. 497–498.

[4]Denis Umstot, Cecil H. Bell, Jr., and Terrence R. Mitchel, "Effects of Job Enrichment and Task Goals on Satisfaction and Productivity: Implications for Job Design," *Journal of Applied Psychology,* Vol. 61 (1976), p. 379.

[5]Adapted from an example presented in Edward E. Lawler, III, *Motivation in Work Organizations* (Monterey, Calif.: Brooks/Cole Publishing Company, 1973), pp. 154–155.

[6]Frederick Herzberg, "One More Time: How Do You Motivate Employees?" *Harvard Business Review,* Vol. 46 (January–February 1968), pp. 53–62.

[7]Ibid.

[8]J. Richard Hackman and Edward E. Lawler, III, "Employee Reactions to Job Characteristics," Vol. 55 (June 1971), pp. 259–286.

[9]This summary is developed from J. Richard Hackman and Greg R. Oldham "Development of the Job Diagnostic Survey," *Journal of Applied Psychology,* Vol. 60 (April 1975), pp. 161–162.

[10]J. Richard Hackman, Jone L. Pearce, and Jane Caminis Wolfe, "Effects of Changes in Job Characteristics on Work Attitudes and Behaviors: A Naturally Occurring Quasi-Experiment," *Organizational Behavior and Human Performance,* Vol. 21 (June 1978), pp. 289–304; Stephen J. Carroll, "Psychological Needs as Moderators in Reactions to Job Enrichment in a Field Setting," *Academy of Management Proceedings* (1978), pp. 55–58; Arthur P. Brief and Ramon J. Aldag, "Employee Reactions to Job Characteristics: A Constructive Replication," *Journal of Applied Psychology,* Vol. 60 (1975), pp. 182–186; Ramon J. Aldag and Arthur P. Brief, *Task Design and Employee Motivation* (Glenview, Ill.: Scott, Foresman and Company, 1979).

[11]From J. Richard Hackman, Greg Oldham, Robert Janson, and Kenneth Purdy, "A New Strategy for Job Enrichment," *California Management Review,* Vol. XVII (1975), pp. 51–71.

[12]Ibid.

[13]Herzberg, op. cit.

[14]Paul J. Champagne and Curt Tausky, "When Job Enrichment Doesn't Pay," *Personnel,* Vol. III (January–February 1978), pp. 30–40.

[15]William W. Winpisinger, "Job Enrichment: A Union View," p. 222 in Karl O. Magnusen, *Organizational Design, Development and Behavior: A Situational View* (Glenview, Ill.: Scott, Foresman and Company, 1977).

[16]Richard M. Steers and Richard T. Mowday, "The Motivational Properties of Tasks," *Academy of Management Review,* Vol. 2 (October 1977), pp. 645–658.

[17]Charles L. Hulin and Milton R. Blood, "Job Enlargement, Individual Differences, and Worker Responses," *Psychological Bulletin,* Vol. 69 (1968), pp. 41–55.

[18]Hackman and Lawler, op cit.; Hackman and Oldham, op. cit.

[19]Greg R. Oldham, J. Richard Hackman, and Jone L. Pearce, "Conditions Under which Employees Respond Positively to Enriched Work," *Journal of Applied Psychology,* Vol. 61 (1976), pp. 395–403.

[20]Aldag and Brief, op. cit., 1979.

[21]Adapted in part from Aldag and Brief, op. cit., 1979, pp. 144–145.

[22]Herzberg, op. cit.

[23]J. Richard Hackman, "Is Job Enrichment Just a Fad?" *Harvard Business Review,* Vol. 56 (September–October 1978), pp. 129–138.

[24]Charles N. Greene, "The Satisfaction-Performance Controversy," *Business Horizons,* Vol. 15 (October 1972), pp. 31–42.

[25]Denis D. Umstot, Terrence R. Mitchell, and Cecil H. Bell, Jr., "Goal Setting and Job Enrichment: An Integrated Approach to Job Design," *Academy of Management Review,* Vol. 3 (October 1978), p. 868.

[26]Edwin A. Locke, "Toward a Theory of Task Motivation and Incentives," *Organizational Behavior and Human Performance,* Vol. 3 (1968), pp. 157–184.

[27]Gary P. Latham and Gary A. Ukl, "A Review of Research on the Application of Goal-Setting in Organizations," *Academy of Management Journal,* Vol. 18 (1975), pp. 824–845.

[28]Ibid.

[29]Allan R. Cohen and Herman Gadon, *Alternative Work Schedules: Integrating Individual and Organizational Needs* (Reading, Mass.: Addison-Wesley Publishing Company, 1978), p. 125.

[30]Ibid., pp. 54–64; William F. Glueck, "Changing Hours of Work: A Review and Analysis of the Research," paper presented at the Academy of Management Meetings, Orlando, Florida, August 1977.

[31]Cohen and Gadon, op. cit., pp. 38–46.

[32]Ibid., p. 33.

[33]Ibid.; Robert T. Golembiewski and Carl W. Prehl, Jr., "A Survey of the Empirical Literature on Flexible Work Hours: Character and Consequences of a Major Innovation," *Academy of Management Review,* Vol. 3 (October 1978), pp. 853–873.

[34]Cohen and Gadon, op. cit., p. 127.

[35]Statement by Nora Watson found in Studs Terkel, *Working* (New York: Avon Books, 1975), p. XXIX.

[36]Developed from ideas presented in Herzberg, op. cit.

[37]From James L. Gibson, John M. Ivancevich, and James H. Donnelly, Jr., *Organizations: Behavior, Structure, Processes,* Third Edition, pp. 299–300. © Business Publications, Inc., 1973, 1976 and 1979. All rights reserved. Used by permission.

# PART THREE

# MANAGING GROUPS IN ORGANIZATIONS

## THE MANAGER'S GOAL

**To Ensure High Levels of Group Task Performance and Human Resource Maintenance.**

## YOUR LEARNING OBJECTIVE

**To Develop a Capability for Systematically Analyzing Group Behavior in Organizations; and to Identify Action Alternatives for Achieving High Group Task Performance and Human Resource Maintenance.**

## Chapters in This Part of the Book

In this part of the book, our focus is on the group as a human resource organization. Several questions to keep in mind are:

What is a group?

Why do groups exist in organizations?

What makes a group successful?

How do groups affect their members?

How do groups affect organizational performance?

The following prediction case helps to put these and related questions in a managerial perspective. Read the case and test your understanding of group behavior in organizations.

# The Case of the Changing Cage[1]

The voucher-check filing unit was a work unit in the home office of the Atlantic Insurance Company. The assigned task of the unit was to file checks and vouchers written by the company as they were cashed and returned. This filing was the necessary foundation for the main function of the unit: locating any particular check for examination upon demand. There were usually eight to ten requests for specific checks from as many different departments during the day. One of the most frequent reasons checks were requested from the unit was to determine whether checks in payment of claims against the company had been cashed. Thus, efficiency in the unit directly affected customer satisfaction with the company. Complaints or inquiries about payments could not be answered with the accuracy and speed conducive to client satisfaction unless the unit could supply the necessary document immediately.

Nine workers staffed this unit. There was an assistant (a position equivalent to a foreman in a factory) named Ms. Dunn, five other full-time employees, and three part-time workers.

The work area of the unit was well defined. Walls bounded the unit on three sides. The one exterior wall was pierced by light-admitting north windows. The west interior partition was blank. A door opening into a corridor pierced the south interior partition. The east side of the work area was enclosed by a steel mesh reaching from wall to wall and floor to ceiling. This open metal barrier gave rise to the customary name of the unit—"The Voucher Cage." A sliding door through this mesh gave access from the unit's territory to the work area of the rest of the company's agency audit division, of which it was a part, located on the same floor.

The unit's territory was kept inviolate by locks on both doors, fastened at all times. No one not working within the cage was permitted inside unless his or her name appeared on a special list in the custody of Ms. Dunn. The door through the steel mesh was generally used for departmental business. Messengers and runners from other departments usually came to the corridor door and pressed a buzzer for service.

The steel mesh front was reinforced by a rank of metal filing cases where checks were filed. Lined up just inside the barrier, they hid the unit's workers from the view of workers outside their territory, including Mr. Burke, the section head responsible for overall supervision of this unit according to the company's formal plan of operation.

## QUESTIONS

1. What level of work performance will be produced by this group? Why?
   high medium low
2. What level of membership satisfaction will exist within the unit? Why?
   high medium low

*Continuing On* On top of the cabinets, which were backed against the steel mesh, one of the male employees in the unit neatly stacked pasteboard boxes in which checks were transported to the cage. They were later reused to hold older checks sent into storage. His intention was less getting these boxes out of the way than increasing the effective height of the sight barrier so the section head could not see into the cage "even when he stood up."

The clerks stood at the door of the cage that led into the corridor and talked to the messengers. The workers also slipped out this door unnoticed to bring in their customary afternoon snack. Inside the cage, the workers sometimes engaged in a good-natured game of rubber-band "snipping."

Workers in the cage possessed good capacity to work together consistently, and workers outside the cage often expressed envy of those in it because of the "nice people" and friendly atmosphere there. The unit had no apparent difficulty keeping up with its work load.

## Our Viewpoint

The voucher-check filing unit is doing its job. The members also seem reasonably well satisfied with their work. The privacy afforded by the filing cases, opportunities to converse with messengers, afternoon snacks, and the rubber-band game all appear to be sources of special enjoyment. The situation seems quite acceptable . . . unless something changes!

*Continuing On* For some time, the controller's department of the company had not been able to meet its own standards of efficient service to clients. Company officials felt the primary cause to be spatial. Various divisions of the controller's department were scattered over the entire twenty-two-story company building. Communication between them required phone calls, messengers, or personal visits, all costing time. The spatial separation had not seemed very important when the company's business volume was smaller, but business had grown tremendously and spatial separation appeared increasingly inefficient.

Finally, in November, company officials began to consolidate the controller's department by relocating two divisions together on one floor. One was the agency audit division, which included the voucher-check filing unit. As soon as the decision to move was made, lower-level supervisors were called in to help with planning. Line workers were not consulted, but were kept informed by the assistants of planning progress. Company officials were concerned about the problem of transporting many tons of equipment and some two hundred workers from two locations to another single location without disrupting work flow. So the move was planned to occur over a single weekend, using the most efficient resources available. Assistants were kept busy planning positions for files and desks in the new location.

Desks, files, chairs, and even wastebaskets were numbered prior to the move, and relocated according to a master chart checked on the spot by the assistant. Employees were briefed as to where the new location was and which elevators they should take to reach it. The company successfully transported the paraphernalia of the voucher check filing unit from one floor to another over one weekend. Workers in the cage quit Friday afternoon at the old stand and reported back Monday at the new.

The exterior boundaries of the new cage were still three building walls and the steel mesh, but the new cage possessed only one door—the sliding door through the steel mesh into the work area of the rest of the agency audit division. The territory of the cage had also been reduced in size. An entire bank of filing cabinets had to be left behind in the old location to be taken over by the unit moving there. The new cage was arranged so that there was no longer a row of metal filing cabinets lined up inside the steel mesh obstructing the view into the cage.

## QUESTIONS

1. How will this change affect work performance? Why?
   increase no change decrease
2. What will happen to membership satisfaction? Why?
   increase no change decrease

***Continuing On*** When the workers in the cage inquired about the removal of the filing cabinets from along the steel mesh fencing, they found that Mr. Burke had insisted that these cabinets be rearranged so his view into the cage would not be obstructed by them. Ms. Dunn had tried to retain the cabinets in their prior position, but her efforts had been overridden.

Mr. Burke disapproved of conversation. Since he could see workers conversing in the new cage, he "requested" Ms. Dunn to put a stop to all unnecessary talk. Attempts by clerks to talk to the messengers brought the wrath of Mr. Burke down on Ms. Dunn, who was then forced to reprimand her workers.

Mr. Burke also disapproved of an untidy work area, and any boxes or papers which were in sight were a source of annoyance to him. He did not exert supervision directly, but would "request" Ms. Dunn to "do something about those boxes." In the new cage, desks had to be completely cleared at the end of the day, in contrast to the work-in-progress piles left out in the old cage. Boxes could not accumulate on top of filing cases.

The custom of afternoon snacking also ran into trouble. Lacking a corridor door, the food-bringers had to venture forth and bring back their snack tray through the work area of the rest of their section, bringing a hitherto unique custom to the attention of workers outside the cage. The latter promptly recognized the desirability of afternoon snacks and began agitating for the same privilege. This annoyed the section head, who forbade workers in the cage from continuing this custom.

Mr. Burke later made a rule which permitted one worker to leave the new cage at a set time every afternoon to bring up food for the rest. This rigidity irked cage personnel, accustomed to a snack when the mood struck, or none at all. Having made his concession to the cage force, Mr. Burke was unable to prevent workers outside the cage from doing the same thing. What had once been unique to the workers in the cage was now common practice in the section.

Although Ms. Dunn never outwardly expressed anything but compliance and approval of superior directives, she exhibited definite signs of anxiety. All the cage workers reacted against Burke's increased domination. When he imposed his decisions upon the voucher check filing unit, he became "Old Grandma" to its personnel. The cage workers sneered at him and ridiculed him behind his back. Workers who formerly had obeyed company policy as a matter of course began to find reasons for loafing and obstructing work in the new cage. One of the changes that took place in the behavior of the workers had to do with their game of rubber-band snipping. All knew Mr. Burke would disapprove of this game. It became highly clandestine and fraught with dangers. Yet shooting rubber bands increased.

Newly-arrived checks were put out of sight as soon as possible, filed or not. Workers hid unfiled checks, generally stuffing them into desk drawers or unused file drawers. Since boxes were forbidden, there were fewer unused file drawers than there had been in the old cage. So, the day's work was sometimes undone when several clerks hastily shoved vouchers and checks indiscriminately into the same file drawer at the end of the day.

Before a worker in the cage filed incoming checks, he or she measured the thickness in inches of each bundle to be filed. At the end of each day input was totalled and reported to Ms. Dunn. All incoming checks were measured upon arrival. Thus, Ms. Dunn had a rough estimate of unit intake compared with file input. Theoretically she was able to tell at any time how much unfiled material she had on hand and how well the unit was keeping up with its task. Despite this running check, when the annual inventory of unfiled checks on hand in the cage was taken, a seriously large backlog of unfiled checks was found. To the surprise and dismay of Ms. Dunn, the inventory showed the unit to be far behind schedule, filing much more slowly than before the relocation of the cage.

### Our Viewpoint

The changes have led to a decline in both group task performance and human resource maintenance. New facilities and supervisory practices prevent many of the nonwork activities which were enjoyed so much. Similarly, group practices which once worked to the benefit of the organization now work to its disadvantage. Ms. Dunn is having difficulty controlling the work group and suffers considerable anxiety as a result.

## SUMMARY

This change in the voucher-check filing unit's location was badly handled. It involves management decisions that could be greatly improved upon with a better understanding of group behavior in organizations. The following three chapters will provide you with a knowledge base that can help you to make good decisions when faced with the many challenges of managing groups in organizations. As you read through the three chapters in this part, you will find an increasing emphasis on management applications of the multiple dimensions of group behavior.

**NOTE**

[1] Adapted from "Topography and Culture: The Case of the Changing Cage," by Cara E. Richards and Henry F. Dobyns. Reproduced by permission of The Society for Applied Anthropology from *Human Organization,* 16(1) 16–20, 1957.

# 7

# BASIC ATTRIBUTES OF GROUPS

# POW's Come Home

Consider two sets of prisoners of war who have just been set free. In the first set, the POW's are filled with jubilation and happiness. In the second set, there is a sullen quietness and many POW's appear highly anxious. In the first set there were many escape attempts, little collaboration with the enemy, and a relatively low death rate from illness. In the second set there were few escape attempts, many deaths from disease, and many instances of apparent collaboration with the enemy.

Indeed, the two sets are so different that it is as if they are from two different countries, yet they are both American POW's. The first was from World War II and was captured by the Nazis. The second was from the Korean conflict and was captured by the Chinese. How could such marked differences between the two sets of POW's occur?

In the first set, the Nazis required the POW's to organize themselves in a military structure similar to that from which they came. Rank was strictly recognized. American officers were responsible for policing and maintaining the POW unit. The prisoners had inferior food, clothing, and shelter. Interrogated prisoners were sent back to their unit to serve as an "example" to other POW's.

Many of the Korean war prisoners were taken after the Chinese entered the conflict. As they were marched into China, the prisoners were constantly reminded of how fortunate they were that they had been captured by their Chinese "friends" rather than the North Koreans who would surely have killed them. Living conditions were not very different between the POW's and their captors. Both were far from comfortable. At the prison camps officers were separated from enlisted men. Sometimes those with lower ranks were placed in charge of those with higher ranks. Units were frequently broken up and reconstituted. Interrogated prisoners were sent to new units.[1]

**MANAGEMENT APPLICATIONS QUESTION**

The Chinese, in the above example, used a knowledge of groups dynamics to serve their purposes. The Nazis were less successful in a similar attempt. As a manager you will work with and in groups. What are the basic attributes of groups which influence their success and functioning in organizations?

## PLANNING AHEAD

**The reading and other learning experiences offered in this chapter will acquaint you with the following aspects of groups in organizations:**



Individuals and groups are the human resource foundations of organizations. We discussed the individual in Part Two. Now it is time to study the collective behavior of individuals in the form of groups. The term "group" raises both positive and negative reactions in the minds of most people. Although it is said that "two heads are better than one," we are also warned that "too many cooks spoil the broth." "A camel is a horse put together by a committee," admonishes the true group skeptic!

Against this humorous background lies a useful point. Groups have advantages and disadvantages for their members and for organizations. As far back as the historic Hawthorne studies (see Supplementary Module B), researchers have noted that employees can develop strong group attachments, and that these attachments may prove functional or dysfunctional for the organization. In this chapter, our purpose is to thoroughly introduce you to groups in the work setting of the organization. The knowledge foundation established here will help you to better understand and manage the multiple and complex dynamics of group behavior.

## WHAT DO WE MEAN BY GROUPS?

Suppose there is an automobile accident and you join a number of other people gathered around the wreck. Or suppose you join several persons waiting for an elevator. Are these "groups?" Not in the way most social scientists define the term. A **group** is a collection of people who interact with each other regularly over a period of time and see themselves to be mutually dependent with respect to the attainment of one or more common goals.[2]

The key elements in the definition are interaction, time, and feelings of mutual dependence for goal accomplishment. Neither the people at the wreck nor those waiting for the elevator would meet all of these characteristics. They would be considered an aggregation or collection of individuals, but not a group.

Some people go further and talk about **"psychological groups."**[3] These extend the above definition one more step by adding the additional criterion that group members are aware of one another's needs and potential resource contributions. Just as we said that not all aggregations are groups, all groups are not psychological groups.

Keeping in mind these notions, let's look at some different types of groups found within organizations.

## TYPES OF GROUPS IN ORGANIZATIONS

Groups appear in various forms within the work setting of the organization. It is especially useful to clearly define work groups, formal groups, and informal groups.

### Work Groups

A **work group** is one created by the formal authority of an organization to transform resource inputs (such as ideas, materials, and objects) into product outputs (such as a report, decision, service, or commodity).[4] Indeed, it is popular to view organizations as interlocking networks of work groups, as shown in Figure 7.1. Notice the "linking pin" function of the managers in such a network. Through managers, acting as superiors in one group and as subordinates in others, all work groups are interconnected to create some sense of totality for the organization.

Work groups may be permanent or temporary. Permanent groups may appear as departments (for example, market research department), divisions, (General Motors Oldsmobile Division), or units (voucher-check filing unit in the Case of the Changing Cage). Permanent work groups will vary in size. They may be as small as two or three members or as large as several hundred members. Regardless of size, formal work groups all share the common characteristic of being created to contribute to the organization's production purpose. It is the highest level manager within a work group who is held accountable for this contribution. Earlier, we called this responsibility "the manager's challenge."

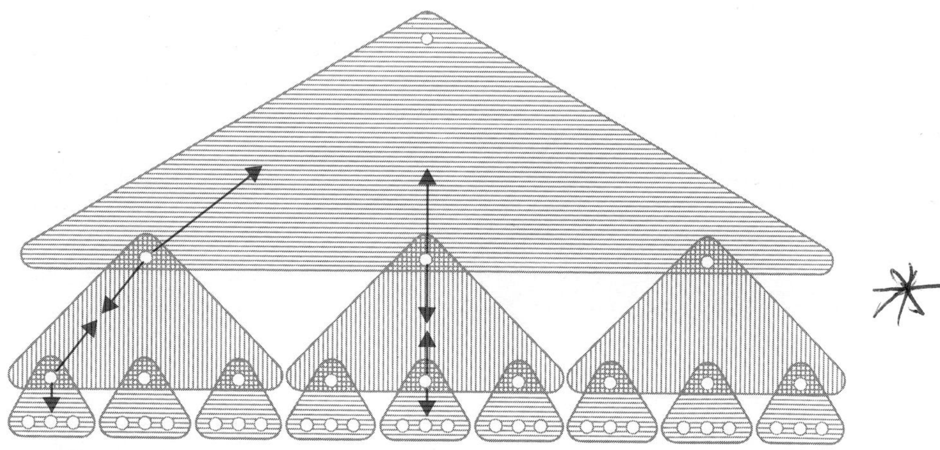
The arrows indicate the linking pin function

**FIGURE 7.1** Likert's linking pin model of an organization. (Source: From *New Patterns of Management* by Rensis Likert. Copyright © 1961, McGraw-Hill. Used with the permission of McGraw-Hill Book Company.)

Committees and task forces represent temporary forms of work groups. They are created for a specific purpose and typically disband with its accomplishment. Temporary work groups will usually have a chairperson who is accountable for results. You have observed these in organizations to which you have belonged.

## Formal and Informal Groups

Social psychologists use the term **formal group** as synonomous with this concept of a work group. Formal groups are created via formal authority for some purpose. They typically have rather clearcut superior-subordinate relationships, and they often appear on formal organization charts.

It is most important for us that theorists make a distinction between formal and **informal groups.** The latter exist without being formally specified by someone in authority. These are often found as subgroups or cliques within formally designated work groups. You may find, for example, that the same people eat together, go on breaks together, or engage in other spontaneous activities on the job. Informal subgrouping can also take place across as well as within formally designated units. For instance, secretaries from one department may eat lunch with those from another. Such informal groups may have their own leaders. The key difference between the informal and formal groups, however, is that informal groups emerge spontaneously, whereas formal ones are designated by an organizational

Formal work groups in an organization.

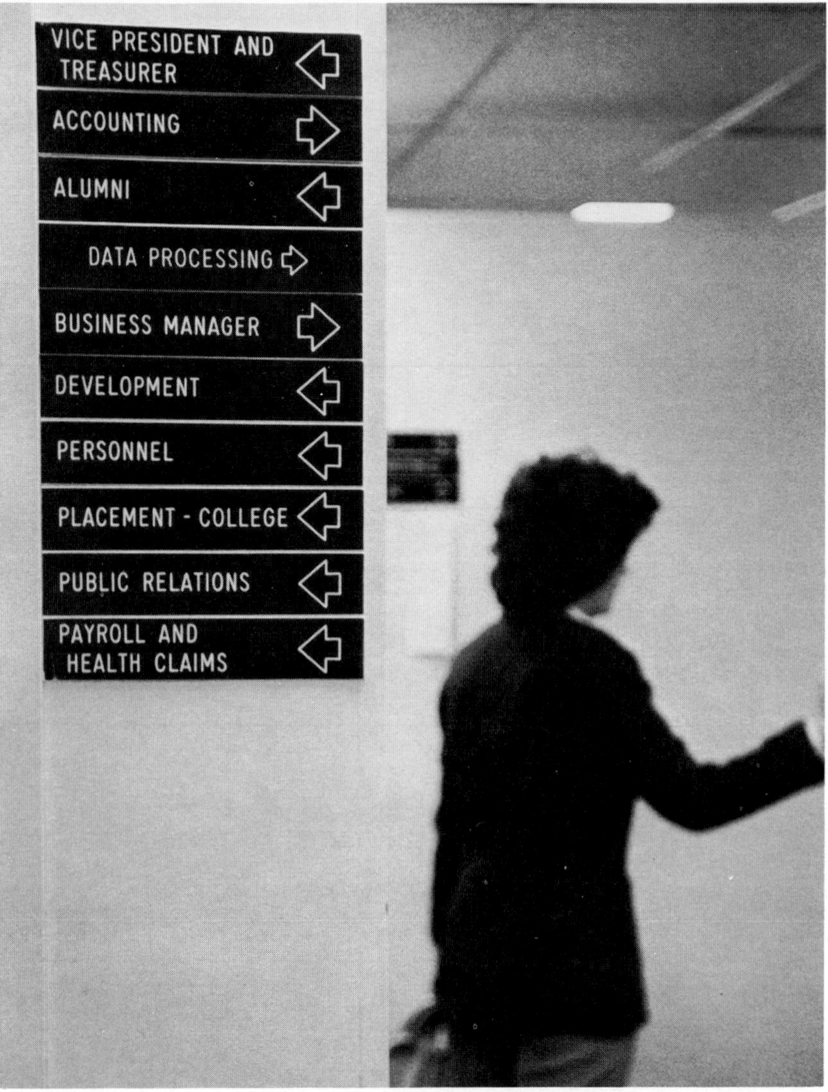


authority. Figure 7.2 illustrates how informal groups add complexity to the linking-pin model of organization discussed earlier. Managers must be skilled at working with both formal and informal groups.

While work groups are formally created by organizations to serve their needs, informal groups exist to satisfy the personal needs of their members. They especially serve social needs, although, as in any group, they are potentially responsive to a full range of individual needs. Often, informal groups provide satisfactions that are denied or thwarted by the formal group affiliations of their members.

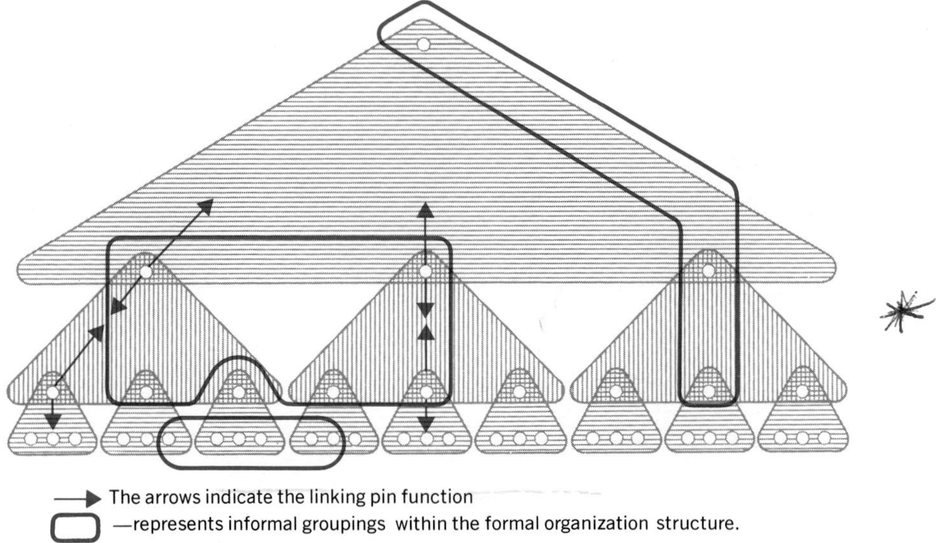

The arrows indicate the linking pin function
—represents informal groupings within the formal organization structure.


**FIGURE 7.2** Informal groups and Likert's linking-pin model of organizations.

As our discussion progresses, you will learn when and under what conditions such informal arrangements can help and hinder organizations.

Returning to our earlier definition of psychological groups, we can see that most informal groups would probably also qualify as psychological groups. However, many formal groups might not. Just being assigned to work together in the same department does not mean group members will share and work toward common goals. Think of group projects you have worked on in your college courses. Each project was designated as a formal group effort by an instructor. But did all of these groups meet the four criteria of psychological grouping defined above? Perhaps group success and your satisfaction would have been higher if they all had.

Managers frequently wish that their formal work groups would act and think as psychological groups. Our study of group behavior in organizations should aid you, as a manager, to help your group make this transition.

## Managerial Implications

Figure 7.3 portrays several of the action settings in which managers find themselves involved with groups. With respect to the formal work group, managers can be either figures of superior authority (department head or chairperson) or of general membership (subor-

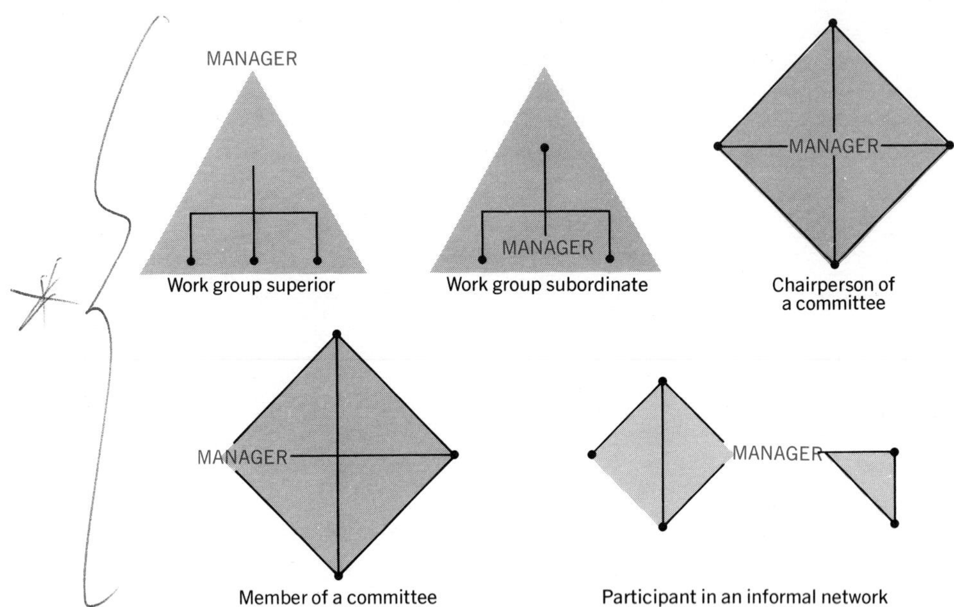


**FIGURE 7.3** Possible group involvements of managers.

dinate or committee member). Managers will also be involved in a variety of informal networks. In each of these action settings, the manager is challenged to help the group achieve success and thereby contribute to the performance and human resource maintenance purposes of the organization.

## USEFULNESS OF GROUPS IN ORGANIZATIONS

Groups are good for organizations and their members. They can make important contributions to organizational task accomplishment and, as our opening vignette shows, they can also exert a strong influence on individual work attitudes and behaviors.

### Groups and Organizational Task Accomplishment

Many things in life are beyond the capabilities of one person. It takes groups efforts, for example, to build a jet airplane or a multi-story office building. It also takes a group to play basketball and to act out a television soap opera. The element common to each of these examples is the benefit of group synergy.

Checkpoint

This concept of synergy is fundamental to our study of OB. In a sense, it represents what a manager is really trying to achieve in mobilizing human and other resources to serve the purposes of the organization. Do you remember the definition of synergy given in Chapter 1? Test yourself and refer back if need be.

If you defined synergy as the creation of a whole that is greater than the sum of its parts, you were right! When synergy occurs, groups accomplish more than the total of their members' individual capabilities. Research shows, for example, that[5]

- When the presence of an "expert" is uncertain, groups make better judgments than would the average individual.
- When problem-solving can be handled by a division of labor and the sharing of information, groups are typically more successful than individuals.
- Because of their tendencies to make more risky decisions than individuals, groups can be more creative and innovative in their task accomplishments.

In sum, a manager must learn when a group is the best human resource configuration for a certain task. Then the manager must know how to ensure that the full benefits of group synergy are achieved.

The challenge, once again, is for you to know how to ensure that such synergy takes place in the groups with which you are affiliated as a manager. Red Auerbach and Bill Russell, two famous professional basketball figures, show their awareness of this in *Newsline 7.1*.

## Groups and Individual Behavior

Formal work groups and informal networks are important aspects of an individual's work setting. Groups are social settings which offer a variety of information, expectations and opportunities which relate to individual need satisfactions. As a result, these groups are major influences on individual work attitudes and behaviors. Figuratively speaking,

Group involvements —offer→ information, expectations, opportunities —which influence→ individual attitudes & behavior

Groups are mechanisms through which people learn relevant job skills and knowledge. Group members can model correct behaviors,

## NEWSLINE 7.1

### All-time NBA Team Built Around Russell

For once, Red Auerbach agreed with the media.

Auerbach, who often has had his differences with the working press during his lengthy tenure in Boston, heartily endorsed the selection of Bill Russell as the greatest player in the 35-year history of the National Basketball Association.

"I don't care how strong your guards or forwards are, you have to build from the middle," said Auerbach, who was Russell's coach on the Celtics and now is the club's president. "If I was starting a team, there's only one player I'd pick: Bill Russell."

Auerbach praised Russell as "one of the brighest, smartest players ever. You might fool him once, but you could never fool him twice—never. He always made the big play. He made the blocked shot into an art form. And he was team oriented—all he wanted to do was win."

"When I signed my first pro contract," Russell recalled, "Red (Auerbach) asked me whether I was concerned about my scoring. I had a reputation as not being much of a scorer in college, and I said I was a little worried. So he told me, 'From this day on, every time we talk about contracts we will never discuss statistics. I want you to think about winning, not about scoring.' That took a lot of the pressure off me.

"I always played to win. And I found out the best way was to play in a style that would make my teammates play better."

"If he played in the NBA today, or tomorrow, he would be a great player," contended Auerbach. "He had the competitive drive you need to be a great player. He was a tough guy then and he would be a tough guy now."

Auerbach was asked whether he would like to have coached the all-time team [made up of Russell and other superstars].

"To be perfectly frank, I wouldn't," he replied. "I think it would be a lousy ballclub. There are too many great stars. You'd have all kinds of internal problems, chemistry problems. I'd only want three or four of these guys—keep the rest."

Source: Adapted from The Associated Press as reprinted in *The Southern Illinoisan* (October 31, 1980), p. 15.

offer feedback on performance, and provide direct instruction and assistance to one another. Often, these relationships among group members assist individuals in building abilities and acquiring competences required to do well at their jobs. These group benefits often make up for deficiencies in the formal training and education practices of the organization.

Individual motivation to expend effort on work tasks can also be affected by group involvements. Groups members communicate expectations to one another regarding work performance. They may encourage or discourage high levels of effort. Members also influence one another's beliefs and predispositions about various aspects of the work setting. A new employee soon learns, for example, who the "bad" supervisors are or whom you can't "trust" as a co-worker. These influences may even extend to the point of communicating how the individual should feel about his or her job and the organization. For example, a co-worker may indicate that "this is a good job to have and a great place to work."

Perhaps the most apparent function of groups is their ability to satisfy the needs of their members. Groups provide for obvious social interactions and interpersonal fulfillments. A group can provide individual security in the form of direct work assistance and technical advice, or emotional support in times of special crisis or pressure. Groups also give their members a sense of identification and offer opportunities for ego involvement by assisting in group activities.

Individual's can find from their group involvements the full range of need satisfactions discussed in Chapter 4. Those satisfactions which are left unfulfilled by the formal work group may be met in the informal group. Whether or not the net result of group influence on the individual is positive or negative for the organization, however, depends on many factors. This is the issue that makes our study of groups in organizations so interesting.

The accompanying *What Managers Do 7.1* gives one example of how groups were mobilized to the benefit of both the organization and its members. You might be thinking, as you read, of how you will act to mobilize the human resource potential of groups in your job as a manager.

## GROUP EFFECTIVENESS

Task performance and human resource maintenance are the key results of interest in our study of groups at work, just as they are with the study of individuals. In the group context, the concept of human resource maintenance represents a group's ability to maintain its social fabric as a working entity over time, and includes the element of member satisfaction.

An **effective work group** is one that achieves high levels of both task performance and human resource maintenance over time.

## WHAT MANAGERS DO 7.1

### Making the Group an Organizational Resource

In the spring of 1973, Rutland (Vermont) Hospital undertook a program to deter the depersonalization among employees that so often accompanies institutional growth. Having just completed a hundred-bed addition, the once-small community hospital now boasted three hundred beds and more than six hundred employees. Specifically, the management was worried that the increase in both size of physical plant and number of employees would lead to a lack of employee identification with the hospital and that patients might pick up this depersonalization to their detriment.

After a series of meetings on the subject, it became apparent that, in order to accomplish the goal, the hospital's administrative staff would have to actually get out into the hospital and meet with all of its employees, no matter how unwieldy such a system might seem on the surface.

The name of the program finally devised was as simple as the underlying concept: Employee Group Meeting Program. The mechanics of the program called for the executive vice-president and personnel director to meet on an informal basis with two groups of employees each week, joined in each instance by the appropriate department head and/or administrative officer. One meeting would be held in a nursing service area and the second in one of the other departments. The meetings were scheduled to allow for personal contact with every employee at least twice a year, for the express purpose of hearing problems, ideas, and requests for information.

Many of the early meetings were taken up with grievance-based items, such as wages, benefits, and other economic factors, and in all cases these were responded to properly. However, today's meetings are more likely to center around well-thought-out suggestions by well-prepared participants who frequently arrive with lists of concerns for consideration.

Source: Excerpted from Robert F. Lagasse, "Hospital Puts Employees on the Management Team," *Hospitals,* Vol. 51 (December 1, 1977), pp. 89–90.

Poor performance and low maintenance have obvious disadvantages for organizations, groups, and their members. These unfavorable results may also indicate fundamental internal problems which may threaten the group's ability to survive and continue functioning over the longer run.

## THE GROUP AS AN OPEN SYSTEM

Every manager should act to promote work group effectiveness. This requires an ability to understand and influence many variables with the potential to affect group behavior.[6] In Figure 7.4 we view the group as an open system transforming various inputs into two outputs, task performance and human resource maintenance, the ultimate criteria of group effectiveness.

A group's ability to be effective depends, in part, upon how well it transforms resource inputs into group outputs. We refer to this transformation stage as the group process and give it detailed attention in Chapters 8 and 9. For now, it is sufficient to recognize **group process** as the means through which multiple and varied resource inputs are aggregated and transformed into group outputs. Stated in other terms,

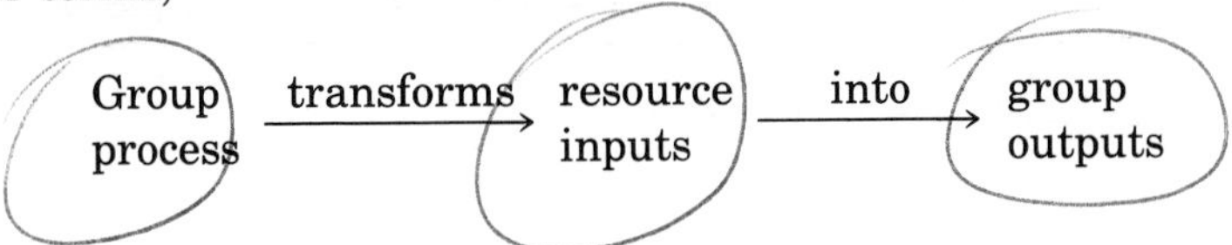


## KEY GROUP INPUTS

Another important influence on group effectiveness is the nature of the inputs themselves. Even the most capable group process will be unable to achieve effective results when inadequate or inappropriate inputs are available. We are concerned with four general categories of group inputs: the organizational setting, the nature of the task, individual attributes, and membership characteristics. The following

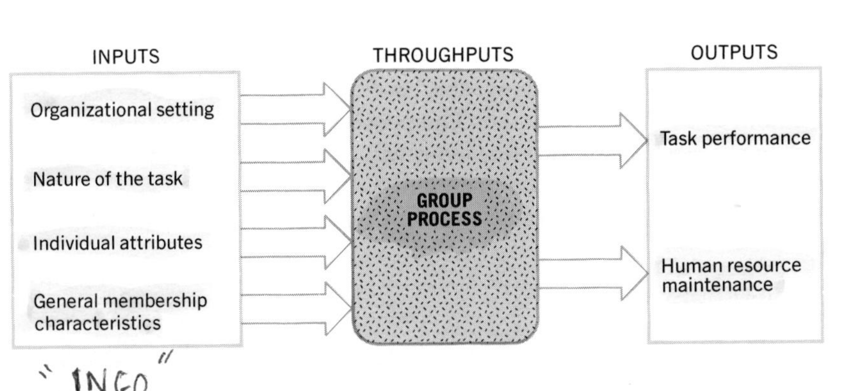


**FIGURE 7.4** The work group as an open system.

sections look in some detail at each input category and the implications which it holds for group effectiveness.

Since our focus here will be on group inputs, with group process reserved for discussion in Chapters 8 and 9, Table 7.1 is presented to summarize the facets of the several group inputs on which our attention now focuses.

## Organizational Setting

The total organization is a major component in the external environment within which work groups operate. The nature of the organization as a work setting thus becomes an important input to groups. Several aspects of the organization are of special importance in this regard. They include characteristics of the established physical environment such as the resources made available, nature of the workflow technology, and spatial arrangements (such as seating and layout of work stations). Research suggests that these factors may influence the degree to which group members get psychologically close to one another, the extent to which they cooperate or compete with one another, and the nature of communication patterns that emerge within the group.[7]

The nature of the organization's reward systems, goals, and structure, as well as its overall size, are also important inputs to the group. Rewards and goal-setting are discussed in Chapters 5 and 6; organizational goals and structures are reviewed in Chapters 10, 11, and 12. You should recognize that these related parts of the book contain insights relevant to the management of groups in organizations. Rather than review the material here, we leave you the responsibility of including the total organization as an environmental input of groups.

## Nature of the Group Task

We have already talked about the usefulness of group task accomplishments to the organization. The specific nature of the task as an input to the group process, however, can place special demands on a work group. Group effectiveness will be affected by how well the group process is able to accommodate these demands.

### Task Complexity

To be effective, a work group must be successful at (1) assessing task demands, and (2) meeting these demands by proper planning, coordination, and utilization of member resources.[8] One useful distinction

**Table 7.1 Important Facets of the Major Group Inputs**

| Input | Facets |
|---|---|
| Organizational setting | Resources, spatial arrangements, technology, structure, rewards, goals, size |
| Nature of the task | Simplicity-complexity |
| Individual attributes | Demographic, competency, and psychological characteristics |
| Membership characteristics | Interpersonal compatibilities, heterogeneity, status congruence, size of group |

when assessing task demands is between simple and complex tasks. Increasing task complexity adds challenge to the group process. Table 7.2 illustrates the various dimensions of task complexity. It includes the technical attributes of task programmability, difficulty, and information diffusion, as well as the social attribute of membership orientation.

Simple tasks place fewer demands on the group process than do tasks of greater technical and social complexity. Managers' concerns

**Table 7.2 Attributes of Simple and Complex Tasks**

| Task Attributes | Characteristics of Simple Tasks | Characteristics of Complex Tasks |
|---|---|---|
| Programmability | Single acceptable solution achieved via a single path and easily verified as correct. | Many alternative solutions and means to solution; any given solution not easily verified. |
| | People who must perform task have experience with the task. | People who must perform the task do not have experience with the task. |
| | Task requirements remain constant. | Task requirements vary. |
| Difficulty | Little effort is required. | Great deal of effort required. |
| | Few operations are required. | Many operations are required. |
| | Involves low-level skills. | Involves complex skills. |
| Information diffusion | Requisite knowledge is centralized. | Knowledge and skills are widely distributed. |
| | Involves few skills or areas of knowledge. | Several skills or areas of knowledge are necessary. |
| Member orientation | Agreement on means and ends. | Ego involved. |
| | | Disagreement over means and ends. |

Source: Adapted from David M. Herold, "The Effectiveness of Work Groups," p. 100 in Steven Kerr (ed.), *Organizational Behavior* (Columbus, Ohio: Grid Publishing, 1979). Reprinted with permission.

for group process, therefore, should increase with task complexity. The challenges facing the supervisor of one segment of an automobile assembly line, for example, will differ greatly from the group process requirements of a research and development laboratory in a high technology electronics firm.

## Research on Task Properties and Group Effectiveness[9]

Tasks of different complexities demand varying amounts of competence and effort on the part of group members. Increasing complexity makes it harder for a group to achieve both high-quality and high-quantity performance. Group members are required to distribute their efforts more broadly than on simple tasks, and greater cooperation and interdependence is required to achieve a common product. When the group process fails to meet these demands, performance suffers accordingly.

In general, membership satisfaction increases as the complexity of the group's task increases. This result assumes that group members have the required competencies and needs appropriate to a

Mission control at NASA: a complex group task.

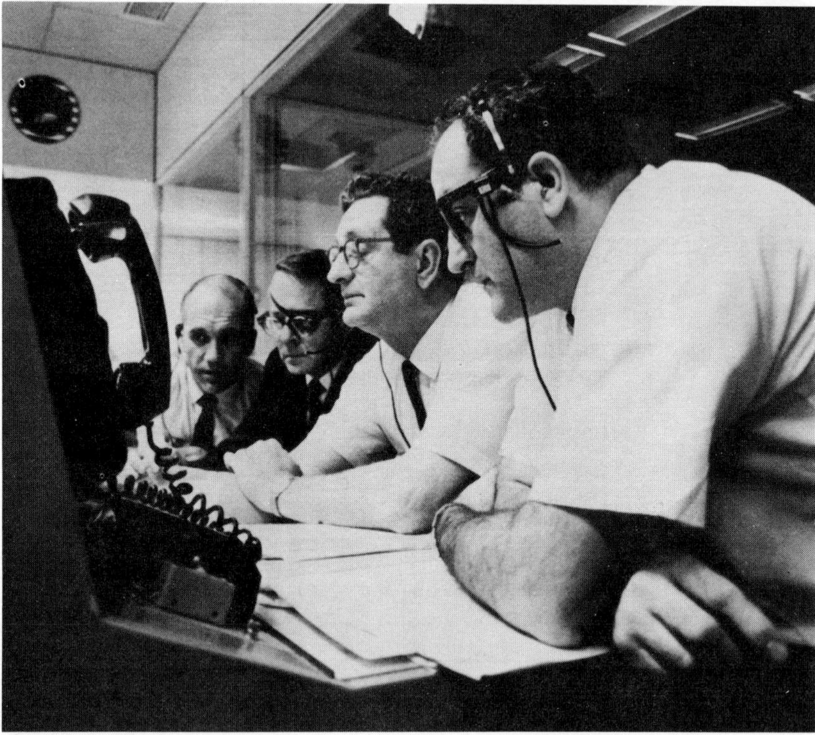

complex task, and that the group process allows for the abilities to be properly aggregated and for individual needs to be fulfilled.

## Individual Attributes

Chapter 3 was devoted to a discussion of the basic attributes of individuals. Although our attention focused at that time on the significance of these attributes for individual performance and human resource maintenance, these same individual attributes are an important input to any group. A group will be influenced in both its process and effectiveness by the demographic, competency, and psychological characteristics of its individual members. To the extent that the right competencies are present, for example, group performance outcomes can be directly enhanced.

To take advantage of the competencies, however, the individuals must function well in the setting of the work group and in harmony with one another. Whether they do or do not achieve this result depends in part on how well individual attributes blend into the general characteristics of the membership as a whole. Before we go on to discuss this "blending" in more detail, recall that the individual as a group resource is the very same individual which we studied very thoroughly in Part Two (Chapters 3–6) of the book.

## Total Membership Characteristics

The willingness of individual members to exert efforts on the group's behalf will be influenced by many factors. Among the most important are the special characteristics of the total membership itself, including interpersonal compatibilities, membership heterogeneity, status congruence, and size.

### Interpersonal Compatibilities

A key element in the functioning of any group is the degree of interpersonal compatibility among its members. The FIRO-B (fundamental interpersonal orientation) theory helps to explain how people orient themselves toward one another.[10] This theory is based on how strongly people need to express and receive feelings of inclusion, control, and affection. These needs are briefly described below.

**Need for inclusion:** Strive for prominence, recognition, and prestige.

**Need for control:** Tendency to rebel and refuse to be controlled, or tendency to be compliant and submissive.

**Need for affection:** Desire to be friendly and seek close emotional ties with others.

The FIRO-B theory argues that groups in which members have reciprocal or compatible needs will be more effective than groups characterized by incompatibilities. Groups of the latter type are predicted to be less likely to have their members work well together. Symptoms of harmful incompatibilities include withdrawn members, open hostilities, struggles over control, and domination of the group by a few members. As you think about what interpersonal compatibilities can mean to a work group, recall these words of advice to managers which were offered by the author of the FIRO-B Theory.

> If at the outset we can choose a group of people who can work together harmoniously, we shall go far toward avoiding situations where a group's efforts are wasted in interpersonal conflicts.[11]

## Membership Heterogeneity

People vary on other attributes in addition to their interpersonal orientations. Homogeneous groups consist of members of similar backgrounds, interests, values, attitudes and traits. Heterogeneous groups include membership diversity on these dimensions.

Research is mixed as to the implications of membership heterogeneity for group effectiveness.[12] Heterogeneity can bring a variety of skills and viewpoints to bear on problems and thus facilitate task accomplishment; but homogeneity increases the chances for harmonious working relationships among group members. Managers must exercise good judgment when selecting members for their work groups so as to balance the advantages of both homogeneity and heterogeneity. The more heterogeneous the membership, the more skilled the manager will have to be in facilitating a successful essential group aggregation process.

## Status Congruence

A person's **status** is his or her total standing on prestige and esteem in a group. This standing can be based on any number of characteristics, including age, work seniority, occupation, education, work accomplishments, or status in other groups. **Status congruence** occurs when a person's standing on each of these factors is consistent with his or her standing on the other factors. Status incongruity occurs when standings vary among the factors.

Figure 7.5 illustrates some of the negative consequences for groups when members experience status incongruities. As shown in the figure, groups whose members experience a range of status in-

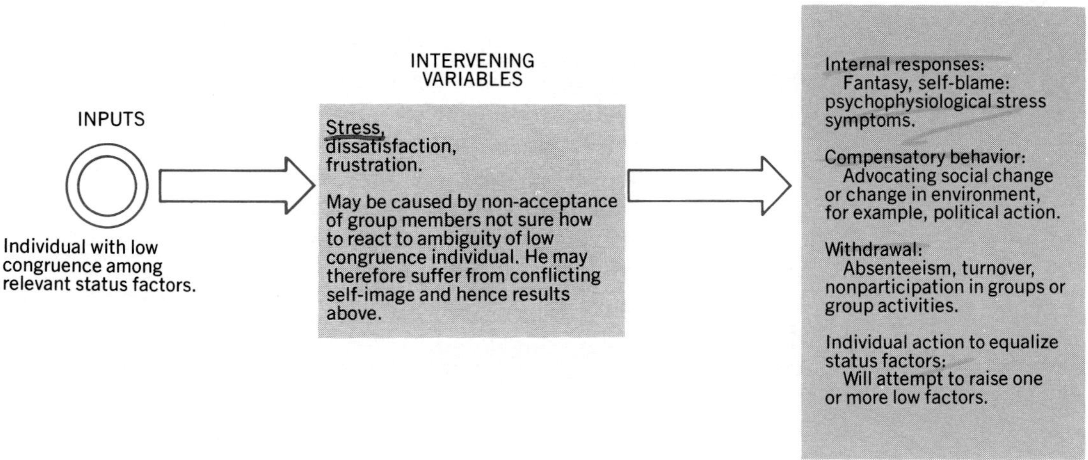
INPUTS
Individual with low congruence among relevant status factors.
INTERVENING VARIABLES
Stress, dissatisfaction, frustration.
May be caused by non-acceptance of group members not sure how to react to ambiguity of low congruence individual. He may therefore suffer from conflicting self-image and hence results above.
OUTPUTS (Responses or actions)
Internal responses:
Fantasy, self-blame: psychophysiological stress symptoms.
Compensatory behavior:
Advocating social change or change in environment, for example, political action.
Withdrawal:
Absenteeism, turnover, nonparticipation in groups or group activities.
Individual action to equalize status factors:
Will attempt to raise one or more low factors.

**FIGURE 7.5** The effects of status incongruity on group members. (Source: Adapted from James G. Hunt "Status Congruence in Organizations: Effects and Suggested Research." In R. W. Millman and M. P. Hottenstein, eds., *Academy of Management Proceedings*, 1976. Reprinted by permission of Hunt and Academy of Management Publications.)

congruities can place further challenges on the manager who seeks to ensure group effectiveness.

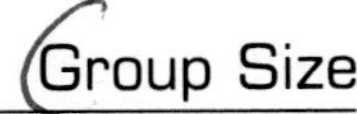

## Group Size

Consider the implications of being in groups of various sizes. As the size of a group increases, the number of possible relationships among its members increases in a geometric progression. In a group of two members there is one possible mutual relationship; in a group of five, this number increases to ten.

As groups grow in size, more communication and coordination are required to aggregate the collective potential of the membership. Although it is difficult to pinpoint an ideal group size, it has been shown that for problem-solving groups[13]

1. Less than five members results in:

- Fewer people to share task responsibilities.
- More personal discussions.
- More complete participation.

2. More than seven members results in:

- Fewer opportunities to participate.
- More member inhibitions.

- Domination by aggressive members.
- Tendency to split into subgroups.

Such findings argue for an ideal problem-solving group size of five to seven members. However, you need to weigh this against the fact that increasing group size offers more human resources to help achieve the desired task accomplishment. At the same time as groups grow larger, however, special efforts must be made in the group process to overcome any disadvantages that may be associated with the increasing size. This impact of size on the resource and communication/coordination tradeoff is shown in Figure 7.6. As groups become larger, more potential resources become available to perform the task. However, the growth in size also increases communication and coordination requirements. The result is a tradeoff as shown in the figure. The same kind of reasoning holds for other membership characteristics, including interpersonal compatibilities and homogeneity-heterogeneity as discussed earlier. Managers must be aware of the existence of these tradeoffs when staffing their work groups or otherwise acting to affect the composition of the membership.

**Research on Group Size and Human Resource Maintenance** Research shows that member satisfaction increases as group size approaches five members, and decreases thereafter. Turnover and absenteeism also increase with group size.[14] In general, it appears that the larger groups suffer some disadvantages in terms of the maintenance criterion of group effectiveness. Smaller groups enable

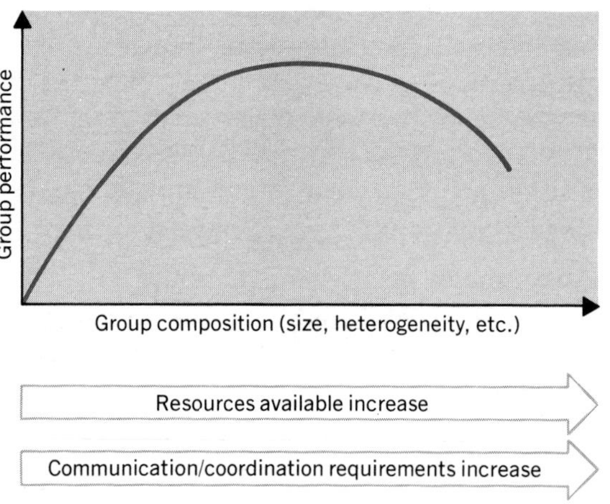


**FIGURE 7.6** Trade-offs in resources and communication coordination. (Source: Adapted from Richard N. Osborn, James G. Hunt, and Larry R. Jauch, *Organization Theory: An Integrated Approach*. New York: John Wiley & Sons, 1980, p. 414.)

members to interact more frequently and to get to know one another better. As a result, membership satisfaction is enhanced.

**Research on Group Size and Task Performance** Conclusions vary as to the impact of size on group performance. In laboratory settings, research indicates performance tends to increase with size; results from field studies show the opposite.[15] A number of complexities may account for these inconsistencies. They include the additional effects of such things as the nature of the task and the other membership factors just discussed. Groups of any size can be well managed and achieve high performance. To do so, however, good decisions must be made on managing the group process.

## MANAGERIAL CHALLENGES OF GROUPS

Work groups enable organizations and their members to accomplish things which individuals can't do alone. This is yet another illustration of synergy and, as a result, the group becomes a key human resource of organizations.

As you conclude this chapter, recall that groups are like double-edged swords. Individuals affect group outcomes by the extent to which their competencies and efforts are applied or withheld in the group's behalf. On the other hand, the group can have a strong influence on individual behavior. Among other things, the group can affect an individual's choice of performance goals, establish expectations regarding the probability of success, influence the choice of work methods, clarify which rewards are to be expected, and reinforce work values consistent with group beliefs and standards. All in all, it is important for the practicing manager to recognize that:

1. Groups are important phenomena in organizations.
2. Groups can have positive and negative effects on both organizations and their members.
3. An understanding of group behavior can help to enhance the desirable consequences and reduce the undesirable consequences of groups as human resources of organizations.

This chapter has concentrated most heavily on the first of the above concerns. Chapters 8 and 9 focus primarily on the second and third points.

## SUMMARY

We have started this chapter with a discussion of the way groups differ from simple aggregations or collections of people. This involves regular interactions of members who see themselves to be mutually dependent in terms of goal accomplishment. To this we have added the criterion of member awareness of one another's needs and potential contributions in order to have a "psychological group."

We have then talked about types of groups in organizations and divided these into formal work groups and such temporary work groups as committees and task forces. These were contrasted with various kinds of informal groups spontaneously arising from the people themselves.

The usefulness of groups in organizations was considered next. We noted some examples of where groups are superior to individuals in terms of task accomplishment. Once again, synergy was shown to be an important contributor in creating this superiority.

Though groups are often necessary for task accomplishment, some are more effective than others. Four basic inputs to the group process are important in this regard—the organizational setting, nature of the group task, individual attributes, and total membership characteristics.

The factors in the organizational setting include structure, technology, goals, and size. These are discussed in detail in Chapter 10. The individual attributes, as reviewed in Chapter 3, include demographic, competency, and psychological characteristics. To function with effectiveness, a work group requires a supportive organizational setting and competent individual members.

We went on to note that the complexity of the task also influences group effectiveness. The greater the complexity, the harder it is for a group to achieve both quantity and quality of performance. On the other hand, satisfaction tends to increase with complexity.

In terms of membership, we have shown some effects of interpersonal compatibilities and size on group outputs. There is a resource and communications coordination tradeoff involved in these, such that an optimum combination of either compatibility or size is reached when the resource and communications requirements are balanced.

Finally, we have concluded this look at groups from a managerial perspective by directing your attention to the importance of group process. This is the subject of the coming chapter.

## THINKING THROUGH THE ISSUES

1. Define and give work examples of formal and informal groups.
2. List and explain some of the advantages and disadvantages of informal groups for (a) their members, and (b) their host organizations.
3. When does a formal group become a psychological group? Should every manager want his or her work unit to become a psychological group? Defend your answer.
4. Describe some of the important characteristics which influence a group's effectiveness in terms of task performance and human resource maintenance.
5. Describe some circumstances under which a group is likely to be superior to an individual in task accomplishment.
6. Describe some membership influences on group effectiveness and relate these to the resource-communications/coordination tradeoff.
7. We argued that the number of potential relationships among group members grows geometrically as group size increases. Explore this argument by calculating and drawing the number of potential relationships for groups of three, six, and nine members. What implications do you see here in terms of the resource-communications/coordination tradeoff?
8. What is the significance of status congruence as far as group members are concerned?

## CASE: PART-TIMERS AT STUDENT TOOL RENTAL[16]

This case is concerned with the student tool rental unit of a large state supported vocational-technical school. In order to minimize the tools and equipment which students must purchase, the school has arranged to charge them a flat per term rental fee and make certain kinds of tools and equipment available to them as needed during a term. The unit has two main responsibilities. The first is to process orders from instructors concerning equipment needed for their classes. The second is to check the equipment in and out to the students as needed during the term.

The organizational hierarchy at tool rental consists of four levels. At the top is A. A. Jones who is responsible for the whole operation of the unit. Under him there are five civil servant workers: four females and one male. Of the four females, two are general secretaries. One is A. A. Jones' chief assistant, and the other one is in charge of a number of part-time workers. The male civil service worker is responsible for a small number of highly specialized tools which are sold rather than rented. However, he also helps with other jobs, as necessary. Of the civil service workers, one has graduated from college, one has flunked out of the vocational school several times, and the others have a high school education. All of these workers have lived within a few miles of the vocational school most of their lives.

Under Mrs. Johnson, who is in charge of the part-time workers, there are three part-time supervisors. Under the supervisors are the rest of the part-time workers. According to the organization chart, Mrs. Johnson should have complete control of the workers. However, this is not the case. Mrs. Lockin tries to act as the part-time worker boss. Whenever these workers are caught doing something wrong, she lets Mrs. Johnson do the "dirty work" in reprimanding them. Mrs. Johnson tries to overlook small faults, but Mrs. Lockin looks for the most unimportant faults. Thus, two people are watching over the part-timers most of the time. As a result, there is a conflict in the hierarchy.

There are thirty-four part-time workers at tool rental. All are vo-tech students. Many are married and badly need the job. The pay starts at the federal minimum wage rate. The only form of promotion present in this system is moving from worker to supervisor. Supervisor positions are kept open for married students. Ten cent an hour pay increases are granted after 1500 hours of work.

Tool rental is currently housed on the fourth floor of the auto repair shop. Its storage area has been moved twice in less than a year. Originally it was located in a temporary building behind the health sciences building. Next it was moved to the basement immediately across from the electronics repair area and finally to its present location. Adequate storage is very important for tool rental. There is a very large tool and equipment inventory necessary. The storage area is also used to handle tool turn-ins at the end of the term. Since all the tools are currently processed by hand, the storage area is also used for this.

Most of the remaining work is done by hand and involves physical and clerical labor by all workers. Among the most important duties of the workers are: shelving tools, processing tools, checking tools in and out, finding special tools for people, and keeping accurate records. Every person is taught how to do every job. The typical working period for a part-timer is four hours per day.

The physical conditions are generally good. Since the service is located on the fourth floor, it is isolated from the rest of the building. There is not much outside traffic, except for laborers who use a freight elevator. Tool rental has a large area in which the workers can work. The area is well lighted, and it is usually neatly kept through the term. The offices are enclosed by glass windows through which the civil service workers can watch the part-timers at all times.

The working conditions are clean most of the time. Part-timers may wear casual clothes unless there is work to be done at the old warehouse. Tool rental keeps obsolete and discarded tools in this old warehouse. It is dirty most of the time. The lighting is very poor there. In the warm months, it is too hot and in the cold months, it is too cold; however, by going to the warehouse, part-timers are out of the sight of the regular supervisors.

There are no written rules for the workers. The rules seem to have come about through the work practices rather than being formally written. Management assumes that every worker will be at work every free hour of the day. In practice this is also assured. If a worker does not show up for work, he or she is supposed to call in and tell the supervisor. Some employees have been fired for not doing this. The rule is strictly enforced. For the first offense there is a strong reprimand. Usually, most excuses given for failure to call in are not taken into consideration. If a person misses work and does not call in, management assumes that this person does not care about his or her job.

It is also assumed that the worker will work every minute he or she is there. The only exception to this is during the worker's break. The rule for a break is that any person who works four straight hours is entitled to a fifteen minute break. If a worker does not work four hours, there is not supposed to be a break; but, in reality, everyone takes a break whether they work four hours or not. However, those workers caught get a reprimand.

Management also assumes that the person is there to work, not talk. This assumption is taken for granted, but management enforces it. If a worker is caught talking too much, he or she is told to stop. If the talking continues, the worker is moved to an isolated spot away from the other workers. However, this rule is not enforced all the time. Its enforcement seems to be a function of the mood of the civil service workers. If they are in a good mood, most workers can converse during work, but if the atmosphere is bad, the worker will get reprimanded. Therefore, workers try to find out the atmosphere on a particular day.

During the beginning and end of the term, tool rental is open from 8 A.M. to 9 or 9:30 P.M. The part-timer is supposed to be at work at 7:30 A.M. and work up to 9:30 P.M., if possible. Thus the typical four-hour work period may stretch to twelve hours a day during the week at the beginning and at the end of each term.

All workers are also supposed to work at least once each school break. If a person does not, the job probably will not be there when he or she gets back.

Workers are expected to conform to the job requirements and rules of tool rental with no back talk. The workers need the job and there are few alternative jobs available for them in the area.

However, there are many things that occur in addition to those mentioned above. One event is playing frisbee with the plastic top to a glue can. Games such as this are typical. They all take place in the storage area. Another game which has developed is baseball played with a frisbee. Each team has as many people as there are workers available. While one team is up to bat, the other team spreads out over the storage area. Consequently, there is a potential problem with the civil service workers. There are two ways they can enter the area. One is by the freight elevator, and the other is by the main elevator. By approaching in either of these ways, it is possible to unlock a door and sneak in behind the part-timers. This happened once, and now one worker is assigned to the door while the game is being played.

The fun of these games for the workers is that they know if they are caught they will be fired. Management knows about the games but hasn't been able to catch one in action. On some days when there is no work to be done the games are played for two or three hours. The only time the game stops is when a civil service worker approaches to check up on the workers, or to take a break. To keep from getting caught, each worker is assigned to a position involving some tool processing. When a civil service worker shows up, the game is stopped, and everyone acts as if some work is being done.

Everyday after work, one of the civil service workers goes upstairs to try to find the frisbees. Whenever the game is finished, the frisbees are hidden in a special place. Occasionally the workers leave one out so the civil service worker will find it. Management is overjoyed and thinks the hiding place has been found.

As previously indicated, workers are supposed to show up for work promptly and regularly. Often, however, a worker will call or have someone else call indicating that he or she won't be in on a particular day. This happens more often during nice weather.

Workers are also not supposed to do any unnecessary talking. However, they try to see how much talking they can get away with without being caught by management. Usually someone watches the office windows to see if a civil service worker is coming to tell them to be quiet. Of course, if a member of management comes along, the part-timers act as if they are working.

Among part-timers, the part-time supervisors have the greatest amount of status and power. If a worker does not follow their orders, that person could be fired very easily. After the supervisors, there is a struggle for status. Usually the people directly under the supervisor are the workers who have been employed the longest. The people who usually get the worst jobs are those who have worked the shortest period of time, or those whom the supervisors do not like.

From this description you might think performance would be low, but it meets management expectations. However, the potential for individual development is low and job satisfaction is low.

## QUESTION

1. How can the various group concepts introduced in Chapter 7 be used to describe or explain the situation presented in this case?

## THE MANAGER'S VOCABULARY

**Effective Work Group** One that achieves high levels of both task performance and membership satisfaction, and is able to maintain itself over time.

**Formal Group** A group created by formal authority for some organizational purpose; synonymous with work group.

**Group** A collection of people who interact with each other regularly over a period of time and see themselves to be mutually dependent with respect to the attainment of one or more common goals.

**Group Process** The means through which multiple and varied resource inputs are aggregated and transformed into product outputs.

**Informal Group** A group which exists without being formally specified by someone in authority.

**Psychological Group** A group whose members achieve a true sharing of goals and values.

**Status** Standing of prestige and esteem of a member in a group.

**Status Congruence** When a person's standing on various status factors is congruent with his or her standing on the other factors.

**Work Group** A group created by the formal authority of an organization to transform resource inputs into product outputs.

## Notes

[1]These descriptions are based on the work of Edgar H. Schein, "The Chinese Indoctrination Program for Prisoners of War," *Psychiatry,* Vol. 19 (1956), pp. 149–172.

[2]K. N. Wexley and G. A. Yukl, *Organizational Behavior and Personnel Psychology* (Homewood, Ill.: Richard D. Irwin, 1977).

[3]See, for example, Edgar H. Schein, *Organizational Psychology,* Second Edition (Englewood Cliffs, N.J.: Prentice-Hall, 1970), p. 81.

[4]David M. Herold, "The Effectiveness of Work Groups," p. 95 in Steven Kerr (ed.), *Organizational Behavior* (Columbus, Ohio: Grid Publishing, 1979).

[5]See Marvin E. Shaw, *Group Dynamics: The Psychology of Small Group Behavior,* Second Edition (New York: McGraw-Hill, 1976).

[6]See Herold, op. cit., for a discussion of the group as a complex social system.

[7]Linda N. Jewell and H. Joseph Reitz, *Group Effectiveness in Organizations* (Glenview, Ill.: Scott, Foresman and Company, 1981), pp. 149, 150.

[8]This discussion is adapted from Herold, op. cit., p. 103.

[9]J. T. Lanzetta and T. B. Toby, "Effects of Work Group Structure and Certain Task Variables on Group Performance," *Journal of Abnormal and Social Psychology,* Vol. 53 (1956), pp. 307–314.

[10]William C. Schutz, *FIRO: A Three-Dimensional Theory of Interpersonal Behavior* (New York: Rinehart & Co., 1958).

[11]William C. Shutz, "The Interpersonal Underworld," *Harvard Business Review,* Vol. 36, No. 4 (July–August, 1958), p. 130.

[12]See Shaw, op. cit.

[13]E. J. Thomas and C. F. Fink, "Effects of Group Size," in L. L. Cummings and W. E. Scott (eds.), *Readings in Organizational Behavior and Human Performance* (Homewood, Ill.: Richard D. Irwin, 1969).

[14]L. W. Porter and R. M. Steers, "Organizational, Work, and Personal Factors in Employee Turnover and Satisfaction," *Journal of Applied Psychology,* Vol. 80 (1973), pp. 151–176.

[15]R. Marriott, "Size of Working Group and Output," *Occupational Psychology,* Vol. 26 (1949), pp. 47–51.

[16]Adapted from a course assignment prepared by James T. Wallace for Professor J. G. Hunt, Southern Illinois University-Carbondale. Copyright © by J. G. Hunt, 1980.

# 8

# GROUP AND INTER-GROUP DYNAMICS

# JIM THOMAS' PROBLEM[1]

Jim Thomas is manager of the Mountain Side plant of the National Alloys Company. He has a tough production schedule that demands solid performance from all of his people in all areas of the plant. Jim wants to do a top-flight job and becomes concerned when production drops, when problems go unsolved, or when morale sags.

After his job and his family, Jim's greatest interest is pro football—particularly as played by the Dallas Cowboys. Being a native Texan, Jim has followed the Dallas team from its inception. He gets to attend an occasional game and watches the team regularly on TV or listens to games on the radio. When a game is over, Jim can give a clear, detailed accounting of the team's success or failure.

What raises Jim's boiling point higher than anything is to watch his team fail to play together. He can spot in an instant when someone misses a block, loafs on the job, fails to pass on obvious information to the quarterback, or tries to "shine" at the expense of the team. He can diagnose the Cowboys' areas of weakness, and, if the coach could only hear him, he would tell him what to do to remedy the situation. But with all his insight into teamwork and football, Jim fails to see the parallels between what is needed to improve the Dallas Cowboys and what is needed to shape up the management team at National Alloys. Many of the problems are exactly the same:

- Some individuals have never really learned what their assignments are, particularly for certain plays or situations.
- Some are afraid of the coach, so they pretend to know things that they should be asking questions about.
- Some want to do things "the old way," while others feel that more modern methods are needed.
- Factions and cliques quarrel and fight among one another.
- The whole unit has not come together to develop common goals to which everyone is committed.
- Decisions are made by someone, but some people either don't "get the word" or they disagree with the decision and drag their feet.
- There is jealousy between units and a lack of playing together.
- Even when people are aware of a problem, they don't know exactly what to do about it.

**MANAGEMENT APPLICATIONS QUESTION**

Collaboration among members is essential in successful work groups. Forces exist, however, which can impair the success of even the most well-staffed and best intentioned groups. The above analogy between the Dallas Cowboys football team and work groups in general is most appropriate. It should lead you to ask: What are the key forces in groups and between groups with which a manager should be concerned?

## PLANNING AHEAD

**This chapter will help you to understand the following dimensions of group and inter-group dynamics in organizations:**

**The Concept of Group Dynamics**
**Homans' Model of Group Dynamics**
**Group Norms and Cohesiveness**
**Interaction Patterns in Groups**
**Decision-Making Methods in Groups**
**Group Task and Maintenance Activities**
**Inter-Group Relations**

The previous chapter introduced task performance and human resource maintenance as the ultimate criteria of work group effectiveness. Figure 8.1 places these criteria in perspective in an open systems view of group operations. This figure shows that the group process transforms various inputs into performance and maintenance as the two key outputs.

Figure 8.1 offers the manager a way of looking at groups and seeking to understand their behavior. Sporting teams such as the Dallas Cowboys work hard in trying to understand their successes and failures, and then to practice ways of improving how well members of the team work together. Work groups in organizations can benefit from similar efforts to review results, analyze group behavior, and make constructive changes.

When you review the work groups with which you are concerned as a manager, you will examine both inputs and group process. In respect to the input factors, you will be concerned about the support offered by the organization setting, the nature of the task demands, attributes of individual members, and the characteristics of the group membership as a whole. These were discussed in detail in Chapter 7.

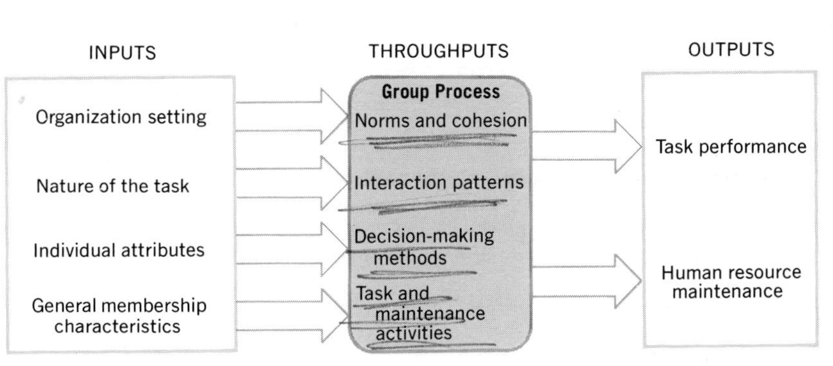


**FIGURE 8.1** The group as an open system.

When attention shifts to the group process, your concern is to ensure that it responds properly to the various inputs and takes full advantage of them in producing the desired outputs. There are four aspects of group process that are especially important—group norms and cohesion, interaction patterns, decision-making methods, and task and maintenance activities. These are the topics of the present chapter and are highlighted in Figure 8.1. Since, together, the process issues are often referred to as the basic elements of group dynamics, we'll begin by clarifying this specific concept.

## THE CONCEPT OF GROUP DYNAMICS

**Group dynamics** are forces operating in groups which affect task performance and membership satisfaction. They include the nature of group norms, cohesion, interaction patterns, decision-making methods, and task and maintenance activities. These factors comprise the essential group process, and, when they fail to operate to the group's benefit, group effectiveness is compromised. Naturally, an informed manager will want to facilitate group dynamics that are positive influences on group effectiveness.

Table 8.1 lists a number of characteristics which research has associated with effective work groups. The list includes insights into

**Table 8.1 The Nature of Highly Effective Groups**

1. The members of the group are attracted to it and are loyal to its members, including the leader.
2. The members and leaders have a high degree of confidence and trust in each other.
3. The values and goals of the group are an integration and expression of the relevant values and needs of its members.
4. All the interaction, problem-solving, decision-making activities of the group occur in a supportive atmosphere. Suggestions, comments, ideas, information, criticisms are all offered with a helpful orientation.
5. The group is eager to help members develop to their full potential.
6. The group knows the value of "constructive" conformity and knows when to use it and for what purposes.
7. There is strong motivation on the part of each member to communicate fully and frankly to the group all the information which is relevant and of value to the group's activity.
8. Members feel secure in making decisions which seem appropriate to them.

Source: Excerpted from Rensis Likert, *New Patterns of Management* (New York: McGraw-Hill, 1961), pp. 166–169.

the group dynamics identified above. As you read Table 8.1, try to anticipate the challenges of creating a group which satisfies each of the items on the list.

## HOMANS' MODEL OF GROUP DYNAMICS[2]

Group dynamics enact the transformation process through which inputs are turned into group outputs. One classic view of these dynamics is offered by George Homans. He feels it is useful to distinguish among the activities, sentiments, and interactions of group members, and to examine the required and emergent forms of each. Because Homans' model can help you to better conceptualize group dynamics, we briefly outline it here.

### Required and Emergent Behaviors

The operational dynamics of groups include both required and emergent forms. **Required behaviors** are those which the organization requests from group members as a basis for continued affiliation and support. They may include such work-related behaviors as being punctual, treating customers with respect, and being helpful to coworkers. **Emergent behaviors** are what group members do in addition to or in place of what is asked by the organization. In "The Case of the Changing Cage" described in the Introduction to Part Two, the afternoon snacks and games of rubber-band sniping were emergent behaviors. Other examples include "punching in" a late coworker and extending the authorized coffee breaks.

What the members do in respect to both required and emergent behaviors constitutes the basic process through which the group turns resource inputs into product outputs. Whereas the required behaviors are formally designed to benefit the organization, emergent behaviors exist purely as products of individual and group choice. In practice, however, both required and emergent behaviors can have their functional and dysfunctional sides. Ideally speaking, the two complement one another to benefit the essential group process.

It may help you to think of the system of emergent behaviors as the "shadow" or informal aspect of any required group behaviors. We show this shadow effect in Figure 8.2, which modifies the open systems model of groups presented earlier. Ideally, the emergent system

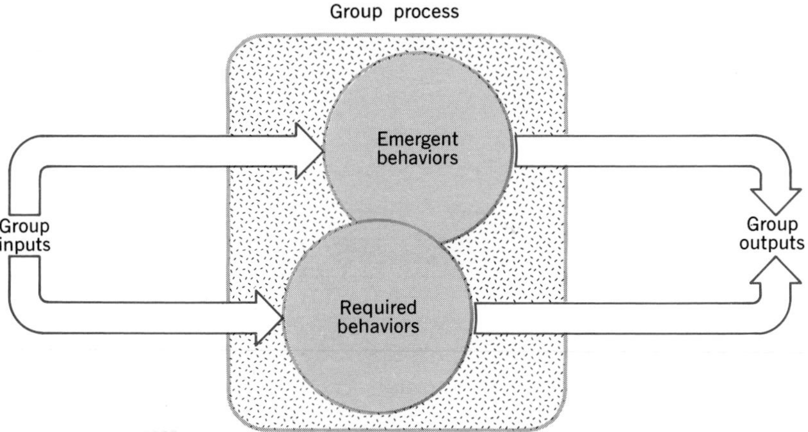


**FIGURE 8.2** Emergent behaviors as a "shadow" for required behaviors in the group process.

will function in support of the required operations, enhance a group's process, and be a positive influence on overall group process.

George Homans identifies activities, interactions, and sentiments as three basic elements of group process which have both their required and emergent forms. These concepts can assist the manager to understand a group and are briefly explained below. As you read on, think back to the "Case of the Changing Cage" and see if you can apply the concepts to this case. Keep in mind that the activities, interactions, and sentiments of any group must be understood in both their required and emergent forms.

## Activities

**Activities** are the verbal and nonverbal behaviors in which group members engage. They are the things people do in groups and include efforts directed toward the group task, social activities, and other forms of physical movement. The required activities of a work group member are often specified by the organization in a written job description. This document outlines the activities which the organization expects the individual to accomplish as a group member and in return for any inducements offered.

Both required and emergent activities will be found in any group. Table 8.2 gives examples of each as taken from the "Case of the Changing Cage." Many other examples can be found in that same case.

**Table 8.2 Examples of Required and Emergent Behaviors: The Case of the Changing Cage**

| Group Element | Required Behavior | Emergent Behavior |
|---|---|---|
| Activities | Cancelled checks are to be filed in numerical order. | Periodic games of rubber band "sniping" take place. |
| Interactions | Clerks take orders from Ms. Dunn, the unit supervisor. | Clerks stand and "chat" with the messengers. |
| Sentiments | Clerks should be polite to persons from other work units. | Clerks held negative feelings toward Mr. Burke. |

## Interactions

**Interactions** are behaviors which group members direct toward other persons. The essence of any interaction is the sending and receiving of information. This occurs by oral conversation as well as in written (such as letters, memos, and signs) and nonverbal media (such as facial gestures and hand signals). Table 8.2 shows by example that interactions also occur in both required and emergent forms. As with activities, they can be both positive and negative in their influence on group functioning and effectiveness.

## Sentiments

**Sentiments** are the feelings, attitudes, beliefs, or values held by group members. These sentiments may be brought into a group from the outside by individual group members, or they may be learned as a result of becoming a group member. A new employee may value hard work and the concept of a "fair day's work for a fair day's pay." To maintain harmonious working relations with other members of the work group, however, this person may learn that it is more important to value restricted efforts and to avoid out-performing other members of the group.

Group sentiments are especially subject to emergent forces. Although it may be easy to require positive attitudes toward work such as a respect for authority and belief in company rules and procedures, it is more difficult to achieve these results in actual practice. When the goals of the emergent system support the required system, their likelihood is greatly increased. The dynamics in the "Case of the Changing Cage" show just how tenuous this desired complement can be between required and emergent group sentiments.

## Summary

Homans' concepts of required and emergent group behaviors, and of activities, interactions, and sentiments as key elements of group dynamics are useful in further describing groups. To the extent that required and emergent group behaviors complement, rather than contradict one another, and to the extent to which the activities, interactions, and sentiments of group members support organizational goals, group process is likely to be more harmonious. Higher group effectiveness is likely to result.

# GROUP NORMS AND COHESIVENESS

Two key aspects of group dynamics which relate to the sentiments described in Homans' model are group norms and group cohesiveness. Consider the following incident as a typical example.

### Frank Jackson[3]

Frank Jackson deftly soldered his last wires in the interconnection. That was eighteen for the morning—not bad, he thought. He moved on to the next computer and began to string out the cable for the next job.

"You're new here, aren't you?" The man was standing beside Frank, soldering iron in hand.

"Yeah. I came over from Consumer Products Division—been with the company for ten years."

"I'm Jim Miller. Been working here in computer assembly for five years."

The men shook hands. Jim walked back to the last job Frank did and looked it over. "Pretty good, Frank, pretty good." He looked back down the assembly floor. "How many have you done this morning?"

"Eighteen."

"Hey, you're quite a rate-buster, aren't you?" Jim laughed. "Most of us here figure fifteen interconnections a day is about par for the course."

"Well, these I'm doing are pretty easy."

Jim frowned. "Yeah, but look what happens. You do twenty, maybe twenty-five easy ones, and the boys stuck with the hard jobs look bad. You wouldn't want that to happen, would you?"

"Well, no, of course not."

"That-a-boy!" Frank smiled. "You know, the boys here have a

bowling team—kind of a company deal. Not everybody is on it—just the interconnection group. Even a few of them don't make it. You know, we like to keep it a friendly bunch." He paused. "Like to come next Wednesday?"

"Why, OK. Sure. Jim, what does the foreman think about the number of jobs a day?"

"Him? He don't know the difference, and if he did, what difference would it make? You can't find good interconnection men right off the street. He goes along—the boys upstairs don't know how fast the work should go, and they don't bother him. So he don't bother us."

Frank looked over his next job. He was doing the toughest kind of interconnection, and he knew that any reasonably skilled man should be able to do at least forty jobs a day on most of the other interconnections. Boy, this was going to be a relaxing job. He didn't like to goof off, but these people were going to be working with him every day—and he wasn't about to get off on the wrong foot with them. Besides, he liked to bowl.

"It's all cost plus anyhow." Jim said. "The company gets plenty from the government for the work. They've got nothing to worry about. Hey, come over to the latrine with me—we can have a smoke. We got plenty of time."

## Norms

Previously, we discussed the proposition that group performance is largely determined by how well the competencies and other attributes of its members are aggregated. In the above incident, a person of ability and motivation has been influenced by the group to withhold work effort. The forces at play in this example include group norms and cohesiveness.

A **group norm** is a behavior that is expected by members of a group. Norms are often referred to as "rules" or "standards" of behavior that apply to group members. When violated, they may be enforced with reprimands and other group sanctions. In the extreme, violating group norms can result in expulsion from the group or social ostracism. In fact, it was just this concern that apparently caused Frank Jackson in the prior case to agree to the group norm of restricted performance.

Norms are among the sentiments which develop as group members interact with one another. They serve the group by allowing members to predict one another's behavior and therefore to be better able to select appropriate behaviors for themselves. Norms help a group to avoid chaotic behavior as the inputs of many different individuals are organized into collective group action. There are many types of norms. For a student project group, there may be norms regarding attendance at meetings, social behaviors, preparedness for meetings, willingness to challenge one another's ideas, and so on. Of course, one of the most important norms relates to the levels of work effort and performance which members are expected to contribute to the group's task.

The performance norm is a key characteristic of work groups. It can be positive or negative in terms of its implications for organizational goals. In the case of Frank Jackson's group, the result was obviously negative. Researchers report that work groups with more positive norms tend to be more successful in accomplishing organizational objectives than groups with more negative norms. Compare and contrast, for example, some of the following norms summarized in one study.[4]

| **Norms of . . .** | **Positive form** | **Negative form** |
|---|---|---|
| Organizational and personal pride | It's a tradition . . . around here for people to stand up for the company when others criticize it unfairly. | In our company . . . they are always trying to take advantage of us. |
| Performance/excellence | In our company . . . people always try to improve, even when they are doing well. | Around here . . . there's no point in trying harder—nobody else does. |
| Teamwork/communication | Around here . . . people are good listeners and actively seek out the ideas and opinions of others. | Around here . . . it's dog-eat-dog and save your own skin. |
| Leadership/supervision | Around here . . . managers and supervisors really care about the people they supervise. | In our company . . . it's best to hide your problems and avoid your supervisor. |
| Profitability/cost effectiveness | Around here . . . people are continually on the lookout for better ways of doing things. | Around here . . . people tend to hang on to old ways of doing things even after they have outlived their usefulness. |

Other norms that may emerge as important sentiments in the work setting include relationships with supervisors, colleagues, and customers, as well as honesty, security, personal development, and change.

## Cohesiveness

Norms vary in the degree to which they are accepted and adhered to by group members. Conformity to norms is strongly influenced by a group's cohesiveness. **Group cohesiveness** is the degree to which members are attracted to and motivated to remain part of a group. Persons in a highly cohesive group value their membership and strive to maintain positive relationships with other group members. The work group which Frank Jackson joined was apparently cohesive. Other members of his team rallied together and restricted their work efforts. This sense of group belongingness apparently had a strong attraction for Frank. Perhaps it was a need for social affiliation that led him to accept this norm, rather than to break it and run the risk of being ostracized from the group.

Cohesion is an important group property. Managers should know the answers to such questions as: (1) What creates group cohesiveness? and (2) What are the results of group cohesiveness?

### Sources of Cohesion

Group cohesiveness is affected by a variety of personal and situational variables. Cohesion tends to be high in groups characterized by members who are homogeneous in terms of attitudes, socio-economic backgrounds, needs, and other individual attributes. When members respect and hold one another's competencies in high esteem, cohesiveness is also likely to be high.[5] Situational factors which enhance group cohesion include agreement on group goals, small size, tasks requiring a high degree of interdependence, physical isolation from other groups, performance success, and performance failure or crisis.

Checkpoint

Many of these sources of cohesiveness are illustrated in the Case of the Changing Cage which introduced Part Three of the book. You might review the case and see if you can identify them.

## Results of Cohesion

Members of highly cohesive groups are concerned about their group's activities and achievements. They tend, as opposed to persons in less cohesive groups, to be more energetic in working on group activities, less likely to be absent, to feel happy about performance success, and to feel sad about failures.[6] Cohesive groups generally have stable memberships and foster feelings of loyalty, security, and high self-esteem among their members. They satisfy a full range of individual needs.

Cohesive groups are good for their members. But the critical remaining question is whether or not cohesive work groups are good for their host organizations. Research answers, "it all depends on the group's performance norm!" A basic rule of group dynamics is that, the more cohesive the group, the greater the conformity of members to group norms. When the performance norm is positive, high conformity has a very beneficial effect; when the norm is negative, however, substantial undesirable results can occur when conformity is high.

Table 8.3 illustrates the performance levels predicted for various combinations of group cohesion and performance norms. Performance is likely to be highest in a highly cohesive group with positive performance norms. In this situation, members with the proper competencies can work hard and achieve both performance success and satisfaction with their group affiliation. The worst situation for a manager is a highly cohesive group with negative performance norms. Once again members will be highly motivated to support one another and experience personal satisfactions. However, the organization will probably suffer as the group restricts its performance to levels consistent with the negative performance norm.

Between these two extremes are mixed situations. In both cases, the lack of cohesion fails to ensure member conformity to the guiding norm. Thus, the strength of the norm is substantially less and the level of outcome is somewhat unpredictable but on the moderate to low side.

**Table 8.3 Group Cohesiveness, Performance Norms, and Predicted Levels of Group Performance**

| | Performance Norms | |
|---|---|---|
| | Positive | Negative |
| Cohesion | | |
| High | High performance | Low performance |
| Low | Moderate performance | Moderate to low performance |

In summary, group cohesion is a source of member satisfaction. Turnover and absenteeism also tend to be low in highly cohesive groups. This should be good for the group. With high cohesion comes high conformity to group norms. When there is a positive performance norm, performance will be high, with little variability among the members. When the norm is low, the performance level will be low and again little variability will occur. As an informed manager you would like to be able to influence group norms and cohesiveness to support the organization's production purposes. In the next chapter we'll offer specific guidelines for building positive norms and influencing group cohesion.

## INTERACTION PATTERNS IN GROUPS

Up to now, we have treated groups as if they were all structured the same way in the patterns of interactions linking members to one another. That is an oversimplification. In fact, it is useful for you to think about three different patterns of interaction employed by groups. As described in Figure 8.3, these are interacting, coacting, and counteracting patterns.

| PATTERN | DIAGRAM | CHARACTERISTICS |
| --- | --- | --- |
| Interacting group | 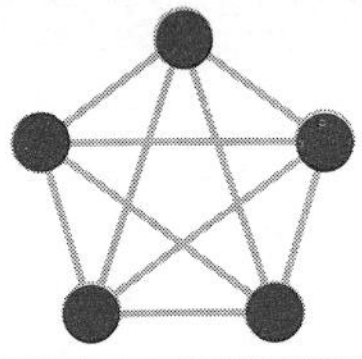 | High interdependency around a common task |
| Coacting group | 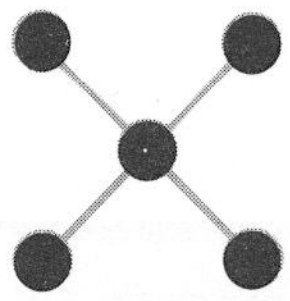 | Independent individual efforts on behalf of common task |
| Counteracting group | 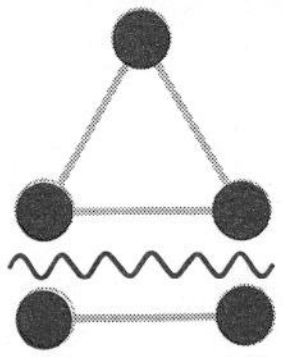 | Subgroups in disagreement with one another |

**FIGURE 8.3** Basic patterns of group interactions.

## Interacting, Coacting, and Counteracting Groups[7]

**Interacting groups** involve high interdependence among members in task performance. Each member interacts regularly with every other. You would expect to find this pattern in a medical team working on an emergency accident victim. Close coordination is required to manage the high level of interdependency and facilitate task performance.

Members of **coacting groups** work independently on common tasks. Members divide up the required labor and then work individually to fulfill this responsibility. A central control point is required to hold each member accountable and to accumulate the individual contributions into a final group product. Department store sales clerks work in coacting groups.

**Counteracting group** formations include the presence of subgroups which disagree on some aspect of overall group operations. These may be issue-specific disagreements, such as temporary debate over the best means to achieve a goal. They may also be of longer-term duration, such as labor management disputes. In either case, the interaction pattern involves polarized subgroups which contest one another's positions and therefore maintain restricted and sometimes antagonistic relations. Some of the implications of counteracting formations will become clearer in our later discussion of intergroup relations.

Checkpoint

Think of a student project group, for example a team completing a required course project, in which you have participated in your OB course or another class. Describe how it functioned in terms of the three interaction patterns above. Was the group successful in its interactions? Or was one or more of the patterns used inappropriately, or not at all?

## Group Communication Networks

**Communication** is discussed at length and defined in Chapter 14 as an interpersonal process of sending and receiving symbols with meanings attached to them. Communication allows group members to interact and complete their business. It enables members to get to know one another, learn norms, and distribute information required to accomplish necessary tasks.

Groups may structure themselves for communication in different

**Table 8.4 Interaction Patterns, Communication Networks, and Group Effectiveness**

| Group Effectiveness Criteria | Coacting or Centralized Networks | Interacting or Decentralized Networks |
|---|---|---|
| Member Satisfaction | Low[a] | High |
| Task Performance | | Low |
| Simple Tasks | High | |
| Complex Tasks | Low | High |

[a]Except for central person.

ways. Researchers have investigated decentralized and centralized communication networks, in particular, for their impact on group effectiveness.[8] These networks correspond to the interacting (decentralized) and coacting (centralized) patterns just reviewed.

Table 8.4 summarizes the key findings of research on communication networks within groups. In general, people tend to be better satisfied in decentralized groups. This results from more opportunities to be involved in information flows associated with work on the group task. The table also shows that the central person in the centralized network tends to be highly satisfied. Again, this is because of access to information.

Performance results vary with the nature of the group task. Centralized networks work better on simple tasks requiring little creativity, information processing, and problem-solving. Here, centralized groups will be faster and more accurate than decentralized groups. The reverse is true under more complex task conditions, where the decentralized group is the top performer.

## DECISION-MAKING METHODS IN GROUPS

One of the key activities in which group members engage is the making of decisions. **Decision-making** is the process of choosing among alternative courses of action. This process is discussed in Chapter 13 as an essential managerial skill. Here, our interest is focused on the alternative ways in which groups can make decisions as they share information and work on tasks. We sometimes criticize groups for their inability to make timely decisions or for making poor decisions. *Newsline 8.1,* in fact, offers an interesting example of the lengths to which people may go to help groups make decisions! Although you will most likely not require the extreme approach

## NEWSLINE 8.1

### Rome's Example

One can only admire the dispatch with which the College of Cardinals settled on John Paul I as the new Pope, and it's interesting to see how this oldest of all bureaucracies evolved such efficient procedures.

In the Middle Ages, we find, the cardinals took their time electing a new Pope because they were free of higher authority during the interregnum. In 1271, after an election that had lasted two years and nine months, the exasperated citizenry locked up the cardinals in a place until they produced a Pope. The new pontiff, Gregory X, thought this such a fine idea that he promulgated a new law of conclave, providing that the cardinals be sequestered and forbidden contact with the outside. Furthermore, he proclaimed that after three days they could be allowed only two dishes of food a day, and after eight days would be reduced to bread, wine, and water. The next conclave lasted a single day, and papal elections have been expeditious since.

Source: *The Wall Street Journal* (August 31, 1978), p. 14.

reported in the newsline, there are several considerations about group forms of decision-making which will be important to you as a manager.

## Types of Decision-Making Methods in Groups[9]

It would be nice if every group had an expert who could provide a correct solution to every problem. Unfortunately, it is not always apparent that an expert exists, and groups may find themselves compromised when a self-avowed or presumed "expert" commits errors. It is also convenient to delegate decision-making authority to a subgroup, such as an executive committee or special task force. This method minimizes the time demands on all group members, but it may result in some members who disagree with or feel they don't understand the final decision which the subgroup makes for them. Similar problems exist with majority voting. On very close ballots the "winners" and "losers" tend to emerge as coalitions. The losing members may or may not feel committed to follow the majority's wishes. In fact, the minority may actively work to undermine the majority and eventually achieve a reversal of the decision. Such dynamics can severely reduce a group's effectiveness.

Let's examine decision-making in groups in more detail. We are most interested in the individual, consultative, and group or consensus methods for arriving at a decision. The three methods are arranged on a continuum in Figure 8.4. Individual decisions tend to be

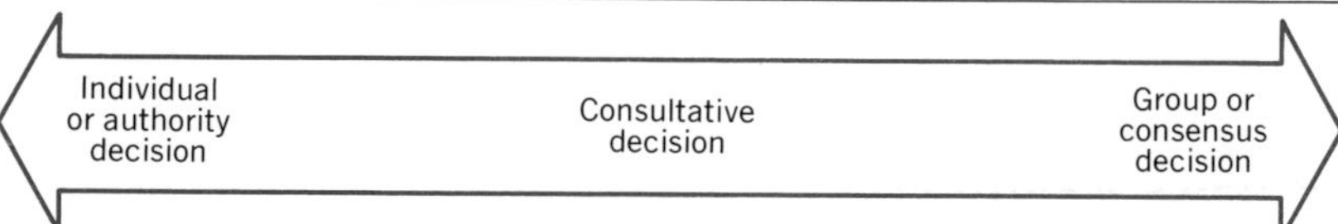


**FIGURE 8.4** A continuum of decision-making methods used by groups.

less time-consuming, while group-oriented decisions increase understanding and acceptance. Thus, a critical question to be answered by groups and by the managers of groups is when and under what conditions a particular method is the most desirable.

Look back to the continuum of methods shown in Figure 8.4. As you move to the right on the continuum, decisions become more group-oriented; as you move to the left, decisions reflect more the prerogatives of one person, perhaps an authority figure such as a chairperson or supervisor. The difference between individual and consultative decision-making is clear-cut. An **individual decision** is made by one person, such as an authority figure, and then communicated as a command to the group. No input is asked of other group members, and the person taking control essentially assumes that he or she has all the information required to make a good decision. Whenever an individual decision is made, the person so doing assumes that he or she is the group "expert" on the issue or task at hand.

A **consultative decision** is one for which each group member provides information, advice, or opinion, and then the authority figure makes a decision for the group. There are two forms of consultation. In one group, members are consulted individually; in the other, a group meeting is convened for purposes of the consultation. Consultation might well be transacted using a coacting group configuration.

In a **group or consensus decision,** everyone participates and finally agrees on the course of action to be taken. Here, complete unanimity is not the goal. Rather, the group process is successful enough that each member is ultimately able to accept the logic and feasibility of the final group decision. Consensus is achieved when any dissenting member is able to say:

> I understand what most of you would like to do. I personally would not do that, but I feel that you understand what my alternative would be. I have had sufficient opportunity to sway you to my point of view but clearly have not been able to do so. Therefore, I will gladly go along with what most of you wish to do.[10]

Groups seeking consensus will use the decentralized communications network and adopt an interacting configuration. The process of ar-

Group decision making.

riving at group consensus, however, is a particularly challenging one that demands participation and discipline from everyone. Some guidelines for persons who seek to facilitate group decisions by consensus are contained in the accompanying *What Consultants Do 8.1*.

## The Vroom-Yetton Decision-Making Model[11]

Victor Vroom and Phillip Yetton have developed a framework for helping managers choose which of the three decision-making methods is most appropriate for the various problem situations encountered in their day-to-day work efforts. Their framework begins by expanding the three basic decision-making methods into the five forms that follow.

*AI (First variant on the authority decision):* Manager solves the problem or makes the decision alone using information available at that time.

*AII (Second variant on the authority decision):* Manager obtains the necessary information from subordinate(s) or other group members, then decides on the problem solution. The manager may or may not tell subordinates what the problem is before obtaining the information from them. The subordinates provide

## WHAT CONSULTANTS DO 8.1

### Facilitating Group Consensus

Group consensus is difficult to reach. The following guidelines are offered by a consultant to group members interested in helping their groups to reach consensus.

1. Avoid blindly arguing for your own individual judgments. Present your position as clearly and logically as possible, but listen to other members' reactions and consider them carefully before you press your point.
2. Avoid changing your mind just to reach agreement and avoid conflict. Support only solutions which you are able to agree with to at least some degree. Yield only to positions that have objectives and logically sound foundations.
3. Avoid "conflict-reducing" procedures such as majority vote, tossing a coin, averaging, or bargaining in reaching decisions.
4. Seek out differences of opinion. They are natural and expected. Try to involve everyone in the decision process. Disagreements can help the group's decision because a wide range of information and opinions improves the chances for the group to hit upon more adequate solutions.
5. Do not assume that someone must win and someone must lose when discussions reach a stalemate. Instead, look for the next most acceptable alternative for all members.
6. Discuss underlying assumptions, listen carefully to one another, and encourage the participation of all members—three important factors in reaching decisions by consensus.

Source: These guidelines are found in "Decisions, Decisions, Decisions," *Psychology Today* (November 1971), pp. 55, 56.

the necessary information but do not generate or evaluate alternatives.

*CI (First variant on the consultative decision):* Manager shares the problem with relevant subordinates or other group members individually, getting their ideas and suggestions without bringing them together as a group. The manager then makes a decision which may or may not reflect subordinates' influence.

*CII (Second variant on the consultative decision):* Manager shares the problem with subordinates or other group members, collectively obtaining their ideas and suggestions. The manager then makes the decision, which may or may not reflect subordinates' influence.

*G (The group or consensus decision):* Manager shares the problem with subordinates as a total group and engages the group in consensus-seeking in order to arrive at a final decision.

The central proposition in the Vroom and Yetton model is that the decision-making method should be appropriate to the problem being solved. Thus, all decision methods are useful and important to a manager and each should be used over time. As a manager, therefore, you need two capabilities:

1. To be able to know when each decision-making method is best for the problem situation at hand.
2. To be able to implement each decision method when required.

Presently, we will help you to master the first of these capabilities. The many discussions of individual and group behavior throughout the book will help you to master the second.

Checkpoint

Assume you are manufacturing manager in a large electronics plant. The company's management wants to find ways to increase efficiency. New machines and a simplified work system have been installed, but the expected rise in productivity has not occurred. In fact, both production and quality have dropped, and employee turnover has risen.

There is evidence that there is nothing wrong with the machine.

You suspect that some parts of the new work system may be responsible for the change, but your immediate subordinates don't generally agree. They are four first-line supervisors and a supply manager. The drop in production has been attributed to: poor operator training, lack of financial incentives, and poor morale. There is considerable depth of feeling and potential disagreement among your subordinates.

This morning, you received a phone call from the division manager. He just saw your production figures. He indicated that you could solve the problem however you wanted, but to let him know within a week the steps you plan to take.

Both you and your subordinates share your boss's concern. How should you proceed in making a decision regarding the production problem? Would you make your decision via

AI? AII? CI? CII? G?

## Problem Attributes

Vroom and Yetton argue that a proper choice of decision-making method will depend on the basic attributes of the problem situation faced by the manager. We describe seven problem attributes in Table 8.5. Note that the table also identifies the diagnostic questions which a manager would ask to clarify each attribute for the various problems faced.

**Table 8.5 Problem Attributes Used in the Vroom and Yetton Decision-Making Model**

| Problem Attributes | Diagnostic Questions |
|---|---|
| *A*. The importance of the quality of the decision. | Is there a quality requirement such that one solution is likely to be more rational than another? |
| *B*. The extent to which the leader possesses sufficient information/ expertise to make a high-quality decision by himself or herself. | Do I have sufficient information to make a high-quality decision? |
| *C*. The extent to which the problem is structured. | Is the problem structured? Do you know what information is required or where it is? |
| *D*. The extent to which acceptance or commitment on the part of subordinates is critical to the effective implementation of the decision. | Is acceptance of decision by subordinates critical to effective implementation? Can you do it finally without their support? |
| *E*. The prior probability that the leader's autocratic decision will receive acceptance by subordinates. | If you were to make the decision by yourself, is it reasonably certain that it would be accepted by your subordinates? |
| *F*. The extent to which the subordinates are motivated to attain the organizational goals as represented in the objectives explicit in the statement of the problem. | Do subordinates share the organizational goals to be obtained in solving this problem? Or do they have personal considerations that might override? |
| *G*. The extent to which subordinates are likely to be in conflict over preferred solutions. | Is conflict among subordinates likely in preferred solutions? |

Source: Reprinted by permission of the publisher as adapted from "A New Look at Managerial Decision-Making" (Victor H. Vroom), *Organizational Dynamics* (Spring, 1973), copyright © 1973 by AMACOM, a division of American Management Associations (pp. 69–70). All rights reserved.

## Choosing a Decision-Making Method

Extensive research on decision-making has led Vroom and Yetton to develop the decision process flow chart shown in Figure 8.5. They offer the chart as a way for managers to analyze the attributes of problem situations and choose the most appropriate decision method.

To use the chart in Figure 8.5, start at the left and sequentially answer each of the diagnostic questions (A through G) for the problem at hand. Highlighted in the figure is the path most appropriate for the problem which we asked you to analyze in the prior Checkpoint. It shows that the problem would be best handled via a G method. That is, you share the problem with your subordinates and arrive at a consensus decision.

**Checkpoint**

Review the solution to the prior Checkpoint as shown in Figure 8.5, and make sure you understand why the diagnostic questions were answered in the stated fashion. Examine the comparability of your "gut-reaction" choice of decision method with the "ideal" choice determined through the Vroom and Yetton approach.

## Feasible Sets of Decision Methods

The "ideal" decision methods shown at the ends of the various paths in Figure 8.5 are the most time efficient methods. For each ideal

**FIGURE 8.5** The Vroom and Yetton decision process flow chart. (Source: Reprinted, by permissiion of the publisher, from "A New Look at Managerial Decision-Making," Victor H. Vroom, *Organizational Dynamics,* Spring 1973. Copyright © 1973 by AMACOM, a division of American Management Associations (pp. 69–70). All rights reserved.

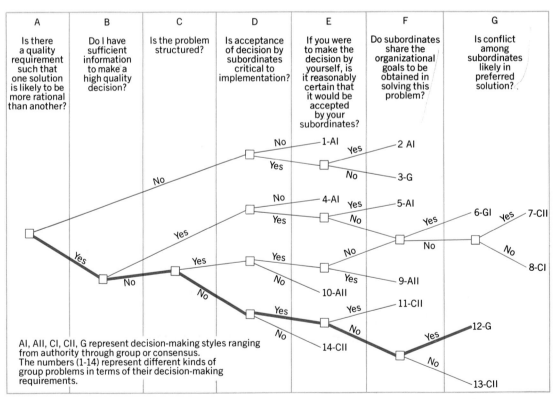

A
Is there a quality requirement such that one solution is likely to be more rational than another?
B
Do I have sufficient information to make a high quality decision?
C
Is the problem structured?
D
Is acceptance of decision by subordinates critical to implementation?
E
If you were to make the decision by yourself, is it reasonably certain that it would be accepted by your subordinates?
F
Do subordinates share the organizational goals to be obtained in solving this problem?
G
Is conflict among subordinates likely in preferred solution?

No
Yes
No
Yes
No
Yes
No
Yes
No
Yes
No
Yes
No
Yes
No
Yes
No
Yes
No
Yes
No
Yes
No
Yes
No
Yes
No
1-AI
2 AI
3-G
4-AI
5-AI
6-GI
7-CII
8-CI
9-AII
10-AII
11-CII
12-G
13-CII
14-CII

AI, AII, CI, CII, G represent decision-making styles ranging from authority through group or consensus.
The numbers (1-14) represent different kinds of group problems in terms of their decision-making requirements.

solution of the A and C type, a feasible set also exists. The A set includes the C and G options; the C set includes G as an option. To the extent that sufficient time is available, Vroom and Yetton suggest that choosing another option in the set allows for subordinate development by increasing opportunities to learn through participation in the problem-solving process.

### Summary Implications

The Vroom and Yetton model has been critized as complex and cumbersome.[13] We would agree, and certainly do not expect you to work through Figure 8.5 for every problem faced. Yet, there is a basic discipline in the model which is most useful. When you face decision situations in the future, a familiarity with this model will help you to recognize where time, quality requirements, information availability, and subordinate acceptance are critical issues affecting decision outcomes. Furthermore, the model helps you to understand that each of the decision methods is important and useful. The key is to implement each well and in situations for which it is the most appropriate response. To further help you develop this discipline, two more problem situations are offered in the case at the end of the chapter. They should be analyzed again using Figure 8.5.

## GROUP TASK AND MAINTENANCE ACTIVITIES

The activities in which group members engage can also be looked at from the perspective of the contributions made to the group process. Research on the social psychology of groups suggests that two broad types of activities are essential if group members are to work effectively together over time.[14] These are task and maintenance activities.

### Task Activities[15]

**Task activities** of group members focus on and contribute directly to the group's production purpose. They include efforts to define and solve problems relating to task accomplishment. Without relevant task activities, groups will have difficulty accomplishing their objectives. Group task performance depends upon members' willingness to contribute to group dynamics activities such as those described in Table 8.6.

**Table 8.6 Sample Group Task and Maintenance Activities**

| Task Activities | Maintenance Activities |
|---|---|
| Initiating | Encouraging |
| Seeking opinion | Harmonizing |
| Giving information | Setting standards |
| Clarifying | Accepting |
| Summarizing | Gate-keeping |

### Maintenance Activities[16]

Maintenance activities support the emotional life of the group as an ongoing social system. They help to strengthen and perpetuate the group as a social entity. These maintenance activities, listed in Table 8.6, help to enhance member satisfaction and thereby contribute, along with the task activities, to group effectiveness. When these activities are well performed, good interpersonal relationships should be achieved and the ability of the group to stay together over the longer term will be ensured.

### Distribution of Group Task and Maintenance Activities

Task and maintenance activities are skills. They can and should be learned by all persons, especially managers, who wish to be successful in helping groups perform.

Both task and maintenance activities are required for groups to be effective over the long run. Every member can assist the group by performing these functions. Although a formal authority, such as chairperson or supervisor, will do these activities, the responsibility for their occurrence is often shared and distributed among all group members. For anyone involved in group dynamics, this responsibility thereby includes

1. Correctly diagnosing group dynamics and recognizing when task maintenance activities are needed.
2. Responding by providing the required activities.

## INTER-GROUP RELATIONS[17]

As groups mature and take control of their internal group processes, attention eventually shifts to include the relationship between the group and others in its external setting. Such inter-group relations are especially important in complex organizations requiring the coordination of many groups in order to achieve their production purposes. The lack of adequate inter-group coordination is often a problem. Take, for example, colleges and universities where numerous separate departments are responsible for teaching specialized subjects. It would be impossible for a student to get a degree if the course offerings and program requirements weren't well coordinated across departments. But we all know that coordination occasionally does break down at considerable inconvenience to students. A common reason for such breakdowns is inter-group competition.

## Consequences of Inter-Group Competition

Managers strive to establish relationships among groups so that each group achieves maximum individual productivity and so that the

A student's view of inter-departmental coordination in a university.

accumulated results of all group efforts contribute to the accomplishment of the total organization's production purposes. This is the desired synergy among groups as human resources of organizations. Unfortunately, there is a tendency for groups to develop rivalries and even antagonisms with one another. The net result may have negative consequences for the organization.

Groups compete for rewards, status, resources, and special privileges, among other things. For groups in competition, the following may be observed.[18]

### WITHIN Each Competing Group:

- Members become closer knit and evidence increased group loyalty; group cohesion increases.
- Concern for the accomplishment of the group's task grows; members become more task-oriented.
- Group members become more willing to accept a single leader.
- Activities become more highly structured and organized.

### BETWEEN the Competing Groups:

- Each group views the other as an enemy.
- Each group tends to develop very positive images of itself and very negative images of the other; one's own group strengths are overestimated while those of the other are underestimated.
- Hostilities increase and communications decrease between the groups.
- When forced into interaction, group members listen only to what reinforces their original predispositions toward one another.

You can imagine the organizational difficulties which result from these inter-group dynamics. Managers walk a thin line as they try to realize some of the advantages of inter-group competition (such as increased cohesion and task orientation), while minimizing its disadvantages.

## Reducing the Disadvantages of Inter-Group Competition[19]

There are two approaches to the managing of inter-group competition. The first is to deal with the competition after it occurs; the second is to take action preventing its occurrence in the future.

## Controlling Existing Competition

Strategies for minimizing negative consequences when groups are in a state of competition include:

1. Identifying a common enemy (for example, another company to be outperformed).
2. Appealing to a common goal (for example, corporate profits or the welfare of students).
3. Bringing representative subgroups into direct negotiations with one another (see the accompanying *What Managers Do 8.1*).
4. Training members of the competing groups in group skills, and then engaging them in structural interactions (see the accompanying *What Consultants Do 8.2*).

## Preventing Future Disadvantages

Additional guidelines for preventing future disadvantages from inter-group competition include the following:

1. Reward groups on the basis of their contribution to the total organization rather than solely on individual group task accomplishment.

## WHAT MANAGERS DO 8.1

### Resolving Inter-Group Problems

One large university had very severe riots on its campus which led to a breakdown of communication between faculty, students, and administration. A planning team decided to hold a three-day conference away from the university for key representatives of the trustees, student body, faculty, and administration. The conference was designed by a group of invited consultants who were expert at group dynamics. Small problem identification teams were established in such a way that each of the key groups would get to know members of the other groups in a more personal, informal setting. The output of the small groups was thus twofold: at the formal level there were lists of priority problems which were then amalgamated into a master set of priorities in a plenary session; at the informal level, trust was reestablished among the various groups within the university, making possible further problem-solving activities back on the campus.

Source: Adapted from Edgar H. Schein, *Organizational Psychology*, Second Edition, © 1970, p 91. Reprinted by permission of Prentice-Hall.

## WHAT CONSULTANTS DO 8.2

### Training in Inter-Group Skills

A large oil refinery was having difficulty in its labor-management relations, and was threatened with having many of its employees vote to join a rather hostile and militant union. Several committees had been set up to find new solutions to the many problems brought up by the employees, but these committees invariably broke down in an antagonistic deadlock after a few meetings, with both labor and management members feeling that the other side was stubborn and recalcitrant.

The refinery instituted a training program devoted specifically to helping trainees become more familiar with problems of being an effective group leader and group member and with obtaining some insight into their own behavior in groups and their impact on other people. The program involved two weeks of full-time training in interpersonal relations and group dynamics, and resulted in considerable attitude change and personal insight for the trainees. The plan was eventually to have all members of management and the professional staff services, like research and engineering, attend the two-week program; but long before the goal had been accomplished, the labor crisis reached new proportions.

Management at this point decided to try still one more set of problem-solving committees, but this time, having gained some insight into group functioning, composed them and launched them in a very different manner. First of all, only management members who had been through the training program, and who were therefore assumed to be more sensitive to group problems, were put on the committees. Second, the groups were instructed not to arrive at decisions (in previous efforts the drive toward decisions had resulted in premature polarization of opinions) but to explore certain of the issues with the aim of identifying alternatives. Third, the management members were carefully instructed to allow the initiative for meeting times, locations, and agenda details to remain with the labor members.

From the outset, these committees had a very different kind of climate. They were oriented far more toward problem-solving than toward worrying about which member had how much status; and indeed, they generated proposals which met the desires of both workers and managers, and thus led to an overwhelming defeat of the militant union's effort to organize the refinery.

Source: Adapted from Edgar H. Schein, *Organizational Psychology,* Second Edition, © 1970, p 90. Reprinted by permission of Prentice-Hall.

2. Reward groups for the help they give one another.
3. Stimulate frequent interaction between groups; avoid tendencies for the groups to withdraw and become isolated from one another.
4. Rotate members among the various groups whenever possible.
5. Avoid putting groups in positions of win-lose competition to obtain desired organizational rewards; emphasize the sharing of resources for maximum benefit to the organization.

## SUMMARY

In this chapter, we have looked intensely at group dynamics, forces present within groups that affect performance and membership satisfaction. We began with Homans' model of group dynamics, which describes a group in terms of required and emergent behaviors, as well as activities, interactions, and sentiments. Our attention then shifted to a more in-depth look at how the latter manifest themselves in the forms of group norms and cohesion, interaction patterns and communication networks, decision-making methods, task and maintenance activities, and inter-group relations.

Norms refer to the behavior expected of other group members. Cohesiveness refers to the degree to which members are attracted to and motivated to remain part of the group. In combination, these two concepts have a substantial influence on group effectiveness, either positively or negatively.

There are three important interaction patterns in groups: (1) interacting (where there is high interdependence on task performance); (2) coacting (where members perform essentially independent task functions); and (3) counteracting (where groups work at cross purposes with each other). These, in turn, influence communication networks. Interacting structures provide for decentralized communication networks and coacting structures provide for decentralized networks. The effectiveness of the two networks varies with the nature of the task to be performed.

Decision-making methods range on a continuum from individual or authority (where the manager makes the decision and then communicates it) through consultative, (where subordinates are consulted but the manager makes the decision) to group or consensus (where everyone in the group agrees on the decision). Vroom and Yetton have developed a model which helps managers to choose the most appropriate decision method depending upon the quality and acceptance needed and the time available to the group.

In terms of group member activities, the manager is especially concerned with those involving task and group maintenance roles. The former facilitates completion of the group's task. The latter is concerned with maintaining the group as a going concern. The chapter discussed these activities and showed that even though performed by the manager, the activities should also be distributed across the group members if a group is to be successful in the long run.

Finally, a manager is not concerned with the work group alone. He or she must be sensitive to inter-group relations. Thus, we have concluded this chapter by looking at inter-group dynamics and examining ways of managing them for constructive rather than destructive results.

## THINKING THROUGH THE ISSUES

1. Apply the concepts of activities, interactions, and sentiments to the "Case of the Changing Cage." Distinguish for each concept its required and emergent forms in the case.
2. List the factors which originally fostered high cohesiveness in the voucher-check filing unit in the "Case of the Changing Cage." Which of these were disrupted after the move? With what result?
3. What can a manager do to increase the cohesiveness of a work group?
4. Suppose you are the manager of a work group which displays a negative performance norm. What would you do to overcome its negative effects? Why?
5. Explain why it is that the variability in group performance will be less in a highly cohesive group, but that the level of performance will depend upon the group productivity norm.
6. Explain why it is that centralized communication networks seem to be better for simple tasks, while decentralized networks are better for more complex tasks.
7. Some people have argued that it is "good" to have participation in decision-making and "bad" for the boss to make the decision alone. React to this in terms of the chapter discussion and the Vroom-Yetton model.
8. Think of one of your class project groups and determine the extent to which task and maintenance activities were distributed among the members over the life of the group.

## CASE: CHOOSING A DECISION-MAKING METHOD[20]

Harold Jones is being considered by top management in his company for promotion to a junior executive position. He is now participating in a formal assessment exercise where he has been asked to respond to various case problems. Harold needs to choose, in particular, which group decision method (authority, consultative, group consensus) he would employ in the two situations that follow. Using the Vroom and Yetton framework as depicted in Figure 8.5 earlier in the chapter, which method would you recommend in each situation and why?

### Situation 1. The Oil Pipeline Gang

You are general foreman in charge of a large gang laying an oil pipeline. It is now necessary to estimate your expected rate of progress in order to schedule material deliveries to the next field site.

You know the nature of the terrain you will be traveling, and have the historical data needed to compute the mean and variance in the rate of speed over that type of terrain. Given these two variables, it is a simple matter to calculate the earliest and latest times at which materials and support facilities willbe needed at the next site. It is important that your estimate be reasonably accurate. Underestimates result in idle foremen and workers, and an overestimate results in tying up materials for a period of time before they are to be used.

Progress has been good, and your five foremen and other members of the gang stand to receive substantial bonuses if the project is completed ahead of schedule.

### Situation 2. The Financial Staff Unit

You are the head of a staff unit reporting to the vice-president of finance. He has asked you to provide a report on the firm's current portfolio to include recommendations for changes in the selection criteria currently employed. Doubts have been raised about the efficiency of the existing system in the current market conditions, and there is a considerable dissatisfaction with prevailing rates of return.

You plan to write the report, but at the moment you are quite perplexed about the approach to take. Your own specialty is the bond market and it is clear to you that a detailed knowledge of the equity market, which you lack, would greatly enhance the value of the report. Fortunately, four members of your staff are specialists in different segments of the equity market. Together, they possess a vast amount of knowledge about the intricacies of investment. However, they seldom agree on the best way to achieve anything when it comes to the stock market. While they are obviously conscientious as well as knowledgeable, they have major differences when it comes to investment philosophy and strategy.

You have six weeks before the report is due. You have already begun to familiarize yourself with the firm's current portfolio and have been provided by management with a specific set of constraints that any portfolio must satisfy. Your immediate problem is to come up with some alternatives to the firm's present practices and select the most promising for detailed analysis in your report.

## THE MANAGER'S VOCABULARY

**Activities** The verbal and nonverbal behaviors in which group members engage.

**Coacting Groups** Work independently on common tasks.

**Cohesiveness** Degree to which members are attracted to and motivated to remain part of a group.

**Communication** Interpersonal process of sending and receiving symbols with meanings attached to them.

**Consultative Decision** One for which each group member provides information, advice, or opinion, and then the authority figure makes a decision for the group.

**Counteracting Groups** Include the presence of subgroups which disagree on some aspect of overall group operations.

**Decision-Making** Process of choosing among alternative courses of action.

**Emergent Behaviors** What group members do in addition to or in replacement of what is asked by the organization.

**Group or Consensus Decision** One in which everyone participates and finally agrees on the course of action to be taken.

**Group Dynamics** Forces operating in groups which affect group performance and member satisfaction.

**Individual Decision** Made by one person, such as an authority figure, and then communicated as a command to the group.

**Interacting Groups** High interdependence among members in task performance.

**Interactions** Behaviors which group members direct toward other persons.

**Maintenance Activities** Support the emotional life of the group as an ongoing social system.

**Required Behaviors** Those which the organization requests as a basis for membership and support.

**Sentiments** Feelings, attitudes, beliefs, or values held by group members.

**Task Activities** Focus directly on the group's production purpose.

## Important Names

**George C. Homans** Offers a model of group dynamics that includes activities, interactions, and sentiments, and which differentiates required and emergent behaviors.

**Victor Vroom and Phillip Yetton** Developed a framework for helping managers to choose among authoritative, consultative, and group decision-making methods.

## Notes

[1]William G. Dyer, *Team Building,* copyright © 1977, Addison-Wesley Publishing Company, Inc., Chapter 4, pages 34, 36, 37, Chapter 6, pages 6, 55, 56, 64–67. Reprinted with permission.

[2]This discussion is based on George C. Homans, *The Human Group* (New York: Harcourt, Brace and World, 1950).

[3]This incident was obtained from Dorothy N. Harlow and Jean J. Hanke, *Behavior in Organizations* (Boston: Little, Brown and Company, 1975), pp. 244–245. The original source cannot be located.

[4]Robert F. Allen and Saul Pilnick, "Confronting the Shadow Organization: How to Detect and Defeat Negative Nouns," *Organizational Dynamics* (Spring 1973), pp. 6–10.

[5]Marvin E. Shaw, *Group Dynamics* (New York: McGraw-Hill, 1971), pp. 110–112.

[6]Ibid., p. 192.

[7]This discussion is based on Fred E. Fiedler, *A Theory of Leadership Productivity* (New York: McGraw-Hill, 1967).

[8]Alex Bavelas, "Communication Patterns in Task-Oriented Groups," *Journal of the Accoustical Society of America,* Vol. 22 (1950), pp. 725–730; see also the Research on Communication Networks as summarized in Shaw, op. cit., pp. 137–153.

[9]Adapted from a discussion by Edgar H. Schein, *Process Consultation: Its Role in Organization Development* (Reading, Mass.: Addison-Wesley, 1969), pp. 53–57.

[10]Ibid., p. 56.

[11]The material in this section is based on Victor H. Vroom, "A New Look in Managerial Decision-making," *Organizational Dynamics* (Spring 1973), pp. 66–80.

[12]This problem situation is from Victor H. Vroom and Phillip Yetton, *Leadership and Decision-Making* (Pittsburgh: University of Pittsburgh Press, 1973).

[13]R. H. G. Field, "A Critique of the Vroom-Yetton Contingency Model of Leader Behavior," *Academy of Management Review,* Vol. 4 (April 1979), pp. 249–257.

[14]Robert F. Bales, "Task Roles and Social Roles in Problem-Solving Groups," in Eleanor E. Maccoby, Theodore M. Newcomb, and E. L. Hartley (eds.), *Readings in Social Psychology* (New York: Holt, Rinehart & Winston, 1958).

[15]This discussion is based on Schein, op. cit., pp. 39–41, and Rensis Likert, *New Patterns of Management* (New York: McGraw-Hill, 1961), pp. 166–169.

[16]Ibid.

[17]This discussion is based on Edgar H. Schein, *Organizational Psychology,* Second Edition (Englewood Cliffs, N.J.: Prentice-Hall, 1970), pp. 96–103.

[18]Ibid., p. 97.

[19]Ibid., pp. 99–102.

[20]The two problem situations are from Vroom and Yetton, op. cit.

# 9

# GROUP DEVELOPMENT AND CREATIVE WORK GROUP DESIGN

# THE ABILENE PARADOX[1]

The July afternoon in Coleman, Texas (population 5,607) was particularly hot—104 degrees as measured by the Walgreen's Rexall Ex-Lax temperature gauge. In addition, the wind was blowing fine-grained West Texas topsoil through the house. But the afternoon was still tolerable—even potentially enjoyable. There was a fan going on the back porch; there was cold lemonade; and finally, there was entertainment. Dominoes. Perfect for the conditions. The game required little more physical exertion than an occasional mumbled comment, "Shuffle 'em," and an unhurried movement of the arm to place the spots in the appropriate perspective on the table. All in all, it had the makings of an agreeable Sunday afternoon in Coleman—that is, until my father-in-law suddenly said, "Let's get in the car and go to Abilene and have dinner at the cafeteria."

I thought, What, go to Abilene? Fifty-three miles? In this dust storm and heat? And in an unairconditioned 1958 Buick?

But my wife chimed in with, "Sounds like a great idea. I'd like to go. How about you, Jerry?" Since my own preferences were obviously out of step with the rest I replied, "Sounds good to me," and added, "I just hope your mother wants to go."

"Of course I want to go," said my mother-in-law. "I haven't been to Abilene in a long time."

So into the car and off to Abilene we went. My predictions were fulfilled. The heat was brutal. We were coated with a fine layer of dust that was cemented with perspiration by the time we arrived. The food at the cafeteria provided first-rate testimonial material for antacid commercials.

Some four hours and 106 miles later we returned to Coleman, hot and exhausted. We sat in front of the fan for a long time in silence. Then, both to be sociable and to break the silence, I said, "It was a great trip, wasn't it?"

No one spoke.

Finally my mother-in-law said, with some irritation, "Well, to tell the truth, I really didn't enjoy it much and would rather have stayed here. I just went along because the three of you were so enthusiastic about going. I wouldn't have gone if you all hadn't pressured me into it."

I couldn't believe it. "What do mean, 'you all'?" I said. "Don't put me in the 'you all' group. I was delighted to be doing what we were doing. I didn't want to go. I only went to satisfy the rest of you. You're the culprits."

My wife looked shocked. "Don't call me a culprit. You and Daddy and Mamma were the ones who wanted to go. I just went along to be sociable and to keep you happy. I would have had to be crazy to want to go out in heat like that."

Her father entered the conversation abruptly. "Hell!" he said.

He proceeded to expand on what was already absolutely clear. "Listen, I never wanted to go to Abilene. I just thought you might be bored. You visit so seldom I wanted to be sure you enjoyed it. I would have preferred to play another game of dominoes and eat the leftovers in the icebox."

After the outburst of recrimination we all sat back in silence. Here we were, four reasonably sensible people who, of our own volition, had just taken a 106-mile trip across a godforsaken desert in a furnace-like temperature through a cloud-like dust storm to eat unpalatable food at a hole-in-the-wall cafeteria in Abilene, when none of us had really wanted to go. In fact, to be more accurate, we'd done just the opposite of what we wanted to do. The whole situation simply didn't make sense.

**MANAGEMENT APPLICATIONS QUESTION**

There are many "roads to Abilene" which can threaten the effectiveness of groups in organizations. What can managers do to facilitate group development and to creatively design group tasks to ensure performance success and human resource maintenance?

## PLANNING AHEAD

**A thorough understanding of the following issues can help you to better manage groups as human resources of organizations:**

**The Stages of Group Development**
**Facilitating Individual Entry**
**Influencing Norms and Cohesion**
**Team-Building**
**Creative Work Group Designs**

Dilemmas such as the one posed in "The Abilene Paradox" which introduced this chapter can sidetrack even the best intentions of work groups. Managers are therefore challenged to both understand the various group dynamics described in Chapter 8 and to direct them toward constructive as opposed to destructive results. To help you to achieve this latter goal, this chapter focuses on the various stages of group development and the key managerial implications of each stage. The chapter concludes with case examples of creative work group designs which have been adopted by organizations.

## THE STAGES OF GROUP DEVELOPMENT

Because newly formed groups show quite different behavior patterns from mature ones, it's important to know the stage of development of a given group. This knowledge should help you predict the kinds of behavior most likely to occur and understand why one group acts one way and another quite different. A synthesis of the research on small groups suggests that there are four distinct phases of group development: (1) forming, (2) storming, (3) initial integration, and (4) total integration.[2]

### Forming Stage

The forming stage involves the initial entry of individual members into the group. At this point individuals ask a number of questions as they begin to identify with other group members and the group itself. What can or does the group offer its members? What will they be asked to contribute? Can individual needs be met at the same time that individual contributions serve the needs of the group?

In the forming stage, people are concerned to discover what is considered acceptable behavior and what the real task of the group is. Defining group boundaries and group rules is important. In a work group, this identification process is likely to be more complicated than in other group settings. The work setting may consist of individuals who have been in the organization for substantial time periods. Such things as multiple group memberships and identifications, prior experience with task group members in other contexts, and impressions of organization philosophies, goals, and policies may all affect newly formed work groups.

### Storming Stage

This second stage of group development is a period of high emotionality. There may be periods of overt hostility and in-fighting. Typically, the storming period involves relatively high tension among the members.

During the storming period, changes occur in the group. Required activities are further elaborated, and attention is shifted toward obstacles standing in the way of group goals. In work groups individuals begin to clarify one another's interpersonal styles. Efforts will be made to find appropriate ways to accomplish group goals while also satisfying individual needs.

Outside demands create pressures. Coalitions or cliques may

form as subgroups on an emergent and informal basis. Conflict may develop over authority as individuals compete to try to impose their preferences on the group and to achieve their desired position in the group's status structure.

## Initial Integration

While the storming phase is characterized by differences among group members, the next phase of group development stresses integration. Here, the group begins to become coordinated as a working unit. The probes and jockeying behaviors of the storming phase lead to a precarious balancing of forces. Group members strive to maintain this balance. The group will try to regulate individual behavior toward this end. Members are likely to develop a sense (although possibly superficial) of closeness, an interacting communication network, a division of labor, and norms designed to protect the group from disintegration. Indeed, holding the group together may become more important than successful task accomplishment.

During initial integration, cohesion is emphasized and minority viewpoints may be strongly discouraged. This stage is perhaps descriptive of the family that went to Abilene even though no one really wanted to go. Although a group may feel a sense of integration at this stage, it may be superficial rather than genuine.

## Total Integration

Total integration characterizes a mature, organized, and well functioning group. The integration is now completed. The group is able to deal with complex tasks and to handle membership disagreements in creative ways. Group structure is stable, and members are motivated by group goals. The primary challenges of this stage are to continue working together as an integrated unit, to remain coordinated with the larger organization, and to successfully adapt to changing conditions over time. A group that has achieved total integration will score high on the criteria of group maturity presented in Figure 9.1.

### Checkpoint

Choose a group to which you belong, perhaps your OB class or project group might serve as an example. Rate this group using Figure 9.1. What needs to be done to help this group achieve or maintain total integration? Students in project groups often mistake stage 3 for stage 4. Has this happened in one of your groups? Why might it happen?

**FIGURE 9.1** Criteria of group maturity. (Source: Edgar H. Schein, *Process Consultation,* Copyright © 1969, Addison-Wesley Publishing Company, Inc., Chapter 6, p. 62, Figure 6.1, "A Mature Group Processes." Reprinted with permission.)

A MATURE GROUP POSSESSES:

1. Adequate mechanisms for getting feedback:

| Poor feedback mechanisms | 1 2 3 4 5 (Average) | Excellent feedback mechanisms |
|---|---|---|

2. Adequate decision-making procedure:

| Poor decision-making procedure | 1 2 3 4 5 (Average) | Very adequate decision-making |
|---|---|---|

3. Optimal cohesion:

| Low cohesion | 1 2 3 4 5 (Average) | Optimal cohesion |
|---|---|---|

4. Flexible organization and procedures:

| Very inflexible | 1 2 3 4 5 (Average) | Very flexible |
|---|---|---|

5. Maximum use of member resources:

| Poor use of resources | 1 2 3 4 5 (Average) | Excellent use of resources |
|---|---|---|

6. Clear communications:

| Poor communication | 1 2 3 4 5 (Average) | Excellent communication |
|---|---|---|

7. Clear goals accepted by members:

| Unclear goals—not accepted | 1 2 3 4 5 (Average) | Very clear goals—accepted |
|---|---|---|

8. Feelings of interdependence with authority persons:

| No interdependence | 1 2 3 4 5 (Average) | High interdependence |
|---|---|---|

9. Shared participation in leadership functions:

| No shared participation | 1 2 3 4 5 (Average) | High shared participation |
|---|---|---|

10. Acceptance of minority views and persons:

| No acceptance | 1 2 3 4 5 (Average) | High acceptance |
|---|---|---|

**Table 9.1 The Stages of Group Development and Their Associated Management Challenges**

| Time | Stages of Group Development | Management Problems |
|---|---|---|
| Immature group; early in its life | Forming | Facilitating individual entry |
| ↓ | Storming | Developing norms |
| | Initial integration | Influencing cohesiveness |
| Mature group; later in its life | Total integration | Team-building |

Table 9.1 summarizes selected managerial problems which are fundamental to each stage of group development. These problems include the management of individual entry (forming stage), norm development (storming stage), cohesiveness (initial integration stage), and team-building (total integration stage). A manager's job is to take action so that these needs are satisfied and group efforts are applied in support of the organization's production purposes. The managerial implications of Table 9.1 are discussed below.

## FACILITATING INDIVIDUAL ENTRY

There are many specific issues facing the members of work groups. Some examples are presented in Table 9.2. The table also relates each specific issue to a set of questions which a concerned group

**Table 9.2 Some Dilemmas Facing Work Groups and Their Members**

| Membership Issue | Individual Questions |
|---|---|
| Participation | Do I want to participate?<br>To what extent? |
| Goals | Do I share any goals with the group? |
| Control | Who values the decisions?<br>To what extent can I influence what takes place? |
| Relationships | How close will we become?<br>How close do I want to get? |
| Processes | Can I disagree?<br>How will conflict be resolved?<br>Is information shared freely? |

member may be led to ask. The questions, in turn, summarize the many dilemmas which may puzzle individuals upon initial entry to a group. Questions regarding atmosphere and relationships, for example, may create the dilemma of "How friendly do I want to be? How close? Will others allow that?" These dilemmas may occur during any stage of group development, but are especially likely in the forming stage or whenever a new member joins the group. We refer to these dilemmas as problems of individual entry. Their importance lies in that

Individual entry dilemmas $\xrightarrow[\text{cause}]{\text{may}}$ operating problems $\xrightarrow[\text{impair}]{\text{that}}$ group effectiveness

## Individual Problems upon Entering Groups[3]

Edgar Schein, a noted social psychologist, offers a set of profiles of individuals who encounter difficulties upon entering groups. The profiles include the "tough battler," "friendly helper," and the "objective thinker." They are associated with coping responses that individuals may adopt in response to the dilemmas described in Table 9.2. These coping responses often include self-serving activities which interfere with, rather than facilitate, group effectiveness.

Consider the profiles described below. Have you seen such people in your course projects or other work groups? Would one of these profiles describe your behavior in a group? What do managers need to do to help individuals to overcome these entry problems and become productive and satisified group members?

**The Tough Battler.** Group members frustrated by identity problems may act aggressive and tend to resist the ideas and authority of others. These "tough battlers" are seeking answers to the question: "Who am I in this group?"

**The Friendly Helper.** Initial entry into a group can create tensions as people try to solve problems of control and intimacy. These tensions may lead to showing support for others, acting dependent, and helping and forming supportive alliances. The "friendly helper" is trying to determine whether or not he or she will be liked by the other group members, and if he or she will be able to exert any control or influence over their behavior.

**The Objective Thinker.** Another anxiety which accompanies individual entry into a group is needs and goals. People join groups for various reasons and seek many types of need satisfactions from their group memberships. Initial passivity, indifference, or oneness of logic or reason in deliberations often characterize the "objective thinker." This person is trying to determine if group goals include opportunities to satisfy personal needs.

### Clarifying Membership Expectations

Individuals are expected to contribute efforts to their groups, and they expect certain inducements in return. The psychological contract of membership is based on a fair and equitable exchange of these values. Problems experienced by individuals upon entering groups often reflect uncertainties regarding expected work roles and opportunities to satisfy needs. Similar problems may occur over time as a group matures or changes to meet challenges in the setting and as individuals personally develop. There is a continuing challenge in any group to maintain clarity of membership expectations. A managerial strategy for accomplishing this both at the point of initial entry and over time is called "role negotiations."

This is a technique sometimes used by consultants who find their client groups unable to coordinate individual efforts for the common good. Managers and concerned group members may follow the steps listed below to facilitate role negotiations.[4]

1. Individuals write lists of things they would like to see other group members (a) do more or do better, (b) do less or stop doing, and (c) keep doing or remain unchanged.
2. These lists are shared and discussed.
3. Individuals negotiate contracts with one another specifying action commitments which will help satisfy the other's needs and enhance group effectiveness.
4. The contracts are summarized in written form as a reminder to all members of their commitments.
5. The contracts are revised at regular intervals to update and further clarify group membership roles.

Sample material from an actual role negotiation is shown in the accompanying *What Consultants Do 9.1*. Note the presence of a true "give and take" in the final written agreements among the participating group members.

## INFLUENCING NORMS AND COHESION

Group norms and the level of cohesion interrelate with one another to affect the behavior of group members. As noted in Chapter 8, this effect can include positive or negative consequences for work group

## WHAT CONSULTANTS DO 9.1

### Role Negotiations

Issue Diagnosis Form

Messages from ______________________

to ______________________

1. If you were to do the following things *more* or *better,* it would help me to increase my own effectiveness:

- BE MORE RECEPTIVE TO IMPROVEMENT SUGGESTIONS FROM THE PROCESS ENGINEERS
- GIVE HELP ON COST CONTROL (SEE 2)
- FIGHT HARDER WITH THE G. M. TO GET OUR PLAN IMPROVED.

2. If you were to do the following things *less,* or were to *stop* doing them, it would help me to increase my own effectiveness:

- ACTING AS JUDGE AND JURY ON COST CONTROL
- CHECKING UP FREQUENTLY ON SMALL DETAILS OF THE WORK.
- ASKING FOR SO MANY DETAILED PROGRESS REPORTS.

3. The following things which you have been doing help to increase my own effectiveness, and I hope you will continue to do them:

- PASSING ON FULL INFORMATION IN OUR WEEKLY MEETINGS.
- BEING AVAILABLE WHEN I NEED TO TALK TO YOU.

**Final agreement between James Farrell and David Sills**

*Jim agrees to let David know as soon as agreed completion dates and cost projections look as though they won't be met, and also to discuss each project's progress fully with David on a bi-weekly basis.*

*In return David agrees not to raise questions about cost details and completion dates, pending a trial of this agreement to see if it provides sufficient information soon enough to deal with questions from above.*

Source: Roger Harrison, "When Power Conflicts Trigger Team Spirit," *European Business* (Spring 1972), pp. 61, 63. Used by permission.

effectiveness. Managers should be skilled both at influencing norms and at controlling cohesion so that group task performance and member satisfaction are best served.

### Building Positive Norms

Group norms are essentially determined by the collective will of group members. As such it is very difficult for organizations and their managers to dictate which norms a given work group will possess. Thus, the concerned manager must use his or her knowledge of group dynamics very wisely to help group members to adopt norms supportive of organizational goals.

In Chapter 8 we discussed various types of group norms. Table 9.3 now equates the focus of norm-building efforts to the stages of group development. In the forming and storming stages, norms relating to membership issues such as expected attendance and levels of commitment are important. By the time a group reaches the stage of total integration, growth-oriented norms relating to adaptability and change become most relevant. Groups which are unable to build norms consistent with the operating problems faced at various stages of development may well compromise their effectiveness.

Among the means which you may use as a manager to help groups build positive norms are the following.[5]

1. Acting as a positive role model.
2. Reinforcing, via rewards, the desired behaviors.
3. Controlling results by performance reviews and regular feedback.
4. Training and orientating new members to adopt desired behaviors.
5. Recruiting and selecting new members who exhibit the desired behaviors.
6. Holding regular meetings to discuss group progress and ways of improving task performance and member satisfaction.
7. Using group decision-making methods to reach agreement on appropriate behaviors.

**Table 9.3 Typical Sequence of Norm Development in Work Groups**

| Stage of the Group | Focus of Group Norms | Illustrative Behaviors Addressed |
|---|---|---|
| Early | Membership | Who is and is not a member, attendance at group meetings, punctuality, commitment. |
| ↓ | Influence | Leadership roles, strategies for doing the work of the group, status, and dominance relations among members. |
| ↓ | Affection | Patterns of intermember liking and disliking, balance between task work and interpersonal relationships. |
| Late | Growth | Experimentation with new behaviors, adaptation of group norms, and processes to a changing environment. |

Source: From David A. Nadler, J. Richard Hackman, and Edward E. Lawler, III, *Managing Organizational Behavior,* p. 124. Copyright © 1979 by David A. Nadler, J. Richard Hackman and Edward E. Lawler, III. Reprinted by permission of the authors and Little, Brown and Company.

## Influencing Cohesion

As pointed out in Chapter 8, there are advantages and disadvantages to high group cohesiveness. Members of highly cohesive groups typically experience satisfaction from the group affiliation. When norms related to performance are positive, high cohesiveness contributes to high levels of task accomplishment. To the extent the performance norms are negative, however, high cohesiveness can restrict task accomplishments and work to the detriment of the organization.

Given these two sides of cohesion, the positive and the negative, there will be times when a manager will want to build cohesiveness in work groups, and there may be times when the objective is to break down cohesiveness. A number of things managers can do to increase and decrease group cohesion are listed in Table 9.4.

## "Groupthink"

There is another, more subtle side to group cohesion that can work to a group's disadvantage. Do you recall the Abilene paradox used to introduce this chapter? Now consider an example of how the paradox actually operates in the world of business.[6]

### The Boardroom

The Ozyx Corporation is a relatively small industrial company whose managers have embarked on a trip to Abilene. The president of Ozyx has hired a consultant to help discover the reasons for the poor profit picture of the company in general, and the low morale and productivity of the R&D division in particular. During the process of investigation, the consultant becomes interested in a research project in which the company has invested a sizeable proportion of its R&D budget.

When asked about the project by the consultant in the privacy of their offices, the president, the vice-president for research, and the research manager each describe it as an idea that looks great on paper but will ultimately fail because of the unavailability of the technology required to make it work. Each of them also acknowledges that continued support of the project will create cash flow problems that will jeopardize the very existence of the total organization.

Furthermore, each individual indicates he or she has not told the others about his reservations. When asked why, the president says he can't reveal his "true" feelings because abandoning the project, which has been widely publicized, would make the company look bad in the press. In addition, it would probably cause his vice-pres-

**Table 9.4 Managerial Strategies for Increasing and Decreasing Group Cohesion**

*Actions to Increase Cohesion:*

Induce agreement on group goals
Increase membership homogeneity
Increase interactions among members
Decrease group size
Introduce competition with other groups
Allocate rewards to the group rather than individuals
Provide physical isolation from other groups

*Actions to Decrease Cohesion:*

Induce disagreement on group goals
Increase membership heterogeneity
Restrict interactions among members
Increase group size
Allocate rewards to individuals rather than the group as a whole
Remove physical isolation
Introduce a dominating member
Disband the group

ident's ulcer to kick up or perhaps even cause her to quit, "Because she has staked her professional reputation on the project's success."

Similarly, the vice-president for research says she can't let the president or the research manager know her reservations because the president is so committed to it that "I would probably get fired for insubordination if I questioned the project."

Finally, the research manager says he can't let the president or vice-president know of his doubts about the project because of their extreme commitment to the project's success.

All indicate that, in meetings with one another, they try to maintain an optimistic facade so the others won't worry unduly about the project. The research director, in particular, admits to writing ambiguous progress reports so the president and the vice-president can "interpret them to suit themselves." In fact, he says he tends to slant them to the "positive" side, "given how committed the brass are."

The scent of the Abilene trail wafts from a paneled conference room where the project research budget is being considered for the following fiscal year. In the meeting itself, praises are heaped on the questionable project, and a unanimous decision is made to continue it for yet another year. Symbolically, the organization has boarded a bus to Abilene.

## Avoiding "Groupthink"

Groups which fall prey to the Abilene paradox have difficulty managing agreement. Their members are prone to publicly agree with courses of action while privately having serious personal reservations. Group cohesion is a key force in these situations. In fact, research documents a tendency for members of highly cohesive groups to lose their willingness and abilities to critically evaluate one another's ideas and suggestions. As a result, desires to hold the group together and to avoid unpleasant disagreements lead to an overemphasis on concurrence and an underemphasis on realistically appraising alternative courses of action. Irving Janis calls this phenomenon **groupthink,** a tendency for highly cohesive groups to lose their critical evaluative capabilities.[7]

Groupthink is attributed by Janis to a variety of well-known historical fiascoes. They include the lack of preparedness of the U.S. Naval forces for the 1941 Japanese attack on Pearl Harbor, President Kennedy's handling of the Bay of Pigs, and the many roads which led to the United States involvement in Vietnam. Groupthink can occur anywhere. It may have led to President Nixon's downfall in the Watergate fiasco.

Table 9.5 lists a number of symptoms of groupthink. Do you recognize any of these signs in groups with which you are familiar? When and if you ever do experience groupthink as a manager, Janis suggests the following action guidelines for avoiding its negative consequences.[8]

1. Assign the role of critical evaluator to each group member; encourage a sharing of objections.
2. Avoid, as a leader, seeming partial to one course of action.
3. Create subgroups operating under different leaders and working on the same problem.
4. Have group members discuss issues with subordinates and report back on their reactions.

**Table 9.5 Symptoms of Groupthink**

| |
|---|
| Illusions of group invulnerability |
| Rationalizing unpleasant and disconfirming data |
| Belief in inherent group morality |
| Stereotyping competitors as weak, evil, and stupid |
| Applying direct pressure to deviants to conform to group wishes |
| Self-censorship by members |
| Illusions of unanimity |
| Mindguarding—members protecting the group from disturbing ideas or viewpoints |

Source: See Irving Janis, *Victims of Groupthink* (Boston: Houghton Mifflin Co., 1972).

5. Invite outside experts to observe group activities and react to group processes and decisions.
6. Assign one member to play a "devil's advocate" role at each meeting.
7. Write alternative scenarios for the intentions of competing groups.
8. Hold "second-chance" meetings after consensus is apparently achieved on key issues.

## TEAM-BUILDING[9]

When we think of the word "teams," sporting teams come to mind. The Dallas Cowboys, New York Yankees, and the U.S. Olympic team are good examples. We know, too, that sporting teams have their problems. Members slack off or become disgruntled, and some get retired or traded to other teams as a result. Even world champion teams have losing streaks, and the most highly-talented players are prone to lose motivation at times, quibble among themselves, and go into slumps. When these things happen, the owners, managers, and players are apt to examine their problems and take corrective action to "rebuild the team" and restore what we have been calling group effectiveness.

Work groups are teams in a similar sense. Like sporting teams, even the most mature work group is likely to experience problems over time. When difficulties do occur, or as a means of preventing them from occurring, team-building activities can help. **Team-building** is a sequence of planned action steps to gather and analyze data on the functioning of a group and implement changes to increase its operating effectiveness.

There are many team-building strategies, but they generally share the steps shown in Figure 9.2. The cycle begins with a sensitivity by one or more members that a group problem may exist or might develop in the future. Group members then work together to gather and analyze data such that the problem is finally diagnosed. Plans are made and corrective action implemented. Results are then evaluated and any difficulties or new problems become reasons to recycle the process. Team-building is a data-based way of assessing a work group's functioning and taking corrective action to improve group effectiveness. It can be done with or without consulting assistance, and can become a regular part of a group's continuing work routine.

The gathering and analysis of data on group functioning is a key element in the team-building cycle. This is the point, in fact, where

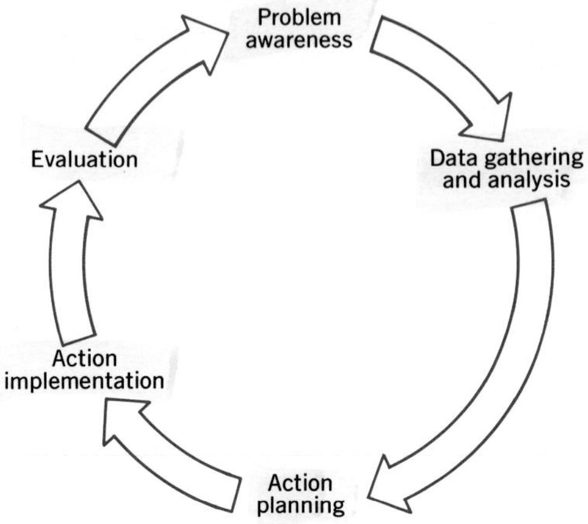


**FIGURE 9.2** A typical team-building cycle.

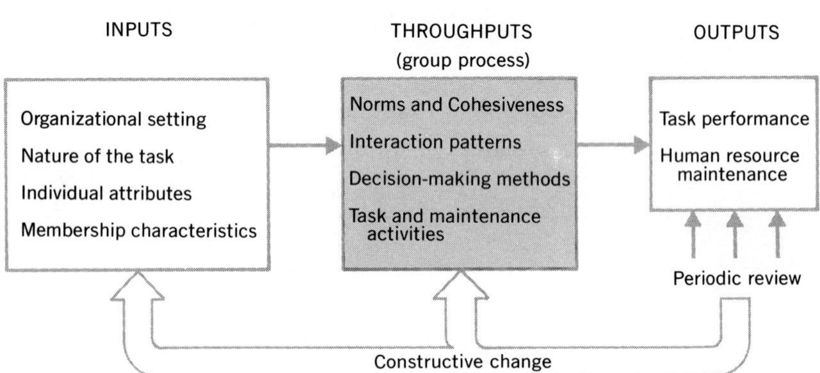


**FIGURE 9.3** A group review-analysis-change cycle.

a manager applies the knowledge of group and intergroup dynamics which we discussed in Chapter 8. To be successful in this stage, group outcomes in terms of task performance and member satisfaction must be carefully assessed. Then decisions can be made regarding the constructive modification of group inputs and throughputs, including any or all of the fundamental structural properties and interpersonal processes already discussed. You can see the major points of attention in this review-analysis-change cycle in Figure 9.3.

There are many ways to gather the required data. Structured and unstructured interviews, questionnaires, group meetings, and written records are all examples. A frequent approach is the survey method using an instrument such as the team-building checklist in Figure 9.4. Regardless of the method used, the principle of team-building requires that all members participate in the data-gathering process, assist in the data analysis, and collectively take action to resolve and/or prevent group problems. One of the more creative means of gathering data for team-building is described in *What Managers Do 9.1*.

Problem identification: to what extent is there evidence of the following problems in your work unit?

| | Low Evidence | | Some Evidence | | High Evidence |
|---|---|---|---|---|---|
| 1. Loss of production or work-unit output. | 1 | 2 | 3 | 4 | 5 |
| 2. Grievances or complaints within the work unit. | 1 | 2 | 3 | 4 | 5 |
| 3. Conflicts or hostility between unit members. | 1 | 2 | 3 | 4 | 5 |
| 4. Confusion about assignments or unclear relationships between people. | 1 | 2 | 3 | 4 | 5 |
| 5. Lack of clear goals, or low commitment to goals. | 1 | 2 | 3 | 4 | 5 |
| 6. Apathy or general lack of interest or involvement of unit members. | 1 | 2 | 3 | 4 | 5 |
| 7. Lack of innovation, risk taking, imagination, or taking initiative. | 1 | 2 | 3 | 4 | 5 |
| 8. Ineffective staff meetings. | 1 | 2 | 3 | 4 | 5 |
| 9. Problems in working with the boss. | 1 | 2 | 3 | 4 | 5 |
| 10. Poor communications: people afraid to speak up, not listening to each other, or not talking together. | 1 | 2 | 3 | 4 | 5 |
| 11. Lack of trust between boss and member or between members. | 1 | 2 | 3 | 4 | 5 |
| 12. Decisions made that people do not understand or agree with. | 1 | 2 | 3 | 4 | 5 |
| 13. People feel that good work is not recognized or rewarded. | 1 | 2 | 3 | 4 | 5 |
| 14. People are not encouraged to work together in better team effort. | 1 | 2 | 3 | 4 | 5 |

*Scoring:* Add up the score for the fourteen items. If your score is between 14–28, there is little evidence your unit needs team building. If your score is between 29–42, there is some evidence, but no immediate pressure, unless two or three items are very high. If your score is between 43–56, you should seriously think about planning the team-building program. If your score is over 56, team-building should be a top priority item for your work unit.

**Figure 9.4** Team-building checklist. *Source:* William G. Dyer, *Team Building: Issues and Alternatives* (Reading, Mass.: Addison-Wesley, 1977), pp. 36, 37.) Reprinted with permission.

Checkpoint

Complete the checklist in Figure 9.4 for a group with which you are familiar. How does the group score? How do you think other members would score this group? What improvements might you suggest, based on the data, that might lead to higher levels of group effectiveness?

## WHAT MANAGERS DO 9.1

### A Team-Building Strategy

After preliminary remarks by the manager, the group members could be asked: in order for us to get a picture of how you see our group functioning, would each of you take a few minutes to describe our group as a kind of animal or combination of animals, a kind of machine, a kind of person, or whatever image comes to mind?

Some groups in the past have been described as:

a. A hunting dog—a pointer: We run around and locate problems, then stop and point and hope somebody else will take the action.
b. A Cadillac with pedals: We look good on the outside, but there is no real power to get us moving.
c. A Rube Goldberg device: Everything looks crazy and you can't imagine anything will ever happen, but, in some way, for some reason, we do get results at the end.
d. An octopus: Each tentacle is out grasping anything it can, but doesn't know what the other tentacles are doing.

As people share these images and explain what elicits the image, the questions are asked: what are the common elements in these images? Do we like these images of ourselves? What do we need to do to change our image? The answering of these questions becomes the major agenda item of subsequent group meetings.

A variation of the above is to have subgroups of two to four people build a collage. They are given magazines and other materials, crayons, magic markers, and a large piece of cardboard and then asked to assemble a collage representing their work unit. The collages are then displayed and explained, and questions similar to those above are asked and then used as a basis for subsequent work.

Source: From William D. Dyer, *Team-Building,* Copyright © 1977, Addison-Wesley Publishing Company, Inc., Chapter 6, pp. 55, 56. Reprinted with permission.

## CREATIVE WORK GROUP DESIGNS

In Chapter 5 we discussed the different kinds of individual job designs and their impact on individual task performance and human resource maintenance. Now our attention shifts to some ideas for creative designs for work groups and their tasks. When the situation and job technology permit, these work group designs can be powerful ways of promoting group effectiveness from both the performance and maintenance perspectives. Our discussion will focus on two recent and innovative work group designs developed in and outside of the United States.

### Illustrative Case: Automobile Assembly

Our first case involves automobile assembly plants in the U.S. and Sweden.

Checkpoint

Let's start by comparing and contrasting the accompanying photographs. The first is of an automobile assembly line somewhere in the United States; the second is taken in an automobile manufacturing plant in Sweden. Given a choice, which work setting would you prefer and why?

It has been said,[10] "The auto assembly line epitomizes the conditions that contribute to employee dissatisfaction: fractionation of work into meaningless activities, with each activity repeated several hundred times each work day, and with the employees having little or no control over work pace or any other aspects of working conditions." Indeed, the principle of the automobile assembly-line process (as shown in the photo) has changed little since introduced by Henry Ford in 1913.

But what are the alternatives? What can we do to protect workers from the alienation and frustration that often accompanies work in such settings? Answers to these questions include job designs of two extremes: (1) increasing the degree of production automation, that is, decreasing the use of human labor; and (2) adopting autonomous work groups as a means of expanding individual participation in the work process.

#### Increasing Automation

The potential benefits of the automobile assembly line job specialization, such as economics of scale and high production volume, must be weighed against potential social costs, which may include high wage levels and individual disenchantment with work. It was largely the goal of realizing these benefits while minimizing social costs that led General Motors in 1966 to construct the most automated automobile assembly plant in the world. It's located at Lordstown, Ohio. Young and experienced workers were hired to work a production line that also included 26 specially designed robots. This line was capable of producing an incredible one hundred cars per hour. Problems soon arose, however, and the Lordstown plant became embroiled in controversy. Poor quality of final products, including some actual sabotage, and labor-management disputes were representative of problems encountered by GM at Lordstown.

## Autonomous Work Grouping

An alternative to increasing the automation of assembly lines is found in the concept of **autonomous work groups.** These are self-managed teams responsible for accomplishing defined production

Autonomous work groups at Volvo's Kalmar Plant in Sweden.

goals, and which have discretion in deciding how tasks will be distributed among individuals and at what pace work will progress in order to meet these goals. Members of autonomous work groups may go so far as to establish pay grades and train and certify members in required job skills.

The physical arrangement of workers and partially finished autos in photo 9.1 indicates the presence of autonomous work groups. This photo, in fact, was taken at the Kalmar plant in Sweden, a production facility for Volvo. This innovative, and also controversial, production facility was specially built to accommodate autonomous work group principles. The result of the Kalmar experience is described by one observer as follows:[11]

> The basic idea of Kalmar is flexibility—how people can choose the way they assemble a car. The facility has fewer supervisors than a normal auto plant.
>
> Whereas assembly-line workers would be rooted in position doing a single specialized chore all day, Kalmar's workers are grouped in about 25 teams of 15 to 25 persons each. Each team handles a general area, such as door assembly, electric wiring, or fitting upholstery.
>
> Members of teams can exchange jobs or change teams when they wish. They can also vary the pace of the work, keeping up with the general flow of production but speeding up or pausing as they wish—because the car-carrying trolleys can be delayed for a while both before entering and after leaving each team's work areas.
>
> While conventional assembly-line workers must perform operations on the undercarriage by the tiring method of working from beneath, the Kalmar worker presses a button and the trolley rolls an auto 90 degrees on its side so the work can be done from a comfortable position.
>
> The resulting building differs markedly from conventional plants. While they tend to look like large rectangles, Kalmar consists of four six-sided structures—three of them two stories tall and the other single-story—that fit together, forming the general shape of a cross.
>
> The windows are big, and the workshop is compartmented so the workers, located along the outer walls, have natural light and the sensation of being in a comfortably small workshop.

The Kalmar plant is an expensive facility (see photo 9.2). To replicate it throughout the United States, literally all of the existing assembly-line facilities would have to be abandoned and new ones constructed. The benefits and costs of such a changeover are issues of continuing debate. Kalmar, for example, can produce only 30,000 cars per year, versus 200,000 for a typical U.S. plant and 400,000 for Lordstown![12] To build a Kalmar-style plant, to produce 60 cars per hour (a standard U.S. goal) a 10-mile-long facility could be required.

The disadvantages of the Kalmar approach thus include reduced

The exterior of Volvo's Kalmar Plant in Sweden.

production rates, increased space requirements, and the need for radically new physical plants. On the other hand, allowing the assembly process to take place under autonomous work group designs is observed to offer a number of advantages, including[13]

- Increased ease of adjusting to individual absenteeism.
- Improved quality of production.
- Lower turnover.
- Improved employee work attitudes.
- Decreased investment in supervisory personnel.

Perhaps the ultimate question is how adaptable the Kalmar alternative is to the U.S. scene. One attempt to answer this question is described in *Newsline 9.1*. Many experiments are presently under way to explore possibilities for autonomous work grouping to improve productivity and employee satisfaction in a variety of other settings. These are typically called "quality of working life projects." One that has been evaluated most thoroughly is described below.

## NEWSLINE 9.1

### An American Look at the Swedish Way

Last November, Professor Arthur Weinberg of the School of Industrial Relations, Cornell University, led a team of six U.S. auto workers to Sweden to see how laborers trained on the conventional production line would take to "industrial democracy." The Ford Foundation put up $50,000 to pay expenses and worker salaries for the four-week "worker exchange program," as it was called.

The group went, not to Kalmar, but to Sodertalje, about 25 miles south of Stockholm, to a Saab auto engine plant where three-person teams assemble the entire engine. As in the Kalmar plant, much is left to the team as to how to operate—individually or together. Their only obligation is to meet a production schedule of 14 engines per assembler daily.

Only one, a 31-year-old Cadillac worker named Ruth Russell, was really enthusiastic. "In Detroit, my job is to insert 10 head bolts and a thermal plus at a rate of 88 an hour, but here I can put the whole engine together," Russell said. "I feel I'm accomplishing something."

Others were cool to the demands of the job. "It doesn't look as if people are working hard at all," said William Cox, 33 from Plymouth. "But when you go to work on the engines yourself, you find out, wow, these people are working their butts off." Another of the auto workers discerned the same boredom at Saab as in Detroit. "My job in Detroit in monotonous," he said, "but it's more relaxed."

But the U.S. workers found much they admired: relaxed relationships between workers and foremen; close attention to safety and working conditions such as good light and low noise levels. "The first day on the job the girls in my team asked why I talked so loud," said William Cox. "I was just talking the way I do in Detroit—it's so noisy you have to shout to make yourself heard." The fact that workers wash up on company time and attend to union matters on company time also impressed the Americans, as did the general informality. "Some people here bring plants and flowers in and out to brighten the place," said one American. "If that happened in my plant, they'd think you were stealing."

Source: *MBA Magazine* (March 1975), p. 42.

## Illustrative Case: Pet Foods in Topeka[14]

In 1968, General Foods Corporation was planning to construct a new dry dog food plant in Topeka, Kansas. The Company's existing plant was experiencing problems. Employees were indifferent and inattentive to their work, waste was high, shutdowns frequently occurred, and there were acts of worker violence and sabotage. General Foods wanted to avoid such problems in the new plant. Richard Walton, a noted social scientist, was asked to serve as a special consultant and evaluator.

## Pet Foods in 1971

Autonomous work groups were created in the new plant. Six teams of 7–14 workers were formed. Each included "operators" and a "team leader." The teams were individually responsible for a large part of the production process. Within teams, individuals were assigned work tasks by group consensus. These tasks were rotated and shared. The team was responsible for handling problems with other teams, coverage of absentees, training members in equipment maintenance, product quality control, and maintenance of the work area.

In addition, pay levels and raises for team members were based on the principle of job mastery; the guiding concept was "pay for learning." Individuals first mastered all jobs within their team and then within the plant. As they did so, their pay levels increased accordingly.

Some difficulties were in evidence as workers adjusted to the ways of this plant. The compensation scheme caused problems. Decisions regarding job mastery were sometimes controversial, and tensions appeared as team members began to qualify for different pay levels. Not all workers liked the increased responsibility of team membership and the atmosphere of mutual help. Some team leaders found their roles difficult.

Still, Walton viewed the experiment positively as of 1971. Product quality and plant safety were high, employee attitudes were generally positive, and absenteeism was low. Prospects looked good for autonomous work groups in this facility. What would you predict?

## Topeka—Six Years Later

Walton revisited the Topeka plant and reassessed the situation in 1977.[15] Again, he observed advantages in terms of employee attitudes, safety, absenteeism, and turnover. However, he also noted that problems still existed.

Group dynamics were a key force in the plant. Some teams developed as working entities more quickly and positively than did others. Different levels of group "skills" among the teams accounted for at least part of this variance. In addition, a growing minority of workers appeared dissatisfied with the position of "team leader," the use of peer evaluations, ways of making pay decisions, levels of interteam cooperation, and plant-wide coordination.

Obviously, the success of such creative work group designs depends on the ability of managers and other personnel to facilitate group effectiveness under innovative conditions. Perhaps these experiments to improve productivity and the quality of work life represent, more than any others, the types of things which you may do to mobilize the full potential of groups as human resources of organizations.

## SUMMARY

This chapter has focused on the way in which managers may apply, in actual practice, insights from the group dynamics concepts developed in the previous two chapters. It has emphasized four stages which groups go through in evolving from a newly formed group to a mature group: (1) forming stage (involves the entry of individual members into the group); (2) storming period (group members are trying to establish themselves and their positions in the group); (3) initial integration stage (group establishes superficial integration and may try to smooth over potential differences); and (4) total integration stage (integration now completed and the group is able to deal with disagreement in constructive ways).

Since there are different managerial implications for each of these stages, it is very important for you to be able to diagnose the stage of group development. The major issues are three: (1) facilitating individual entry to a group, (2) influencing norms and cohesion, and (3) team-building.

In terms of individual entry, the manager is concerned about resolving dilemmas which beset members unfamiliar with the group and its pattern of operations. The clarification of what members expect of one another can be done informally, or by written role negotiations which managers and subordinates revise at regular intervals, as necessary.

Concerning norms and cohesiveness, a key issue is how the manager may influence them to increase the performance and human resource maintenance of a work group. The specific steps which need to be taken to affect norms and cohesiveness vary according to the group's stage of development. Cohesiveness, as we also argued in Chapter 8, can be a double-edged sword for the manager, depending upon the extent to which group norms encourage performance. It can also lead to groupthink, where the members fail to be sufficiently critical of group decisions for fear of lowering group cohesiveness. Once again, we have outlined strategies which the manager can take to avoid groupthink.

Managers can also engage in team-building, a sequence of planned action steps to gather and analyze data on group functioning and implement changes to increase its operating effectiveness. Team-building is especially useful at periodic intervals to help a work group assess its progress and decide on appropriate plans for improving its future effectiveness.

In addition to the ideas summarized above, a most intriguing group management issue concerns designing creative work teams. It is sometimes possible to move job enrichment techniques (studied in Chapter 6) beyond individual jobs and apply them to work groups as a whole. Two such applications have been discussed for their strong and weak points. Other creative applications of this group-level approach to job design are certainly possible.

## THINKING THROUGH THE ISSUES

1. Think about a time when you saw the Abilene paradox in operation. Be prepared to discuss this in class.

2. Analyze a group which you have recently joined in terms of the stages of group development. Show evidence supporting your assessment.

3. Give some examples, which you have actually experienced, illustrating each of the management problems summarized in Table 9.1.

4. Discuss how you would explain the contention that groups often mistake the third stage of group development, initial integration, for the fourth, total integration.

5. Discuss the interaction between norms and group cohesiveness in influencing performance. Discuss where groupthink fits into this interaction, and state some strategies for avoiding groupthink.

6. Discuss some things a manager can do to influence cohesiveness both positively and negatively. Why would a manager even want to decrease group cohesion?

7. Think of an automobile assembly line. Compare and contrast the way the line might be set up to provide for individual job enrichment and group job enrichment.

8. Choose a work group or project group with which you are familiar. Apply to it the team-building checklist in Figure 9.4. How might you go about using a team-building approach for the group?

## CASE: URIS HALL DORMITORY KITCHEN[16]

### Part 1

The history of the dormitory began many years ago. The building was built to house 30 men, provide food service to these men, and contain the needed room for office space. At that time the cafeteria staff included 11 women and 1 male student worker. The organization of work was as follows: one woman worked during the morning and early afternoons as cashier; 5 of the remaining 10 worked from 5:00 A.M. until 1:00 P.M.; and the other 5 worked from 1:00 P.M. until 8:00 P.M.

The male student worked in the evenings as a cashier and dishwasher. Two of the women, Mrs. A and Mrs. B, served as the head cooks. One worked in the morning, the other worked in the evening. Their duties were limited to preparing food according to the menus, and assigning work. Each of the women under the head cook had a specialty, such as baking, salad making, or dishwashing, and each ordered her own supplies in light of the scheduled menus.

Because of the relatively small number of people served, the women were not pressured to prepare large quantities of food. The student cashier was looked upon as an outsider, but generally he was accepted, especially if some strenuous task was necessary. The cooks prepared 20 meals a week (Sunday night being the exception).

The menu was known because it repeated itself weekly, with only occasional variations. With but two exceptions, the workers had ten or more years of duty in the dormitory when the case observer first came upon the scene. He was impressed with the quality of the food which, although repetitious, was very good, as everyone agreed.

The organization of work was as follows. The head cooks supervised the other cooks, the dishwasher, and the cashier. The setup was identical with each of the two crews. The student worker was treated well by the women because he was helpful when they needed him; he also happened to be the dormitory director's son. The women were all in their middle or late sixties, except the cashier who was about 50 years old. They were all either married or widowed, and all had one or more children who were no longer living at home.

The women were all skilled in their work, as evidenced by the good food. All but one of them, the eldest who did the baking, had completed grade school. Although only five had finished high school, none had attended college. They were all of Protestant background, and all lived in the city or just outside it. The women got along together extremely well and were always willing to help each other. They took turns serving at meal time so everyone had a chance to eat, and they frequently rode to and from work together. When any of them became sick, the others would always give everyone a day-by-day account of the stricken individual's condition.

Several of the women attended the same church in town. They all conversed freely and at length at meal time or any other time, and in the case observer's two years at that dorm, he never knew of any hard feelings among them.

The head cook pretty much let the other cooks carry out their assignments as they wished. Troubles encountered in the job were typically blamed on the dorm director. Working conditions were adequate although not modern. Much of the equipment installed in 1947 was still being used at the time of the case. Many time-saving devices, such as electric can openers and electric dishwashers, were not available. The cafeteria was not air conditioned although two large fans were utilized in the summer, and the cafeteria was always warm in winter.

In spite of these less than ideal conditions, the women rarely complained. They seemed to be accustomed to the old equipment and were comfortable using it. As for the activities of the people, all of the cooks did part of the buying, and all took turns serving.

The other activities will be described for each group. At 5:00 P.M. when the morning crew arrived, all turned their attention to getting breakfast ready by 7:00 o'clock. The women were assigned typical breakfast preparation duties. After breakfast, and after eating and helping the dishwasher get started, each woman began preparing her own part of the noon meal. One woman had sole responsibility for making the various salads, two others prepared the vegetables, one cooked the meat, and the fifth made the desserts. This routine was strictly followed unless someone was ill. In this case, one of the women in the evening group worked all day, or all of the women of the morning crew shared their stricken comrade's duties.

The activities of the evening crew were similar. They did specialized jobs, much like the morning crew, in preparing the evening meal. However, after the meal was over at 7:00 P.M., they all helped clean the kitchen for the next day. In the cleaning process the women assumed the job of cleaning the area in which they worked in preparing their specialty. There were some strong sentiments among the women about their work and their relationship to each other. These women had worked together for a long time, and had built strong and lasting friendships. Although each jealously protected her individual independence in her specialty, there were strong feelings that each owed it to the others to make sure her part was done well and on time. During the few times when someone did not have her part of the meal ready when it was time to begin serving, the sanctions of the other women were overt, verbal, and sharp.

The dorm was recently purchased by State University and then rebuilt and considerably enlarged. Some two years later, it emerged from the expansion with facilities for 278 men and women, a recreation hall, a large dining hall, a library, and a chapel.

All of the old crew were invited to work in the new kitchen, and they all accepted the invitation. To accommodate the increased volume, additional people were required, as were clearer lines of organization. Initially, all of the old crew were put together in one group along with one new person. This group worked in the morning. In addition, ten more women were hired to work the evening shift. Six male students were hired to operate the new automatic dishwasher and to take out garbage during the rush periods. A new organizational structure was developed for the growing organization.

A cafeteria supervisor was hired to head the entire cafeteria operation. This woman had a number of years of experience in running large food service facilities. She was given the responsibility for planning all menus, buying the food, assigning jobs and scheduling workers. The only authority she was not given was the right to hire and fire workers and to make her own budget. These two functions were assumed by the dormitory director. The work remained divided on a functional basis. The only change was that more women were assigned to each specialty. The work was divided among the following categories: meats, vegetables, salads, desserts, and dishwashing. The morning crew moved its working schedule back an hour. They started at 4:00 A.M. and worked until 1:00 P.M. The evening crew worked from 1:00 P.M. until 9:00 P.M. A head cook was chosen in each group. She was responsible for seeing that things were done when the supervisor was not present.

The kitchen duties now called for the combined efforts of more than one woman. The interactions were very limited because the women rarely saw each other, and the two groups prepared their own meals. Thus, the evening crew started making the evening meal from scratch rather than serving what was prepared in the morning. The only exception was that the desserts were all made in the morning.

Brand-new equipment was placed in the cafeteria. An emphasis was placed on obtaining equipment capable of preparing large quantities of food in the most efficient manner. The building was air conditioned, well lighted, and carpeted.

The workers were no longer allowed to order their own supplies. The new supervisor assumed this function entirely. It was necessary to order different kinds and different quantities of food now that 300 were being fed instead of 30. The old crew was accustomed to cooking rather small roasts, for instance, but in the new building they were asked to cook very large roasts. Soon a lot of trouble was evident concerning the kinds of food being ordered. The old crew felt that the supervisor was not doing a creditable job. They made their sentiments well known in verbal discussions with the supervisor and in written statements to the director. They claimed the food was impossible to cook, of inferior quality, and a waste of money.

Their second gripe concerned the hiring of a woman to work in the morning who was not of the old group. The women objected to her presence for two reasons. First, she was loud. She was not belligerent or profane, but she had a husky, bellowing voice. She was also given to lengthy seizures of singing at the top of her booming voice. None of the other women possessed these characteristics and objected rather strongly to the noise.

This was not their most serious objection, however. This woman, whom we shall call Mrs. Loud, also frequently extolled her own great skill in large kitchens though she had had only one year of experience. Not only did Mrs. Loud boast of her own abilities, she also tried to instruct the other women in the proper method of cooking. Mrs. Loud felt that her supposed expertise qualified her to boss the other women. A long succession of incidents followed in which Mrs. Loud became an increasingly bad influence on the morning crew. Finally, two of the women went to the supervisor and explained that they could no longer tolerate Mrs. Loud and would quit if she was not replaced.

There also was a problem concerning the dishwasher. One woman was assigned the entire job of washing dishes at the old dormitory and the old crew accepted this as proper procedure. However, the volume of business and the mechanics of the automatic dishwasher at the new cafeteria necessitated that the women sometimes help the woman assigned to the dishwasher. This was especially true when the student helpers were not available. Many of the women did not like or accept this situation and were rather upset about it.

They first objected because they felt that the woman assigned to the job was not doing her job properly. It soon became evident that this was not the case. Rather, at times the volume of dishes simply was too much for one woman to handle. The student workers alleviated the problem to a great extent, but there were still times when the cooks were required to help. Scraping and washing dishes is not the most desirable or satisfying job in a kitchen, or anywhere else for that matter. Each woman was assigned a specialty and took pride in her work, so broadening these duties to include this kind of activity did not go over well. Long and sad grumbling was often voiced by the cooks who had to wash dishes.

The evening crew was also plagued by some problems. First, there was the problem of adjustment for the new employees. As previously stated, all the old employees were put on the morning shift, so all the evening crew was new. Three of the women had no previous experience working in a large cafeteria, so they had much to learn. The part of the job involving the cleaning of the cafeteria each night also became a problem. The women felt that they were being imposed upon because the morning crew had no such duties. Several of the women had expressed displeasure at the cleaning chore and had said that they would quit "if the opportunity arose for another job."

A more serious problem involved the head cook of the evening crew, who was black. Mrs. Jones was an extremely hard worker and a very good cook. She also possessed a pleasing personality. She was hesitant to take the job as head cook because she felt the other women, who were all white, would object to the assignment. The dorm director indicated to the case observer that he was afraid that trouble would result from the arrangement, but that Mrs. Jones was best qualified for the job, and he needed her in the position. Mrs. Jones finally took the job after much persuasion.

The reaction of the other women was quick and quite strong. The resentment grew almost visibly while Mrs. Jones tried to ignore it. The displeasure displayed itself in such things as tardiness, slovenly work, and frequent bad meals. The situation worsened with time. Finally, the circumstances became so desperate that the director felt some action had to be taken. The last straw came when Mrs. Smith, an avid segregationist, was asked to clean up a mess made by Mrs. Jones, and promptly left the job.

The third group of people working in the new dormitory was the student workers. At the old dormitory, only one student was working, but the new dormitory required the part-time help of six students. These workers were all young men who lived in the dorm. They worked mainly at the noon and evening meals when as many as 325 people were served. Their work was done almost entirely on the automatic dishwasher, which was used to capacity during these peak hours. They also did some cleaning chores and stocking, but were generally limited to washing dishes.

Although these students were generally aware of the problems in the cafeteria, they did not take sides or engage in any way in the squabbling. Their consensus seemed to be to come in, do the work, and get out as fast as possible. The cooks and other staff considered these students as welcome help. As one put it, "I don't know what we'd do without them."

## Questions

1. How do you explain the differences evident in Part 1 and Part 2 of the case?
2. What do you predict for employee task performance and human resource maintenance for the situation described in Part 2? Why?
3. What changes, if any, do you recommend to the director and why?

# THE MANAGER'S VOCABULARY

**Autonomous Work Groups** Self-managed teams, responsible for accomplishing defined production goals, which have discretion in deciding how tasks will be distributed among individuals and at what pace work will progress in order to meet these goals.

**Abilene Paradox** Individual group members respond to what they think other group members want, without actually finding out what the others really want.

**Groupthink** A tendency for highly cohesive groups to lose their critical evaluative capabilities.

**Team-Building** A sequence of planned action steps to gather and analyze data on the functioning of a group and implementing changes to increase its operating effectiveness.

## Important Names

**Irving Janis** Identified the phenomenon of "groupthink."

**Edgar Schein** A noted social psychologist who has established a series of profiles characterizing people entering groups.

**Richard Walton** A management consultant and scholar who helps organizations implement and evaluate creative work group designs.

## Notes

[1]Reprinted by permission of the publisher, from "Managing Agreement in Organizations: The Abilene Paradox," by Jerry Harvey, *Organizational Dynamics* (Summer 1974), copyright © 1974 by AMACOM, a division of American Management Associations, pp. 63–80. All rights reserved.

[2]J. S. Heinen and E. Jacobson, "A Model of Task Group Development in Complex Organizations and a Process of Supplementation," *Academy of Management Review*, Vol. 1 (1976), pp. 98–111.

[3]This discussion is based on Edgar H. Schein, *Process Consultation: Its Role in Organization Development* (Reading, Mass.: Addison-Wesley, 1969), pp. 32–37.

[4]This example is taken from Roger Harrison, "When Power Conflicts Trigger Team Spirit," *European Business* (Spring 1972), pp. 57–65.

[5]Robert F. Allen and Saul Pilnick, "Confronting the Shadow Organization: How to Select and Defeat Negative Norms," *Organizational Dynamics* (Spring 1973), pp. 13–17.

[6]Harvey, op. cit.

[7]Irving L. Janis, "Groupthink," *Psychology Today* (November 1971), pp. 43–46.

[8]Ibid.

[9]This discussion is based on Edgar H. Schein, *Organizational Psychology* (Englewood Cliffs, N.J.: Prentice-Hall, 1970), pp. 96–103.

[10]William F. Dowling, "Job Redesign on the Assembly Line: Farewell to Blue-Collar Blues," *Organizational Dynamics* (Autumn 1973), p. 51.

[11]Bowen Northrup, "Auto Plant in Sweden Scores Some Success with Worke Teams," *The Wall Street Journal* (March 1, 1977), p. 1.

[12]Ibid.

[13]Ibid.; Dowling, op. cit., pp. 51–67.

[14]See Richard E. Walton, "How to Counter Alienation in the Plant," *Harvard Business Review* (November–December 1972), pp. 70–81.

[15]See Richard E. Walton, "Work Innovations at Topeka: After Six Years," *Journal of Applied Behavior Science,* Vol. 13 (1977), pp. 422–431.

[16]Adapted from a course assignment prepared by Charles I. Cash for Professor J. G. Hunt, Southern Illinois University at Carbondale. This case also appears in John E. Dittrich and Robert A. Zawacki, *People and Organizations: Cases in Management and Organizational Behavior* (Plano, Texas: Business Publications, Inc., 1981), pp. 301–306. Used with permission.

# PART FOUR

# MANAGING ORGANIZATIONS

## THE MANAGER'S GOAL

**To Understand the Organization as a Complex System; and, to Use This Knowledge to Help the Organization Accomplish Its Tasks and Maintain Its Human Resources.**

## YOUR LEARNING OBJECTIVE

**To Become Familiar with the Common Features of Organizations; and, to Identify Action Guidelines for Designing Appropriate Organization Structures.**

## Chapters in This Part of the Book

The organization is every manager's work setting, and it is the goals of organizations that managers are expected to serve. A smaller component of the organization, the work unit, is that part over which the manager is given formal authority. Both the larger organization and the work unit must be designed to take maximum advantage of the human and physical resources at their disposal. When the design of either the organization, the work unit, or both is inappropriate to meet situational demands, performance and human resource maintenance may suffer.

Thus, you as a manager must press beyond a knowledge of individuals and groups to learn about the organization as a social phenomenon. In this part of the book we will study organizations. Before getting down to business, however, let's put this interest in the organization into a true managerial perspective. In fact, let's look in at Jaccob Jaccober and a dilemma he recently faced.

## The Middle States Manufacturing Case

Jaccob Jaccober is the president of Middle States Manufacturing. The firm, while not particularly efficient, has been highly profitable. Its emphasis is on innovation and maintaining the technical quality of its products at or above competitive levels. At the moment, Jaccob didn't feel much like a corporate tycoon as he sat slumped into the soft leather sidechair in his office overlooking the city. "How long will it be," he wondered, "before Susan Rice, my Vice-President of Finance, will call about the West Coast financing package?" The lights of the city glowed uniformly in the same neat grid of rows and columns some city planner had specified over a hundred years ago. "Oh, if only I could design such a logical, permanent structure for my rapidly growing organization," thought Jaccob.

His thoughts turned to a quick review of the hectic day of meetings. Opportunities were turning into problems. Each new piece of business only seemed to further cloud the distribution of roles and responsibilities among Middle States' managers. Orders were not getting processed promptly. Two important accounts were recently sent incomplete shipments, and both shipments were late at that! Of course, there were many new people in new jobs, and most were working long hours to overcome their inexperience. But nobody seemed able to agree with anybody on anything!

Joan Wood (Vice-President of Production), for example, had convincingly argued that longer production runs were needed to reduce machine setup time, increase quality control, cut wear and tear on expensive machinery, and simplify the order delivery process. To provide these longer runs, a reduction in specialized orders was the key. Pat Vincent (Vice-President of Marketing), however, strongly resisted this recommendation. Marketing, he explained, had carefully nurtured a company image of quick delivery of quality products engineered to the unique needs of major customers. Joan's recommendations would force Marketing to sell a standardized product line. Pat foresaw immediate lost sales and a longer term decline in market acceptance if this were done.

Then there was Howard Teebs, Assistant to the Vice-President of Finance. He was concerned over the financing of inventories. Howard had argued for a stricter budgeting process that stressed weekly targets for purchasing, in-process goods, and finished goods inventory. Variations over 10% of the plan would be subject to direct control by the Assistant to the Vice-President of Production.

As the meeting of the executive committee droned on, it was apparent to Jaccob that the Middle States management team had numerous ideas for improving performance. Everyone seemed willing to recommend changes, particularly if the changes affected someone else's department.

As Jaccob stared out into the city lights, he argued to himself that the problems of growth had to be manageable. He reviewed things again. Business from three key customers—Chicago Distributing, Ohio Wholesalers, and Blake, Inc.—accounted for 50% of total sales and 75% of gross profits. Substantial new growth from these three appeared questionable. The potential lay with Profab. Profab was already used by the big three. It used slightly different production methods than current products and required a lot of handcrafting from a few highly skilled people. Longer production runs with a more flexible design could cut costs by 30%. This would increase the profitability of the existing market. Then, by starting a second shift and by using commission salespersons selling specialized lines related to Profab, new opportunities in the East and West Coast markets could be captured.

Yes, Profab was the future of the company. Yet the management staff was already overworked. Jaccob was already "passing off" direct day-to-day relations with the big three to Pat. And the engineering requirements of the new direction might yield even more production problems in serving the big three. "How could Middle States capitalize on this opportunity without losing its major customers?"

Before Jaccob could try to answer his own question, the phone rang. It was an excited Susan Rice. She announced that within six months Middle States would have two million dollars to market Profab and its derivatives nationally. Susan chided Jaccob that Middle States would no longer be an appropriate name. She suggested Profab National. Jaccob countered with Profab International.

Once again the grid of city lights, with neat rows and columns expanding to the horizon, caught Jaccob's eye as he congratulated Susan. It was time for a change—a change which would create the proper organization and establish the management team for Profab International.

## Viewpoint

Well, Jaccob seems to have his goals clearly in mind. He's going to reconfigure his company, that is, establish a new organizational structure, so as to meet new challenges successfully. Assuming that Jaccob has studied OB, or at least has access to an informed consultant, he should be able to design a structure that can facilitate profitable growth and still maintain the firm's technical leadership capability.

Deep down inside organizations, however, it is still people who work within the structure to perform the required tasks. We should wonder at this point what Jaccob's ideas mean to lower-level managers who are already trying hard to fulfill their current obligations and generally do a good job!

***Continuing On*** While the future for Middle States seemed promising to Jaccob, Sam

Ford's prospects didn't appear too bright at the moment. Sam was a junior executive in charge of finished goods and delivery. He reported to Joan Wood and he was on the hot seat.

For the second time in four weeks, two orders were shipped incomplete. Neither Ron Cloud, in charge of production line A, nor Sandy Rivers, in charge of production line B, had checked with each other. Chicago Distributing got only "A" items and Blake, Inc., got only the "B" items. Sam knew that the problem had been mentioned in a recent executive committee meeting, and he experienced firsthand that Joan had been livid when the error was discovered. Just switching incomplete shipments would not have been so bad, had they not also been four days late!

Now Sam sat pondering a phone message from Joan's secretary. It called for a meeting on scheduling and delivery problems, but it sure looked like it had "pink slip" potential.

Sam had to get his work unit organized to process adequately the delivery requests which called for both A and B items. These orders always came from one of the big three. But he didn't know how to proceed. He was new and both Ron and Sandy had been with the company since Jaccob Jaccober had founded it. Today was Tuesday; the meeting sealing his fate was the following Thursday. "Three months on the job and already a failure?" he thought. "How to proceed? What can be done?" Barking orders and asking for cooperation had failed. "What can be done?"

### Viewpoint

Jaccob and Sam appear to have quite different problems. But do they really? Both share the problem of experiencing the pitfalls of inappropriate organizational structures, and each must respond as a manager to the challenge of finding a better way.

Sam has yet to learn some fundamental principles of organizational structure. There are various approaches to solving problems such as incomplete deliveries. They do require, though, an understanding of different ways to divide up work. While Jaccob's prospects appear brighter, his problem is far more complex. It requires a more complete understanding of organizational design. Both Sam and Jaccob need to understand the basics, but Jaccob must also study the theory of organizational design and choose an overall strategy based on his objectives. Perhaps the design Jaccob chooses will be as neat and orderly as his grid of city lights, perhaps not.

## SUMMARY

This part of the book offers a knowledge base that will help you solve problems similar to those facing Jaccob and Sam. As you read on, keep in mind your concern is to perform well in respect to two very specific managerial responsibilities:

1. As a manager, you must successfully interface your work unit with the rest of the organization. This requires that you understand the logic of the total organizational system. Such understanding can help you take effective action to ensure that proper resource support is obtained for the work unit, and that the efforts of the work unit contribute to the purposes of the overall organization.

2. As a manager, you must also be successful in coordinating the many different activities, roles, interactions, and programs of your work unit. This is necessary if you are to achieve synergy in the combining

of human and physical resource inputs into product or service outputs. To achieve such coordination, you must be familiar with alternative organization structures and recognize the special pressures imposed on these structures by differences in environment, size, and technology. Coordination also requires that you know how to design and maintain, over time, appropriate structures that provide a good fit with these environmental, size, and technological differences.

The case shows clearly that both Jaccob and Sam face these two responsibilities. Jaccob faces them as the chief executive officer, while Sam faces them as a lower-level department manager. Both men could benefit from the insights that follow. Our discussion in the coming chapters will largely adopt the top manager's viewpoint, but the principles and implications are also relevant to managers like Sam whose responsibilities exist at middle and lower management levels. Remember, an organization is a collection of people working together in a division of labor to achieve a common purpose. It is time now to learn more about how to divide the labor, coordinate the results, and thereby facilitate accomplishment of the common purpose.

# 10

# BASIC ATTRIBUTES OF ORGANIZATIONS AND THEIR ENVIRONMENTS

# WPPSS (WOOPS)—WE JUST LOST ANOTHER BILLION

Washington Public Power Supply System (WPPSS) is building five nuclear power plants for some 34 utilities in the Northwest. This is one of the largest construction projects ever attempted by a single organization, and the cost for the five plants is billions over budget. High interest rates, strikes, and changes in regulations are partially to blame. But WPPSS has also tried a new way of administering the construction of power plants. First, engineering design work was far from complete when WPPSS asked for competitive bids from construction firms. Later, designs were changed in midstream. These constant changes have driven up costs and building delays are typical. For instance, walls were constructed, torn down, and reconstructed. Second, WPPSS tried to co-manage construction with each of the five "lead" contractors. The lead contractors, in turn, subcontracted to more specialized firms, such as cement contractors. When problems occurred, WPPSS blamed the lead contractors and the lead contractors blamed WPPSS. While each was blaming the other, construction work all but stopped.[1]

**MANAGEMENT APPLICATIONS QUESTION**

The previous example highlights an organization in trouble. What do you need to learn about organizations and their overall characteristics in order to help avoid such operating difficulties?

## PLANNING AHEAD

**After reading this chapter and participating in the recommended learning experiences, you will be familiar with the following topics:**

**Organizations as Bureaucracies**
**Organizations as Seen by Their Members**
**Organizations as Open Systems**
**The Environment of Organizations**
**Organizational Context: Size and Technology**

Organizations are a major force in our society. In Chapter 1 we defined an **organization** as a collection of people working together in a division of labor to achieve a common purpose. The opening example in the present chapter portrays WPPSS as an organization in which the division of labor is unclear, the people are sometimes not working together, and the common purpose is threatened with failure. Managers throughout organizations such as WPPSS are responsible for helping to avoid these breakdowns. The material to be covered in this fourth part of the book will help you to answer this challenge. In this chapter we introduce the basic attributes of organizations and their environments. Chapter 11 reviews various organization structures, and Chapter 12 presents an integrated approach to organizational design.

Checkpoint

Before reading further, make sure you recall the following definitions from Chapter 1. They are fundamental to our treatment of organizations in this and subsequent chapters.

**Organizational Purpose** To produce a good or service.
**Division of Labor** The process of breaking work into small components that serve the organization's purpose and to be done by individuals or groups.
**Authority** The right to command other persons.
**Hierarchy of Authority** The arrangement of work positions in order of increasing authority.

## ORGANIZATIONS AS BUREAUCRACIES

Table 10.1 presents a sample of organizations and their product outputs. These are the types of organizations in which you may work as a manager. Let's begin our look at these work settings by recog-

**Table 10.1 Sample Types of Organizations and Their Products**

| Organizations | Products |
|---|---|
| Hospitals, nursing homes | Health services |
| Restaurants, hotels | Hospitality services |
| Welfare agencies, child care centers | Social services |
| Manufacturers | Consumer goods |
| Libraries, museums | Artistic and cultural services |
| Universities, technical schools | Educational services |

nizing that you, your subordinates, your superiors, and your peers may view organizations in different ways. Some people, for example, think of organizations as characterized by red tape, inefficiency, and endless lines. Their image is of a large and impersonal "bureaucracy."

A **bureaucracy** is an ideal form of organization whose characteristics were defined by the German sociologist Max Weber.[2] Many people, perhaps even yourself, view the concept of "bureaucracy" as a negative term. In fact, to call someone a "bureaucrat" is often considered a disparaging remark. For Weber, however, a bureaucracy was the best possible form for an organization, and bureaucrats were the people who made it work.

Table 10.2 summarizes the major characteristics of Weber's ideal bureaucracy. It is an organization based on legal authority, logic, and order. As a result, it is supposed to be rational, fair, and efficient in

**Table 10.2 The Characteristics of Weber's Ideal Bureaucracy and Some Associated Dysfunctions**

| Characteristics of Weber's Ideal Bureaucracy | Associated Dysfunctions Identified by Critics |
|---|---|
| 1. Labor is specialized so that each person has clear-cut authority and responsibility. | 1. Over specialization stimulates a divergence of interests that lead to conflict.[3] |
| 2. Offices and positions are arranged in a hierarchy of authority. | 2. A very formal hierarchy creates inflexibility.[4] |
| 3. Members are selected and promoted on the basis of technical competence. | 3. Bureaucracies become political systems serving an elite corps of managers.[5] |
| 4. Members have administrative careers and work on a fixed salary. | 4. Conformity to the organization's ways can be detrimental to one's mental health.[6] |
| 5. Members are subject to rules and controls which are strict, impersonal, and applied universally. | 5. Rules become ends in themselves;[7] rules can only specify minimum requirements.[8] |

its operations. Certainly, these are outcomes which even today can be considered desirable for any organization!

The table also indicates, though, that certain dysfunctions have been associated with bureaucracies by their critics. It is because of these problems that bureaucracies often suffer a negative image, particularly in the minds of their clients or customers. See *Newsline 10.1* for an example of how these negative images can develop.

It is important for you to recognize the potential dysfunctions of a bureaucracy. However, it is also important to understand the essence of Weber's ideal bureaucracy as a cornerstone concept in OB. Given this as a foundation, we can explore some of the more recent viewpoints on organizations and their basic attributes.

An employee's view of bureaucracy.
© Sidney Harris.

## NEWSLINE 10.1

### It's Illegal! But New Yorkers Persist in Cleaning Their Subway Station

NEW YORK—(AP)—Oliver Leeds and some of his friends are defying the Transit Authority and scrubbing their Brooklyn subway station each Saturday.

They have been notified that they are breaking the law, but they are washing just the same.

"The station is dirty and we want it clean," Leeds said yesterday.

Bob Huber, a spokesman for the Transit Authority, said: "They're hardly criminals, just good neighbors and good citizens doing a job that is potentially dangerous."

Huber would not say what steps the authority might take. But he said that it was illegal for private citizens to clean public property for two reasons.

"There is a very real safety problem," he said. "Someone could get hurt in a station and then someone is going to be held liable."

Determining liability usually means courts and courts cost money.

"That seems kind of silly. But, if you're talking about litigation, you're talking maybe millions of dollars," Huber said. "There's no way we can insulate ourselves."

He observed also that the Transit Authority had a contract with the Transport Workers Union to maintain the subways and 458 stations.

"It's an exclusive contract and these people are professional cleaners."

Leeds and his friends began cleaning the Broadway GG line station in Williamsburg early this spring.

"We kept at it every Saturday and there was a real improvement," he said. "When the people who desecrated the walls saw that their markings wouldn't last more than a few days, they stopped."

Source: The Associated Press, as printed in *The Seattle Times*, (May 15, 1981), p. 2. Reprinted by permission of AP News Features.

## ORGANIZATIONS AS SEEN BY THEIR MEMBERS

While most people share a perspective on organizations as bureaucracies, employees tend to describe their work organizations in other terms. For them, an organization is a **structure** or configuration of positions, job duties, and lines of authority among its component parts. This structure represents the division of labor and the lines of communication which link the various individual and group components of the organization to one another. While the structure forms the internal anatomy of an organization, people constitute its muscle and tissue. A manager works to combine human and material resources to give life to the basic structure. Thus, structure is a framework for action within which the basic managerial functions of planning, organizing, staffing, directing, and controlling are carried out.

## Organization Charts and the Principles of Management

**Organization charts** are diagrams that depict the formal structures of organizations. A typical chart will show the various positions, the position holders, and the lines of authority linking them to one another. Figure 10.1 is a partial organization chart for a university. The total chart allows university employees to locate their positions in the structure, and to identify the lines of authority linking them with others in the organization.

We can use this concept of an organization chart to review some of the classical **management principles.** These principles emerged from the work of Henri Fayol and others (see Supplementary Module A) and were offered as guidelines for action which should not be violated without substantial reasons.[9] The principles are:

**Unity of Command** Each person in a hierarchy of authority should have one and only one boss.
**Chain of Command** Each person in a hierarchy of authority should have a clear understanding of his or her linkages with the highest and lowest levels in the hierarchy.
**Span of Control** A manager should have no more immediate subordinates than he or she is capable of supervising.
**Authority and Responsibility** A manager should be given the authority required to execute the responsibilities of his or her position.

These four principles have added much to our understanding of organizations and of how they can be used to mobilize the efforts of many people to accomplish common goals. For many years, in fact, they have served as guidelines for the creation of organization charts, such as the one shown in Figure 10.1

Checkpoint

The organization chart in Figure 10.1 actually violates one of the above four management principles. Can you identify which one?

*Answer:* Unity of command is violated. The college deans are shown as reporting to two bosses—the Assistant Provost for Graduate Affairs and the Assistant Provost for Undergraduate Affairs.

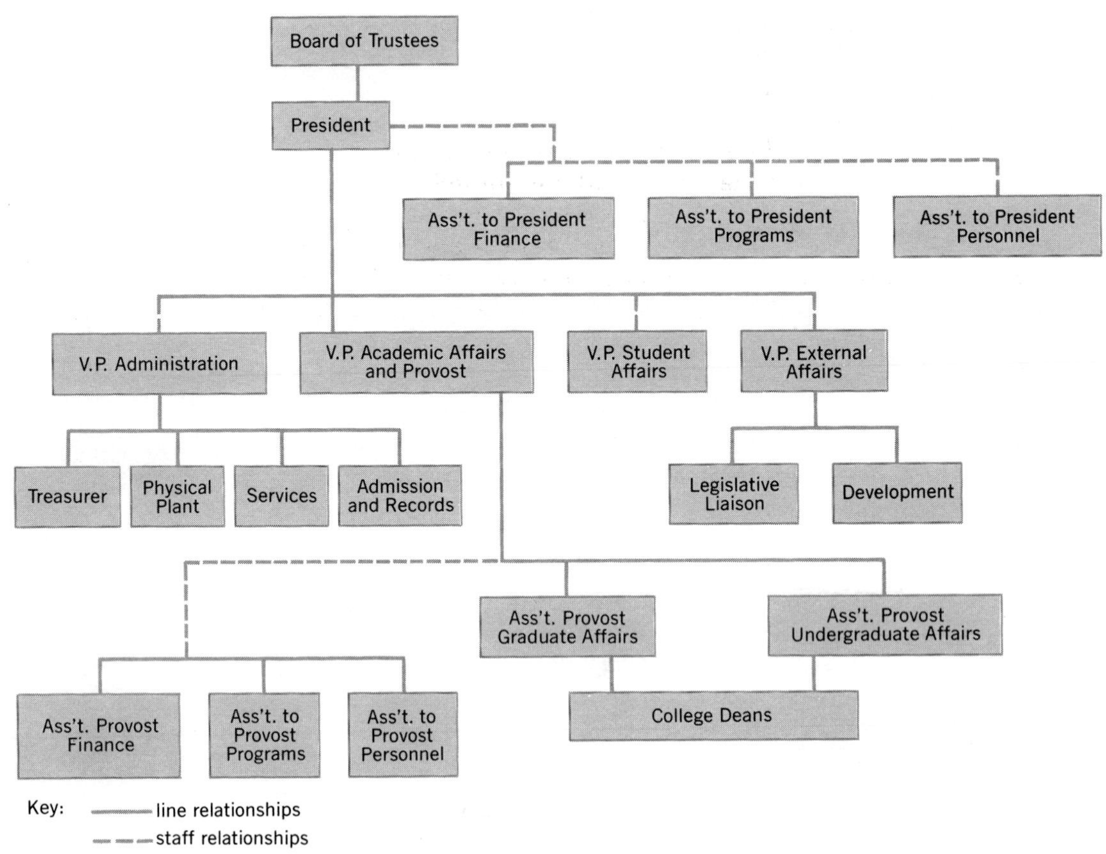


**FIGURE 10.1** A partial organization chart for a state university.

## Vertical and Horizontal Divisions of Labor

Organizations of any size have three levels of vertical action—top, middle, and bottom.[10] These levels generally represent a vertical division of labor in an organization's hierarchy of authority. Top managers, that is executives, plan the overall strategy of the organization and plot its long-term future. They also act as final judges for internal disputes and serve to certify promotions, reorganizations, and the like. Middle managers guide the day-to-day operations of the organization, help formulate policy, and translate top management decisions into more specific guidelines for action. Lower-level managers supervise the actions of subordinates to ensure implementation of the strategies authorized by top management and compliance with the related policies established by middle management.

The division of labor works horizontally in organization as well. Through task specialization, individual jobs become defined. These jobs are then grouped through departmentation into work units with a manager at their head.

Another aspect of the division of labor is the distinction between line and staff functions. **Line units and personnel** conduct the major business of the organization. The production and marketing functions are two examples. In contrast, **staff units and personnel** assist the line units by providing specialized expertise and services. The dotted lines on the chart in figure 10.1 denote staff relationships, while the solid ones denote line relationships. For example, the Vice-President of Administration heads a staff unit, as does the Vice-President of Student Affairs. All academic departments in the figure are line units since they constitute the basic production function of the university.

A useful distinction to be made for both line and staff units concerns the amount and types of contacts they maintain with outsiders to the organization. Some units are mainly internal in orientation, while others are more external in focus. Figure 10.2 briefly summarizes the differences between them.

## Centralization-Decentralization of Decison Making

For employees in general, and managers in particular, a critical issue in organizations relates to the locus of authority for decision-making. As managers and employees look upward in a hierarchy, the question

| | | |
|---|---|---|
| *Line Units:* | | |
| Internal (e.g., production) | Focus → on | Transforming raw material and/ information into products and/or services. |
| External (e.g., marketing) | Focus → on | Linking clients and/or suppliers to the organization. |
| *Staff Units:* | | |
| Internal (e.g., accounting) | Focus → on | Assisting line units in the technical areas of budgeting and fiscal control. |
| External (e.g., public relations) | Focus → on | Linking the organization to its environment through the conveyance of a positive public image. |

**FIGURE 10.2** Internal and external line and staff units in organization. (Source: Based on a discussion in Richard N. Osborn, James G. Hunt, and Lawrence R. Jauch, *Organization Theory: An Integrated Approach.* New York: John Wiley & Sons, 1980, pp. 277–280.)

specifically becomes one of how many and which types of decisions can be made at a given level. The farther the discretion to spend money, hire people, and make similar decisions is moved down the hierarchy of authority, the greater the degree of **decentralization.** Generally speaking, greater decentralization yields higher subordinate satisfaction and a quicker response to problems. Decentralization also assists in the on-the-job training of subordinates for higher level positions.[11]

Closely related to decentralization is the notion of participation. Many people want to be involved in decisions affecting their work. Participation results when a manager delegates some authority for such decision-making to subordinates. The planning function is a good example of how participation can yield very positive benefits for the organization and its managers. See *What Managers Do 10.1* for a current example.

## Formalization of Rules and Policies

When asked to describe their organizations, employees often complain about the degree to which their actions are prescribed by higher-level managers and about the large number of written rules, policies, and procedures that are to be followed. Such **formalization** varies in degree among organizations. As with other attributes of organizations, formalization has both advantages and disadvantages.

Rules, policies, and procedures are substitutes for managerial direction. They may be used to help specify the goals of the worker, indicate the best method for performing tasks, show which aspects of task accomplishment are most important, and outline how individuals will be rewarded. They allow "management by exception." That is, the formalization of rules, policies, and procedures allows managers to concentrate their energies on important, unusual conditions which may affect performance and/or satisfaction.[13] Remember,

| Rules, procedures, and policies | may be → viewed as | impersonal and inflexible | but → | they free the manager for other choices |
|---|---|---|---|---|

Usually we think of a policy as a guideline for action which outlines important objectives and indicates broadly how an activity is to be performed. A policy allows for individual discretion and minor adjustments without direct clearance by a higher-level manager. Rules and procedures, on the other hand, are more rigid and impersonal and they are often negatively stated. The problem is, of course, that

## WHAT MANAGERS DO 10.1

### Participatory Planning

The following excerpts are from a recent *Wall Street Journal* article which describes how Dr. Charles Ping, President of Ohio University, uses participatory planning to avoid financial chaos.

When Dr. Ping arrived in 1975, enrollment had fallen 32% from the 1970–71 high. "Morale was low, anxiety was high and the place was $6 million out of balance," he says. "It seemed necessary to establish a rational, participatory process for decision-making and planning." . . .

The university's financial condition was spelled out in abysmal detail to the deans and other administrators, who were expected to pass the word to faculty members. It was a new tactic at the school, where decision-making authority in the past had been closely guarded at the top. Dr. Ping explains his reasons for the change: "A university is an odd place to manage. There's clearly a shared responsibility for decision making between administration and faculty." . . .

The deans and administrators were asked to trim their base budgets over a three-year period and were given considerable leeway how they did it. Cuts resulted in savings of $1.1 million. The key was the faculty's attitude, explains Dean William Dorrill of the College of Arts and Sciences. "You can't order a faculty around, especially a tenured faculty. They have to be persuaded, which takes some doing when the proposal is that they act against their own short-term self interests."

Source: John A. Prestbo, "Pinching Pennies: Ohio University Finds Participatory Planning Ends Financial Chaos," *The Wall Street Journal* (May 27, 1981), pp. 1, 18. Reprinted by permission of The Wall Street Journal, 

few employees and lower-level managers clearly distinguish between policies and rules. Policies are often seen as rules with the result of too much inflexibility and an aura of impersonality. *Newsline 10.2* illustrates some responses to an organizational policy that is of direct interest to you.

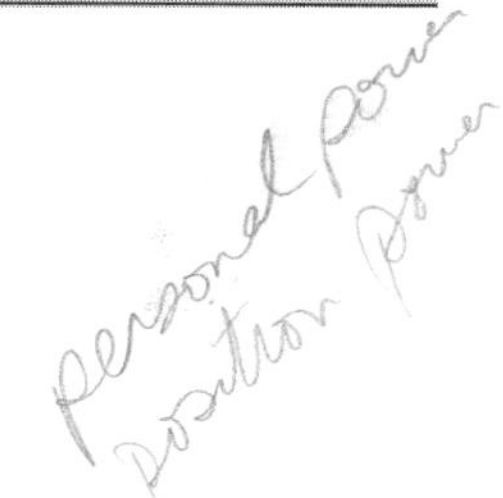


## Summary

People within organizations view them as structures of formal authority relationships. These structures are vertically differentiated into lower and higher levels of authority; they are also horizontally differentiated into separate departments and individual jobs having line and staff responsibilities. Organization charts depict this internal anatomy of organizations. They locate positions of managerial responsibility and show the formal authority relationships through which these positions are linked to one another.

Organization charts also illustrate the use of some of the classic management principles such as unity of command, chain of com-

## NEWSLINE 10.2

### Dean Urged to Comply with Policy

*Finals said to be 'part of the course'*

As the end of the semester rolls around, many students are getting anxious to finish their final exams as soon as possible.

There is one problem with that. Instructors who don't hold class during final exam week are in violation of University policy, Vice President for Academic Affairs John Guyon said.

"Our institutional finals policy requires instructors to hold class during final exam week in accordance with the University finals week schedule," Guyon said.

"Finals week is a part of the course," he said. "Students are not getting the full academic package when an instructor cuts a class short."

Guyon said that although he has urged that classes be held during final exam week, he is "a long way away" from using disciplinary action to enforce the policy.

Guyon has tried to enforce the policy by urging deans to ask department heads to request that instructors hold class according to schedule, he said.

C.B. Hunt, dean of the College of Communication and Fine Arts, said he sent out letters to each department chairman in his college telling them to comply with the University policy.

However, he said that finals for some classes can't always be held at the time given on the schedule.

"Some of our classes, especially in theater and music have projects for finals instead of tests. In cases like that we make allowances," Hunt said.

He added that an instructor needs approval from himself and the respective department head to hold final exams at any time other than finals week.

"When instructors start changing schedules, it throws off students' schedules," he said.

Seymour Bryson, dean of the College of Human Resources, said he hasn't had many problems with instructors not holding class during finals week.

"Normally the problem we have had is that some students have requested that they be allowed to take their final exams early," Bryson said. Exceptions are made sometimes with the approval of a department chairman, he said.

"Norman Doorenbos, Dean of the College of Science, said that although he is aware of instructors in other colleges violating the policy, all the classes in his college are in compliance.

Source: Southern Illinois University at Carbondale, *Daily Egyptian* (December 11, 1980), p. 1.

mand, span of control, and authority and responsibility. In addition, they visually represent for the individual employee two special aspects of the organization's division of labor. One is the centralization of decision-making, that is, how many and what kinds of decisions can be made at a given organization level. The second is the formalization of rules, policies, and procedures.

These basic attributes of organizations as seen by their members are often reflected in answers to the following questions. In the organization,

1. Are any management principles violated?
2. What are the vertical and horizontal divisions of labor?
3. How centralized or decentralized is decision-making authority?
4. How formalized are the rules, procedures, and policies?

When used in conjunction with an organization chart, answers to these questions can give a good description of the basic setting within which you as a manager will have to work.

## ORGANIZATIONS AS OPEN SYSTEMS

In the late 1950s and early 1960s, the more traditional views of management and organization such as "scientific management," "the management principles," and "the human relations" schools (see supplementary Module A) were challenged by a new group of scholars. The new developments resulted in a number of innovative, insightful investigations.[14] A revolution in management thought was virtually begun, with its underpinnings in an open-systems view of organizations.

In Chapter 1 we characterized the organization as an open system which transforms resource inputs into product outputs and human resource maintenance. One such view of a typical organization is shown in Figure 10.3. Note that the external environment is important both as a source of resource inputs and as a consumer of outputs.

When theorists recognized this interdependency between the organization and its environment, they introduced a dynamic element into our thinking about organizations. Managerial success became predicated on an ability to structure organizations in a manner best fitting a variety of environmental factors, as well as fitting the requirements of their size and production technologies.

Among the many different roots for this revolution in organizational theory, the work of Burns and Stalker is important.[15] They investigated 20 manufacturing firms in England and Scotland and concluded that two quite different organizational forms could be successful. A more traditional bureaucratic form thrived where the environment was stable and the firm was using a well-understood

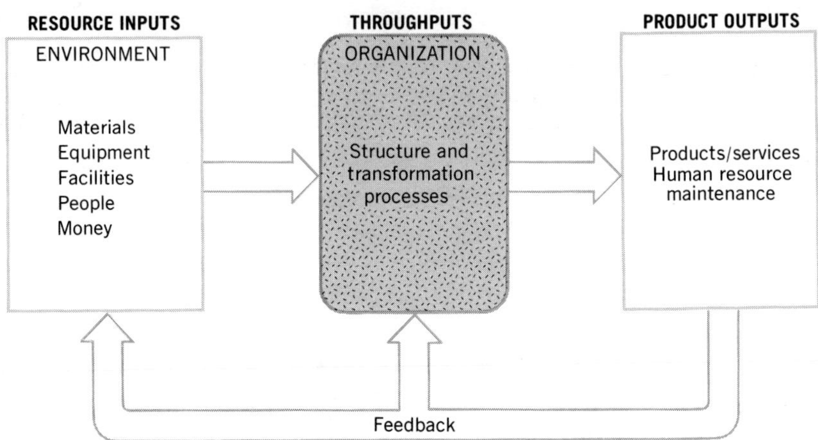


**FIGURE 10.3** An organization as an open system.

production technology. Where the environment and technology were rapidly changing, however, the vertical command structure of the more traditional bureaucratic form suffered difficulties. Here successful organizations stressed horizontal relations and managerial discretion.

Later studies in the United States and elsewhere seem to confirm the general notions of Burns and Stalker.[16] The term "contingency" has now crept into the literature. That is, we recognize that different problems and opportunites call for different organizational structures. There are many ways to run an organization, not just one. Indeed, for an organization to survive and be successful it must continuously adapt to its environment, modify its methods of production, and develop a structure which meets the opportunities and problems at hand.

While an open-systems view of an organization now appears obvious, it created a radical departure from the ways in which scholars traditionally looked at the attributes of organizations. We can summarize this revolution in two respects. First, we can examine the environment as a contingency variable; second, we can examine the context for action, technology, and size, in similar terms.

## THE ENVIRONMENT OF ORGANIZATIONS[17]

As "open systems," organizations must obtain resources from and exchange their outputs with their external environments. The external environment of any organization can be analyzed for its general and specific aspects.

## The General Environment

Organizations conduct most of their business within one common geographic area. This area bounds the general environment.[18] The cultural values, economic, legal-political, and educational conditions within a region comprise the **general environment** for organizations in that area. These conditions have a profound and often unseen effect on the internal operations and performance of organizations. See, for example, *Newsline 10.3*.

### Cultural Values

The most subtle aspects of the general environment emanate from cultural values. They tell us what actions are important, right, and proper, as well as what are considered desirable. Cultural values change slowly and often come in contradictory pairs. Table 10.3 outlines some dominant and contradictory American values.

In the United States we prize individualism, initiative, democracy, the family, among other values. But we recognize that these ideals cannot always be guides for action. Organizations, as a result, have relied upon contradictory values, including collectivism, leadership, authoritarianism, and economic achievement.

**Table 10.3 Selected Dominant and Contradictory American Values**

| Dominant Value | Contradictory Value |
|---|---|
| *Individualism* The secret of American greatness. | *Collectivism* People should stand together and work for common purposes. |
| *Initiative* People can be trusted if left alone to guide their conduct wisely. | *Leadership* You cannot simply afford to sit and wait for people to make up their minds. |
| *Democracy* The ultimate form of living together. | *Authoritarianism* Nothing would get done if everything were left to a popular vote. |
| *Goal attainment* Everyone should attempt to be successful. | *Method* What kind of person you are is more important than success. |
| *Family orientation* The family is the basic institution of the society. | *Economic orientation* Other institutions must conform to the needs of economic organizations since the national welfare depends on them. |
| *Equality of opportunity* America is the land of opportunity and all people should get a fair chance. | *Unequal opportunity* Not everybody is equal and the best should be put in charge. |

Source: Adapted from R. Lynd, *Knowledge for What? The Place of Science in American Culture* (Princeton, N.J.: Princeton University Press, 1939).

## NEWSLINE 10.3

### Foreign Firms: Outer Space or the Citibank Way?

With a dramatic increase in foreign investment in the U.S. (an increase of some 20% in 1979), foreign corporations are seeking American managers to head their probes into the U.S. Working for a foreign corporation dramatically illustrates some of the hidden cultural influences embodied in organizations. As one former executive said, "It's really like becoming an astronaut. You get to visit the other side of the moon." The executive described how Japanese organizations prefer a slow, deliberate, consensual approach that can frustrate American managers. Another former high level executive claims that "I think Japanese companies think Japanese companies are best run by Japanese."

European firms have fewer problems, but generally their approach stresses a "family responsibility for employees," and they place more emphasis on stature, school degrees, reputation in the community, and intelligence. Both European and Japanese firms have problems with American style compensation for top executives. Performance bonuses, stock options, and short-term financial performance are not given the emphasis in foreign corporations to the extent they are in many U.S. firms. To many European and Japanese firms, stock options are as foreign as McDonalds.

Several who follow international conglomerates see a new approach developing. A new cadre of "international managers" is emerging. Shared business experiences and a common business approach are beginning to overcome national cultural bonds. The movement toward a global corporate culture may replace national allegiance. In one professor's view, the company would be run "the Citibank way" or "the Sony way." The American, German, or Japanese way should be archaic.

Source: John Andrew, "Hiring American: More Foreign Firms Seek U.S. Executives for Their U.S. Units, but Snags Can Arise." *The Wall Street Journal* (February 3, 1981) p. 1. 

## Economic Conditions

While cultural values are important, organizations rely upon an economic surplus to thrive and prosper. With larger surpluses, more organizations get the resources they need to grow and develop. At the same time, economic growth means more people have the money to buy products and services. As the economy grows, organizations not only become larger, but also more specialized.

Comparatively small changes in the pattern of economic growth can have a dramatic impact on financial performance for even the largest firms. For instance, in 1980, the American economy was sluggish with exceptionally high interest rates. For the first time since 1921, General Motors lost money, as did Ford and Chrysler.[19] But, despite the huge losses in the auto industry, the U.S. economy did not collapse. Unlike the economies of many developing nations, it could continue to grow despite a decline in a major industry. Economic development encourages both more specialized organizations and a wider range of products and services. Firms may be more dependent upon one another, but the economy as a whole is less dependent upon one or a few major products and services.

## Educational Conditions

While economic conditions may have dramatic effects on the short-term financial health of firms, organizations also need educated individuals for survival. In more developed nations, economic and educational development move hand in hand. A larger proportion of white-collar professionals reflects a more favorable climate for organizations since more complex organizations need the specialized skills provided by more educated employees. Furthermore, few organizations can afford to fully train individuals for today's complex business operations. They rely upon colleges and universities to provide a pool of skilled professionals.

## Legal-Political Conditions

The fourth leg of the organization's general environment is the legal-political system. It allocates power among various groups in the society by developing, administering, and enforcing laws. For analyzing the general environment of organizations, three issues are particularly important. One issue concerns the range of governmental activity. A second deals with the capacity of the legal-political system to perform its functions. A third issue centers on stability.

There is considerable variation in the scope of governmental activity across nations. At one extreme sit governments that confine their activities strictly to protecting the nation from internal and external threats and establishing a few rules or laws to limit the actions of individuals and organizations. At the other extreme are governments which attempt to permeate virtually all aspects of the society. The broader the domain of government, the less attractive the general environment becomes to non-government organizations because their freedom of action is too constrained.

Just as organizations benefit from economic success, a developed legal-political system can provide important services. As legal entities, organizations enjoy protection under the law. A government which facilitates a balanced, rational allocation of power backed by legislation with efficient administration and enforcement provides an invaluable service to organizations. For instance, U.S. corporations benefit directly from federal economic forecasts, a national banking system, and international economic treaties.

Stability in the legal-political system is also critical. Stability can reinforce a narrow scope of governmental action backed by the capacity to provide legal-political services. Constant changes in laws and their interpretations seriously undermine the efforts of organizations to provide goods and services. Organizations need to know the rules of the game and be assured they will not change dramatically.

### Summary

Table 10.4 summarizes key attributes of the general environment of organizations and shows the preferred conditions for each attribute.

## The Specific Environment

Organizations position themselves within one or a series of organizational networks. They buy materials, hire workers, and secure financial backing from one another. They sell their products and services under the influences of competitors and government agencies. The set of suppliers, distributors, government agencies, and competitors with which an organization must interact to grow and survive constitutes its **specific environment.** Figure 10.4 highlights the distinction and linkage between the general and specific aspects of organizational environments.

**Table 10.4 The General Environment of Organizations**

| Dimension | Importance | Most Desirable Condition |
|---|---|---|
| Cultural values | Basis for acceptance and evaluation | Acceptance of contradictory values |
| Economic conditions | Source of resources needed for growth and survival | Rich economy with stable growth and a broad range of economic activity |
| Educational conditions | Source of skilled workers | Balance of white- and blue-collar workers with skills |
| Legal-political conditions | Provide rules of the game and the privilege to exist | A limited range of governmental activity; minimum changes in laws and regulations |

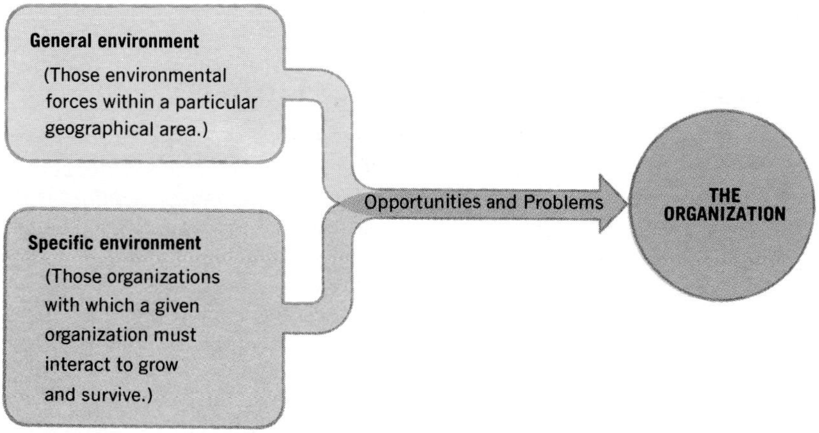

General environment

(Those environmental forces within a particular geographical area.)

Specific environment

(Those organizations with which a given organization must interact to grow and survive.)

Opportunities and Problems

THE ORGANIZATION

FIGURE 10.4 The organization environment.

An organization may have little choice about its general environment, but it can have substantial choice over its specific environment. By selecting the type of business it pursues, an organization really makes a broad choice of a specific environment. Within its industry, the organization also has some choices regarding suppliers and distributors. It has less immediate choices concerning labor unions, regulatory agencies, and competitors. Nonetheless, how the organization links itself to other organizations is partially under the discretion of top management.

## Environmental Complexity

A basic question in analyzing the environment of an organization is its complexity. This is especially true of the specific environment. As the specific environment becomes more complex, it provides an organization with more opportunities and more problems. **Environmental complexity** is a measure of the magnitude of the problems and opportunities in the organization's environment as evidenced by the degree of richness, interdependence, and uncertainty.

### Richness

The specific environment is richer and more developed when the firm's suppliers, distributors, competitors, and regulators are growing in numbers and resources. In a specific environment which is rich, organizations invest in each other for the future and thus help the industry grow. The opposite cycle occurs in a declining specific environment. *Newsline 10.4* illustrates the feedback one organization

## NEWSLINE 10.4

### School Closures Will Make City Furious

In a meeting held to discuss an environmental impact study of school closures, the School Board of Seattle was told again that the community will not accept closure of 14 school buildings at the end of this spring. Mayor Charles Royer urged the closing of fewer schools than in the plan developed by Superintendent David Moberly. Members of a planning commission, selected to represent all areas in Seattle, agreed with the Mayor.

A spokesperson for Save Lincoln High and the North Seattle Coalition charged in a press conference that the board was not using the most up-to-date population studies. These groups are considering legal action. Comments from interested citizens included, "I think school closures are wrecking Seattle; the School Board is just trading lower heating bills for higher gasoline costs."

Source: Adapted from "School Closures Will Make City Furious, Board Told," *Seattle Post-Intelligencer,* Seattle Washington (February 10, 1981), pp. 1–15.

received as it responded to a decline in the richness of its environment.

The richness or leanness of the environment is under only the partial control of the organization. A business firm is often driven by general economic conditions. For government agencies, the overall growth of the legal-political system appears to be a driving factor; and so it goes for educational and cultural organizations. The overall richness of the specific environment is heavily influenced by conditions in the general environment. However, each organization has some choice. It may select a richer or leaner set of specific environment organizations than the ones chosen by competitors.

### Interdependence

While richness is important, equally critical is the nature and type of interdependence established by an organization with environmental elements. The critical questions become—Who does the organization need? Who has the upper hand?

Exchanges between organizations typically yield benefits to each party. But the terms of trade may favor one organization more than another. Each organization would prefer to deal with outsiders that are isolated from one another and over which it has some control. In reality, the degree of control varies. An organization may have the upper hand with distributors, be on even terms with suppliers, and play a less powerful role with financial institutions and government regulatory agencies.

### Uncertainty

James D. Thompson wrote one of the most influential volumes in organization theory.[20] He stressed the importance of uncertainty in the organization's environment and argued that managing such uncertainty was one of the most critical tasks facing an organization. Larger organizations with rigid internal operations are particularly vulnerable to environmental uncertainties and external change. Investments can become outmoded, internal operations no longer work properly, and the organization loses the ability to direct itself.

Particularly important is the combined effect of higher interdependence and uncertainty. When most of the outsiders are changing dramatically, the environment becomes turbulent.[21] The organization can lose control, or become a tool of outside interests. It can become internally frozen by constantly changing directives. Most larger organizations spend considerable resources on forecasting and planning to minimize external uncertainty. They want to anticipate changes and prepare appropriate responses.

### Implications

In summary, managers need to be able to identify, understand, and successfully relate to the important elements in an organization's environment. In addition, they must recognize that,

1. The greater the richness, interdependence, and uncertainty in these elements, the greater is environmental complexity.
2. The greater the environmental complexity, the more problems and opportunities the organization has to deal with, and the greater the demand for a responsive organizational structure.

Chapters 11 and 12 will explain more precisely how organization structures should vary in response to environmental complexity.

## ORGANIZATIONAL CONTEXT: SIZE AND TECHNOLOGY

In addition to the external environment, a manager must be prepared to analyze the **organizational context** for action which includes its size and technology. Each of these factors is an additional attribute of organizations which may influence their structure and outcomes. However, within the research on size and technology, there exists a controversy.

One group of scholars argues that the size of an organization is the single most important factor influencing its structure. As size increases, the organization's structure is predicted to become more complicated.[22] On the other hand, a second group argues that there is a "technological imperative." That is, successful organizations are felt to arrange their internal structures to meet the dictates of their dominant technologies or work flows.[23] Some of the major issues in this debate are explained below.

## Technology

**Technology** is the combination of resources, knowledge, and techniques that creates a product or service output for an organization. The term is used in various ways in the OB literature. Thus, it will help you to become acquainted with two of the more common classification schemes used by theorists and managers to describe the technologies of organizations.

### Thompson's View of Technology[24]

James D. Thompson classifies technologies as intensive, mediating, or long-linked. Each type is described in Figure 10.5. In the intensive technology there is uncertainty as to how to produce desired outcomes. A group of specialists must be brought together to use a variety of techniques to solve problems. There is high interdependence among the members of such teams. Examples might be found in a hospital emergency room, or a research and development laboratory. Standard operating procedures are difficult to develop for this

| INTENSIVE | MEDIATING | LONG-LINKED |
|---|---|---|
| a. Cause-effect relations not well known. | a. Cause-effect known. | a. Cause-effect known. |
| b. Interdependence extensive across many members and/or units. | b. Interdependence pooled. | b. Interdependence sequential, step-by-step. |
| c. Utility—form, time, place, and information. | c. Utility—time, place, and information. | c. Utility—primarily form. |

**FIGURE 10.5** Major characteristics of three types of technologies. (Source: Adapted from Richard N. Osborn, James G. Hunt, and Lawrence R. Jauch, *Organization Theory: An Integrated Approach*. New York: John Wiley & Sons, 1980, p. 240.)

technology, and coordination is achieved by mutual adjustment among those trying to solve the problem.

The mediating technology links parties desirous of becoming interdependent. Banks, for example, link creditors and depositors, and store money and information to facilitate such exchanges. While all depositors and creditors are interdependent, the reliance is pooled through the bank. Thus, if one creditor defaults on a loan, no one depositor is injured. Wholesalers, retailers, and insurance companies are other organizations that use a mediating technology.

The long-linked technology is also called mass production or industrial technology.[25] Because it is known how to produce the desired outcomes, the task is broken down into a number of sequential and interdependent steps. A classic example is the automobile assembly line. The long-linked technology is relatively inflexible and a high volume of output is required to justify its use.

## Woodward's View of Technology[26]

Joan Woodward divides technology into three categories—small-batch, mass production, and continuous-process manufacturing. In small-batch production a variety of custom products are tailor made to fit customer specifications. The machinery and equipment used are generally not very elaborate, but considerable craftsmanship is often needed. In mass production the organization produces one or a few products with an assembly-line type system. The work of one group is highly dependent upon another, and the equipment is typically sophisticated and accompanied by very detailed instructions for workers. Mass production is similar to Thompson's long-linked technology. Organizations, using continuous-process technology produce a few products with considerable automation. Classic examples are automated chemical plants and oil refineries.

## The Technological Imperative

Joan Woodward conducted a now famous study of technologies and structures in English manufacturing firms. In her examination of some one hundred plants, she found systematic changes in structure as technologies varied from small-batch to mass production to continuous-process. The number of administrative levels increased, for example, as did the spans of control at the top management levels of the organizations. Most interesting was the similarity which emerged between small-batch and continuous-process manufacturers. Firms in both groups evidenced flexibility in their structures, work groups at lower levels were small, and there was very little

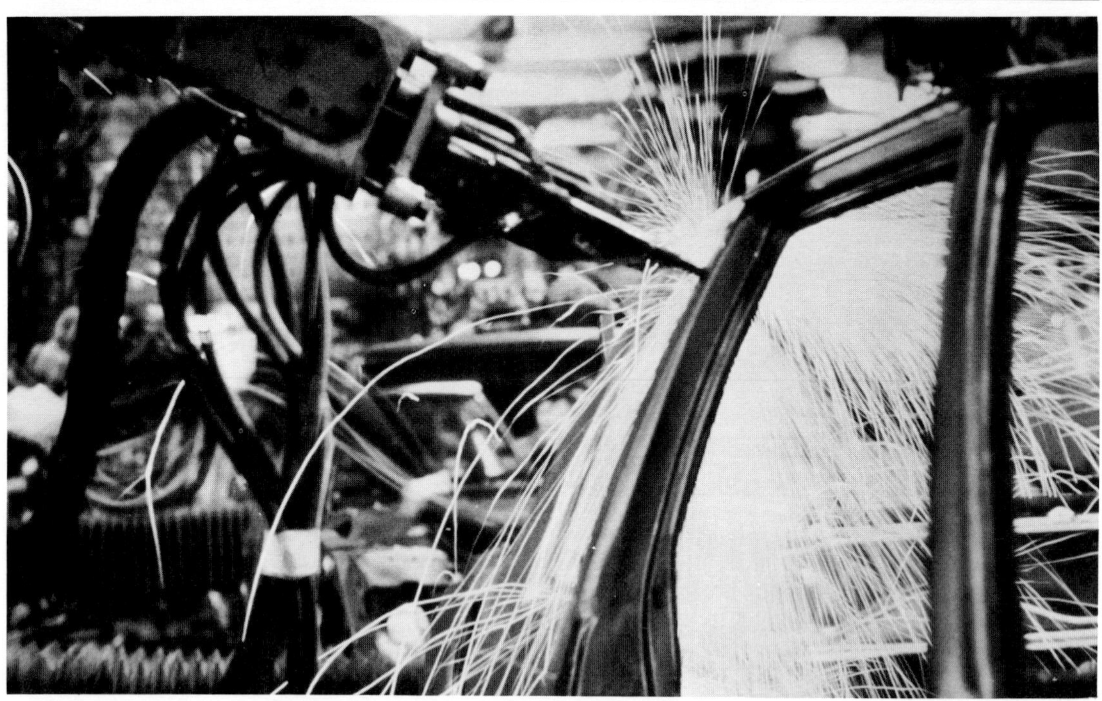

Using robots on an automobile assembly line.

line-staff conflict. The opposite was true for firms with mass-production operations.

Even more significant is Woodward's conclusion that the combination of structure and technology was critical in the success of the organizations. When technology and structure were properly matched, a firm was more successful. That is, successful small-batch and continuous-process plants had flexible structures with small work groups at the bottom; more rigidly structured plants were less successful. Successful mass-production operations, by contrast, were rigidly structured and had large work groups at the bottom. This **technological imperative** has since been supported by other investigations.[27]

## Size

Woodward's technological imperative has been challenged by two groups of researchers in particular. One group, the Aston researchers, conclude that organization size and interdependency in the environment are more important determinants of structure than is technology.[28] Another group of American sociologists, led by Peter Blau, argues that there are quite fundamental differences in the structures of small versus large organizational units.[29]

Research still continues along both the above lines. When support is found for size as an important influence on structure, it doesn't seem to make a lot of difference how size is measured. Similar results are obtained whether **size** refers to total number of employees, total assets, or still other alternative measures.[30]

### Size and Technology in Perspective

Even though this controversy continues about the relative importance of size and technology, several points can be made. As an organization grows, it has the opportunity to increase the number and types of specialists it uses. It may substitute rules, policies, and procedures for some managers and reserve judgmental roles for only very specialized managers. Growth does cause control problems. Managers must learn to administer the system without being able to directly observe all activity. Some control problems can be eliminated by grouping units in special ways, by using sophisticated information systems, or by some creative use of administrative assignments. We believe that successful organizations do change their structures as they grow in order to adapt to changing conditions. But there are many different ways in which they may adjust, and much of the adjustment is guided by top management.

As for technology, the more sophisticated it becomes in terms of required discretionary judgments or automated equipment and craftsmanship, the more difficult to manage it will be. This, too, will require more elaborate structural arrangements. Then, too, organizations often have multiple technologies. Huge conglomerates, for example, operate in several different industries and may produce over a hundred different products and services. Firms with a very large range of products and services will require different structures than those producing a narrower range of outputs. Thus technological sophistication and technological variability, in combination with size, have an important impact on structure.

## SUMMARY

People view organizations in different ways. They are often considered as bureaucracies, with attributes based upon a framework of legal authority and rationality. Organization members also view them in terms of organization charts, the division of labor, locus of decision-making, and the presence of governing rules, procedures, and policies. Organizations of any size have three vertical levels of action—top, middle, and bottom. Each level makes its own contribution, from setting goals and strategy, to the interpretation of strategy, to its implementation. Horizontal specialization often emerges in terms of line and staff personnel. Ideally, line units conduct the major business of the organization, while staff assists with special services and expertise.

The open-systems perspective has been the basis for a revolution in studying organizations. It focuses attention beyond the internal workings of the organization and asks the manager to analyze environment, size, and technology as important contingency variables. The external environment of the organization is divided into two major segments—the general environment and the specific environment. The general environment contains the cultural, economic, educational, and legal-political forces common to all organizations which operate within a given geographical area. The specific environment is unique to a particular organization and includes the other organizations with which it must interact. As an organization's environment becomes more complex, structural adaptations are required to ensure success.

The technology and size constitute an organization's context for managerial action. While scholars quibble over which is more important, managers must consider the impact of both on structure and outcomes. Schematically,

| | | | | |
|---|---|---|---|---|
| As context & environment | become complex → | organization structures must adapt | to ensure → | task performance & human resource maintenance |

## THINKING THROUGH THE ISSUES

1. Suppose you had an interview for a management trainee position with a large manufacturing operation. What could you predict about the firm before you even started the interviews?

2. You are about to have lunch with the assistant to the president of a wholesale drug company. What kinds of questions might you ask to show you understand the type of position the assistant holds?

3. If forces in the general environment are common to all or-

ganizations in a given geographical area, why should you even consider them?

4. Would you work for a foreign-owned company? Why or why not? What differences might you expect?

5. Identify those units which you think would be considered important parts of the specific environment by the president of your college or university. See if you can assess the complexity of this environment.

6. Some people claim that, when cuts are made within an organization, individuals will cooperate to minimize potential loss to the organization as a whole. Assume each unit is an organization and that budget cuts reduce the richness of the environment for each unit. What would you predict? Why?

7. Select a work unit with which you are familiar. Describe in detail the technology.

8. See if you can classify the technology of this same unit in Woodward's terms and in Thompson's terms. Which seems more useful and why?

## EXERCISE: ORGANIZATIONAL ANALYSIS—PART I

### Purpose:

To apply, as clearly and thoroughly as possible, the concepts developed in Chapter 10 to a real-world organization. This will give you and your group a chance to apply the concepts and share your findings with those of your classmates.

### Time:

50 minutes or more in class, plus at-home group preparations.

### Procedure:

**A.** Do the following before coming to class:

1. Form a group of four or five people. Assume the group is a management consulting team required to prepare a written report following the format indicated by your boss (the instructor).
2. Select an organization for analysis. In addition to work organizations, student organizations provide another possibility. Thus, student government organizations, fraternities, sororities, professional organizations, or clubs are possibilities. So

are scouting organizations, churches, and various volunteer organizations with which someone in your group may be familiar. Grocery stores, dry cleaners, or eating establishments are still other candidates. It is important to select an organization from which you can obtain observational and interview information and perhaps even some company records (such as organizational charts). If someone in your group is at least somewhat familiar with the organization, that is likely to be helpful. Finally, the organization should not be too large, since your group will be asked to discuss it from both the bottom up and the top down. If the organization is large, your instructor may want your group to focus on a major subsystem within it.

3. Using observations, interviews, and company records as necessary, your group has been assigned to do the following for its organizational report.

   **a.** Discuss the open-systems aspects of the organization. Try to apply such notions as equilibrium, hierarchy of systems, feedback, and boundaries.

   **b.** Discuss the major goals and objectives of the organization and trace an example of a means-ends chain. Discuss the extent to which human resources maintenance seems to be emphasized. Tie this discussion into a discussion of Weber's bureaucratic characteristics as they apply to the organization.

   **c.** Identify and discuss the organization's line and staff units.

   **d.** Specify the size of the organization and its major subunits.

   **e.** Discuss the organization's dominant technology in terms of one of the categorization schemes used in this book.

   **f.** Define and justify the boundaries for the organization's general environment. Briefly assess the complexity of the general environment and justify your assessment. Discuss cultural values and the impact they seem to have.

   **g.** Briefly assess the complexity of the organization's specific environment and defend your assessment.

**B.** Be prepared to turn in this part of the group report to your instructor and to discusss the group's findings and their implications.

## CASE: EAGLE AIRLINES I

Turn to the Eagle Airlines case at the end of Chapter 12. Then answer the following questions.

## Questions

1. Discuss the ideal and dysfunctional bureaucratic characteristics summarized in Table 10.2 as they apply to this case.
2. Discuss vertical and horizontal division of labor, centralization of decision-making authority, and formalization as they apply to the case.
3. Making any necessary assumptions (and clearly identifying them), describe Eagle Airline's general and specific environments. Try to arrive at an overall assessment of complexity for each of these environmental components.
4. Discuss the technology in Dodds' and Edwards' units in Thompson's terms and in Woodward's terms.

## THE MANAGER'S VOCABULARY

**Bureaucracy** An ideal form of organization whose characteristics were defined by the German sociologist Max Weber.

**Decentralization** The degree to which authority to make decisions is given to lower levels in an organization's hierarchy.

**Environmental Complexity** The magnitude of the problems and opportunities in the organization's environment as evidenced by the degree of richness, interdependence, and uncertainty.

**Formalization** The written documentation of work rules, policies, and procedures.

**General Environment** The set of cultural, economic, educational, and legal-political forces common to organizations operating within a given geographical area.

**Line Units** Conduct the major business of the organization.

**Management Principles** Guidelines for action which should not be violated without substantial reason.

**Organization Charts** Diagrams depicting the formal structures of organizations.

**Organizational Context** The size and technology of the organization.

**Specific Environment** The set of suppliers, distributors, competitors, and government agencies with which a particular organization must interact to grow and survive.

**Staff Units** Assist the line units by performing specialized services to the organization.

**Structure** A configuration of positions, job duties, and lines of authority among the component parts of an organization.

**Technology** The combination of resources, knowledge, and techniques that creates a product or service output for an organization.

**Technological Imperative** The idea that if an organization does not adjust its internal structure to the requirements of the technology it will not be successful.

## Important Names

**Burns and Stalker** Contingency theorists who argued that the structure of the organization should match its environment and technology.

**James D. Thompson** Provided an integrated theory of how and why organizations fear and respond to uncertainty; developed a framework for classifying technology.

**Max Weber** Specified the characteristics of an ideal bureaucracy.

**Joan Woodward** Developed the technological imperative and a framework for classifying technology.

## Notes

[1]J. Connelly, "N-Plants' Cost Will Jump by 300 Million: WPPSS Bungling Leads to the Latest Satsop Hikes," *Seattle Post-Intelligencer* (March, 2, 1981), p. 30; used by permission.

[2]Max Weber, *The Theory of Social and Economic Organization,* translated by A. M. Henderson and H. T. Parsons (New York: Free Press, 1947).

[3]John Jackson and Cyril Morgan, *Organization Theory: A Macro Approach for Management* (Englewood Cliffs, N.J.: Prentice-Hall, 1978).

[4]Victor A. Thompson, *Modern Organizations* (New York: Alfred A. Knopf, 1961).

[5]Richard N. Osborn, James G. Hunt, and Lawrence R. Jauch, *Organization Theory: An Integrated Approach* (New York: Wiley & Sons, 1980).

[6]Robert K. Merton, "Bureaucratic Structure and Personality." *Social Forces, 18* (1940), pp. 560–568.

[7]Alvin Gouldner, *Patterns of Industrial Bureaucracy* (New York: Free Press, 1954).

[8]Charles Perrow, *Organizational Analysis: A Sociological View* (Monterey, Calif.: Belmont/Cole, 1970).

[9]For instance, see Harold Koontz, Cyril O'Donnell, and Hans Weihrich, *Management,* Seventh Edition (New York: McGraw-Hill, 1980); and R. Thierauf, R. Klekamp, and D. Greiding, *Management Principles and Practices* (New York: John Wiley & Sons, 1977).

[10]Daniel Katz and Robert Kahn, *The Social Psychology of Organizations,* Revised Edition (New York: John Wiley & Sons, 1978); and H. T. Parsons, *Structure and Process in Modern Societies* (New York: Free Press, 1960).

[11]Ross Webber, *Management: Basic Elements of Managing Organizations* (Homewood, Ill.: Richard D. Irwin, 1975).
[12]See, for example, Rensis Likert, *The Human Organization* (New York: McGraw-Hill, 1967).
[13]Osborn, Hunt, and Jauch, op. cit., pp. 274–302.
[14]For details see, Arthur Bedeian, *Organization: Theory and Analysis* (Hinsdale, Ill.: Dryden Press, 1980).
[15]T. Burns and G. Stalker, *The Management of Innovation* (London: Tavistock, 1961).
[16]See, for example, Paul R. Lawrence and Jay W. Lorsch, *Organization and Environment: Managing Differentiation and Integration* (Homewood, Ill.: Richard D. Irwin, 1967).
[17]This section is based on Osborn, Hunt, and Jauch, op. cit., pp. 128–215.
[18]Richard Farmer and Barry Richman, *Comparative Management and Economic Progress* (Homewood, Ill.: Richard D. Irwin, 1965).
[19]*The Wall Street Journal* (July 25, 1980), p. 1.
[20]James D. Thompson, *Organizations in Action* (New York: McGraw-Hill, 1967).
[21]For instance, see Lawrence and Lorsch, op. cit.
[22]Richard H. Hall, *Organizations: Structure and Process* (Englewood Cliffs, N.J.: Prentice-Hall, 1977), pp. 181–193.
[23]Joan Woodward, *Industrial Organization: Theory and Practice* (London: Oxford University Press, 1965).
[24]James D. Thompson, op. cit.
[25]William Scott, "Organizational Structure," *Annual Review of Sociology,* (1975), pp. 1–20.
[26]Woodward, op. cit.
[27]See Osborn, Hunt and Jauch, op. cit., p. 236.
[28]The Aston studies include: David S. Pugh, David J. Hickson, C. R. Hinings, and C. Turner, "Dimensions of Organizational Structure," *Administrative Science Quarterly,* Vol. 13 (1968) pp. 65–105; C. R. Hinings and G. L. Lee, "Dimensions of Organizational Structure and Their Context: A Replication," *Sociology,* Vol. 5 (1971) pp. 83–93; and J. Inkson, David S. Pugh, and David J. Hickson, "Organizational Context and Structure: An Abbreviated Replication," *Administrative Science Quarterly,* Vol. 15 (1970) pp. 318–329.
[29]Peter M. Blau and R. A. Schoennerr, *The Structure of Organizations* (New York: Basic Books, 1971); and Peter M. Blau, C. Falbe, W. McKinley, and P. Tracy, "Technology and Organization in Manufacturing," *Administrative Science Quarterly,* Vol. 21 (1976), pp. 26–30.
[30]Hall, op. cit.

# 11

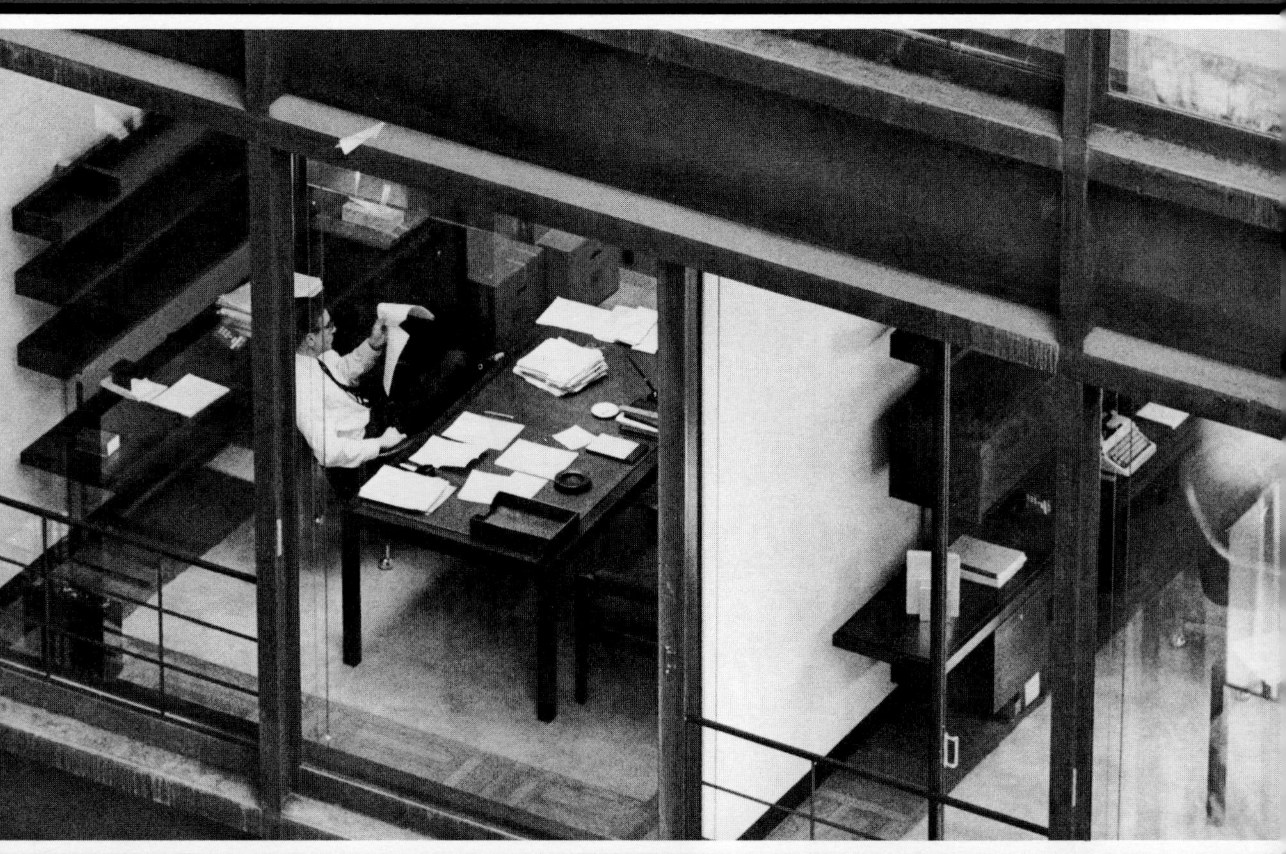

# ORGANIZATION STRUCTURES

# MONASTIC ORDER PUTS ITS FAITH IN CONTEMPORARY BUSINESS HABITS

The above headline from a recent *Wall Street Journal* article caught our attention.[1] The article begins with the following statement,

> Each morning after matins, the hour-long liturgical service which begins at 7 A.M.; a monk wearing the black cassock and round black hat of the Monastery of the Glorious Ascension walks into a specially air-conditioned room, flips two toggle switches, and punches a button marked "load." He waits for a low hum and a green glow.
>
> The hum comes from an IBM System/34 computer, and the glow comes from the computer's video-display terminal. The five Russian Orthodox monks hope to set up a computerized records service at their two-story house on a hill here in Resaca, Georgia. The name of the enterprise is MGA Computer Services.

In essence, the monks are entering the business world in hopes of generating income for the order by selling specialized computer services. They were negotiating with nine potential clients—four hospitals, three child-care centers, a professional association, and a medium-sized college. When asked about the new venture, the abbot Father Damian said, "A computer isn't a plow or an oven or a spatula, but it's still a tool that can be used for the greater glory of God."

**MANAGEMENT APPLICATIONS QUESTION**

How would you suggest that the monks organize themselves as MGA Computer Services in order to be successful in this business venture? Suppose, too, that the company really is a success and business expands. What should they do to meet the pressures of growth up to the level of 50, 100, or even 250 employees?

## PLANNING AHEAD

**The learning activities of this chapter will help you better understand the structural aspects of organizations.**
**Key topics are:**

**The Concept of Structure**
**Departmentation by Function**
**Departmentation by Division**
**Departmentation by Matrix**
**Mixed Forms of Departmentation**
**Vertical Specialization**
**Coordination and Control**

To work effectively in organizations, managers must understand organizational structures. The monks in our introduction to the chapter are good examples. MGA Computer Services will not succeed unless it is structured properly. Moreover, as it grows, different structures may be required to meet the special challenges of increasing size, advancing technology, and changing environmental conditions.

In Chapter 10 we defined structure as a configuration of positions, job duties, and lines of authority among the component parts of an organization. It may also be thought of as a formal pattern of activities and planned interrelationships among the various subunits of an organization and their managers. The present chapter examines in detail some of the alternative structures that may be implemented to help organizations achieve their purposes.

# THE CONCEPT OF STRUCTURE

The two core issues in the concept of organizational structure are (1) specialization and (2) coordination and control. Although you were introduced to these topics in Chapter 10, we now take the opportunity to review them in greater detail. Without a reasonable knowledge of these topics, you will find it difficult as a manager to understand the structures within which you work and to modify them to best fit the needs of the organization.

## Specialization

**Specialization** deals with the division of labor. It represents the grouping of people and material resources to accomplish the important tasks of the organization. **Horizontal specialization** involves the formation of work units or groups. We call this the process of **departmentation,** that is, dividing necessary duties and grouping jobs and people into administrative units. These are the work units needed to obtain, transform, produce, and market the products or services of the organization. There are several choices of departmentation in organizations. Here we will describe the functional, divisional, and matrix forms.

The division of labor also involves **vertical specialization.** This involves establishing who will manage the departments or work units and determining how they will make critical decisions. Put another way, vertical specialization creates various levels in the hierarchy of authority and indicates how plans will be set, results evaluated, and corrective action taken when outcomes do not meet expectations.

Two major considerations in vertical specialization are the use of sophisticated managerial techniques and the specification of line and staff units. After we have examined the various forms of departmentation, we will review these aspects of vertical specialization in some detail.

## Coordination and Control

Once the division of labor has been accomplished along both the vertical and horizontal dimensions, an organization needs coordination and control to link the specialized activities of people and departments to one another. It is only when such coordination and control are successful that the means-end chains of the organization become integrated and synergy occurs.

**Coordination** is concerned with ensuring proper communication among the components of the organization. It enables the units to understand one another's activities and to work well together. **Control** involves establishing goals and plans, measuring results, rewarding or sanctioning results, and taking corrective action.

Checkpoint

Means-end chains and synergy are terms initially introduced in Chapter 1. They are fundamental to your appreciation of organizations and for understanding why specialization, coordination, and control are such important aspects of organization structures. Remember the definitions:

**Means-end chains** Link the work efforts of individuals and groups to an organization's purpose.

**Synergy** The creation of a whole that is greater than the sum of its parts.

## Summary

The management of every organization develops its own means of accomplishing specialization, control, and coordination. The results constitute the structure of the organization. Before studying some alternative structures in more detail, recognize that the ideal structure has yet to be formulated. Selecting one type of specialization over another can yield both benefits and problems. A given type of control or coordination can help in some ways but hurt in others. Thus, each possible structure has strengths and weaknesses which need to be evaluated and then matched with the challenges posed by environmental and contextual factors. *What Consultants Do 11.1* shows the importance which one organization attaches to such structural evaluation.

## WHAT CONSULTANTS DO 11.1

### Evaluating the Structure of the NRC

Early in 1981, the Nuclear Regulatory Commission asked for proposals to "perform an independent review of the NRC's management structure, processes, procedures, and operations as applied to the management of its resources." The agency specifically asked that four tasks be accomplished. The approximate budget for the four tasks enumerated below was some $300,000.

**Task 1** Identify important NRC programs related to statutory responsibility with large (or growing) backlogs and length (or lengthening) processing times, and identify the resources associated with these programs.

**Task 2** Describe NRC's management practices for (a) defining acceptable levels of backlogs and establishing objectives for processing times, (b) forecasting and planning to deal with backlogs or processing time problems, and (c) allocating and managing resources to deal with these problems.

**Task 3** Evaluate the effectiveness of NRC's management practices in each area described in Task 2, considering factors within and outside NRC control, recommend improvements where warranted, and indicate potential resource savings where applicable.

**Task 4** Assuming that recommended improvements are implemented, identify areas where resource requirements, backlogs, and processing times should be declining, leveling off, or increasing in the future. Identify the factors causing these changes.

Source: RFP RS MPA-81-312, p. 21.

Before reading on, we can summarize the previous thoughts as follows,

| | | |
|---|---|---|
| To accomplish means-end chains and achieve synergy | organizations ⟶ require | structure in the form of horizontal specialization, vertical specialization, coordination, and control |

Let's turn now to examine three basic forms of horizontal specialization—departmentation by function, division, and matrix.

## DEPARTMENTATION BY FUNCTION

When dividing the total task into separate duties, management attempts to group similar people and resources together. Grouping by skill, knowledge, and action yields a **functional pattern of departmentation,** such as shown in Figure 11.1. In business, marketing, finance, production, and personnel are important functions. Middle States Manufacturing Company, described in the introduction to this part of the book, has a functional pattern of organization.

Table 11.1 summarizes the advantages of the functional pattern.[2] With all these advantages, it is not surprising that the functional form is extremely popular. It is used in most organizations, particularly toward the bottom of the hierarchy. Of course, the functional structure also has some disadvantages, as summarized in Table 11.1.

Organizations which rely heavily upon the functional structure may expect the following tendencies to emerge over time: (1) an emphasis on quality from a technical standpoint, (2) rigidity to change, particularly if change within one functional area is needed

**FIGURE 11.1** A functional pattern of departmentation.

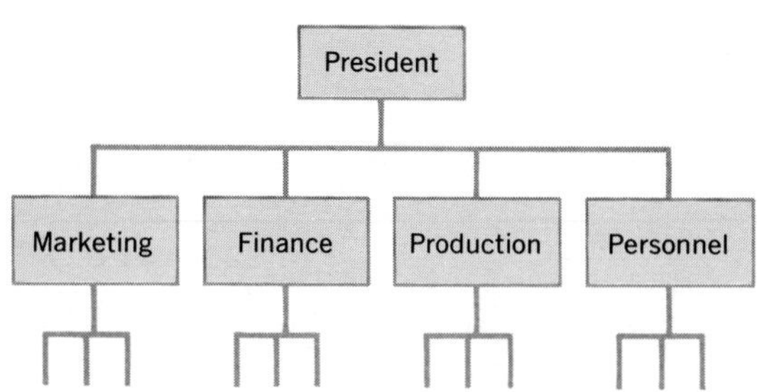

**Table 11.1 Major Advantages and Disadvantages of Functional Structure**

| Advantages | Disadvantages |
|---|---|
| 1. It can yield very clear task assignments that are consistent with an individual's training.<br><br>2. Individuals within a department can easily build upon one another's knowledge, training, and experience. Facing similar problems and having similar training facilitates communication and technical problem solving.<br><br>3. It provides an excellent training ground for new managers who must translate their academic training into organizational action.<br><br>4. It is easy to explain. Most employees can understand the role of each unit, even though many may not know what individuals in a particular function do. | 1. It may reinforce the narrow training of individuals and lead to narrow, boring, and routine jobs. Communication across technical areas is difficult, and thus conflict between units may increase. If the organization relies exclusively upon the functional structure, the lines of communication across the organization can become very complex. For instance, to find a common supervisor for a salesman and a credit review employee it may require going all the way to the top of the organization.<br><br>2. A problem related to the complex communication channels is that of "top management overload." Top management may spend too much time and effort.<br><br>3. There is a tendency for individuals to look up to the organizational hierarchy for direction and reinforcement or outside the organization to those having similar jobs. Rarely is the focus of attention on products, services, or clients. Guidance is typically sought from functional peers or superiors. |

to help other functional areas, and (3) difficulty in coordinating the actions of different functional areas, particularly if the organization must continually adjust to changing external conditions.

## DEPARTMENTATION BY DIVISION

The **divisional pattern of departmentation** groups individuals and resources by products, services, clients, territories, and/or legal entities.[3] Figure 11.2 shows a divisional pattern of organization grouped around products.

The divisional pattern is often used to meet diverse external threats and opportunities. Many larger, geographically dispersed organizations selling to national and international markets use departmentation by territory. The savings in time, effort, and travel

FIGURE 11.2 A divisional pattern of departmentation based on product.

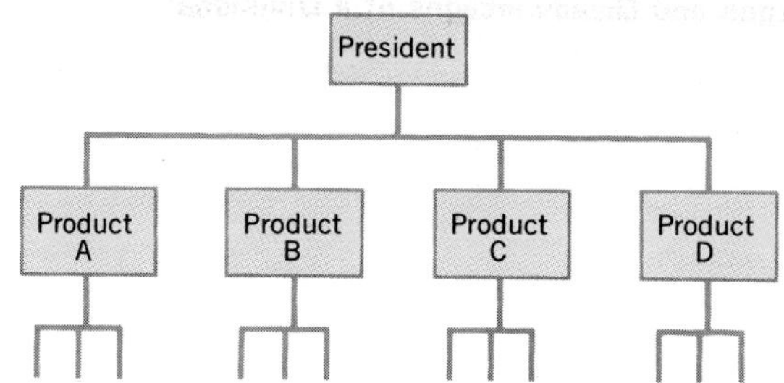


can be substantial; and, each territory can adjust to regional differences.

Organizations which rely upon a few major customers may organize their people and resources by client. Here, the idea is to focus attention on the needs of the individual customer. To the extent that customer needs are unique, departmentation by client can also cut costs, reduce confusion, and increase synergy.

Some organizations have a divisional structure as a result of their history. They have acquired firms or developed new legal entities to limit their liability in new risky ventures. Organizations expanding internationally may also departmentalize by legal entity to meet host country ownership requirements. For some large organizations, the maze of subsidiaries, joint ventures, and holding agreements would confuse even the brightest lawyer. Many government agencies also have a legal form of organization, primarily because of the legislation which authorizes their activities.

The major advantages and disadvantages of a divisional structure are summarized in Table 11.2.[4]

Organizations which rely heavily upon the divisional structure can generally expect the following tendencies to occur over time: (1) an emphasis on flexibility and adaptability to the needs of important external units, (2) a lag in the technical quality of products and services vis-à-vis functionally structured competitors, and (3) difficulty in coordination across divisions, particularly where divisions must work closely or sell to each other. In organizations where satisfying the demands of outsiders is particularly important, the divisional structure may provide the desired capabilities. This pattern can help cut costs in organizations with diverse operations which operate in many territories, produce quite different products and services, or serve a few major customers. It is the most popular form among large, multinational conglomerates. For instance, see *Newsline 11.1*.

**Table 11.2 Major Advantages and Disadvantages of a Divisional Structure**

| Advantages | Disadvantages |
|---|---|
| 1. Provides adaptability and flexibility in meeting the demands of important external groups. | 1. Does not provide a pool of highly trained individuals with similar expertise to solve problems and train new employees. |
| 2. Allows for spotting external changes as they are emerging. | 2. It can lead to a duplication of effort as each division attempts to solve similar financial, operating, personnel, and marketing problems. |
| 3. Provides for the integration of specialized personnel deep within the hierarchy. | 3. With the focus of attention on outsiders, divisional goals may be given priority over the health and welfare of the overall organization. Divisional organizations may have difficulty responding to corporate-wide threats. For instance, a functionally organized company may respond to a regulatory requirement by (a) establishing a new department, (b) developing a response to the regulations, and (c) implementing the response throughout all functions. The divisional organization may tend to respond on a division-by-division basis. Such multiple responses may make the total organization's response appear confusing and contradictory. |
| 4. Focuses on the success or failure of particular products, services, clients, or territories. | 4. Divisional firms may also have conflict problems across divisions when divisions attempt to develop joint projects, exchange resources, or share individuals. An example of this problem is known as the "transfer pricing" problem. How much should one division charge another for goods and services? What if the division price is greater than that of competitors? |
| 5. To the extent that this pattern yields separate "business units," top management can pit one division against another. For instance, Proctor and Gamble has traditionally promoted friendly competition among product groups. | |

## DEPARTMENTATION BY MATRIX

Some 25 years ago, NASA faced an apparently overwhelming challenge: to put a man on the moon by the end of the decade. The effort called for a management structure that placed an emphasis both on technical development and product development. An emphasis on

## NEWSLINE 11.1

### Structural Redesign at Swift

Esmark, Inc., a large conglomerate, is revamping Swift and Co. It is selling the meat packing operations which accounted for some two billion in sales in 1980.

Swift's new president, Joseph Sullivan, has made a number of changes in the design of the remaining Swift operation. He has reorganized Swift, changed the emphasis from marketing to commodities, and upped the budget for research.

Swift had been organized on a functional basis, with operations sorted into accounting, marketing, and the like. Now Swift has business groups, including processed meats, poultry, cheese, and dry groceries. The switch was to make group executives more responsive to market changes and aware of customer preferences. Marketing executives are upset, but those with commodity expertise call the change a brilliant move. Said one executive, "It's so easy (now) to talk with someone who understands what you're saying."

In explaining the shift, Sullivan stressed the importance of commodity prices and supply. "Butterball (Swift's turkeys) is a great brand, but you also have to have terrific commodity management. You have to buy your soybean meal at the right price. And if you're planning a big promotion on turkeys, you have to know how long it takes to raise a turkey."

Source: "Esmark Trims Fat From Swift Unit, Reorganizing It Along Product Lines," February 11, 1981, by Meg Cox. Reprinted by permission of The Wall Street Journal, 

one at the expense of the other would spell failure. The NASA solution was called the matrix organization. The dual reporting relationship is the hallmark of **departmentation by matrix,** as shown in Figure 11.3. Note that each group member reports to both a functional manager (production, marketing, engineering) and a project manager.

The major advantages and disadvantages of this structure are summarized in Table 11.3.

During the seventies the matrix structure was a fad. Many progressive, well-managed organizations used the matrix structure. Thus, some organizations adopted this form to appear similarly progressive and well-managed. Furthermore, many firms have adopted elements of the matrix arrangement without using the term "matrix." Special project teams, coordinating committees, task forces, blue-ribbon commissions—all these are the beginnings of the matrix structure.

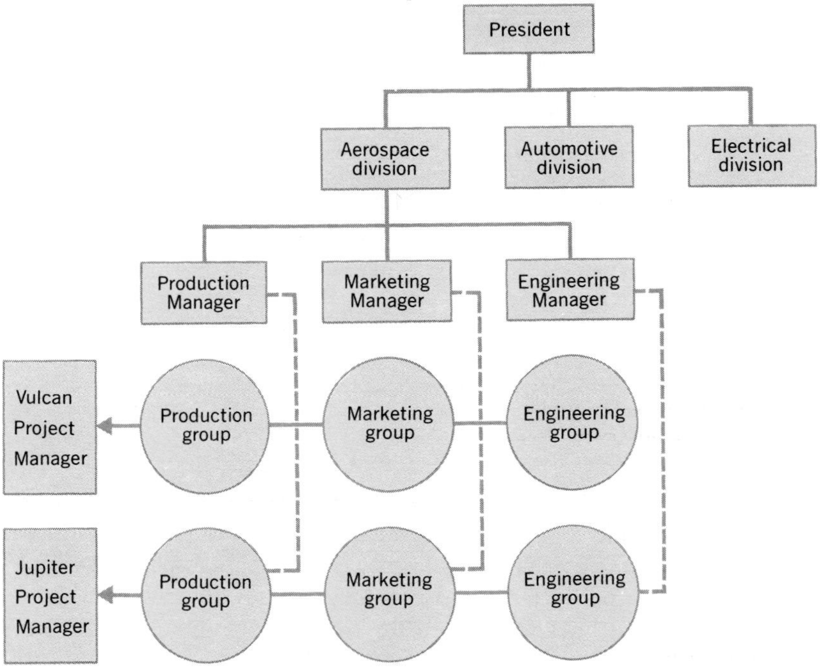

President

Aerospace division | Automotive division | Electrical division

Production Manager | Marketing Manager | Engineering Manager

Vulcan Project Manager ← Production group — Marketing group — Engineering group

Jupiter Project Manager ← Production group — Marketing group — Engineering group

**FIGURE 11.3** A matrix pattern of departmentation at NASA.

## MIXED FORMS OF DEPARTMENTATION

Which form of departmentation should be used? As the matrix structure suggests, it is possible to departmentalize by two different methods at the same time. Actually, organizations often use a mixture of departmentation forms. In fact, it is often desirable to divide the effort (group people and resources) by two methods at the same time to balance the advantages and disadvantages of each.

### Combined Functional and Divisional Patterns

Let's start with an example involving the combined use of functional and divisional departmentation.[5] Northwest Manufacturing and Wholesale produces filters for autos, ships, and, most recently, for the elimination of toxic and nuclear waste. Its plant in Tacoma, Washington, produces marine filters. The Walla Walla, Washington works specializes in nuclear and toxic waste filters. All auto filters are manufactured in Los Angeles. The firm is active in both the new

**Table 11.3 Major Advantages and Disadvantages of a Matrix Structure**

| Advantages | Disadvantages |
|---|---|
| 1. Combines strengths of both functional and divisional departmentation. | 1. Very expensive. |
| 2. Helps provide a blending of technical and market emphasis in organizations operating in exceedingly complex environments. | 2. Unity of command is lost (individuals have more than one supervisor). |
| 3. Provides a series of managers able to converse with both technical and marketing personnel. | 3. Authority and responsibilities of managers may overlap, causing conflicts, gaps in effort across units, and inconsistencies in priorities. |
| | 4. Difficult to explain to employees. |

Source: Summarized from S. Davis, P. Lawrence, H. Kolodny, and M. Beer, *Matrix* (Reading, Mass.: Addison-Wesley, 1977); and L. Sayles, "Matrix Management: The Structure with a Future," *Organizational Dynamics,* Vol. 5 (1976) pp. 2–17.

equipment market for auto filters and the replacement market. Most auto filters are sold in the replacement market via discount stores and auto supply outlets. This is a highly competitive market in which success depends upon providing inventory control and restocking for hundreds of retail outlets. Filters for toxic waste, nuclear applications, and marine use must be specifically tailored to individual customers. The president also sees substantial growth opportunities in Europe. Now European sales, mainly in the United Kingdom, account for 22 percent of total sales and 29 percent of gross profits.

Checkpoint

Review the functional and divisional patterns. How would you structure Northwest Manufacturing and Wholesale to obtain the advantages of each? Draw your organization chart on a separate sheet of paper and then compare it to Figure 11.4.

Figure 11.4 shows a possible organization chart for this successful and growing regional firm. It has three divisions, each of which is a separate legal entity. The largest division is Northwest Manufacturing which produces all the filters and markets for industrial consumers. Note that it is functionally organized below the President with Vice-Presidents of Finance, Personnel, R&D, and Operations. Due to the close coordination required between manufacturing and industrial sales, both plant managers and the director of industrial sales report to the Vice-President of Operations. As you might expect, both regional and product differences separate the plants. Note the technical thrust of this division, with its emphasis on a functional structure at the top and with product groups in sales and operations.

Eurofilter, a separate division, is structured to serve the Euro-

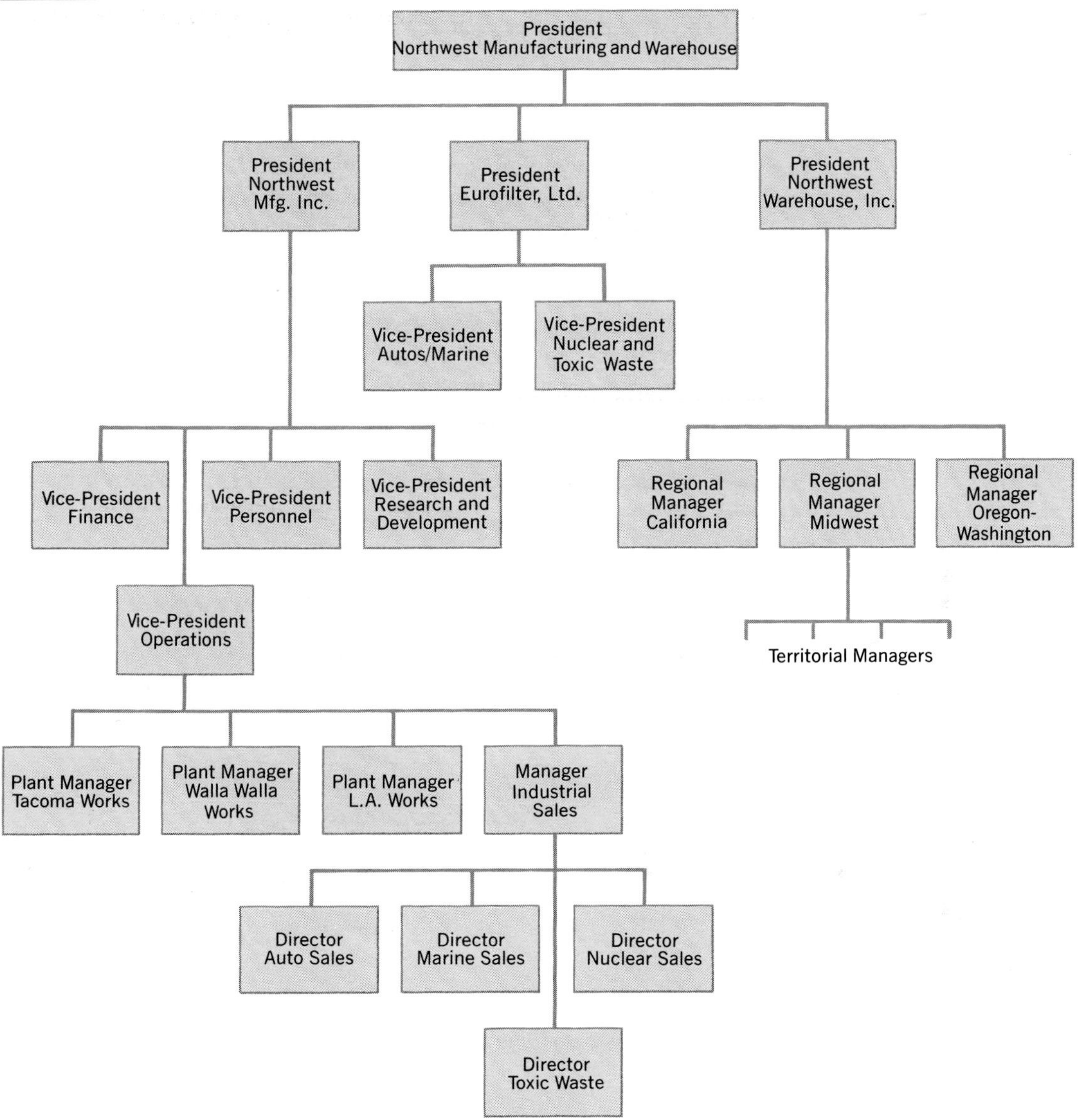


**FIGURE 11.4** Partial organizational chart for Northwest Manufacturing and Wholesale.

pean market. Note that the divisional form dominates. In a similar fashion, the wholesaling company is dominated by divisional departmentation, since the key to this business is service. Maintaining retailer inventories and ensuring prompt delivery are important. Thus, customers are grouped into territories, and the territories form regions headed by a regional manager.

## Combined Matrix and Functional Patterns

Now let's take a look at a research organization which utilizes a matrix structure. The firm offers research services to a broad range of clients, but the majority of its business is with three large government agencies. Quality Research employs specialists in management, psychology, economics, sociology, law, and health care. Technical quality and responsiveness to the client are considered equally important and should be facilitated by the organization structure.

This firm solves the problem in two ways, as shown in Figure 11.5. First, financial and administrative functions are separated from research. This is a functional division. Within the research function, functional heads are assigned for each discipline. These individuals are charged with the responsibility of hiring qualified personnel and encouraging professional development. Coordinators are designated for each of the key agencies to help define client research needs, respond to client requests, and coordinate projects performed by the research staff.

For each project there is a principal investigator (PI). The PI is drawn from one of the functional areas and manages a particular project. Since individuals may work on several projects, they could

**FIGURE 11.5** A partial organization chart for Quality Research Associates.

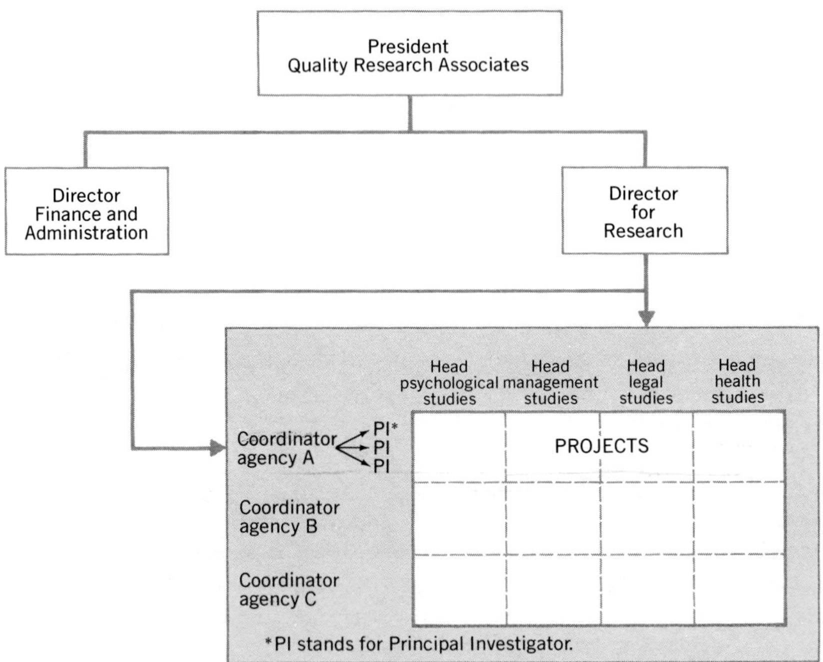

be a PI on one and a researcher on another. Note that all individuals have two immediate superiors. One is the functional head. The other is an agency coordinator for PIs or a PI for a researcher assigned to a particular project. Note also that both the coordinators and functional heads report directly to the director for research.

### Summary

The first example of a manufacturing and wholesaling firm showed the use of functional and divisional patterns. The second example of the research organization involved functional and matrix forms. An emphasis on the divisional and matrix patterns provides a structure which is more fluid and responsive to external pressures and opportunities. A pure functional pattern, on the other hand, provides a more rigid structure, often centering on technical quality.

As we will see in Chapter 12, the departmentation of an organization should fit the demands and constraints placed on it by environmental and contextual factors. The choice of functional, divisional, and matrix patterns will influence the organization's ability to respond to outside demands, produce high-quality products and services, and efficiently manage people and resources. No one pattern or combined form is best for all organizations. The best choice is the one in tune with the goals of the organization, technological requirements, the magnitude of its operations, and the external pressures and opportunities facing the system.[6] See *What Managers Do 11.1* for two recent examples of how organizations modify their structures to meet such challenges.

## VERTICAL SPECIALIZATION

Grouping individuals and resources into departments is only half of the specialization issue. The other half is concerned with determining who will manage the work units and how critical choices will be made. This is a question of vertical specialization.

Traditionally, the central issue in vertical specialization was span of control. It was viewed as mainly a question of how many subordinates should report to a manager. Now managers and consultants realize that the issue is more complex. Most organizations use a combination of managerial techniques and line and staff units to vertically specialize the division of labor.

## WHAT MANAGERS DO 11.1

### Structural Changes at Sears and Paine Webber

Rapid changes just aren't possible with some 400,000 employees, 2,300 locations, and a sales volume of over 24 billion. But to quicken the pace of change, Sears has restructured itself. It now has three operating groups: retailing (Sears), insurance (Allstate), and real estate and financial (Seraco). Within the retailing group the number of territories (regions) will be cut from five to four. An attempt will be made to develop a spirit of "sibling rivalry" among the three divisions. Yet Sears will "cross pollinate" across divisions by moving top executives from division to division. For instance, a former Vice-Chairman in Allstate becomes a Vice-Chairman in the retailing group (Sears).

Paine Webber, Inc., known publically as a New York-based stock broker, is also undergoing reorganization. Three operating groups are being formed, one centering on investment-research, a second involved in investment banking, and the third consisting of brokerage operations. Paine Webber plans to spend substantial sums on information systems to increase control while establishing a "collegial" management team comprising officials from the three major operating groups.

Top management at both Sears and Paine Webber believe their reorganizations will substantially increase the chances of survival, growth, and future profitability.

Source: Excerpted from "Identity Crisis: Sears Finds Broadening Its Image Takes Time, Presses Staff to Adjust," *The Wall Street Journal* (October 31, 1980), pp. 1, 18; and "Don Marron is Revitalizing Paine Webber with a Goal of More than Just Survival," *The Wall Street Journal* (November 5, 1980), p. 48. Reprinted by permission of The Wall Street Journal, 

## Managerial Techniques

**Managerial techniques** are the systematic methods managers use for detecting problems and opportunities, selecting among alternatives, evaluating, and instituting corrective action. They typically relate to the technical aspects of marketing, operations, finance, and personnel management. They are the means of showing how managers can make better decisions. For instance, marketing managers can make better decisions with market forecasts. Other common and useful techniques are budgeting, elaborate planning models, sophisticated capital investment models, and computerized inventory control systems. These techniques are used to expand the volume and scope of the operations that a manager can administer. They replace intuitive judgments and provide ordered, detailed processes for obtaining data and combining apparently disparate sets of information.

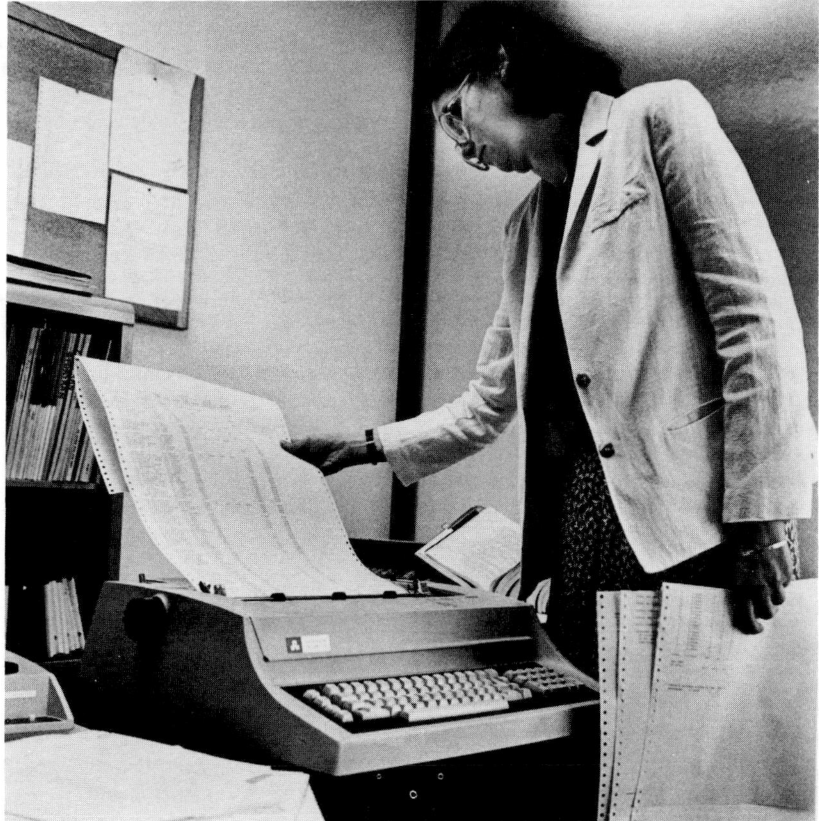

Computerization in the workplace.

The mix of managers and managerial techniques adopted by a particular organization should rest on a number of factors.[7] First are the problems and opportunities facing the system. A second is the extent to which management understands how to combine raw materials, people, and equipment to produce desired products and services. A third is the consistency and range of outputs. Table 11.4 provides guidelines for the use of managerial judgment versus managerial techniques.

## Line and Staff Units

No manager can be an expert in all areas. As individuals move up the organizational ladder they become, of necessity, generalists. They lose touch with new developments in the technical and functional areas. To expand the competency of executives, organizations often develop specialized staff units. The placement of these staff units is particularly important. Grouping many staff units at the top rein-

**Table 11.4 Some Guidelines Concerning the Use of Managerial Judgment Versus Managerial Techniques**

- *As the environment of the organization becomes more uncertain, managerial judgment and initiative should be prized over decision techniques.* The uncertainty may be positive, due to possible opportunities. It may be negative, due to deterioration in economic conditions, increases in regulation, or problems with suppliers, distributors, and unions. In stable settings, firms can cut costs, improve the consistency of response, and expand the capabilities of existing managers using managerial techniques. Investments in the hardware (equipment) and software (programs and training) may be extensive. However, the stable environment allows heavy initial costs to be spread over many years.

- *Organizations with well-defined and stable technologies have more opportunity to substitute techniques for managers than firms relying upon more volatile processes.* Volatility in the technology may be due to a number of factors. Of major importance in the electronics industry, for instance, is new technical development. In primary and secondary education, the volatility in methods of teaching emanates from our lack of understanding. We appear to know more about building bridges across rivers than bridging the gap between ignorance and knowledge. Without a clear understanding, organizations are forced to rely more upon judgments than techniques.

- *Organizations that must produce small quantities of many different products and/or services usually opt for managers over managerial techniques.* Again, the heavy fixed costs of developing and implementing these techniques are difficult to recover. For similar reasons, smaller organizations often opt for managers even where they produce few products with stable technologies in a predictable setting.

forces the expertise and managerial scope of top level decison makers. Placement lower in the organization puts these specialized units toward the interface between planning and implementation.

Take another look at the partial organization chart for Northwest Manufacturing and Wholesaling (Figure 11.4). Some obvious staff specialities are missing. These include legal, planning, auditing, and labor relations, among others. As organizations grow, specialists in these areas more than pay for themselves. They provide the needed technical assistance in areas where managerial techniques cannot substitute for judgment.

When these specialists are placed at the top of the organization, they expand top management capabilities. This tends to yield comparatively little vertical specialization. As an employee or lower level manager, you are likely to see this as a centralized pattern of decision making. For instance, in the case of Northwest Manufacturing, staff could be attached to the office of the president.

When staff specialists are moved down under divisional heads in the Northwest example, the action capacity of these managers is expanded and each can begin to operate more as an independent operation. More expertise for planning, adjusting to external threats, evaluating action, and instituting corrective measures is available to each division head. Commensurate with the additional assistance, we would expect divisional managers to expand their range, scope, and depth of action. Further planning, adjustment to external threats, and instituting corrective action can be tailored to the specific problems of each division.

Rarely does an organization place all staff units at the top or bury them deep within the hierarchy. Most often some are elevated to the top while others remain farther down. Where the firm needs corporate-wide action to confront a specific threat or opportunity, staff specialists may be placed toward the top. For instance, in the 1970s some firms developed an affirmative action staff to guide corporate efforts to reduce discrimination. In the 1980s, these units are being dispersed down into the hierarchy. Figure 11.6 illustrates how placement of staff changes the look of the pyramid we visualize when we traditionally think of an organizational hierarchy.

There may be secondary effects associated with staff units at the top of the organization.[8] Staff personnel may use their high level position to increase the attention given to their area. Top level units may attempt to get operating managers to obtain clearances before taking action. And, of course, few top level staff units can avoid the temptation to keep detailed written records, routinize staff work via standardized forms, and improve their performance with more staff and a larger budget. Heads of such expanding staff units may be called "empire builders."

## Vertical Specialization in Summary

From the view of top management, vertical specialization centers on two related questions. One, who manages, and how will they manage? Two, where should staff specialists be placed? The most appropriate pattern of vertical specialization depends upon the environment of the organization, its size, its technology, and its goals. Generally, as organizations grow, vertical specialization increases.

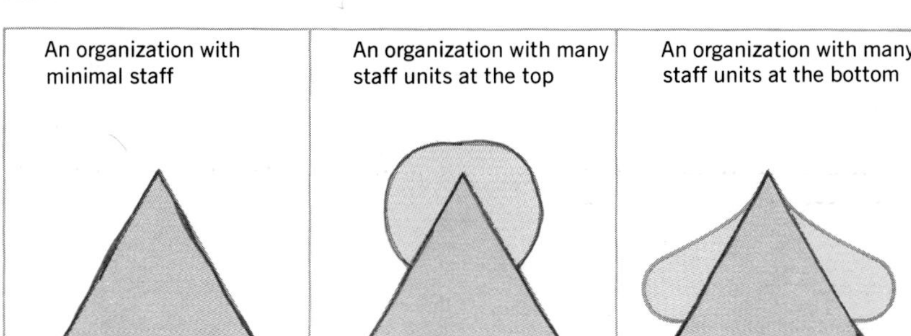


**FIGURE 11.6** How placement of staff changes the visual look of an organization.

More stable settings and more stable, well-controlled technologies also produce greater vertical specialization. Often too, increasing vertical specialization takes the form of more elaborate managerial techniques.

## COORDINATION AND CONTROL

Our discussion to this point in the chapter indicates that there are many ways of grouping people and resources into operating departments. Horizontally, we looked at functional, divisional, and matrix patterns of departmentation. Vertically, we examined the use of managerial techniques and the placement of line and staff units.

Specialization divides the labor in organizations and differentiates people and work units from one another. Given this differentiation, a means is then needed to provide for the integration of the multiple and varied specialized activities, and to minimize any weaknesses resulting from the organization's patterns of specialization. When management selects a functional pattern of departmentation, for example, the need for coordination and control across products, services, territories, and clients quickly emerges. Conversely, if the divisional pattern is selected, coordination and control across functional areas are needed. Now we need to specify exactly what we mean by coordination and control and show how organizations can successfully coordinate and control diverse and specialized activities.

### Coordination

**Coordination** is the mechanism an organization uses to link the actions of its units into a consistent pattern. Much of the coordination within units is handled by the manager. Smaller organizations, using simple technologies and operating in stable settings, may rely upon their management hierarchy to provide the necessary consistency. But as the environment becomes more complex, as technologies become increasingly sophisticated, and as the organization grows, managers become overloaded. The organization then needs to develop more efficient and effective ways of linking units.

The organization often uses a mix of personal and impersonal methods of coordination. Some of these methods are quite obvious; some are not. They are summarized in Table 11.5[9]

### Control

While coordination is concerned with meshing the actions of units across the organization, control is more vertical in character. Control

**Table 11.5 Personal and Impersonal Methods of Coordination**

**Personal Methods**

*Common values* Built into management through selection, socialization, training, and reinforcement. Examples: a company dress code or business philosophy.

*Grapevine* Informal communications. Though fast, these are often inaccurate and need to be supplemented with more formal means.

*Committees* Allow for participation and mutual adjustment across units. Good for communicating complex, qualitative information. Especially useful between two managers whose units must work together.

**Impersonal Methods**

*Written rules, policies, and procedures* Schedules, budgets, and plans are examples.

*Specialized staff units* Often used to coordinate functions where there is divisional departmentation. An example is a personnel staff unit to ensure policy consistency across divisional units. In a matrix structure the staff coordinating function often develops into a line decision-center.

*Management information systems* Originally were such things as suggestion systems, newsletters, etc. Now are often computerized information and record keeping systems. Particularly useful where timing of efforts is important.

is the set of mechanisms used to keep action and outputs within predetermined limits. **Control** deals with setting standards, measuring results versus standards, and instituting corrective action.[10] As with coordination, much of the control within a unit is the responsibility of the manager. But organizations typically use a variety of impersonal control mechanisms.

The most popular control technique is probably the planning-budgeting process. Corporations often develop five-year rolling plans where the latest year is used to develop a detailed budget. Businesses may also employ Management by Objectives (MBO) to ensure that managers set specific measurable goals, monitor progress toward these goals, and receive rewards based on their accomplishments. For an example of MBO in practice, see *What Managers Do 11.2*.

Controls establish specific standards, systematically measure individual performance, and adjust rewards or sanctions to measurable performance. Toward the bottom of the organization, management may integrate its procedures into its controls. Managers may specify exactly how a particular series of duties is to be performed. For instance, in one case we know, mail sorters are advised by the postal service to hold letters at a 45-degree angle to sort mail more efficiently. One clerk who held the mail at a 90-degree angle was given a five-day suspension for violation of the control procedure. Rarely is such "process control" applied in middle and upper management ranks.

## WHAT MANAGERS DO 11.2

### MBO at the Department of Energy

Management by objectives (MBO) is embodied in the federal government's Senior Executive Service (SES). The Department of Energy (DOE) is instituting the government approach to management by objectives in order 3430.2 (1980). An excerpt from the order shows the control process of MBO via performance appraisal of senior managers.

#### *Step 1 Identification of Critical Elements and Subelements*

- On or before the beginning of each rating period the rating official shall review with the incumbent executive the duties and responsibilities of his/her position, the critical elements, subelements and performance objectives that will be used to measure the executive's performance. Unless otherwise provided, the rating official's opinion must prevail in any disagreement between executive and rating official as to critical elements, subelements and performance objectives.
- Two critical elements have been determined to be common to all SES positions in the department: 1 Achievement of Organizational Goals and 2 Managerial Effectiveness
- Other critical elements relevant to a specific position may be identified. To the extent any subelement listed under managerial effectiveness reflects a critical measure of successful performance, it may become a critical element that is further subdivided into its appropriate subelements.

#### *Step 2 Mandatory Interim Performance Review*

- By at least April 1 of each year, rating officials and their SES subordinates must review and, if necessary, update or add any critical element, subelement or performance objective that will be used to measure the subordinate executive's performance at the end of the rating period.
- Interim reviews may be made more frequently at the option of the rating official, but must be completed whenever a significant change in program priority of reorganization occurs.
- A copy of any changes in critical elements, subelements or performance objectives following an interim review will be furnished to the executive as they are made.

#### *Step 3 Performance Appraisal*

- At the end of the rating period (normally September 30) each rating official must initiate a performance appraisal for each subordinate executive. The appraisal should be completed no later than 30 days after the end of the rating period.
- The rating official shall assign an overall performance rating based upon the extent to which the executive's critical element summary ratings meet the performance rating definitions.
- The rating official shall also include appropriate recommendations for performance bonuses, incentive awards, pay adjustments, designations of rank for executives who have demonstrated exceptional performance or achievement, reassignment, or removal from the SES.

#### *Step 4 Appraisal Review and Executive Response*

- When the rating official has completed the Performance Appraisal, a copy shall be given to and discussed with the executive.
- The executive shall be given the opportunity to submit a written response to the rating official's appraisal and any accompanying recommendations.

A post office letter sorter: is she holding the letters at the correct angle?

The controls evident in *What Managers Do 11.2* are unusually detailed. You may be surprised at the lack of control in the top management ranks of many organizations. Probably less surprising is the lack of effective "output controls" at the bottom of the organization.[11] Unions, for instance, often push very hard for uniform work quotas backed by uniform salary increases and benefits. Even where elaborate goals are specified and measured, the organization may lose control because it does not provide differential rewards. For instance, pay and promotions for professors may follow years of experience more closely than research or teaching excellence.

Given constraints in linking rewards to measured performance, organizations must often base their control efforts on specifying the priority placed on different goals. They monitor processes which have been associated with success in the past, and they may expand the budgetary discretion of units with a record of success. Often committee meetings, information systems, and elements of the matrix structure may be used to try to boost unit performance. Rarely are such attempts very successful since they fail to provide all the important ingredients to effective control: attainable standards, accurate measurement of performance, and rewards (sanctions) based on performance.[12]

Efforts to exert control in organizations can involve limiting action, reducing rewards, increasing output targets with existing resources, and eliminating poor performers. Thus, control efforts often yield a series of difficult side effects. Some of these problems are summarized in Table 11.6.[13]

## Coordination and Control In Summary

Coordination helps organizations achieve synergy. Personal and impersonal mechanisms can be used to provide needed linkages among and across components of the organization. Personal methods of coordination include common values, grapevine, and committees. Impersonal methods are used by many organizations and include sched-

**Table 11.6 Some Side Effects of Organizational Controls**

*Imbalance* Concentrating on one goal neglects others. For example, rewards based on volume may lower quality. In emphasizing short-term efficiency, equipment maintenance, human resource maintenance, and research and development may be minimized.

*Lack of patience* Managers attempt a "quick fix," and when that doesn't work try one short-term fix after another without allowing time for any to be successful.

*Across the board cuts* Common in public institutions as politically acceptable; they don't focus where needed. The organization loses growth opportunities and may not reduce unnecessary expenditures.

*Confusing documentation with action* Concern for performance may lead to a stack of impressive-sounding plans.

*Vague and unrealistic expectations* Chapter 6 indicated the problems of "do your best goals" in comparison with more specific ones. Also; goals asking for more than a 10 percent improvement are often unrealistic.[14]

*Panic* This often ensues when effective control is suddenly established over a unit. Communication accompanied by participation helps avoid panic.

*Standard increasing* Without increasing resources, changing methods, or giving better rewards, higher standards are set. This tends to lead to long-term problems.

ules and staff units; they are often used as cheaper mechanisms to link unstable units. As the organization favors impersonal methods, the structure of the organization becomes more bureaucratic in orientation.

Control is another means for ensuring synergy in organizations. Three elements are needed for effective control. They are the establishment of measurable standards, measurements against standards, and rewards or sanctions based on measured performance. Organizations have difficulty in developing effective control systems. In some it may be virtually impossible to measure an individual's or unit's actual contribution. In others, institutional conditions such as union contracts may limit the use of rewards and sanctions. Thus, control in many organizations boils down to a mixture of methods and may be accompanied by negative side effects.

Organizations which attempt to emphasize controls of methods and means have a more bureaucratic structure than those stressing control of outputs. Specifying in detail exactly how duties are to be performed and basing controls on these procedures also yields a more rigid structure. Conversely, if managers are allowed to develop their own methods but are held accountable for results, the structure is more flexible.

## SUMMARY

This chapter has focused on four key aspects of organization structure: horizontal and vertical specialization, coordination and control. Horizontal specialization centers on the kinds of departments needed to obtain, transform, and market an organization's products and services. Functional grouping (by skill, knowledge, or action) is one kind of departmentation. Divisional grouping (by products, services, clients, territories, and/or legal entities) is a second major kind. The matrix (a unique combination of functional and divisional forms) is a third form of departmentation. Each of these has its own strengths and weaknesses, and most organizations of any size use some combination of them.

Vertical specialization centers on who will manage the departments and how critical choices will be made to plan, implement plans, evaluate activities, and institute corrective action where necessary. It involves the use of managerial techniques for detecting problems and opportunities, selecting among alternatives, evaluating, and instituting corrective action in lieu of or in addition to managerial intuitions. It also involves the use of staff units to aid line units or to replace managerial techniques.

Coordination and control are twin concerns in structuring an organization. They are needed to minimize the weaknesses resulting from the organization's choices of specialization. Coordination consists of the personal and impersonal mechanisms an organization uses to link the action of its component units into a consistent pattern. These include common values, grapevine, and committees as personal mechanisms. Impersonal mechanisms are written rules, policies and procedures, specialized staff units, and management information systems.

Control deals with setting standards, measuring results versus standards, and instituting corrective action. Some widely used control mechanisms are the planning-budgeting process and management by objectives (MBO). Control techniques vary widely in their comprehensiveness and tend to be less precise as you move up the managerial hierarchy and into functions where the means of obtaining objectives are not clearly known.

## THINKING THROUGH THE ISSUES

1. Which pattern of departmentation appeals to you the most as a potential manager and why?

2. Can you devise a better design for Quality Research (see Figure 11.5) than it presently has?

3. If you were president of Quality Research, what coordination and control strategies would you emphasize to keep the balance between functional heads and area coordinators?

4. From other courses in business or administration, provide a list of three managerial techniques and the major goals embodied in each technique.

5. Draw the organization chart of your university and talk with several administrators to isolate the major coordination and control mechanisms used. Compare your findings with those of others in the class.

6. Computers and computerized management information systems are touted as "saviors" of management. As coordination mechanisms what are their basic advantages and disadvantages?

7. Review the MBO system being used by the Department of Energy. What flaws does it have built into it?

8. Some have argued that the designs and managerial techniques used in efficient manufacturing operations should be applied to the administration of hospitals. What problems do you see in such a transfer?

## EXERCISE: ORGANIZATIONAL ANALYSIS—PART II

### Purpose:

To apply, as clearly and thoroughly as possible, the concepts developed in Chapter 11 to the organization your group selected for Part I of this exercise in Chapter 10. This will give you and your group a chance to apply the concepts and share your findings with those of your classmates.

### Time:

50 minutes or more in class, plus at-home group preparation.

### Procedure:

**A.** Do the following before coming to class:

1. Form the same group used for Part I of this exercise. Assume the group is a management consulting team required to prepare a written report following the format indicated by your boss (the instructor).
2. Use the same organization your group selected for Part I of this exercise.
3. Using observations, interviews, and company records as necessary, your group has been assigned to do the following for its organizational report:
    **a.** Discuss the kind of horizontal specialization used at each level of the organization.
    **b.** Discuss the kind of vertical specialization used at each level and in each department of the organization. Make sure you include details concerning the use of managers, staff, managerial techniques, and the trade-offs involved.
    **c.** Discuss the coordination and control mechanisms used at each level and in each department in the organization.
    **d.** Go back to the report your group prepared in Part I. Discuss to what extent this organization seems to have adapted its structure, in terms of horizontal and vertical specialization and coordination and control, to environment, size, and/or

technology. Do you see an environmental, size, or technological imperative operating? Why or why not?

**B.** Be prepared to turn in this part of the group report to your instructor and to discuss the group's findings and their implications.

## CASE: EAGLE AIRLINES II

Turn to the Eagle Airlines case at the end of Chapter 12. Then answer the following questions.

### Questions

1. Discuss the kind of departmentation used in the case. What are its apparent advantages and disadvantages, especially in terms of top management's expressed philosophy of "decentralization"?
2. Discuss the important aspects of vertical and horizontal specialization as they are applied to both sales and service.
3. Discuss the appropriateness of this specialization in terms of your assessment of the firm's environment.
4. Discuss the coordination and control mechanisms used by Eagle Airlines, and evaluate their appropriateness in terms of top management's "decentralization" philosophy and the kind of departmentation used.

## THE MANAGER'S VOCABULARY

**Control** The means of establishing goals and plans, measuring results, and taking corrective action.

**Coordination** Personal and impersonal means of communication among the components of the organization.

**Departmentation** Dividing duties, and grouping jobs and people together to form administrative units.

**Divisional Departmentation** Grouping individuals and resources by product, service, client, territory, or legal entity.

**Functional Departmentation** Grouping individuals and resources by skill, knowledge, and action.

**Horizontal Specialization** A division of labor through the formation of work units or groups within an organization; the process of departmentation.

**Matrix Departmentation or Matrix Structure** A combination of functional and divisional patterns wherein an individual is assigned to more than one type of unit.

**Specialization** The division of labor within an organization that groups people and resources together in order to accomplish important tasks.

**Structure** A configuration of positions, job duties, and lines of authority among the component parts of an organization; the formal pattern of activities and the planned interrelationships among the various subunits of an organization and their managers.

**Vertical Specialization** A division of labor that establishes who will manage the departments or work units of the organization and determines how they will make critical decisions.

## Notes

[1]Anthony Ramirez, *The Wall Street Journal* (December 15, 1980), p. 21.

[2]Richard N. Osborn, James G. Hunt, and Lawrence R. Jauch, *Organization Theory: An Integrated Approach* (New York: John Wiley & Sons, 1980), pp. 291–292.

[3]Ibid.

[4]S. Davis, Paul Lawrence, H. Kolodny, and Michael Beer, *Matrix* (Reading, Mass.: Addison-Wesley, 1977).

[5]See Osborn, Hunt, and Jauch, op. cit., p. 289.

[6]Richard Cyert and James March, *A Behavioral Theory of the Firm* (Englewood Cliffs, N.J.: Prentice-Hall, 1963); and J. Sutherland, *Administrative Decision-Making: Extending the Bounds of Rationality* (New York: Van Nostrand-Reinhold, 1977).

[7]Osborn, Hunt, and Jauch, op. cit., pp. 284–288.

[8]Ibid., pp. 350–354.

[9]Ibid., pp. 293–296.

[10]Arlyn J. Melcher, *Structure and Process of Organizations: A systems Approach* (Englewood Cliffs, N.J.: Prentice-Hall, 1976), pp. 219–223.

[11]Osborn, Hunt, and Jauch, op. cit., pp. 282–284.

[12]Melcher, op. cit., pp. 219–223.

[13]Ibid., p. 226.

# 12

# ORGANIZATIONAL DESIGN

# WANTED: AN APPROPRIATE ORGANIZATION STRUCTURE!

Do you remember the Middle States Manufacturing Company case which introduced Part Four? As we left him, the president Jaccob Jaccober was concerned with how to redesign the structure of the firm to meet the new challenges facing the organization. He wanted a structure that wasn't necessarily efficient, but that would facilitate profitable growth while maintaining the firm's tradition of technical leadership at or above competitive levels.

Jaccob was feeling pressure, On the one hand, he was being counseled to reduce specialized orders and to provide longer production runs. On the other hand, it was argued that a standardized product line would hurt the company's image. There was also pressure for a tighter and more formalized budgeting and control process.

Business from three key customers accounted for 50 percent of Middle States' total sales and 75 percent of gross profits. Profab, an extremely important product, had just been developed. It used a slightly different production process than did the current products and required lots of handcrafting from a few highly skilled people. Longer production runs with a more flexible design could cut costs by 30 percent. A second shift would also be feasible. Two million dollars would be available over the next six months to market Profab.

**MANAGEMENT APPLICATIONS QUESTION**

What would you do if you were in Jaccob's shoes? What kind of structure would you design to best meet the needs of the Middle States manufacturing firm?

## PLANNING AHEAD

**After reading and participating in the learning experiences offered in this chapter, you will be familiar with the following topics:**

**Mechanistic and Organic Organizations**
**A Manager's View of Organizational Design**
**Strategic Factors in Organizational Design**
**Mechanistic Designs**
**Organic Designs**
**Diverse Designs**

In Chapter 11 we discussed the various aspects of organizational structures. We emphasized the many alternatives for accomplishing vertical and horizontal specialization, and coordination and control. It is now time to ask how managers choose among these alternatives to establish a structural configuration that best meets an organization's needs. This process of choosing and implementing a structural configuration is what we refer to as **organizational design.**

# MECHANISTIC AND ORGANIC ORGANIZATIONS

Some 20 years ago British scientists, Tom Burns and G. M. Stalker, introduced the notions of mechanistic and organic organizations to the field of OB.[1] We can view these two ideal types as opposite extremes on a continuum of organizational design strategies, such as the one shown in Figure 12.1.

Burns and Stalker argued that **mechanistic organizations** tend to favor what we have called vertical specialization and control. These configurations stress rules, policies, and procedures, specify the techniques for decision-making, and develop elaborate and well-documented control systems backed by centralized staff. In mechanistic organizations, staff units will typically be placed toward the top. This reinforces a heavy vertical emphasis. In smaller organizations, a functional form of departmentation is common. Visually the mechanistic configuration resembles the mushroom shown in Figure 12.2.

We can describe **organic organizations** in opposite terms. Here, the design strategy emphasizes horizontal specialization and coordination, over vertical specialization and control. Rules, policies, and procedures are loose, since the organization favors personal means of coordination. When controls are used, they tend to rest heavily on socialization, training, and personal reinforcement. Staff units tend to be placed toward the middle of the organization. Divisional and matrix structures are common forms of departmentation in organic configurations.

FIGURE 12.1 A basic comparison of mechanistic and organic organizations.

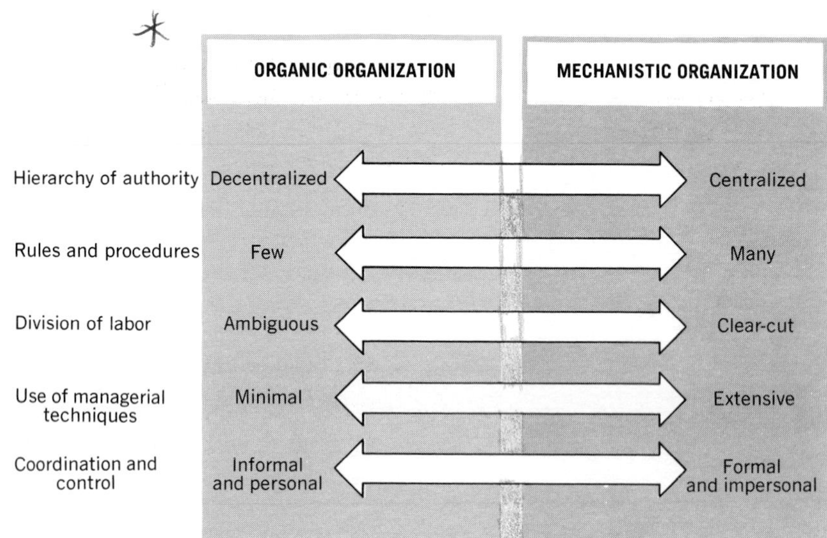


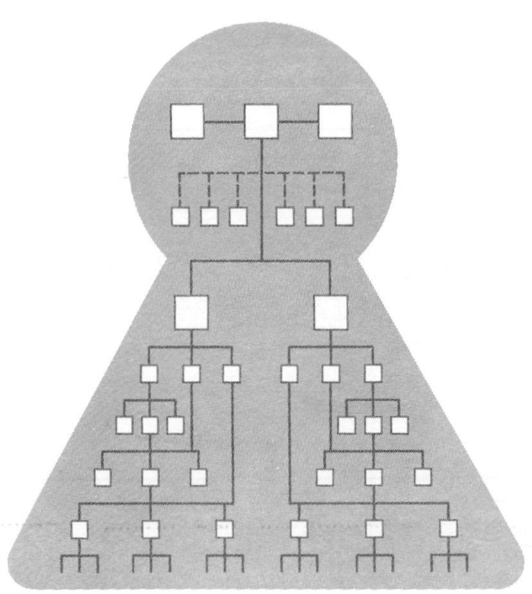

FIGURE 12.2 The "mushroom effect" in a mechanistic structural configuration.

Schematically, we can say the following to summarize the two types of organizational designs.

| | | |
|---|---|---|
| A mechanistic configuration | involves → | much vertical specialization and control; tight rules, policies, procedures; a centralized staff |
| An organic configuration | involves → | much horizontal specialization; personal coordination; few rules, policies, and procedures; a decentralized staff |

## A MANAGER'S VIEW OF ORGANIZATIONAL DESIGN

These two ideal forms of structural configuration serve as the core concepts for our treatment of organizational design in this chapter. Our basic theme in this regard is quite simple. The structural configuration of the organization should be consistent with the organization's goals and the problems and opportunities posed by its environment, size, and technology. Although there are a vast number of ways in which organizations can be configured, we'll use "ideal types" to characterize a few basic patterns. As we discuss them, remember the key question in organizational design is: How should structure be adjusted to meet major problems and opportunities, and thereby allow the organization to accomplish its goals? To help you answer this question in actual managerial practice, we'll rely heavily on Jaccob Jaccober's firm as our example.

Checkpoint

The Middle States Manufacturing case will be used throughout this chapter to highlight the concepts and practice of organizational design. Make sure you recall the case; refer back to the Part Four introduction if necessary.

### Middle States Manufacturing: A Recap

A key concern for Jaccob is to exploit the new product—Profab. Customers want Profab, and lower-level managers and employees are willing to see the implementation of this new product succeed.

So, what's the problem? Why is Jaccob fretting so much? Why not just go ahead and schedule production, hire the needed workers, and make the appropriate sales and marketing arrangements? Some managers would simply charge ahead in this situation without seriously analyzing the structure of the organization. Let's not be so hasty.

Look at the problems and opportunities confronting Jaccob. Middle States historically stressed innovation, while maintaining the technical quality of its products at or above competitive levels. Although the firm has not been particularly efficient, innovation has provided growth and high profits. Should Jaccob continue to develop this comparative advantage? If so, how?

Currently, the new product, Profab, requires slightly different production methods than existing products. There is a lot of handcrafting, and successful production rests heavily upon the skilled work of a few key people. Profab calls for more than minor adjustments to the existing methods, and the engineers can't yet specify how to produce it in large quantities.

Jaccob must also consider the new customers gained because of the success of Profab. Certainly the firm would be less dependent upon a few key customers. But would it be able to detect small yet important changes in a large number of customers? Currently there is a market, but will there continue to be one in the future? Also, the sale of Profab is likely to call for clearances by any number of government regulatory agencies.

Finally, there is the force of expanding volume. Jaccob knows that adding Profab means more than just using another production shift. Current personnel will have to cope with additional employees, and this growth will put a heavy strain on staff units. For instance, just training a new production crew might take two months.

All of these issues mean that Jaccob must consider changes in specialization, as well as new forms of coordination and control. He needs a means of gaining an overall perspective on this situation so that good decisions on organizational design can be made.

## STRATEGIC FACTORS IN ORGANIZATIONAL DESIGN

Management must consider several competing factors in selecting an overall structural configuration for an organization. Many of these factors relate to the organization's goals, environment, size, and technology. Let's review these strategic factors by starting with the bottom line: What does management really want? What are the goals for the organization?

## Goals[2]

The process of organizational design begins with a strategic decision concerning an organization's goals. Over the long run, organizations must provide returns to society and satisfy investors, suppliers, distributors, and customers, while operating within governmental, union, and labor constraints. Over time, many organizations develop a set of goals capable of satisfying these competing groups. Some organizations operate as if flexibility and adaptability were the keys to survival. Some emphasize technical superiority. Others place the major emphasis on efficiency. Growth with consistently high profits is a common theme among U.S. corporations. Thus, the relative emphasis of an organization's goals on flexibility, technical superiority, or efficiency is crucially important when its managers select an overall structural configuration for the organization.

## External Environment[3]

A second important factor, emphasized in Chapter 10, is the external environment of the organization. What is the potential for success? What other organizations must the organization rely upon to reach its goals? How predictable and stable is the environment? Generally, as more opportunities arise, the structure should facilitate change and growth. Where the organization faces a few powerful outsiders, the structure should help the organization target its responses. Conversely, where the organization faces many powerful outsiders, the structure should facilitate frequent adjustments to external demands.

## Size and Technology[4]

Managers should also recognize the important role of size and technology in selecting an overall structural configuration. Growth creates both new opportunities and problems. The structure needed for smaller organizations often becomes inadequate with the onset of growth. In high technology firms operating on the frontiers of technical development, structure should facilitate technical problem solving and risk taking. Conversely, firms operating with more well know and stable processes should consider structures which facilitate efficiency. As the range of products and services increases, the structure of the organization should accomodate differences across products and services.

## Case Application: Middle States Manufacturing

Table 12.1 summarizes the design issues facing Middle States Manufacturing. Since Jaccob Jaccober is president, let's take his perspective. What does Jaccob want? While only he can answer this question, the history of the firm provides an outside view of the goals Jaccob has chosen in the past. Specifically, Middle States has pursued innovation as a path to longer-term profits and survival. In doing so, it has placed efficiency and flexibility farther down the priority list. While the firm was small, efficiency and flexibility were not major problems since Jaccob had direct contact with most of his managers and employees. The scope of operations was small enough for him to deal with major customers and still keep tabs on internal operations.

Can Jaccob keep the existing emphasis on technological innovation and still make adequate profits to ensure long-term survival? The case description suggests that the answer is yes. But why even ask this question? Can't the skill and hard work of the chief executive and the team of managers dictate goal priorities that will ensure profits and survival? In some cases we can answer yes to this question, and in some cases no. The answer for a particular organization rests on contingencies in its environment and context, in addition to the skills of its management.

In the case of Middle States, the general and specific environments are complex. The firm is small in size and may become moderately large with the planned expansion. The technology is sophis-

**Table 12.1 Major Design Issues Facing Middle States Manufacturing**

| Strategic Factors | Case Applications |
|---|---|
| A. Goals | What does Jaccob really want? |
| B. External environment: general and specific characteristics | Possible expansion nationwide; many new customers, suppliers, distributors, government agencies, and financial backers. |
| C. Context: size and technology | Anticipated growth in size; new production process required for Profab. |
| D. Structure | |
| 1. Horizontal specialization | Existing use of functional structure (Vice-Presidents for Marketing, Finance, Production, and Personnel). |
| 2. Vertical specialization | Need for new managerial levels; budgeting techniques important; assistant managers used as staff aides. |
| 3. Coordination and control | Problems occurring in product delivery and service to existing customers. |

ticated and makes it difficult for Jaccob to stress efficiency. The need for even more sophisticated technology to produce Profab may also restrict flexibility.

## MECHANISTIC DESIGNS

We can now match the strategic factors of goals, environment, size, and technology with the major structural configurations available to managers. Remember, we will emphasize the mechanistic-organic continuum as representing the basic range of choices in organizational design.

Earlier, we described the mechanistic configuration as one emphasizing vertical specialization, the extensive use of managerial techniques, and use of top-level staff. Managers acting within such a structure would be given clear assignments, precise methods, and very specific targets. The resources available to their units would be detailed in budgets, and deviations from budgets would result in required explanations to a superior.

The mechanistic configuration is consistent with a desire for efficiency. It works best when the external environment is stable and when the organization relies upon few influential suppliers, distributors, and regulatory agencies. It also presumes the technology of the organization is well known and that only a limited range of products or services are produced. This configuration is often found in basic industries, such as steel, automobile manufacturing, and utilities.

### Why They Work

Why does this configuration work in such situations? It works because it has a vertical emphasis. Procedures developed by centralized staff can be readily implemented throughout the system. Changes in standards can be used to redirect managerial effort. Careful attention to following well-defined processes allows management to plan ahead in detail and make minor corrections before they become serious problems.

There is another advantage to the mechanistic structure. When an organization faces periodic crises, such a configuration can provide the vehicle for action. Action is needed quickly in a crisis situation. The vertical emphasis of the mechanistic configuration facilitates control and generates quick responses by subordinates to top management orders. Thus, it is no wonder it is the preferred configuration in military organizations and that variations of mechanistic structure are often embodied in emergency response plans.[5] For instance, nuclear power plants have voluminous manuals outlining formal procedures for averting disaster in the event of crisis. Of course, using this configuraton in a crisis presumes that a capable person is in charge and is willing to make the required decisions.

## Problems

One problem sometimes associated with mechanistic structures is low job satisfaction and poor human resource maintenance.[6] Mechanistic organizations tend to be seen by employees as rigid, centralized, nonparticipative, and very bureaucratic. Another problem is that mechanistic organizations are not very good at spotting small but potentially important variations in their environments. The attention of too many managers, and their managerial techniques, is directed toward vertical affairs. External communications within and outside the organization are sacrificed for responsiveness to top management.

## Case Application: Middle States Manufacturing

Table 12.2 summarizes some of the conditions that favor the mechanistic structure and contrasts them with the actual conditions facing Middle States. It is pretty obvious that a mechanistic configuration

**Table 12.2 A Comparison of Selected Conditions Favoring a Mechanistic Configuration and the Conditions Facing Middle States Manufacturing**

| | Conditions Favoring a Mechanistic Configuration | Conditions Facing Middle States Manufacturing |
|---|---|---|
| 1. Goals | Oriented toward efficiency. | Oriented toward technical innovation. |
| 2. External environment | Generally rich in several areas; specifically reliant upon few outsiders; low in uncertainty. | Generally rich in one narrow area; specifically reliant upon many outsiders; high in uncertainty. |
| 3. Size | Moderate to large. | Small. |
| 4. Technology | Known meansof production; extensive substitutability of capital; output quality easy to measure. | Means of production not well known; little substitutability of capital; output quality moderately easy to measure. |

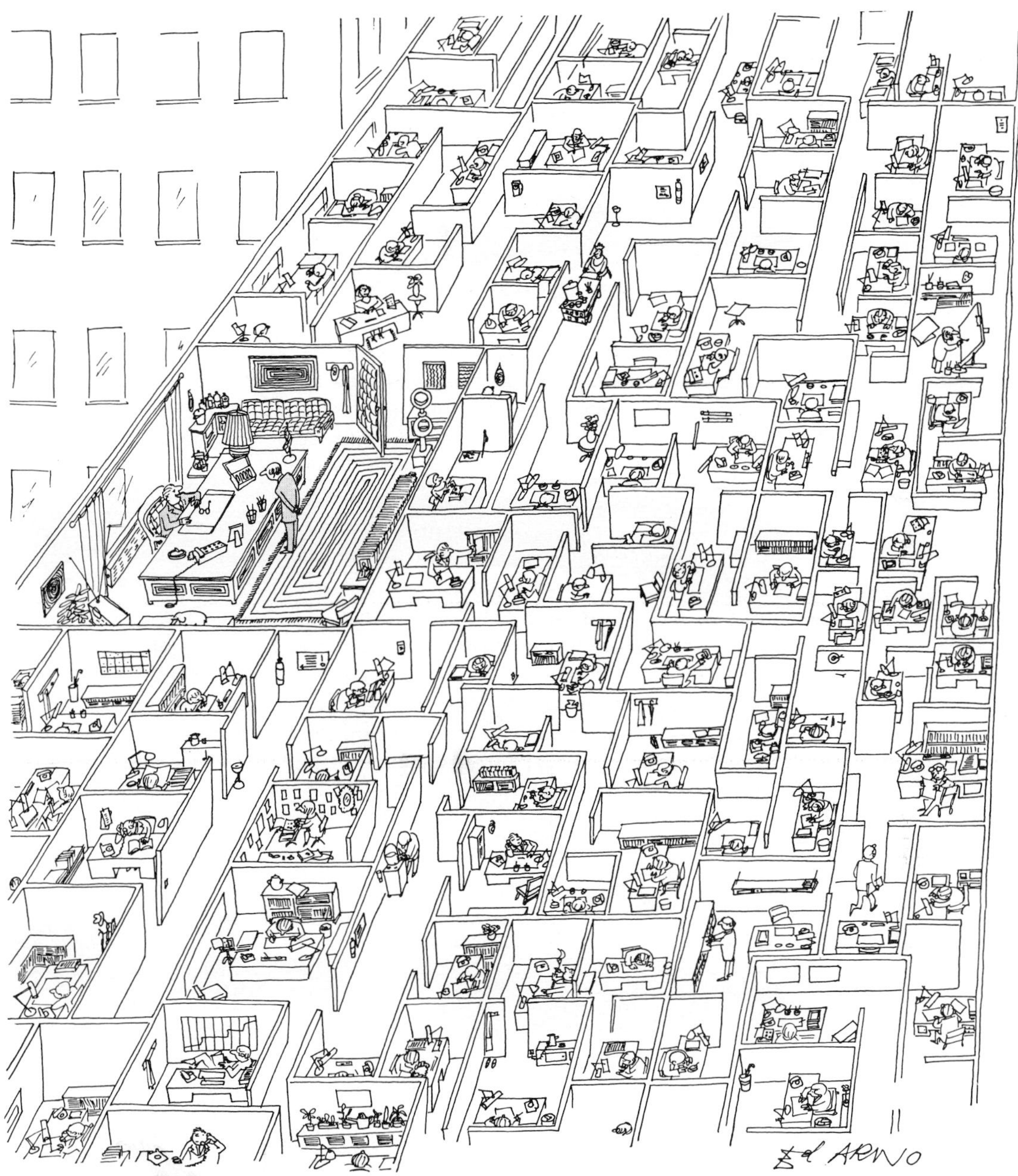


*"I'm afraid a raise is out of the question, Benton, but in view of your sixteen years of service we are advancing you two spaces."*

A mechanistic organization.

Drawing by Ed Arno; © 1977 The New Yorker Magazine, Inc.

doesn't fit Middle States very well. Jaccob would do well to seek an alternative in his organizational design efforts.

## ORGANIC DESIGNS

Now let's change the setting. Assume that an organization can't completely engineer production operations, but must rely upon the judgment, craftsmanship, and professionalism of employees. Let's also assume that the quality of the major product or service is difficult to judge. Picture the environment as unstable and difficult to predict. The organization must rely upon many different suppliers, distributors, customers, unions, and regulatory agencies, each of which places slightly different demands on it. No single opportunity appears to offer the best path toward growth and profits.

This combination of environment and technology calls for an adaptive and responsive organization. It favors the organic configuration with its emphasis on horizontal specialization and coordination. Managers in such structures are given broad objectives with only general notions of how to proceed. They are expected to work closely with fellow managers and subordinates. Although guidance from superiors would be available, there would be few written documents outlining procedures. In organic organizations, successful managers are particularly aware of minor changes in the needs and desires of outsiders. A lot of their time is devoted to external relations.

### Why They Work

Why does the organic configuration work in such situations? It works because information can easily penetrate the organization and be circulated among managers. Subunits can make small adjustments to particular clients. Even though successful performance by one unit may be offset by poor performance in another, the "law of averages" produces an overall success rate. When and where success occurs, the organization can quickly add resources to exploit the opportunity. Research and development organizations, contract research firms, and engineering and construction corporations typically use this softer, organic structure. Employees tend to view the organic structures as decentralized, participative, and nonbureaucratic. Generally, we expect lower turnover and absenteeism and more highly committed employees than in mechanistic settings.[7]

## Problems[8]

The organic configuration does have its disadvantages. It is not very efficient in producing large quantities of standardized products or services. It is also difficult to maintain in larger organizations. Furthermore, even if organizations with this configuration can detect changes in their environment, it may be difficult to implement an organization-wide response. Finally, the organic configuration is vulnerable to empire building when a reduction in external opportunities occurs. Few managers or employees, for example, are willing to recommend their own termination for the good of the organization.

## Case Application: Middle States Manufacturing

Table 12.3 shows that the organic configuration fits the major characteristics of Middle States pretty well. Yet, the organic form does not automatically guarantee an emphasis on innovation.

# DIVERSE DESIGNS

Organizations can develop a history of prosperity, growth, and long-term survival from either the mechanistic or organic structural foundations. Growth can also allow top management to slowly shift the

**Table 12.3 A Comparison of Selected Conditions Favoring an Organic Configuration and the Conditions Facing Middle States Manufacturing**

| | Conditions Favoring an Organic Configuration | Conditions Facing Middle States Manufacturing |
|---|---|---|
| 1. Goals | Oriented toward flexibility. | Oriented toward technical innovation. |
| 2. External environment | Generally rich in one narrow area; specifically reliant upon many outsiders; high in uncertainty. | Generally rich in one narrow area; specifically reliant upon many outsiders; high in uncertainty. |
| 3. Size | Small to moderate. | Small. |
| 4. Technology | Not a well known means of production; little substitutability of capital; output quality difficult to measure. | Not a well known means of production; little substitutability of capital; output quality moderately easy to measure. |

overall configuration of the organization from mechanistic to organic, or vice versa. For example, the auto divisions of General Motors once operated under an organic structure with considerable engineering, production, and marketing autonomy. While there were strict financial controls from the top, this so-called "decentralized" approach helped GM become the largest auto maker in the world. In the seventies, however, GM's structure began to become mechanistic as engineering and production decisions were made on a corporate-wide basis. While the divisions lost some autonomy, GM gained economies of scale and was able to respond more quickly than competitors to the market for small cars.

In contrast, General Electric once operated under a mechanistic structure. To respond more quickly to varied market opportunities, GE decided to develop a softer structure with over 500 identifiable "businesses." Note that GE produces a much wider variety of products than the GM auto divisions and must compete directly with a larger number of smaller, flexible manufacturers.

Selecting between the mechanistic and organic configurations would be comparatively easy if all the performance, environmental, and technological pressures of a given organization called for the same structure. Often this is not the case, and a diverse form of structural configuration is chosen. Some of the diverse configurations are weighted toward the mechanistic, while others are made more organic. Some of the more common diverse designs are described below.

## Mechanistic Core within an Organic Shell

Perhaps the most common conflict situation is when an organization produces only one or a few basic products, but begins to face a more uncertain environment. The technology would favor a mechanistic configuration; the changing environment calls for more flexibility and adaptability than that structure easily tolerates. One solution is to develop a series of externally oriented, organic line and staff units to protect the mechanistic production units. Such a configuration is shown in Figure 12.3.

The line and staff units in Figure 12.3 are there to scan the environment in an attempt to provide an early warning system for top management. They can also explain the actions of internal units and convince outsiders that some of their demands are illegitimate or that the organization is already serving others. This approach is useful in protecting the basic production organization from minor changes and unwanted intrusions from external forces.

The diverse configuration of a mechanistic core and an organic

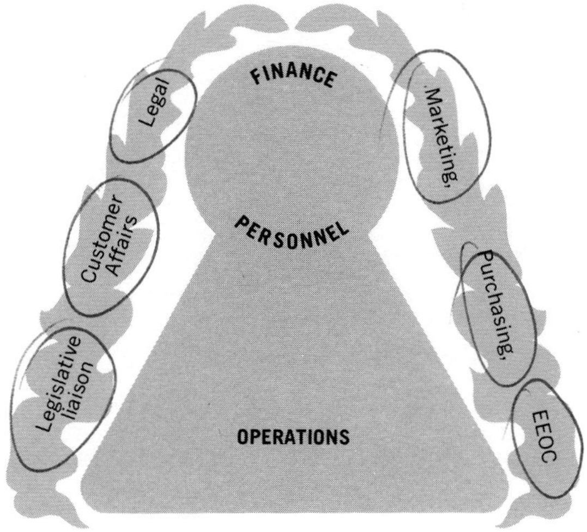

FIGURE 12.3 A mechanistic core wrapped by an organic shell.

shell does not meet Middle States' needs as well as the simple organic configuration. A key reason is Jaccob's desire for technical innovation and the need for a responsive production process.

## Organic Core with a Mechanistic Shell

Conflicting pressures are also found in large organizations that must rely upon a nonroutine and intensive technology. Universities, larger research organizations, and research hospitals are examples. In such cases a possible design strategy is to allow the internal line units to maintain an organic configuration, while the staff units become mechanistic. Figure 12.4 shows such an organic core protected by a mechanistic shell. This configuration allows line managers to develop a whole series of comparatively small, quasi-autonomous departments that can detect and adjust to relevant technical developments. Each department can proceed with few internally induced rules, policies, and procedures. Staff units, on the other hand, can be designed to improve efficiency, increase the chances of immediate response, and buffer the organic core from nontechnical concerns.

There are advantages and disadvantages to this form of diverse configuration. It does allow top managers to plan and control more carefully the actions of staff units. Unfortunately, staff units in these organizations may lag behind their counterparts working in the more organic configuration. Attempts from the top to redirect the organic line units can also meet with resistance unless excess resources are available. The quasi-autonomous departments are likely to fight at-

FIGURE 12.4 An organic core protected by a mechanistic shell.

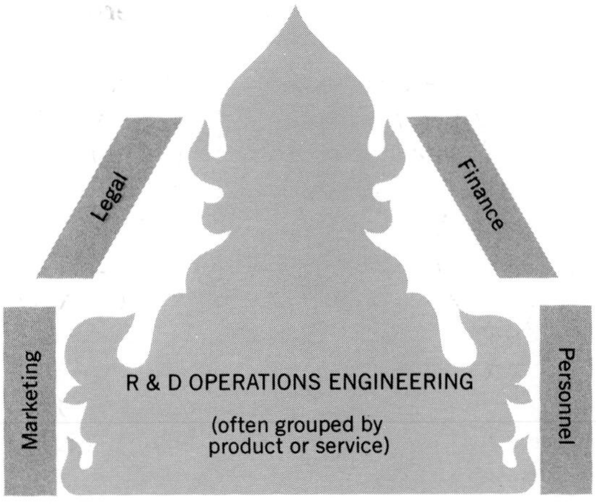


tempts to reduce their budgets, staff, or authority. Thus, these systems may be responsive and adaptable to technical matters, but may also be very resistant to other administrative changes.

This diverse configuration is likely to be preferred by Jaccob Jaccober for his Middle States Manufacturing firm. It helps provide a mix of flexibility and innovation, while retaining some emphasis on efficiency. Figure 12.5 shows a partial organization chart for Mid-

FIGURE 12.5 From Middle States Manufacturing to International Manufacturers.

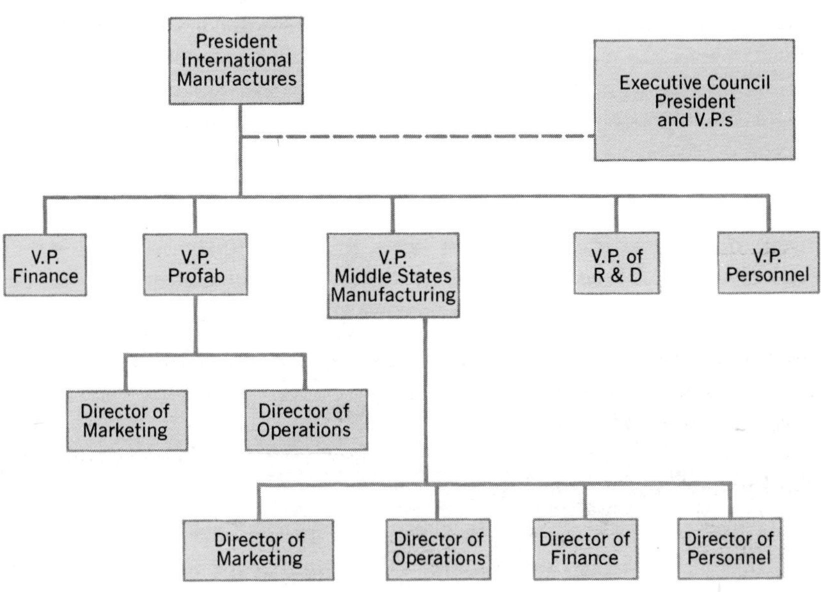

dle States in the new configuration with a new name —International Manufacturers.

To establish Profab as a viable product separate from existing product lines, the figure indicates that Jaccob should create two operating divisions. A new Profab division will be headed by a vice-president and will have two major units within it—marketing and operations. The second division will be the old Middle States Manufacturing, with the name kept the same to maintain its identification with existing customers. Here Jaccob will place the various functional heads as subordinate to the current Vice-President of Manufacturing. To maintain an innovative thrust, he will create the position of Vice-President for Research and Development. These three vice-presidents and their units will constitute the more organic core of the new configuration.

By separating the more innovative and technically sophisticated Profab from other operations, Jaccob is able to maintain the functional structure his employees are most familiar with. Although the functional departmentation within the Middle States Manufacturing division provides a mechanistic flavor, it will be moderated by the small size of the unit.

Finance and personnel staffs at the corporate level create a mechanistic shell for the organic core. They will act to protect the operating units from two problems associated with growth and expansion. First, Personnel will select and train any new employees to be added. This specialized staff unit will be able to do the job quickly, in an efficient manner, and be consistent with state and federal requirements. The acquiring of financial resources for the expansion will be managed by the Corporate Vice-President of Finance. Again, the existence of specialized expertise will facilitate the job.

To help resolve coordination problems among subunits, and to deal with the outside regulatory agencies significant to Profab, Jaccob will create an executive council with himself as chairperson. The vice-chairperson will deal with the federal agencies and act as Jaccob's chief of staff. This unit, too, will act to protect the operating divisions from outside interference.

## The Conglomerate

So far we have looked at two types of compromises between the mechanistic and organic structural extremes. One had a mechanistic core surrounded by more organic units. The other hand a mechanistic shell with an organic center. A third alternative is also very common. We know it as the conglomerate.

Conglomerates are typically huge businesses that produce products and services in many different industries. Some are merely large holding companies; that is, one corporation owns all or large parts of others. Each subsidiary may be structured differently. A parallel is found in the public sector in federal and state government agencies. Neither the federal nor state governments are designed to be either mechanistic or organic. Instead, they are conglomerates. Even large departments in the federal bureaucracy defy simple classification, in part because their structure is indirectly set by Congress.

## SUMMARY

The key issue in organizational design is the choice of structural configuration. We have explained the mechanistic configuration and shown how it can provide profits, growth, and technical superiority under certain environmental and technological conditions. The organic configuration is also explained. It is preferred under a different combination of environmental and technological conditions. Since the pressures and opportunities from environment and technology may not be consistent, we have also analyzed a number of diverse configurations. These diverse configurations incorporated size as another important design variable. Larger organizations need more specialization, coordination, and control and may be difficult to categorize as purely mechanistic or organic in configuration.

It is also important to recognize the managerial implications of the various organizational design decisions. Mechanistic organizations involve tight control based on careful planning and detailed record keeping. Managers and other employees tend to experience centralization, little participation, and considerable bureaucracy. The opposite is the case with organic configurations. In the final result, you will probably manage in organizations that have diverse configurations and that offer multiple and varied challenges.

## THINKING THROUGH THE ISSUES

1. Explain why being able to categorize organizational structures in terms of overall configuration is useful for organizational design purposes.

2. Obtain a copy of the organization chart for your college or

university. Describe the overall structural configuration and comment on its appropriateness.

3. Contrast an academic department with the registrar's office in a college or university in terms of the kinds of control and coordination mechanisms used. Which design (organic or mechanistic) is more suitable for each of these units and why?

4. Return to the monks' computerized record-keeping firm described in the introduction to Chapter 11. Design a structural configuration for it, assuming it has 50 employees. Make any necessary assumptions concerning the major considerations influencing the configuration.

5. Describe how you as a manager might function in an organic configuration. What might your day be like? How do you think you would feel about this? Consider whether you might feel better or worse operating in a mechanistic configuration.

6. Explain the differences between a diverse configuration with a mechanistic core and organic shell, and one with an organic core and mechanistic shell.

7. Explain in your own words why an organic design is a better fit than a mechanistic design for a complex environment.

8. Discuss in some detail why a mechanistic structure has been the traditionally preferred one for the military. What about an organization such as the Catholic church? What type of design exists and why?

## EXERCISE: ORGANIZATIONAL ANALYSIS—PART III

### Purpose:

To apply, as clearly and thoroughly as possible, the concepts developed in Chapter 12 to an actual organization. This will give you and your group a chance to apply the concepts and share your findings with those of your classmates.

### Time:

50 minutes or more in class, plus at-home preparations.

### Procedure:

**A.** Do the following before coming to class:

1. Form the same group used for Part I of this exercise. Assume the group is a management consulting team required to pre-

pare a written report following the format indicated by your boss (the instructor).

2. Use the same organization your group selected for Part I of this exercise.
3. Using observations, interviews, and company records as necessary, your group has been assigned to do the following for its organizational report:
   - **a.** Using relevant material from the first two parts of this analysis (which were assigned in Chapters 10 and 11) along with concepts from Chapter 12, summarize the structural configuration of this organization.
   - **b.** Discuss the appropriateness of this configuration in light of the material covered in Chapter 12.
   - **c.** Discuss one possible alternative configuration and justify your choice.

**B.** Be prepared to turn in this part of the report to your instructor and to discuss the group's findings and their implications.

## CASE: Eagle Airlines III[9]

Eagle Airlines was a medium-sized regional airline serving the southwest quarter of the United States. The company had been growing rapidly in the last fifteen years, partially as a result of dynamic company activity, but also as a result of the rapid economic growth of the area which it served.

The most outstanding of the areas was Bartlett City. Bartlett City's growth since the middle 1940s had rested on two primary developments. One of these was the very rapid growth of manufacturing and research establishments concerned with defense work. Some firms located here at the urging of government agencies to build new defense plants and laboratories away from coastal areas. Others moved to this location because of the attractive climate and scenery, which was considered an advantage in attracting technicians, engineers, and scientists for work on advanced military projects. Once some plants and research laboratories were developed, smaller, independent firms sprang up in the community for the purpose of servicing and supplying those which were established first. These developments encouraged the rapid growth of local construction and the opening of numerous attractive housing developments. The second basis for growth was the completion, also in the 1940s, of a major irrigation project that opened a large area for intensive cultivation.

While the economy of Bartlett City had grown rapidly, it was in many ways tied to coastal areas, where parent firms or home offices of many of the local establishments existed. Also, since many of its industries serviced the national defense effort, they consequently had to be closely connected with matters decided on in Washington, or other places distant from Bartlett City. Lastly, it had many strong financial and business ties with major coastal cities, such as San Francisco and Los Angeles. As a result, executives, engineers, and scientists in Bartlett City industries were frequently in contact with the major business, political, and scientific centers of the country, particularly those on the West Coast. In making a trip, for example, to Los Angeles from Bartlett City, one was faced with using one of three alternative modes of travel: auto, private corporate jet, or commercial jet flight. Eagle Airlines had the sole route between Bartlett City and Los Angeles, which was found to be a most lucrative run and to which it gave a great deal of attention.

### *Company Management*

The rapid growth of Eagle Airlines was held by many to be in no small degree a result of the skill of its management. It should be pointed out that its top management had been particularly skillful in obtaining and defending its route structure and had been particularly successful in financing, at advantageous terms, the acquisition of modern aircraft, particularly jet-powered airplanes. Top management emphasized "decentralization," in which the lower members of management were given as much freedom as possible to fulfill their responsibilities in whatever way they thought best. This policy was thought to have built a dynamic, aggressive, and extremely able group of middle- and lower-level executives who had been particularly imaginative in finding ways to expand and improve the operation of the firm. This decentralization had always been accompanied by the understanding that the individual manager must "deliver." This policy, or actually philosophy, was conveyed and reinforced through letters, personal conversations, and example, Executives who increased sales or reduced costs, or in some manner made their operations more efficient, were rewarded in a number of ways. Praise, both public and private, was given to executives who improved their unit's performance. Bonuses for increased sales or cost reduction were both generous and frequent, and promotions came rapidly to those who managed outstanding units. The chairman of the board, who was also chief executive officer during this period of growth, frequently used words that were only half-jokingly claimed by other executives to be the company motto, "This company's success rests upon expansion and efficiency."

### *The Local Unit*

Eagle Airlines was organized as shown in Figure 12.6. The three major divisions were: operations, which was involved in scheduling and operating the planes over the entire route system; sales, which was concerned with advertising all phases of airline service, maintaining ticket offices in all cities and airports, and also selling to institutional customers such as companies and government agencies; and service, which was concerned with activities at the airport, maintenance, handling baggage, loading passengers, and similar functions.

For all practical purposes, operations had no local offices in that it had to operate the entire system. Sales and service had both district and local or regional offices. The sales manager in Bartlett City, for example, was responsible for the ticket sales at the airport and in maintaining a downtown ticket office, as well as for institutional sales to the local companies and agencies. Service was usually broken into a number of subdivisions at the local level, so that at Bartlett City there was a ramp service manager who was responsible for handling everything pertaining to the airplane while it was on the ground, but not while it was under maintenance. The manager would, therefore, be responsible for the loading and unloading of all baggage, mail, and passengers. That individual was also responsible for cleaning the planes between flights, having food put on board, getting baggage to the customers and picking up from them, guiding passengers on and off the aircraft, and checking their tickets when they arrived at the terminal.

Consistent with company policy of decentralization and individual accountability, each of these local people had an individual budget and standards of performance. A sales manager, for example, was given complete authority to hire, train, and fire whatever salespeople or any other personnel he or she thought necessary. The sales manager knew what his or her budget was and was expected to stick within it and reduce it if possible. Furthermore, the sales manager knew what the standards of performance relevant to sales volume were. The company placed great emphasis on an increase in sales rather than in absolute volume of sales. Hence, the sales manager at Bartlett City, as at all other local units, knew that individual performance would be evaluated, not on matching past sales volume, but by increasing it a certain percentage. The percentage would vary from one location to another depending upon the number of condi-

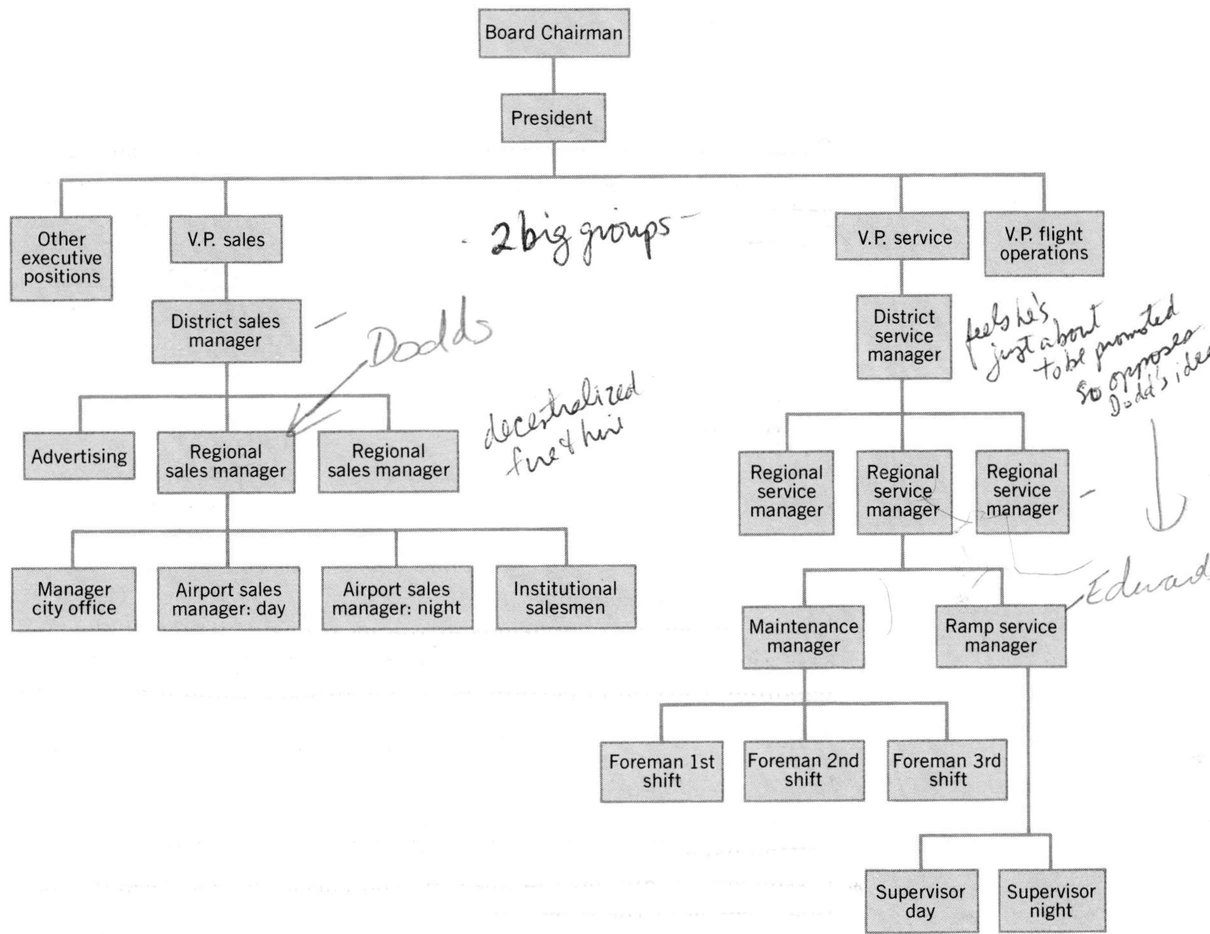


**FIGURE 12.6** Partial organization chart of Eagle Airlines.

tions: market potential, absolute volume, and similar terms. Although the percentage increase might vary, it was always there and was known by the company as the "ratchet." The regional service manager had no actual sales figure to be held accountable for, but that manager did have costs that were expected to be controlled, and if at all possible, reduced. While there was no similar "ratchet," such as a percentage reduction of costs expected each year, there was continual pressure on the local ramp manager in the form of exhortation, suggestions, and illustrations of managers who had successfully found ways to reduce costs.

### *Plan of the Sales Manager*

Carl Dodds, sales manager in Bartlett City, had been with Eagle Airlines seven years, during which time he had had three promotions. Upon graduation from a western state university, he had started working for Eagle Airlines in the San Francisco office as a ticket clerk at the local airport. Within a year he had been made accounts salesman, selling airline service to local companies and institutions. Within two years he had become a local sales manager at San Jose, the smallest of the company's sales offices. Six months ago he had received his promotion to Bartlett City, the second largest sales office and, until recently, the one growing most rapidly. Dodd's superior looked at him as a particularly dynamic, inventive salesman and sales manager. He seemed gifted at finding spectacular ways of substantially increasing sales. In previous positions he had developed a number of attention-getting promotion packages that met with spectacular results. Higher management looked to him to again increase sales at Bartlett City, which had leveled out about a year ago with the decline in the economy. It was not known how long the decline would continue.

Some of Dodd's previous associates in the other parts of the company agreed that he had been imaginative in developing some spectacular promotion schemes, but also felt that success had always been of the short-run variety: he had made sudden bursts at the expense of long-term growth. They further claimed that he had been fortunate in always being promoted out of a position before the consequences of his activity caught up with him.

Since coming to Bartlett City, Dodds had been intensively studying the local market situation, making contacts with the various companies and big business executives, hiring some new salesmen, and training them after having, as he called it, weeded out some deadwood. He had also increased advertising and redecorated the downtown sales office. In spite of this activity, in his own mind, he had been largely getting ready for his major effort.

Dodds defined his sales situation this way. The airline had done well attracting customers who wanted speed and convenience. However, a considerable number of business executives drove or used a company plane. He adopted and embellished a popular local image of the Bartlett City executive as a dynamic, imaginative, administrator-scientist who represented a new type of business tycoon. In Dodd's mind, what he had to do was sell this young dynamic, new type of tycoon the comfort and gracious service that, apparently, such a person thought should come to him or her in this new role. His new plan then was to do everything possible to give the "new tycoons" this sort of service. He therefore developed a plan to set up *Tycoon*

*Specials* on certain of the flights carrying the greatest number of these business executives. This plan was to begin with the flight between Bartlett City and Los Angeles.

In this plan the customer-executive upon arriving at the ticket-checking counter for the *Tycoon Special* flight would be asked to select his or her own seat. This then would be reserved in the customer's name. Upon arriving at the ramp for boarding, the customer would be greeted by name by the gate attendant, usually dressed plainly but neatly in a white top, blue cap, and slacks, but now in a gold coat and a simulated turban. Stretching between the gate and the aircraft was to be a wide, rich-red carpet. Upon arrival, the customer's name would be announced through a special intercom to the plane. As the individual walked down the red carpet, the customer-executive would note that the flight hostess would appear smiling at the door, ready to greet him or her by name before being ushered to the appropriate seat, identified by a card with the executive's name, indicating, "This seat is reserved for Tycoon _____."

Once in flight this deluxe service would continue, with the hostesses changing into more comfortable and feminine-looking lounge dresses and serving a choice of champagne, wine, and other cocktails along with exotic and varied hors d'oeuvres. There were other details to the plan, but this will give you some idea of its general nature. In this way, Dodds thought surely that he would be able to not only match but exceed the services and comfort some executives thought they obtained by alternative means of transportation.

Dodds' great problem was in getting the plan operational. Almost all of the service had to be provided by people who did not report to him. This would be supplied by the local ramp service manager, to whom the gate clerk reported, and who would have to provide the red carpet, the additional gold uniforms, turbans, and the other paraphernalia necessary to create the impression that Dodds had in mind. The local ramp service manager, Chris Edwards, had been particularly abrupt in rejecting this proposal, insisting that it did not make sense and that he was going to have absolutely nothing to do with it. Dodds had in several meetings attempted to "sell," persuade, pressure, and finally threaten Edwards into accepting the plan. Edwards refusal had become more adamant and pointed at every step. Relationships between the two, never close or cordial, had deteriorated until there was nothing but the most unrestrained hostility expressed between them.

### *Reaction of the Service Manager*

Chris Edwards was a graduate engineer who had worked for the company for about ten years. He had first started in the maintenance department of the firm and had gradually risen through several supervisory positions before being given this position as service manager with Eagle. It was the first position he had had in which he had an independent budget and was held individually accountable. After three years in this capacity, he personally felt and had been led to believe by several higher executives in the company that he had acquired as much experience in this position as was necessary. He was, therefore, looking forward to a new assignment, which probably involved a promotion in the very near future. He realized that this promotion would probably be based upon his earlier proven technical competence and his more recent experience in his present position, where he had run a particularly efficient operation. This was evidenced by several reductions in his operating expenses, due to efficiencies he had installed, and by other measures of performance, such as reduction in the time necessary to service, fuel, and load aircraft.

After having met with increasingly adamant refusals by Edwards, Dodds had gone to his superior, pointing out that he was being hampered by Edwards in his effort to increase sales and advance the company. Dodd's supervisor had made a point of seeing his counterpart, in the service area, asking if something could not be done by the service people at Bartlett City to support the sales effort. Upon inquiry, Edwards' superior learned the details of the request from Edwards and the reasons for his refusal. Dodds kept insistent pressure on his superior, asking to have something done about the local service manager's obstinacy. Eventually, word of the continued arguments between Dodds and Edwards went up the chain of command to the vice-president of sales and later to the vice-president in charge of service. One day while discussing this issue, their conversation was overheard by the president. Upon hearing the story, he made the comment that these personality clashes would either have to be straightened out or one or both of the men either transferred or, for that matter, fired. He emphatically insisted that the company could not operate efficiently with an unnecessary expenditure of energy going into personal disputes.

## Questions

Analyze Eagle Airlines from the perspective of a consultant on organizational design.

1. Is the present design appropriate? Why or Why not?
2. What design changes do you recommend? Why?

## THE MANAGER'S VOCABULARY

**Diverse Configuration** Where the organization stucture embodies a mix of the mechanistic and organic configurations among subunits.

**Mechanistic Organization** Where the structure emphasizes vertical specialization and control, an extensive use of managerial techniques, impersonal coordination and control, and a heavy reliance on rules, policies, and procedures.

**Organic Organization** Where the structure emphasizes horizontal specialization, an extensive use of personal coordination, and loose rules, policies, and procedures.

**Organizational Design** The process of choosing and implementing a structural configuration for an organization.

### Important Names

**Burns and Stalker** Developed the concepts of mechanistic and organic structures for organizations.

### Notes

[1] Tom Burns and G. M. Stalker, The *Management of Innovation* (London: Tavistock, 1961).

[2] See J. Anderson and W. Duncan, "The Scientific Significance of the Paradox in Administrative Theory," *Management International Review,* Vol. 17 (1977), pp. 99–106; and, Charles Perrow, *Organizational Analysis: A Sociological View* (Belmont, Calif.: Brooks/Cole, 1970).

[3] See Jeffrey Pfeffer and Gerald Salanick, *The External Control of Organizations: A Resource Dependence Approach* (New York: Harper & Row, 1978); and, Richard N. Osborn, R., James G. Hunt, and Lawrence R. Jauch, *Organizational Theory: An Integrated Approach* (New York: John Wiley & Sons, 1980), pp. 335–360.

[4] See Osborn et al., op. cit., p. 217.

[5] Ibid., pp. 298–300.

[6] Peter Blau and Richard Schoenner, *The Structure of Organizations* (New York: Basic Books, 1971); and J. Woodward, *Industrial Organization: Theory and Practice* (London: Oxford University Press, 1965).

[7] A. G. Kidron "Individual Differences, Job Characteristics, and Commitment to the Organization," (Doctoral Dissertion, The Ohio State University, 1976).

[8] Osborn, Hunt, and Jauch, op. cit., pp. 298–300.

[9] This case has been reproduced with the permission of its author, J. A. Litterer. Copyright © J. A. Litterer. As reported in Osborn, et al., *Organizational Theory: An Integrated Approach* (New York: John Wiley & Sons, 1980).

# PART FIVE

# MANAGING THE PROCESSES OF ORGANIZATIONAL BEHAVIOR

## THE MANAGER'S GOAL

**To Facilitate High Levels of Organizational Task Performance and Human Resource Maintenance.**

## YOUR LEARNING OBJECTIVE

**To Develop an Awareness of and Comfort with the Interpersonal Processes through which Managers Do Their Work, Including: Perception, Decision-Making, Communication, Conflict, Power, Politics, Change, and Leadership.**

## Chapters in This Part of the Book

Hardly anyone works alone in organizations, and managers never do. As shown throughout our earlier discussions, managers maintain a complex network of interpersonal relationships as part of their day-to-day work routines. It is through and with other people that managers get their own jobs accomplished.

This part of the book focuses your attention on the interpersonal processes with which every manager becomes heavily involved. Our emphasis will be on helping you understand skills that are important if you are to continue throughout your career to be successful at managing organizational behavior.

The prediction case that follows involves one manager who has just taken a great leap forward in his career. Read the case and think about the very demanding and complex challenges which he faces.

## The Jim Donovan Case[1]

Jim Donovan, 37, the new president and chief executive officer of Famous Products, was suddenly in the toughest spot in his life. Having just been selected by Omega Corporation, a huge conglomerate, to take over as president of their latest acquisition, he had been feeling very good about himself. Having grown up on "the wrong side of the tracks," worked his way through engineering college, earned an MBA from Harvard Business School, worked for 10 years as a management consultant and for two years as a successful president of a small company, he felt that he had arrived. The company he was going to manage was known throughout the world, had a good reputation, and would provide a good opportunity for visibility in the parent company. The pay would be the highest he had ever earned, and while the money itself was not that important (though he'd be able to assure his wife and four children financial security), he enjoyed the indicator of success a high salary provided. And Jim was eager to manage a company with over a thousand employees; the power to get things done on such a large scale was very attractive to him.

When Omega had selected him, they had told him that Don Bird, the current president of Famous Products, was close to retirement and would be moved upstairs to chairman of the board. Bird had been president of Famous for 22 years and had done reasonably well, building sales steadily and guarding quality. The top management group was highly experienced, closely knit, very loyal to the company, and its members had been in their jobs for a long time. As long-term employees, they all were reported to be good friends of Don Bird. They were almost all in their early 60s and quite proud of the record of their moderate-sized but successful company. Famous had not, however, grown in profits as rapidly as Omega expected of its operating companies, and Omega's president had told Jim that he wanted Jim to "grab a hold of Famous and make it take off."

With this challenge ringing in his ears, Jim flew out to Milwaukee for his first visit to Famous Products. He had talked briefly with

Don Bird to say that he'd be arriving Thursday for half a day, then would be back for good after ten days in New York at Omega. Bird had been cordial but rather distant on the phone, and Jim wondered how Bird was taking Jim's appointment. "I've only got a few hours here," thought Jim. "I wonder how I should play it."

## QUESTIONS

1. How would you "play it" if you were Jim?
2. How do you anticipate the current top management staff of Famous Products will react to the real Jim Donovan?

### Our Viewpoint

Jim exemplifies a "fast-track" pattern of success for the young executive. At 37, he is named to the top management post at Famous Products. He had worked hard, achieved performance levels highly valued by Omega, and is now being well rewarded.

If we were Jim, this prior work and educational experience would lend considerable confidence to our facing up to the tasks ahead. Being brought into Famous Products from the outside, he also has the advantage of not being intertwined in company politics, rumor mills, or social cliques. He is starting "fresh," and this can be to his distinct advantage.

Of course, Jim has a lot to learn about Famous Products and its people. Many of his early efforts will probably be devoted to this end. If he's smart, he'll learn before he acts.

Jim should also remember that his early actions and efforts will largely determine how people will think about and react to him in the future. This first staff meeting, therefore, can't be taken too lightly. People will be watching him very closely!

***Continuing On*** When Jim pulled up to Famous Products headquarters in his rented car, he noticed the neat grounds and immaculate landscaping. To his surprise, Don Bird met him at the door. Bird had on a very conservative blue business suit, black tie, black shoes, and white shirt. He peered out at Jim through old-fashioned steel-rimmed glasses and said, "Welcome to our plant. You're just in time for our usual Thursday morning executive meeting; would you like to sit in on that and meet our people?" Jim thought that the meeting would give him a chance to observe the management group in action, and he readily agreed, planning to sit back and watch for as long as he could.

Jim was ushered into the most formal meeting room he could remember ever having seen. The dark-paneled room was dominated by a long, heavy table, with 12 high-backed chairs around it. Seven of the chairs were filled with unsmiling executives in dark suits.

Bird led Jim to the front of the room, indicated an empty chair to the left of the seat at the head of the table, then sat down in the place that was obviously his. Turning to the group, he said:

> Gentlemen, I want you to meet Mr. Donovan, but before I turn the meeting over to him, I want you to know that I do not believe he should be here; I do not believe he's qualified and I will give him no support. Mr. Donovan . . .

### Our Viewpoint

Zap! Jim is on the griddle and he has to come up with a solution to this problem fast. "Why," he is probably saying to himself, "didn't I anticipate this thing? Why wasn't I prepared?" Surely Jim could have expected some resistance and perhaps even some resentment to his appointment. Not once did he stop and try to see things through the eyes of the "old guard" at Famous Products.

Now he is in a situation where he has to learn quickly to deal with the perceptions of these people, to communicate with them, and to be able to work with them to make decisions, handle conflict, and implement change. This is where his knowledge of individual and group behavior in organizations will be put to the true test! Can he, Jim Donovan, come out of this crisis and emerge as a true source of leadership for these and all other operating personnel at Famous Products? This is the ultimate managerial question.

## SUMMARY

Jim Donovan's dilemma clarifies the direction which our study of OB now takes. Managers must be able to achieve success in the interpersonal processes through which individual and group behavior is mobilized in support of an organization's production purpose. The four chapters in this part delve deeply into the topics of perception, decision-making, communication, conflict, power, politics, change, and leadership. You will find an emphasis in each chapter on understanding the concepts and learning how to apply them in actual managerial practice.

## NOTE

[1]This case is a synthesis of Jim Donovan (A) and (B) written by Allan R. Cohen and Michael Merenda, University of New Hampshire, for purposes of classroom discussion. Copyright 1979, Whittemore School of Business and Economics, University of New Hampshire. Reproduced with permission.

# 13

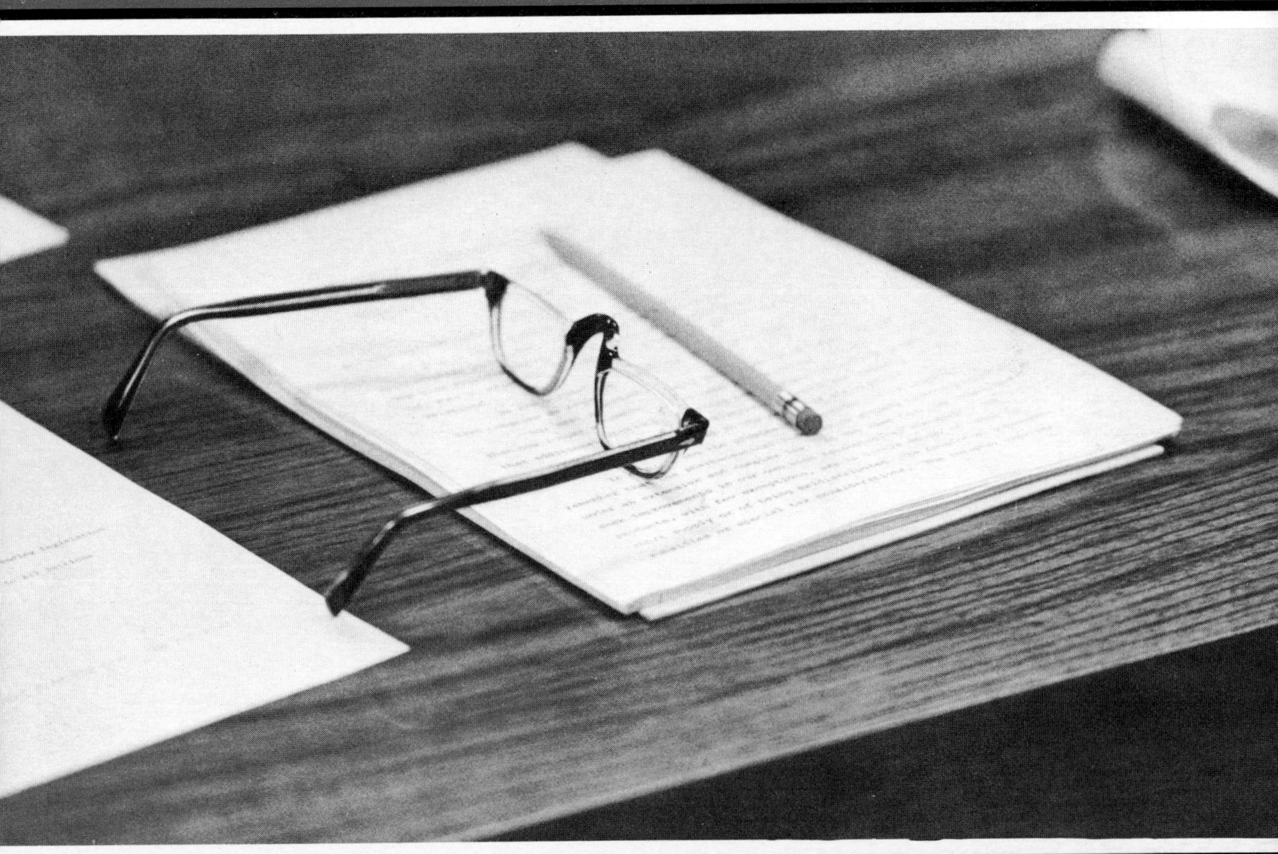

# PERCEPTION AND DECISION-MAKING

# A SHORT-SHORT STORY[1]

The lights in a store had just been turned off by a businessman when a man appeared and demanded money. The owner opened a cash register. The contents of the cash register were scooped up, and the man sped away. A member of the police force was notified promptly.

*Quiz:* Answer the following questions about the story.

1. A man appeared after the owner turned off his store lights. T F ?
2. The robber was a man. T F ?
3. The man who appeared did not demand money. T F ?
4. The man who opened the cash register was the owner. T F ?
5. The store owner scooped up the contents of the cash register and ran away. T F ?
6. Someone opened a cash register. T F ?
7. After the man who demanded money scooped the contents of the cash register, he ran away. T F ?
8. While the cash register contained money, the story does not state how much. T F ?
9. The robber demanded money of the owner. T F ?
10. A businessman had just turned off the lights when a man appeared in the store. T F ?
11. It was broad daylight when the man appeared. T F ?
12. The man who appeared opened the cash register. T F ?
13. No one demanded money. T F ?
14. The story concerns a series of events in which only three persons are referred to: the owner of the store, a man who demanded money, and a member of the police force. T F ?
15. The following events occurred: someone demanded money; a cash register was opened; its contents were scooped up; and a man dashed out of the store. T F ?

Each of us forms impressions about the world in which we live. These impressions affect our decisions and actions. Inaccurate impressions can lead to biased decisions and inappropriate actions. Managers cannot afford to make errors of impression when dealing with subordinates and other persons in the work setting.

**MANAGEMENT APPLICATIONS QUESTION**

How will you, as a manager, ensure that your decisions and actions will be based on truly accurate impressions of the work situation and the persons who comprise it?

## PLANNING AHEAD

**This chapter is designed to help you respond to the Management Applications Question just posed. The topics to be discussed include:**

**The Perception Process**
**Perception and Decision-Making**
**Perceptual Distortion by Generalization**
**Perceptual Distortion by Anticipation**
**Managing the Perception Process**

Managers make decisions about the employment of human resources in their work units. To make good decisions that actually promote job performance and human resource maintenance, the manager must be capable of drawing accurate impressions of the work situation. Then, and only then, can OB theories be used to their full advantage.

It is not always easy to derive accurate impressions of a situation. This is especially true of situations that are somewhat ambiguous. The anecdote that opens this chapter, in fact, is good proof of this. How well did you do? Look back at your responses. There are only three questions that have a factual frame of reference: 3 false, 6 true, and 13 false. All other questions should be marked "?". Study the story to learn why this is the case. Then ask yourself whether or not you can afford to look at work situations and make similar errors in the accuracy of your impressions!

## THE PERCEPTION PROCESS

**Perception** is the process through which people receive, organize, and interpret information from their environment.[2] This process is diagrammed in Figure 13.1. Through perception, people process information inputs into decisions and actions. It is a way of forming impressions about yourself, other people, and day-to-day life experiences. Perception is a screen or filter through which information

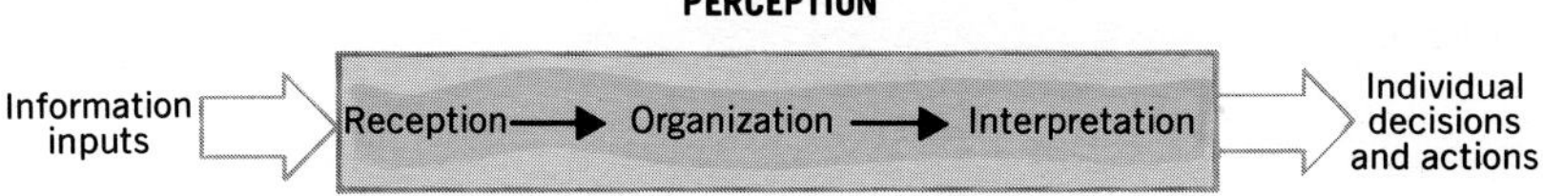


**FIGURE 13.1** The perception process.

must pass to achieve impact on human thought processes and behaviors.

People can perceive the same situation quite differently. In Figure 13.2, do you see the young woman or the old lady? Look again and find both faces in the picture. The following discussion will help you understand why it may be easier for you to see one face and not the other. This tendency for perceptions to vary among people is most important for managers to recognize, anticipate, and understand.

## Perceptual Differences

The data in Figure 13.3 show perceptual differences between managers and subordinates in one work setting. At issue is the frequency with which recognition is allocated as a work reward. Managers perceive that they give recognition frequently; subordinates view recognition as being less frequently available as a work reward.

The consequences of these different perceptions can be severe. Since perception links information with behavior, we might expect the managers' and subordinates' reactions to the same situation to be inconsistent with one another. This result is described in Figure

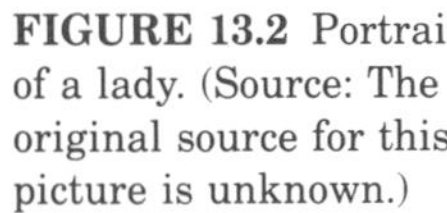

**FIGURE 13.2** Portrait of a lady. (Source: The original source for this picture is unknown.)

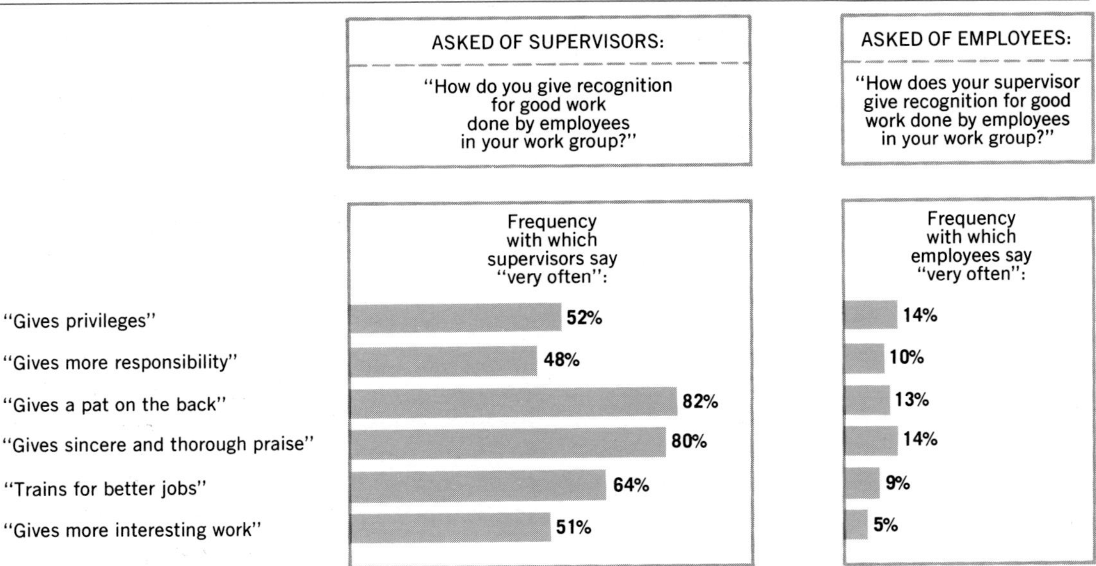
ASKED OF SUPERVISORS:
"How do you give recognition for good work done by employees in your work group?"
ASKED OF EMPLOYEES:
"How does your supervisor give recognition for good work done by employees in your work group?"
Frequency with which supervisors say "very often":
Frequency with which employees say "very often":
"Gives privileges"
52%
14%
"Gives more responsibility"
48%
10%
"Gives a pat on the back"
82%
13%
"Gives sincere and thorough praise"
80%
14%
"Trains for better jobs"
64%
9%
"Gives more interesting work"
51%
5%

**FIGURE 13.3** Perceptual differences between managers and their subordinates. (Source: From *New Patterns of Management* by Rensis Likert, p. 91. Copyright © 1961, McGraw-Hill. Used with the permission of McGraw-Hill Book Company.)

13.4. It could lead to problems if the managers reduce their attention to subordinates' needs for recognition and focus instead on other concerns. The subordinates' desires would remain frustrated, and the unfortunate result could well be declining job performance and satisfaction!

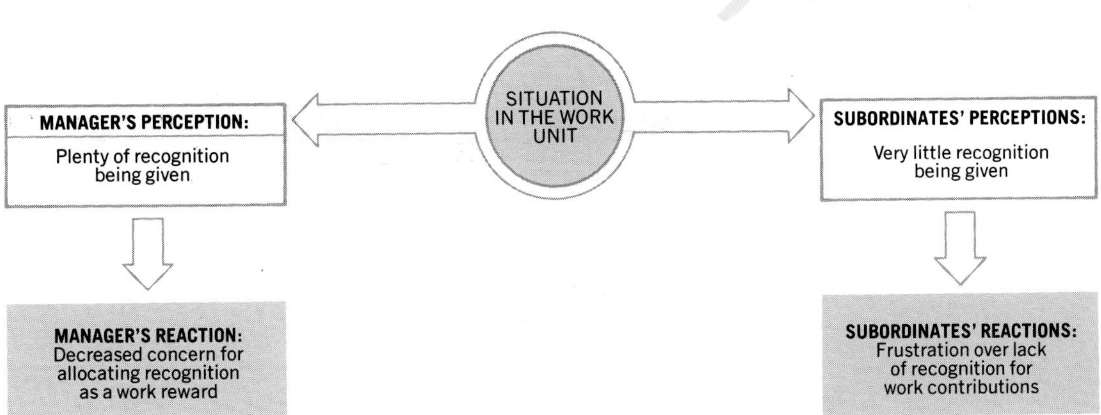
SITUATION IN THE WORK UNIT
MANAGER'S PERCEPTION:
Plenty of recognition being given
SUBORDINATES' PERCEPTIONS:
Very little recognition being given
MANAGER'S REACTION:
Decreased concern for allocating recognition as a work reward
SUBORDINATES' REACTIONS:
Frustration over lack of recognition for work contributions

**FIGURE 13.4** Contrasting definitions of the work situation and their consequences for managers and subordinates.

Perception is a screen through which information passes before having an effect on people. As such, perception is a dynamic that has important consequences for managers and their subordinates. Figuratively speaking,

Perception —affects→ the manager's view of a work situation —which affects→ the manager's decisions and actions

By the same token,

Perception —affects→ the subordinate's view of a work situation —which affects→ the subordinate's decisions and actions

Successful managers are in control of their perception processes. They are also able to understand the perceptions of other people. To achieve these capabilities, you need to know more about the process of perception and how it applies to managers in their work settings.

Checkpoint

Make sure you can define the concept of perception. Remember that perception links information inputs from a person's environment to their eventual effects on individual actions and decisions.

## Understanding the Perception Process

An individual's perception process is influenced by many forces. These include a number of techniques for organizing perceptual data, as well as certain situational variables.

### Organizing Perceptual Data

The way we organize information received from our settings affects its meaning. Four organizing devices which influence the perception process are figure and ground, set, Gestalt, and attribution. Definitions and work-related examples of each device follow.[3]

| Term/Definition | Work Example |
|---|---|
| **Figure and Ground:** The tendency to distinguish a central object from its surroundings. | Some people "stand out" more than others in work situations. As performance appraisal time approaches, the actions of your boss may become "accented," or especially visible, in day-to-day office routines. |

| | |
|---|---|
| **Set:** The tendency to respond to a situation in terms of anticipations rather than in terms of what actually exists. | While preparing to interview a job applicant, a manager reads a note from the personnel department. The note says the candidate lacks interpersonal skills. Throughout the interview, the manager notices where these skills are deficient. A decision is made not to hire the applicant. |
| **Gestalt:** The tendency to avoid the discomfort of unorganized information by assigning to it overall meaning. | A number of people are observed lingering around the coffee machine in the company cafeteria. You see this not as a random event, but as a "meeting" of a group of people, all from your office. |
| **Attribution:** The tendency to try to predict the behavior or intentions of other people or groups. | In the previous example, the manager notes a "meeting" of his subordinates. Now, he concludes, they are griping about his decision to require overtime work for the coming weekend. |

Everyone's perceptions are affected by organizing devices such as those noted above. As a manager, you will want to recognize when and how these devices affect your interpretation of key events. Care must be exercised to ensure accurate rather than inaccurate impressions. Managers should also recognize that these devices affect the perceptions of other people in the work setting. The astute manager, for example, may take special care to make her behavior appear nonthreatening and positive as performance appraisal time approaches for subordinates. In this way, the potentially negative effects of subordinates' figure and ground tendencies (as noted in the earlier example) may be avoided.

## Situational Variables

A number of situational variables also have the potential to influence an individual's perceptions. Consider the following incident involving former President of the United States Richard Nixon and one of his aides.[4]

> The President was working alone, very late at night, in a hotel room while on a trip. He opened the door, beckoned to a waiting aide, and ordered, "Get me coffee." The aide immediately responded to the request.

> Most of the activities of the hotel including the kitchen were not operating at such a late hour. Hotel personnel had to be called in and a fresh pot of coffee brewed. All of this took time and the President kept asking about "coffee" while waiting. Finally a tray was made up with a carafe of coffee, cream, sugar, and some sweet rolls and was rushed to the President's suite. It was only at this point that the aide learned that the President did not want coffee to drink, but rather wanted to talk to an assistant whose name was Coffee.

The misperceptions of the President's aide may be accounted for as follows.[5] The situation took place late at night, and the President's physical appearance suggested a person who was getting sleepy while working alone. Through past experience, the aide had learned that the President disliked being questioned and liked immediate service. The aide wanted to please the President. These various factors affected the aide's perception of the situation. His decision was to order the President coffee to drink. Unfortunately for both parties, the decision was wrong!

Among the situational variables active in the prior case were the characteristics of the perceiver, the characteristics of what was being perceived (in this case the person of the President), and the situational context within which the incident occurred. Figure 13.5 includes these situational variables, along with the preceding organizing devices, as multiple influences on the perception process. The situational variables of most significance are

**Characteristics of the perceiver:** needs, past experience, habits, personality, and organizational affiliations.

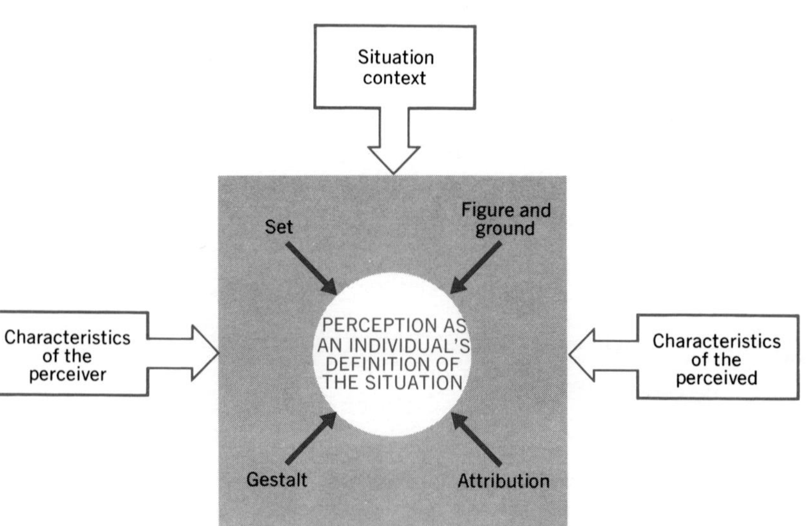


**FIGURE 13.5** Multiple influences on the perception process.

**Characteristics of the perceived:** a person's age and sex.

**Situational context:** physical surroundings, social setting, and time frame.

## PERCEPTION AND DECISION-MAKING

To make good decisions, a manager must first get good information from his or her setting and then interpret it accurately via the perception process. Picture yourself receiving information from many sources, including such people as your boss, subordinates, and other people in the organization. This information is needed if you are to make good decisions about the management of your work unit. Perception, as a screen or filter, may work to your advantage or disadvantage as you interpret this information. Given inaccurate perceptions, your decisions can be as erroneous as the one made by the President's aide in the case above.

### The Decision-Making Process

**Decision-making** is the process of choosing among alternative courses of action. The four basic steps in the decision-making process are:[6]

Define problem ⟶ Identify action alternatives ⟶ Choose among alternatives ⟶ Take action

OB theorists identify two alternative approaches to decision-making, classical and behavioral. A discussion of each will help you further understand the important relationship between perception and the processes through which managers make decisions.[7]

### Classical Decision Theory

Classical decision theory views the manager as acting in a world of complete certainty. The manager faces a clearly defined problem, knows all possible action alternatives and their consequences, and then chooses the alternative giving the best or "optimum" resolution of the problem. Clearly, this is an ideal way to make decisions.

Classical theory is often used as a model for how managers should make decisions.

Behavioral scientists are cautious regarding classical decision theory. They recognize that the human mind is a wonderful creation, capable of infinite achievements. But they also recognize that we each have cognitive limitations. The human mind is limited in its information-processing capabilities. Information deficiencies and overload both compromise the ability of managers to make decisions according to the classical model. As a result, it is argued that behavioral decision theory gives a more accurate description of how people make decisions in actual practice.

## Behavioral Decision Theory

Behavioral decision theory says that people act only in terms of what they perceive about a given situation. Furthermore, such perceptions are frequently imperfect. Rather than facing a world of complete certainty, the behavioral decision-maker is seen as acting under uncertainty and with limited information. Managers make decisions about problems that are often ambiguous, have only a partial knowledge about the available action alternatives and their consequences, and choose the first alternative that appears to give a satisfactory resolution of the problem. This is referred to by Herbert Simon, who has since won a Nobel Prize for his efforts, as a "satisficing" style of decision-making.[8] Simon and a colleague state,[9]

> Most human decision-making, whether individual or organizational, is concerned with the discovery and selection of satisfactory alternatives; only in exceptional cases is it concerned with the discovery and selection of optimal decisions.

## Cognitive Limitations and Decision-Making

The key difference between a manager's ability to make an optimum decision in the classical style and the tendency to make a satisficing decision in the behavioral style is the presence of cognitive limitations and their impact on our perceptions. Cognitive limitations impair our abilities to clearly define problems, identify action alternatives, and choose alternatives with ideal and predictable consequences. Figure 13.6 shows how these limitations differentiate between the two decision-making approaches.

You can see why it is so important for managers to understand the perception process. In fact, there are several perceptual distortions to which all persons are especially susceptible as a result of their cognitive limitations. The remainder of this chapter discusses

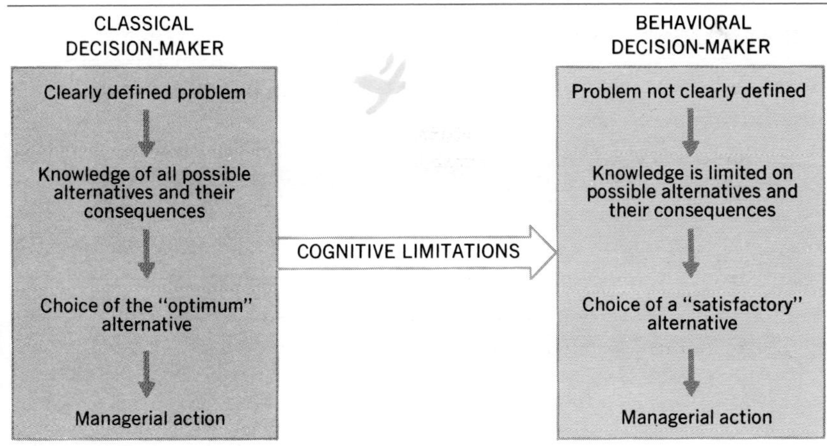


**FIGURE 13.6** Decision-making in the classical and behavioral perspectives.

these distortions as they fall into two categories: distortion by generalization and by anticipation. If you can learn to recognize the distortions, they can be controlled and their negative consequences minimized. As you read further, think about how each distortion might prevent you from understanding the work situation as it is viewed by other people, especially your subordinates.

Checkpoint

The distinction between classical and behavioral decision theory is important. Answer the following questions. Check the preceding discussion to verify your responses.

T F Because of our cognitive limitations, the influence of the perception process on individual decisions is increased.

T F "Satisficing" is a characteristic of classical decision theory.

T F In behavioral decision theory, only a limited amount of information is perceived and used as part of the decision-making process.

## PERCEPTUAL DISTORTION BY GENERALIZATION

Two perceptual errors that result from distortion by generalization are the stereotype and halo effect. Each applies with special relevance to the work setting.

## Stereotypes

Because of our cognitive limitations, we are able to attend to only a small portion of the infinite stimuli made available to us by the environment. To reduce the complexity of the environment, we often try to classify people and events into already known categories. Prior experience with the category then tells us what we need to know about the person or event in question. This is a process of generalization from the category to the specific event or person. It results in a stereotype.

A **stereotype** occurs when an individual or event is assigned to a group or category, and then the attributes commonly associated with the group are associated with the individual or event in question. They are common in interpersonal relations. There are stereotypes of young people, old people, teachers, students, union members, males, and females, among others. The phenomenon, in each case, is the same. A person is classified into a group on the basis of one piece of information (for example, young in age). Then characteristics commonly associated with the group ("young people dislike authority") are assigned to the individual. The problem is that what may be true about the group as a whole may or may not be true about the individual!

Stereotypes tend to obscure individual differences. When this happens in a manager's perceptions of a subordinate, for example, erroneous decisions can result. Two common stereotypes to which the manager may fall prey are those of age and sex. They deserve our special attention.

### Sex-Role Stereotypes

*Newsline 13.1* illustrates a classic sex-role stereotype. The case depicts Mrs. Lowe as having to "prove" herself to be capable as the branch manager of a bank. As a person she is prejudged to be a

Breaking the stereotype.

## NEWSLINE 13.1

### Mrs. Lowe Has to Deal with Stress and Sexism as a Bank-Branch Head

"Your secretary came outside to inspect the no-parking signs we put up at the drive-in teller," the police lieutenant told Martin Hartmann, an assistant branch manager for Continental Bank. "Hey, that was no secretary," objected Mr. Hartman, "that was my boss."

His boss is Challis M. Lowe, a 31-year-old black woman who earns more than $25,000 a year running the bank's first branch office, which opened last September in a skyscraper lobby at the north end of Chicago's financial district. Well aware that Mrs. Lowe is in charge, her staff of 26 bankers, tellers, and clerks have dubbed the branch "Challis's palace." But outsiders, unaccustomed to dealing with a woman executive, sometimes mistake her for a secretary.

Mrs. Lowe was Continental Bank's first black woman officer. Now the bank employs about 100 women executives—up from only 30 in 1973—three of whom are black. Altogether, the bank has 1,123 individuals in management.

Sometimes customers were also skeptical of her authority, refusing to talk to her and insisting that they be allowed "to see an officer." One elderly man was finally persuaded to confer with her and was so pleased with the results that he told her, "You can be my secretary any time." Mrs. Lowe coolly replied, "I don't think you can afford me."

Her quick adaptation to office politics and her smooth operation of the new office (its deposit volume is running four months ahead of schedule) are winning her praise. Staff morale is high, customers are pleased, "and we're getting a good business there," says John H. Perkins, Continental Bank's president. "It's got to be because she's running the place well."

Source: Excerpted from Joann S. Lublin, "Mrs. Lowe Has to Deal with Stress and Sexism as a Bank-Branch Head," *The Wall Street Journal* (April 26, 1977), p. 1. Reprinted by permission of The Wall Street Journal, 

secretary. After all, "management" is and has been viewed as the domain of males. Research shows that both male and female students view successful managers as possessing traits more commonly attributed to men than women.[10]

The logic and beliefs underlying the use of stereotypes are almost as damaging as the effects of prejudgement.[11] To justify the use of a stereotype some untested explanation is frequently offered. For instance, women may be considered too emotional and submissive to be successful managers. However, such justifications are rarely accurate. Emotionality and submissiveness, for example, are poor predictors of managerial success. Even if women were more emotional and submissive than men it does not follow that they would make poorer managers.

In attempting to remedy a deeply ingrained stereotype though, well intentioned managers may actually reinforce negative prejudgements.[12] Examine *What Consultants Do 13.1.* This piece presumes women may need special help. Should the advice that is given be restricted to women, or is it sound for all managers? Data from real organizations suggest only that women are disadvantaged in pay and career opportunities.[13] Men and women can be equally successful as managers.

Actions to debunk stereotypes can take valuable organizational resources. Actions based on stereotypes may yield opportunity losses. *Newsline 13.2* shows the experiences of some firms with women professionals. How many qualified female professionals for example, have been denied opportunites as a result of the myth that they would leave the company after only a short period of employment?

## Age Stereotypes

Age is another basis for stereotypes that affect people at work. Research suggests that negative stereotypes can bias managers against older workers.[14] The following summarizes how age stereotypes can place the older worker at a disadvantage in various problem situations.

| Problem | Older Worker Stereotype | Biased Decision by Manager |
|---|---|---|
| Individual work performance is declining. | Older workers are resistant to change. | Reassign the older worker, rather than encourage improvement in the present job. |
| Who should be promoted to fill an important, challenging job? | Older workers lack creativity, are cautious, and tend to avoid risk. | Don't promote the older worker. |
| Individual requests reassignment to a job requiring substantial physical strength. | Older workers are weak; their physical strength has declined with age. | Ask the older worker to withdraw the request for transfer. |

Any stereotype can prevent a manager from getting to know people and from accurately assessing individual differences at work. Sex and age stereotypes are most unfortunate in a time when equal

## NEWSLINE 13.2

### Debunking a Myth

*Women managers don't leave jobs more often than men*

With a few exceptions, most companies report their experiences don't support the oft-expressed suspicion that turnover rates among women professionals are higher than those for men. Motorola Inc. says management turnover rates for its men and women managers are identical. At a Chicago bank—Continental Illinois—the rate is higher for men than for women.

Ryder System Inc., the truck-leasing operation, reports that, among all employees, women leave at a faster rate (28%) than men (23%). But at the company's Miami headquarters, the rates are identical at 11%. General Electric, however, reports a differential—6% for men, 9% for women—which the company says hampers efforts to increase the number of women in upper-level jobs.

The G.E. differential is most pronounced among employees with high technical expertise. Some attribute this in part to the intense competition for such workers.

Source: "Debunking a Myth, Women Managers Don't Leave Jobs More Often Than Men," *The Wall Street Journal* (November 14, 1978), p. 1. Reprinted by permission of The Wall Street Journal, 

opportunity for all persons is a positive value. Stereotypes can compromise your decisions as a manager. They are a perceptual distortion which should be closely disciplined and controlled.

## The Halo Effect

A **halo effect** occurs when one attribute of a person or situation is used to develop an overall impression of the individual or situation. This is a process of generalization from one attribute to the total person or event. Halo effects are common in our everyday lives. When meeting a new person, for example, one trait such as a pleasant smile can lead to a positive first impression. The result of a halo effect, however, is the same as with a stereotype; individual differences become obscured.

Halo effects can influence a manager's evaluations of subordinates' work performance. Research shows that people with good attendance records are viewed as intelligent and responsible. Similarly, workers with poor attendance records are considered poor performers.[15] Such conclusions may or may not be true. It is the manager's

## WHAT CONSULTANTS DO 13.1

### Making Room at the Top as a Woman Manager

1. Decide objectively whether you really want a career. Do you expect to continue working whether or not you are married, or have children? What do you want out of work?

2. Make a specific list of every job you have ever held, including how well you did at each, and the skills, knowledge and experience you gained.

3. Make a five-year plan. Take a good look at where you want to be in five years. What skills and experience will you need, and what jobs must be held between now and then? Work out a detailed plan for progressing through those jobs. Check the plan with your boss, or someone else in a position to give you a realistic evaluation of your chances and knowledgeable advice on how to achieve your goal.

4. Try to find ways to increase your experience in planning, problem solving and group leadership—all crucial skills for a successful career in management. Ask your boss to assign you projects that will give you such experience, and then ask him to criticize your performance. Read books on these subjects or take courses in them, either in your company's in-house training program or at a nearby business school.

5. Study the informal system of personal relationships that exists in your company. Try to develop relationships with a broad range of your colleagues, and with key individuals whose friendship could be important in gaining subsequent jobs.

6. Try to establish an informal system of relationships with other women in the company. You can help each other identify job opportunities in other areas of the firm. Such a group can also help identify bosses who are particularly supportive of career advancement for women.

7. When dealing with male colleagues, don't try to engage in their male joking and camaraderie. Keep your relations with them revolving around job-related issues. Stress your competence rather than your personality. When dealing with men who treat you as a woman rather than as a fellow executive, try to bring the relationship back to the task at hand.

8. Learn to control your emotions, and the way you express them at work. Make a list of situations that caused you to become emotionally upset. Describe what happened: did you cry, express anger, or become visibly defensive? Look for patterns in these events. Did they occur when you were criticized, or when you were challenged? Was there some warning signal before each occasion? If so, learn to watch for those warnings and then excuse yourself and go somewhere where you'll have a chance to compose yourself.

9. Ask yourself why you are so vulnerable to criticism. Have you failed to do something you should have done? Do you balance the criticism by crediting yourself with all the things you have done well? Try to realize that

criticism is a necessary ingredient in learning. When you're criticized, don't assume it's directed at you personally.

10. Are you having difficulty trying to be a perfect employee as well as a perfect wife, or mother, or woman? Stop trying to separate the worlds of work and home. Discuss your job with your husband and your family. Make sure they understand your commitment to your career, and your responsibilities at work. Try to reduce potential conflicts by setting clear priorities for your life at home and on the job. Some jobs at home may have to be let go. Your husband or your children might be able to take on more responsibilities at home, or household help could relieve you of some of the burden.

11. Stop waiting to be chosen, and start letting people at work know what you want. Ask questions about promotions and job opportunities. Start asking to take on new or extra projects that will give you a chance to learn new skills. Stop being reactive, and start initiating. Start trying to take control of your career.

Source: Excerpt from *The Managerial Woman* by Margaret Hennig and Anne Jardim. 

job to get true impressions, rather than allowing halo effects to result in biased and erroneous evaluations.

We often kid our students that the halo effect can be used to one's career advantage. How? Well, to get good performance evaluations from your boss, be the first person to work and the last person to leave work every day. Through the halo effect, your colleagues and boss may come to consider you a high performer as well. Anyone who starts work so early and leaves so late must surely be a high performer! By the way, *Newsline 13.3* suggests that this advice shouldn't be taken too lightly.

## NEWSLINE 13.3

### The Early Bird Gets Not Only the Worm But Also a Better Job

In his Air Force days in Nome, Alaska, John Kern came close to winning a sleeping contest. He spent 17 hours in the sack but finished second to another airman who put in 19 hours conked out in the land of the midnight sun.

Today, Mr. Kern, now personnel manager at Prudential Insurance Co. of America's Western office in Los Angeles, finds it impossible to sleep past 6 a.m. even on work-free weekends.

Mr. Kern is up at 3:45 every morning. From his home in the Torrance section of Los Angeles, he drives to an all-night doughnut stand for a breakfast of black coffee. When he arrives at his office at 5:15, he is already one-up on nearly everybody else in town: he has beaten the legendary L.A. rush-hour traffic. By 6:00, he is on the phone with Prudential's Newark, N.J. headquarters. "There's a three-hour time difference, but the people there are still fresh at that time," he says. Thanks to his early start, Mr. Kern also finds that he doesn't need to take work home anymore because he finishes it at the office.

The alarm rings even earlier for Robert Hyland, CBS regional vice president in charge of radio station KMOX in St. Louis, who gets up at 2:15 in order to get to work at 3:30, fully five hours before his fellow executives. He says he prefers to start early "because I work more effectively in the morning and I like to have my evenings free for my family."

Benjamin Franklin, of course, said it all long ago with his dictum: "He that riseth late must trot all day," as well as "Early to bed and early to rise." But a surprising number of executives are discovering fresh reasons to join the dawn patrol. Not only do they beat the commuter rush, but also they can get more work done in the hours before the telephone starts to ring and the normal distractions of the day begin to crowd in on them.

J. Robert Harman, Jr., senior vice president in charge of executive recruitment for Booz, Allen & Hamilton, Inc., a Chicago-based management-consulting firm, says the majority of corporate chief executives he deals with get to work early. He contends that there is a "high correlation between executive success and early arrival at the office," and he says he uses arrival time as one criterion in judging an executive's qualifications.

"Educators and lawyers tend to be late starters, but if you are talking about a guy in a publicly held corporation who's dealing with the bottom line every day, he's usually in early, leading the pack," Mr. Harman asserts.

Source: Excerpted from John R. MacArthur, "The Early Bird Gets Not Only the Worm But a Better Job," *The Wall Street Journal* (September 20, 1977), p. 1. Reprinted by permission of The Wall Street Journal, copyright © Dow Jones & Company, Inc., 1977. All rights reserved.

## PERCEPTUAL DISTORTION BY ANTICIPATION

**Distortion by anticipation occurs in three possible ways: as selective perception, as projection, and as expectancy. Each of these perceptual tendencies is an additional source of error as managers make decisions that affect their work situations.**

### Selective Perception

It's time for a parable.

## The Parable of the Spindle[16]

There once was a large restaurant chain. The president of this chain became concerned about inefficiencies and ill tempers among employees. She called in a sociologist, a psychologist, and an anthropologist as consultants. The charge given the consultants was to find reasons for and identify solutions to these problems: why waitresses break down in tears, why cooks walk off the job, and why managers get so upset that they summarily fire employees on the spot. The consultants decided to pursue their tasks separately.

After they each studied the problem in a different city, the consultants returned with their reports to the president.

**The Sociologist's Report** The problems appear during rush hours. There is a stress problem. Stress exists between the customers and the waiters, the waiters and the cook, the waiters and the manager, the manager and the cook, and the manager and the customers. Furthermore, there is a status problem. The manager is of the highest status. Next come the cooks, waiters, busboys, and dishwashers, in descending order. But the waiters actually give orders to the cook, and it isn't right for a lower status person to give orders to one of higher status.

I suggest you put a "spindle" on the order counter. This spindle is a wheel on a shaft. The wheel has clips so that waiters can simply put their orders on the wheel rather than calling out orders to the cook.

**The Psychologist's Report** Your problems occur during rush hours. In the restaurant, the manager is the parent figure, the cook is the child, and the waiter another child. Now we know that in our culture it isn't good to have children giving orders to one another. It louses up their ego structures.

We need a way to break up this face-to-face relationship between cook and waiter. The idea I have is to put a "spindle" on the order counter. A spindle is. . . .

**The Anthropologist's Report** It is during rush hours that your problems arise. We anthropologists know that people behave because of their value systems. The manager holds as a central value the continued growth and development of the restaurant organization. The cooks share these values, but the waiters do not. Most of them are working to supply income to their families. They couldn't care less whether the organization thrives or not as long as it's a decent place to work. Now, you can't have a noncentral value system giving orders to a central value system.

What is needed is some way of breaking up the face-to-face contact between the waiters and the cook. One suggestion is to place on the order counter an adaptation of the old-fashioned spindle. . . .

## Continuing On

Thus, it came to pass that the spindle, the very same spindle we all know, was introduced into restaurants! Even though each consultant looked at the problem from a different perspective and came up with a unique perception of its root causes, a common solution was found. Inherent in this parable lie examples of both selective perception and one means of reducing its negative consequences in the work setting.

**Selective perception** is the tendency to single out for attention those aspects of a situation or person which reinforce or emerge consistent with existing beliefs, values, and needs. In the parable of the spindle, the consultants selectively perceived the restaurant problem in terms consistent with their academic backgrounds. A similar tendency is found among executives working in different departments in a business corporation, as we have shown in Chapter 10.[17] No harm was done in the restaurant example, since the consultants' conlusions were the same. Such is not always the case.

A manager must test whether or not situations and individuals are being selectively perceived. The easiest way to do this is to gather additional opinions from other people. This is what the president did in the parable. When these opinions are contradictory, an effort should be made to check the original impression. This tendency toward selectivity is one which a manager must be able to control in terms of his or her own behavior, as well as recognize in the behavior of others.

## Projection

**Projection** is the assignment of personal attributes to other individuals. You have heard the familiar admonition: "Do unto others as you would have them do unto you." In all due respect to its enduring wisdom, managers should be cautious in applying this maxim in the work setting. The reason is the fallacy of projection.

A classic projection error is the manager who assumes that the needs of subordinates are the same as his or her own. Suppose, for example, that you enjoy responsibility and achievement in your work. Suppose, too, that you are the newly appointed manager of subordinates whose work seems dull and routine. You might move quickly to redesign these jobs and help your subordinates achieve higher-level satisfactions. Why? Because you want them to experience things that you personally value in work.

This may not be a good decision. By projecting your needs on subordinates, individual differences are lost. Rather than designing the subordinates' jobs to best fit their needs, you have designed their jobs to fit yours. The problem is they may be quite satisfied and productive doing jobs that, to you, seem dull and routine.

Projection is a perceptual distortion that compromises a manager's ability to respond to individual differences in the work setting. It can be controlled through a high degree of self-awareness and by a willingness to enter the frame of reference of the other person and come to see the situation through their eyes. This is called **empathy.**

## Expectancy

Another perceptual distortion is **expectancy.** This is the tendency to create or find in another situation or individual that which you expected to find in the first place. Expectancy is sometimes referred to as the "pygmalion effect."[18] Pygmalion was a mythical Greek sculptor who created a statue of his ideal mate and then made her come to life. His expectations came true! By committing expectancy errors, you may also create in the work situation that which you expect to find.

Expectancy can have both positive and negative results for the manager. Let's consider an example. Suppose that the manager assumes that his or her subordinates basically prefer to satisfy most of their needs outside the work setting and only minimal involvement with their jobs. Therefore, the manager will try to provide simple, highly structured jobs designed to require little involvement.

Can you predict the response of the subordinates to this situation? Their most likely response is to show the lack of commitment which the manager assumed in the first place. Thus, the manager's initial expectations are confirmed as a self-fulfilling prophecy.

Is this result positive or negative? For those workers wanting challenging jobs and a lot of workplace need satisfaction, the result is clearly negative. For those who like narrow, unenriched jobs, the result is positive. Whether positive or negative though the example demonstrates the self-fulfilling prophecy effect which initial expectations can have.

Some additional research on the positive side of expectancy may further stimulate your thinking. Psychologists, for example, have found that rats identified to their handlers as "maze bright" run mazes more quickly than rats introduced to their handlers as being "dumb"; students identified to their teachers as "intellectual bloomers" do better on achievement tests than counterparts who lack such a positive introduction; job trainees pointed out to their supervisors as having "special potential" have higher job performance than trainees not so identified.[19]

The expectancy effects in the above cases are not easy to explain. It does appear, though, that certain conditions may facilitate the confirming of expectancies.[20] Managers, for example, who perceive their subordinates under conditions of positive expectancy may

- Create a warmer interpersonal climate between themselves and subordinates.
- Give more performance feedback to subordinates.
- Spend more time helping subordinates to learn job skills.
- Give subordinates more opportunities to ask questions.

**Checkpoint**

We have just discussed five perceptual distortions that can have a significant impact on the quality of a manager's decisions. For the following columns, match each type of distortion on the left with its correct description from the list on the right. Check your answers by referring back to the preceding pages.

| | |
|---|---|
| ____ Halo effect | a. Using one trait to bias a total evaluation of the individual. |
| ____ Projection | b. Anticipating the presence of something and then creating it by a self-fulfilling prophesy. |
| ____ Stereotype | c. Drawing a self-reinforcing conclusion from an ambiguous situation. |
| ____ Expectancy | d. Attributing personal needs to someone else. |
| ____ Selective perception | e. Generalizing attributes of a group to an individual group member. |

## MANAGING THE PERCEPTION PROCESS

The importance of this chapter lies in the following logic.

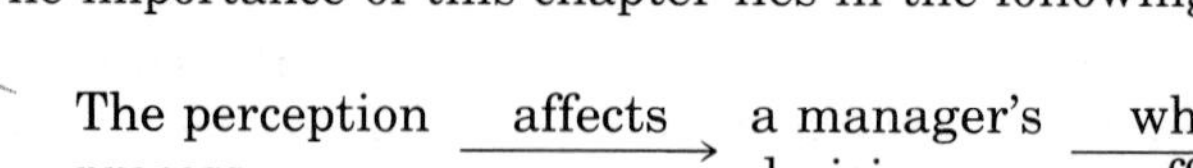
The perception process
affects
a manager's decisions
which affect
work unit results

Successful managers will be in control of their perceptions. They will be sensitive to the perception processes of other people and know how perception affects attitudes and behaviors at work. Such managers will make decisions and take action with a true understanding of the work situation as viewed by all persons concerned.

Perception is an important interpersonal skill of managers. The following guidelines will help you to develop this capability. A manager who is skilled in the perception process will[21]

1. Have a high level of self-awareness. Individual needs, experience, and expectations can all affect perceptions. The successful manager knows this and is able to identify when a situation is inappropriately distorted by perceptual tendencies.
2. Seek information from various sources to confirm or disconfirm personal impressions of a decision situation. Selectivity is an important perceptual tendency. The successful manager will avoid the biases of selective perception by seeking out the viewpoints of others and using these insights to gain additional perspective on problems.
3. Be empathetic, that is, be able to see a situation as it is perceived by other people. Since people tend to define the same situation differently, a manager must be capable of rising above personal impressions to view problems as seen by other people.
4. Influence the perceptions of other people when they are drawing incorrect impressions of events in the work setting. Because people act in terms of their perceptions, a manager must be able to influence others' perceptions so that the work situation is interpreted to the advantage of the work unit.
5. Seek to avoid perceptual distortions that can obscure individual differences and bias performance evaluations. A manager's success in applying OB theories to real problems depends on an accurate assessment of people and their work circumstances.

## SUMMARY

Managers depend upon information received from their environment to make decisions. Much of this information is gathered through interpersonal relationships with the manager's boss, subordinates, and other persons inside and outside of the work unit. Perception is the process through which a manager receives, organizes, and interprets information from these sources. As the accuracy of the perception process increases or decreases, the quality of a manager's decisions and actions will be affected accordingly.

Perception is a cognitive process. It is affected by a variety of situational variables as well as certain organizing tendencies shared by all people. Important situational variables are the characteristics of the perceiver, the social setting, and what is being perceived. The organizing tendencies include the dynamics of Gestalt, figure and ground, set, and attribution. A manager who is aware of the influence of these forces on perceptions can recognize when they are contributing to inaccurate perceptions of people or situations.

Perception influences the way people make decisions. Limited cognitive abilities to receive and process information result most often in a behavioral style of decision-making. Only a limited number of action alternatives are considered, and the first satisfactory, rather than optimum one, is selected for action. The use of a behavioral style of decision-making reminds all managers that their perceptions must be especially accurate in order to ensure that good results are achieved.

Several perceptual distortions pose special threats to decision-makers. They include stereotypes, halo effects, selective perception, projection, and expectancy. Each distortion, once recognized, can be controlled by the informed manager.

## THINKING THROUGH THE ISSUES

1. Describe why perception is a key variable in the manager's attempt to meet his or her work responsibilities.

2. Identify the situational variables that may have influenced your perceptions of a work experience. What could be done to control these perceptions and possibly change your attitudes or behavior toward this work situation?

3. What are the key differences between the classical and behavioral decision theories? How does perception contribute to these differences?

4. What is the major difference between the stereotype and the halo effect? Give an example of how each might have a negative effect on a manager's relationships with his or her subordinates.

5. Explain how expectancy effects may account for the behavior of students in the classroom. Be sure to include examples of where an instructor's use of initial assumptions about students may create self-fulfilling prophecies.

6. Define and give an example of projection as a perceptual distortion sometimes made by managers.

7. Consider Chapter 4 on motivation. Explain how key aspects of perception can influence components in the various motivational models.

8. Summarize the importance of the perception process to the manager who seeks to take full working advantage of OB theories.

## EXERCISE: ALLIGATOR RIVER STORY[22]

### Purpose:

To help you realize the different perceptions, values, and attitudes which people have even on common, everyday happenings.

### Time:

50 minutes plus out-of-class preparation.

### Procedure:

1. Read the Alligator River Story which follows.

After reading the story, rank the five characters in the story beginning with the one whom you consider as the most offensive and end with the one whom you consider the least objectionable. That is, the character who seems to be the most reprehensible to you should be entered first in the list following the story, then the second most reprehensible, and so on, with the least reprehensible or objectionable one being entered fifth. Of course, you will have your own reasons as to why you rank them in the order that you do. Very briefly note this down too. Bring this material to class with you.

2. Form groups as assigned by your instructor (at least four persons per group; at least one female per group and as close to an equal mix of males and females, if this is possible).

3. Each group should:

- **a.** Elect a spokesperson for the group.
- **b.** Tabulate how your group members ranked each of the characters that appear in the story.
- **c.** Examine the reasons as to why the characters got the rankings that they did. That is, what was the primary reason why each member of the group ranked individuals in the order that they did?
- **d.** Try to arrive at a group consensus on the rankings.

(1) If you can, be prepared to tell the class later the basis on which you arrived at the agreement and what the final rankings were.

(2) If you cannot, what were the main reasons that blocked a consensual ranking? Be prepared to discuss this with the class later and share the final rankings of your group with the class.

4. Reassemble for debriefing at the time specified by your instructor. The spokesperson for each group should first indicate the group's outcomes during the debriefing session. There will be a general discussion thereafter.

## The Alligator River Story[23]

There lived a woman named Abigail who was in love with a man named Gregory. Gregory lived on the shore of a river. Abigail lived on the opposite shore of the same river. The river which separated the two lovers was teeming with man-eating alligators. Abigail wanted to cross the river to be with Gregory. Unfortunately, the bridge had been washed out by a heavy flood the previous week. So she went to ask Sinbad, a riverboat captain, to take her across. He said he would be glad to if she would consent to go to bed with him prior to the voyage. She promptly refused and went to a friend named Ivan to explain her plight. Ivan did not want to get involved at all in the situation. Abigail felt her only alternative was to accept Sinbad's terms. Sinbad fulfilled his promise to Abigail and delivered her into the arms of Gregory.

When Abigail told Greogry about her amorous escapade in order to cross the river, Gregory cast her aside with disdain. Heartsick and rejected, Abigail turned to Slug with her tale of woe. Slug, feeling compassion for Abigail, sought out Gregory and beat him brutally. Abigail was overjoyed at the sight of Gregory getting his due. As the sun set on the horizon, people heard Abigail laughing at Gregory.

| Rank | Name | Reasons |
|---|---|---|
| First | | |
| Second | | |
| Third | | |
| Fourth | | |
| Fifth | | |

| Character | First | Second | Third | Fourth | Fifth |
|---|---|---|---|---|---|
| | Frequency of Being Ranked: | | | | |
| Abigail | | | | | |
| Gregory | | | | | |
| Sinbad | | | | | |
| Ivan | | | | | |
| Slug | | | | | |

## THE MANAGER'S VOCABULARY

**Attribution** The tendency to predict the behavior or intentions of other people or groups.

**Decision-Making** The process of choosing among alternative courses of action.

**Empathy** A willingness to enter the frame of reference of another person and see the situation through their eyes.

**Expectancy** The tendency to create or find in another situation or individual that which one expected to find in the first place.

**Figure and Ground** The tendency to distinguish a central object from its surroundings.

**Gestalt** The tendency to avoid the discomfort of unorganized information by assigning it an overall meaning.

**Halo Effect** One attribute of a person or situation is used to develop an overall impression of the person or situation.

**Perception** The process through which people receive, organize, and interpret information from their environment.

**Projection** The assignment of personal attributes to other individuals.

**Satisficing** Choosing the first satisfactory rather than the optimal decision alternative.

**Selective Perception** The tendency to single out for attention those aspects of a situation or person that reinforce or emerge and are consistent with existing beliefs, values, and needs.

**Set** The tendency to respond to a situation in terms of anticipations rather than in terms of what actually exists.

**Stereotype** Assigning an individual or event to a group or category, and then ascribing to that individual or event the attributes commonly associated with the group or category.

## Notes

[1]William V. Haney, *Communication and Interpersonal Relations: Text and Cases,* Fourth Edition. (Homewood, Ill.: Richard D. Irwin, Inc., 1979), pp. 250–251. Copyright ©Richard D. Irwin, Inc., 1960, 1967, 1973, 1979. All rights reserved. Used by permission.

[2]Blair J. Kolasa, *Introduction to Behavioral Science for Business* (New York: John Wiley & Sons, 1969).

[3]Ibid., pp. 212–218; and John Seager, "Seeing Eye to Eye: Practical Problems of Perception," *Personnel Journal,* Vol. 53 (October 1974), pp. 744–751.

[4]Dan Rather and Gary Paul Gates, *The Palace Guard* (New York: Harper & Row, 1970), p. 109.

[5]See John M. Ivancevich, Andrew D. Szilagyi, Jr., and Marc J. Wallace, Jr., *Organizational Behavior and Performance* (Santa Monica, Calif.: Goodyear Publishing Company, 1977), pp. 90–91, for another discussion of this incident.

[6]For a discussion of these variables and related research, see Sheldon S. Zalkind and Timothy W. Costello, "Perception: Some Recent Research and Implications for Administration," *Administrative Science Quarterly,* Vol. 7 (September 1962), pp. 218–235; J. Bruner and C. Goodman, "Value and Need as Organizing Factors in Perception," *Journal of Abnormal and Social Psychology,* Vol. 42 (1947), pp. 22–44; Dewitt C. Dearborn and Herbert A. Simon, "Selective Perception: A Note on the Departmental Identification of Executives," *Sociometry,* Vol. 21 (1958), pp. 140–144; Barry M. Staw, "Attitudinal and Behavioral Consequences of Changing a Major Organizational Reward: A Natural Field Experiment," *Journal of Personality and Social Psychology,* Vol. 29 (1974), pp. 742–751; and, Gerald R. Salancik and Jeffrey Pfeffer, "A Social Information Processing Approach to Job Attitudes and Task Design," *Administrative Sciences Quarterly,* Vol. 23 (June 1978), pp. 224–253.

[7]This discussion is based on James G. March and Herbert A. Simon, *Organizations* (New York: John Wiley & Sons, 1958), pp. 137–142.

[8]For a sample of Simon's work see Herbert A. Simon, *Administrative Behavior* (New York: Free Press, 1947); and, March and Simon, op. cit.

[9]March and Simon, op. cit., pp. 140–141.

[10]Virginia Ellen Schein, "Relationships Between Sex Role Stereotypes and Requisite Management Characteristics Among Female Managers," *Journal of Applied Psychology,* Vol. 60 (1975), pp. 340–344.

[11]Margaret Hennig and Anne Jardim, "Women Executives in the Old-Boy Network," *Psychology Today,* Vol. 10 (January 1977), pp. 76–81; see also Hennig and Jardim, *Managerial Woman* (New York: Doubleday and Company, 1976).

[12]See Benson Rosen and Thomas H. Jerdee, "The Influence of Sex-Role Stereotypes on Evaluations of Male and Female Supervisory Behavior," *Journal of Applied Psychology,* Vol. 57 (1973), pp. 44–48; "Influence of Sex-Role Stereotypes on Personnel Decisions," *Journal of Applied Psychology,* Vol. 59 (1974), pp. 9–14; "Sex Stereotyping in the Executing Suite," *Harvard Business Review,* Vol. 52 (March–April 1974), pp. 45–58; "On-

the-Job Sex Bias: Increasing Managerial Awareness," *Personnel Administrator,* Vol. 16 (January 1977), pp. 15–18.

[13]See Richard Osborn and William Vicars, "Sex Stereotypes: An Artifact in Leader Behavior and Subordinate Satisfaction Analysis," *Academy of Management Journal,* Vol. 19 (1976), pp. 439–449.

[14]Benson Rosen and Thomas H. Jerdee, "The Influence of Age Stereotypes on Managerial Decisions," *Journal of Applied Psychology,* Vol. 61 (1976), pp. 428–432.

[15]See Zalkind and Costello, op. cit.

[16]Adapted from Elias Porter, "The Parable of the Spindle," *Harvard Business Review,* Vol. 40 (May–June 1962), pp. 58–66.

[17]Dearborn and Simon, op. cit.

[18]J. Sterling Livingston, "Pygmalion in Management," *Harvard Business Review,* Vol. 47 (July–August 1969), pp. 81–89; Robert Rosenthal, "The Pygmalion Effect Lives," *Psychology Today,* Vol. 7 (September 1973), pp. 56–63.

[19]Rosenthal, op. cit.

[20]Ibid., p. 60.

[21]Some of these ideas can be found in Zalkind and Costello, op. cit.

[22]Adapted from an exercise by Uma Sekaran and William Coscarelli appearing in *Exchange: The OB Teaching Journal,* Vol. 5 (Winter 1980) pp. 46–47.

[23]This story is with 78 other thought-provoking situations in Sidney Simon, Leland Howe, and Howard Kirschenbaum, *Values Clarification* (New York: Hart Publishing Company, 1972).

# 14

# COMMUNICATION AND CONFLICT

# CORPORATE COVERUPS[1]

*The Wall Street Journal* reports there is a widespread coverup at work in society. It is a conspiracy to hide unpleasant truths about problems and mistakes from the eyes and ears of senior managers. Although individual circumstances may vary, the pattern is similar: "Something is wrong. Some people know it is wrong. The people who should find out it is wrong are not told until too late."

*Example 1.* The president of a large machinery producer ordered work to begin on a new kind of photocopying machine. Though those with direct responsibility for the machine knew the job would take two years, a report to the president stated that the machine could be developed in a matter of months. The reason: each layer of management shaved a few weeks off the original estimate to please superiors. Working day and night, the staff managed to construct a prototype to meet the truncated timetable. The president inspected it and left with assurances it was "ready to roll." Hardly had he left the lab when the prototype burst into flames and was destroyed.

*Example 2.* The chief executive of an electronics company on the West Coast discovered that shipments were being predated and papers falsified to meet sales targets that his managers knew were unrealistically high. At least 20 persons in the organization cooperated in the deception, but it was months before anyone at the top found out.

The "problem" underlying corporate coverups is the presence of communication gaps between higher-level managers and their subordinates. Perhaps one cause of the gaps is the fear of being punished for bearing bad news; another reason could be a fear of conflict.

**MANAGEMENT APPLICATIONS QUESTION**

What will you do, as a manager, to ensure an open flow of information between yourself and other persons in the work setting?

## PLANNING AHEAD

**The learning activities of this chapter will help you gain insight into the processes of interpersonal communication and conflict. Key topics include:**

**Communication and the Manager**
**Communication as a Process**
**Guidelines for Effective Communication**
**The Communication of Roles**
**Interpersonal Conflict**
**Conflict Resolution**

"Communication" is a word like "organization." Everyone knows what it means until they are asked to formally state its definition. It is useful to think of **communication** as an interpersonal process of sending and receiving symbols with meanings attached to them.

## COMMUNICATION AND THE MANAGER

When problems arise in organizations, their cause is frequently identified as poor communication. This is because communication is the source of information used by managers in making decisions that affect the organization. When poor decisions result, bad communication is frequently to blame.

Managers depend on their communication skills to get the information required to make decisions, and to transmit the results and intentions of these decisions to other people. Research indicates managers spend as much as 80% of their time in verbal interactions with other people.[2] Figure 14.1 shows how the time of five chief executives was distributed among various types of communications: telephone calls, scheduled and unscheduled meetings, plant tours, and desk work. You may be surprised that only 33% of the managers' time was spent on desk work! Obviously, these executives spent the large majority of their work days in direct interaction with other people.

The information-processing skills required of a manager include the abilities to send and to receive information when acting as a monitor, disseminator, spokesperson, and strategy-maker. Figure 14.2 summarizes these responsibilities in the manager's role as an information-processing system.

**FIGURE 14.1** The distribution of managers' time among various communication media. (Source: Abridged and adapted text from chart on p. 39 in *The Nature of Managerial Work* by Henry Mintzberg. Copyright © 1973 by Henry Mintzberg. Reprinted by permission of Harper & Row Publishers, Inc.)

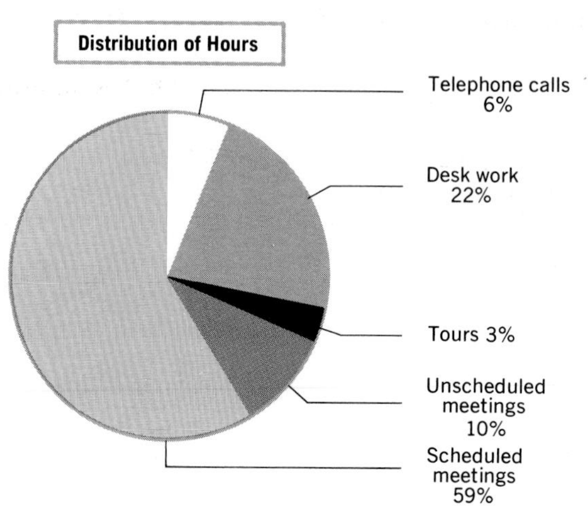


Managers are the nerve center of information flows. They stand at the intersection of information that flows upward, downward, and laterally in the organization's hierarchy of authority. The quality of these information flows can help or hinder the manager's attempts to promote high levels of job performance and human resource maintenance in the work unit.

**FIGURE 14.2** The manager as an information-processing system. (Source: Abridged and adapted text from chart on p. 72 in *The Nature of Managerial Work* by Henry Mintzberg. Copyright © 1973 by Henry Mintzberg. Reprinted by permission of Harper & Row Publishers, Inc.)

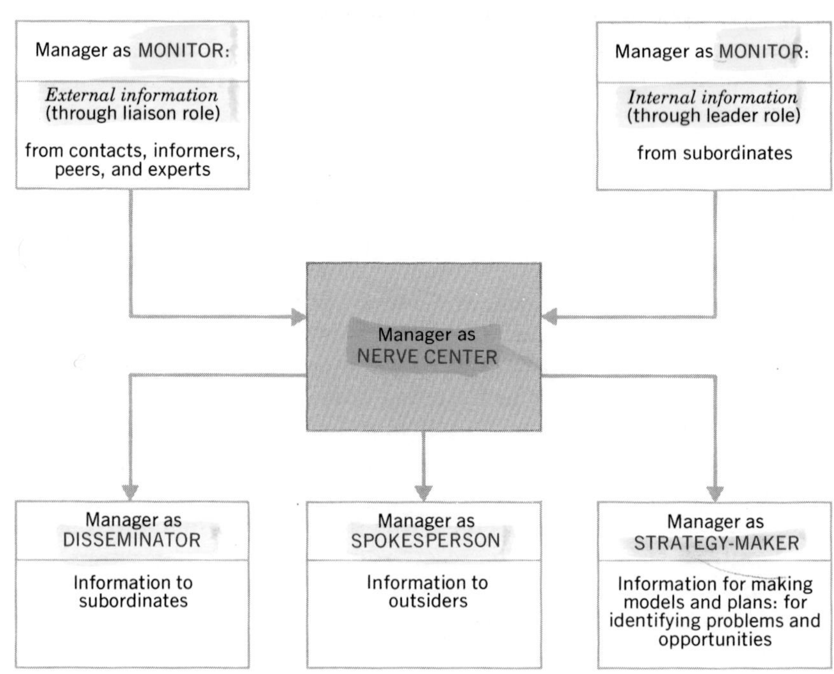

In downward communications, the manager transmits job instructions, organizational goals, and performance feedback, along with a variety of other information, to subordinates. On the lateral dimension, the manager seeks to keep the activities of the work unit well coordinated with other units in the organization and with clients or consumers. Upward communications contain opportunities for the manager to transmit to higher organization levels information on work unit activity and personal needs. Unless each of these responsibilities is done well and honestly, "cover-ups" such as those described in the chapter introduction may well occur. As we move on in our study of the communication process, keep this description of a manager's information-processing responsibilities clearly in mind.

## COMMUNICATION AS A PROCESS

The key elements in the communication process are diagrammed in Figure 14.3.[3] They include a source, who is responsible for encoding an intended meaning into a message, and a receiver, who decodes the message into a perceived meaning. Feedback from receiver to source may or may not be given.

Frequently, the intended meaning of the source and the meaning as perceived by the receiver differ. How would you react, for example, to this well-intentioned roadside sign advertising a combination diner and gasoline station?[4]

**FIGURE 14.3** The communication process and possible sources of "noise."

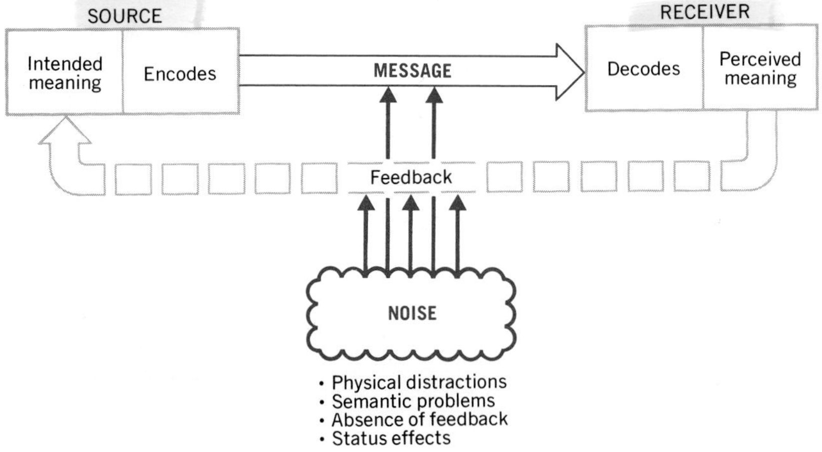

SOURCE
Intended meaning
Encodes
MESSAGE
RECEIVER
Decodes
Perceived meaning
Feedback
NOISE

- Physical distractions
- Semantic problems
- Absence of feedback
- Status effects

EAT HERE AND GET GAS

Don't let the hilarity of this example fool you. It is a challenging task to communicate accurately. Managers, like owners of roadside diners, can make mistakes. A more specific look at the key elements in the communication process can help us to analyze the causes of such communication errors.

The information source is a person or group of persons with a reason for communicating with someone else, the receiver. The reasons for the source to communicate include changing the attitudes, knowledge, or behavior of the receiver. As a manager, for example, you may want to communicate with your boss in order to make him or her understand why your work unit needs more time to finish an assigned project.

To communicate with the receiver, the source translates his or her intended meaning into symbols. This translation is an encoding process that results in a message that may consist of verbal (such as written) or nonverbal (such as gestures) symbols, or some combination of both. The receiver decodes the message into meaning. This process of translation may or may not result in the assignment of the same meaning intended by the source.

## Effective Versus Efficient Communication

**Effective communication** occurs when the intended meaning of the source and the perceived meaning of the receiver are one and the same. This should be the manager's goal in any communication attempt. It is not always achieved. Even now, we worry whether or not you are interpreting our written words as we intend. Our confidence would be higher if we were face to face in class together and you could ask clarifying questions. This opportunity to question is one advantage of face-to-face communication as opposed to the use of written memos, letters, posted bulletins, or reports.

**Efficient communication** occurs at minimum cost in terms of resources expended. Time is an important resource in the communication process. Picture your instructor taking the time to communicate individually with each student. It would be virtually impossible to do and, even if possible, it would be very costly in terms of time. For reasons like this, managers will often choose to write memos rather than visit their employees personally and to hold group rather than individual meetings.

Efficient communications are not always effective. A low-cost communication such as a posted bulletin may save time for the sender, but it doesn't always achieve the desired results in terms of the receiver's perceived meaning. Similarly, an effective communication may not be efficient. For a manager to visit each employee and explain a new change in procedures may guarantee that everyone truly understands the change. It may also be prohibitively expensive in terms of the required time expenditures.

Managers are busy people who depend on their communication skills to remain successful in their work. You need to learn how to maximize the effectiveness of your communications with other people and to achieve maximum efficiency in the process. Figure 14.4 portrays a comedy of errors that could happen to managers who fail to develop these important skills.

## Barriers to Effective Communication

**Noise** is anything that interferes with the effectiveness of a communications attempt. Four special sources of noise are physical dis-

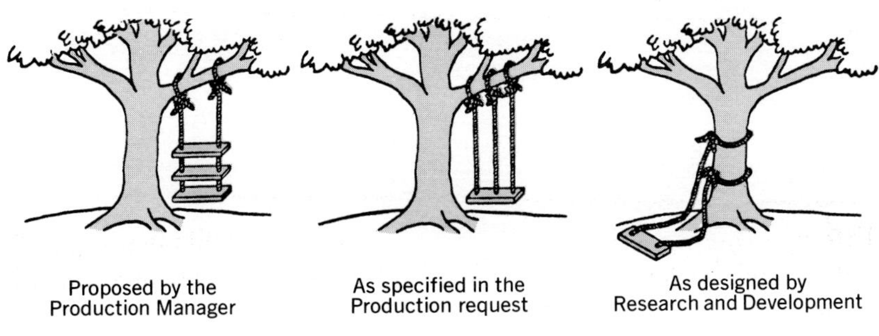

Proposed by the
Production Manager
As specified in the
Production request
As designed by
Research and Development

**FIGURE 14.4** A case of ineffective communication. (Source: The original source is unknown.)

tractions, semantic problems, the absence of feedback, and status effects. Each of these sources of noise should be recognized and subjected to special managerial control. They are included in Figure 14.3 as potential threats to any communication process.

## Physical Distractions

Any number of physical distractions can interfere with the effectiveness of a communications attempt. Some of these distractions are evident in the following conversation between an employee, George, and his manager.[5]

> Okay, George, let's hear your problem (phone rings, boss picks it up, promises to deliver a report, "just as soon as I can get it done"). Uh, now, where were we—oh, you're having a problem with your secretary. She's (. . . secretary—the manager's—brings in some papers that need immediate signature, so he scribbles his name where she indicates; secretary leaves) . . . you say she's depressed a lot lately, wants to leave . . . is she pregnant, maybe (laughter)? I tell you what, George, why don't you (phone rings again, lunch partner drops by) . . . uh, take a stab at handling it yourself . . . I've got to go now.

Besides what may have been poor intentions in the first place, George's manager was suffering from physical distractions which created information overload. He or she was letting too many requests for information processing occur at once. As a result, the communication with George suffered.

The mistake of processing too much information at once can be eliminated by setting priorities and planning. If George has something to say, his manager should set aside adequate time for the meeting. In addition, interruptions such as telephone calls, secretarial requests, and drop-in visitors should be prevented. All of these things physically distracted both parties in their attempt to communicate in the example. Each distraction, in turn, could have been avoided by proper managerial attention.

## Semantic Problems

Semantic barriers to communication occur as encoding and decoding errors and as mixed messages. Symbols, such as the words "Eat Here and Get Gas," are selected by the source and interpreted by the receiver. Communications will only be effective to the extent that the source makes good choices when creating messages.

We generally don't realize how easily encoding and decoding errors occur. They abound, however, as the following examples illustrate. Consider the following sign posted in a University of Colorado cafeteria:[6]

| SHOES ARE REQUIRED TO EAT IN THE CAFETERIA |
|---|

A perceptive student added to this sign the gratuitous comment: "socks can eat wherever they want."

How about this sign appearing in a nightclub?[7]

| CLEAN AND DECENT DANCING EVERY NIGHT EXCEPT SUNDAY |
|---|

The sign carried an unsolicited addition: "You must do a big business on Sundays!"

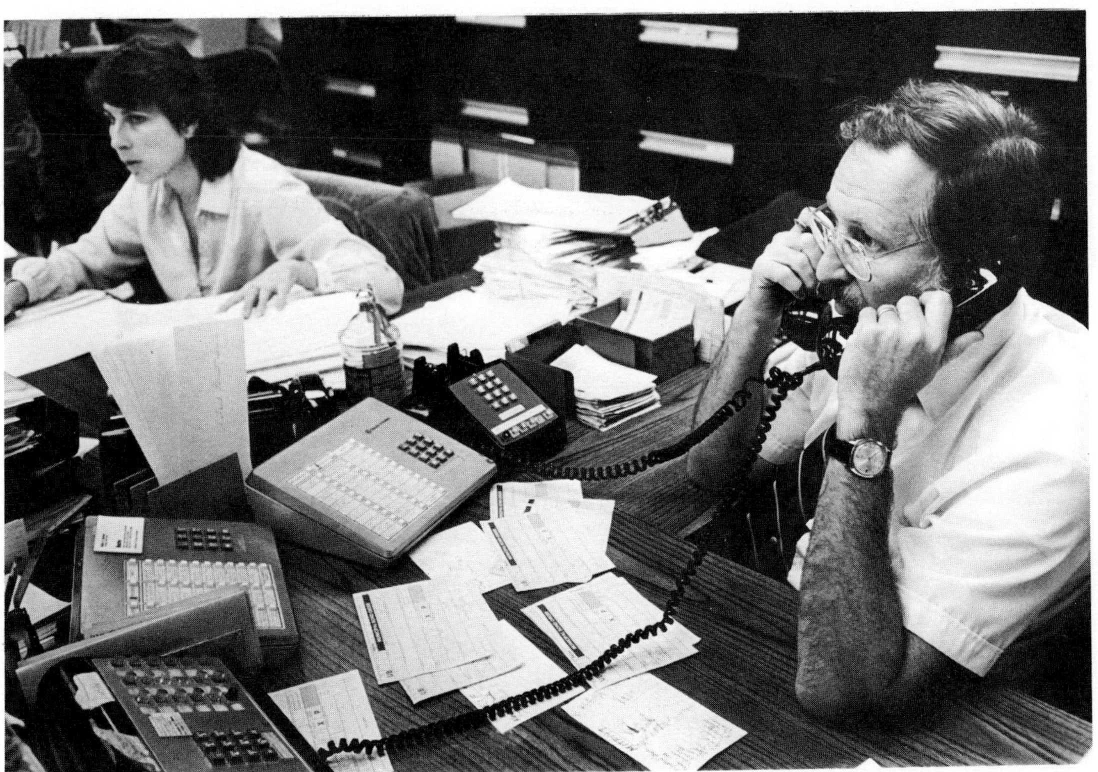

Information overload: a communications barrier.

Each of the prior examples is a case of an encoding and decoding error. The source chose poorly when putting the intended meaning into words. Managers must be careful in this regard, especially in respect to their written communications. *What Consultants Do 14.1* explains how encoding and decoding problems affected communications in one company and how a consultant intervened to correct the situation.

Another semantic problem is the conflict between verbal and nonverbal communications. Mixed messages result when a person's words communicate one message while their actions or "body language" communicate something else. Facial and hand gestures, body postures, and eye positions can all communicate. We also communicate by the way in which we arrange the furniture in our offices.

## WHAT CONSULTANTS DO 14.1

### Eliminating Misunderstood Memos

A vice-president in a large U.S. corporation was having trouble with his division managers, who occasionally responded inappropriately to his memos. The vice-president had the choice of (a) sending his subordinates to a communications course, (b) attending a communications course himself, (c) both (a) and (b), (d) trying to live with the problem, or (e) working on the problem directly. He chose the last alternative. A hired consultant designed a work session to be held from 9:00 A.M. to lunch on a regular workday in the staff meeting room.

Before the meeting, several memos from the vice-president to the division managers were selected to be shown on a screen via a projector. After reading each memo on the screen the division managers were asked three questions: (1) What do you think the message says? (2) What priority would you give to the message: (a) *high,* take care of the matter immediately; (b) *medium,* take care of the matter relatively soon; or (c) *low,* take care of it when I can get to it. (3) What action would you take?

After everyone responded to the three questions by writing their answers, each manager was asked to read his response to the total group. Considerable differences occurred among the managers. Later, the vice-president explained what he meant the memo to say, what priority he desired, and what action he wanted. As might be expected, a number of misunderstandings were corrected.

Source: This incident is reported in W. Warner Burke and Warren H. Schmidt, "Management and Organization Development: What is the Target of Change?" *Personnel Administration* (March–April 1971), pp. 44–57.

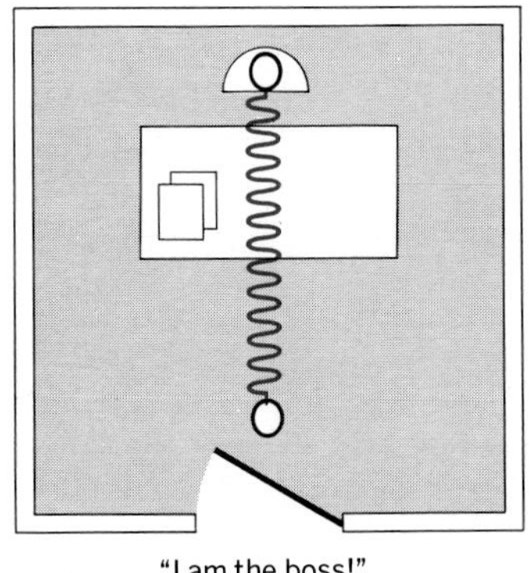

"I am the boss!"

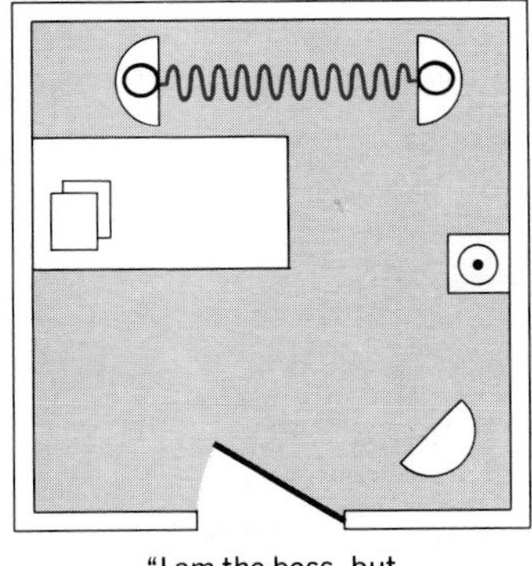

"I am the boss, but let's communicate."

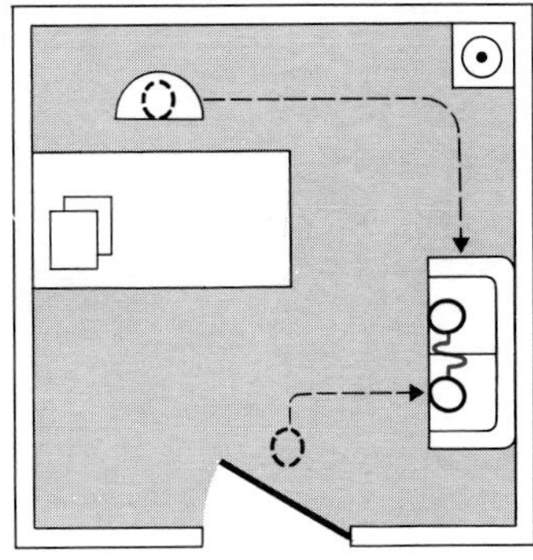

"Forget I'm the boss, let's communicate."

**FIGURE 14.5** Furniture placement as a non-verbal message.

Checkpoint

Figure 14.5 shows three different office layouts and the messages they may communicate to visitors. Check this diagram against the arrangement in your office, your instructor's, or that of a manager with whom you are familiar. What are you/they saying to visitors by the choice of furniture placement?

## The Absence of Feedback

In one-way communications there is no feedback from receiver to source. Two-way communications include such feedback and are characterized by the normal interactive conversations in our day-to-day experiences. Figuratively speaking, two-way communication is of the form

$$\text{Source} \quad \begin{matrix} \longrightarrow \text{ sends messages } \longrightarrow \\ \longleftarrow \text{ returns feedback } \longleftarrow \end{matrix} \quad \text{Receiver}$$

Research indicates that two-way communication is more accurate and effective than one-way. One-way communication is more time efficient, more frustrating for the receiver, and less threatening to the sender.[8] Many of your interactions as a student with your instructors, for example, are frustrating because of one-way communications. Examinations are good illustrations of this. How often have you labored over the interpretation of a question and wished you could get clarification from the instructor? Sometimes you can't even ask; sometimes you can ask, but still don't get clarification. One-way communications are frequent in our work settings. Sometimes they protect the source from threat or discomfort; always they result in the receiver being left unsure as to the actual intentions of the source.

### Status Effects

The hierarchy of authority in organizations can create another barrier to effective communication. Research indicates that the situation depicted in Cartoon 14.1 is often reality; communication is frequently biased when flowing upward in organizational hierarchies.[9]

Status differentials create special barriers between managers and their subordinates. Given the authority of their positions, managers may be inclined to do a lot of "telling," but not much "listening." Subordinates, on the other hand, may tell their superiors only what they expect the boss wants to hear. Whether the reason is a fear of retribution for bringing bad news, an unwillingness to identify personal mistakes, or just a general desire to please, the result is the same. The manager ends up making poor decisions because of a biased and inaccurate information base! The "corporate cover-ups" reported in the chapter introduction illustrate just how severe the effects of status barriers on effective communications can be.

## GUIDELINES FOR EFFECTIVE COMMUNICATION

The following item appeared sometime ago in the *London Times*. It holds a lesson for managers interested in becoming effective communicators.

*From Our Correspondent*[10]

Mr. Thor Heyerdahl, the Norwegian scientist of Kon Tiki fame, declared here last night that the mystery of the great stone statues of Easter Island is a mystery no longer. Mr. Heyerdahl has just led another archaeological expedition into the South Pacific, including several weeks on Easter Island.

Easter Islanders engaged by Mr. Heyerdahl and his party transported and erected one of the giant statues in what Mr. Heyerdahl is convinced is the same manner in which their forebears did. The team of 180 Easter Islanders had no difficulty in towing the statue over level grass from the quarry where it lay. On the selected site it was raised by levering the other side similarly. When the base of the statue reached the height of the plinth the levering and wedging process was applied only to the upper portion of the statue, which was thus raised gradually to a position from which it could be hauled vertically by ropes.

With 12 hired islanders Mr. Heyerdahl raised the 30-ton statue to

# Backing Off

HI, JAKE. WELL, THE BOSS IS ASKING FOR THE ANNUAL UPWARD APPRAISAL. IT'S DUE TOMORROW. WHAT ARE YOU GOING TO INCLUDE?

REALLY? MINE'S QUITE THE OPPOSITE. CANDID. TO THE POINT. FOR EXAMPLE, I'M GOING TO SAY THAT HE'S ALWAYS ASKING ME TO DO STUPID THINGS, LIKE THIS UPWARD APPRAISAL...

HE TREATS HIS SUBORDINATES LIKE CHILDREN. TOTALLY LACKS COMMUNICATION SKILLS. IS RELUCTANT TO DELEGATE ANYTHING BEYOND TYPING ASSIGNMENTS, ETC., ETC., ETC.

WHAT DO YOU MEAN I DON'T DARE TO WRITE THOSE THINGS. I'M GOING TO HANG UP AND WRITE IT RIGHT NOW, WHILE IT'S STILL FRESH IN MY MIND.

MEMO TO T.J. WHIPPLEWORTH:

DEAR SIR, YOU ASKED FOR AN UPWARD APPRAISAL. HERE GOES. CANDID AND STRAIGHTFORWARD. YOU ARE AN EXCELLENT COMMUNICATOR. YOUR LEADERSHIP STYLE FITS YOUR SUBORDINATES...

DELEGATION IS YOUR STRONG SUIT HOWEVER. YOU TREAT EVERYONE WITH DIGNITY AND RESPECT. YOU WRITE APPRAISALS VERY WELL...

The difficulties of upward communication.

Reprinted from Mgr. Magazine. AT&T Long Lines.

> the vertical in 18 days by this ancient method. This statue now ornaments the island skyline as the only one of the great monoliths standing as in ancient days. . .
>
> Mr. Heyerdahl and his fellow archaelogists have a modest explanation of their discovery of the system by which ancient monuments were raised without mechanical aids. Previous expenditions to Easter Island have returned without the answer. Mr. Heyerdahl sought the opinion of the island's mayor on the methods used by ancient Islanders to erect their statues, and the answer was immediately forthcoming. "Why did you not tell this to previous expeditions?" asked Mr. Heyerdahl. "They never asked me," vouchsafed the phlegmatic old mayor.

Managers, as did the archeologists who preceded Mr. Heyerdahl to Easter Island, may sometimes fail to get accurate information from their subordinates because they fail to ask. Other times, though, the manager may ask and still not find out!

Being an effective communicator is a skill. Part of the skill lies in recognizing and controlling communication barriers. Another part is to simply become good at encouraging the flow of information in your direction, i.e., being an "active listener," and also to become good at giving constructive feedback in a non-threatening way to others. It is through these skills that the manager acts to take full advantage of two-way communication.

## Active Listening[11]

Active listening is a term popularized by persons in the service professions, such as counselors and therapists. It recognizes that when someone "talks," they are trying to communicate something. That "something" may or may not be what they are saying. The manager's job in **active listening,** therefore, is to take action by helping the source of a message to articulate what he or she really means.

One of the two conversations below involves active listening by the supervisor. Read each and think through how you would feel as the foreman in the case.[12]

### Example No. 1

**Foreman:** Hey, Al, I don't get this production order. We can't handle this run today. What do they think we are?

**Supervisor:** But that's the order. So get it out as soon as you can. We're under terrific pressure this week.

**Foreman:** Don't they know we're behind schedule already because of that press breakdown?

**Supervisor:** Look, Kelly, I don't decide what goes on upstairs. I just have to see that the work gets out and that's what I'm gonna do.

**Foreman:** The guys aren't gonna like this.

**Supervisor:** That's something you'll have to work out with them, not me.

### Example No. 2

**Foreman:** Hey, Ross, I don't get this production order. We can't handle this run today. What do they think we are?

**Supervisor:** Sounds like you're pretty sore about it, Kelly.

**Foreman:** I sure am. We were just about getting back to schedule after that press breakdown. Now this comes along.

**Supervisor:** As if you didn't have enough work to do, huh?

**Foreman:** Yeah, I don't know how I'm gonna tell the guys about this.

**Supervisor:** Hate to face'em with it now, is that it?

**Foreman:** I really do. They're under a real strain today. Seems like everything we do around here is rush, rush.

**Supervisor:** I guess you feel like it's unfair to load anything more on them.

**Foreman:** Well, yeah. I know there must be plenty of pressure on everybody up the line, but—well, if that's the way it is . . . guess I'd better get the word to 'em.

The supervisor in Example 2 possesses active listening skills. He responded to the foreman's communication attempt in a way which increased the flow of information. The supervisor ended up receiving important information about the work situation, and should be able to use this information for constructive results. The foreman also feels better after having been able to really say what he felt, and after being heard!

There are five guidelines for active listening.

1. Listen for message content: try to hear exactly what is being said in the message.
2. Listen for feelings: try to identify how the source feels in terms of the message content. Is this something pleasing or displeasing to the source? Why?
3. Respond to feelings: let the source know that his or her feelings, as well as the message content, are recognized.
4. Note all cues, verbal and non-verbal: be sensitive to the non-

verbal communications as well as the verbal ones; identify mixed messages which need to be clarified.

5. Reflect back to the source, in your own words, what you think you are hearing: restate the verbal and non-verbal messages as feedback to which the source can respond with further information.

## The Art of Giving Feedback

Managers frequently give feedback to other people, often in the form of performance appraisals. There is an art to giving feedback in such a way that it is accepted and used constructively by the receiver. Feedback poorly given can be threatening and become a basis for resentment and alienation.

**Feedback** is the process of telling someone else how you feel about something they did or said, or about the situation in general. The first requirement in giving feedback is to recognize when it is intended to truly benefit the receiver and when it is purely an attempt to satisfy a personal need. A manager who berates the secretary for typing errors, for example, may actually be mad about personally failing to give clear instructions in the first place.

Given that the sender's intent is to give feedback helpful to the receiver, a manager should recognize that constructive feedback is[13]

- Given directly and with real feeling, and based on a foundation of trust between the giver and the receiver.
- Specific rather than general, with good, clear, and preferably recent examples.
- Given at a time when the receiver appears to be in a condition of readiness to accept it.
- Checked with others to be sure they support its validity.
- In respect to things that the receiver might be expected to be able to do something about.
- Not more than the receiver can handle at any particular time.

## Avoiding Communication Gaps

Effective communication is a two-way process between source and receiver. The skilled manager will have a high degree of self-awareness, be sensitive to various types of communication barriers, and act responsibly as both an active listener and as a giver of feedback.

One manager's attempt to create and maintain a free flow of information is described in *What Managers Do 14.1*. Think about how you might act to avoid communication gaps in your work setting.

## WHAT MANAGERS DO 14.1

### One Organization's Experience with Communications

SMC is a 487-bed hospital with 2,600 employees. In an effort to open communications between employees and top management, SMC developed four special programs.

***Open Office Hours***
The hospital director holds open office hours every Wednesday afternoon from 4:00 p.m. to 5:00 p.m. Any employee wishing to speak in private with the director may do so at that time.

***Employee Meetings***
Each week, the hospital director holds a 60-minute morning meeting and a 90-minute evening meeting for 25–30 hospital employees who are selected at random from departments and divisions throughout the hospital. These meetings have a fairly structured format which includes reports from the director on current and future programs to improve services. Most of the time is given to employees who wish to ask questions or talk about their concerns or ideas.

***Employee Advisory Council***
The Employee Advisory Council is composed of 30 employees who are elected by their fellow employees. The Council acts in an advisory capacity to the hospital director. The hospital director holds monthly meetings with the group's executive committee to discuss issues raised by the Council. He also asks for reactions to policies or programs currently being developed by top management that will affect hospital employees.

***The Suggestion Box***
SMC encourages employees to submit their ideas to the director's office. Employees who identify themselves receive a letter of acknowledgment. Staff then review ideas that seem promising. Employees whose ideas for improving service are implemented are given public recognition. When these ideas lead to savings in dollars or to increased revenues, the authors may receive cash awards.

Source: Adapted from Robert B. Smith, "Bridging the Management Employee Gap," *Health Care Management Review,* Vol. 2 (Spring 1977), pp. 9–10.

## THE COMMUNICATION OF ROLES

One of the most important communications in which managers become involved is the sending and receiving of role expectations. A **role** is a set of activities expected of a person holding a particular office or position in a group or organization.[14] The various people who have these expectations regarding the behavior of someone in a role are considered members of the **role-set.**

Consider the role of the instructor in the OB course in which you are enrolled. You have certain expectations of this instructor, for example, setting course objectives, giving lectures, and grading exams. Similarly, the instructor's boss and other faculty have expectations regarding your instructor's classrom behavior. You, the boss, and these colleagues are members of the instructor's role-set.

Managers are part of the role-sets of their subordinates. For a subordinate, the role expectations communicated by the manager are likely to include instructions about desired behavior and behavior to be avoided, intentions regarding the allocation of rewards, and evaluations about past performance.[15]

When the communication of role expectations is distorted by barriers such as those discussed above, role ambiguity and role conflict may occur. These role dynamics deserve your attention as one of the many reasons why every manager should work hard at interpersonal communication skills. Remember

The communication of role expectations —creates→ role dynamics —which affect→ work attitudes and behaviors.

## Role Ambiguity

**Role ambiguity** occurs when the person in a role is uncertain about the role expectations of one or more members of the role-set. To do their jobs well, people need to know what is expected of them. Sometimes these expectations may be unclear because the manager has not tried to communicate them to the subordinate, or has done so inadequately. Or, it may be a failure of the subordinate to listen that creates the lack of understanding. In either case, the resulting role ambiguity can be stressful for the individual. Research indicates it may cause a loss of confidence in the role sender, lowered self-confidence, or decreased job satisfaction.[16]

## Role Conflict

**Role conflict** occurs when the person in a role is unable to respond to the expectations of one or more members of the role-set. The role expectations are understood but, for one reason or another, they cannot be complied with. Role conflict is another source of potential tension that may result in a loss of job satisfaction, decreased confidence in one's boss, and a tendency to avoid the unpleasant work situation.[17]

A common form of conflict is **role overload.** This is a situation in which there are simply too many role expectations being communicated to a person at a given time. There is too much to be done and too little time to do it. Managers may create role overload for their subordinates, especially when they rely on one-way communication. When cut off from valuable feedback, it is hard for these managers to learn when or why a subordinate is experiencing stress.

Of course, the busy manager, or student for that matter, frequently experiences role overload. In fact, many consultants now specialize in teaching people how to manage time and overcome these overloads. See *What Consultants Do 14.2* for one example of a time management seminar.

Role conflicts also occur when the expectations of one or more members of the role-set are incompatible. The four basic incompatibilities are intra-sender, inter-sender, person-role, and inter-role conflicts. A definition and example of each type of role conflict follows.[18]

## WHAT CONSULTANTS DO 14.2

### The Time-Management Seminar

Most time-management seminars, which range in length from a few hours to three days, take one or two approaches to teaching time management. One is the gimmick approach, in which hundreds of time-saving tips are tossed out for managers to pick and choose. For example: don't face your desk toward an open door because it invites interruptions; don't eat a lot or drink booze at lunch because you'll become sleepy; cut down the number of meetings by 10% to 15% because meetings are notorious time-wasters; hire a good secretary who can screen your mail and phone calls.

The other is the systematic approach, which is aimed at developing effective work habits rather than saving a few minutes here and there. These suggestions are psychologically rooted and for some are much easier said than done: learn how to say no to people (including the boss) who want to divert you from the work you should be doing; don't waste time regretting failures or the things you didn't accomplish; don't let subordinates manipulate you into doing their thinking for them on jobs you've delegated to them; learn both how to concentrate intently and how to relax.

Source: Adapted from John A. Prestbo, "Don't Waste Time," *The Wall Street Journal* (December 11, 1978), p. 28. Reprinted by permission of The Wall Street Journal. 

| Types of Role Conflict | Examples |
|---|---|
| **Intra-Sender:** The same role-set member sends conflicting expectations. | A purchasing agent is asked to buy special material unavailable through normal channels; the boss also says that company procedures should not be violated. |
| **Inter-Sender:** Different role-set members send conflicting expectations. | A manager's boss expects her to be very direct and to exercise close control over subordinates; the subordinates want more freedom in their work. |
| **Person-Role:** The values and needs of the individual conflict with the expectations of the members of the role-set. | There is growing pressure on a senior executive to agree secretly to fix prices with competing firms; this violates the personal ethics of the executive. |
| **Inter-Role:** The expectations of two or more roles held by the same individual become incompatible. | As workload increases, a manager finds himself spending evenings and weekends at work; his family is upset because they feel he is not meeting husband and father responsibilities. |

### Managing Role Dynamics

Role ambiguities and conflicts can create tensions which reflect adversely on individual work attitudes and behaviors. The informed manager will seek to minimize these negative consequences by opening and maintaining effective two-way communications with all members of his or her role-sets. This same manager will use active listening to solicit feedback from others on their understandings of any reactions to role expectations.

## INTERPERSONAL CONFLICT

Our review of roles and role conflicts introduces another key aspect of a manager's interpersonal skills, the ability to deal with conflict.

**Interpersonal conflict** occurs whenever two or more people disagree over an issue of substance and/or when they experience

emotional antagonisms with one another.[19] **Substantive conflicts** involve disagreements over such things as group goals, the allocation of resources, distribution of rewards, policies and procedures, and the assignment of roles. **Emotional conflicts** result from feelings of anger, trust, dislike, fear, and resentment, as well as from personality clashes.[20]

Managers spend up to 20% of their time dealing with conflict.[21] These include conflicts in which the manager is a principal party, one of the persons actively in conflict with one or more others. They also include conflicts in which the manager acts as a mediator, or third party, to try and resolve the conflicts between other people to the benefit of the organization and the individuals involved.

Both as a principal party and as a third party, the manager must be a skilled participant in the dynamics of interpersonal conflict. He or she must be able to recognize situations that have the potential for conflict. Then the manager should be capable of diagnosing the situation and taking action through communications to ensure that the goals of the organization are best served.

## Constructive and Destructive Conflict

Interpersonal conflict can be upsetting to the persons experiencing the conflict, and to others who may observe or who are affected by

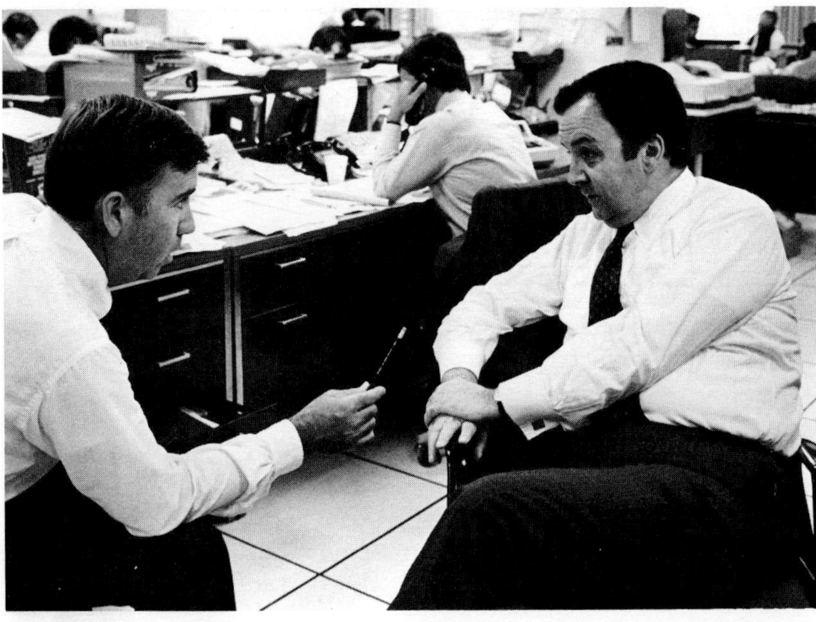

Conflict in the making.

its occurrence. It can be quite uncomfortable, for example, to be in an environment where two co-workers are continually hostile toward one another. There are two sides to conflict, however, as it relates to organizational outcomes. Conflict that results in positive benefits to the group or organization is constructive; conflict that works to the group's or organization's disadvantage is destructive.

Destructive conflict occurs, for example, when two employees are unable to work together due to interpersonal hostilities (a destructive emotional conflict) or when the members of a committee fail to act because they can't agree on group goals (a destructive substantive conflict). Destructive conflicts reduce group effectiveness by decreasing work productivity and member satisfaction and increasing absenteeism and turnover.[22]

Conflict can be beneficial. Constructive conflict offers groups opportunities to recognize otherwise neglected problems and opportunities, and thereby can increase their creative capacities. Indeed, the following example illustrates how the lack of conflict can compromise organizational effectiveness when such creativity is lacking.[23]

> The bankruptcy of the Penn Central Railroad has been generally attributed to mismanagement and a failure of the company's board of directors to question actions taken by management. The board was composed of outside directors who met monthly to oversee the railroad's operations. Few questioned the decisions made by the management. Apathy and a desire to avoid conflict allowed poor decisions to stand unquestioned. It can only be postulated how differently things might have turned out for the Penn Central if it had an inquiring board which demanded that the company's management discuss and justify key decisions.

Due to its two sides, destructive and constructive, conflict is an especially challenging interpersonal dynamic. Managers should be comfortable with conflict so that its destructive side can be controlled and its constructive side enhanced.

## Understanding Conflict Processes

Let's take an example as a way of building your sensitivity to the challenges of conflict processes.[24] The president of a small company is in favor of immediately introducing a new computerized record-keeping system. The head of the accounting department is quite opposed to it. There is a definite difference of opinion between the two regarding this possible change of procedures.

The president in this case is a principal party in the conflict. She is also the organizational superior of the other principal party. Although we don't know all the facts, the accountant could be quite

**Table 14.1 Key Differences of Opinion on the Computerized Record-Keeping System**

| | Nature of the Difference | | | |
|---|---|---|---|---|
| | Over Facts | Over Methods | Over Goals | Over Values |
| *President* | "The new system will save money." | "It should be installed at once." | "We want rapid and accurate data retrieval on demand." | "Efficiency is the key." |
| *Head of accounting department* | "The new system will be more expensive." | "Let's move slowly." | "We need a flexible system managed by accountants who can solve unexpected problems." | "We must consider the welfare of loyal workers." |

Source: Adapted from Warren H. Schmidt and Robert Tannenbaum, "Management of Differences," *Harvard Business Review*, Vol. 38 (November/December, 1960), p. 110.

threatened by the way the president handles the situation. He has already taken some risk to communicate his views upwards, and the response of the president may well determine his willingness to do so again in the future. This is a conflict that could prove constructive in getting the best decision made for the company or become destructive by alienating a key employee.

To manage this situation, the president should begin by analyzing the various conflict ingredients. Key factors to be considered include apparent differences over facts, methods, goals, and values. Table 14.1 lists how differences in each of these factors could be operating in the case.

After such differences are identified, the reasons for them can be established. Once the reasons for the differences are clarified and understood, steps can be taken to constructively address them and resolve the conflict. Table 14.2 presents some possible explanations for the differences based on information, perceptions, and roles.

| **Difference** | **Managerial Action** |
|---|---|
| Facts | Information could be shared; steps could be taken to check the validity of the data; more data could be gathered from mutually respected outside sources. |
| Methods | The common goals of the company's well-being should be remembered; the current disagreement should be viewed as a difference of means, not ends; |

| | |
|---|---|
| | alternatives to the automated system as proposed should be explored. |
| Goals | The goals of the president and the accountant should be clarified; each should be discussed and revised relative to the company's goals. |
| Values | The president and the accountant should share their values on the record-keeping functions; the reality of any real value differences should be clarified; attempts should be made to find areas where the values overlap and contain consistencies. |

If steps such as the above are successful, the original conflict may prove very constructive for the company. Perhaps a new computerized system will be implemented, with resulting cost savings. Or maybe the manual system will be retained and a costly "mistake" avoided. In either event, the important result is that the best interests of the company are served.

**Table 14.2 Reasons for the Differences of Opinion on the Computerized Record-Keeping System**

| | Reasons for the Difference | |
|---|---|---|
| | Explanation of the President's Position | Explanation of the Head Accountant's Position |
| *Information* (Having different information) | She has read articles describing the savings brought about by automation. Sales representatives have given her savings estimates. | He has heard about the "hidden costs" in automation. He estimates the cost to be much higher than the salaries of workers to be replaced. |
| *Perception* (Interpreting the same data differently) | She regards the sales representatives as knowledgeable and feels their analysis of the company's needs can be trusted. | He feels the representatives are just trying to sell machines and regards their analysis with suspicion. |
| *Role* (Pressures of the position) | She feels the company looks to her as the person responsible for keeping systems up-to-date. | He feels responsible for the morale and security of the accounting personnel. |

Source: Adapted from Warren H. Schmidt and Robert Tannenbaum, "Management of Differences," *Harvard Business Review,* Vol. 38 (November/December, 1960), p. 110.

## The Stages of Conflict

Conflict develops in stages, as shown in Figure 14.6. These stages include antecedent conditions, perceived and felt conflict, manifest conflict, conflict resolution or suppression, and conflict aftermath.[25]

Some of the antecedents which establish the conditions from-which conflict can develop are role ambiguities, competition for scarce resources, communication barriers, unresolved prior conflicts, and individual differences in needs, values, and goals. In effect, when these conditions exist, the stage is set for conflict to develop. Any person who works in a situation characterized by one or more of these conditions, therefore, should be sensitive to the conflict potential they represent.

When the antecedents are recognized as a basis for substantive or emotional differences between people, perceived conflict exists. Of course, this perception may be held by only one of the conflicting parties. There is also a difference between perceived and felt conflict. When conflict is felt, we give it meaning, in the sense that a tension exists such that we are motivated to reduce feelings of discomfort. Sometimes we feel conflict, but can't pin down its source or cause.

For conflict to be resolved, all parties should both perceive and feel the need to do something about the conflict. When conflict is openly expressed in behavior it is said to be manifest. Once a state of manifest conflict exists, it must be traced back to its antecedent conditions in order to plot strategies for resolving it constructively. Manifest conflict can be resolved in the sense that its antecedent conditions are corrected. It can also be suppressed in that, although

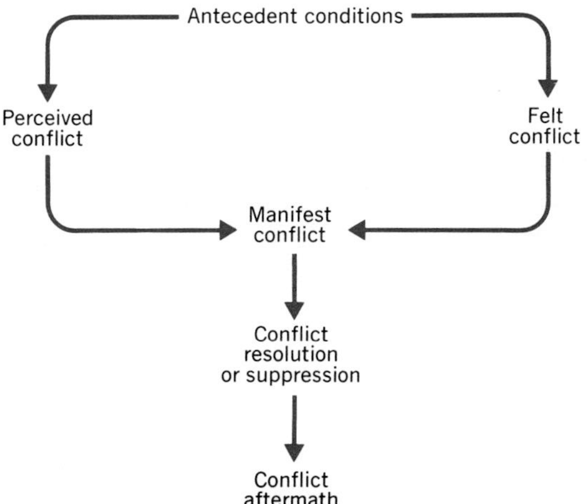


**FIGURE 14.6** The stages of conflict.

no change in antecedent conditions occurs, the manifest conflict behaviors are controlled.

Finally, the way a given conflict is handled can affect future conflicts. Unresolved conflicts continue to fester and promote future conflicts over similar issues. Truly resolved conflicts may establish conditions that reduce future conflicts of a similar nature and which help other eventual conflicts to be resolved in a constructive fashion. Thus, any manager should be sensitive to the influence of conflict aftermath on future conflict episodes.

This model of the conflict process points the manager's attention in several directions.

1. To promote conflict, establish antecedent conditions under which it is likely to occur.
2. To resolve conflict, work back from the manifest stage to understand antecedent conditions, and ensure that all principal parties both perceive and feel the conflict.
3. To take action to resolve rather than merely to suppress the conflict, establish a stage of conflict aftermath that works to the advantage of the organization.

## CONFLICT RESOLUTION

Interpersonal conflict can be met with nonattention, suppression, or resolution. Nonattention means what it says; there is no direct attempt to deal with a manifest conflict. The conflict is left to develop on its own into a constructive or destructive force within the organization.

Suppression results in a decrease in the negative consequences of a conflict, but does not address and/or eliminate the root causes. It is a surface treatment that allows the reasons for the original conflict to remain as antecedent conditions for future ones. **Conflict resolution** occurs when the reasons, substantial and/or emotional, for a conflict are eliminated.[26] No lingering issues or antagonisms remain to generate more conflicts in the future.

Interpersonal conflicts in groups may be addressed through lose-lose, win-lose, and win-win strategies. Only in the win-win case does true conflict resolution occur.[27]

### Lose-Lose Conflict

Lose-lose outcomes occur as a result of managing conflict by avoidance, smoothing, and/or compromise. No one achieves their true desires, and the underlying reasons for conflict remain unaffected. Future conflict of a similar nature is likely to occur.

**Avoidance** is an extreme form of nonattention. Everyone pretends that conflict doesn't really exist, and hopes that it will simply go away. **Smoothing** plays down differences among the conflicting parties, and highlights similarities and areas of agreement. Peaceful coexistence through a recognition of common interests is the goal. Smoothing may ignore the real essence of a given conflict.

"Let's compromise" is a phrase frequently heard in a group setting. The classic example occurs whenever representatives of unions and management meet to prepare new labor contracts. **Compromise** occurs when accommodations are made such that each party to the conflict gives up something of value to the other. As a result, neither party gains its full desires and the antecedent conditions for future conflicts are established. Although a conflict may appear to be settled for awhile through compromise, it may well reappear again at some future time.

## Win-Lose Conflict

In win-lose conflicts, one party achieves its desires at the expense and to the exclusion of the other party's desires. This may result from **competition,** where a victory is achieved through force, superior skill, or domination, or as a result of **authoritative command.** In the latter circumstance, a formal authority simply dictates a solution and specifies what is gained and lost and by whom. When the authority is a party to the conflict, it is easy to predict who will be the winner and the loser. Each of these strategies also fails to address the root causes of the conflict and tends to suppress the desires of at least one of the conflicting parties. As a result, future conflicts over the same issues are likely.

## Win-Win Conflict

Win-win conflict is achieved by **confrontation** of the issues and the use of **problem-solving** to reconcile differences. This positive approach to conflict involves a recognition by all conflicting parties that something is wrong and needs attention. When success is achieved in problem-solving, the conflict has truly been resolved. Win-win conditions eliminate reasons for continuing or resurrecting the conflict, since nothing has been avoided or suppressed. All relevant issues are raised and openly discussed. The ultimate test for a win-

win solution is whether or not the conflicting parties are willing to say to each other.[28]

> "I want a solution which achieves your goals and my goals and is acceptable to both of us."
>
> "It is our collective responsibility to be open and honest about facts, opinions, and feelings."

Research indicates that problem-solving and confrontation are the more successful approaches to conflict resolution. Organizations that tend to use more confrontation have been found to outperform those that don't.[29] Managers identified as being constructive users of conflict are more likely to make use of confrontation as opposed to the avoidance or competitive strategies.[30]

## The Conflict Grid

The five conflict management styles of avoidance, authoritative command, smoothing, compromise, and problem-solving are depicted on the conflict grid in Figure 14.7. The grid classifies each style as evidencing low or high concerns for the people involved and low or high concerns for the production goals of the work unit or organization. Only the problem-solving style scores high both on concerns for people and production. This is one reason why theorists argue that only problem-solving strategies lead to true conflict resolution. Problem-solving is an attempt by the manager to locate and treat the causes of conflict, not merely to suppress them temporarily.

### Checkpoint

Suppose that you are a manager who allows subordinates to participate in decisions relating to the design of their jobs.[31] A situation now makes it possible for the employees to split up a task for purposes of job rotation. Two want to change to the rotation design; one does not.

Listed below are four approaches you might take to remedy this conflict. Write, in the space provided, the name of the conflict management style best describing each approach.

______________ Simply tell all three that job rotation will begin immediately.

______________ Convince all three that their good feelings toward one another are more important than any job design; get them to agree to rotate jobs or not, depending on what will maintain harmony in the group.

_____________ Work out an arrangement where job rotation occurs for a while, and then is stopped for a while, and so on; this allows each of the conflicting parties to have their way part of the time.

_____________ Drop the idea about making any job design changes; forget you ever raised the possibility in the first place.

If you have learned your lesson well, none of these approaches represents a problem-solving style. In fact, the correct answers are, in order, authoritative command, smoothing, compromise, and avoidance.

True problem-solving would require bringing the conflicting parties together to discuss the decision. Through direct communication an attempt would be made to identify where fact, values, methods, and/or goal differences contribute to the conflict. Then, reasons for the conflict in terms of such things as information, goals, and perceptions could be identified. Once these reasons are clear, steps can be taken to eliminate or minimize them as sources of conflict.

Each of the five conflict management styles has some potential value to the practicing manager. Although only problem-solving results in true conflict resolution, there may be times when the other styles yield adequate outcomes. Sample situations in which the chief executives of several organizations use the various styles are reported in *What Managers Do 14.2*.

## Additional Conflict Management Techniques

Managers can support their problem-solving efforts by additional conflict management techniques. There are times when an appeal to superordinate goals can focus the attention of conflicting parties on one mutually desirable end state. This offers all parties a common frame of reference against which to analyze differences and reconcile disagreements. Conflicts whose antecedents lie in competition for scarce resources can also be resolved by expanding the resources available to everyone. Although costly, this technique removes the reasons for the continuing conflict. By altering one or more human variables in a situation, or by replacing or transferring one or more of the conflicting parties, conflicts caused by poor interpersonal relationships can be eliminated. The same holds true if a manager can alter structural variables. Rearranging the physical work setting or putting incompatible persons on different work shifts are approaches common to this latter technique.

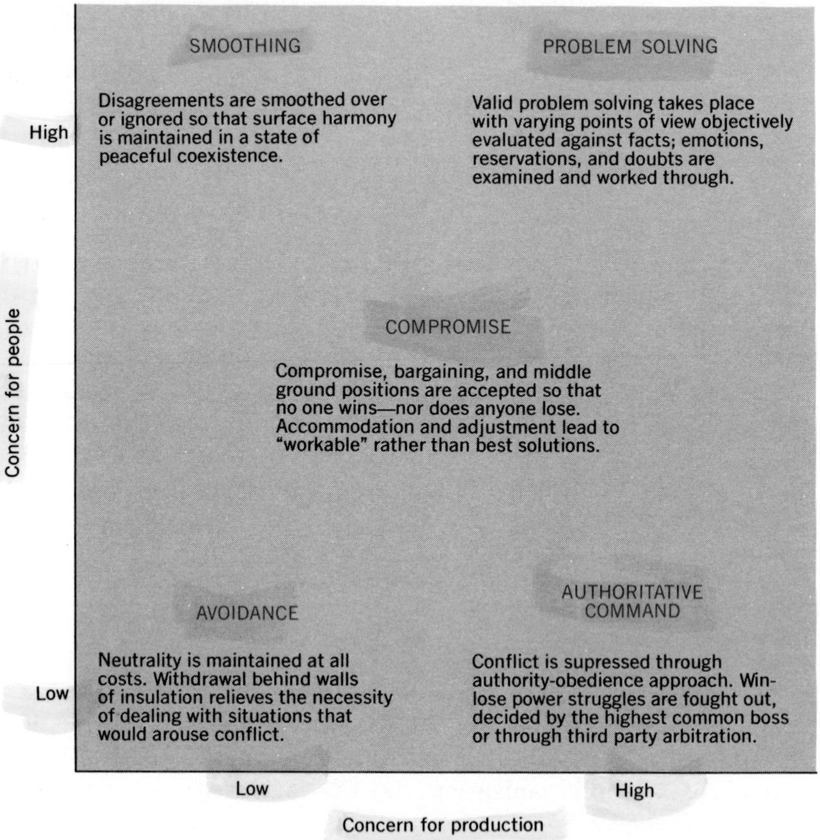

Concern for people (High)

**SMOOTHING**

Disagreements are smoothed over or ignored so that surface harmony is maintained in a state of peaceful coexistence.

**PROBLEM SOLVING**

Valid problem solving takes place with varying points of view objectively evaluated against facts; emotions, reservations, and doubts are examined and worked through.

**COMPROMISE**

Compromise, bargaining, and middle ground positions are accepted so that no one wins—nor does anyone lose. Accommodation and adjustment lead to "workable" rather than best solutions.

Concern for people (Low)

**AVOIDANCE**

Neutrality is maintained at all costs. Withdrawal behind walls of insulation relieves the necessity of dealing with situations that would arouse conflict.

**AUTHORITATIVE COMMAND**

Conflict is supressed through authority-obedience approach. Win-lose power struggles are fought out, decided by the highest common boss or through third party arbitration.

Low — High

Concern for production

**FIGURE 14.7** The conflict grid. (Source: Reproduced by special permission from *The Journal of Applied Behavioral Science,* "The Fifth Achievement," by Robert R. Blake and Jane Strygley Mouton, Volume 6, No. 4, p. 148, copyright 1970, NTL Institute.)

# SUMMARY

This chapter has built on two basic premises. First,

A manager's communication skills —affect→ the information flows —upon which→ managerial decisions are based

## WHAT MANAGERS DO 14.2

### Situations in Which Chief Executives Use the Five Conflict Management Styles

***Avoidance***

1. When an issue is trivial, or more important issues are pressing.
2. When you perceive no chance of satisfying your concerns.
3. When potential disruption outweighs the benefits of resolution.
4. To let people cool down and regain perspective.
5. When others can resolve the conflict more effectively.
6. When issues seem tangential or symptomatic of other issues.

***Authoritative Command***

1. When quick, decisive action is vital (emergencies).
2. On important issues where unpopular actions, such as cost-cutting, enforcing unpopular rules, and discipline need implementing.
3. On issues vital to company welfare, when you know you're right.

***Smoothing***

1. When you find you are wrong—to allow a better position to be heard, to learn, and to show your reasonableness.
2. When issues are more important to others than yourself—to satisfy others and maintain cooperation.
3. To build social credits for later issues.
4. To minimize loss when you are outmatched and losing.
5. When harmony and stability are especially important.

***Compromising***

1. When goals are important, but not worth the effort or potential disruption of more assertive modes.
2. When opponents with equal power are committed to mutually exclusive goals.
3. To achieve temporary settlements to complex issues.
4. To arrive at expedient solutions under time pressure.
5. As a backup when problem-solving or authoritative-command is unsuccessful.

***Problem-Solving***

1. To find an integrative solution when both sets of concerns are too important to be compromised.
2. When your objective is to learn.
3. To merge insights from people with different perspectives.
4. To gain commitment by incorporating concerns into a consensus.
5. To work through feelings that have interfered with a relationship.

Source: Adapted from Stephen P. Robbins, " 'Conflict Management' and 'Conflict Resolution' are not Synonymous Terms!", *The Dynamics of Organization Theory* by John F. Veiga and John N. Yanouzas, copyright © 1979, West Publishing Company. All rights reserved.

Second,

A manager's conflict skills —lead to→ conflict that is constructive —or→ conflict that is destructive

Simply put, good managers possess the communication and conflict skills which enable them to implement decisions in support of the organization's production purposes. The manager who is a good communicator will be effective in sending information to others and at encouraging accurate information feedback in return. To do so managers should recognize the various barriers that can threaten the effectiveness of their communication attempts. They should also be aware that efficient communications are not always effective, and should practice the specific skills of active listening and the art of giving feedback.

Among the most important communications in which managers become involved are the sending and receiving of role expectations. Managers should work hard to understand the dynamics of their own roles and to help subordinates to understand the dynamics of theirs. Role ambiguities and conflicts can create tensions that affect people's work attitudes and behaviors. Good communication skills can help to clarify ambiguities and conflicts when they occur, and can minimize their negative consequences for individuals and the organization.

To successfully manage interpersonal conflicts such as those which develop from incompatibe role expectations, managers need to understand the nature of the conflict process. Conflict situations must be diagnosed to locate the specific substantive and emotional differences upon which they are based, and to identify the reasons for these differences.

People attend to conflicts in different ways, but only a problem-solving approach results in true conflict resolution. Managers should be aware of the five different styles of conflict management, and of their personal tendencies to use each. Managers can also use additional conflict management techniques such as superordinate goals, expanded resources, and altering human and/or structural variables.

In the final result, a manager's interpersonal relationships present opportunities to increase or decrease his or her personal performance success. Being skilled at the communication and conflict processes can help you maintain these relationships on their most positive footing.

## THINKING THROUGH THE ISSUES

1. Make a list of the communication barriers that might limit the effectiveness of a manager's communications with subordinates. Give examples of each barrier as they might be found in the work setting in which you expect to practice as a manager.

2. Analyze the communication skills of a person for whom you work. (Your instructor would be a good choice.) What does he or she do well as a communicator? What could he or she do to improve communications with other persons?

3. Reread the communications techniques described in *What Managers Do 14.1*. What is your opinion regarding these attempts to improve communications in an organization? Will you try to use them both in actual practice? Why or why not?

4. Diagram the role-set for your instructor.

5. Identify where role ambiguities and conflicts might develop. What can your instructor do to minimize the negative consequences of these role dynamics? What can his or her boss do?

6. Whose responsibility is it to take action to eliminate undesirable role ambiguities and conflicts? Is it the person in the role or the role sender? Defend your choice.

7. Select an interpersonal conflict in which you have recently been involved. Adopt a diagnostic approach to identify the reasons for this conflict. How could problem-solving have been used to resolve the conflict?

8. When would a manager want to promote conflict within the work unit? How can this be done in a way that ensures a constructive rather than destructive result?

## EXERCISE: UPWARD APPRAISAL[32]

### Purpose:

To practice the art of giving feedback to an organizational superior and to observe the dynamics of status as a communication barrier; to allow the instructor to practice and demonstrate the techniques of active listening and to receive constructive feedback on the course.

### Time:

50–75 minutes.

## Procedure:

1. Form work groups as assigned by your instructor.
2. The instructor will leave the room.
3. Convene in your assigned work groups for a period of 10 minutes. Create a list of comments, problems, issues, and concerns you would like to have communicated to the instructor in regard to the course experience to date.
4. Select one person from the group to act as spokesperson in communicating the group's feelings to the instructor.
5. The spokespersons should briefly convene to decide on what physical arrangement of chairs, tables, and so forth is most appropriate to conduct the feedback session. The classroom should then be rearranged to fit the desired specifications.
6. While the spokespersons convene, persons in the remaining groups should discuss how they expect the forthcoming communications event to develop. Will it be a good experience for all parties concerned? Be prepared to critically observe the actual communication process.
7. The instructor should be invited to return, and the feedback session will begin. Observers should make notes so that they may make constructive comments at the conclusion of the exercise.
8. Once the feedback session is completed, the instructor will call upon the observers for comments, ask the spokespersons for their reactions, and open the session to general discussion.

## Remember:

Your interest in the exercise is twofold: (1) to communicate your feelings to the instructor, and (2) to learn more about the process of giving and receiving feedback.

# CASE: COMMUNICATING PAY RAISE DECISIONS

Refer back to the exercise "Managing Merit Pay" at the end of Chapter 5. Assume that your task is now to communicate your pay raise decisions to the affected employees.

## Questions

1. Will you communicate the raises through written or oral messages? Why?

2. If you choose a written message, draft a copy of the letter, memo, or bulletin. Defend its content.
3. If you choose an oral message, describe the physical arrangements you will make for the communications to take place. Defend your choice.
4. Make a series of notes on any special messages you may want to convey to each employee.
5. In general, what are you doing to minimize "noise" and increase the probability that effective communication will take place?

## THE MANAGER'S VOCABULARY

**Active Listening** Communication (verbal and non-verbal) that helps the source of a message articulate what he or she really means.

**Communication** An interpersonal process of sending and receiving symbols with meanings attached to them.

**Conflict** When two or more people disagree over issues of organizational substance and/or when they experience some emotional antagonisms with one another.

**Conflict Resolution** Occurs when the reasons, substantial and/or emotional, for a conflict are eliminated.

**Effective Communication** When the intended meaning of the source and the perceived meaning of the receiver are one and the same.

**Efficient Communication** Minimum cost in terms of resources expended.

**Feedback** The process of telling someone else how you feel about something they did or said, or about the situation in general.

**Noise** Anything that interferes with the effectiveness of a communication attempt.

**Role** A set of activities expected of a person holding a particular office or position in a group or organization.

**Role Ambiguity** When the person in a role is uncertain about the role expectations of one or more members of the role-set.

**Role Conflict** When the person in a role is unable to respond to the expectations of one or more members of the role-set.

**Role Overload** A situation in which there are simply too many role expectations being communicated to a person at a given point in time.

**Role-Set** The various people who hold expectations regarding the behavior of someone in a role.

## Notes

[1]Adapted from John and Mark Arnold, "Corporate Coverups," *The Wall Street Journal* (June 5, 1978), p. 18. Reprinted by permission of The Wall Street Journal, copyright © Dow Jones & Company, Inc., 1978. All rights reserved.

[2]Henry Mintzberg, *The Nature of Managerial Work* (New York: Harper & Row, 1973), p. 38.

[3]A classic model of the communication process is presented by Claude E. Shannon and Warren Weaver, *The Mathematical Theory of Communication* (Urbana, Ill.: University of Illinois Press, 1949). Figure 8.2 is a derivative of this original model.

[4]William J. Haney, *Communication and Interpersonal Communication: Text and Cases,* Fourth Edition (Homewood, Ill.: Richard D. Irwin, 1979).

[5]Richard V. Farace, Peter R. Monge, and Hamish M. Russell, *Communicating and Organizing* (Reading, Mass.: Addison-Wesley, 1977), pp. 97–98.

[6]Haney, op. cit., p. 316.

[7]Ibid.

[8]See, for example, Harold J. Leavitt and Ronald A. H. Mueller, "Some Effects of Feedback on Communication," *Human Relations,* Vol. 4 (1951), pp. 401–410; Harold J. Leavitt, *Managerial Psychology,* Third Edition (Chicago: University of Chicago Press, 1972).

[9]This research is reviewed by John C. Athanassiades, "The Distortion of Upward Communication in Hierarchical Organizations," *Academy of Management Journal,* Vol. 16 (June 1973), pp. 207–226.

[10]"An Easter Island Mystery Solved," *The Times* (London) (August 1, 1956).

[11]This discussion is based on Carl R. Rogers and Richard E. Farson, "Active Listening" (Chicago: Industrial Relations Center of the University of Chicago).

[12]Ibid.

[13]Adapted from John Anderson, "Giving and Receiving Feedback," pp. 103–111 in Paul R. Lawrence, Louis B. Barnes, and Jay W. Lorsch, *Organizational Behavior and Administration,* Third Edition (Homewood, Ill.: Richard D. Irwin, 1976), p. 109.

[14]See, for example, Robert L. Kahn, Donald M. Wolfe, Robert F. Quinn, and J. Diedrick Snoek, *Organizational Stress: Studies in Role Conflict and Ambiguity* (New York: John Wiley & Sons, 1964).

[15]Daniel Katz and Robert L. Kahn, *The Social Psychology of Organizations,* Second Edition (New York: John Wiley & Sons, 1978), p. 191.

[16]Kahn et al., op. cit., pp. 94–95.

[17]Ibid., p. 71.

[18]See Kahn et al., op. cit., pp. 19–20.

[19]Richard E. Walton, *Interpersonal Peacemaking: Confrontations and Third-Party Consultation* (Reading, Mass.: Addison-Wesley, 1969), p. 2.

[20]Ibid., p. 73.

[21]Kenneth W. Thomas and Warren H. Schmidt, "A Survey of Managerial Interests with Respect to Conflict," *Academy of Management Journal,* Vol. 19 (1976), pp. 315–318.

[22]Stephen P. Robbins, " 'Conflict Management' and 'Conflict Resolution' are not Synonymous Terms," in John F. Veiga and John N. Yanouzas (eds.), *The Dynamics of Organizational Theory* (St. Paul, Minn.: West Publishing Company, 1979), p. 301.

[23]Ibid.

[24]Reprinted by permission of the *Harvard Business Review*. "Management of Differences" by Warren H. Schmidt and Robert Tannenbaum, Vol. 39, November/December 1960. Copyright © 1960 by the President and Fellows of Harvard College. All rights reserved.

[25]These stages are generally consistent with the conflict models described by Alan C. Filley, *Interpersonal Conflict Resolution* (Glenview, Ill.: Scott, Foresman and Company, 1975) and Louis R. Pondy, "Organizational Conflict: Concepts and Models," *Administrative Science Quarterly*, Vol. 12 (September 1967), pp. 269–320.

[26]Walton, op. cit., p. 2.

[27]This discussion is based on Filley, op. cit., pp. 21–30.

[28]Ibid., pp. 27, 29.

[29]Paul R. Lawrence and Jay W. Lorsch, *Organization and Environment* (Homewood, Ill.: Richard D. Irwin, 1969).

[30]R. J. Burke, "Methods of Resolving Superior-Subordinate Conflict: The Constructive Use of Subordinate Differences and Disagreements," *Organizational Behavior and Human Performance*, Vol. 5 (1970), pp. 393–411.

[31]This example is from Filley, op. cit., p. 24.

[32]Adapted from an exercise reported by Eugene Owens, "Upward Appraisal: An Exercise in Subordinate's Critique of Superior's Performance," *Exchange: The Organizational Behavior Teaching Journal*, Volume III, Number 1, (1978), pp. 41–42.

# 15

# POWER, POLITICS, AND CHANGE

# CAN REAGAN COPE WHERE CARTER DIDN'T?[1]

When Jimmy Carter took over the Oval Office in January, 1977, one of his first orders was that all federal management regulations—those setting our correct procedures for circulating mail and filing documents, for example—be rewritten in simple English and that unnecessary or redundant regulations be eliminated.

That was a simple enough idea, and a logical one for the man who had campaigned as a "Washington outsider" against the excesses of big government.

But the outcome of his directive is one that Ronald Reagan and his aides should observe: After three years and nine months of bureaucratic battering, Carter's regulators have finally come up with, not the changes themselves, but only a process by which the regulations could be changed in the future.

"Senior Civil Service people told us flatly three years ago that this simply couldn't be done," one of Carter's aides recalled. "They were saying that if you changed this word or that phrase the consequences would be 'serious and unpredictable.' "

"And the problem is, you're so busy organizing your office and following through higher priority directives, you just don't have the time to figure out what the effects will be of doing something like that. So it tends not to get done very fast—or at all." . . .

The term "executive order" implies a simple, clean, directive from the chief executive, but usually the action is neither clean nor simple. Most executive orders are drafted by the White House staff, then circulated to agency heads for comment. Agency heads usually pass them along to staff lawyers for review.

"Once that happens, you get into months of wrangling, memos, and counter-memos," a weary Carter administration official said.

"Then when the incoming administration wants to abolish an order, it has no idea what all those bureaucratic considerations were," the official said. "You don't know whether rescinding the previous administration's order would have the effect you want, or just the remainder of executive branch regulations might be frustrated as well, because such cuts are already in the works."

**MANAGEMENT APPLICATIONS QUESTION**

Why is it that an order from even the President of the United States may not be carried out as that person intended or may not even be carried out at all? Think about this question and then ask yourself: to what extent can I expect subordinates and other persons in the work setting to carry out my directives?

## PLANNING AHEAD

**This chapter offers learning activities which will acquaint you with the following topics.**

**Power and Influence**
**Obedience**
**Organizational Politics**
**Planned Change in Organizations**
**Organization Development**

"Power is America's last dirty word"—so begins a recent article in the *Harvard Business Review.*[2] The implication is that we are uncomfortable with the concept of power, perhaps that we are even somewhat offended by it. But the author of this provocative sentence then goes on to explore power in organizations and to suggest how managers can act to ensure that they have the power required to be successful in their jobs. This theme is consistent with that in the introductory segment to this chapter. It argues strongly for you to understand the concept of power and to become comfortable with its place in organizations and managerial roles.

# POWER AND INFLUENCE

**Power** is the ability to get someone else to do something you want done, or the ability to make things happen in the way you want. The essence of power is control over the behavior of others.[3] One of the peculiar things about power is that it has no verb form. You don't "power" something. You can, however, "influence" something. Power is the force which makes things happen. This force is activated in the influence process.[4] Thus, we also say that power is the capacity to exert influence.[5]

**Influence** is a behavioral response to the exercise of power. Managers use power to achieve influence over other people in the work setting. Figure 15.1 summarizes this linkage between power and influence. It also identifies the key sources or bases of power.

## Sources of Power

Managers derive power from both organizational and individual sources. We call these sources position power and personal power, respectively.

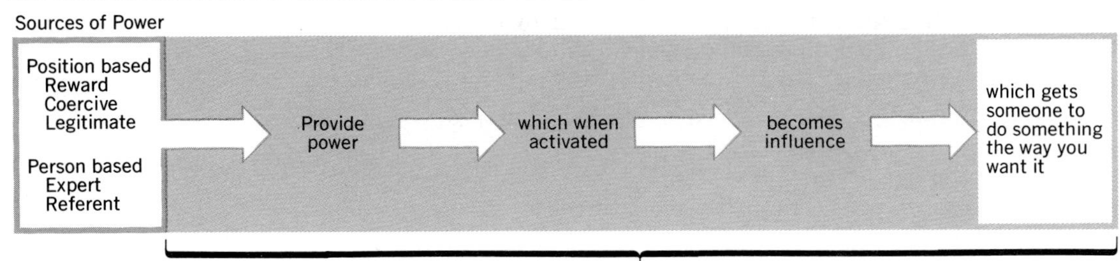


**FIGURE 15.1** Power sources and the influence process.

## Position Power

Three bases of power are available to a manager because of his or her position in the organization: reward, coercive, and legitimate power.[6] **Reward power** is the extent to which a manager can use extrinsic and intrinsic rewards in order to control other people. Examples of such rewards include money, promotions, compliments, or enriched jobs. These types of rewards are discussed in detail in Chapters 5 and 6. Although all managers have some access to rewards, success in accessing and utilizing them to achieve influence varies according to the skills of the manager.

Power can also be founded upon punishment, as opposed to reward. A manager may, for example, threaten to withhold a pay raise or recommend the firing of a subordinate who does not act as desired. Such **coercive power** is the extent to which a manager can deny desired rewards or administer punishments in order to control other people. The availability of coercive power also varies from one organization and manager to another. The presence of unions and other restrictions on employee treatment can weaken this power base considerably.

The third base of position power is **legitimate power.** It stems from the extent to which a manager can use subordinates' internalized values or beliefs that the "boss" has a "right of command" to control their behavior. A classic example is in the armed forces where officers have legitimate power over enlisted personnel.

## Personal Power

Two bases of personal power are expertise and reference.[7] **Expert power** is the ability to control another's behavior due to the possession of knowledge, experience, or judgment which the other person does not have but needs. In the case of a supervisor having expert power, a subordinate would obey because the boss is felt to know more about what is to be done or how it is to be done than the subordinate.

**Referent power** is the ability to control another's behavior because of their wanting to identify with the power source. In this case, a subordinate would obey the boss because he or she wants to behave, perceive, or believe as the boss does. This may occur, for example, because the subordinate likes the boss personally and therefore tries to do things the way the boss wants them done. In a sense, the subordinate behaves in order to avoid doing anything that would interfere with the pleasing boss-subordinate relationship.

### Authority

At this point, you may be thinking that the concept authority should fit somehow into the present discussion of power. In Chapter 1, we defined authority as the right to command. Consider once again the power bases described above. Is there a similarity between any of them and the concept of authority?

In fact, formal authority and legitimate power are one and the same. The two terms represent a special kind of power that a manager has because subordinates believe it is legitimate for a person occupying the managerial position to have the right to command. In practice it is often hard to separate authority, or legitimate power, from the use of reward and coercive power. This is because persons with authority usually have special access to rewards and punishments.

## OBEDIENCE

Power is the potential to control the behavior of others. But we all know that people who seem to have power don't always get their way. This fact leads us to the subject of obedience. Why do some people obey directives, while others do not? More specifically, why should subordinates respond to a manager's "right to command"? Furthermore, given that they do, what determines the limits of the response? Answers to these questions lie with the psychological contract, a concept introduced in Chapter 3, and with its implications for what is called the zone of indifference.

### Obedience and the Psychological Contract

The psychological contract, you should recall, is a set of expectations held by the individual and specifying what the individual and the organization expect to give and to receive from each other in the course of their working relationship. These expectations cover how much work is to be performed for how much pay. They also summarize the broader rights, privileges, and obligations accruing to the individual-organization relationship.

Most people seek a balance between what they put into the organization (contributions) and what they get from the organization in return (inducements). Within the boundaries of the psychological contract, therefore, employees will agree to do many things in and for the organization because they think they should. That is, in exchange for certain inducements, they recognize the authority of the organization and its managers to direct their work-related behavior in certain ways.

Each of us learns to respond to authority early in our lives. You are most likely responding to your instructor's authority right now by reading this textbook! Through interactions with parents, teachers, and other authority figures, and through such means as movies, books, and television which show acquiescence to authority, people come to learn what is the "right" or socially acceptable behavior in various circumstances.[8] This feeling about what is "right" also sets limits beyond which people typically will not go in obeying commands or following the wishes of someone else.

Thus, within the boundaries of the exchange of values defined by the individual's psychological contract with an organization and within the boundaries of what the individual considers morally right, she or he is prone to obey the orders of authority figures in the organization. Chester Barnard, a former president of the New Jersey Bell Telephone Company and a renowned management scholar, calls this area in which directions are obeyed the "zone of indifference."[9]

## Zone of Indifference

A **zone of indifference** is the range of authoritative requests to which a subordinate is willing to respond without subjecting the directives to critical evaluation or judgment, hence to which he or she is indifferent.[10] Directives falling within the zone are obeyed. Requests or orders falling outside the zone of indifference are not considered part of the authority relationship defined as acceptable by the terms of the psychological contract. Such "extraordinary" directives will receive critical consideration from the subordinate and may or may not be obeyed. We clarify this link between the zone of indifference and the psychological contract through the example shown in Figure 15.2.

The secretary whose psychological contract is shown in the figure may be expected to perform, in return for various inducements and

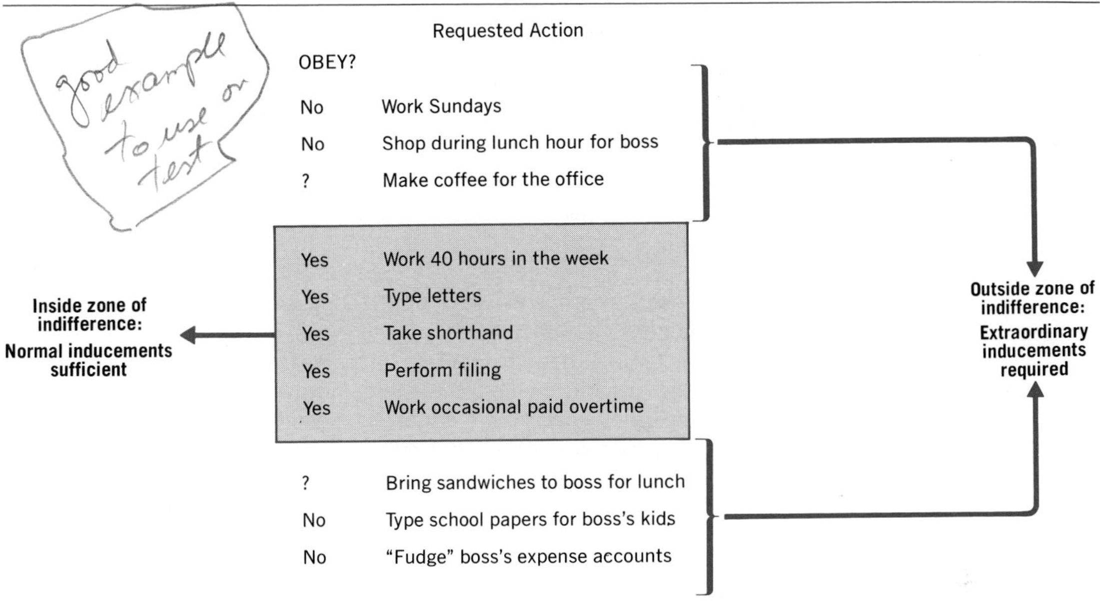


**FIGURE 15.2** Hypothetical psychological contract for a secretary.

with no questions asked, a number of activities falling within the zone of indifference. This response tendency will satisfy the manager most of the time. There may be times, however, when the boss would like the secretary to do things falling outside the zone. This requires efforts to enlarge the zone to accommodate additional behaviors.

It might not be difficult, for example, to broaden the zone a bit and influence the secretary to regularly make coffee and even bring in luncheon sandwiches from time to time. The secretary might even be convinced to work Saturday mornings if the boss is willing to provide extra inducements of special value. In these attempts to broaden the zone, the boss will most likely have to use power sources beyond formal authority or position power. In some instances, such as Sunday work and "fudging" expense accounts, no power base may be capable of accomplishing the desired result.

*Newsline 15.1* describes the viewpoints of one major corporation's executives regarding the zone of indifference of company personnel. Note the potential strain between company expectations and personal ethics or preferences. This is a situation most of us will occasionally face throughout our work careers. We wonder: what are the limits to your zone of indifference? When will you say "no"? What is your predisposition to obey?

## NEWSLINE 15.1

### The Corporation

In November of 1972, CBS News journeyed to the Bartlesville, Oklahoma, headquarters of the Phillips Petroleum Corporation, with a proposal guaranteed to leave even the most adventurous public relations man breathless. CBS wanted to "look at the Phillips Corporation from the viewpoint of the Executive Suite . . . to explore the so-called 'corporate mind' . . . what loyalties are demanded?—and where is the dividing line between loyalty to one's own self and loyalty to corporate objectives?"

"The Corporation" is a journalistic foray, made timely by the course of events, into the age-old discipline of ethics. In broad terms, it suggests that as corporations grow larger, more aggressive, and encompass more functions in our society, their demands on employees also grow. Corporations can become the focal point of life for many people, if they have not done so already. Employee loyalty may be transformed into an unhealthy, even dangerous, blind allegiance.

Phillips officials concede they run a disciplined business. Dissent is permitted, but once corporate policy is established it must be adhered to. Loyalty is required, greater loyalty rewarded. Attitudes are screened carefully before an employee is hired. Some clerks, once on the payroll, even have their performance monitored by computers. Everything is geared toward making the employee part of the overall corporate profit-making effort. "The worst thing that can happen," says company president William Martin, "is to have an employee that doesn't fit." A corporation has to have regimentation in order to run.

Phillips personnel say forthrightly that they like the life they lead for its security and monetary compensation. Ethics isn't a problem. "It's a simple trade-off" says employee Henry Fox. "If you want them to feed, clothe and maintain you and keep you with all the sustenance of life that you want, you simply have to cooperate with them and conform with their rules and conform with their policies."

Source: Excerpted from Michael J. Connor, "CBS Brings in a Lucky Gusher," *The Wall Street Journal* (December 6, 1973), p. 14. Reprinted by permission of The Wall Street Journal, 

## The Milgram Experiments

The later questions point directly toward Stanley Milgram's seminal research on obedience.[11] Milgram designed an experiment to determine the extent to which people tend to obey the commands of an authority figure, even if believing that they are endangering the life of another person. The subjects were 40 males, ranging in age from 20 to 50 and representing a diverse set of occupations (engineers, salespeople, school teachers, laborers, and others). They were paid a nominal fee for participation in the project, which was conducted in a laboratory at Yale University.

The subjects were falsely told that the purpose of the study was to determine the effects of punishment on learning. They were to be the "teachers," and the "learner," a confederate of Milgram's, was strapped to a chair in an adjoining room with an electrode attached to his wrist. The "experimenter," another confederate of Milgram's, was dressed in a gray laboratory coat. Appearing impassive and somewhat stern, he instructed the teacher to read a series of word pairs to the learner, and then reread the first word along with four other terms. The learner was supposed to indicate which of the four terms was in the original pair. This was accomplished by pressing a switch which caused a light to flash on a response panel in front of the teacher.

The teacher was instructed to administer a shock to the learner each time a wrong answer was given. This shock was to be increased one level of intensity each time the learner made a mistake. The teacher controlled switches which ostensibly administered shocks ranging from 15 to 450 volts. The voltage and degree of shock were labeled on the switches. In reality, there was no electric current in the apparatus, but the learners purposely "erred" often, and responded to each level of "shock" in progressively distressing ways. A summary of the switch markings and the learner's fake responses to the various levels of shock is shown in Figure 15.3.

If a teacher proved unwilling to administer a shock, the experimenter used the following prods to get him to perform as requested: (1) "please continue" or "please go on," (2) "the experiment requires that you continue," (3) "it is absolutely essential that you continue," and (4) "you have no choice, you must go on." Only when the teacher refused to go on after the fourth prod would the experiment be stopped.

Checkpoint

Keep in mind what you have learned about the responsiveness of people to the directives of others. Write in the shaded area in Figure 15.3 the number of the 40 "teachers" that you think would *refuse* to obey the "experimenter's" order to shock the "learner" at each shock level.

Milgram asked some of his students and colleagues the same question. Most felt that few, if any, of the subjects would go beyond the "Very Strong Shock" level.[12] How do your answers in the *Checkpoint* compare?

In actual fact, 26 subjects (65%) continued to the end of the experiment and shocked the "learners" to the XXX level! None

| Switch Voltage Marking (Volts) | Switch Description | "Learner's" Responses | Number of "Teachers" Refusing to Go On |
|---|---|---|---|
| 15–60 | Slight | No sound | ______ |
| 75–120 | Moderate | Grunts and moans | ______ |
| 135–180 | Strong | At 150 volts asks to leave; at 180 volts can't stand the pain | ______ |
| 195–240 | Very strong | Can't stand the pain | ______ |
| 255–300 | Intense | At 300 volts pounds on wall | ______ |
| 315–360 | Extreme intensity | No sound | ______ |
| 375–420 | Danger: severe shock | No sound | ______ |
| 435–450 | XXX | No sound | ______ |

**FIGURE 15.3** Shock levels and programmed learner responses in the Milgram experiment.

stopped prior to 300 volts, the point at which the learner pounds on the wall. The remaining 14 subjects refused to obey the experimenter at various intermediate points.

Most people, as was Milgram, are surprised by these results. They wonder just why other people would have a tendency to accept or comply with authoritative commands under such extreme conditions Milgram conducted further experiments to try to answer these questions. We have summarized his findings in Table 15.1.

## The Acceptance Theory of Authority

An acceptance theory of authority helps us to understand when people will and will not obey the directives of others. It holds that a manager's orders will be accepted when, and only when:[13]

1. The subordinate truly understands the directive.
2. The subordinate feels capable of carrying out the directive.
3. The subordinate believes the directive to be in the best interests of the organization.
4. The subordinate believes the directive to be consistent with personal values.

You will want other persons in the work setting to comply with your requests. The acceptance theory can help you to plan your commu-

**Table 15.1 Summary of Possible Determinants of Obedience in Milgram's Experiments**

| Determinants of Obedience | Frequency of Subjects Obeying Through XXX Level |
|---|---|
| *Background Authority* (two variations: Yale University lab or office in run-down office building in downtown shopping area) | Dropped from 65% to 48%. |
| *Closeness of Victim* (four variations: from in another room and not heard or seen to in same room 1½ feet away) | Dropped from 65% to 30%. |
| *Closeness of Authority Figure* (three variations: from in same room a few feet away to not present, with instructions given by tape recorder) | Obedience three times more frequent when experimenter present; when experimenter absent several subjects administered lower shocks than required. |
| *Group Influences* (four variations: naive subject and two trained actors who refused to go on in middle of experiment; actors followed orders obediently; actor shocked, subject watched; subjects themselves determined shock level, with actors suggesting more) | When actors refused, 90% of subjects did as well; when actors followed orders, subjects obeyed about the same as in original study; where subject watched, only 3 of 40 refused at some point; results mixed in last condition. |

Source: Summarized from Stanley Milgram, "Behavioral Study of Obedience," *Journal of Abnormal and Social Psychology,* Vol. 67 (1963), pp. 371–378; "Group Pressure and Action Against a Person," *Journal of Abnormal and Social Psychology,* Vol. 69 (1964), pp. 137–143; "Some Conditions of Obedience and Disobedience to Authority," *Human Relations,* Vol. 18 (1965), pp. 57–76; *Obedience to Authority* (New York: Harper and Row, 1974).

nications in this regard. Ultimately, too, you should understand the psychological contracts and subsequent zones of indifference of others. Then and only then will you be complete in recognizing when position power becomes inadequate and person power becomes necessary if the desired influence is to be achieved.

Before leaving this discussion, there is another side to obedience with which you should be familiar as a manager. That side is your own zone of indifference and tendency to obey. When will you say "no" to your boss? When should you be willing to say "no"?

History is replete with examples of loyal subordinates who failed to say "no" and were then led to commit socially undesirable acts. The "Watergate" crimes are but one example of illegalities committed by people who felt they were "just following orders." Saying "no" can be tough and a price may have to be paid at times to protect that in which you believe. *Newsline 15.2* reports on one person who was willing to stand up for personal values by saying "no" to a legitimate authority.

## NEWSLINE 15.2

### Board Fires Teacher After Disagreement Over Evaluation Forms

SHELBURNE—Shelburne Middle School teacher James Reid was fired by the Shelburne School Board, effective today, because he refused to complete district-mandated student progress evaluation forms.

In a letter couched in legal terms, School Board Chairman Sheara Billado called for Reid's dismissal because he refused to "carry out a reasonable order" of the superintendent.

"James Reid has rejected all opportunities for compromise and has chosen to stand by his refusal to keep district records in any form," the letter said.

Reid was suspended with pay Feb. 17 by district Superintendent Theodore Whalen.

At two public hearings held to consider Reid's dismissal, Shelburne teachers and parents rose to defend Reid. In often emotional testimony teachers charged that the system was of little value to students and could even be detrimental to the teaching process.

They praised Reid for his courage in "laying his job on the line" and said that only fear for their jobs convinced them to complete the forms.

At a subsequent meeting held on March 2 to discuss the record-keeping system, 31 of the 35 Sheiburne Middle School teachers went on record in opposition to the system.

At that meeting the School Board decided to establish a committee of teachers and parents to re-examine and, if necessary, revise the record-keeping system.

At the same time, however, the board stipulated that student progress still be evaluated one step at a time—the key element of Reid's objections to the system.

Reid expressed disappointment with this decision, and accused the board of "sandbagging the issues."

"The changes are only going to be cosmetic. I don't see the study as possibly accomplishing what is needed," Reid said.

But Ms. Billado defended the evaluation system. "It is important to know where the students stand. Before we instituted the present system Shelburne schools had no uniform way to keep track of student progress," she said.

In a letter submitted to the board Monday Reid pleaded with the board to listen to the "good instincts and judgment (of the teachers)."

He said the evaluation cards were "a knee-jerk reaction to the sort of paranoia which has been contaminating schools throughout the country," and emphasized that Shelburne's defense of that reaction "does not befit a school system which has always been in the forefront of education."

Reid warned that a "streamlined" version of the system would "be merely a better edition of a bad idea" and would in the long run drive out good teachers.

Reid did not rule out the possibility of an appeal. He said, however, that it would be no light matter and he would need time "to weigh the possibilities."

Source: Excerpted from The *Burlington [Vt.] Free Press* (March 15, 1978).

## ORGANIZATIONAL POLITICS[14]

Any study of power and influence inevitably leads to the subject of "politics." This word may conjure up thoughts of illicit deals, favors, and special personal relationships in your mind. But to the extent that **organizational politics** is the art of gaining and maintaining power for action through and with one's peers, managers engage in political action much more than most are willing to admit.

### Functions of Politics in Organizations

Organizations are collections of individuals pursuing personal goals and some common purposes. They are also networks of individuals with widely different interests attempting to deal with a host of inconsistent demands from within and outside the organization. Organizational politics helps these people to adapt and helps the organization to succeed in ways that the formal structure alone can't guarantee. Rather than something to be avoided or denied, we argue that "organizational politics" helps give life to the skeleton of an organization. More specifically, organizational politics serves a number of functions, including helping managers to:

1. Overcome personnel inadequacies. As a manager, you should expect some mismatches between people and positions in organizations. Even in the most well-managed firms, mismatches arise among managers who are learning, burned out, lacking in needed training and skills, overqualified, or lacking resources needed to accomplish their assigned duties. Organizational politics provides a mechanism for circumventing these inadequacies and getting the job done.

2. Cope with change. Changes in the environment and technology of an organization often come more quickly than an organization's ability to restructure. Even in organizations known for detailed planning, unanticipated events occur. To meet unanticipated problems, people and resources must be moved into place quickly before small headaches become major problems. Organizational politics can surface such problems and move ambitious, problem-solving managers into the breach.

3. Channel personal contacts. In larger organizations, it is all but impossible to know the persons in every important position. Yet managers need to influence individuals throughout the organization. The political network of the organization can provide the necessary access.

## Political Action and the Manager

Junior executives, especially, may gain a better understanding of political behavior by placing themselves in the positions of other persons involved in critical decisions or events. Each action and decision can be seen as having benefits and costs to all parties concerned. Where the costs exceed the benefits, the manager may act to protect his or her position.

Figure 15.4 shows a sample payoff table for two managers, Lee and Leslie, in a problem situation involving a decision whether or not to allocate resources to a special project. If both authorize the resources, project X gets completed on time and their company keeps a valuable client. Unfortunately, by doing so both Lee and Leslie will overspend their budgets. Taken on its own, a budget overrun would be bad for their performance record. Assume that the overruns will be acceptable if the client is kept. Thus, if both act, both they and the company win. This is the upper left hand block in Figure 15.4. Obviously, it is the most desirable outcome for all parties concerned.

Assume Leslie acts, but Lee does not. The company loses the client and Leslie overspends the budget in a futile effort, but Lee ends up within budget. While the company and Leslie lose, Lee wins.

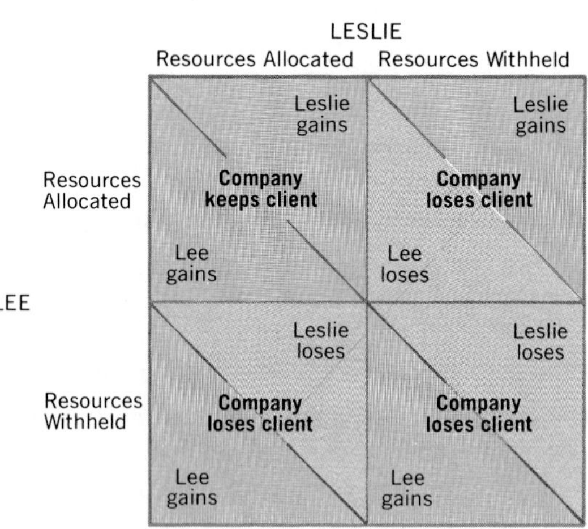


**FIGURE 15.4** Political payoff matrix for the allocation of resources on a sample project.

This is the lower left hand block of the figure. The upper right hand block shows the reverse situation, where Lee acts but Leslie does not. Leslie wins, and the company and Lee lose. Finally, if both fail to act, they each stay within the budget and therefore gain, but the company loses the client.

The company clearly wants both Lee and Leslie to act. But will they? Would you take the risk of overspending the budget, knowing full well that your colleague may refuse? Suppose further that Lee and Leslie will be promoted on the basis of their budgetary performance. A political analysis would presume that each will seek to maximize his or her comparative performance at minimal risk. We would predict in such an instance that both would fail to act. When estimating the political behavior of other managers, calculating a simple payoff matrix such as the one in Figure 15.4 may be most helpful.

## Political Action and Subunit Power

The prior discussion of political action involved power and influence in person-to-person interfaces. Another level of political action links people more formally to one another as representatives of their work units. When the relations fall outside of the formal authority of the vertical chain of commad, we refer to them as lateral relations among subunits. Table 15.2 highlights five of the more typical lateral relations in which you might engage as a manager—work flow, service, advisory, auditing, and approval. The table also shows how lateral relationships among subunit representatives challenge even further the political skills of a manager. Note that each of the examples in the table requires the manager to achieve influence on some other means than formal authority.

To explore this notion further, refer to Figure 15.5, which outlines some of the key relationships among Legal, EEO, Fabrication, Purchasing, and Data Processing for a sample organization. It would appear from this mapping that Legal has the upper hand, has the greater power, because it has an approval relationship with all other units. But while legal does have approval rights, they are limited. Would you recognize this? To be effective in political action, managers should understand how to estimate the relative power of other units in the organization.

First, let's start with a few basics about estimating subunit power, a first step in understanding the politics of subunit relations. Line units are typically more powerful than staff groups. This is because the power of a unit is often limited by the degree to which its function is an integral part of the organization's mission. Thus,

**Table 15.2 Typical Lateral Relations Engaged in by Managers and Their Associated Influence Requirements**

| Type of Relationship | Sample Influence Requirements |
|---|---|
| *Work flow*—contacts with units that precede or follow in a sequential production chain. | An assembly line manager informs another line manager responsible for a later stage in the production process about a delay that must be taken. |
| *Service*—contacts with units established to help with problems. | An assembly line manager asks the maintenance manager to fix an important piece of equipment on a priority basis. |
| *Advisory*—contacts with formal staff units having special expertise. | A marketing manager consults with the personnel manager to obtain special assistance in recruiting for a new salesperson. |
| *Auditing*—contacts with units having the right to evaluate the actions of others. | A marketing manager tries to get the credit manager to retract a report criticizing marketing's tendency to open bad-credit accounts. |
| *Approval*—contacts with units whose approval must be obtained before action may be taken. | A marketing manager submits a job description to the company affirmative action officer for approval before recruiting for a new salesperson can begin. |

Source: Adapted from James L. Hall and Joel L. Leidecker, "Lateral Relations in Organizations," pp. 213–223 in Patrick E. Connor (ed.), *Dimensions in Modern Management* (Boston: Houghton-Mifflin Company, 1974) which was based in part on Leonard Sayles, *Managerial Behavior* (New York: McGraw-Hill, 1964).

line units have more power than staff, and units toward the top of the hierarchy are often more powerful than those toward the bottom.

Units gain power as more of their relations with others are of the approval and auditing types. Work flow relations are more powerful than advisory associations, and both are more powerful than service relations. Units can also increase power by incorporating new actions into their task domains. Specifically, units which tackle and resolve difficult problems can gain power. A difficult problem is one that presents uncertainty to the organization, calls for unique skills, affects many organizational units, and requires immediate attention before it becomes a very serious matter.

## Political Action and Organizational Design

Although politics is common to all organizations, its nature may differ among organizations adapting different structural configura-

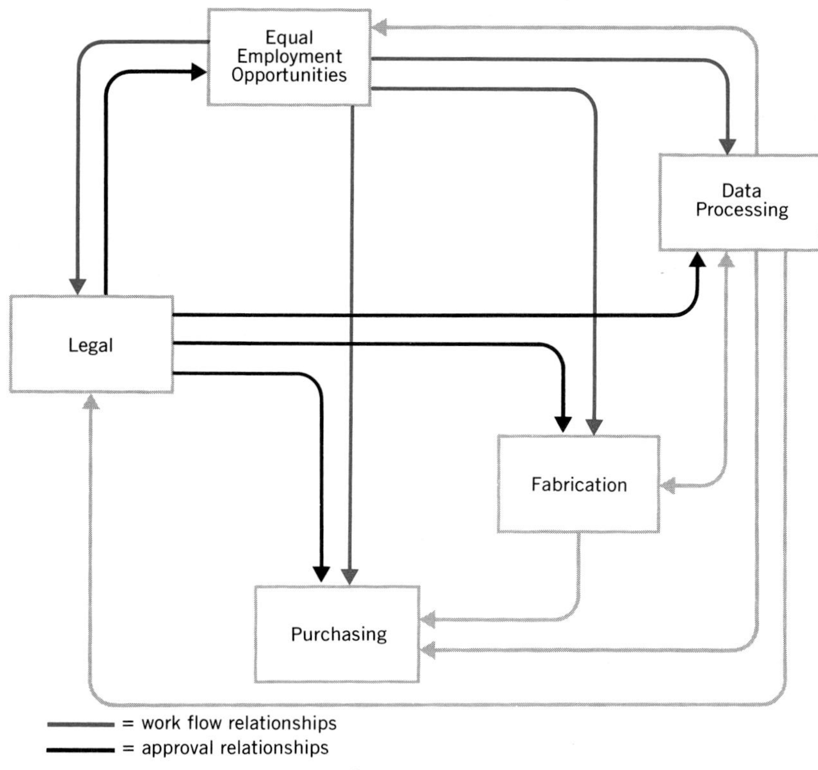


**FIGURE 15.5** Selected subunit relationships among legal, EEO, fabrication, purchasing, and data processing departments in a sample organization.

tions. Chapter 12 introduced you to the mechanistic, organic, and diverse forms of organizations. Let's review the political implications of each.

## Politics in the Mechanistic Structure

Organizations using a mechanistic structure may find particular problems with auditing and approval relationships. The presence of many explicit rules and procedures provides these units with numerous standards for judgment and control. Auditing groups can enforce the adherence to rules, policies, and procedures by other units in great detail. As a result, their relative power is increased.

## Politics in the Organic Structure

With less emphasis on the vertical hierarchy, organic structures put more weight on work flow and advisory relations to resolve problems between operating units. Staff units become powerful with success in selling their advice to line managers, while work flow partners must consider the impacts of their actions when dealing with other units. Without a formal structure to resolve conflicting needs, the political games in organic organizations tend to stress trust and cooperation.

### Politics in Diverse Structures

In organizations with a diverse structure, much of the political action is likely to move toward the interface between mechanistically and organically structured units. Substantial potential for conflict exists at this interface. The structural differences promote mistrust and misunderstanding. Managers in the mechanistic units see the others as loose, out of control, and needing central direction. Organic unit managers see the others as bureaucratic, inflexible, and bogged down in unnecessary paperwork.

### Summary

Organizational politics flows with and supplements the design of the organization. It allows the organization to respond to a variety of changes and pressures without having to restructure. The ultimate function of organizational politics is to allow the power of different units to wax and wane while the overall design of the organization remains consistent over time. Thus, organizations need managers capable of using political action to fill the breach between subunits and formal structures over time.

## PLANNED CHANGE IN ORGANIZATIONS

This discussion of organizational politics leads directly into the final topic of this chapter—planned change. A **change agent** is an individual or group who takes responsibility for changing the existing pattern of behavior of a person or social system. Every manager must be prepared to act as a change agent in the work situation. Indeed, power and politics are essentially change phenomena.

### Planned and Unplanned Change

**Unplanned changes** are those that occur at random or spontaneously and without a change agent's direction. They may be disruptive, such as a wildcat strike that results in a plant closure, or beneficial, such as a machine breakdown that forces an innovative procedure which turns out to be a better way to run the production process. Your goal in managing unplanned change is to act immediately once it is recognized so as to minimize any negative consequences and maximize any possible benefits.

We are particularly interested in **planned change,** that which happens as a result of specific efforts in its behalf by a change agent. The accompanying *Newsline 15.3* gives an example of a planned change in working hours initiated by higher management in one company. As the example indicates, the change was implemented by management as a solution to an experienced problem. It is useful to think of most planned changes as problem-solving efforts initiated by managers who then act in a change agent capacity.

Many of the ideas discussed elsewhere in this book represent potential planned changes in one or more aspects of organizational behavior. They include changes in reward systems, job designs, group dynamics, work flow technology, and organization structure, among others.

## The Phases of Planned Change

Change is a complicated process, at the heart of which lies people. Consider, for example, two situations found in the history of England which have implications for the introduction of planned changes in organizations.

> The British created a civil-service job in 1803 calling for a man to stand on the cliffs of Dover with a spyglass. He was supposed to ring a bell if he saw Napoleon coming. The job was abolished in 1945.[15]
>
> The Royal Artillery was giving a demonstration to some visiting Europeans on Salisbury plain in the 1950s. Visitors were most impressed with the speed and precision of the light artillery crew, but one asked about the duty of the man who stood at attention throughout the demonstration.
>
> "He's number six," the adjutant explained.
> "I, too, can count. But why is he there?"
> "That's his job. Number six stands at attention throughout."
> "But why then do you not have five?"
>
> No one knew. It took a great deal of research through old training manuals, but finally they discovered his duty. He was the one who held the horses.[16]

The organization in each situation could have benefited from change long before the need for change was finally recognized. The examples highlight the tendency of people to act habitually in stable and

## NEWSLINE 15.3

### Costly Problem

*Firms try newer way to slash absenteeism as carrot and stick fail*

NORTHAMPTON, Mass.—The midmorning sunshine darted through the windows as Jerry Hathaway, his wife and his three-year-old daughter ("she's a great little camper") prepared for a weekend outing along the shimmering Quinebaug River.

With their gear assembled, one detail remained. Mr. Hathaway's wife, Donna, had to telephone a message to the local box-board plant of Tenneco Inc.'s Packaging Co. of America. The message: "Jerry will be out sick today."

This popular lie plus legitimate absences adds up to a monumental headache for U.S. industry. Statistics suggest that absenteeism costs workers and the economy $20 billion a year in lost pay alone. In addition, industry spends $10 billion a year in sick pay and $5 billion on fringe benefits that continue whether or not the worker is there.

Absenteeism also can cripple production and profits. A computer analysis at the University of Nebraska for a major manufacturer showed that a 1% rise in absences could slash profits by 4%. Once when Mr. Hathaway and six co-workers failed to report for the 40-man night shift at the packaging-company plant here, the evening's target of one million square feet of corrugated box-board was sliced by 20%. . . .

Eli Kwartler, the plant manager, last year drafted a 100-item questionnaire on workers' attitudes. Among other things, the survey showed that night-workers wanted a four-day week of 10-hour shifts, Monday through Thursday, instead of a five-day week of eight-hour shifts. So the company switched last June to a four-day night shift and reaped a double reward: Not only did absences fall, but the shift's production climbed 9%.

Even Mr. Hathaway, a fork-lift operator whose predilection for absences was common knowledge, took fewer days off after the changeover. He no longer had to skip Fridays to take long weekends.

Source: Excerpted from James Robins, "Firms Try Newer Way to Slash Absenteeism as Carrot and Stick Fail," *The Wall Street Journal* (March 14, 1979). Reprinted by permission of The Wall Street Journal, 

predictable patterns over time. As a manager, you will need to recognize such inertia and learn how to deal with it in order to be successful in implementing planned changes.

Kurt Lewin, a famous psychologist, recommends that any change effort be viewed as a three-phase process: Unfreezing, changing, and refreezing.[17] This process is diagrammed in Figure 15.6.

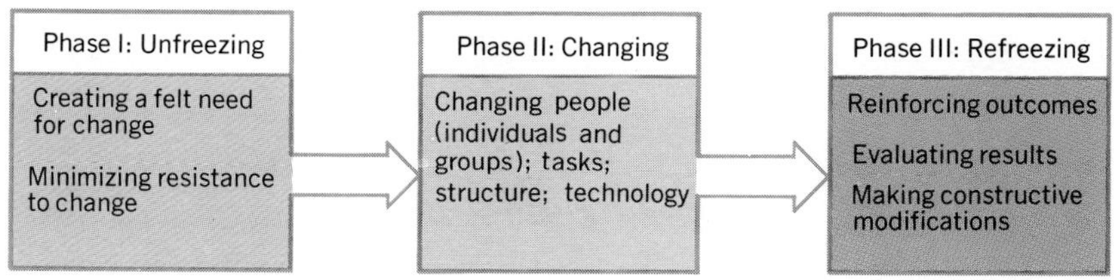


**FIGURE 15.6** The three phases of planned change in organizations.

### Unfreezing

This is the stage of preparing a situation for change. Unfreezing involves disconfirming existing attitudes and behaviors to create a felt need for something new. It is facilitated by environmental pressures, declining performance, the recognition of a problem, and awareness of a better way, among other things. Unfreezing was noticeably absent in the two situations previously stated.

### Changing

This stage in the process involves the actual modification in people, task, structure, and/or technology. Lewin feels that many change agents enter this stage prematurely, are too quick to change things, and therefore end up creating resistance to change in a situation that is not adequately unfrozen.

### Refreezing

The final stage in the planned change process is refreezing. Designed to maintain the momentum of a change, refreezing tactics include positively reinforcing desired outcomes and providing extra support when difficulties are encountered. Evaluation is a key element in this final step. It provides data on the costs and benefits of a change and offers opportunities to make constructive modifications in the change over time. Improper refreezing results in changes that are abandoned or incompletely implemented.

## Planned Change Strategies

Managers use various means for exerting influence to get other persons to adopt a desired change. We summarize these means in Figure 15.7 as force-coercion, empirical-rational, and normative-reeducative change strategies.[18]

### Force-Coercion

A **force-coercive strategy** uses legitimacy, rewards, and punishments as primary inducements to change. The change agent acts

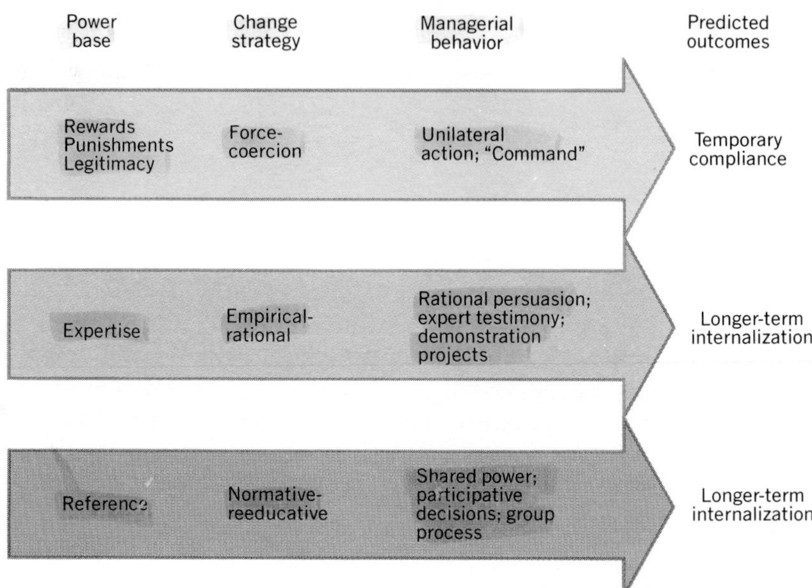


**FIGURE 15.7** Power, bases, change strategies, managerial behavior, and predicted change outcomes.

unilaterally to try to "command" change through the formal authority of his or her position, to induce change via an offer of special rewards, or to bring about change via threats of punishment. People respond to this strategy mainly out of the fear of punishment or desire for reward. Compliance is usually temporary in nature and will continue only so long as the change agent remains visible in his or her legitimate authority, or so long as the opportunity for rewards and punishments remain obvious.

## Empirical-Rational

Change agents using an **empirical-rational strategy** attempt to bring about change through persuasion by special knowledge and rational argument. Use of this strategy assumes that rational people will be guided by reason and self-interest in deciding whether or not to support a change. Expert power is mobilized to convince others that the cost/benefit value of a proposed change is high; that the change will leave people better off than before. When successful, this strategy results in a longer-lasting more internalized change than does the force-coercion strategy.

## Normative-Reeducative

A **normative-reeducative strategy** identifies or establishes values and assumptions such that support for a proposed change naturally emerges. This strategy builds essential foundations such as personal values, group norms, and shared goals to support change. Managers using normative-reeducative approaches emphasize personal reference, and share power by allowing other persons to participate in change planning and implementation. Given this high level of involvement, the strategy is likely to result in a longer lasting and internalized change.

## Resistance to Change

"Resistance" is usually viewed by change agents as something to be overcome in order for change to be successful. Consider, though, the viewpoint that resistance to change is really feedback which can be used constructively by the astute change agent.[19] The essence of this notion is to recognize that when people resist change, they are defending something important and which appears threatened by the change attempt.

Shown in Table 15.3 are examples of why people might resist the introduction of a new management practice. As also shown, an informed change agent can take steps to deal with such points of resistance if they are recognized early enough in the change process.

We divide the possible sources of resistance into three categories: resistance to the change itself, resistance to the change strategy, and resistance to the change agent.

**Table 15.3 Potential Sources of Resistance to a New Management Practice and Suggested Change Agent Responses**

| Source of Resistance | Suggested Response |
|---|---|
| Fear of the unknown | Information and encouragement |
| Need for security | Clarification of intentions and methods |
| No felt need to change | Demonstrate problem or opportunity |
| Vested interests threatened | Enlist key people in change planning |
| Contrasting interpretations | Disseminate valid information, facilitate group sharing |
| Poor timing | Await better time |
| Lack of resources | Provide supporting resources and/or reduced performance expectations |

## Resistance to the Change

People may reject a change because it does not appear as something worth their time, effort, and/or attention. To minimize such resistance, you should be careful to ensure that any changes which you sponsor as a manager

1. Have a positive relative advantage; that is, their benefits are clearly apparent to the persons you are asking to change.
2. Are compatible with existing values and experiences.
3. Are not too complex, that is, they are easy to understand and to learn how to use.
4. Are triable on an incremental or experimental basis before a total commitment has to be made.

## Resistance to the Change Strategy

Resistance is sometimes focused on the strategy rather than on the change itself. Attempting change via force-coercion, for example, may create resistance among persons who resent management by "command" or the use of threatened punishment. People may also resist an empirical-rational strategy in which expertise is not clearly demonstrated, and a normative-reeducative strategy that appears manipulative and insincere.

## Resistance to the Change Agent as a Person

Resistance may also reflect inadequacies in the person of the change agent. Change agents who are isolated from other persons in the change situation, who appear self-centered, and who have a high emotional involvement in the change are especially prone to such problems. Research also indicates that change agents who are largely dissimilar to other key persons in such dimensions as age, education, and socio-economic factors are likely to experience greater resistance to change.[21]

## Summary

Resistance to change is something to be recognized and used by the manager of a planned change program. The presence of resistance typically suggests that something can be done to achieve a better "fit" among the change, the situation, and the people the change will affect. Change agents who are open to feedback and consultative in their behaviors are most likely to become aware of resistance in time to make constructive modifications in the change, the change strategy, or themselves as change agents.

## ORGANIZATION DEVELOPMENT

Behavioral scientists have been experimenting with a comprehensive approach to change that is designed to improve the effectiveness of organizations as a whole. This approach, called **organization development** (OD for short) is "the application of behavioral science knowledge in a long-range effort to improve an organization's ability to cope with change in its external environment and increase its internal problem-solving capabilities."[22] The essence of OD as a planned change effort is found in the various types of interventions and the action-research model used by most OD practitioners.

### Types of OD Interventions

OD interventions are programs, activities, or things done by consultants and/or managers in support of a comprehensive OD program. Table 15.4 classifies the more popular interventions into those focusing on the individual, group, and organizational levels of action. The various interventions are based upon principles discussed throughout this book.

OD is a comprehensive approach to organizational change that typically involves many interventions chosen for specific reasons and systematically used over time within any one organization. Figure 15.8 shows a hypothetical example of one such OD effort. Note its coverage of all organizational levels and the use of data feedback, along with T-groups, team-building, and management training sessions.

**Table 15.4 Types of OD Interventions**

| Focus | Interventions |
|---|---|
| Individual | Sensitivity training (T-groups) |
| | Career planning |
| | Management training |
| | Role analysis |
| | Transactional analysis |
| | Job redesign |
| Group | Team-building |
| | Inter-group team building |
| | Survey-feedback |
| | Confrontation meeting |
| | Grid OD |
| Organizational | Managerial grid |
| | Survey-feedback |
| | Confrontation meeting |
| | Organization redesign |
| | Management by objectives |

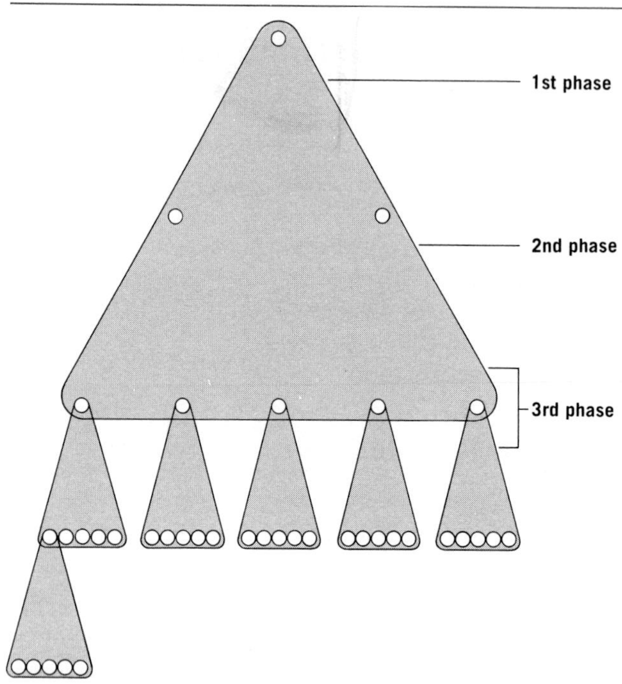
1st phase
2nd phase
3rd phase
1st Phase. Data gathering, feedback, and diagnosis—consultant and top executive only.
2nd Phase. Data gathering, feedback, and revised diagnosis—consultant and two or more key staff or line people.
3rd Phase. Data gathering and feedback to total top executive team in "team-building" laboratory, with or without key subordinates from level below.
4th and Additional Phases. Data gathering and team-building sessions with second or third level teams.
Subsequent Phases. Data gathering, feedback, and interface problem-solving sessions across groups.
Simultaneous Phases. Several managers may attend "stranger" T-Groups; courses in the management development program may supplement this learning.

**FIGURE 15.8** Organization development phases in a hypothetical organization. (Source: Copyright 1969 by the Regents of the University of California. Reprinted from *California Management Review,* Volume XII, p. 27, by permission of the Regents.)

## Action Research

The shared foundation for most OD efforts is **action research,** a process of systematically collecting data on an organization, feeding it back for action planning, and evaluating results by collecting and reflecting on more data.[23] Action research is a data-based approach to problem-solving that helps to identify the specific OD interventions which may enhance organizational effectiveness. A typical action research sequence is illustrated in Figure 15.9.

Data gathering is a major element in the action research process. A number of techniques are available for this, including survey questionnaires, interviews, collages, drawings, nominal grouping, and the delphi technique.[24] Collages and drawings are among the most creative and less familiar of the many options. *What Consultants Do 15.1.* illustrates how each is used to gather data for OD.

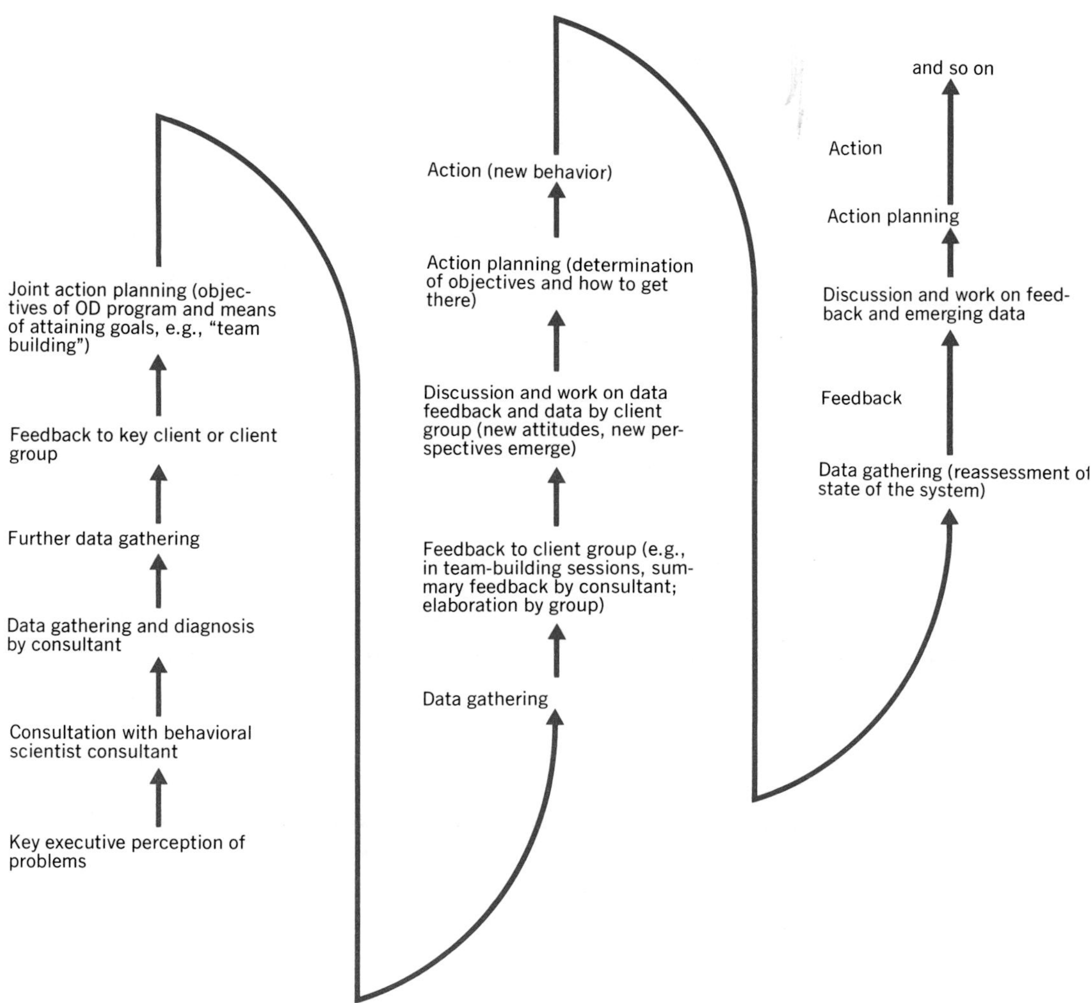


**FIGURE 15.9** An action research model for organization development. (Source: Copyright 1969 by the Regents of the University of California. Reprinted from *California Management Review,* Vol. XII, No. 2, p. 26, Figure 1, by permission of the Regents.)

## OD in Perspective

OD is an exciting application of behavioral science in general and OB in part cular. It is a tool with which any manager concerned about achieving and maintaining high levels of organizational effectiveness will want to be familiar. Still, you should recognize that OD is a relatively new approach to organizational change. Researchers

## WHAT CONSULTANTS DO 15.1

### Using Collages and Drawings as Data-Gathering Methods in OD

***Drawings***

One member of the group (or some, or all members) is asked to make a drawing about an aspect of the individual's life, or something about the nature of the organization. The drawings are made on large sheets of paper posted on the walls. The authors are then asked to discuss their drawings in the presence of the group. Members of the group may ask questions to clarify the author's intent. Common themes and problems, or significant differences of opinion, are then culled from the drawings and posted on chart pads.

Here is an example of an instruction given to all members of a group:

> Draw a circle for each person in the group, including your boss and his boss. Make the circle proportionately larger for those individuals who seem to have greater influence over the way the group does its work.
> Place the circles near or far apart, depending on how closely you feel those individuals must work together to get their job done.
> Label the circles with the names of the people.
> With a blue line, connect those people who are personally close to one another. Connect with a red line those people who are far apart (i.e., individuals who communicate very little with one another or between whom you feel there is friction).

***Collages***

Individuals, subgroups, or groups may be asked to prepare collages around a theme (e.g., "How do you feel about this team?" "How do you feel about yourself in this organization?" "What is happening to this organization and the team?"). Materials for the collage include large sheets of paper, magazines from which pictures and words may be clipped, crayons, felt pens, glue, scissors, etc. Each finished collage is then described for the total group by the individual or subgroup preparing it. If a single, large collage is prepared by the total group, it becomes the focal point for a total group discussion.

Source: Excerpted from Jack Fordyce and Raymond Weil, *Managing With People* (Reading, Mass.: Addison-Wesley Publishing Company, 1971), pp. 127, 128.

are still trying to determine when, under what conditions, and why it works.[25] Nonetheless, OD remains an important integrating concept for managers interested in working comprehensively, collaboratively, and over time to introduce planned changes and improve their organizations.

A management training session.

## SUMMARY

We started this chapter by concentrating on the concept of power. It was defined as the ability to get someone else to do what you want. Influence was introduced as the process by which power is activated. We talked about power vested in both the position and the person of the manager, and of the different sources or bases of these points of power. Position power included reward, coercive, and legitimate power bases; person power included expert and referent power bases. Authority was described as a special kind of position power, one which relies on legitimacy and the right of command.

Next, we used the notion of the psychological contract to help define the zone of indifference, the arena of action within which subordinates will routinely do what they are asked to do by the boss. We discussed ways of "stretching" this zone to expand a manager's influence and we inquired into the boundaries or limits which might characterize your personal zone of indifference as a manager. These concepts led to a detailed discussion of the famous Milgram experiments on obedience.

Ultimately, our thoughts turned to the extension of power into the realms of organizational politics and change. Defined as the act of gaining and maintaining power for action through and with one's peers, organizational politics was viewed as a functional activity. Several examples were used to clarify its implications for junior executives, subunit relations, and organization design.

Power, politics, and change are really inseparable phenomena. Managers act as change agents to bring about planned changes in their work settings. To be successful at change, managers must be aware of unfreezing, changing, and refreezing as the phases of change; as well as the force-coercion, empirical-rational, and normative-reeducative change strategies. Resistance is a frequent byproduct of change and may be indicative of problems with the change itself, the change strategy, and/or the person of the change agent.

Organization development (OD) is a comprehensive approach to implementing change and fostering organizational effectiveness. Based on action research and drawing on a wide range of possible interventions, OD is a rather new and promising application of behavioral science in general and OB in particular. It represents an ultimate application of OB to improve organizations and the work lives of their members.

## THINKING THROUGH THE ISSUES

1. Why is it that an order from the President of the United States may not be carried out?

2. Explain how the various bases of position and person power do or do not apply to the classroom relationship between instructor and student. What sources of power do students have over their instructors?

3. Put yourself in the shoes of one of the subjects in Milgram's experiment on obedience. Diagram a psychological contract for a

typical subject, and show where you think the boundaries of the zone of indifference might be. What power bases did the experimenter have at his disposal, and how did these narrow or widen the boundaries?

4. Think again about the President of the United States. Why might the President have difficulty getting his orders carried out when people readily obeyed the directives of Milgram's experimenter in the gray lab coat?

5. Is organizational politics a dirty, unethical, but essential part of the organization game or is it an activity which is as legitimate for managers as painting is to an artist? Why?

6. Name the three phases of planned change and clarify the managerial requirements of each.

7. When would each of the three major change strategies be useful for a manager? What are the risks of using each?

8. Define the concept of OD and show how it has the potential to work constructively with individuals and groups, as well as total organizations.

## CASE: MACHIAVELLIAN TACTICS FOR B-SCHOOL STUDENTS

Consider the following situation experienced by a graduate student working on a summer internship for a New York bank.

> The 30-year-old hotshot New York banker was dominated by ambition and willing to take calculated risks. Though experienced only as a systems analyst, he was scheming to land a training director's job in a big New York bank. He would then report directly to an influential senior vice-president, whom he regarded as capable of speeding his promotions. But the young comer never got the job. He was foiled—out Machiavellied, as it were—by a 25-year-old summer intern, fresh from a controversial new seminar on Machiavellian behavior, who torpedoed the banker's chances just for practice—and for fun.

The above excerpt is from a *Business Week* article with the same title as this case.[26] The article goes on to quote the intern from Cornell University's Graduate School of Business & Public Administration Program as saying,

> "It was clear that this guy was only interested in the job so he could impress the senior v-p, and there were others far more qualified."
>
> "But I couldn't speak right out against him because things like that have a way of getting back to a person. So when the personnel vice-

president asked for my recommendation of the guy, I decided to say nothing. By saying nothing, I blocked him without making an enemy."

The intern practiced what he learned in a controversial seminar taken at Cornell and based on Machiavelli, the sixteenth century author of *The Prince* and *The Discourses*. These handbooks for gaining and using power have been debated for centuries. They are simultaneously praised and abhorred by politicians, executives and scholars alike. Machiavelli's books offer tactics for self-advancement by taking advantage of circumstances that serve one's self interest. As the article points out, a Machiavellian measures rivals and exploits their weaknesses.

### Questions

Is a course on Machiavelli and his tactics truly appropriate in a business school curriculum? Why or why not?

## THE MANAGER'S VOCABULARY

**Action Research** The process of systematically collecting data on an organization, feeding it back for action planning, and evaluating results by collecting and reflecting on more data.

**Change Agent** An individual or group that takes responsibility for changing the existing pattern of behavior of a person or social system.

**Coercive Power** The extent to which a manager can deny desired rewards or administer undesirable outcomes in order to control other people.

**Empirical-Rational Change Strategy** Attempts to bring about change through persuasion by special knowledge and rational argument.

**Expert Power** The ability to control another's behavior due to the possession of knowledge, experience, or judgment which the other person doesn't have but needs.

**Force-Coercion Change Strategy** Uses legitimacy, rewards, and punishments as primary inducements to change.

**Influence** A behavioral response to the exercise of power.

**Legitimate Power** The extent to which a manager can use the internalized values of a subordinate that the "boss" has a "right of command" in order to control other people.

**Normative-Reeducative Change Strategy** Attempts to bring about change by identifying or establishing values and assumptions such that support for the change naturally emerges.

**Organizational Politics** The art of gaining and maintaining power for action through and with one's peers.

**Organization Development (OD)** The application of behavioral science knowledge in a long-range effort to improve an organization's ability to cope with change in its external environment and increase its internal problem-solving capabilities.

**Person Power** The extent to which a manager can use extrinsic and intrinsic rewards in order to control other people.

**Planned Change** Change that happens as a result of specific efforts in its behalf by a change agent.

**Power** The ability to get someone else to do something you want done; the ability to make things happen or get things done the way you want; the capacity to exert influence.

**Referent Power** The ability to control another's behavior because of their wanting to identify with the power source.

**Reward Power** The extent to which a manager can use extrinsic and intrinsic rewards to control other people.

**Unplanned Change** Change that occurs at random or spontaneously, and without a change agent's direction.

**Zone of Indifference** The range of authoritative requests through which a subordinate is willing to respond without subjecting the directives to critical evaluation or judgment; hence, to which he or she is indifferent.

## Important Names

**Chester Barnard** Famous executive and management scholar who identified the zone of indifference.

**Kurt Lewin** A social psychologist who identified unfreezing, changing, and refreezing as the three phases of planned change.

**Stanley Milgram** Performed important experiments on obedience.

## Notes

[1]Excerpted from David Wood, "Can Reagan Cope Where Carter Didn't," *Southern Illinoisan* (December 15, 1980), p. 4.

[2]Rosabeth Moss Kanter, "Power Failure in Management Circuits," *Harvard Business Review* (July-August 1979), pp. 65–75.

[3]John R. P. French, Jr. and Betram Raven, "The Bases of Social Power," in Darwin Cartwright (ed.), *Group Dynamics: Research and Theory* (Evanston, Ill.: Row, Peterson and Co., 1962), pp. 607–623.

[4]Stephen J. Carroll and Henry L. Tosi, *Organizational Behavior* (Chicago: St. Clair Press, 1977), p. 215.

[5]Allan R. Cohen, Stephen L. Fink, Herman Gadon, and Robin D. Willits, *Effective Behavior in Organizations,* Revised Edition (Homewood, Ill.: Richard D. Irwin, 1980), p. 252.

[6]French and Raven, op. cit.

[7]Ibid.

[8]Stephen J. Carroll and Henry L. Tosi, *Organizational Behavior* (Chicago: St. Clair Press, 1977), p. 212.

[9]Chester Barnard, *The Functions of the Executive* (Cambridge, Mass.: Harvard University Press, 1938).

[10]Richard R. Ritti and Ray G. Funkhouser, *The Ropes to Skip and The Ropes to Know* (Columbus, Ohio: Grid Inc., 1977), p. 197.

[11]Stanley Milgram, "Behavioral Study of Obedience," in Dennis W. Organ (ed.), *The Applied Psychology of Work Behavior* (Dallas: Business Publications, Inc., 1978), pp. 384–398.

[12]Stanley Milgram, "Behavioral Study of Obedience," *Journal of Abnormal and Social Psychology,* Vol. 67 (1963), pp. 371–378.

[13]Barnard, op. cit.

[14]Although the work on organizational politics is not extensive, useful reviews include a chapter in Robert H. Miles, *Macro Organizational Behavior* (Santa Monica, Calif.: Goodyear Publishing Company, 1980); and Bronston T. Mayes and Robert W. Allen, "Toward a Definition of Organizational Politics," *Academy of Management Review,* Vol. 2 (1977), pp. 672–677. A good discussion of the manager's role in shaping and using informal relations with others is found in Leonard Sayles, *Managerial Behavior* (New York: McGraw-Hill, 1964).

[15]Robert Townsend, *Up the Organization; How to Stop the Corporation from Stifling People and Strangling Profits* (New York: Alfred A. Knopf, 1970), p. 93.

[16]Anthony Jay, *Management and Machiavelli: An Inquiry Into The Politics of Corporate Life* (New York: Holt, Rinehart and Winston, 1967), p. 96.

[17]Kurt Lewin, "Group Decision and Social Change," pp. 459–473 in G. E. Swanson, T. M. Newcomb, and E. L. Hartley (eds.), *Readings in Social Psychology* (New York: Holt, Rinehart and Winston, 1952).

[18]Robert Chin and Kenneth D. Benne, "General Strategies for Effecting Changes in Human Systems," pp. 22–45 in Warren G. Bennis, Kenneth D. Benne, Robert Chin, and Kenneth E. Corey (eds.), *The Planning of Change,* Third Edition (New York: Holt, Rinehart and Winston, 1969).

[19]Donald Klein, "Some Notes on the Dynamics of Resistance to Change: The Defender Role," pp. 117–124 in Bennis et al., op. cit.

[20]See Everett M. Rogers with F. Floyd Shoemaker, *Communication of Innovations,* Second Edition (New York: The Free Press, 1971), pp. 136–172.

[21]Ibid., pp. 210–215.

[22]Edgar F. Huse, *Organization Development and Change,* Second Edition (St. Paul, Minn.: West Publishing Company, 1980), p. 508.

[23]Wendell L. French and Cecil H. Bell, Jr., *Organization Development,* Second Edition (Englewood Cliffs, N.J.: Prentice-Hall, 1978), p. 88.

[24]See Jack K. Fordyce and Raymond Weil, *Managing With People* (Reading, Mass.: Addison-Wesley, 1971) and Andre L. Delbecq, Andrew Van de Ven, and David Gustafson, *Group Techniques in Program Planning* (Glenview, Ill.: Scott-Foresman, 1974).

[25]Wendell L. French, Cecil H. Bell, Jr., and Robert A. Zawacki (eds.), *Organization Development: Theory, Practice and Research* (Dallas: Business Publications, Inc., 1978), pp. 3, 473.

[26]"Machiavellian Tactics for B-School Students," *Business Week* (Oct. 13, 1975), p. 86.

# 16

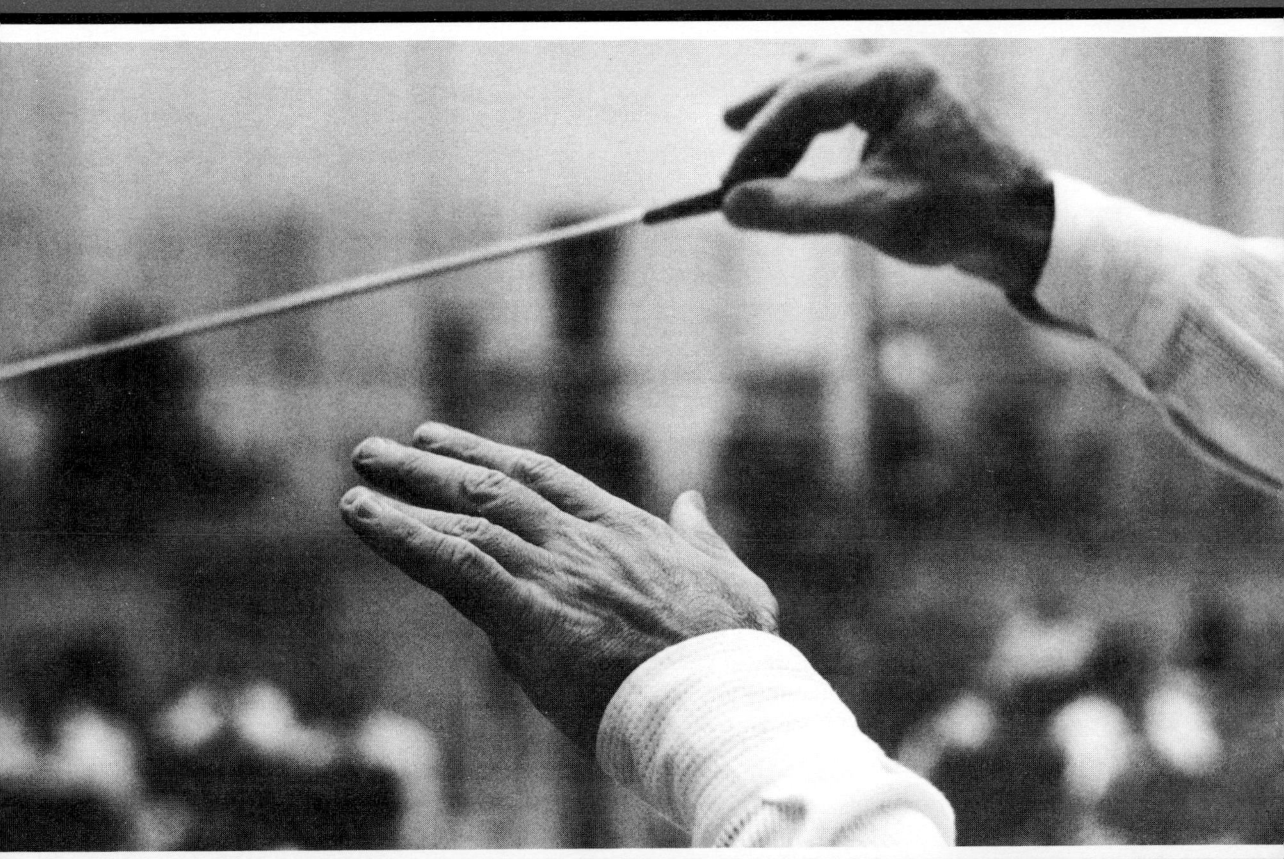

# LEADERSHIP

# VINCE LOMBARDI AND THE GREEN BAY PACKERS

Some say the Green Bay Packers teams under Vince Lombardi were the greatest football dynasty ever created. In 1968, Lombardi moved up to general manager and Phil Bingstone became head coach. The team went six and seven.

A number of people said flatly the sole difference was the absence of Vince Lombardi. Others weren't so sure. At the beginning of the season nobody thought Phil would be another Lombardi. He was a gentler man, a calmer man, but every bit as dedicated to perfection as Lombardi was. The defensive line had always been a reflection of Phil's brilliance. And the defensive players and others as well loved him and wanted to win for him.

However, some of the players took advantage of Phil. He gave them water breaks, things they had never had before. Before long, sometimes some would sneak over in the shade and lie on the ground. That never happened when Vince was around.

Lombardi made the players hate him much of the time, but this hatred, the half-serious suspicion among the players that he treated them like dogs, served to unify them. They had a single target for all their frustrations and they lost it when Lombardi left.

Early in the year, Lombardi suggested to Phil that somebody had to be an S.O.B., and that if Phil wasn't going to be an S.O.B. then one of his assistants should be. But nobody picked up this responsibility.

Lombardi was the genius of the locker room speech; he always knew how to talk to the players. Phil, on the other hand, was very calm, very matter of fact. As a result the '68 team lacked emotion. It was not being provided by Phil. The players had forgotten how to motivate themselves. Lombardi had pushed them so hard they had never had to push themselves; they'd gotten lazy under Lombardi.[1]

**MANAGEMENT APPLICATIONS QUESTION**

Clearly, Lombardi and Bingstone acted differently as coaches. In what ways did their leadership behaviors differ, with what impact on team effectiveness, and what are the wider implications for other kinds of organizations?

## PLANNING AHEAD

**This chapter considers a number of different aspects of leadership. The learning activities of the chapter will make you familiar with the following topics:**

**Leadership as a Concept**
**Different Approaches to Studying Leadership**
**Fiedler's Situational Theory**
**House's Path-Goal Theory**
**Managerial Perspectives on the Contingency Theories**
**Horizontal Leadership**
**The Multiple-Influence Leadership Theory**

Mention the word "leadership" and what comes to mind? Many people think of it as an almost mystical quality which some have and others don't. Some say they can't define it but they know it when they see it. Others tend to treat it more specifically, arguing, for example, that "good" leaders behave more considerately toward their subordinates or supervise their subordinates loosely rather than closely.

Regardless of the way leadership is viewed, most managers consider it so important that library shelves are replete with books on the subject, and millions of dollars a year are spent on leadership training. Let's see if we can strip away some of the mystique in the concept of leadership and related to other aspects of OB.

## LEADERSHIP AS A CONCEPT

The first part of Chapter 15 was devoted to various forms of power and influence. A natural extension of this discussion is the subject of leadership. We define **leadership** as the process of using power to obtain interpersonal influence.[2]

Important as it may be, leadership is but one part of managerial behavior, just as it is but one kind of influence. Planning a budget is something managers do, and it will probably influence subordinates, but it is not leadership. In Chapter 1 we discussed 12 managerial skills. Leadership was one of them. As a manager, you will want to keep leadership in proper perspective as an important part, but not the only part, of a manager's job.

Within organizations, leadership occurs in two forms. **Formal leadership** is exerted by persons appointed to or elected to positions of formal authority in organizations. **Informal leadership** is exerted by persons who emerge as influential over others because of special skills or resources which they have to meet the needs of a work unit or its members.

While we typically think of the formal aspects of leadership, most work situations also contain informal leaders. Research suggests, as you might expect, that when subordinates see their supervisors as inadequate in important ways, an informal leader will step in to fill the vacuum.[3] Both formal and informal leadership are important, but the evidence indicates that if one category of leadership is more important than the other, the dominant one is likely to be formal leadership.[4]

## DIFFERENT APPROACHES TO STUDYING LEADERSHIP

Research on formal leadership falls into three general categories. They include studies of leadership traits, leader behaviors, and leadership contingencies.

### Leadership Traits

The earliest studies of leadership tried to identify those traits which differentiated the great persons in history from the masses.[5] This led to an emphasis on research that tried to identify profiles of traits which would separate leaders from non-leaders.[6] Sarge, in the cartoon, is using a trait approach in his view of the true leader. Table 16.1 lists some of the traits used in this research tradition.

Think of how valuable a trait profile would be for you as a manager. You could use it to identify people with the right traits and

The trait approach to leadership. 

**Table 16.1 Illustrative Traits Which Researchers Considered in Separating Leaders from Non-Leaders**

| | |
|---|---|
| Height | Knowledge |
| Weight | Judgment and decision |
| Physique | Insight |
| Energy | Originality |
| Health | Adaptability |
| Appearance | Dominance |
| Fluency of speech | Initiative |
| Intelligence | Persistence |
| Scholarship | Ambition |
| | Self-confidence |

Source: Ralph M. Stogdill, *Handbook of Leadership* (New York: The Free Press, 1974), Chapter 5.

appoint them as leaders. Of course, you might be quite unhappy to find out that you don't fit the right profile! Fortunately or unfortunately, leadership researchers failed to find the trait approach to be as useful as they had hoped.[7] Problems exist in determining and measuring the traits. Furthermore, no consistent set of traits emerged to differentiate leaders from non-leaders in any theoretically meaningful way. For example, in one study an extroverted, tall, dynamic person might emerge as a leader; in another a quiet, intelligent, deliberative person might be the leader.

This result is not surprising if you think about it for a minute. Would you expect the same traits to characterize the successful leaders of a construction crew, an army combat squad, and a university research and development group? If your answer is "no," you're right. Given this general lack of success in identifying universal traits, a different approach to studying leadership came to be emphasized more heavily.

## Leadership Behaviors

In the late 1940s, researchers moved away from an emphasis on traits and toward the study of leader behaviors. This new approach differed from the trait-oriented research in two major ways. First, actual leader behaviors rather than personal traits were the focus. Second, whereas most trait studies sought to separate leaders from non-leaders, leader behavior studies wanted to determine how various kinds of specific behaviors affect the performance and satisfactions of followers. You might remember this difference as follows.

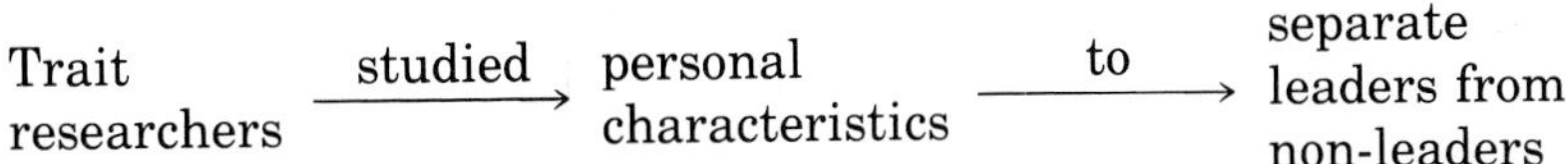
Trait researchers
studied
personal characteristics
to
separate leaders from non-leaders

| Leader behavior researchers | —studied→ | how a leader's behaviors | —affected→ | followers' performance and satisfactions |
|---|---|---|---|---|

The earliest leader behavior studies considered leadership to be a continuum. A typical continuum viewed leaders as ranging from human-relations oriented at one extreme, to task oriented at the other.

Checkpoint

Mark an "X" on the continuum below at the point that best illustrates what you consider to be your typical leadership behavior. Ask yourself if other people with whom you have worked would score you the same way.

Human-relations oriented |______|______|______|______| Task oriented

One of the problems with such a continuum is that it does not allow a leader to be high on both types of behaviors simultaneously. This implies that neither you nor any other leader is capable of showing both human-relations behavior and task behavior in your relationships with followers.

Researchers from the University of Michigan recognized that leader behaviors were not opposite and mutually exclusive points on a continuum. They studied employee-centered and production-centered leadership behaviors and concluded that a leader could be high on both at the same time.[8] Of course, a leader was not necessarily high on both. Leaders could fall in any one of the four different combinations of behaviors shown below. We have labelled each combination with a term often used in popular conversations about leadership.

| | **Leader Behaviors** | |
|---|---|---|
| **Conversational Label** | **Employee-Centered** | **Production-Centered** |
| Democratic | high | high |
| Human relations | high | low |
| Autocratic | low | high |
| Laissez-faire | low | low |

Another important research program at Ohio State University investigated two similar dimensions of leader behavior—consideration and initiating structure.[9] A highly considerate leader is sensitive to people's feelings and tries to make things pleasant for followers. A leader high in initiating structure is concerned with spelling out task requirements and clarifying other aspects of the work agenda. These terms are still in popular use today. They are similar to what people sometimes refer to as socio-emotional and task leadership respectively.[10] They also encompass what we discussed in Chapter 8 as maintenance and task activities on the part of group members.

At first, it looked to the researchers as if being high on consideration or socio-emotional warmth (in other words, showing a high concern for people) resulted in a leader having more highly satisfied and/or better-performing subordinates. Later results, however, indicated that leaders should be high on both these people-oriented behaviors and those of a more task-oriented nature, that is initiating structure, as well.[11]

The leader behavior research was viewed as particularly promising by practicing managers. If the findings were generally true, training and educational programs could be established to try to teach managers the leadership behaviors in which they were weak. For example, people could be taught to be more considerate and/or to be better at initiating task structure. Having been so trained, performance and human resource maintenance within their work units could be expected to improve. Unfortunately, further studies did not confirm the original findings, and disillusionment again beset the leadership researchers.[12]

## Leadership Contingencies

In the 1960s, the emphasis of leadership research shifted to the contingency approaches that are still with us today. Figure 16.1 summarizes the focus of this new research perspective. Although still concerned with leader behaviors, the new approach also focuses on "contingency variables" such as the nature of the task, subordinate attributes, and group characteristics. These contingency variables are felt to influence the relationship between various leader behav-

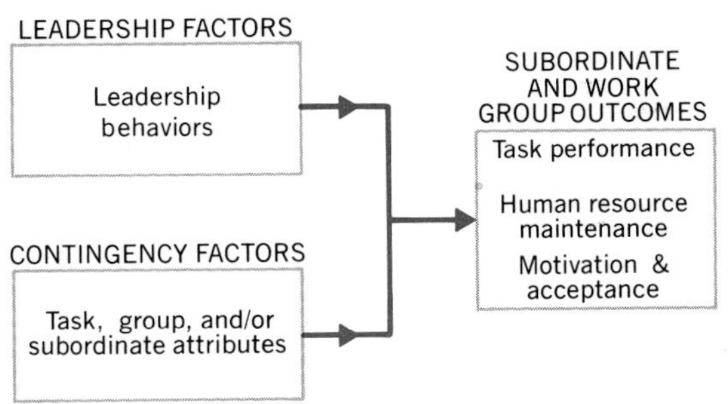


**FIGURE 16.1** Key relationships in contingency approaches to leadership.

iors and outcomes for followers. You may want to contrast the logic of this figure with the underlying premises of the trait and leader behavior theories just discussed.

The term contingency is used here to mean, "dependent upon the happening of something else."[13] In other words, this research approach posits that the relationship between leadership and the performance and human resource maintenance of followers depends upon what happens to the important contingency variables. In the scientific terminology reviewed in Supplementary Module B, the contingency variables "interact" with or "modify" the effects of leader behavior on follower outcomes.

In summary, the various contingency theories argue that what is successful leadership behavior will depend upon the situation. It is the contingency variables that describe how situations vary and thereby affect the choice of appropriate leadership behavior. For example, we might say that directive behavior is appropriate when subordinates' tasks are unclear, but inappropriate when tasks are very clear. The contingency variable in this argument is task clarity. As the task changes from clear to unclear, the argument goes, the relationship between directive leadership and performance changes from positive to negative. Later, we will recognize this as a hypothesis with good research support.

We will concentrate on two well-known contingency approaches in this chapter. At the same time, the Vroom and Yetton decision-making model discussed in Chapter 8 can also be considered a leadership contingency model. You should refer back to that discussion if need be to familiarize yourself once again with the theory.

## FIEDLER'S SITUATIONAL THEORY[14]

The first contingency leadership approach we consider is Fiedler's situational theory. It is presented here for two reasons. First it is the one that ushered in the new era of contingency leadership research. Second, Fiedler has developed the model to the point where you can be introduced to situational leadership thinking in a very systematic way. This *discipline of situational thinking* is extremely important if you are to be able to make the most of what the contingency leadership approaches as a group have to offer.

Fiedler's concern is to predict work-group effectiveness (task performance). His theory holds that group effectiveness depends on a successful match between the style of the leader and the demands of the situation. Specifically, Fiedler is interested in the amount of control and influence that the situation provides the leader. **Situational control** is defined as the extent to which a leader can determine what the group is going to do, and what the outcomes of its actions and decisions are going to be. In situations of high control, leaders can predict with a high degree of certainty what will happen when they want something done.

Checkpoint

Fiedler's theory is best understood by working through some examples. But first he would want to measure your leadership style. Let's do the same.[15] Complete the Least Preferred Co-worker Scale in Figure 16.2. Then read on.

## Understanding Your Leadership Style

The LPC (Least Preferred Co-worker) scale, which you just completed, is used by Fiedler to measure people's leadership styles. Fiedler interprets it as a leader's primary motivation or predisposition to act in a work situation. To determine your LPC score, turn back to the scale and write the numbers you checked in the column shown at the right of the page. Add these numbers, and put the total at the bottom of the page.

If your score is 64 or higher, Fiedler considers you to be a high LPC person. The high LPC person essentially says of his or her least preferred co-worker, "Even if I can't work with you, you may still be an okay person." Because of this sensitivity for relationships with others, the high LPC person is considered to be "relationship-motivated" as a leader.

If your score is 57 or lower, you are a low LPC leader. A low LPC person describes the least preferred co-worker in very negative terms. Essentially he or she says, "Work is extremely important to me; therefore, if you are a poor co-worker and prevent me in my efforts to get things done, then I can't accept you in other respects either." This low LPC individual is termed "task-motivated" as a leader.

A score of 58 to 63 indicates a possible mix of motivations and goals. If you fall in this range, Fiedler argues that you will need to decide for yourself where you fit between task and relationship motivations.

Now, you should be asking whether or not one of these two leadership motivations is superior to the other. Fiedler's answer is "no." The essence of contingency leadership thinking is that the most effective style will vary with the situation. In the case of Fiedler's theory, the critical aspect of the situation is the amount of control

Throughout your life you will have worked in many groups with a wide variety of different people—on your job, in social groups, in church organizations, in volunteer groups, on athletic teams, and in many other situations. Some of your co-workers may have been very easy to work with in attaining the group's goals, while others were less so.

Think of all the people with whom you have ever worked, and then think of the person with whom you could work *least well*. He or she may be someone with whom you work now or with whom you have worked in the past. This does not have to be the person you liked least well, but should be the person with whom you had the most difficulty getting a job done, the *one* individual with whom you could work *least well*.

Describe this person on the scale which follows by placing an "X" in the appropriate space.

Look at the words at both ends of the line before you mark your "X". *There are no right or wrong answers*. Work rapidly; your first answer is likely to be the best. Do not omit any items, and mark each item only once.

Now describe the person with whom you can work least well.

| | | | | | | | | | | Scoring |
|---|---|---|---|---|---|---|---|---|---|---|
| Pleasant | 8 | 7 | 6 | 5 | 4 | 3 | 2 | 1 | Unpleasant | ____ |
| Friendly | 8 | 7 | 6 | 5 | 4 | 3 | 2 | 1 | Unfriendly | ____ |
| Rejecting | 1 | 2 | 3 | 4 | 5 | 6 | 7 | 8 | Accepting | ____ |
| Tense | 1 | 2 | 3 | 4 | 5 | 6 | 7 | 8 | Relaxed | ____ |
| Distant | 1 | 2 | 3 | 4 | 5 | 6 | 7 | 8 | Close | ____ |
| Cold | 1 | 2 | 3 | 4 | 5 | 6 | 7 | 8 | Warm | ____ |
| Supportive | 8 | 7 | 6 | 5 | 4 | 3 | 2 | 1 | Hostile | ____ |
| Boring | 1 | 2 | 3 | 4 | 5 | 6 | 7 | 8 | Interesting | ____ |
| Quarrelsome | 1 | 2 | 3 | 4 | 5 | 6 | 7 | 8 | Harmonious | ____ |
| Gloomy | 1 | 2 | 3 | 4 | 5 | 6 | 7 | 8 | Cheerful | ____ |
| Open | 8 | 7 | 6 | 5 | 4 | 3 | 2 | 1 | Guarded | ____ |
| Backbiting | 1 | 2 | 3 | 4 | 5 | 6 | 7 | 8 | Loyal | ____ |
| Untrustworthy | 1 | 2 | 3 | 4 | 5 | 6 | 7 | 8 | Trustworthy | ____ |
| Considerate | 8 | 7 | 6 | 5 | 4 | 3 | 2 | 1 | Inconsiderate | ____ |
| Nasty | 1 | 2 | 3 | 4 | 5 | 6 | 7 | 8 | Nice | ____ |
| Agreeable | 8 | 7 | 6 | 5 | 4 | 3 | 2 | 1 | Disagreeable | ____ |
| Insincere | 1 | 2 | 3 | 4 | 5 | 6 | 7 | 8 | Sincere | ____ |
| Kind | 8 | 7 | 6 | 5 | 4 | 3 | 2 | 1 | Unkind | ____ |
| | | | | | | | | | Total | ____ |

**FIGURE 16.2** Least preferred co-worker (LPC) scale. (Source: Adapted from Fred E. Fiedler, Martin M. Chemers, and Linda Mahar, *Improving Leadership Effectiveness* (New York: John Wiley and Sons, 1976), pp. 7.)

which it provides the leader. Let's now look at this notion in more detail.

## Situational Control and Task-Motivated Leaders

According to Fiedler, task-motivated individuals need to get things done. They gain self-esteem from tangible, measurable evidence of performance and achievement. They are strongly motivated to successfully accomplish any task to which they have committed themselves, even if there are few or no external rewards.

In situations over which they have little control, task-motivated leaders feel most comfortable working from clear guidelines and standard operating procedures. When these are missing, the leaders try to develop them. They will move in and take charge early to increase the amount of control in the situation, even to the point where they don't worry very much about subordinates' interpersonal problems and conflicts. When they are in complete control of the situation and don't have to worry as much about getting the job done, task-motivated leaders tend to be considerate and pleasant. They are content to let their group handle the job, but tend to resist interference from those in higher levels of authority.

It is in moderate control situations, especially those with interpersonal conflicts, that task-motivated leaders tend to feel out of their element. They are likely to concentrate so heavily on the task that they ignore group members' needs, as well as any conflicts that may exist. Hence, the performance of the group may suffer.

In summary, Fiedler's theory states that **task-motivated leaders will be most successful in situations of high leadership control and in situations of low leadership control.** They are likely to be less successful in situations of moderate control.

## Situational Control and Relationship-Motivated Leaders

While relationship-motivated leaders are concerned with doing a good job, their primary orientation is toward good interpersonal relations with others. Their self-esteem is affected by how other people relate to them. These leaders tolerate different viewpoints and are good at dealing with complex problems requiring creative and resourceful thinking.

In stressful and challenging low-control situations, these relationship-oriented behaviors may become exaggerated. These leaders may become so involved in subordinate consultations and friendly conversations that they don't pay enough attention to the job. Group support is so important that they may be reluctant to do things that,

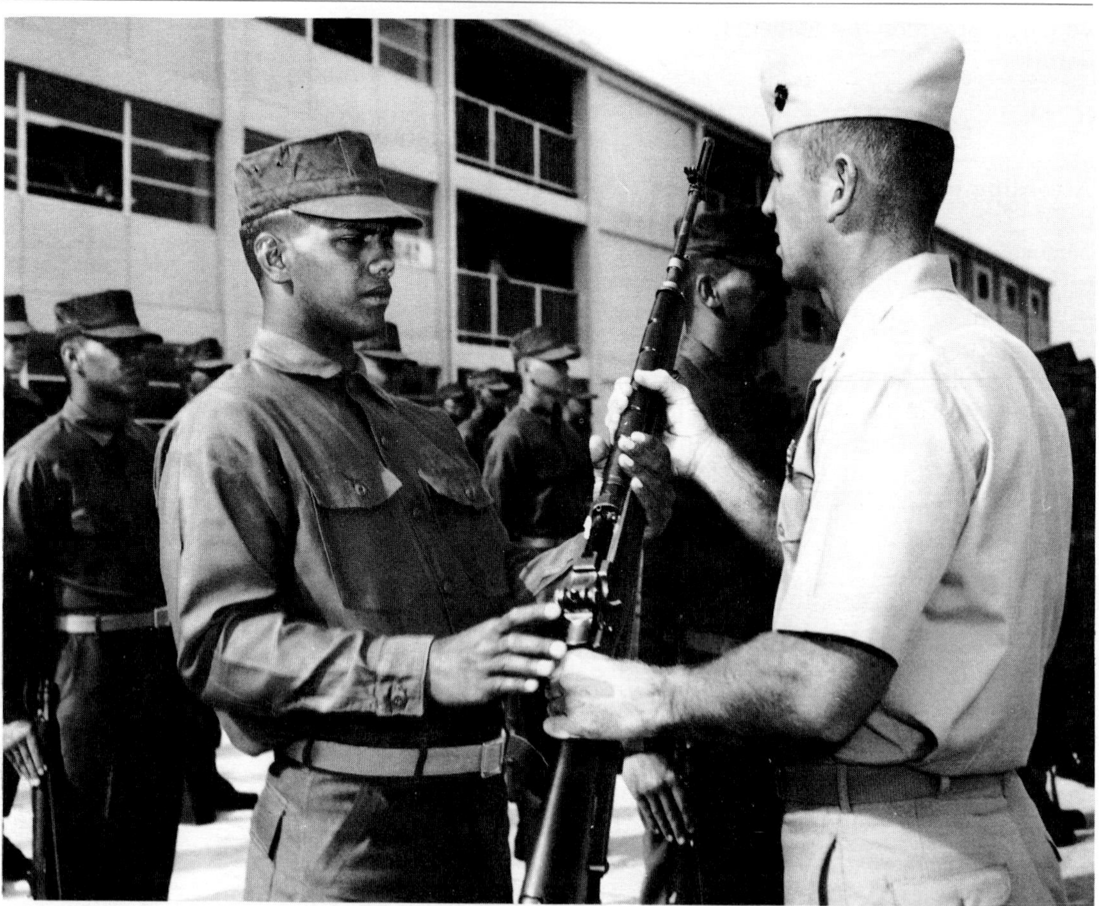

Task-oriented leader behavior.

although annoying to the members, are necessary job requirements. Thus, the group's performance is likely to suffer.

Similarly, these leaders tend not to be at their best in high-control situations. Here, they don't need to worry much about relations with the group. They may, therefore, become more concerned with how they appear to their boss and to others outside the group. In their eagerness to impress outsiders, they may push ahead with a task and be less considerate of subordinates' feelings. Because the high-control situation is so relaxed for the leader, they are not likely to be challenged much and may even appear bored and aloof to group members.

Thus, **the relationship-oriented leader is at his or her best in moderate-control situations.** Here, the leader's concern with interpersonal relations is appropriate and he or she knows how to deal with the uncertainties and problems that occur. Because of their strong interpersonal sensitivities, these leaders can deal with difficult group members. Their creativity and imaginations are challenged by tasks needing innovation. Relationship-oriented leaders do *not* do well in either high- or low-control situations.

## Diagnosing Leadership Situations

Figure 16.3 summarizes the predicted relationship between each style of behavior and leadership success in situations of varying degrees of control. The figure is a useful summary of Fiedler's theory. But, now you should be asking, "how do I know how much control various situations offer me as a leader?" This is an important question. You must learn how to diagnose leadership situations if you are to use Fiedler's theory effectively.

Relationship-oriented leader behavior.

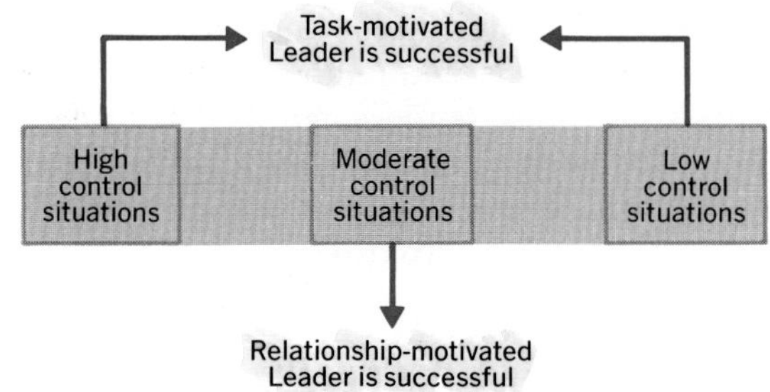


**FIGURE 16.3** Predictions from Fiedler's contigency theory of leadership.

Fiedler specifies three variables which define the amount of control and influence a situation allows the leader: **leader-member relations** (good/poor)—the degree to which the group supports the leader; **task structure** (high/low)—the extent to which task goals, procedures, and guidelines are clearly spelled out; and **position power** (strong/weak)—the degree to which the position gives the leader power to reward and punish subordinates. By using these three variables in the combinations shown in Figure 16.4, you can describe any leadership situation as high, moderate, or low in control for the leader. Let's look at some examples.

Suppose you are the supervisor of a production line. Your subordinates are highly supportive. The production operation is clearly structured in terms of the tasks that need to be done and how they are to be done. Your workers are not unionized and you have the authority to evaluate performance and make pay and promotion recommendations. You have a thorough knowledge of the production process that allows you to instruct your subordinates clearly.

Since your subordinates are supportive, leader-member relations would be good. Task structure would also be high. Finally, your authority and job knowledge give you high position power. In this situation Fiedler would consider you to have a high degree of control as a leader.

Suppose you are serving as chairperson for a student council committee made up of volunteers who are not very happy that you are chairperson. The committee is to organize a "Parents' Day" program to help improve university-parent relations. Here the task goal is clear, but the means to achieve it are uncertain. Who can say exactly what activities will promote the "improved relations"? Task structure is therefore low. Because the volunteer committee members can quit if they don't like the way the meetings are going or what is being planned, you as chairperson have little position power. Furthermore, because the members aren't happy that you are chairperson, leader-member relations are poor. Here you are in a low-control situation.

How about a moderate-control situation? Let's assume you are a university department chairperson responsible for "enhancing the teaching, research, and service missions of the department." Being strongly supported by your faculty members offers good leader-member relations. But it's difficult to predict exactly how to carry out the mission (task structure is low), and the leader's position power over tenured faculty is not very high. According to Fiedler, this situation offers the leader only a moderate degree of control.

Figure 16.4 clarifies the previous three examples and their preferred leadership styles according to Fiedler's prediction.

## Managerial Implications

In summary, the managerial implications of Fiedler's theory can be stated as follows:

1. Understand your leadership style in terms of task and relationship orientations.
2. Understand how to diagnose the degree of control offered by various leadership situations (that is, according to leader-member relations, task structure, and position power).
3. Act to match your leadership style with leadership situations for which it is appropriate (a task-oriented style is appropriate for high- or low-control situations; a relationship-oriented style is appropriate for moderate-control situations).
4. When a mismatch between your style and situational control occurs correct the match by (in priority order):
   (a) Changing the situation to increase or decrease control.
   (b) Changing your leadership style.

**FIGURE 16.4** Summary of Fiedler's situational variables and their preferred leadership styles.

Situational Characteristics

| | | | | | | | | |
|---|---|---|---|---|---|---|---|---|
| Leader-member relations | Good | Good | Good | Good | Poor | Poor | Poor | Poor |
| Task-structure | High | High | Low | Low | High | High | Low | Low |
| Position power | Strong | Weak | Strong | Weak | Strong | Weak | Strong | Weak |
| Text examples | PRODUCTION SUPERVISOR | | | DEPARTMENT HEAD | | | | COMMITTEE CHAIR |
| Preferred leadership styles | Task-motivated (low LPC) | | | Relationship-motivated (high LPC) | | | | Task-motivated (low LPC) |

Let's look more closely at this last point of being able to match your leadership style and the situation. Fiedler feels that it is very difficult to change a person's leadership style, since it really means trying to change an underlying psychological characteristic or personality. Thus, he advocates "situational engineering" by the manager to increase or decrease situational control in a direction which makes the existing leadership style much more favorable. Table 16.2 illustrates some of the things Fiedler believes can be done to change situational characteristics in a direction more favorable to the leader.

### The Research

Fiedler's model of leadership effectiveness was the earliest of the contingency theories. Its roots are now more than 25 years old and there has been considerable research on it. As with other OB theories, there is controversy surrounding Fiedler's work and it is easy to find research that is both pro and con.[16] Perhaps the greatest controversy surrounds the meaning of a person's LPC score[17]. It does not directly measure leader behavior, but measures a person's feeling about his or her least preferred co-worker. Yet, Fiedler interprets the LPC in terms of behavior. This interpretation and the lack of consistency in the scores of some people who complete the instrument more than once have been subjected to serious question.

Given the controversy surrounding the model, we use the theory here mainly to emphasize the usefulness of "situational" or "contingency" thinking. Such thinking is required in the theories that follow and will certainly help you apply them in actual managerial situations. Fiedler's "situational engineering" and "leadership match" concepts are also useful alternatives to the more traditional advice and training based on earlier leadership theories.

## HOUSE'S PATH-GOAL THEORY

A second well-known approach to leadership contingencies is one developed by Robert House and based on the earlier work of others.[18] This approach has its roots in the expectancy model of motivation which we discussed in Chapter 4. The term "path-goal" is used because of its emphasis on how a leader influences subordinates' perceptions of work goals and personal goals, and the linkages or paths found between these two sets of goals.

The theory assumes that a leader's key function is to act in ways that complement the work setting in which subordinates operate.

**Table 16.2 Summary of Things Which Can Be Done to Change Situations**

**Modifying Leader-Member Relations**

1. Spend more—or less—informal time with your subordinates (e.g., lunch, leisure activities, etc.).
2. Organize some off-work group activities which include your subordinates (e.g., picnics, bowling, softball teams, excursions, etc.).
3. Request particular people for work in your group.
4. Volunteer to direct difficult or troublesome subordinates.
5. Suggest or effect transfers of particular subordinates into or out of your unit.
6. Raise morale by obtaining positive outcomes for subordinates (e.g., special bonuses, time off, attractive jobs).
7. Increase or decrease your availability to subordinates (e.g., open door policy, special gripe sessions, time available for personal consultation).

**Modifying Task Structure**

If you wish to work with a less structured task, you can:

1. Ask your boss, whenever possible, to give you the new or unusual problems and let you figure out how to get them done.
2. Bring the problems and tasks to your group members and invite them to work with you on the planning and decision-making phases of the task.
3. Where possible, leave the task in relatively vague form.

If you wish to work with a more highly structured task you can:

1. Ask your superior to give you whenever possible the tasks which are more structured or to give you more detailed instructions.
2. Learn all you can about the task so that you can prepare a detailed plan for performing the job, and get additional instruction and expert guidance if needed.
3. Break the job down into smaller subtasks which can be more highly structured.

**Modifying Position Power**

To raise your position power, you can:

1. Show your subordinates "who's boss" by exercising fully the powers which the organization provides.
2. Become, as quickly as possible, an expert on the job (e.g., through training).
3. Make sure that information to your group gets channeled through you.

To lower your position power, you can:

1. Try to be "one of the gang" by socializing, by playing down any trappings of power and rank the organization may have given you.
2. Call on members of your group to participate in planning and decision-making functions.
3. Let information from the organization reach all group members as quickly and directly as possible and permit group members easy access to your boss.
4. Let your assistants exercise relatively more power.

Source: Adapted from Fred E. Fiedler, Martin M. Chemers, and Linda Mahar, *Improving Leadership Effectiveness* (New York: John Wiley & Sons, Inc., 1976), pp. 154–158.

Suppose, for example, that a subordinate's job is ambiguous. The path-goal theory argues that the manager should try to offset this ambiguity by providing clarity and structure, unless other factors make this unnecessary. This might occur, for example, if the subordinate has a lot of job-related experience and expertise. In this case, or when jobs are well defined, clarifying behavior from the manager will be redundant.

House's theory argues that when the leader is able to compensate for things lacking in the setting, subordinates are likely to be satisfied with the leader. Performance should benefit as the paths by which effort leads to performance (expectancy) and performance leads to valued rewards (instrumentality) become clarified. Once again, though, redundant behavior by the leader won't help and may even hinder performance. Who needs a boss telling you how to do something that you already know how to do!

## Details of the Theory

The details of House's approach are summarized in Figure 16.5. Remember that this theory, like Fiedler's, is a contingency approach to leadership. The figure shows four different kinds of leader behavior

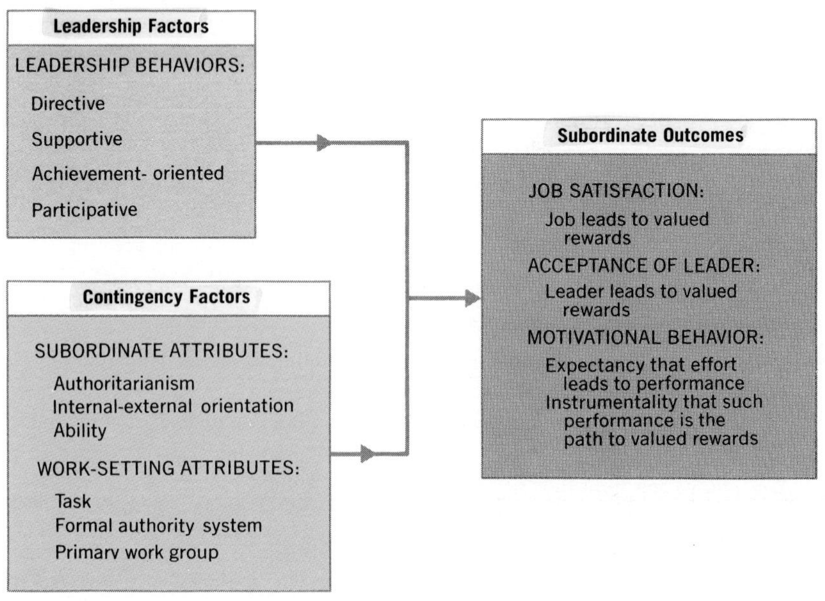


**FIGURE 16.5** Summary of major-path-goal relationships in House's path-goal leadership approach. (Source: Adapted from Richard N. Osborn, James G. Hunt, and Larry R. Jauch, *Organization Theory: An Integrated Approach*. New York: John Wiley & Sons, 1980, p. 464.)

and two categories of contingency variables. Together, the behaviors and contingencies influence the motivation for task performance and satisfaction of subordinates.

The four dimensions of leader behavior are directive, supportive, achievement-oriented, and participative. The true meaning of these dimensions as they would be reflected in actual leader behaviors is illustrated in Table 16.3. Note that these four dimensions include, but then go beyond, the task and relationship orientations used in Fiedler's work.

The contingency variables include subordinate attributes and the work setting. Important subordinate attributes are authoritarianism (close-mindedness, rigidity), external-internal orientation, and ability. The key work setting factors are the nature of the subordinates' tasks, the formal authority system, and the primary work group. The most well-researched issues deal with how clear-cut and repetitive tasks are, as compared with being ambiguous and nonrepetitive.

**Table 16.3 Leader Behavior Dimensions in House's Path-Goal Approach**

*Leader directiveness*

- Letting subordinates know what is expected.
- Providing specific guidance as to what should be done and how it should be done.
- Making his or her part in the group understood.
- Scheduling work to be done.
- Maintaining definite standards of performance.

*Leader supportiveness*

- Showing concern for the status, well-being, and needs of subordinates.
- Doing little things to make the work more pleasant.
- Treating members as equals.
- Being friendly and approachable.

*Leader achievement-orientedness*

- Setting challenging goals.
- Expecting subordinates to perform at their highest level.
- Continuously seeking improvement in performance *and* showing a high degree of confidence that subordinates will assume responsibility, put forth effort, and accomplish challenging goals.
- Constantly emphasizing excellence in performance and simultaneously displaying confidence that subordinates will meet high standards of excellence.

*Leader participativeness*

- Consulting with subordinates.
- Soliciting subordinate suggestions.
- Taking these suggestions seriously into consideration before making a decision.

Source: Adapted from Robert J. House and Terence R. Mitchell, "Path-goal Theory of Leadership," *Journal of Contemporary Business* (Autumn 1974), pp. 81–97.

## Predictions from the Theory[19]

Leader directiveness is predicted to have a positive relationship with subordinates' satisfactions, expectancies, and instrumentalities when the task is ambiguous, and to have just the opposite effect for clear tasks. When task demands are ambiguous and clarification does not come from elsewhere, leader directiveness is needed to compensate for the lack of structure. When clarification is otherwise available, directiveness is viewed as a hindrance by subordinates. In addition, the theory predicts that ambiguous tasks being performed by highly authoritarian and close-minded subordinates call for even more directive leadership than do ambiguous tasks alone.

Leader supportiveness is predicted to increase the satisfaction of subordinates who work on highly repetitive tasks or on tasks considered to be unpleasant, stressful, or frustrating. The leader's supportive behavior helps to compensate for these conditions.

Leader achievement-orientedness is predicted to cause subordinates to strive for higher performance standards and to have more confidence in their ability to meet challenging goals. For subordinates in ambiguous non-repetitive jobs, achievement-oriented leadership should increase subordinates' expectancies that effort will lead to desired performance.

Leader participativeness is predicted to promote satisfaction on non-repetitive tasks which allow for the ego-involvement of subordinates. On repetitive tasks, open-minded or non-authoritarian subordinates will be satisfied with a participative leader.

## The Research

The research so far supports the path-goal model in general and the above predictions in particular.[20] However, if you turn back to Figure 16.5, you will note some contingency variables that are not included in the above predictions—namely, subordinates' external-internal orientation and ability, and the nature of the work group. So far there is no evidence available concerning the place of these variables in the theory, but they do seem intuitively important. Why, for example, do you think ability might be important? (*Answer*: Because it can help provide task clarity.) What about the role of external-internal orientation? (*Answer*: Because those with high internal orientation, who feel in charge of their own destiny, should respond better to participation.) Furthermore, you learned in Part Three that there are many ways in which group variables can affect leader behavior and its outcomes. Thus, even though not all of the contingency variables have been tested, path-goal theory is a promising avenue of inquiry for the continued study of leadership.

## MANAGERIAL PERSPECTIVES ON THE CONTINGENCY THEORIES

As noted earlier, the contingency theories are receiving the predominant attention of leadership researchers as of this moment. This is important for the manager, since the contingency approaches offer a number of potentially useful managerial implications. First, the contingency theorists are telling you that there is no one best way to lead. The successful way to lead varies according to the situation. Second, to be successful as a leader, managers must (1) understand their personal style or behavior, (2) be able to diagnose situations, and (3) know how to modify the situations and/or their style to create a perfect leader-situation match.

Consider the three examples of successful leader-situation matching that follow.[21]

> *Foremen on the automobile assembly line* can allow their subordinates only the most limited opportunities for participation. Here the good foreman is the person who shows concern for the inevitable frustrations induced by the work process (consideration) as well as the person who is able to obtain adequate supplies and support for the workers (facilitation).
>
> *University deans* must allow broad opportunities for participation. If they fail to do this, their personal efforts to be considerate may be wasted or resented and largely irrelevant.
>
> *The symphony conductor* must be a close supervisor; there is little opportunity for independent decision making in a symphony orchestra (as opposed to a jazz combo). Technical competence and an ability to coordinate activities is what counts here. Concern with subordinates' feelings is a desirable plus, but it is essentially secondary—some of the best conductors have been unfeeling autocrats.

## HORIZONTAL LEADERSHIP

The previous contingency leadership theories deal with relations between a manager and his or her subordinates. They focus on **vertical leadership**—the use of power to influence persons within the range of the manager's formal authority. Figure 16.6, as well as our previous treatment of lateral relations and politics in Chapter 15, reminds you, however, that horizontal leadership is also of great

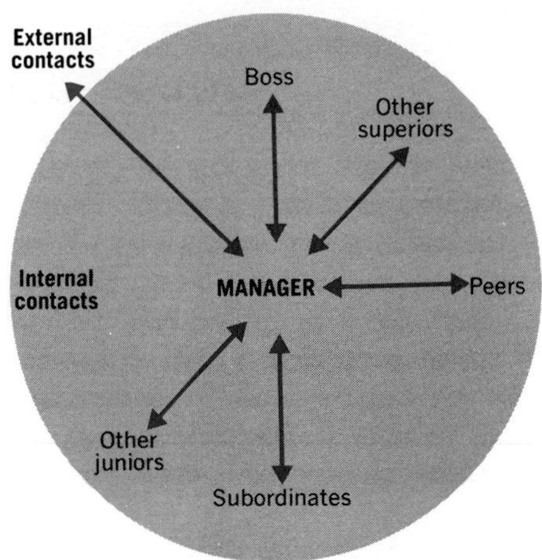


**FIGURE 16.6** The interpersonal relations of managers.

importance for managers. **Horizontal leadership** is the use of power to influence persons over which the manager has no formal authority. It includes the manager's involvement in lateral relations inside the organization and in external relations with outsiders.

## Leadership in Lateral and External Relations

Virtually all managers have to be successful in lateral relations within the organization. Some also have the added responsibility of maintaining external relations. Those that do so are called upon to act in a boundary-spanning capacity.[22]

An obvious boundary-spanner is the chief executive officer (CEO) of any organization. Although other roles such as personnel director, purchasing agent, strategic planner, sales manager, and public relations director develop similar responsibilities, the CEO is a classic example of a person who must be good at external leadership.

The CEO sets the stage for the environmental relations of his or her organization. The emphasis can range from ignoring external contacts to pursuing them very aggressively. Externally oriented CEOs get actively involved with persons from other important organizations. They try to influence these people in order to buffer their organization against outside pressures and take advantage of environmental opportunities.

## The Research

In spite of its importance, much less research has been done on horizontal leadership than on vertical leadership.[23] There is evidence, however, that the higher a leader's scores on the lateral or external relations dimensions, the better the performance and human resource maintenance of his or her work unit is likely to be.[24] One of the interesting things about these findings is that lateral relations were found to be more important for managers at higher levels in organizations. Further research is called for to examine more thoroughly horizontal leadership issues. A new generation leadership theory offers a first step in this direction.

## THE MULTIPLE-INFLUENCE LEADERSHIP THEORY

Current leadership approaches give primary emphasis to concerns inside the manager's own work unit. Our discussion of horizontal leadership, though, shows that such a view is too narrow to really meet the needs of managers in today's complex and dynamic organization.

As a manager you need to broaden your concerns to include the problems and opportunities that will exist outside as well as inside your work unit. The multiple-influence theory assumes that the organization's environment, its context for action (size and technology), and its structure, as well as conditions within the work unit, affect the manager's challenge. They do this in the first place by influencing the manager's behavior as a leader. In the second place they serve as contingencies which act in combination with leader behavior to affect work unit task performance and human resource maintenance.

### Background of the Theory

To understand the essence of the multiple-influence leadership theory, first think of the way in which a work unit is designed. It is set up to deal with expected or intended conditions. However, as we all know, actual day-to-day events frequently deviate from those originally anticipated. In other words, there is a gap between predicted and actual conditions. For example, as complexity in the organization's environment, context, and/or structure increases, the gap between predicted and actual conditions also increases. At the same time, the problems and opportunities facing the leader become greater. This puts the leader in a position that the other leadership approaches fail to consider in developing theories and action guidelines.

The multiple-influence theory recognizes the inevitability of this gap, and points out that it is the manager's job to act as a leader by stepping in to narrow the gap through appropriate behaviors. To the extent that he or she is successful in this regard, there will be greater task performance and human resource maintenance in the work unit. The intent of the multiple-influence theory is to prepare managers to act in this expanded leadership capacity. Figuratively speaking, the theory recognizes that

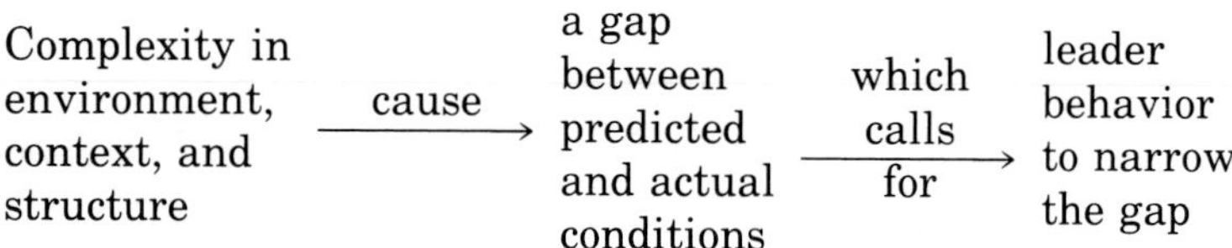


## Details of the Theory

The details of the multiple-influence leadership approach are summarized in Figure 16.7. As shown by the shaded areas in the figure, the theory moves beyond other approaches to include the organization's environment, context, and structure as variables impacting on the leader's behavior. Another modification is the classification of leader behavior into required and discretionary components. Let's begin our look at the theory's details with these two aspects of leader behavior, and then return to examine complexity in the organization's environment, context, and structure.

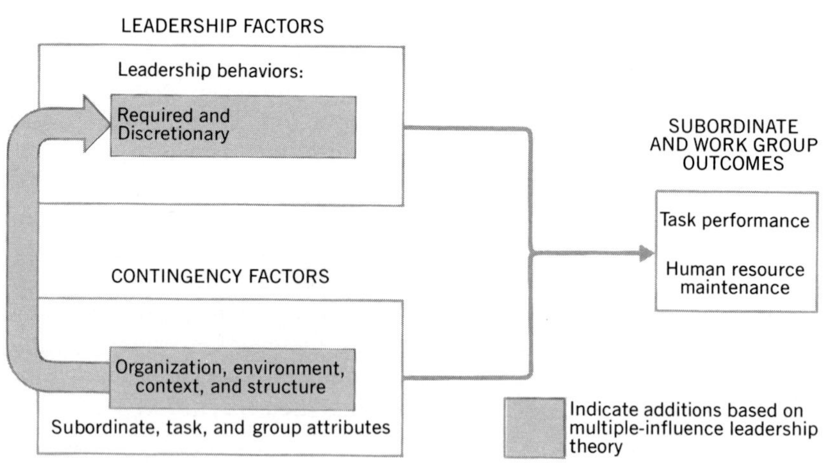


**FIGURE 16-7** The multiple-influence leadership approach compared with other contingency leadership approaches.

## Required and Discretionary Leadership

You can think of one aspect of a manager's job as involving required duties that would be expected of anyone who holds the position. These duties are prescribed through the design of the organization as formal role requirements. **Required leadership** is the use of power to accomplish duties that must be performed by any leader in a position of formal managerial authority. We can represent this schematically as

$$\text{Organizational design} \xrightarrow[\text{forth}]{\text{calls}} \text{required leadership}$$

The required aspects of a managerial position involve both vertical and horizontal leadership. The manager links the work unit to the total organization. Managers pass communications up and down the hierarchy. For instance, many organizations require quarterly reports on activity, including the volume of and quality of output, as well as changes in personnel, manpower plans, job estimates, and budgeting are often parts of the leader's job requirements. The leader also communicates the desires of higher management to the work group through scheduling, job assignments, performance reviews, and group meetings. He or she may also be asked to represent the group in discussions with others, such as in conferences with members of staff units. The leader is the formal representative of his or her work unit both in the vertical hierarchy and in horizontal relationships with other staff and line units in the organization.

A manager successful in required leadership may achieve satisfactory task performance and human resource maintenance. But both higher management and subordinates typically expect more. They want discretionary leadership as well. **Discretionary leadership** involves the use of power in influence attempts over and above those required by the position. It can make the difference between satisfactory and extraordinary job performance for a manager.

What kinds of actions above and beyond requirements can the leader take? We have argued that a manager's job is both vertical and horizontal in its leadership demands. Discretionary leadership applies to both, as shown in Table 16.4. The table shows three vertical leadership roles for the leader, matched by three horizontal roles. Vertically, he or she may act to more carefully manage rewards, reduce uncertainty by providing direction, and strengthen inter-unit linkages through network development. Horizontally, the leader may establish a more favorable climate for the unit by more carefully managing the rewards given to other units. He or she may also resolve uncertainty facing the unit by pressuring other managers for

**Table 16.4 Corresponding Vertical and Horizontal Dimensions of Discretionary Leadership**

| Vertical Leadership | Horizontal Leadership |
|---|---|
| *Reward management*<br>Altering and interpreting intrinsic rewards. More carefully targeting extrinsic rewards. Example behaviors: consideration, supportiveness, orientation toward achievement. | *Reward management*<br>Rewarding other units by adjusting actions of his or her unit to those of others. Leader's willingness to adapt to pressures. |
| *Uncertainty reduction*<br>Interpreting the relationship between current conditions and desired outcomes. Example behaviors: initiating structure, directiveness. | *Uncertainty reduction*<br>Reducing uncertainty by pressuring other unit heads to provide a more predictable flow of resources to the leader's unit. |
| *Network development*<br>Linking individuals to the group (team building, group member participation). Linking the unit to the organization (upward influence). | *Network development*<br>Establishing linkages to other units to broaden and deepen organizational connections. |

action. Here the leader makes agreements with others so that the flow of resources, information, and inputs to his or her unit is more predictable. Finally, he or she may develop a broader and deeper network of ties with managers in other line and staff units.

## Complexity in the Environment, Context, and Structure

We introduced the notions of environmental, contextual, and structural complexity in Part Four. Now complexity becomes a contingency variable in the multiple-influence theory. Briefly, the major contingencies as they relate to the theory are outlined below.

**Environmental Complexity** Environmental complexity is an overall indicator of the conditions outside the unit. Here a manager needs to assess the amount of resources held by others (the more the better), the reliance of the group on others (the less the better), and the extent to which he or she can predict the actions of others (the more the better). A more complex environment is one where there are plenty of resources but where a manager's unit is heavily dependent on other units which are themselves changing.

For instance, picture yourself as the head of a line unit that is in the midst of a reorganization. Now your unit will be in direct contact with a new staff V.P. in company headquarters. No one is quite sure how your unit should be treated (uncertainty), but resources for growth are available (richness) and the new staff V.P. will tightly monitor the unit's activities and resources (high interdependence). Both you and your boss see new demands, some problems, and quite a few opportunities for growth.

**Contextual Complexity** The context for action also needs to be assessed. Again, you can start with an overall estimate of complexity. The context is more complex when your unit is larger, uses a more sophisticated technology, and produces more varied products and services than others.

**Structural Complexity** Finally, the theory asks you to assess the structure of the unit, particularly in comparison to others like yours. Look for subtle differences such as the addition of a staff assistant or an expansion of duties by subordinates (horizontal specialization). Vertically, check the number of levels in the hierarchy. Then analyze the coordination and control mechanisms.

## Predictions, Research, and Implications

Although there are many specific propositions in the theory, the core prediction is that as complexity (from environment, context, or structure) increases, a response in discretionary leadership is called for. Success in this response will enhance task performance and human resource maintenance; a poor response, or none at all, will impair these outcomes. Potential responses would include activities detailed in Table 16.4, involving reward management, uncertainty reduction, or network development.

This is a new theory that so far has been tested only once. Results of that test provided considerable support for the general logic of the theory as represented in the above prediction.[25] The theory provides a simple general guideline for the leader. He or she should complement environmental, contextual, and structural complexity with discretionary leadership. When the action setting becomes more complex, the work unit is being asked to operate at the outer limits of its design specifications. Like an airplane in a dive, the unit experiences stresses and strains. Required leadership is insufficient. The leader must step in to provide rewards, build linkages, and resolve uncertainties that the organizational design leaves unattended. In other words, the leader acts to fill the gap between intended and actual conditions. Through appropriate discretionary behavior he or she can seize upon opportunities and solve specific problems which meet the demands placed upon the work unit as a whole.

The fact that the multiple-influence approach considers factors outside of the work unit as variables affecting leadership behavior and outcomes has some important implications. Traditional theory recommends training to solve leadership problems. This often takes the form of trying to change a manager's behavior. For instance, training might be devoted to making a task-oriented manager more considerate. Fiedler's theory argues in favor of training leaders to diagnose a situation and orchestrate an appropriate leader-situation match. The multiple-influence theory offers the opportunity to broaden this diagnosis and matching process to include an analysis of environmental, contextual, and structural variables and the utilization of discretionary as well as required leadership behaviors.

## SUMMARY

We started this chapter by defining leadership as the process of using power to obtain interpersonal influence. We also differentiated between leadership and managerial behavior and between formal and informal leadership. The history of leadership research has been traced, from an early emphasis on traits and leader behaviors, to the current interest in contingency theories. The latter are most useful for their attempt to identify situational variables that affect which "style" or set of behaviors will result in leadership success.

Two contingency approaches have been discussed in detail. These are Fiedler's situational theory and House's path-goal theory. Our step-by-step application of Fiedler's theory has been designed to help you to become familiar with situational diagnosis as a managerial skill. House's theory has been linked to expectancy motivational theory, of which it is a cousin.

We then discussed ways in which both the Fiedler and House approaches might be applied by a manager. Through study and training, the concerned manager can learn how to change situations in a way that increases their favorability to the leader. House argues, and Fiedler disagrees, that managers can also benefit by learning to change their behaviors to fit the challenges of the situation. Resolution of this controversy lingers as a continuing challenge to OB researchers.

We extended our discussion by arguing that contingency theories, as useful as they are, fail to recognize the lateral relations in which managers engage. Nor do they emphasize the environment, technology, and structure facing a manager. The multiple-influence model of leadership recognizes all of these as an important part of the manager's challenge. It treats both vertical and horizontal leadership, and separates these into required and discretionary aspects. Discretionary leadership is potentially quite important because of its emphasis on influence attempts beyond those required in the leader's role.

## THINKING THROUGH THE ISSUES

1. Describe how leadership is related to the broader concepts of power and influence treated in Chapter 15.
2. Think of a work situation and describe at least one instance of informal leadership.
3. Based on your understanding of earlier chapters, describe the difference between traits and behaviors. Based on these differences, which might managers be more interested in?
4. Explain how contingency leadership theories differ from leader behavior theories.
5. Give examples of managerial jobs requiring differing combinations of vertical and horizontal leadership skills. Use Figure 16.3 to guide your thinking.
6. Define leadership in lateral relations as it differs from leadership in external relations. Which form of horizontal leadership is most likely to dominate a manager's concerns in the early stages of his or her career? Why?
7. Show by diagram how the multiple-influence leadership theory moves beyond the existing contingency theories.
8. Explain the concepts of required and discretionary leadership. Give examples of how they apply to a managerial situation with which you are familiar.

## EXERCISE: APPLYING CONTINGENCY LEADERSHIP[26]

### Purpose:

To develop your skill in applying a contingency approach to a real leadership situation.

### Time:

50 minutes in class, plus at-home preparations.

## Procedure:

1. Do the following before coming to class:
   - **a.** Make sure you have reviewed the discussion of Fiedler's model and completed and scored the LPC questionnaire in Figure 16.2.
   - **b.** Think of a current or recent assignment in which you are functioning or have functioned as a leader. It can be a paid or unpaid position (such as a student organization committee, or the like).
   - **c.** For that assignment, complete and score the Leader-Member Relations Scale that follows.
   - **d.** Do the same for Parts 1 and 2 of the Task Structure Scale that follows.
   - **e.** Do the same for the Position Power Rating Scale that follows.
   - **f.** Complete the Situational Control Summary that follows.

2. Form groups as assigned by your instructor (at least four persons per group).

3. Share and discuss your Situational Control Summaries and LPC scores one at a time.

4. Develop a summary of each individual's case example and its implications in terms of the type of leadership style needed.

5. Have a spokesperson prepared to report to the class on the summary in (4) in terms of:
   - **a.** Differences and similarities in the situational control found in each case.
   - **b.** How well each person's LPC scores seem to agree with that person's intuitive feelings about his or her leadership style.
   - **c.** The degree of match or mismatch between leadership style and situational control in the cases of group members.
   - **d.** Some steps that might be taken to address any mismatches in the various cases.

6. Reconvene as a total class to discuss results and examine the implications of the exercise.

### LEADER-MEMBER RELATIONS SCALE

| *Circle the number which best represents your response to each item.* | Strongly agree | Agree | Neither agree nor disagree | Disagree | Strongly disagree |
|---|---|---|---|---|---|
| 1. The people I supervise have trouble getting along with each other. | 1 | 2 | 3 | 4 | 5 |
| 2. My subordinates are reliable and trustworthy. | 5 | 4 | 3 | 2 | 1 |
| 3. There seems to be a friendly atmosphere among the people I supervise. | 5 | 4 | 3 | 2 | 1 |
| 4. My subordinates always cooperate with me in getting the job done. | 5 | 4 | 3 | 2 | 1 |
| 5. There is friction between my subordinates and myself. | 1 | 2 | 3 | 4 | 5 |
| 6. My subordinates give me a good deal of help and support in getting the job done. | 5 | 4 | 3 | 2 | 1 |
| 7. The people I supervise work well together in getting the job done. | 5 | 4 | 3 | 2 | 1 |
| 8. I have good relations with the people I supervise. | 5 | 4 | 3 | 2 | 1 |
| Total Score | ☐ | | | | |

## Scoring

Simply add the circled numbers for each item above and write in the total. The highest possible score is 40. A score of 25 or above indicates good leader-member relations, a score of 20–25 indicates moderate leader-member relations, and a score below 20 indicates poor leader-member relations.

## TASK STRUCTURE RATING SCALE—PART 1

| *Circle the number in the appropriate column.* | Usually true | Sometimes true | Seldom true |
|---|---|---|---|
| Is the goal clearly stated or known? | | | |
| 1. Is there a blueprint, picture, model, or detailed description available of the finished product or service? | 2 | 1 | 0 |
| 2. Is there a person available to advise and give a description of the finished product or service, or how the job should be done? | 2 | 1 | 0 |
| Is there only one way to accomplish the task? | | | |
| 3. Is there a step-by-step procedure, or a standard operating procedure which indicates in detail the process which is to be followed? | 2 | 1 | 0 |
| 4. Is there a specific way to subdivide the task into separate parts or steps? | 2 | 1 | 0 |
| 5. Are there some ways which are clearly recognized as better than others for performing this task? | 2 | 1 | 0 |
| Is there only one correct answer or solution? | | | |
| 6. Is it obvious when the task is finished and the correct solution has been found? | 2 | 1 | 0 |
| 7. Is there a book, manual, or job description which indicates the best solution or the best outcome for the task? | 2 | 1 | 0 |
| Is it easy to check whether the job was done right? | | | |
| 8. Is there a generally agreed understanding about the standards the particular product or service has to meet to be considered acceptable? | 2 | 1 | 0 |
| 9. Is the evaluation of this task generally made on some quantitative basis? | 2 | 1 | 0 |
| 10. Can the leader and the group find out how well the task has been accomplished in enough time to improve future performance? | 2 | 1 | 0 |

Total Score ☐

### TASK STRUCTURE RATING SCALE—PART 2
### *Training and Experience Adjustment*

(a) Compared to others in this or similar positions, how much *training* has the leader had?

| 3 | 2 | 1 | 0 |
|---|---|---|---|
| No training at all | Very little training | A moderate amount of training | A great deal of training |

(b) Compared to others in this or similar positions, how much *experience* has the leader had?

| 6 | 4 | 2 | 0 |
|---|---|---|---|
| No experience at all | Very little experience | A moderate amount of experience | A great deal of experience |

Add lines (a) and (b) of the training and experience adjustment, then *subtract* this from the subtotal given in Part 1. NOTE: Do not adjust jobs with Part 1 task structure scores of 6 or below.

Subtotal from Part 1 ☐

Subtract training and experience adjustment ☐

Total Task Structure Score ☐

## Scoring

Simply add the circled numbers for each item in Part 1 and write in the subtotal. Then subtract the training and experience adjustment (if any) from Part 2 to provide a total task structure score. The total possible score is 20, half as much as the leader-member relations scale. A score of 14 or above is high in task structure, a score of 7–13 is medium in structure, and a score below 7 is low in structure.

**POSITION POWER RATING SCALE**

*Circle the number which best represents your answer.*

1. Can the leader directly or by recommendation administer rewards and punishments to his subordinates?

| 2 | 1 | 0 |
|---|---|---|
| Can act directly or can recommend with high effectiveness | Can recommend but with mixed results | No |

2. Can the leader directly or by recommendation affect the promotion, demotion, hiring, or firing of his subordinates?

| 2 | 1 | 0 |
|---|---|---|
| Can act directly or can recommend with high effectiveness | Can recommend but with mixed results | No |

3. Does the leader have the knowledge necessary to assign tasks to subordinates and instruct them in task completion?

| 2 | 1 | 0 |
|---|---|---|
| Yes | Sometimes or in some aspects | No |

4. Is it the leader's job to evaluate the performance of his subordinates?

| 2 | 1 | 0 |
|---|---|---|
| Yes | Sometimes or in some aspects | No |

5. Has the leader been given some official title of authority by the organization (e.g., foreman, department head, platoon leader)?

| 2 | 0 |
|---|---|
| Yes | No |

Total Score ☐

## Scoring

Simply add the circled numbers for each item above and write in the total, which can range from 0 to 10, half as much as the task structure score. A score of 7–10 indicates high position power, 4–6 indicates moderate position power, and 3 or below indicates low position power.

**SITUATIONAL CONTROL SUMMARY**

*Write in below your score for each of the diagnostic instruments.*

| | | |
|---|---|---|
| LPC score | | ____ |
| Leader-member relations total | ____ | |
| Task structure total | ____ | |
| Position power total | ____ | |
| Grand total for leader-member relations, task structure, and position power | | ____ |

## Scoring

If your total score is from 10–30, you have described a low-control situation calling for a task-motivated (LPC score of 57 and below) leadership style. If it is from 31–50, you have described a moderate-control situation calling for a relationship-motivated (64 and above) style. If your score is from 51–70, you have described a high-control situation which again calls for a task-motivated style of leadership.

# THE MANAGER'S VOCABULARY

**Contingency Leadership Approach** Posits that the relationship between leadership and the task performance and human resource maintenance of followers depends upon selected contingency variables.

**Discretionary Leadership** The use of power in influence attempts over and above those required by the managerial position.

**Formal Leadership** Persons exercising influence from a position of formal authority in an organization.

**Horizontal Leadership** The use of power to influence persons over whom the manager has no formal authority.

**Informal Leaders** Persons who emerge as influential because of special skills or resources which they have to meet the needs of the work unit and/or its members.

**Leadership** The process of using power to obtain interpersonal influence.

**Required Leadership** The use of power to accomplish duties which must be performed by anyone in the managerial position.

**Situational Control** The extent to which leaders can determine what their group is going to do and what the outcomes of their actions and decisions are going to be.

**Vertical Leadership** The use of power to influence persons over whom the manager has formal authority.

## Important Names

**Fred Fiedler** Developed a situational theory of leadership effectiveness.

**Robert House** Developed a path-goal theory of leadership effectiveness.

## Notes

[1] Summarized from Jerry Kramer, "Death by Inches," *Sports Illustrated* (August 4, 1969), pp. 31–34.

[2] This definition is consistent with the treatment of William M. Fox, "An Analysis of Military Leadership in a Realistic Field Setting," ONR Technical Report 70-6, 70-7. Organizational Effectiveness Research Programs, Office of Naval Research, Code 452, Arlington, Va., 1974; and Carroll and Tosi, op. cit., p. 215.

[3] D. Katz and R. L. Kahn, "Human Organization and Worker Motivation," in L. R. Tripp (ed.), *Industrial Productivity* (Madison, Wis.: Industrial Relations Research Association, 1952).

[4] Lars L. Larson and Arnold E. Allen, "The Relationships of Formal and Peer Leadership to Job Satisfaction," in Andrew F. Sikula and Raymond L. Hilgert (eds.), *Proceedings of the Nineteenth Annual Midwest Academy of Management Conference* (St. Louis, Mo.: Washington University, 1975).

[5] Ralph M. Stogdill, *Handbook of Leadership* (New York: Free Press, 1974). Strictly speaking, some of these studies were not of formal leaders, since the studies tried to find traits separating leaders from non-leaders. However, this makes no difference in the conclusions.

[6] Stogdill, op. cit.

[7] Ralph M. Stogdill, "Personal Factors Associated with Leadership: A Survey of the Literature," *Journal of Psychology,* Vol. 25 (1948), pp. 35–71.

[8] Rensis Likert, *New Patterns of Management* (New York: McGraw-Hill, 1961).

[9] Stogdill, 1974, op. cit., Chapter 11.

[10] Robert F. Bales, "Task Roles and Social Roles in Problem-Solving Groups," in Eleanor E. Maccoby, Theodore M. Newcomb, and E. L. Hartley (eds.), *Readings in Social Psychology* (New York: Holt, Rinehart and Winston, 1958).

[11] Likert, op. cit.

[12] Lars L. Larson, James G. Hunt, and Richard N. Osborn, "The Great Hi-hi Leader Behavior Myth: A Lesson from Occam's Razor," *Academy of Management Journal,* Vol. 19 (1976), pp. 628–641.

[13] David B. Guralnik, *Webster's New World Dictionary,* Second Edition (New York: The World Publishing Company, 1970), p. 307.

[14] The discussion in this section is based on Fred E. Fiedler, Martin M. Chemers, and Linda Mahar, *The Leadership Match Concept* (Newark: John Wiley & Sons, 1978).

[15] Fiedler et al., op. cit., pp. 6–8.

[16] Chester Schriesheim and Steven Kerr, "Theories and Measures of Leadership: A critical Appraisal of Current and Future Directions," in James G. Hunt and Lars L. Larson (eds.), *Leadership: The Cutting Edge* (Carbondale, Ill.: Southern Illinois University Press, 1977), and Michael J. Strube and Joseph E. Garcia, *A Meta-Analytic Investigation of Fiedler's Contingency Model of Leadership Effectiveness,* unpublished manuscript, Department of Psychology, University of Utah, 1980.

[17] Schriesheim and Kerr, op. cit.

[18] Robert J. House, "A Path-goal Theory of Leader Effectiveness," *Administrative Sciences Quarterly,* Vol. 16 (1971), pp. 321–338; Martin G. Evans, "The Effects of Supervisory Behavior on the Path-goal Relationship," *Organizational Behavior and Human Performance,* Vol. 5 (1970), pp. 277–298.

[19] Robert J. House and Terrence R. Mitchell, "Path-goal Theory of Leadership," *Journal of Contemporary Business* (Autumn, 1977), pp. 81–97.

[20] House and Mitchell, op. cit.

[21] J. Richard Hackman and J. Lloyd Suttle, *Improving Life at Work: Behavioral Science Approaches to Organizational Change* (Santa Monica, Calif.: Goodyear Publishing Company, 1977).

[22] For a good review of the recent research on boundary spanning see Howard Aldrich and Diane Herker, "Boundary Spanning Roles and Organization Structure," *Academy of Management Review,* Vol. 2 (1977), pp. 217–230; and J. Stacy Adams, "The Structure and Dynamics of Behavior in Organization Boundary Roles," pp. 1175–1199 in M. D. Dunnette (ed.), *The Handbook of Industrial and Organizational Psychology* (Chicago: Rand-McNally, 1976).

[23] Richard N. Osborn, James G. Hunt, and Lawrence R. Jauch, *Organization Theory: An Integrated Approach* (New York: John Wiley & Sons, 1980), pp. 453–454.

[24] Osborn et al., op. cit.

[25] James G. Hunt, Richard N. Osborn, and Harry M. Martin, *A Multiple Influence Model of Leadership* (Alexandria, Va.: Army Research Institute, 1981).

[26] The scales are from Fiedler et al., op. cit., pp. 39, 53, 69, 77, 92 (New York: John Wiley & Sons, Inc., 1976).

# PART SIX

## CONCLUSION

### THE MANAGER'S GOAL

**To Establish and Maintain a Productive and Personally Satisfying Managerial Career.**

### YOUR LEARNING OBJECTIVE

**To Summarize the Managerial Implications of OB as a Knowledge Base; and to Explore Career Planning as a Means of Helping Achieve Continuing Success as a Manager.**

## Chapter in This Part of the Book

**CHAPTER 17**
**Managerial Futures, OB, and You**

This is the final part of the book. It is written to help bring closure to your introductory study of OB. It is also written to stimulate you to think about your future career as a manager. We want you to look ahead and ask "Where do I go from here?" and, "How can this knowledge of OB help me along the way?" The following case and Chapter 17 will help you consider appropriate answers to each question.

# Career Planning Contrasts Case[1]

Harlan Cleveland is a successful executive. He views career planning for managers in the following perspective.

> A career as an executive is not something you plan for yourself. It's a series of accidental changes of job and shifts of scenery on which you look back later, weaving through the story retroactively some thread of logic that was not visible at the time.
>
> If you try too carefully to plan your life, the danger is that you will succeed—succeed in narrowing your options and closing off avenues of adventure that cannot now be imagined, perhaps because they are not yet technologically possible. When a student asks me for career advice, I can only suggest that he or she opt for the most exciting "next step" without worrying where it will lead, and then work hard on the job in hand, not pine for the one in the bush. When your job no longer demands of you more than you have, go and do something else. Always take by preference the job you *don't* know how to do.

William O. Grabe is also a successful executive. Some of his views on career planning follow.

> . . . an aspiring executive should not make the personal investment in a career without some basic planning. Career planning is more art than science and highly individualized. Nonetheless, some form of plan can greatly enhance the evaluation of various opportunities and enable you as a manager to make better career decisions. A career plan allows you to identify how to use your basic strengths to maximum advantage, set major career objectives, and establish immediate milestones to measure personal development and advancement. . . .
>
> A fundamental requirement of successful career planning is self-awareness—the ability to bring out your own best effort. The path to the top can be hard. So you as a manager should assess your physical and mental strengths and your willingness to concentrate on the fulfillment of your career plan.

## QUESTION

Which approach to career planning do you favor—Cleveland's or Grabe's? Why?

## Our Viewpoint

Cleveland and Grabe have very contrasting perspectives on career planning. While Cleveland suggests one should let his or her career develop in a random and opportunistic way, Grabe sees a career as something to be programmed and planned very rationally. Interestingly enough, each man seems to have found executive success in his own way.

It may be best not to see the two points of view as "either-or" alternatives. In fact, each of us may end up doing some of what each suggests. A well thought out plan can point you in a general career direction; an eye for opportunity can fill in the details along the way.

The essence of any successful career, no matter how well planned, is for a person to be good at his or her work. It is through a record of accomplishment that the potential to advance arises. Thus, we refer you back once again to the study of OB. First and foremost, it is intended to help you become good at being a manager.

## SUMMARY

There is only one chapter in this final part of the book. The title speaks for itself—Managerial Futures, OB, and You. The ideas contained in this chapter will help you to summarize and integrate your thinking about OB. They also offer opportunities for you to further examine some of the problems and prospects of planning for a managerial career.

### Note

[1]These viewpoints are found in the *Advanced Management Journal* (Summer 1975).

# 17

# MANAGERIAL FUTURES, OB, AND YOU

# LOOKING FOR LONGER HORIZONS

No one has held the title of CEO of a U.S. firm longer than J. Peter Grace. Since 1945, he has headed the $5 billion-a-year conglomerate of W.R. Grace founded by his grandfather. J.P.G. has completely revamped the firm. He took it out of Latin American shipping, airlines, and banking and entered the firm into retailing, chemicals, and restaurants, mostly in the U.S. and Western Europe. He is 66 and he will not slow down or let go. What drives Peter Grace? What is this most senior U.S. executive really thinking?[1]

I work almost all the time. We have 78,000 employees and 80,000 shareholders and thousands of pensioners, and I feel a tremendous responsibility to all of them. We made a mistake in Ireland a couple of years ago by not keeping in touch with a company that we had over there. We threw 175 people out of work in a small town. You do that once, and see how you feel. That's the sort of thing that haunts me. Therefore, I can't stand not paying attention.

Like tonight. I'll leave the office, be driven from Manhattan to Long Island, dictate to a secretary all the way out, have dinner with my wife for 90 minutes at the yacht club, then work all the way back to Manhattan, go to my apartment, and work over sales charts and company books until 1 A.M. Tomorrow, I'll be back in the office at 7:50 in the morning and go into a budget meeting at 8:20. I give 8% of my time to charity. I work with Cardinal Cooke; I raised about $300,000 last year for Father Bruce Ritter who takes the kids off the streets in Times Square, and I'm treasurer of the National Jewish Hospital in Denver. . . . What do I do for fun? Work is my fun. I love it. I'm not recommending it. I just feel that it is my obligation.

**MANAGEMENT APPLICATIONS QUESTION**

Clearly, Peter Grace is one of a select few who make it to the top of a major corporation. He does, however, indicate that this accomplishment is not without its price. What do you expect in a managerial career and how can a knowledge of OB help you to succeed?

## PLANNING AHEAD

**The reading and learning activities provided in this final chapter will help you to review and synthesize your thinking around the following topics:**

**Managerial Skills: A Recap**
**OB: The Manager's Knowledge Base**
**Career Planning and Development**
**Final Advice**

OB is a knowledge base used by managers to effectively utilize individuals and groups as the human resources of organizations. When this goal is achieved, the manager can feel satisfied with a job well done. We think the many previous topics and learning experiences offered in this book will help you become a fine manager. Now it is time to pull things together and point you in the direction of this exciting future!

## MANAGERIAL SKILLS: A RECAP

Throughout this book we have been talking about managers, people to whom one or more other persons report in organizations. We have highlighted the importance of managers being able to work with subordinates, individually and in groups, to encourage high levels of task performance and provide for human resource maintenance. We have also emphasized the importance of understanding organizations and their design. In the last chapter we reminded you, too, that managers must be able to work with and influence persons in and outside of the organization over whom they have no formal authority. We called this horizontal leadership and differentiated it from vertical leadership, which links managers with their subordinates.

Shown in Figure 17.1 are some of the various vertical and horizontal capacities in which managers act. Listed below are insights into the nature of the demands associated with each of these action roles.[2]

### Interpersonal Roles

| | |
|---|---|
| Figurehead | To attend ceremonies and represent the organization/work unit to external constituencies. |

**FIGURE 17.1** The manager's roles. (Source: Chart on p. 59 in *The Nature of Managerial Work* by Henry Mintzberg. Copyright © 1973 by Henry Mintzberg. Reprinted by permission of Harper & Row Publishers, Inc.)

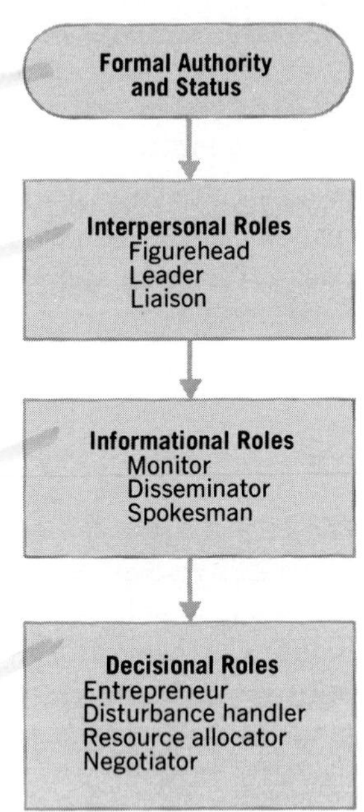


| | |
|---|---|
| Leader | To motivate subordinates and integrate the needs of subordinates and the needs of the organization/work unit. |
| Liaison | To develop and maintain contacts with outsiders to gain benefits for the organization/work unit. |
| **Informational Roles** | |
| Monitor | To seek and receive information (mail, reports, observations, reading, etc.) of relevance to the organization/work unit. |
| Disseminator | To transmit to organization members information relevant to the organization/work unit. |
| Spokesperson | To transmit to outsiders information relevant to the organization/work unit. |
| **Decisional Roles** | |
| Entrepreneur | To seek problems and opportunities and to initiate action in the best interests of the organization/work unit. |
| Disturbance handler | To resolve conflicts among persons within the organization/work unit or between |

| | |
|---|---|
| | the organization/work unit and external parties. |
| Resource allocator | To make choices allocating resources within the organization/work unit. |
| Negotiator | To represent the organization/work unit in formal negotiations with third parties such as union officials or government regulators. |

Checkpoint

Table 17.1 recreates the very first table presented in this book—"Some 'Teachable' Managerial Skills." Look at this set of skills once again, think carefully about the above managerial roles, and record your degree of mastery over the various skills.

We hope you feel more confident about these managerial skills now than you did back in Chapter 1. Hopefully, too, you also recognize that OB is a knowledge base that helps managers master such skills and maintain high levels of competency in all aspects of the managerial role.

**Table 17.1 Some "Teachable" Managerial Skills**

| | Mastery? | |
|---|---|---|
| | Yes | No |
| *Interpersonal relations*—Ability to enter into and maintain effective peer relationships with other persons in the work setting. | ___ | ___ |
| *Leadership*—Ability to deal with subordinates, to motivate and train, to help, and to deal with authority and dependency problems. | ___ | ___ |
| *Conflict-resolution*—Ability to mediate between conflicting parties, resolve disturbances, and negotiate differences with others. | ___ | ___ |
| *Information-processing*—Ability to collect information, organize information for decision-making purposes, and disseminate information. | ___ | ___ |
| *Decision-Making*—Ability to know when a decision is needed, diagnose situation, plan an approach, search for solutions, evaluate potential consequences, and select an alternative. | ___ | ___ |
| *Resource-allocation*—Ability to distribute physical, financial, human, and personal resources among competing demands. | ___ | ___ |
| *Entrepreneurism*—Ability to recognize problems, implement solutions, and take advantage of opportunities for constructive change. | ___ | ___ |
| *Introspection*—Ability to understand one's job and staff and to learn through self-study and awareness. | ___ | ___ |

Source: Developed from discussions by Henry Mintzberg, *The Nature of Managerial Work* (New York: Harper & Row, 1973), pp. 188–193; and Robert L. Katz, "Skills of an Effective Administrator," *Harvard Business Review,* Vol. 42 (September–December 1974), pp. 90–102.

## OB: THE MANAGER'S KNOWLEDGE BASE

Figure 17.2 reviews the basic elements in the study of OB: individuals, groups, organizations, and managerial processes. Each topic listed in the diagram is covered by a chapter in this book. It is through a knowledge of these topics that managers can develop their skills and become successful in meeting the basic managerial challenge. Remember,

$$\text{OB is a knowledge base} \xrightarrow[\text{by}]{\text{used}} \text{managers} \xrightarrow[\text{achieve}]{\text{to}} \text{good human resource utilization}$$

Let's briefly review the discussions we've had on these OB topics.

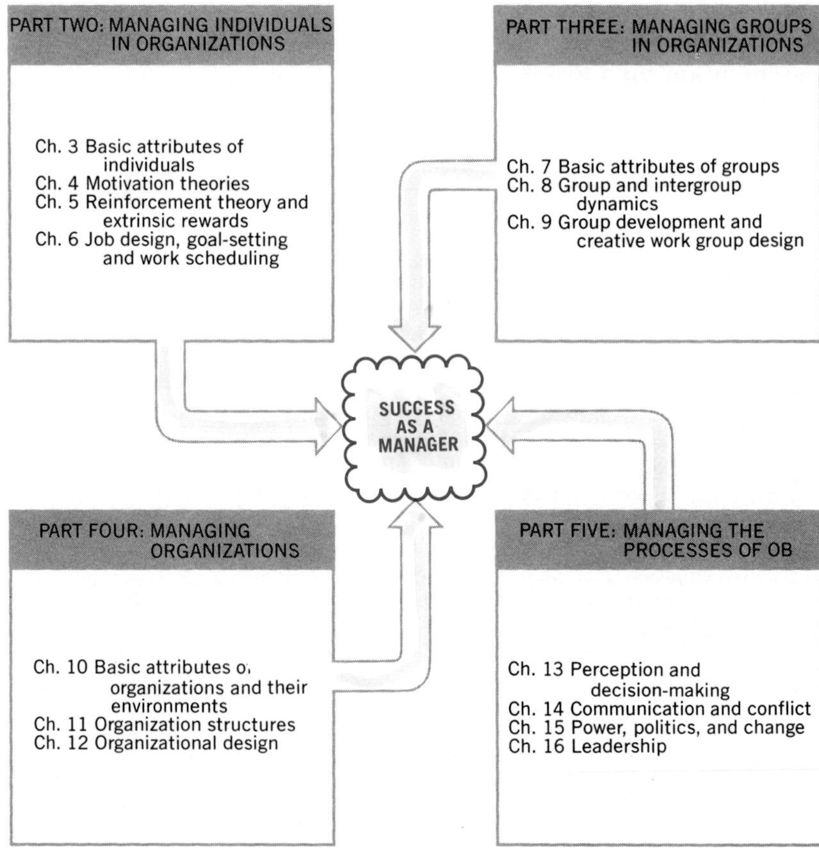


**FIGURE 17.2** The major elements in the study of OB.

## Introduction

Our introduction to OB in Part One began with an initial look in Chapters 1 and 2 at managers, organizations, and people at work. We explored the nature and meaning of work for individuals, and used the psychological contract to emphasize the importance of a balance between the work contributions of people and the inducements they receive from the organization. Task performance and human resource maintenance were then introduced as key results sought by managers. After detailed consideration of the "job satisfaction-performance controversy," it became obvious that the statement "satisfied workers are productive workers" is an oversimplification. At the very least, managers must strive to create both satisfaction and performance.

## Managing Individuals in Organizations

Part Two of the book provides a knowledge of individuals. Chapter 3 presented the individual performance equation and noted how differences in individual attributes combine with effort and organizational support to influence task performance and human resource maintenance. The individual performance equation looked like this.

$$\text{Performance} = \begin{array}{c}\text{individual}\\ \text{attributes}\end{array} \times \begin{array}{c}\text{work}\\ \text{effort}\end{array} \times \begin{array}{c}\text{organizational}\\ \text{support}\end{array}$$

The next three chapters concentrated on various motivation theories and the management of rewards, reinforcements and job designs. These topics contain insights that can help managers derive maximum work efforts from subordinates and to provide them with personally satisfying work settings.

## Managing Groups in Organizations

Part Three showed that another important part of OB as a knowledge base is the study of groups. Chapter 7 discussed the major types of groups in organizations and presented a model of group behavior. Chapter 8 went on to discuss the major dimensions of group dynamics including norms, cohesion, membership roles and intergroup relations. Finally, Chapter 9 showed how these concepts could be applied in group development and creative work group design to help meet the challenges of managing groups at work.

## Managing Organizations

Part Four of the book focused on a knowledge of organizations as work settings. Organizations are work instruments that require managers if they are to achieve success. Chapter 10 introduced an open systems view of organization, stressing environment, technology, and size as important influences on organizational dynamics. Basic organizational concepts were introduced and a number of different organizational perspectives were discussed. Chapter 11 reviewed the basic components of organizational structure and showed the impact of environment, size, and managerial goals on structure. Chapter 12 then took these ideas and applied them in designing organizations for effective mission accomplishment.

## Managing the Processes of OB

In Part Five of the book, a number of basic processes in OB were covered in detail. It is through these processes that managers enact their day-to-day roles and responsibilities. It is also through these processes that managers put their knowledge of individuals, groups, and organizations to work. The processes include perception, decision-making, communication, conflict resolution, power, politics, change, and leadership. It is easy to see how they relate directly to the managerial skills listed in Table 17.1.

Special attention has been given to the subject of leadership, an all-encompassing and frequently talked-about managerial skill. Chapter 16 treated leadership in vertical superior-subordinate relations. This is an important concept, and a number of key theories were discussed to stimulate your thinking. Throughout the book, however, we have stressed that a manager's success requires more than an ability to work with subordinates. Thus, Chapter 16 also introduced the concept of horizontal leadership and summarized a comprehensive treatment of leadership in the multiple influence theory. This theory can help managers take a broader and more integrated view of their leadership behaviors and responsibilities.

## Conclusion

Well, here we are—Part Six and Chapter 17! This is the last chapter of a journey we hope has been very worthwhile. Where do you go from here? This important question needs to be answered in two ways. First, you will probably embark on a managerial career. Second, you will need to continue to learn, throughout this career, about OB and its managerial applications. Simply put, you must become a life-long learner to ensure long term success as a manager. To help you face this responsibility, let's close with a look ahead toward your career.

## CAREER PLANNING AND DEVELOPMENT

A **career** is a set of work choices and activities representing what a person does for a living. It is through this concept of a career that the needs of people and organizations are inevitably mixed together. One noted theorist and consultant states,[3]

> Organizations are dependent on the performance of their people, and people are dependent on organizations to provide jobs and career opportunities. . . . The problem for society, for organizations, and for people is how to match their respective needs, not only at the point of entry into the organization, but also throughout the career or life history of the person in the organization.

A person's career is an important component of their total life experience. The following quotes from a recent study about people and their careers should cause you to think about your career, as well as the careers of those persons who will some day become your subordinates.[4]

> "Years ago I made a bad mistake, and now I'm paying for it; I'm trapped in this job."

> "I should have found out how this firm was run before taking their offer. I had other good prospects at the time."

> "They led me down the garden path, and I was damn fool enough to be taken in."

Such pessimistic statements suggest that everyone should think seriously about their careers, and think ahead! Managers should also share this concern for the continued development of their personnel. Listed below are suggested actions for individuals interested in their careers, and for managers who are interested in the career development of subordinates.[5] Table 17.2 summarizes even more specifically a number of organizational methods for promoting career development.

| Individual Responsibilities | Managerial Responsibilities |
|---|---|
| Establish a personal career plan. | Establish a human resource plan. |
| Take a personal skills inventory. | Take a human resource inventory. |
| Set specific personal development objectives. | Establish human resource development objectives. |
| Maintain a dialogue with higher-level managers. | Maintain a dialogue with subordinates. |
| Take advantage of development opportunities. | Supplement development activities. |
| Evaluate and constructively modify personal development efforts over time. | Evaluate and constructively modify development activities over time. |

**Table 17.2 Summary of Organizational Methods of Promoting Career Development**

I. *Entry: Changing employee inputs*
1. Better links between school and employer personnel functions.
2. Training students in job-related skills.
3. Realistic job previews in recruiting.
4. Better selection methods to identify development candidates.

II. *The Job: Development through the work environment*
1. Challenging initial jobs.
2. Periodic job rotation.
3. Colleague stimulation.
4. Frequent feedback and performance review.
5. Rewarding good performance.

III. *Changing the boss's role*
1. Making managers career developers.
2. Training managers in job design and career planning.
3. Rewarding managers for subordinate development.

IV. *Changing organization structures and procedures*
1. The matrix organization structure.
2. Accounting for human resources.
3. Career-planning services.

V. *Changing personnel policies.*
1. Rotation of managers through "people departments."
2. Ending job-rotation training; creating life-long job rotation.
3. Legitimizing downward transfers.
4. "Tenure" and identification of marginal performers.
5. Fallback position for promoted employees.
6. Incentives for leaving.
7. Involvement of families in career decisions.

Source: From *Careers in Organizations* by Douglas T. Hall, p. 177. Copyright © 1976 by Goodyear Publishing Co., Inc. Reprinted by permission.

Many things will command your attention over time as you grapple with the problems and prospects of a managerial career. Three issues of special interest are initial entry, adult transitions, and dual-career families.

## Initial Entry

Choosing a job and a work organization are difficult decisions to make. They inevitably exert a lot of influence over our lives. Whenever a job change is contemplated, the best advice is to know yourself and learn as much about the job and organization as you can. This helps to ensure the best person-job-organization match. One example of such an assessment is provided in the accompanying *What Managers Do 17.1*. Such thoughtful attention to the critical joining-up decision can help in the successful implementation of a career plan.

## Adult Life Cycles

As people mature, they pass through adult life stages which present somewhat different problems and prospects. It's helpful for you to recognize these transitions and to prepare to face them in the course of your managerial career. It is also useful to recognize the effects of these transitions on other people with whom you work. Understanding their special problems and pressures can help you to better work with them in a leadership capacity.

Several popular and scholarly books discuss adult life cycles.[6] Shown in Figure 17.3 is one portrayal of the developmental periods of adulthood. Note the three transition points: early adult transition, mid-life transition, and late adult transition. Each transition involves special challenges as described in the following list.[7]

| | |
|---|---|
| The move to early adulthood | This is a period of completing one's education, entering an occupation, and becoming married. Parenthood follows, with new family and job responsibilities. It is a time of vitality, self-determination, and perhaps one or more job changes. |
| Mid-life transition | In the late 30's and early 40's, the career is all-important. Family complications stress this orientation, and personal crisis can occur. Some frustrations in the career may occur and bring with them added questions of confidence, goals, and identity. For the first time health and age become relevant concerns. |

| Middle and later adulthood | Settling in begins here, with a knowledge of the "system" and a mellowing of goals. Concerns turn toward making a real impact at work, being a mentor to others, and balancing goals and reality. This is a time of consolidating personal affairs and accepting career limitations. The next step is retirement and, perhaps, a new career. |
|---|---|

Table 17.3 relates these adult life stages to both task requirements and socio-emotional needs. This table gives you a good opportunity to consider how you might plan to ensure a productive and satisfying career for yourself and subordinates in each of the adult life stages.

**FIGURE 17.3** Developmental periods in early and middle adulthood. (Source: Daniel J. Levinson, The Seasons of a Man's Life New York: Alfred A. Knopf, 1978, p. 57. Used by permission.)

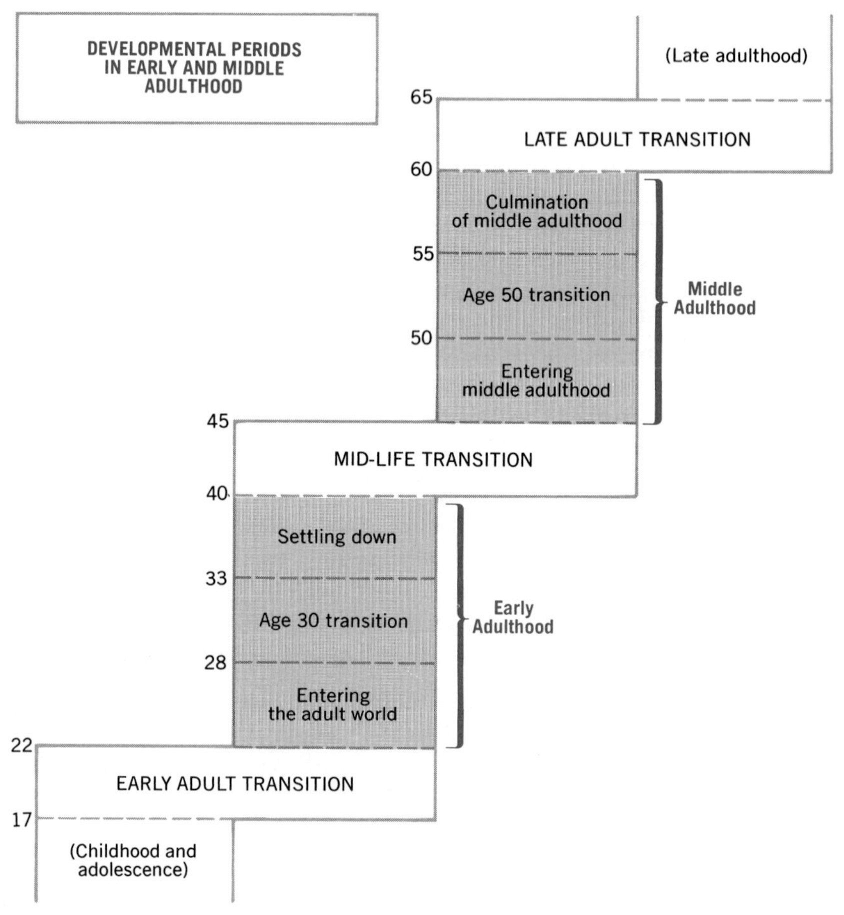

## WHAT MANAGERS DO 17.1

### A Manager's Balance Sheet

The grid lays out the pros and cons of one alternative facing a production manager at a large manufacturing plant who is contemplating a job change: whether or not to remain in his present position. Balance sheets would be filled out for all other alternatives as well—for example, whether to seek a lateral transfer within the company.

| | Positive Anticipations | Negative Anticipations |
|---|---|---|
| Tangible gains and losses for *self* | 1. Satisfactory pay.<br>2. Plenty of opportunities to use my skills and competencies.<br>3. For the present, my status in the organization is okay (but it won't be for long if I am not promoted in the next year). | 1. Long hours.<br>2. Constant time pressures—deadlines too short.<br>3. Unpleasant paper work.<br>4. Poor prospects for advancement to a higher-level position.<br>5. Repeated reorganizations make my work chaotic.<br>6. Constant disruption from high turnover of other executives I deal with. |
| Tangible gains and losses for *others* | 1. Adequate income for family.<br>2. Wife and children get special privileges because of my position in the firm. | 1. Not enough time free to spend with my family.<br>2. Wife often has to put up with my irritability when I come home after bad days at work. |
| Self-approval or self-disapproval | 1. This position allows me to make full use of my potentialities.<br>2. Proud of my achievements.<br>3. Proud of the competent team I have shaped up.<br>4. Sense of meaningful accomplishment when I see the products for which we are responsible. | 1. Sometimes feel I'm a fool to continue putting up with the unreasonable deadlines and other stupid demands made by the top managers. |
| Social approval or disapproval | 1. Approval of men on my team, who look up to me as their leader and who are good friends.<br>2. Approval of my superior who is a friend and wants me to stay. | 1. Very slight skeptical reaction of my wife—she asks me if I might be better off in a different firm.<br>2. A friend in another firm who has been wanting to wangle something for me will be disappointed. |

Source: Irving Janis and Dan Wheeler, "Thinking Clearly About Career Choices," *Psychology Today* (May 1978), p. 75. 

**Table 17.3 Developmental Needs in Early, Middle, and Late Career**

| Stage | Task Needs | Socio-Emotional Needs |
|---|---|---|
| Early Career | 1. Develop action skills.<br>2. Develop a specialty.<br>3. Develop creativity, innovation.<br>4. Rotate into new area after 3–5 years. | 1. Support.<br>2. Autonomy.<br>3. Deal with feelings of rivalry, competition. |
| Middle Career | 1. Develop skills in training and coaching others (younger employees).<br>2. Training for updating and integrating skills.<br>3. Develop broader views of work and organization.<br>4. Job rotation into new job requiring new skills. | 1. Opportunity to express feelings about mid-life (anguish, defeat, limited time, restlessness).<br>2. Reorganize thinking about self (mortality, values, family, work).<br>3. Reduced self-indulgence and competitiveness.<br>4. Support and mutual problem-solving for coping with mid-career stress. |
| Late Career | 1. Shift from power role to one of consultation, guidance, wisdom.<br>2. Begin to establish self in activities outside the organization (start on part-time basis). | 1. Support and counseling to help see integrated life experiences as a platform for others.<br>2. Acceptance of one's one and only life cycle.<br>3. Gradual detachment from organization. |

Source: From *Careers in Organizations* by Douglas T. Hall (p. 90). Copyright © 1976 by Goodyear Publishing Co., Inc. Reprinted by permission.

## Dual-Career Families

More and more families find both spouses entering the work force and seeking rewarding careers. In these cases, individual career problems and prospects become magnified due to the added challenge of managing separate careers on the part of a husband and a wife. A recent survey of corporate chief executives summarizes the challenges faced by dual-career couples.[8]

> In one of every 10 of the survey cases, the executive's spouse is employed full-time outside the home. Among couples in that category, about 18% report that the wife or husband of the respondent to the survey turned down a promotion or job offer from another organization within the past two years. Most often, the reason cited was conflict with the respondent's career.

How are career conflicts resolved? About 42% of the respondents who have experienced such a conflict said the career with the higher compensation takes priority. Another solution mentioned frequently: Give precedence to the career that offers greater long-term potential.

One final point regarding the dual-career couple is highlighted in *Newsline 17.1*. If, as the previous quote suggests, a popular resolution to dual-career conflicts is to follow the route of higher compensation, it may well be the woman who gets compromised. It appears that the pay of women managers still lags behind that of their male counterparts.

"Why should my husband mind if I work? I don't mind if he works."



## NEWSLINE 17.1

### Women Managers Get Paid Far Less Than Males, Despite Career Gains

A recent survey of female executives in U.S. companies shows that women have made career gains in recent years. However, their pay is still less than most male counterparts. Only 8.6% of women in the survey earn $100,000 a year or more; one in five earns $70,000+; six in ten earn $50,000 or less; and nearly three in ten earn less than $30,000. These results compare to an average of $134,500 annual cash compensation for male senior executives.

Source: Data reported in Frank Allen, "Women Managers Get Paid Far Less Than Males, Despite Career Gains," *The Wall Street Journal* (October 7, 1980), pp. 27, 30.

## FINAL ADVICE

Many problems and prospects await you in a managerial career. The issues discussed here merely set the stage for the excitement to come. As you look ahead to an exciting future, remember your study of OB and these final career commandments.[9]

- Good performance that pleases your superiors is the basic foundation of success.
- Manage your career; be active in influencing decisions about you.
- Develop relations with a senior executive who can be your sponsor.
- Learn your job as quickly as possible and train a replacement so you can be available to move and broaden your background in different functions.
- Nominate yourself for other positions.
- Before taking a position, carefully assess your strengths and weaknesses; what you like and don't like. Don't accept a promotion if it draws on your weaknesses and entails mainly activities that you dislike.
- Leave at your convenience, but on good terms, without parting criticism of the organization.
- Don't be trapped by formal, narrow job descriptions. Move outside them and probe the limits of your influence.
- Accept the fact that responsibility will always somewhat exceed authority and that organizational politics are inevitable.
- Get out of management if you can't stand being dependent on others and having them dependent on you.

## SUMMARY

The future is unlimited for good managers. Today's dynamic environment requires people and organizations to be highly productive in order to successfully meet the challenges of the twentieth century. Everywhere we turn, concern is expressed about solving problems and taking advantage of the opportunities in our world. Managers are cornerstones in the quest for productivity and its good to be a manager. We hope that you've gained a lot from this study of OB. We hope, too, that this learning experience will help you be truly successful in a managerial career.

## THINKING THROUGH THE ISSUES

1. Think of Peter Grace, corporate executive, who introduced this chapter. Do you expect to work under similar time constraints and pressures? Why and with what result?

2. Which of the managerial skills listed in Table 17.1 is most difficult for you? Why?

3. Write a plan of action for reaching and maintaining high mastery of each skill listed in Table 17.1.

4. Summarize the most important managerial implications which you derived from (A) Part Two: Managing Individuals in Organizations, (B) Part Three: Managing Groups in Organizations; and (C) Part Four: Managing Organizations.

5. Explain which of the OB processes discussed in Part Five will be most important to you in the next managerial position you expect to hold.

6. What is the advantage of a systematic approach to career planning?

7. List the responsibilities of individuals and organizations in career planning and development.

8. Choose persons with whom you are familiar and who are at early, mid-, and late adult transitions. What are their special problems, needs, and concerns? How would you handle each of these people as their manager?

## EXERCISE: CAREER PLANNING

### Purpose:

To help you look ahead and establish the foundations for a career plan. (These foundations can be especially helpful when you are considering your initial job upon leaving college.)

### Time:

30–40 minutes in class; one hour at home.

### Procedure:

**A. Home Preparation**

1. Write down your responses to the following questions:

a. Where would I like to be in five years as a manager? (Be as specific as possible and list job title, name, and/ or type of organization, and geographical location.)

b. What salary do you hope to earn in the above position?

2. Think carefully about your answers in question 1. List your current (a) strengths and (b) limitations in achieving these goals.

3. For each strength, write a plan of action for maintaining and/ or increasing it over a five-year period.

4. For each weakness, write a plan of action for removing or reducing it over a five-year period.

5. Make a summary list of the people who you feel will need to help you if you are to succeed during this five-year time period.

**B. In Class**

1. Convene in small groups of 3 to 5 persons to share career goals and action plans.

2. Have a spokesperson ready to report to the class the goals of persons in the group, the salaries expected, and some highlights from the various action plans.

3. The instructor will lead a discussion of the values and limitations of career planning.

## CASE: CAREERS THE JAPANESE WAY

There is growing interest in the United States and other countries in learning more about the Japanese ways of doing business. With their tremendous productivity gains in recent years and the demonstrated success of their automobile and electronics industries, for example, it is logical to wonder, "Just what are the Japanese doing so right?"

One answer to this question is that the Japanese are good managers and that the personnel policies of their firms promote productivity. One of the most interesting policies is the unique approach taken by Japanese companies toward the careers of their work force. Three aspects of the approach include:[10]

1. *Lifetime employment:* Almost 35% of the work force in Japan is covered by lifetime employment practices. When recessions or other threats occur, this means that all workers will sacrifice

some, for example through reduced wages, in order to protect employment for all.

2. *Promotion:* Promotions may be as infrequent as every ten years in some companies.
3. *Nonspecialized careers:* Japanese executives do not specialize, but rotate among all departments in a company. This makes them eventually familiar with all aspects of a firm's operations.

## Questions

1. Which of the above career management practices of Japanese companies do you feel are especially positive influences on productivity? Why?
2. Do you feel each of the above practices could be readily transferred into U.S. industry or that of other Western countries? Why or why not?
3. Would you want to work under each of the above practices? Why or why not?

# THE MANAGER'S VOCABULARY

**Career** A set of work choices and activities representing what a person does for a living.

## Notes

[1]From Marshall Loeb, "Executive View," *Time* (February 4, 1980), p. 4.

[2]Summarized from Henry Mintzberg, *The Nature of Managerial Work* (New York: Harper & Row, 1973), pp. 54–99.

[3]Edgar H. Schein, *Career Dynamics: Matching Individual and Organizational Needs* (Reading, Mass.: Addison-Wesley, 1978), p. 1.

[4]Irving Janis and Dan Wheeler, "Thinking Clearly About Career Choices," *Psychology Today* (May 1978), p. 67.

[5]Summarized in part from a discussion by Kae H. Chung and Leon C. Megginson, *Organizational Behavior: Developing Managerial Skills* (New York: Harper & Row, 1981), pp. 539–540 as based on Schein, op. cit., pp. 189–199.

[6]See for example, Douglas T. Hall, *Careers in Organizations* (Santa Monica, Calif.: Goodyear Publishing Co., 1975); Schein, op. cit.; and Daniel J.

Levinson, *The Seasons of a Man's Life* (New York: Alfred A. Knopf, 1978).

[7]Based on Levinson, op. cit., pp. 56–63; and others mentioned in note 6.

[8]Frank Allen, "Mobile Managers Get Greater Pay, Especially If They Join New Firms," *The Wall Street Journal* (October 6, 1980), p. 31.

[9]Modified from Ross A. Webber, "13 Career Commandments," *MBA* (May 1975), p. 47.

[10]See Christopher Byron, "An Attractive Japanese Export," *Time* (March 2, 1981), p. 74.

Supplementary Module A

# HISTORICAL FOUNDATIONS OF ORGANIZATIONAL BEHAVIOR

One of the delightful aspects of contemporary society is a reawakening interest in our past. Many people are investigating their ancestries and trying to learn as much as possible about their "roots." To better understand what OB is today, it is also useful to identify its roots from the past.

## SCIENTIFIC MANAGEMENT

In 1911, Frederick W. Taylor published a short book called *The Principles of Scientific Management.* This classic book is one you will still find to be provocative (and quick) reading today. The book begins with the following statement.

> The principle object of management should be to secure maximum prosperity for the employer, coupled with the maximum prosperity for the employee.[1]

Taylor's statement is still defensible and consistent with the thoughts developed in this book. He offers managers four "principles of scientific management" as guidelines for meeting this managerial responsibility:[2]

1. Develop a "science" for every job. This science should include such things as rules of motion, standardized work implements, and proper working conditions.
2. Carefully select workers who have the right abilities for the job.
3. Carefully train these workers to do the job; then offer them proper incentives to cooperate with the job science.
4. Support the workers by taking responsibility for work planning and by smoothing the way as they go about their jobs.

### The Pig-Iron Study[3]

Taylor reported a pig-iron study conducted at the Bethlehem Steel Company to illustrate these principles. The year was 1899, and the company had a problem. There were 80,000 tons of iron to be loaded on freight cars for shipment. This iron was in the form of 92-pound "pigs" that workers hand carried up inclined planes to freight cars. A worker typically loaded 12½ tons of pig-iron to earn a daily wage of $1.15. There were 75 persons in the loading gang available to do the work.

Taylor determined that it was possible for one worker to load 47½ tons per day if the principles of scientific management were followed. To prove his point, a study was conducted.

The principal actor was a man Taylor called "Schmidt." He was described as a person

> . . . observed to trot back home for a mile or so after his work in the evening about as fresh as when he came trotting down in the morning . . . upon wages of $1.15 a day he had succeeded in buying a small plot of ground, and he was engaged in putting up the walls of a little house for himself in the morning before starting work and at night after leaving . . . he also had a reputation of . . . placing a high value on a dollar."[4]

Taylor reports that under scientific management Schmidt earned $1.85 per day while loading 47 tons, never failed to work at the new pace during a three-year period, and that one worker after another was picked out of the gang and similarly trained.

## Implications

Over the years, Taylor's work has been expanded upon, modified, and criticized. In fact, his pig-iron study is the subject of a recent exposé that reveals it to be more fiction than fact! Among the discrepancies found between Taylor's original report and newly discovered data are the following.[5]

- Taylor presented at least three different versions of the study during the period 1903–1911.
- There were only 10,000 tons of iron in the Bethlehem Steel Company's yard at the time of the study, not 80,000, as Taylor said.
- The pig-iron was handled in gangs of 5–25 people, not 75 persons, as Taylor said.
- Workers did not walk up an inclined plank to load their "pigs" onto freight cars; the planks were level.
- "Schmidt" was not scientifically selected. He volunteered along with four other men after having been "convinced" by his supervisor to do so. "Schmidt" was the only worker to remain on the project until its completion.

Even though his scientific methods are now in doubt, Taylor has had an impact on the development of OB. His early work initiated interest in many issues that still concern OB scholars today. They include

- The role of compensation as an incentive to increased production.
- The design of jobs and specification of methods for their accomplishment.
- The proper match between individuals and jobs.
- Procedures for selecting and training employees.
- The role of managers in supporting the production process.

## THE HAWTHORNE STUDIES[6]

Not long after Taylor's book was published, in 1924, to be exact, the Western Electric Company began a study of individual productivity in its Cicero (a suburb of Chicago) plant known as the Hawthorne Works. The company was interested in the effects of physical working conditions on output. This concern reflects a direct interest in Taylor's first principle of scientific management.

### The Illumination Studies

Between 1924 and 1927, a series of studies was conducted to determine how various levels of illumination affected the output of workers. After varying the intensity of light for different work groups, measuring changes in output, and then analyzing the results, the researchers were disappointed. They failed to find any relationship between level of illumination and production. In some groups, output moved up and down at random; in others it increased steadily; and in one, it increased even as illumination was reduced to the level of moonlight! Perplexed by these results, the researchers concluded that unforeseen "psychological factors" had somehow interfered with the experiments.

### The Relay Assembly Test Room Studies

In 1927, a new group of researchers from Harvard University led by Elton Mayo began another series of studies. Their objective was to establish the effects of worker fatigue on productivity. Care was taken to design a test of this relationship that would be free of the "psychological effects" thought to have confounded the illumination studies.

Six operators who assembled relays were isolated for intensive study in a special test room. The operators were subjected to various rest pauses, lengths of work day, and lengths of work week, while their production was regularly measured.

Once again, the Hawthorne researchers were unable to find any direct relation between changes made in physical working conditions and worker outputs. Overall, the productivity of the relay assemblers increased over time and regardless of the specific changes made in the work setting by researchers.

Mayo and his colleagues concluded that the new "social setting" created in the test room accounted for the increased productivity. Two factors were singled out as having special importance in this regard. First, there was a positive group development in the test room. The operators shared both good social relations with one another and a common desire to do a good job. Second, supervision was more participative than that otherwise experienced by the operators. Operators in the test room were made to feel important, given a lot of information, and frequently consulted for their opinion on what was taking place.[7] This was not the case in their normal work situation.

## Further Studies

Until worsening economic conditions forced their termination in 1932, Mayo and his group of researchers continued their Hawthorne studies. After the relay assembly test room experiments, however, their interest shifted from physical working conditions to such aspects of the "social setting" of work as employee attitudes, interpersonal relations, and group relations.

Two further studies were conducted. In one, 21,126 Western Electric employees were interviewed to learn what they liked and disliked about their work. The researchers felt that this knowledge could help management to make changes that would improve productivity. The interviews also yielded "complex" and "baffling" results which led researchers to conclude that the same things (work conditions, wages) can be sources of satisfaction for some people and dissatisfaction for others. In other words, people are different! Interestingly enough, this thesis was also advanced by Frederick Taylor.

The second of the final Hawthorne studies was conducted in the Bank Wiring Room. This time the researchers specifically set out to examine the behavior of the work group. One of their "surprises" was to find individuals willing to sacrifice pay that could by earned by increasing output, that is to restrict their output, in order to avoid the displeasure of the group. This finding complemented the earlier relay assembly study and suggested that the work group can have strong negative, as well as positive, influences on individual productivity.

## Implications

The Hawthorne studies shifted the attention of managers and researchers away from physical work planning and the application of monetary incentives toward the social setting of workers and their individual attitudes. They gave birth to a body of literature now referred to as the "Human Relations Movement," a movement characterized by its concern for the creation of good human relationships between managers and their subordinates.[8] Many of the more humanistically-oriented writers whose theories are studied in this book received stimulation from this area in OB's history. They include Abraham Maslow and Frederick Herzberg, among others.

The Hawthorne studies have been criticized for their scientific methods.[9] A common concern is summarized in the **Hawthorne effect,** a term now used to describe situations in which persons who are singled out for special attention end up performing as anticipated only because of the expectancies created by the special situation. This term is a constant reminder that Mayo's test room operators may have improved their performance, not because of any subtle group dynamics or supervisory practices, but simply because they felt increased output was what the researchers and the company wanted.

Like Taylor's work, it is what the Hawthorne studies led to in terms of future research, rather than what they actually achieved as research, that counts most. They stimulated an interest in human relationships that complemented the physical/economic impetus in Taylor's work. As a result, the Hawthorne studies have had a major impact on what we study as part of OB. This legacy includes an interest in

- The group as an important force in the work setting.
- The sources of individual job satisfaction and dissatisfaction.
- Different "styles" of supervision, with a special emphasis on employee participation.
- The need for good interpersonal skills of managers.
- The importance of social relationships as a determinant of individual behavior at work.

## THE MANAGEMENT FUNCTIONS

Perhaps you have already had a course or done some reading in an area called "management" or "administrative theory." If so, you are familiar with the classical axiom: good managers will do five things well—planning, organizing, staffing, directing, and controlling (POSDC for short.) These five "functions" of management derive from another important root of OB. This root includes a body of early literature that does not pretend to rigorous scientific foundations, but which is derived from the systematic reflections of practicing managers on their work experiences. This "grass roots" approach to management is often criticized for being based on "armchair" rather than scientific evidence. We have discussed this problem more generally in a section on scientific thinking in Chapter 1. Nonetheless, the ideas of these early writers on management and administration have also had a significant impact on OB.

The classics among these works were written by Henri Fayol, Mary Parker Follett, James Mooney, and Lyndall Urwick.[10] We will limit our attention to Fayol, a successful executive in French industry.[11] In 1916, he published *Administration Industrielle et Generale* outlining his reflections on the proper management of organizations and the people within them.[12] His book offered the five "rules" listed in Table A.1. These rules, as shown in the table, have led to the formulation of what are now known as the five functions of management—planning, organizing, staffing, directing, and controlling.

## OB AND THE BEHAVIORAL SCIENCES

The three components of science deal with physical, biological, and behavioral phenomena, respectively. The **behavioral sciences** are particularly concerned with the study of human behavior. They would like to predict how people will behave in various settings.[13] OB is an applied behavioral science which has a special interest in human behavior in organizations.

OB is closely related to three behavioral sciences: psychology and its concern for the individual, sociology and its concern for people

**Table A.1 Henri Fayol's Rules for Managers and Their Relationship to the Five Functions of Management**

| Fayol's Rules | Management Function |
| --- | --- |
| *Foresight* To complete a plan of action; to scheme for the future. | Planning |
| *Organization* To provide the resources needed to implement the plan; to mobilize effort in support of the plan. | Organizing<br>Staffing |
| *Command* To get the best out of people working toward the plan; to lead; to properly select and evaluate workers. | Directing |
| *Coordination* To ensure that the efforts of subunits fit together properly; that information is shared and any problems solved. | Controlling |
| *Control* To verify progress; make sure things happen according to plan; take any necessary corrective action. | Controlling |

Source: M. B. Brodie, *Fayol on Administration* (London: Lyon, Grant and Green, 1967), pp. 12–14.

in interaction with one another, and anthropology and its concern for people in their respective cultural settings. The Hawthorne studies, for example, can be viewed from the perspective of each of these disciplines. A psychologist would look at the relay assembly test room and be most interested in the feelings and behavior of the individual operators; a sociologist would be studying the group of six operators as they interacted and worked with one another; an anthropologist would be looking at the total social system created by the test room environment and the behaviors of the operators and observers within it.

There is a natural bridge between OB and the behavioral sciences. As a result, OB is an interdisciplinary body of knowledge which draws insights from many other sciences. OB is different from these parent sciences, however, because it seeks to integrate insights available from all levels of analysis, (individual, group, and social system) and then to apply these insights to help resolve problems relating to human behavior in organizations. Thus, when you think of OB's heritage, you can now identify not only a set of distinct historical roots, but a direct linkage to the behavioral sciences as well. These linkages are summarized in Figure A.1.

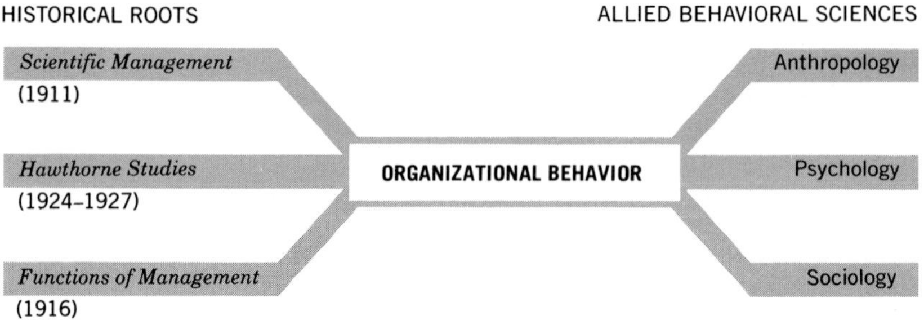


**FIGURE A.1** The heritage of OB as an academic discipline.

## THINKING THROUGH THE ISSUES

1. It is possible to criticize the work of Frederick W. Taylor, the Hawthorne studies, and the work of Henri Fayol for their scientific rigor. What impact do you feel these criticisms of OB's "roots" have had on the field of OB as it exists today?

2. How would you differentiate among the responses Frederick Taylor, Elton Mayo, and Henri Fayol would give to the question: "What should a manager do to ensure a high level of work unit performance?"

## EXERCISE: THE GREAT OB HISTORY DEBATE

### Purpose:

To increase your understanding of the historical "roots" of OB and to provide an opportunity to critically examine these roots for their managerial implications.

### Time:

50 minutes.

### Procedure:

1. Form work groups as assigned by your instructor.

2. Each group will be assigned or allowed to choose one of the following responses to the question: What should a manager do to ensure a high level of work unit performance?

*Response A:* "Frederick Taylor offers the best insight into this question. His advice would be to . . ." (advice to be filled in by the group).
*Response B:* "The Hawthorne studies are the true source of insight into this question. They suggest that a manager should ". . . (advice to be filled in by the group).
*Response C:* "Henri Fayol is the best source of insight into this question. His advance would be to . . ." (advice to be filled in by the group).

3. Each group will have 20 minutes to prepare a five-minute response for oral presentation to the rest of the class.

4. The instructor will reconvene the class and a debate will take place according to the following format:

   **a.** Each group makes an opening statement.
   **b.** Each group is allowed to ask questions and/or offer rebuttals to the other groups.
   **c.** Each group makes a final one-minute closing statement.

5. After time is called, the instructor will lead an open discussion on the three responses. This discussion will end with confrontation of the question: "Where does OB go from here?"

## THE MANAGER'S VOCABULARY

**Behavioral Sciences** Sciences such as anthropology, psychology, and sociology that are particularly concerned with the study of human behavior.

**Hawthorne Effect** Situations in which persons who are singled out for special attention end up performing as anticipated only because of the expectancies created by the "special" situation.

### Important Names

**Henri Fayol** The author of the book *Administration Industrielle et Generale,* in which five basic rules of management were described: foresight, organization, command, coordination, and control.

**Elton Mayo** The head researcher in the Hawthorne studies.

**Frederick W. Taylor** The author of the book *The Principles of Scientific Management* and reporter of the famous pig-iron study.

### Notes

[1] Frederick W. Taylor, *The Principles of Scientific Management* (New York: W. W. Norton, 1967), p. 9. (Note: The original version of this book was published in New York by Harper, 1911).

[2] Ibid., pp. 36–37.

[3] Ibid., pp. 43–47.

[4] Ibid., p. 44.

[5] Charles D. Wrege and Amedeo G. Perroni, "Taylor's Pig-Tale: A Historical Analysis of Frederick W. Taylor's Pig-Iron Experiments," *Academy of Management Journal,* Vol. 17 (March 1974), pp. 6–27.

[6] The Hawthorne Studies are described in detail in F. J. Roethlisberger and William J. Dickson, *Management and the Worker* (Cambridge, Mass.: Harvard University Press, 1966); and G. Homans, *Fatigue of Workers* (New York: Reinhold, 1941). Both sources were used in preparing the synopsis.

[7] F. J. Roethlisberger and W. J. Dickson, op. cit., p. 59.

[8] For a representative of this school of thought see Willart E. Parker and Robert W. Kleemeier, *Human Relationships in Supervision: Leadership in Management* (New York: McGraw-Hill, 1951).

[9] Alex Carey, "The Hawthorne Studies: A Radical Criticism," *American Sociological Review,* Vol. 32 (June 1967), pp. 403–416.

[10] For representatives of this school of thought see Henry C. Metcalfe and L. Urwick (eds.), *Dynamic Administration: The Collected Papers of Mary Parker Follett* (New York: Harper & Brothers, Publishers, 1940); James D. Mooney, *The Principles of Administration,* Revised Edition (New

York: Harper & Brothers, Publishers, 1947); L. Urwick, *The Elements of Administration* (New York: Harper & Brothers, Publishers, 1943).

[11] The primary source for this discussion of Fayol's work is M. B. Brodie, *Fayol on Administration* (London: Lyon, Grant and Green, 1967).

[12] Available in the English language as Henri Fayol, *General and Industrial Administration* (London: Sir Isaac Pitman & Sons, 1949).

[13] See Harold M. Rush, "The World of Work and the Behavioral Sciences: A Perspective and an Overview," Chapter 1 in *Behavioral Sciences Studies in Personnel Policy* (National Industrial Conference Board, 1969). p. x.

Supplementary Module B

# SCIENTIFIC FOUNDATIONS OF ORGANIZATIONAL BEHAVIOR

The field of OB takes care to ensure that the knowledge base from which you will derive managerial applications is built by acceptable scientific methods.

## THE SCIENTIFIC METHOD

The **scientific method** involves four steps.[1]

1. Observations are made regarding real-world events and occurrences.

   *Example* Company officials become concerned that productivity in a plant is not as high as possible.

2. An explanation for the events and occurrences is formulated.

   *Example* These officials agree that productivity probably suffers because the physical working conditions are not as conducive to high production as they could be; one aspect that seems especially important is the level of illumination in the work place.

3. Statements are made that use the explanation to predict future events and occurrences.

   *Example* Company officials and a team of researchers predict that changes made in levels of illumination will directly affect work output. As illumination increases, output should increase; as illumination decreases, output should decrease.

4. The predictions are verified by an examination conducted under systematic and controlled conditions.

   *Example* Two groups of workers are selected for study and their existing levels of output measured. In one group, light intensity is increased; in the other, it is held constant. Output is measured again for both groups. The prediction that illumination will directly affect output is tested against the data.

The previous example shows how the scientific method was followed as company officials moved from an initial observation that a problem may exist, to the point of eventually testing a plausible explanation for the problem and/or a means of resolving it. In actual practice, OB research is sometimes criticized because of the inability of researchers to completely meet the requirements set forth in step 4. It is very difficult to conduct a true experiment when the subjects are people working in organizations. Consequently, when you evaluate an OB research study and the managerial insights it claims to offer, you must have a basic understanding of the strengths and weaknesses of various research designs.

## RESEARCH DESIGNS[2]

The three basic research designs are experimental, quasi-experimental, and non-experimental. Each design has its strengths and weaknesses for OB research.

### Experimental Research

The best way to verify an explanation of the type, "an increase in illumination will cause an increase in productivity," is to perform a true experiment. A **true experiment** exists when the subjects of a research investigation are randomly assigned to one or more treatment and control groups. The key to the prior statement is the word "random." Unless a subject has an equal chance of being assigned to the treatment group (for example, the one where light intensity is varied) and the control group (for example, the one where light intensity remains the same), a variety of explanations alternative to the one advanced by researchers could account for any changes observed. Randomization equalizes the chances and simplifies the process of drawing conclusions.

A diagrammatic example of a true experiment is provided below. In the diagram the "R" stands for random assignment of subjects, "O" for measures taken (e.g. production output), and "X" for the treatment being investigated (e.g. increased illumination). In the illumination study discussed earlier, there was no randomization in the research procedure!

| | | | | |
|---|---|---|---|---|
| R | O | X | O | treatment |
| R | O | | O | control |

Most true experimental research in OB is accomplished in the laboratory setting. Because it is often hard to randomize subjects in the real-world work situation, "field" studies are most often not true experiments. This lack of true experimentation can lead to problems in trying to draw research conclusions and establish "cause-effect" relationships.

Suppose in the illumination study that output actually increased only in the treatment group as the researchers orginally predicted. Would that have meant that increased light intensity caused an increase in productivity? Not necessarily! In addition to the possibility that the results were due to increased illumination, one or more of the following explanations could have accounted for the observed differences in productivity.

- The workers in the treatment group might have been better workers than those in the control group to begin with.
- Something may have occurred in the treatment group that facilitated higher output—for example, new workers added, change in machinery, salary increased, and so on.
- Something may have occurred in the control group that inhibited higher output—for example, loss of workers, change in machinery, salary decrease, and so on.

Whenever a true experiment is not done, alternative explanations such as the above should always be very carefully ruled out. Then, and only then, can observed support for the original explanation be accepted as a basis for decision making and action.

## Quasi-Experimental Research

It is possible to approximate true experimental conditions in field settings. In the illumination studies, for example, non-random treatment and control groups were formed, measures were taken before and after the treatment was administered, and the results were then analyzed systematically. This is a good research approach, but its strength relies very heavily on the ability of researchers to deal with alternative explanations.

A typical quasi-experimental design is diagrammed below. Although treatment and control groups exist, they are not created by randomization. This lack of random assignments makes them easier to do in work settings than true experiments. With good attention given to rival explanations, the quasi-experimental design can make a fine contribution to OB knowledge.

| | | | |
|---|---|---|---|
| O | X | O | treatment |
| O | | O | control |

## Non-Experimental Research

The least rigorous research designs are non-experimental. In them, researchers simply observe events or occurrences of interest and then draw conclusions from the results. Still, non-experimental designs are a source of OB knowledge. They exist in the form of case studies, questionnaire surveys, and reports on systematic interviews. When well-accomplished and interpreted, non-experimental research can be as insightful as research accomplished with the more rigorous designs. The burden of proof, however, is on the investigator to demonstrate that truly logical and defensible interpretations are being made from the research.

One of the most common of the non-experimental designs is for data to be gathered from a number of persons. Then correlational statistics are used to establish the empirical relationships in the data. In such cases, researchers rely on the strength of the statistical argument to overcome the built-in weaknesses of the research design. Much OB research is conducted using this method.

# THE VOCABULARY OF SCIENCE

The previous discussion sets up the necessary groundwork for you to understand the OB research we discuss throughout the book. To further help you to become comfortable with the scientific vocabularly of OB, the following terms are introduced with clarifications as to how we use them.

**Variable** A measure used to describe a real-world phenomenon.

*Example* Researchers counted the number of parts produced by workers in a week's time as a measure of their individual productivity.

*Clarification* How well variables are measured is an important criterion of good research. Measures are often criticized and debated; good measures get used repeatedly by many researchers. You need to be able to judge how well researchers have measured their variables. It is far easier to count the number of parts produced and call that productivity, than it is to measure how the worker feels about the job and call that job satisfaction.

**Hypothesis** "A tentative explanation about the relationship between two or more variables."[3]

*Example* One historical hypothesis of OB researchers was that an increase in the number of rest pauses allowed workers in a work day would increase productivity. Confirmation of this hypothesis would lead to the action implication: If you want to increase individual productivity in a work unit, give the subordinates more frequent rest pauses. This hypothesis has not been confirmed by scientific research.

*Clarification* A hypothesis is what becomes formulated during step 3 of the scientific method. Hypotheses are "predictive" statements. Once verified through empirical research, an hypothesis can be a source of direct action implications. Hypotheses are sometimes called "propositions."

**Dependent Variable** The event or occurrence expressed in a hypothesis which indicates what the researcher is interested in explaining.

*Example* In OB research, individual performance is often the dependent variable of interest; that is, researchers try to determine what factors cause increases in production. One hypothesized relationship between a causal factor and this dependent variable is

Increased rest periods —lead to→ increased performance (dependent variable)

**Independent Variable** An event or occurrence that is presumed by hypothesis to affect one or more other events or occurrences as dependent variables.

*Example* In the previous example, increased rest periods was the independent variable.

**Intervening Variable** An event or occurrence that provides the linkage through which an independent variable is presumed to affect a dependent variable.

*Example* It is sometimes hypothesized that participative supervisory practices (independent variable) improve worker satisfaction (intervening variable) and therefore increase performance (dependent variable). This relationship would be depicted as

Participative supervision ⟶ improves satisfaction (intervening variable) ⟶ increases performance

**Moderator Variable** An event or occurrence that specifies the condition under which an independent variable affects a dependent variable.

*Example* The previous example hypothesizes that participative supervision would lead to increased productivity. It may well be that this relationship will hold only when the employees feel their participation is real and legitimate (a moderator variable). This role of a moderator variable can be diagrammed as

Participative supervision ⟶ increased performance

↑

participation viewed as real and legitimate (moderator variable)

**Theory** A set of systematically interrelated concepts, definitions, and hypotheses that are advanced to explain and predict phenomena.[4]

*Example* One current theory of leadership effectiveness argues that task-oriented leaders will have more effective work groups when the leader has very much or very little situation control; and that relationship-oriented leaders will have more effective work groups when the situation affords the leader an intermediate amount of control.[5]

*Clarification* Theories tend to be abstract and to involve multiple variables. They usually include a number of hypotheses, each of which would be based on clearly articulated concepts and definitions. Most, if not all, of the previously discussed kinds of variables would probably be involved. We should also note that many things called "theories" in OB do not strictly meet the definition above. Actually, they represent viewpoints, explanations, or perspectives that have logical merit and that are in the process of being scientifically verified. Theories are frequently referred to as "models" in OB.

**Empirical Research** The use of objective measurements of research variables as a basis for investigating and verifying theories and hypotheses.

*Example* Researchers collected data on the output of a work unit on a daily basis. These were objective "facts" because the same results would have been obtained by anyone who used the same measuring procedures. These "facts" are quite different from the "opinion" of an observer who may have watched the workers perform and then made a purely personal judgment.

## SCIENTIFIC RESEARCH IN REVIEW

The scientific method is an important criterion used to evaluate research contributions to OB. Although it is not perfect, you will find the knowledge base in OB to be closely scrutinized for its scientific rigor, as well as for its practical merit. The study of OB is a self regenerating process in which initial knowledge helps you to identify problems and a number of possible solutions. The true student of OB will test these alternative solutions scientifically to learn which best fits the need of the specific problem situation. Typically, new problems will be uncovered in the process, and the cycle will start over again. Because of this vitality in OB, you need to learn both what OB currently has to offer and how to continue to learn more about OB in your managerial future.

Ultimately, you need to become a good consumer of other people's research. A familiarity with the scientific foundations of OB and with the scientific research process summarized in the Figure B.1 are your first steps on the way.

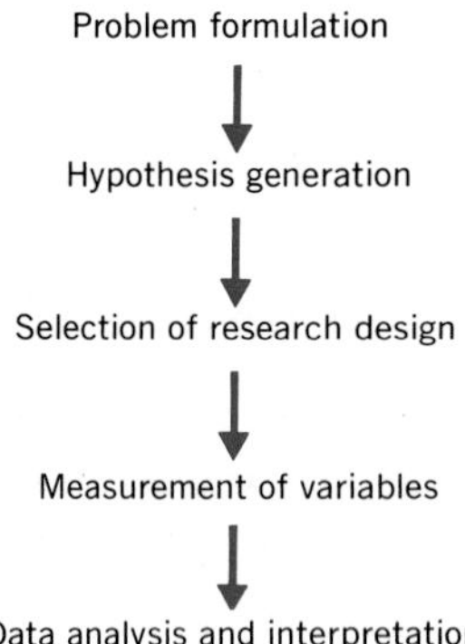


**FIGURE B. 1** The scientific research process.

## THINKING THROUGH THE ISSUES

1. Because their subject is human behavior in organizations, OB researchers are often unable to perform true experiments. Given this reality of OB research, what types of deficiencies would you anticipate finding in the research results that are discussed in this book?

2. Use each of the terms in The Vocabulary of Science section as they might be found in a work conversation between two managers.

## CASE: TRAINING SUPERVISORS AND CONVINCING MANAGEMENT

Shane Alexander is the personnel director of the Central State Medical Center. One of her responsibilities is to oversee the hospital's supervisory training programs. Recently, Shane attended a professional conference where a special "packaged" training program was advertised for sale. The "package" includes a set of videotaped lectures by a distinguished management consultant plus a workbook containing readings, exercises, cases, tests, and other instructional aids. The subjects covered in the program include motivation, group dynamics, communication skills, leadership effectiveness, performance appraisal, and the management of planned change.

In the past, Shane felt that the hospital had not lived up to its supervisory training goals. One of the reasons for this was the high cost of hiring external consultants to do the actual instruction. This packaged program was designed, presumably, so that persons from within the hospital could act as session coordinators. The structure of the program provided through the videotapes and workbook agenda was supposed to substitute for a consultant's expertise. Because of this, Shane felt that use of the packaged program could substantially improve supervisory training in the hospital.

The cost of the program was $3,500 for an initial purchase of the videotapes plus 50 workbooks. Additional workbooks were then available at $8 per copy. Before purchasing the program, Shane needed the approval of the senior administrative staff.

Upon returning from the conference, Shane proposed such a purchase at the next staff meeting. She was surprised at the response. The hospital president was noncommital; the vice-president was openly hostile; and the three associate administrators were varied in their enthusiasm. It was the vice-president's opinion that dominated the discussion. He argued that to invest in such a program on the assumption that it would lead to improved supervisory practices was unwise. "This is especially true in respect to the proposed program," he said. "How could such a package possibly substitute for the training skills of an expert consultant?"

Shane argued her case and was left with the following challenge. The administrators would allow $1,000 to be spent to rent the program with 30 workbooks. It would be up to Shane to demonstrate through a trial program that an eventual purchase would be worthwhile.

There were 160 supervisors in the hospital. The program was designed to be delivered in eight 2½ hour sessions. It was preferred to schedule one session per week, with no more than 15 participants per session.

Shane knew that she would have to present very strong evidence to gain administrative support for the continued use of the program. Given the opportunity, she decided to implement a trial program in such a way that conclusive evidence on the value of the "packaged" training would be forthcoming.

### Questions

1. If you were Shane, what type of research design would you use to test this program? Why?
2. How would the design actually be implemented in this hospital setting?
3. What would be your research hypothesis? What variables would you need to measure to provide data that could test this hypothesis? How would you gather these data?
4. Do you think the administrator's request for "proof before purchase" was reasonable? Why or why not?

## THE MANAGER'S VOCABULARY

**Dependent Variable** The event or occurrence, expressed in an hypothesis, which indicates what a researcher is interested in explaining (e.g., work performance or job satisfaction).

**Empirical Research** The use of objective measurement of research variables as a basis for investigating and verifying theories and hypotheses.

**Hypothesis** A tentative explanation about the relationship between two or more variables.

**Independent Variable** The event or occurrence that is presumed in the statement of an hypothesis to affect one or more other events or occurrences.

**Intervening Variable** An event or occurrence that provides the linkage through which an independent variable is presumed to exert an effect on a dependent variable.

**Moderator Variable** An event or occurrence that specifies the condition under which an independent variable affects a dependent variable.

**Theory** A set of systematically interrelated concepts, definitions, and hypotheses that are advanced to explain and predict phenomena.

**True Experiment** When the subjects of a research investigation are randomly assigned to one or more treatment and control groups.

**Variable** A measure used to describe a real-world phenomenon.

## Notes

[1]Adapted from Eugene Stone, *Research Methods in Organizational Behavior* (Santa Monica, Calif.: Goodyear Publishing Company, 1978), p. 8.

[2]For complete discussions of the three categories of research designs, see Donald T. Campbell and Julian C. Stanley, *Experimental and Quasi-Experimental Designs for Research* (Chicago: Rand McNally, 1969); and Stone, op. cit.

[3]Stone, op. cit., p. 19.

[4]C. William Emory, *Business Research Methods,* Revised Edition (Homewood, Ill.: Richard D. Irwin, 1980).

[5]Based on Fred E. Fiedler, Martin M. Chemers, and Linda Mahar, *Improving Leadership Effectiveness: The Leader Match Concept* (New York: John Wiley & Sons, 1976).

# Photo Credits

**Chapter 1** Page 7: Burk Uzzle/Magnum. Page 13: Everett C. Johnson/ Leo de Wys. Page 19: Peter Southwick/Stock Boston.

**Chapter 2** Page 33: Ken Karp. Page 46: Jackniewicz Photo/Chase Manhattan Archives.

**Chapter 3** Page 69: Stephen L. Feldman/Photo Researchers. Page 73—Cartoon 3.1: Reprinted from Mgr. Magazine, 1977. Page 75: Stan Levy/ Photo Researchers. Page 80: Chuck Fishman/Leo de Wys.

**Chapter 4** Page 103: Sherry Suris/Photo Researchers. Page 104—Cartoon 4.1: Reprinted from Mgr. Magazine, 1977. Drawing by Bill Basso. Page 111—Photo 4.1: Ken Karp.

**Chapter 5** Page 135: Ken Karp. Page 136: Copyright, 1978 by Chicago Tribune-N.Y. News Syndicate. Inc. All Rights Reserved. Page 145: Ken Karp. Page 156: Bettye Lane/Photo Researchers.

**Chapter 6** Page 169: Christopher Morrow/Stock Boston. Page 172: Arthur Tress/Photo Researchers. Page 173: Copyright, 1973, G. B. Trudeau. Reprinted with Permission of Universal Press Syndicate. All Rights Reserved. Page 178: Leo de Wys.

**Chapter 7** Page 211: Stan Goldblatt/Photo Researchers. Page 216: Ellis Herwig/Stock Boston. Page 225: NASA.

**Chapter 8** Page 239: Robert E. Murowchick/Photo Researchers. Page 256: Catherine Ursillo/Leo de Wys. Page 263: David Hurn/Magnum.

**Chapter 9** Page 273: Jon Allen/Photo Researchers. Page 292—Photo 9.2 and Page 294—Photo 9.3: Courtesy of AB Volvo, Gothenburg, Sweden.

**Chapter 10** Page 313: Peter Gridley/FPG. Page 317: © Sidney Harris. Page 336: David Franklin/Time Magazine.

**Chapter 11** Page 345: Bruce Davidson/Magnum. Page 361: Ken Karp. Page 367: Rhoda Sidney/Monkmeyer.

**Chapter 12** Page 375: Ken Karp. Page 385: Drawing by Ed Arno. © 1977 The New Yorker Magazine, Inc.

**Chapter 13** Page 407: Sylvia Johnson/Woodfin Camp. Page 418: Hazel Hankin/Stock Boston.

**Chapter 14** Page 437: Ellis Herwig/Stock Boston. Page 445: Richard Kalvar/Magnum. Page 449: Reprinted from Mgr. Magazine. AT&T Long Lines. Page 457: Richard Kalvar/Magnum.

**Chapter 15** Page 475: Stephen L. Feldman/Photo Researchers. Page 503: U.S. Postal Service.

**Chapter 16** Page 511: John Ross/Photo Researchers. Page 514: Copyright King Features Syndicate, Inc. 1975. World Rights Reserved. Page 522: Marine Corps Photo/Photo Researchers. Page 523: Alex Webb/Magnum.

**Chapter 17** Page 553: Richard Frear/Photo Researchers. Page 567: Rhoda Sidney/Monkmeyer. Page 568: Reprinted by Courtesy of NEW WOMAN magazine from Best Cartoons from NEW WOMAN. © 1979 by NEW WOMAN. ALL RIGHTS RESERVED THROUGHOUT THE WORLD.

# MANAGER'S VOCABULARY INDEX

# NAME INDEX

# SUBJECT INDEX